EXPERIMENTAL PSYCHOLOGY
Methodology, Psychophysics, and Learning

McGRAW-HILL SERIES IN PSYCHOLOGY

Consulting Editors
NORMAN GARMEZY
RICHARD L. SOLOMON
LYLE V. JONES
HAROLD W. STEVENSON

EXPERIMENTAL PSYCHOLOGY

METHODOLOGY, PSYCHOPHYSICS, AND LEARNING

M. R. D'AMATO

Professor of Psychology
Rutgers, The State University

McGRAW-HILL BOOK COMPANY

New York   St. Louis   San Francisco
Düsseldorf   London   Mexico
Panama   Sydney   Toronto

This book was set in Garamond by The Maple Press Company, printed on permanent paper by Halliday Lithograph Corporation, and bound by The Book Press, Inc. The designer was Joan O'Connor; the drawings were done by Russ Peterson. The editors were Walter Maytham, Nat LaMar, and Susan Gamer. Stuart Levine supervised the production.

EXPERIMENTAL PSYCHOLOGY: METHODOLOGY,
PSYCHOPHYSICS, AND LEARNING

Library of Congress Catalog Card Number 72-99197

15230

1234567890 HDBP 79876543210

PREFACE

When I began work on this book after some eight years of experience in teaching undergraduate experimental psychology, I had a number of aims in mind. First, I was convinced from my teaching experience that the undergraduate student in psychology is capable of absorbing and using to advantage far more material having to do with experimental and quantitative concepts and techniques than is represented in the usual levels of accomplishment. I could remember my own problems as an undergraduate student trying to master material that was far too inadequately "programmed." Thus, in Part 1 of the text, which is devoted primarily to methodological and quantitative matters, I have tried to make the material entirely self-contained so that any well-intentioned reader could master virtually all the topics presented there. For a reader to whom logarithmic and power functions mean little, Fechner's law and Stevens' law will mean less. Consequently, these functions are developed and discussed in some detail before the related substantive issues are introduced. Similarly, the normal distribution, which plays such a versatile role in theoretical matters, is introduced and discussed in Chapter 4, before it is used in subsequent chapters. The exercises which occur in Chapters 3 to 6 are an integral part of the plan to develop more than a passing understanding of the subject matter presented in these chapters. Nothing reinforces learning more than learning itself, and I am optimistic that even the student who has a low opinion of his quantitative abilities can with application master most if not all of the material of Part 1, however forbidding some of it might first appear. There is perhaps one exception. It was not possible to develop a background in probability theory that would ensure a thorough understanding of the concepts presented in the section on signal detection theory. But even here I think it likely that a student who has achieved command of the earlier material will come away from this section with a reasonable understanding of its contents.

I am well aware that it is poor pedagogy to attempt to stuff a student with a broad array of methodological and quantitative concepts before turning him loose on actual experimental work. Developing an involvement in experimental problems is as important as cultivating a knowledge of how to go about performing an experiment. The second without the first is dull, dry, and academic. A good case can be made for plunging into experimental work at the earliest possible moment. Still, at some point the researcher must begin to acquire the requisite methodological and quantitative skills, without which he is likely to develop into no more than a laboratory dilettante.

The purpose of Part 2 is to supply content areas upon which meaningful laboratory experiments can be based. It was my aim and hope to present this material in such a way as to constitute interesting and informative background material. Because I felt this goal was better served by stressing contemporary research, I went to some length to draw from the most recent materials available. Close to 50 percent of the references cited in the text bear publication dates of 1965 or later. A large number of researchers were kind enough to allow me to see prepublished copies of their work, much of which has been incorporated into the text.

Another objective that I had in mind was to point to common threads connecting areas of research that have been kept far too distinct from each other because of separate labels, proliferation of specialized professional journals, and other fragmenting influences. Selective perception, discussed in Chapter 11, is one such integrating concept, as it plays an important role in verbal learning, conditioning, and even in psychophysical scaling. A more impressive illustration is signal detection theory, which first arose as an alternative to classical psychophysical theory but soon found important applications in conditioning, discrimination learning, generalization, and human retention. It is clear to me, however, that in this endeavor I have fallen far short of the mark. I am convinced that there are illuminating connections between many of the research areas discussed in the text that now remain isolated from one another, and I regret that I can do little more in this connection than pass the challenge on to the reader.

Finally, I have attempted to point out how certain laboratory findings and the concepts based upon them have found application in the real world. The demand for "relevance" is perhaps stronger today than ever before, and I think it both useful and desirable to point out explicitly such instances as do exist. On the other side of the coin, one must learn to be tolerant of scientific activities that appear completely remote from any worthwhile application. I can remember a fellow graduate student protesting to a professor that it was utterly senseless to keep beating the "dead horse" of Fechner's law and its surrounding psychophysics. Justified as the student's comments may have appeared at the time, Fechner's law shortly gave way to Stevens' law, which, as is mentioned in Chapter 6, has led to a number of unanticipated and useful applications. Although some areas of research described in the text now appear to be far from having any value in the affairs of men, doubtless some of them will eventually lead to valuable applications. It was not so long ago that operant conditioning was branded the "psychology of the white rat," and yet there have been few developments in experimental psychology that have had an equal impact outside of the laboratory. In my view there is no necessary contradiction between being devoted to "pure" scientific research and maintaining an appreciation of useful applications of the fruits of the laboratory. It is my hope that this text will assist in cultivating such an attitude.

Although the chapters in both parts of the book follow a logical development, there is no necessity that they be read in sequence. Chapter 1 should be read first. Chapter 2, which is heavy with methodological considerations, may be skimmed initially to afford the student an overview of some of the methodological problems he may encounter in his research. Chapters 3 and 4, which deal with descriptive statistics, are self-contained to the point that the student should be able to handle them on his own. The material presented in these chapters may therefore be called upon as required by the needs of laboratory experimentation. The remaining chapters of Part 1 and those of Part 2 can be used in virtually any order to conform to the experimentation being performed in class, but it is best not to invert the order of Chapters 5 and 6, 7 and 8, or 10 and 11.

M. R. D'Amato

ACKNOWLEDGMENTS

During the years that this book was under preparation, I had the benefit of critical evaluations from a number of people. Portions of the manuscript were read by Drs. Peter L. Carlton, Peter L. Derks, Harry Fowler, Harry F. Harlow, Geoffrey Keppel, Elijah Lovejoy, N. J. Mackintosh, William F. Prokasy, Joseph Sidowski, Sally E. Sperling, S. S. Stevens, and Thom Verhave. I profited greatly from many of their comments, and I warmly appreciate the generous and constructive spirit in which they were offered. Michael Etkin and James Fazzaro checked the problems and answers of Part 1 of the text; they were helpful to me in many other ways, for which I am very grateful. Mrs. Libby Brusca bore the brunt of the endless typing and proofing with skill and patience. I am pleased to acknowledge my debt to her and to Mrs. Gerry Hansen, who carried the burden earlier.

The research from my laboratory which I had occasion to cite in the text was supported by the National Science Foundation. Those of us who have seen firsthand the crucial role that the enlightened policies of the National Science Foundation and other federal granting agencies have played in the development of scientific psychology cannot help but be alarmed at the prospect that budgetary considerations will force a serious attenuation of their efforts.

This project was initiated and completed while I was a faculty member at New York University and Rutgers, The State University. I am grateful for the use of their facilities, tangible and intangible, which made my research and writing possible.

Chapters 7 and 8 are expanded and updated versions of a section on instrumental conditioning which appeared in *Learning: Processes*, edited by Melvin Marx and published by The Macmillan Company, 1969. I am grateful for their permission to incorporate portions of that material in the present text. Many individual investigators and publishing organizations have given me permission to use various copywrited materials. Acknowledgments have been provided in appropriate places, but I wish here to thank these individuals and organizations for their cooperation and support.

I owe a special debt of gratitude to Dr. Norman E. Spear, who prepared Chapter 12, Verbal Learning and Retention. Aside from the fact that he produced a chapter that I could not hope to equal, his undertaking of the task gave me time to revise and update the manuscript to a degree that would not have otherwise been possible.

Finally I wish to thank my family—Nancy, my wife; and my children, Vivian, Mark, and Erik—who in lost weekends and evenings paid their price for this undertaking.

M. R. D'Amato

CONTENTS

PART II   LEARNING AND BEHAVIOR

EXPERIMENTAL PSYCHOLOGY

Methodology, Psychophysics, and Learning

PART 1

METHODOLOGY AND PSYCHOPHYSICS

1 EXPERIMENTATION IN PSYCHOLOGICAL RESEARCH

This initial chapter has two major aims. First, we shall locate experimental psychology within the context of psychological research in general. Second, we shall introduce and define a number of indispensable concepts; some of these concepts, which form a foundation for future developments, will be used to further the first aim.

PSYCHOLOGICAL RESEARCH

"Research" is a word much used these days but probably no longer conveys meaning of useful precision. It will be of some help in later discussions to make certain distinctions now among "research," "experimentation," and related terms.

We may include under the term "psychological research" all inquiries into problems within the sphere of psychology. Psychological research, in turn, may be subdivided into two distinguishable, though interrelated, categories: *theoretical research* and *empirical research*.

Theoretical Research

Theoretical research subsumes those inquiries which deal primarily with the development of theory in psychology. Such inquiries often take the form of (1) what may be called "library research" and (2) theory construction.

LIBRARY RESEARCH.　In library research one attempts to integrate the findings or data in a particular problem area of psychology around a set of empirical principles or attempts to derive hidden generalizations from seemingly diverse data. Examples of such research are found in the frequent "review" articles that are published in the journal *Psychological Bulletin*. In these articles the accumulated research in a circumscribed problem area of psychology is examined in detail, and an attempt is made to glean generalizations or formulate hypotheses from the data which help one organize and understand them. Thus some theory construction, limited in depth and scope, is often involved in library research.

THEORY CONSTRUCTION.　The development in psychology of systematic theories does not, of course, occur in isolation from empirical research; rather, theory construction and empirical research are complementary activities. One may nevertheless distinguish activities that are primarily theoretical in nature; the goal of these is the elaboration of a theoretical structure which will account for a substantial body of data. Such theories may be informal, stated completely in verbal terms with no attempt at rigorous definition of the basic theoretical concepts and their interrelations, or, much less frequently in psychology, they may be quite rigorously developed. Psychoanalytic theories, for example, generally fall into the former category. A classic example of the latter type of theories may be found in the rather formidable *Mathematico-Deductive Theory of Rote Learning* by Hull and others (1940) and in Hull's later, more manageable *Principles of Behavior* (1943). More recently, psychology has seen the development of thoroughly mathematical theories, as in the field of learning (e.g., Estes, 1959). This new approach quickly built up the momentum to justify the launching of the three-volume *Handbook of Mathematical Psychology* in 1963 (Luce, Bush, & Galanter, 1963, 1965) and the inauguration of the *Journal of Mathematical Psychology* in 1964. However, rigorous quantitative models need not be cast in mathematical terms; information-processing models in the form of computer simulation programs have also been used to achieve these ends (cf. Gregg & Simon, 1967).

Empirical Research

Within empirical research we can distinguish three general and closely related research approaches: (1) observation (in a natural or in a laboratory setting),

(2) correlational research, and (3) experimentation. A large portion of this chapter will be devoted to a discussion of these research approaches.

OBSERVATION. The antiquity and power of observation as a research method are illustrated by the fact that astronomy, the oldest and one of the most precise of sciences, was founded by inquisitive man with little more than his curiosity and his eyes. This is not to say that observation alone can sustain the development of a science; at the very minimum, correlational research is a necessary accompaniment. But observation is very often the source of interesting and important problems as well as the origin of the hypotheses leading to their solution.

Strictly speaking, observation involves the noting and recording of events *without formal manipulation of variables operating in the events under study*. To illustrate within a hypothetical situation, suppose that a researcher wishing to learn something about group processes in children observes a group of children in schoolyard play. From his observations he might arrive at the hypothesis that individual aggressiveness and group leadership are positively related; that is, the more aggressive children tend to engage in group leadership behavior more frequently than the less aggressive children. Thus far, the research, involving no formally manipulated variables, may be classified as observation.

Going further, the researcher, as a first step in the verification of his hypothesis, would obtain some measure of the aggressiveness of an individual child, either by means of an appropriate psychological test or by a rating procedure. On the basis of such a measure, he very likely would *select* for particular attention in future observations those children scoring high and those scoring low on aggressiveness. And if his hypothesis were correct, the former should engage more often in group leadership behavior than the latter. We may consider the psychological test, or the rating procedure, to constitute a means of "manipulating," through selection, the variable of aggressiveness. Thus the researcher, in manipulating this variable and relating it to another variable, group leadership, is no longer engaged in observation only, but rather has advanced to what is called "correlational research."

When observation is employed on events in their natural setting, we speak of *natural observation*. Our researcher, in his study of the children, was initially involved in natural observation. Many studies in animal behavior are grounded in natural observation, as are a good many sociological and anthropological researches.

However, where feasible, natural observation often gives way to *laboratory observation*. The reasons are simple. Control over relevant factors is more practicable in a laboratory setting. Phenomena observed under natural conditions are constantly subjected to the operation of factors which the researcher cannot control and which might greatly complicate the events under observation. Further, in natural observation one must seek out or await the events he wishes to observe, whereas, on the other hand, in laboratory observation it is often possible to initiate the events of interest through manipulation of environmental and related factors.

CORRELATIONAL RESEARCH. A very important segment of psychological research makes use of correlational techniques. Cronbach (1957), dividing scientific psychology into experimental and correlational psychology, includes in the latter such areas as construction and application of psychological tests, differential and developmental psychology, and some instances of comparative psychology. An important defining feature of correlational research is that *the variables under study are not directly (experimentally) manipulated by the researcher.* Rather, variation in the variables of interest is achieved by some sort of *selection procedure*. In psychology, selection procedures often take the form of psychological tests. Thus, if one were interested in the relationship between intelligence and problem-solving ability, the variable of intelligence would be manipulated by using some reasonable test of intelligence to select out individuals of different levels of intelligence. Quite clearly the researcher could not directly (experimentally) manipulate intelligence in his subjects. He could not convert one group of subjects into highly intelligent individuals and a second group into subnormally intelligent individuals. Special aptitudes and many personality variables are other examples of classes of variables that can be manipulated by the researcher only through selection procedures.

The advance of correlational research over observation lies in the *focusing of interest on specific aspects (variables) of the phenomena under study.* The question asked in this kind of research is: Are variables A and B related, and if so, how? Answers to such questions require means of measuring A and B and methods of manipulating A or B or both. By manipulating A we mean *arranging for different quantities or different values of A to appear.* As previously stated, correlational research is characterized mainly by the way variables are manipulated, which is never *directly*, as in experimentation, but rather through a *selection* procedure. Thus, if we wish to manipulate (arrange for different quantities of) scholastic aptitude, we cannot do so directly. We cannot with any means at our disposal—drugs, training techniques, or surgical intervention—establish at will in an individual an arbitrary level of scholastic aptitude. We can only, through the use of some indicator of scholastic aptitude, choose or select among individuals in whom differences with respect to this variable already exist. As a general statement, we may say that research is likely to be correlational in nature whenever *all* the variables under study concern properties of the subject which are either inherent to the subject (e.g., age, sex, phylogenetic level) or are the result—wholly or in part—of prolonged experience (e.g., aspects of personality).

Although correlational research often suffers certain limitations, particularly with respect to controlling relevant variables and rendering conclusions concerning cause-and-effect relations, important areas of investigation exist where its use is unavoidable. Further, in the hands of an able researcher, the advanced statistical tools (factor analysis, for example) developed in some areas of correlational research can prove to be powerful instruments in the dissection and analysis of complex phenomena, such as human intelligence (Guilford, 1959, 1966).

Cronbach, himself an arch-correlational psychologist, said this about the potentialities of correlational research:

> The well-known virtue of the experimental method is that it brings situational variables under tight control. It thus permits rigorous tests of hypotheses and confident statements about causation. The correlational method, for its part, can study what man has not learned to control or can never hope to control. Nature has been experimenting since the beginning of time, with a boldness and complexity far beyond the resources of science. The correlator's mission is to observe and organize the data from Nature's experiments. As a minimum outcome, such correlations improve immediate decisions and guide experimentation. At the best, a Newton, a Lyell, or a Darwin can align the correlations into a substantial theory (Cronbach, 1957, p. 672).

Cronbach and others (e.g., Gulliksen, 1968; Owens, 1968) have urged that experimental and correlational techniques be combined to form a powerful attack on difficult research problems. As yet, however, these suggestions seem not to have been heeded widely by experimental psychologists.

In summary, correlational research, unlike observation, involves the *manipulation of specific variables* chosen from the area of research interest. Manipulating a variable means *arranging for the appearance of different quantities or different values of the variable*. In correlational research the manipulation is always accomplished by some sort of selection procedure.

EXPERIMENTATION. The *sine qua non* of most sciences, including psychology, is experimentation. Even astronomy, which relies heavily on correlational research, owes much of its viability to the improvement in observational techniques and apparatus constantly emerging from experimentation in allied sciences. In an ideal experiment, the investigator controls and *directly* manipulates the important variables of interest to him. Through careful manipulation of variables, the experimenter is able to show that changes in A result in (cause) changes in B: mere concomitance is replaced by cause-and-effect relations. Because the variables with which the experimenter deals are usually within his province of direct manipulation, he is able to achieve a measure of control over relevant experimental factors not easily obtained otherwise, a control which enables him to untangle and isolate from nature's complexity the particular effects of specific variables.

The major criterion, then, for experimentation is that the variables of interest are subject to *direct* manipulation, as contrasted with manipulation through selection procedures. A few examples of variables that allow for direct manipulation may be cited from psychology; in fact, most variables relating to the experimental situation and to the experimental task are of this nature—for example, temperature, humidity, lighting, task instructions, materials, and procedures. Many "subject variables" also permit direct manipulation, such as anxiety level (when manipulated through the application of such aversive stimuli as shock), hunger and thirst drives, states induced through the use of drugs, and variations in (limited) previous experience brought about by different training procedures.

The distinction between direct manipulation of variables and manipulation through selection procedures is important for several reasons. First, when a variable is manipulated through selection, often other, possibly quite relevant, variables are *concomitantly manipulated* with the variable of interest. Such concomitant manipulation of variables can lead to very misleading interpretations of research results, as illustrated by the following example. Suppose a researcher interested in the relationship between height and amount of food intake initiates a study comparing the food intake of people of various heights. He would undoubtedly find that the two variables are positively related; that is, taller people eat more than shorter people. Although this empirically obtained result may be unassailable, would the researcher be correct in concluding that there was something about height *itself* that influences the amount eaten? Consider, for example, the hypothesis that in taller people the heart must work harder to pump the blood into the head region and that this added work expends extra energy, requiring, in turn, greater food intake. A little thought will make it clear that probably height is not the important relevant variable. The relationship obtained by the researcher most likely results from the close relationship of height and *weight*. In manipulating height, through selection of individuals of different heights, the researcher concomitantly manipulated weight, because taller people tend to weigh more. Thus, the tall people were not only taller than the short people, but they also weighed more—and it is quite likely that the latter variable is the important one. This conclusion, it may be noted, could be checked by measuring the food intake of one group of individuals who vary in height but not in weight and of a second group who vary in weight but not in height.

Of course, the danger of erroneous conclusions in matters of interpretation arises primarily when the concomitantly manipulated variable is subtle and goes unnoticed by the researcher—not an uncommon occurrence. For this reason, as well as others, it is often difficult in correlational research to make confident statements concerning cause-and-effect relations. To illustrate, a major reason for the widespread controversy concerning the causal connection between smoking and lung cancer may be traced to the correlational nature of most of the pertinent research. On the other hand, with direct manipulation of variables there is inherently much less of a problem with concomitant manipulation which, when it occurs in conjunction with direct manipulation, is generally more easily detected and eliminated.

A second reason for distinguishing between direct manipulation and manipulation through selection relates to the precision of manipulation attained by the two methods. Although with some variables manipulation through selection is very precise, with others a considerable margin of error is involved.

By "error" we refer to the discrepancy between the value of the variable assumed to have been obtained by manipulation and its actual or "true" value. Thus, any error committed in manipulating age as a variable is likely to be small, but this is not true for variables emanating from research dealing with aptitudes, intellectual ability, and personality. It is generally true, by way of contrast, that directly manipulated variables are normally subject to very little error in their manipulation.

The third difference between the two methods of manipulation is that certain powerful research techniques, developed with directly manipulated variables, are inapplicable to most variables manipulated by selection procedures. Among the more important of these is the *single-group* or *within-subjects* design, a technique in which each subject serves as his own control. For present purposes we shall define single-group (within-subjects) designs as the method in which *a single group of subjects serves under all conditions of the research.* For example, suppose we want to determine whether nicotine has a deleterious effect on motor coordination. One powerful means of attacking this problem is as follows. We would choose a group of subjects and submit them to a series of motor coordination tests, one test daily. Before some of the tests the subjects would be given a dose of nicotine, and before others they would receive a placebo, an innocuous substance administered in the same way as the drug in order to control for suggestion. Hence, *all subjects are tested under both the drug and no-drug conditions.* If the drug has a harmful effect on motor coordination, we should observe that, in general, the performance of our subjects is poorer when tested under the drug than when tested after receiving the placebo. Note that because each subject is tested under both conditions, we need not concern ourselves with individual differences in motor-coordination ability.

Now imagine that the only way in which we could obtain subjects with different amounts of nicotine in them was to choose smokers and nonsmokers from the general population. In this instance we would be forced to use a *separate-groups* (or *between-subjects*) design; that is, one group of subjects (smokers) would be tested under the drug condition, and a second group of subjects (nonsmokers) would be tested under the no-drug condition. More generally, with separate-groups (between-subjects) designs, *a separate group of subjects serves under each of the conditions of the research.* By comparing the performance of the two groups of subjects, we can evaluate the effect of nicotine on motor coordination. Note that the situation with respect to individual differences in motor-coordination ability is radically changed. We are now vitally interested in any dimension of individual differences that might significantly affect motor coordination, such as age, sex, and occupation. Obviously we would want the smokers (drug group) and nonsmokers (no-drug group) to be well equated with respect to such individual characteristics. However, such precautions are not necessary with a single-group design because every subject is tested under all conditions of the research.

In summary, the cardinal feature of experimentation is that the variables under study are *directly* manipulated by the researcher. And it may be stated as a general principle that the more directly the researcher can manipulate his variables of interest, the more reliable and precise his results are likely to be. Direct manipulation of variables possesses several advantages over manipulation by selection: (1) The dangers of *concomitant manipulation* of relevant but extraneous variables are considerably less potent with direct manipulation; (2) there is generally *less error of manipulation* involved when variables are directly manipulated; and (3) certain powerful research techniques, such as single-group designs, are possible with many variables that are manipulated directly but are possible with few variables that are manipulated by selection. In single-group (within-subjects) designs, a single group of subjects serves in all conditions of the research; in separate-groups (between-subjects) designs, a separate group of subjects serves under each of the conditions of the research.

The progress from natural observation to laboratory experimentation is characterized by the researcher's winning increasing control over the events with which he is concerned. Experimentation, however, is not limited to a laboratory setting; it is, in some disciplines, most often practiced within a natural setting.[1] Similarly, correlational research may be conducted within a laboratory or natural setting. It will be possible to make more precise statements about these interrelationships after we have introduced the concepts of independent and dependent variables later in this chapter.

PSYCHOLOGY AND THE CONCEPT OF VARIABLES

Consider the following experiment. A subject (S)[2] is seated before a table on which appear a small telegraph key and, next to it, a white electric light bulb. The S is fitted with earphones and instructed by the experimenter (E) to press the telegraph key as quickly as possible whenever he sees the white light illuminate or hears a tone through the earphones. The stimuli, the white light and the tone, are presented individually in an irregular order so that S cannot predict whether the next stimulus will be the light or the tone. During each stimulus presentation, E accurately measures S's reaction time (RT), that is, the time elapsing between the onset of the stimulus and the time S presses the telegraph key. After 50 presentations of each stimulus, the experimental session is terminated.

Although relatively simple, the preceding situation contains many of the important features common to most experiments in psychological research. Our present interest is the concept of variables, in particular *independent* variables, *dependent* variables, and *relevant* variables.

Before proceeding, however, we shall state more explicitly what is meant by the term *variable*, namely, *any measurable attribute of objects, things, or beings.*

[1] Indeed, a recent volume has been dedicated to the view that "naturalistic research . . . is the only appropriate or suitable way to answer some investigative questions and fulfill certain investigative purposes [Willems & Raush, 1969, p. 3]."
[2] Symbols introduced in the text are defined in *Symbols and Abbreviations*.

The term has a very wide application, but it is not all-inclusive. For example, extrasensory perception is thought by some to be an attribute of human beings, but as it is apparently incapable of reliable measurement (cf. Hansel, 1966), we would not call it a variable. The measurability required of an attribute need not be quantitative. Race, sex, and religion, for example, are variables that are only "qualitatively" measurable. Later in this chapter we will return to a discussion of quantitative and qualitative variables.

Independent Variables

It may be apparent in the illustrative reaction-time experiment that E's interest lies in determining whether the type of stimulus employed, tone or light, has an effect on S's reaction time. The experimental question being asked is: Does, in general, an individual's RT depend on whether the stimulus used is a tone or a light? To answer this question, E systematically manipulates the stimulus presented to S and observes whether S's RT is faster with the light or the tone. Because the *type of stimulus employed* (tone or light) is a variable manipulated by E in order to determine the effects on the aspect of S's behavior in which E is interested (in this case S's RT), it is called an "independent variable."

Note that in the present case E is able to manipulate *directly* the type of stimulus, tone or light, presented to S. However, E may deal with independent variables that he can manipulate only through a selection procedure. As an illustration, suppose E wished to investigate the question, Does the RT of an individual depend on his age? In order to manipulate the variable of interest—age—E would of course select Ss on the basis of their ages, obtaining representation from perhaps 20 to 40 years of age. Age, or more precisely S's age, is a variable manipulated by E by means of selection in order to determine the effects on S's reaction time; it is therefore an independent variable.

In general, then, an independent variable is any variable manipulated by E, either directly or through selection, in order to determine its effects on a behavioral measure (dependent variable).

Because the method of manipulation is, as we have seen, of considerable significance, we want to distinguish between independent variables that are directly manipulated and those that are manipulated through selection. We shall refer to the former as "type-E" (manipulated directly or experimentally) independent variables; those manipulated through a selection procedure we shall refer to as "type-S" independent variables.

Dependent Variables

Any measured behavioral variable of interest in a psychological investigation is called a "dependent variable." In our illustrative experiment, for example, it is clear that S's reaction time is the behavior of interest to E and is subjected to measurement by the latter. Thus, the S's RT is a dependent variable.

The requirement that a dependent variable be a behavioral variable is simply recognition that in psychological research the investigator is always interested in some aspect of the behavior of a living organism. However, the term "behavior" is meant to apply in its most general sense and includes not only overt, directly observable responses, such as reaction time and choice behavior, but also language responses—from which we may infer facts concerning perception, imagery, and similar phenomena—and relevant physiological reactions, such as pulse rate and the galvanic skin response.

By saying that the measured behavioral variable is "of interest" to *E*, we mean, more exactly, that *E*'s concern is in observing the effects of manipulation of the independent variable on the measured behavioral variable. The reason for this requirement is that we do not wish to include as dependent variables all measured behavioral variables.

In summary, a dependent variable is any behavioral variable measured by *E* to assess the effects of a manipulated (independent) variable.

Interdependence of Independent and Dependent Variables

It is clear from the definitions of independent and dependent variables that neither concept is defined independently of the other. One might surmise, therefore, that in the absence of specification of the dependent variable it would not be possible to identify positively the independent variable and vice versa. However, in all but the most poorly conceived research there is little doubt as to the identity of the independent and dependent variables.

There is, on the other hand, good reason for the interdependence of the two definitions. With independent variables, *E* often manipulates certain variables solely for the purpose of control, i.e., to eliminate differential effects of the variables from the research results. In such cases *E* is not at all directly interested in the effects of the manipulated variables on the dependent variable. In our illustrative reaction-time experiment, *E* manipulated the stimulus sequence, that is, the order of presentation of the light and tone. As indicated in the description of the experiment, *E* presented the stimuli in an irregular order until 50 presentations of each stimulus were completed. Suppose *E* first presented the tone on trials 1 to 50 and then the light on trials 51 to 100, adopting this procedure with all *S*s. If it turned out that in general *S*'s *RT* to the light was faster than to the tone, could this result confidently be attributed to differences in the stimuli themselves? Could not the differences in *RT* be assigned as well to the fact that all 50 trials with the light as stimulus came *after* the 50 tone trials and, therefore, had the benefit of any practice effects which might have accumulated over the 50 tone trials? In other terms, had the light stimulus been employed on all 100 trials, it is quite likely that the *RT* on the last 50 trials would have been faster than the *RT* on the first 50 trials, simply because of practice effects. "Order of stimulus presentation," then, is a variable manipulated directly by *E* to control its effects on the experimental results but not to determine its influence on the dependent variable; hence, it is not an independent variable.

The necessity of controlling variables—often through direct manipulation—that might obscure interpretation of the experimental results is an aspect of paramount importance in experimental psychology and will receive detailed treatment later. It is sufficient for present purposes to note that a variable manipulated by E is not classified as an independent variable unless manipulation is for the purpose of observing its effects on the dependent variable.

A complementary situation exists for measured behavioral variables. It sometimes occurs that E will carefully measure a behavioral variable for the one reason of using the data thus obtained for control purposes, for example, to equate groups of subjects for certain characteristics. To illustrate, suppose E wished to determine the effects on the *retention of task* A of learning task B, the latter task being learned *after* task A was acquired. One group of Ss, call it the experimental group, would learn task A, then learn B, and finally be tested on the retention of task A. A second group of Ss, the control group, would also learn task A and, perhaps after a short rest period, be tested on retention of A. The effect of learning task B on the retention of task A would be revealed by comparing the retention scores of the experimental and control groups. Because, in general, the amount *retained* by an individual might vary with the speed with which the individual *learned* the material, E would want to have the experimental and control groups fairly equal with respect to the speed of learning task A. One simple way of accomplishing this is for E to assign the Ss to the two groups *after* all Ss learned task A. He could then assign Ss to the experimental and control groups taking into consideration each S's speed of learning task A.[3]

It is clear that *speed of learning task* A is a measured behavioral variable, but it is also clear that E is not directly concerned with its effect on the dependent variable, retention of task A. Thus, it is not a dependent variable.

Relevant Variables

We have already seen that variables other than the independent variable can exert an effect on the dependent variable. To return to the reaction-time experiment, there are a number of variables, other than order of presentation of the stimuli, whose variation could be expected to affect RT. Intensity of the tone and light stimuli, force required to close the telegraph key, and location of the visual stimulus in the visual field are but a few such variables. However, there are innumerable variables, such as atmospheric pressure and S's income and religion, that within wide limits of variation have no discernible effect on RT.

[3] The terms "experimental group" and "control group" are commonly employed in psychology and related sciences; they are especially applicable to separate-groups-design experiments involving a single independent variable. If in such experiments one group of Ss serves under zero amount of the independent variable or under a value that is in some sense a standard value, it is called the "control group"; the other groups are referred to as "experimental groups." Thus in an experiment involving a drug and a no-drug group, the former is the experimental group and the latter the control group.

The class of variables that have an effect on the dependent variable are called "relevant variables." The class that have no discernible effect on the dependent variable are called "irrelevant variables." The purpose of much psychological research can be described as the classification of independent variables as either relevant or irrelevant variables. The question asked in the reaction-time experiment, for example, could be stated as: Is the type of stimulus, tone or light, a relevant variable with respect to *RT*?

We may now state one of the most critical tasks facing **E**: *the identification and control of all relevant variables operating in the research situation*. This is a challenging and difficult task whose accomplishment in psychological research is usually, to a greater or lesser degree, only approached. The identification and control of relevant variables are topics which receive repeated emphasis in a course in experimental psychology, and, in the present text, they will receive their fair share of attention. A detailed treatment of the historical aspect of this general topic has been presented by Boring (1954).

INTERRELATIONS AMONG RESEARCH APPROACHES, TYPE OF INDEPENDENT VARIABLES, AND RESEARCH SETTINGS

Now that the concepts of independent and dependent variables have been introduced, we return to a more detailed discussion of the three research approaches: observation, correlational research, and experimentation.

Table 1-1 summarizes the results of classifying the three research approaches in terms of the location in which the research takes place (in a natural or a laboratory setting) and the type of independent variables employed (type E, type S, or none). It should be made clear that dichotomizing all research locations into two categories is for purposes of simplicity and is not meant to imply that all laboratory settings permit equally rigorous control over the research being performed. However, once external controls or constraints are brought to bear on the events one is studying, one is no longer conducting research in a natural setting, though the nature of the controls may vary enormously in their extent and in the degree of their rigorousness. Although the dimension of research location could, as indicated, be more faithfully represented by a series of categories rather than only two, the simplification imposed by the dichotomy will not invalidate our conclusions.

Research Employing Type-E Independent Variables

As indicated in the first row of Table 1-1, any research employing *at least one experimentally manipulated independent variable* is classified as experimentation, *irrespective of the research location*. Incorporation of a single type-E independent variable is, therefore, a sufficient condition for experimentation. Of course, the experimentation is likely to be more precise and reliable as the research setting becomes more controlled, but true experimentation can be, and often is, performed under natural conditions.

Table 1-1 Classification of Research Approaches by Research Location and Type of Independent Variables Employed

INDEPENDENT VARIABLES	NATURAL SETTING	LABORATORY SETTING
(1) At least one type E	Experimentation	Experimentation
(2) All type S	Correlational research	Experimentation or correlational research
(3) None	Natural observation	Laboratory observation

Numerous examples of the latter may be furnished from ethology which, like comparative psychology, deals with the objective study of animal behavior. In the following illustration, Tinbergen, the well-known ethologist, investigated the development of brooding behavior in herring gulls by directly manipulating the time at which (artificial) eggs were available to the gulls. However, as so often happens in science, his experiment provided information about an entirely different problem:

> Herring-gulls . . . show a special reaction to food that is too hard to be crushed with the bill; they take it up into the air and drop it. An accident showed us that hardness is the property that releases the reaction in herring-gulls. In order to study the maturation of the incubation drive, I put a wooden egg on the territory of a gull before it had any eggs of its own. Until very shortly before the eggs were laid, the wooden egg did not release brooding behavior. However, in some cases it released feeding responses, and once I observed that a gull, after giving a vigorous peck at the egg, at once took it in its bill, flew up in the characteristic way so commonly observed on the beach, and dropped the egg from a height of about 10 yards . . . (Tinbergen, 1951, pp. 160–161).

A second illustration is taken from psychological research. The general research question was: Are IQ scores of children affected by prenatal nutritional factors? A study several years ago (Harrell, Woodyard, & Gates, 1955) attacked this question by directly manipulating vitamin supplements in the diets of several hundred pregnant women from low-income groups. Four comparable groups of pregnant women were chosen from a maternity clinic in Norfolk, Virginia. Three of the groups had their regular diets supplemented with vitamin pellets (vitamin C, B-1, or B-complex). The fourth group received pellets containing an inert substance (placebos).

Apart from the contents of the pellets, the women received similar treatment, and in their periodic visits to the clinic for routine examinations, they replenished their supply of pellets. When about three years of age, the offspring of these mothers were tested with the Stanford-Binet Intelligence Scale, and a small but highly reliable difference in IQ scores was observed in favor of the children whose mothers had, during pregnancy, received vitamin supplements.

Furthermore, as shown by later testing, this difference in IQ scores was still present at 4 years of age. (A second part of the experiment suggests, however, that such vitamin supplementation has no effect on IQ scores when prenatal diet is naturally adequate.)

It will be noted that in both the preceding examples a type-E independent variable was manipulated—presence of the wooden eggs in the gull's territory and vitamin supplementation of the pregnant women's diets—and the research took place under natural conditions—the herring gulls were not interfered with and the pregnant women's behavior was not modified apart from ingestion of the pellets.

Turning now to research performed in a laboratory situation, it hardly seems necessary to present illustrations of experimentation that result from the use of type-E independent variables in a laboratory setting. For most people this sort of research is the very essence of experimentation. Although the bulk of experimentation probably takes place under such conditions, it should be remembered that important experimental research occurs outside the type-E independent variable–laboratory setting combination.

Research Employing No Independent Variables

Skipping now to the third row of Table 1-1, we see it is clearly possible for research to involve no formally manipulated variables, that is, to involve no independent variables. Such is the case of the researcher who, interested in the mating behavior of gulls, observes them from a distance by the hour in the hope of snatching clues to the important factors underlying their behavior. Such also was the case with our hypothetical researcher who was interested in group leadership behavior of young children (before he introduced an independent variable). Thus we may succinctly define *observation* as *research activity that involves no independent variables*. Observation often serves as a means of detecting promising relevant variables; the next step is the manipulation of these variables, which, depending on the nature of the manipulation, carries the researcher into correlational research or experimentation. Although observation is often identified with research in a natural setting, it is frequently encountered in a laboratory setting and is then called "laboratory observation."

Research Employing All Type-S Independent Variables

IN A NATURAL SETTING. When research employs only type-S independent variables (Table 1-1, second row) and occurs in a natural setting, we classify it as "correlational research." Consider the following research problems:

1. Investigation of the relationship between high school grade averages and scholastic achievement in college
2. Evaluation of the relationship between incidence of schizophrenia in parents and in their offspring

3. Investigation of the relationship between season of the year and incidence of juvenile delinquency

In these examples the independent variables (high school grade average, incidence of schizophrenia in parents, and season of the year) are manipulated through selection, and the research takes place in a natural setting, unrestricted by the researcher. We therefore classify these studies as correlational research. As indicated by the independent variable of the third example (season of the year), type-S independent variables can be variables other than those relating to the subjects of the research, though in psychology they are most often "subject variables."

A special case. A special case of research which employs only type-S independent variables merits our attention. Consider the question, Do people who rate high in "mathematical ability" also tend to rate high in "verbal ability"? To obtain data relevant to this question, one would secure a group of representative subjects and submit each subject to a reasonable test of mathematical ability and to one of verbal ability. If there were a positive relationship between the two variables, people who scored high on one test would, in general, score high on the other, and those who scored low on one test would tend to score low on the other. Now how shall we classify this research? It certainly is not observation, because two variables, mathematical and verbal ability, are manipulated through selection procedures (the psychological tests). But which one is the independent variable and which one is the dependent variable? Certainly, mathematical ability *could* be the independent variable in that the researcher might be interested in observing what happens to verbal ability as mathematical ability is manipulated, as, for example, if the researcher, given the mathematical ability scores of individuals, wished to predict their verbal ability. In this case, verbal ability qualifies as the *dependent* variable, and our definitions are satisfied. But the researcher could just as well be interested in the reverse situation, observing changes in mathematical ability that result from manipulation of verbal ability. With the roles of the two variables reversed, verbal ability and mathematical ability now fulfill our definitions of independent and dependent variables, respectively. We are forced to the conclusion that in certain situations, including the present one, the same variable can serve with equal rationality as an independent or a dependent variable, its role determined by the researcher's point of view. The principle may be stated that *all research involving only variables that qualify with equal appropriateness both as independent and dependent variables is classified as correlational research.* As a matter of fact, correlational research is identified by some with only this last class of research, but as we have seen, it has a much more general application.

Note that in the earlier illustrations duality in the roles of the variables was not a problem; e.g., high school grade average, incidence of schizophrenia in parents, and season of the year do not qualify as dependent variables.

IN A LABORATORY SETTING. We now arrive at the one set of circumstances where classification is equivocal: namely, where the research employs only type-S independent variables and takes place in a laboratory setting (Table 1-1, second row). The problem may be highlighted by an example.

Using a highly controlled laboratory situation, D'Amato and Jagoda (1960) studied how simple discrimination learning in rats was affected by three independent variables: age, sex, and rearing conditions. Each animal was reared from weaning either alone or with a single cage-mate. Now, age and sex are clearly type-S independent variables, but because of the third variable, which was manipulated directly, we would classify the research as experimentation.[4] However, suppose that the third variable had not been included in the study. The research would have then involved type-S independent variables alone. Still it would seem quite arbitrary and artificial to classify this study as correlational research, in view of the fact that intuitively the research retains much of its "experimental" character, even after deletion of the one type-E independent variable. There are two reasons for our intuitive preference to classify this study as experimentation rather than correlational research. First, the research setting is a highly controlled laboratory situation. Second, the type-S independent variables employed, age and sex, enjoy a high degree of precision in their manipulation. Very little error is involved in manipulating age (for example, an animal claimed to be 90 days old might actually be 89 to 91 days old), and none at all in manipulating sex (it is virtually impossible for an experienced E to mis-sex an adult rat). The guiding principle, then, is that research utilizing only type-S independent variables may nevertheless be classified as experimentation when it takes place within a well-controlled laboratory setting and when the type-S independent variables allow for very little error of manipulation.

We may summarize the preceding criteria of classification as follows:

1. Observation is research that involves no independent variables; it is called either natural observation or laboratory observation depending on whether the observation takes place in a natural or laboratory setting.

2. All research involving at least one type-E independent variable is

[4] It is interesting to observe that the independent variable *rearing condition* could also be manipulated by selection. Imagine that our animals' caretaker, in assigning newly weaned infant rats to cages, performed his task somewhat indifferently, housing some animals alone and others in pairs. Suppose that, wishing to investigate the rearing variable, we took advantage of the caretaker's small dereliction and chose (selected) as Ss for our study a group of animals reared alone and a group raised in pairs. Clearly, we would then be dealing with a type-S independent variable, because manipulation is not direct but rather occurs through a selection procedure. With respect to the three differences between type-E and type-S independent variables discussed earlier, the major advantage of direct manipulation over selection is, in the present instance, that it is easier to avoid *concomitant manipulation* of potentially relevant variables. For example, suppose that unknown to us the caretaker had developed the habit of housing aggressive animals alone, pairing off the more timid rats. Consequently, in manipulating rearing condition, we would also unwittingly be manipulating aggressiveness or "fearfulness."

classified as experimentation and constitutes the bulk and body of experimental research.

3. All research employing only type-S independent variables in a natural setting is considered correlational research.

4. All research making use of only variables that with equal appropriateness qualify both as independent and dependent variables is also classified as correlational research.

5. Research employing only type-S variables in a laboratory setting may be classified as experimentation or correlational research depending on the rigorousness of the laboratory situation and the degree of error involved in the manipulation of the independent variables.

It is not difficult to generalize and apply the preceding concepts to research in sciences other than psychology. We need only adjust our interpretation of that portion of the definition of dependent variables that reads: *a dependent variable is . . . any behavioral variable measured by* **E**. *Behavioral variable* would simply be interpreted as any variable relating to the appropriate behavioral aspects of the objects or things with which the science deals. Psychology, then, is the special case in which the "objects" are living, usually higher, organisms and the "appropriate behavioral aspects" encompass such processes as sensing, perceiving, and learning. Within this generalization, research in astronomy is largely, if not solely, correlational because its independent variables cannot at present be manipulated directly and the events which it studies are as yet incapable of being controlled or constrained in any way by **E**; that is, its research occurs in a natural setting. Physics and chemistry, however, are among those sciences whose accomplishments in recent times form the foundation of the widespread faith in the power and efficacy of experimentation.

CLASSIFICATION OF VARIABLES

It will be recalled that a variable was very generally defined as any measurable attribute of objects, things, or beings. Despite the requirement of measurability, the inclusion of such qualitative variables as sex, race, and religion was specifically noted. The purpose of this section is to clarify the distinction between *qualitative* and *quantitative* variables and to consider the subdivision of the latter into *continuous* and *discrete* variables.

Qualitative and Quantitative Variables

In psychology, qualitative variables often relate to aspects or properties of the organisms under study, for example, species and strain membership in animals and race, religion, occupation, and personality classification in humans. Qualitative variables are, however, also encountered elsewhere. A qualitative stimulus variable was employed in the reaction-time experiment described earlier, namely, type of stimulus presented S, tone or light. The essential feature of qualitative variables is that they are composed of categories which do not bear a quantitative relationship (one of magnitude) to each other. Or, what is essentially the same thing, the categories of a qualitative variable do not lie on a dimension that lets us make such statements as "Category A possesses a greater magnitude of the variable than category B." Thus, for example, a researcher studying how emotionality and strain membership are related in rats has strain membership (for example, Wistar strain versus Sprague-Dawley) as his independent variable, the separate categories of which cannot be placed into an order based on magnitude. It is meaningless to assert that the Wistars have more "strain membership" than the Sprague-Dawleys, or that Catholics have greater "religious denomination" than Mohammedans. We therefore define *qualitative variables* as *those variables composed of categories which cannot be ordered with respect to magnitude*.

Quantitative variables, on the other hand, always refer to attributes of objects or things which embody magnitude as an essential characteristic; therefore, questions relating to "how much" make sense with these variables. Thus age, intelligence, number of trials to learn an experimental task, and intensity of an auditory stimulus are all quantitative variables because individuals may vary in magnitude of age, intelligence, and number of trials to learn a specific task, and an auditory stimulus can differ in the magnitude of its intensity. In summary, *any variable that can be ordered with respect to magnitude is a quantitative variable*.

Needless to say, quantitative variables are preferred in scientific work for the simple reason that they lend themselves to much more precise and fruitful measurement than qualitative variables. There is, in addition, little explanatory power in qualitative variables. When a qualitative independent variable influences a quantitative dependent variable, one quite naturally seeks to attribute the effect on the latter to a quantitative variable that is somehow associated with the manipulated qualitative variable. To illustrate, it is well established that reaction time to sound is usually faster than reaction time to light. One possible interpretation of this result is that sound stimuli activate their receptors in the cochlea faster than light stimuli excite their corresponding receptors in the retina (rods and cones) because relatively slow photochemical processes are involved in the latter (Woodworth & Schlosberg, 1954, p. 18). Thus, differences in RT brought about by manipulation of a qualitative independent variable, type of stimulus, are explained by referring to differences in an associated quantitative variable, time to excite the respective receptors.

Continuous and Discrete Variables

Quantitative variables are separable into *continuous* and *discrete* variables, the majority of quantitative variables in psychology falling in the former category. A continuous variable may be defined as *a quantitative variable which can be measured* (i.e., ordered with respect to magnitude) *with an arbitrary degree of fineness*, usually depending only on the precision of the available measuring instrument. Reaction time is plainly a continuous variable; it can be measured with any degree of fineness or exactness that one chooses, subject only to the limitations of the currently available measuring tools. At one time, because of the limitations of the then existing instruments, *RT* could be measured at best in milliseconds; today, if required, it could be measured in microseconds, a thousandfold reduction in the size of the measuring unit.

Consider, however, number of siblings as a variable. This is a discrete variable because no amount of refinement of measuring instruments or techniques can produce a value of, say, $2\frac{1}{2}$ children. Similarly, the number of digits that can be immediately recalled, as well as the number of heads obtained in 10 tosses of a coin, are also discrete variables. As a general rule, in psychology discrete variables are variables *whose values are obtained by counting*, so that the specification of the variable normally begins with "the number of." One must be careful, though, to distinguish between the basic nature of the quantitative variable in question and the means by which it is measured. For example, level of achievement in a college algebra course can be measured by the number of items correctly answered on a final examination. Clearly, the underlying variable, level of achievement in the course, is a continuous variable, even though it is measured by the *number* of items correctly answered on a final examination. In fact, the physical measurement of all continuous variables can be interpreted to involve counting. Age, height, and weight, all of which are continuous variables, are often measured in terms of the number of months of age, the number of inches in height, and the number of pounds of weight. But unlike true discrete variables, the measurement of these variables can be refined almost endlessly so that, if one wished, their measurement could be in terms of the number of days of age, the number of hundredths of an inch in height, and the number of grams of weight.

In summary, all variables in psychology may be classified as either *qualitative* or *quantitative*. Qualitative variables are composed of categories that cannot be ordered with respect to magnitude. Quantitative variables, in contrast, do lend themselves to ordering with respect to magnitude. Quantitative variables may be classified into those that can be measured with an arbitrary degree of fineness and those that cannot. The former quantitative variables are called *continuous* variables; the latter, *discrete* variables. It follows that type-E independent variables may be qualitative, continuous, or discrete variables, and the same holds true for type-S independent variables. Dependent variables are sometimes qualitative, as often found in studies involving personality projective tests, though most often they are quantitative, in particular, continuous, variables.

OPERATIONAL DEFINITION OF VARIABLES

The purpose of this section is to point out that descriptions of variables, independent and dependent, can vary widely in their degree of generality. To illustrate, suppose *E*, employing a separate-groups design, performs an experiment in which hungry rats run down an alleyway at the end of which they find food in a goal box. One group of rats always finds a single food pellet in the goal box, a second group finds two pellets on all trials, and a third group, four pellets. The experimenter is interested in how speed of running is affected by the number of food pellets that *S* finds in the goal box.

The independent variable of this study may be described in several different ways. "Number of food pellets" is a reasonable description, but "amount of food reward" and even "amount of reward" are also possibilities. Note that these descriptions differ in their generality. When *E* varies number of food pellets, he is of course varying amount of food reward; but, and this is the important point, he could have manipulated amount of food reward by means other than varying the number of food pellets, for example, by varying the concentration of a sucrose solution. Amount of reward is a still more general description of the independent variable, including, as it does, manipulations of amount of food reward, water reward, and any other commodity which could serve as a reward for rats.

To distinguish descriptions which are couched in terms of the actual operations performed by *E* from other, more general, descriptions, we refer to the former as "operationally defined," or more briefly, "operational" independent variables. Thus number of food pellets is the operational independent variable in the previous illustration. Of course one can argue that even this definition contains a residue of generality, because food pellets can differ in composition, size, etc. Although a more precise operational definition would specify the latter properties of the food pellets, experience is often a reasonable guide as to which properties can be safely ignored.

In most cases *E*'s interest lies less in operationally defined independent (and dependent) variables than in generalizations thereof. In the previous example, *E*'s concern might be how *amount of reward* influences behavior in the runway. Although much psychological research is stimulated by hunches or hypotheses about relationships between independent and dependent variables defined in general terms, to submit such hypotheses to empirical tests one must resort to operationally defined variables. Ordinarily the transition from a generally defined variable to its operationally defined counterpart presents little difficulty. What does present a major problem is showing that different operationally defined realizations of the same variable act in a reasonably consistent way. To cite one illustration, there are several ways of operationally defining *hunger drive:* for example, hours of food deprivation, maintaining a certain percentage of free-feeding body weight, and the use of drugs. The effects of these various methods of manipulating hunger drive on behavior are, however, by no means equivalent.

It is not our purpose here to pursue this very critical problem. It is sufficient to realize that different levels of description of independent and dependent variables exist and to note the level of generality of the independent and dependent variables encountered.

SUMMARY

The summary of this chapter and later chapters is left to the student, although a guiding outline is provided. It is important that the student complete the summary, not only because it serves as an informal test of his grasp of the chapter's content, but also because the summaries will later provide a convenient means of review.

1. Psychological research may be subdivided into two interrelated categories:

2. The first category consists of two major activities:

3. Within the second category three major research approaches may be distinguished:

4. (a) A *variable* is defined as:
(b) *To manipulate a variable* means:

5. A *relevant variable* is defined as:

6. An *independent variable* is defined as:

7. (a) A *type-E independent variable* is:
(b) A *type-S independent variable* is:

8. Three advantages that type-E independent variables often have over type-S independent variables are:

9. (a) Single-group designs differ from separate-groups designs as follows:
(b) The illustrative reaction-time experiment is an example of:

10. A *dependent variable* is defined as:

11. When research is classified in terms of the nature of the independent variables employed and the research location, five criteria result by means of which we may assign a given piece of research to one of the three major research approaches. These five criteria are:

12. All variables are either qualitative or quantitative.
(a) *Qualitative variables* are defined as:
(b) *Quantitative variables* are defined as:

13. Quantitative variables may be either discrete or continuous.
(a) The definition of discrete variables is:
(b) The definition of continuous variables is:

14. Operationally defined independent and dependent variables are:

2 CONTROL OF RELEVANT VARIABLES

THREE TYPES OF CONTROL TECHNIQUES

As stated in Chap. 1, the identification and control of relevant variables are two of the most critical tasks confronting the researcher and, in particular, the experimenter. Although the control of known or potentially relevant variables is often not difficult to accomplish, their identification frequently requires insight and ingenuity. This is not to say that methods of controlling relevant variables are cut-and-dried. Quite the contrary. What constitutes an adequate control group is a topic frequently debated (e.g., Church, 1964; Rescorla, 1967; Seligman, 1969; Solomon & Lessac, 1968). Still, there are a number of control techniques that are reasonably well formulated whereas the matter of detecting unrecognized relevant variables rests entirely with the experimenter's perceptiveness.

The reason the experimenter wishes to control known and potentially relevant variables is clear. (To avoid repetition, the term "relevant variables" will refer to both relevant and *potentially* relevant variables.) The goal of all experimental research is to determine how the independent variable of the study affects the dependent variable. In the ideal case, all relevant variables are held constant throughout the experiment and only the independent variable varies. The experimenter may then be confident that the variations in the dependent variable that accompany his manipulations of the independent variable are a result of the effects of the latter and not a result of any extraneous variables. In psychological experimentation, rarely, if ever, can all important relevant variables be held constant; thus, other methods of control must be employed.

Most control measures fall into one of three general types of control techniques: *matching; randomizing* (or *randomization*); and *counterbalancing.* Each of these three general methods receives detailed treatment later. But at the moment let us note an important and fundamental difference between matching and randomizing techniques. With matching techniques the experimenter obtains full control of the relevant variable *for the particular experiment being performed; control is achieved by equalization of the effects of the relevant variable over all values of the independent variable of the study.* With randomizing techniques, in contrast, the controlled relevant variable might not, due to chance fluctuations, be well equated in a particular experiment, especially if the number of Ss involved is small. But good equalization *over the long run* (over a very large number of Ss or over a series of experiments) is guaranteed. Counterbalancing techniques, it turns out, can provide either type of control, equalization of the effects of the relevant variable in the single experiment or over the long run.

In brief, then, control techniques aim to equalize the effects that the relevant variable has on the dependent variable, and this equalization is achieved for the single experiment or over the long run.

USING A TABLE OF RANDOM DIGITS

Randomization has been indicated as one of three general types of control techniques. Because its application often involves the use of a table of "random digits" (also called a table of "random numbers") and because knowledge of the proper use of such tables is valuable for an understanding of the randomization technique itself, we now discuss this topic.

Everyone has had the experience of basing a decision between two alternatives on a toss of a coin. In tossing the coin, the decision is left to "chance"; more precisely, the two decisions are made equally likely, or equally probable. In most experimental situations, the necessity of leaving certain decisions to chance also arises, but because the number of decisions involved is often large, the tossing of a coin would be slow and inefficient. This is where a table of random digits enters. By use of such a table, necessary assignments—for example, assignment of subjects to groups—can be put on a chance (random) basis.

Suppose, more specifically, that we wish to determine which set of instructions, A, B, or C, leads to faster solution of a problem-solving task, and we have available a list of 60 subjects for the experiment, 20 of whom are to be tested under each of the instructions. The question arises: Which 20 subjects (Ss) shall be assigned to receive instruction A, which 20 shall be assigned to instruction B, and which 20 to instruction C? Would it do, for example, to assign the first 20 Ss on the list to instruction A? Obviously not—because the more eager, hence presumably more motivated, Ss might have been first to put their names on the list. Suppose, instead, the first subject on the list is assigned to instruction A, the second to B, and the third to C, and this order is repeated for the fourth, fifth, and sixth Ss, and so on through the list. This is by far a better method than the previous one, and in many cases it is an acceptable procedure. However, assigning each S to one of the instructions *at random* is often a more valid method, and because it is a simple technique to employ, its use ought to be routine in all cases such as the present one.

Table A in the Appendix is composed of nothing but digits, arranged in groups of five. These digits, however, have the special property of being *randomly selected*. This means that they were selected by a process which ensured that the likelihood of a 9 occurring in any position was exactly the same as the likelihood of a 4 occurring, or a 3 or a 5, or indeed any of the other digits, and this likelihood or probability is 0.10. Note, for example, that the group of five digits occupying the first row and columns 00 to 04 is 83474. The process that generated these digits was such that every digit had the same likelihood of being the first digit on the page; actually the digit 8 was selected. Again, all digits were equally likely to be selected next, and a 3 was selected. This process of random selection was repeated over and over again, generating all the digits in the table. Hence, the table of digits is called a table of random digits or random numbers. The arrangement of the digits into groups of five is simply for convenience in using the table.

Returning to the problem at hand, random assignment of the 60 Ss to the three instructions, A, B, and C, would proceed as follows. First, let the digit 1 stand for the instruction A, the digit 2 for instruction B, and 3 for C. Then, starting with the very first digit in the table, 8, assignments are made in accordance with the digits that occur in the first column of the table. Because 8 is not a digit that is relevant to the problem, we look down to the next digit in the column which, being zero, is again not relevant. The next digit in the column is 1, and this means that the first S on the list is assigned to instruction A. The next digit, 8, is again not relevant, and the next, 3, signifies that the second S on the list is assigned to instruction C. The third S on the list is assigned to instruction A, as is the fourth, because the next two relevant digits are both 1. This process is repeated until 20 Ss have been assigned to one of the three instructions. (When the end of a column of digits is reached, assignment is continued from the top of the next column.) From that point on, the unallotted Ss are assigned to the two remaining instructions, until a second instruction reaches its quota of 20 Ss. Then, of course, the assignment is complete because any remaining Ss must be assigned to the last of the three instructions.

If two digits were required for assignments, as would be the case if there were 11 or more different sets of instructions in the experiment, one can construct two-digit random numbers from any two adjacent columns of digits. Thus the digits in columns 00 and 01 or 01 and 02 provide random numbers running between 00 and 99. Three-digit random numbers can be obtained from any three adjacent columns of random digits, and so on.

One refinement remains. You will use the limited table in your book repeatedly. Would it be valid in using the table always to start at the same place, say at the first row and column? Such a procedure you may guess is not advisable because it would invalidate, in part, the randomness assumed for separate assignments. This requirement may be satisfied in some measure by making the point at which the table is entered itself a random process, as, for example, entering the table at the row and column specified by 2 two-digit numbers drawn from the table.

Randomness among separate assignments can be further facilitated by varying the method by which successive random numbers are chosen. Thus from the starting point, one may proceed up and down columns, working either from right to left or from left to right, across rows, working downward at times and upward at other times.

The reason for such meticulousness is that the observance of strict randomness in the processes of random selection is an essential requirement of the statistical analyses that are widely used to evaluate experimental results. If a list were compiled of the research results that have been contaminated by violations of the requirements of random selection, it would be long indeed. [See Underwood (1957b, pp. 93–96) for several examples of such infractions.]

THREE CLASSES OF RELEVANT VARIABLES

In the opening paragraphs of this chapter, three types of control techniques were discussed, namely, matching, randomization, and counterbalancing. The purpose of the present section is to identify three major classes of relevant variables whose control is an important consideration in every psychological experiment. The balance of this chapter will be devoted to a discussion of how relevant variables from each of the three classes can be brought under control by methods from one or more of the three types of control techniques.

There are many feasible ways of classifying the innumerable relevant variables (RVs) that can occur in psychological experiments. It will prove convenient for our purposes to classify them in terms of where they originate. Thus, we distinguish three major classes of RVs: (1) those that arise from characteristics of the subjects of the experiment; (2) those emanating from within the experimental situation itself; and (3) those that occur whenever the subject is observed under more than one condition, i.e., those having to do with sequence effects. The major problem then becomes one of devising control techniques for the *RV*s arising from these three sources. These relevant variables may conveniently be referred to as (1) subject relevant variables, (2) situational relevant variables, and (3) sequence relevant variables. A further description of each of these three classes of *RV*s follows.

Subject Relevant Variables

In Chap. 1 a distinction was drawn between type-S and type-E independent variables, and it will be recalled that the former independent variables were manipulated through selection procedures whereas the latter were directly or experimentally manipulated. This distinction may be generalized to variables other than independent variables. Thus, one may speak of type-S and type-E subject relevant variables, or of type-S and type-E situational relevant variables. Type-S subject relevant variables are those relevant variables arising from the subject that are manipulated by means of selection procedures. Doubtless they include the vast majority of important subject *RV*s: age, sex, race, religion, occupation, intelligence, aptitudes, personality classification, and phylogenetic membership. Type-E subject relevant variables are *RV*s relating to characteristics of the subject which are *directly* manipulable. As an illustration of the latter, S's motivation is a subject *RV* of some importance and can sometimes be directly manipulated as, for example, through instructions given to S by the experimenter. When so manipulated, this variable qualifies as a type-E subject relevant variable. As it turns out, there are comparatively few type-E subject relevant variables, and therefore they are infrequently encountered. (Type-E subject variables are more frequently met as *independent* variables.)

It will simplify matters to include within the category of subject *RV*s only subject variables of the type-S variety, subsuming the type-E subject relevant variables under situational relevant variables. Apart from the organizational simplification which it permits, this arrangement is reasonable because the appearance of a type-E subject relevant variable may be attributed in most cases to manipulation of some aspect of the experimental situation, being therefore directly related to a situational *RV*.

Situational Relevant Variables

Included under this heading are (1) all environmental variables operating in the experimental situation, (2) most variables having to do with the experimental task facing the subject, and (3) all type-E subject relevant variables.

The environmental variables include all physical aspects of the experimental situation, e.g., temperature, humidity, noise and lighting level, and time of day. Another aspect of the experimental environment that contains an important source of situational *RV*s is the experimenter himself. Rosenthal (1966) has devoted an entire text to the problem of identifying the effects of the experimenter in behavioral research and to describing measures for their evaluation and control.

"Task" variables refer to the innumerable relevant variables that are associated with the behavioral task presented the subject, including many physical aspects of the apparatus employed and most features of the task procedures. Type-E subject relevant variables have already been discussed, and, as mentioned, S's motivational "set" induced by instructions from the experimenter is an example of such variables.

Sequence Relevant Variables

It is convenient to classify separately all relevant variables in the experimental situation that have to do with sequence effects, i.e., RVs that arise when Ss are tested under two or more conditions of the experiment (not necessarily different values of the independent variable). Since S is exposed to two or more conditions in sequence, it is quite possible that such factors as adaptation, practice effects, and fatigue—examples of sequence relevant variables—will affect S's performance under one condition more than under another, because of the different ordinal positions that the conditions occupy in the sequence. As an example, the first condition in a sequence is likely to profit least from practice effects. Sequence RVs such as those listed are subject to control by counterbalancing techniques.

SOME GENERAL METHODOLOGICAL CONSIDERATIONS

Before turning to a detailed consideration of how the three types of control techniques relate to the control of the three classes of relevant variables, we wish to comment on a few matters of general methodological significance.

Single-group versus Separate-groups Designs

Recall from Chap. 1 that in handling the independent variable, two fundamentally different types of experimental designs exist, namely, single-group (or within-subjects) and separate-groups (between-subjects) designs. In single-group designs a single group of Ss serves under *all* values of the independent variable; in separate-groups designs a separate group of Ss serves under *each* of the values of the independent variable. The earlier definitions, introduced before the development of the concept of variables, made reference to serving under "conditions of the research" rather than under "values of the independent variable."

In recent years it has become clear that this distinction can have more than methodological significance; it can exert a profound influence on the type of empirical relationships obtained. In some cases a given independent variable has a more pronounced effect when manipulated in single-group designs than when manipulated in separate-groups designs, which may actually fail to show the independent variable under study to be effective. The range of situations over which this disparity has been noted is wide, running from the influence of reward magnitude on the strength of secondary reinforcers in rats (e.g., D'Amato, 1955) to the effect of stimulus intensity on eyelid conditioning in human Ss (Grice & Hunter, 1964).[1] To cite another example, monkeys' performance on visual discrimination tasks has been shown to be more sensitive to reward magnitude when manipulated within a single-group-design paradigm than when a separate-groups design is employed (Schrier, 1958).

There are a number of instances, moreover, in which the form of an empirical relationship is reversed under the two types of experimental designs. D'Amato, Lachman, and Kivy (1958) found that a partial reinforcement acquisition schedule resulted in a stronger or weaker secondary reinforcer than a continuous reinforcement schedule in accordance with whether a separate-groups or a single-group design was employed. The partial reinforcement effect itself (the greater resistance to extinction of partially reinforced Ss as compared to continuously reinforced Ss—see Chap. 7) may be reversed when a single-group design is employed (e.g., Pavlik, Carlton, Lehr, & Hendrickson, 1967).

The obvious point of these examples is that empirical relationships are not independent of the type of experimental designs employed in their investigation. This fact must be kept in mind both in designing research and evaluating research results. [See Grice (1966) for a recent discussion of this point.]

That we do not necessarily obtain the same results when S is exposed to one value of the independent variable as when he experiences two or more values should come as no surprise. In the latter case S has a chance to make comparisons among the different values of the independent variable presented him, and such processes as contrast effects (Chap. 7) and related perceptual processes come into play which are not likely to be significant within separate-groups designs.

SINGLE-SUBJECT DESIGNS. There is a special case of single-group designs that deserves mention here. In some experimental situations it is possible to expose an individual S to all values of the independent variable in such a manner that the effects of the independent variable may be evaluated separately for each subject. In a sense, each subject constitutes a replication of the entire experiment. This extremely powerful design is referred to as a "single-subject" design. Later, in our discussion of the control of sequence RVs, we shall have more to say about such designs.

Experimental versus Statistical Designs

The results of most experiments in psychology require statistical analysis of some kind for their evaluation and interpretation. For this reason *experimental*

---

[1] A "secondary" or "conditioned" reinforcer is a stimulus situation whose reinforcing ability —capacity to *strengthen* behavior—is established by past learning, in particular by pairing the secondary reinforcer with primary reinforcement—such as food and water (see Wike's [1966] and Hendry's [1969] recent volumes on the topic).

design and *statistical design* go hand in hand in experimental psychology; **E** must be on guard that the experimental design of his experiment is such that the data resulting from the study can be properly analyzed by appropriate statistical techniques. A separate-groups experimental design, for example, requires a different type of statistical design than that required by a single-group design.[2] More to the problem at hand, the type of control technique employed frequently has implications for the kinds of statistical designs that are appropriate. It is possible to discuss each control technique in conjunction with its appropriate statistical designs, but this approach requires much more knowledge of statistics than the student in introductory experimental psychology is likely to have. Hence, although the ensuing discussion of control techniques will be free of complementary statistics, illustrations of appropriate statistical designs will be given in occasional parenthetical notes, which may be skipped without loss of continuity.

The student should not get the impression from this chapter that all experimental research is carefully planned to the smallest detail. True enough, when the aims of an experiment are clear in advance or when substantial numbers of subjects are involved—as is usually the case in separate-groups techniques— the experimental design to be employed should be carefully thought out in advance. Often, however, particularly in "exploratory" research, an experimenter will grope his way through an experiment, changing strategy as the data come in. The results of one phase of the experiment may suggest modifications or a change in direction which could not have been anticipated earlier. Such research is often fruitful and exciting. In some cases, because of the nature of the research, certain variables, particularly sequence *RV*s, may not have been adequately controlled, and in order to feel confident about the obtained results, a follow-up study may be necessary. In others, the data may be sufficiently consistent across **S**s to be persuasive without immediate confirmation. But even "free-wheeling" research profits from an appreciation of the kinds of confounding of experimental results that can arise from uncontrolled *RV*s. Knowledge of the nature of the latter and the means to control them helps **E** to anticipate, recognize, and perhaps remedy contamination from this source.

Control of Relevant Variables in Experiments Employing a Single Independent Variable

The discussion thus far has been restricted to research involving a single independent variable. It is apparent, however, that within a single experiment or a single piece of research, two, three, or even several independent variables may be studied simultaneously. In fact, the multiple-independent-variable study is

---

[2] Although we have used the terms "within-subjects" and "between-subjects" designs as equivalents of single-group and separate-groups designs, respectively, a distinction is possible on the basis that the latter apply to *experimental* designs whereas the former apply to the corresponding *statistical* designs. Inasmuch as our emphasis is on experimental designs, we shall favor the "single-group, separate-groups" terminology.

the rule rather than the exception in psychological experimentation. Nevertheless, the basic techniques of control are best discussed and illustrated within the context of experiments involving a single independent variable. This is the procedure we shall adopt, deferring consideration of the multiple-independent-variable experiment until the final sections of the chapter.

The discussion will proceed by considering how control of each of the three classes of relevant variables (subject, situational, and sequence RVs) is managed for the single-group and separate-groups designs. The resulting organizational arrangement is shown in Table 2-1, which may be considered a summary table of much of what follows in this chapter. It will be observed that listed in the first column of Table 2-1 are the three classes of relevant variables to be controlled. The control techniques (matching, randomizing, or counterbalancing) that are appropriate for each class of relevant variables are indicated in one column for separate-groups designs and in another for single-group designs.

Table 2-1 Classification of Control Techniques According to Class of Relevant Variables Controlled and Type of Experimental Design Employed

CLASS OF RVS	SEPARATE–GROUPS DESIGN	SINGLE–GROUP DESIGN
Subject (type S)	1. Matched groups (a) Hold the RV constant over all values of the independent variable. (b) Equate the RV over all values of the independent variable. 2. Randomized groups	These RVs are automatically controlled.
Situational	1. Matched conditions (a) Hold the RV constant over all values of the independent variable. (b) Equate the RV over all values of the independent variable. 2. Randomized conditions	Same techniques apply.
Sequence	These RVs do not arise with respect to the independent variable. Where they do occur, however, the same techniques apply.	1. Intrasubject counterbalancing 2. Intragroup counterbalancing (a) Complete counterbalancing (b) Incomplete counterbalancing (c) Randomized counterbalancing

CONTROL OF SUBJECT RELEVANT VARIABLES

Consider the following experiment. We wish to determine whether reaction time, as in the simple key-pressing task described in Chap. 1, is influenced by the intensity of the stimulus employed, a tone. Three tonal stimuli, I_1, I_2, and I_3, of increasing intensity but otherwise identical are to be used in the experiment. If the intensity of the stimulus affects reaction time, presumably RT will be fastest when I_3, the most intense stimulus, serves as the stimulus, slowest when I_1 is the stimulus, and of an intermediate value when the stimulus is I_2. (There are reasons for believing that the reverse relationship is unlikely.) It is easily recognized that the independent variable of the experiment, intensity of the tonal stimulus, is a type-E independent variable and, furthermore, is of a nature that permits employment of either a single-group or a separate-groups design. First we consider how subject RVs are controlled in separate-groups designs.

Control of Subject *RV*s in Separate-groups Designs

Because in the present type of design, a separate group of Ss serves under each value of the independent variable, three groups of Ss are required for the reaction-time experiment, one group to be tested under each of the three values of the independent variable. For identification these groups are called Group I_1, Group I_2, and Group I_3.

1. MATCHED GROUPS

(**a**) *Hold the RV Constant over All Values of the Independent Variable.* One means of controlling subject *RV*s is by matching techniques, i.e., by matched groups. As may be seen in Table 2-1, there are two ways of matching groups, the first of which is to hold the relevant variable in question constant over all values of the independent variable. To illustrate, because sex has been found to be an *RV* in studies of reaction time (Woodworth & Schlosberg, 1954, p. 36), one simply could use only males in the preceding *RT* experiment, thereby equalizing the effect of this *RV* over all values of the independent variable (I_1, I_2, and I_3). Similarly, age, a continuous variable, could be held virtually constant by choosing as Ss only individuals between the ages of 21 and 22. The technique of controlling *RV*s of this class by holding them constant over all values of the independent variable is widely employed and very useful; however, there are two drawbacks.

The first is that experimental Ss often become difficult to obtain because the restrictions that apply preclude their efficient utilization. For example, if the two preceding subject *RV*s were controlled as indicated, the Ss would have to consist only of males between the ages of 21 and 22 years, which might seriously limit the pool of reasonably accessible subjects.

Interaction of variables. The second disadvantage is more subtle and of considerable theoretical significance. Suppose that the reaction-time experiment were conducted with the sex and age variables controlled by employing only male Ss 21 to 22 years of age. Suppose further that the expected relationship between the independent variable and the dependent variable emerged, that is, *RT* decreased as the intensity of the tonal stimulus increased. The difficult question now arises: To what extent can this result be generalized? Does the same relationship between *RT* and intensity of the tonal stimulus hold for *females* of that age? Or for 40-year-old males? In the present case there are reasons to believe that the general form of the relationship, i.e., decreased *RT* with increased intensity of tonal stimulation, will apply to females and to age levels other than 21 to 22 years. Unfortunately, however, there are many other instances in psychology where the relationship between an independent variable and a dependent variable has turned out to depend on the particular value at which a subject *RV* happened to have been held constant. For example, the strain of rats used as experimental Ss, a subject *RV* almost always controlled by being held constant, has been shown more than once to influence the type of relationship obtained between an independent and a dependent variable (e.g., Myers, 1959). When the nature of the relationship between an independent variable, V_1, and a dependent variable turns out to be different for different values of a second variable, V_2 (which may be an *RV* or a second independent variable), there is an "interaction" between variables V_1 and V_2. If, for example, it turned out that the expected relationship between *RT* and intensity of the tonal stimulus was obtained for males, but a reverse relationship was observed for females (*RT increased* with increased stimulus intensity), we would say that, with respect to *RT*, an interaction existed between intensity of the tonal stimulus and sex.

Thus, although controlling a relevant variable by holding it constant (the classical method of the physical sciences) has much to recommend it, one must keep in mind the limitations that the method might entail for the generalization of experimental results. Or, to phrase this somewhat differently, one must guard against the possibility of interaction between the independent variable of the experiment and the *RV* controlled by this method. Such interactions may arise from any of the three classes of relevant variables.

(When control of subject *RV*s is by the above procedure, a single, undifferentiated, group of Ss serves under each of the values of the independent variable, for example, Groups I_1, I_2, and I_3 in the *RT* experiment. Granting that certain statistical assumptions can be met, an appropriate statistical design for determining whether the independent variable has an effect on the dependent variable is the well-known *one-way analysis of variance*. This design, described in most statistical textbooks, is applicable to any number of groups of Ss, i.e., to any number of values of the independent variable. When only two groups of Ss are involved, the one-way analysis of variance is closely related to the widely used "*t* test.")

(**b**) *Equate the RV over All Values of the Independent Variable.* By equating the subject *RV* over all values of the independent variable rather than holding

Table 2-2 Equating Sex over All Values of the Independent Variable (Percents)

SUBJECTS	GROUP I_1	GROUP I_2	GROUP I_3
Males	50	50	50
Females	50	50	50

it constant, one may equalize the effect of the RV on the dependent variable and at the same time evaluate whether it interacts with the independent variable. One equates a subject RV by assigning two or more values of the RV in the same respective percentages, or proportions, over all values of the independent variable. In the preceding RT experiment, for example, the sex variable could be equated by having Groups I_1, I_2, and I_3 consist of 50 percent males and 50 percent females (Table 2-2). Other percentages may be used, e.g., 40 percent males and 60 percent females, but the respective percentages should be the same for all groups of Ss, that is, for all values of the independent variable. It may be apparent from Table 2-2 that the "equating" method equalizes the effects of sex on the dependent variable in much the same way as the method of holding the RV constant. The difference is that in the equating method, the RV is, so to speak, held constant at more than one of its values. In the present context, this method has the advantage that by comparing the relationship obtained between the independent and dependent variables for males with that obtained for females, one can determine whether these differ, that is, determine whether or not sex interacts with the intensity of tonal stimulus.

Now consider age which, unlike sex, is a continuous variable. It too can be controlled by the equating technique. To achieve this type of control with a RV that is continuous, one merely establishes arbitrary *levels* of the variable. In the present case two age levels might be employed, for example, 21 to 22, and 41 to 42 years of age. Assuming that only males were used in the RT experiment, 50 percent of the Ss in each of the three groups would be drawn from the first age level and 50 percent from the second level, though other percentages are permissible. As many levels of the RV as deemed necessary may be employed, and the range encompassed by the individual levels may be relatively narrow, as in the present illustration, or rather wide, for example, 21 to 25 years of age. The important facts are that by so equating the age variable, (1) the effect of this RV on the dependent variable is equalized for the several values of the independent variable and (2) the effects of the independent variable on the dependent variable can be separately determined for the different age levels, permitting evaluation of the interaction between age and the intensity of tonal stimulus in determining RT.

[Unlike the method of holding the RVs constant, the equating method results in groups composed of differentiated Ss. Thus, for example, Group I_1

of Table 2-2 is composed of subgroups of males and females, the same being true for the other two groups. Consequently the one-way analysis of variance, which was suitable when the groups were composed of undifferentiated Ss, does not apply here. An appropriate statistical design is the *two-way analysis of variance*. Applied to the experimental design of Table 2-2, the latter would enable one to evaluate (1) how the independent variable affects *RT* when males are considered alone, when females are considered alone, and when males and females are considered together; and (2) whether the effect of the independent variable on *RT* is similar for males and females, i.e., whether the independent variable (intensity of the tonal stimulus) and the relevant variable (sex) interact.]

Table 2-3 shows how both *RV*s, sex and age, can be equated in the same experiment. Note that 50 percent of the Ss in each of the three groups are males and 50 percent are females; similarly, 50 percent are 21 to 22 years of age and 50 percent are 41 to 42 years old. Thus both subject *RV*s are equated over the three values of the independent variable.

[Because the Ss in the groups of Table 2-3 have been classified with respect to *two RV*s (sex and age), a two-way analysis of variance is now inadequate, and a *three-way analysis of variance* design is required. Note that there are three manipulated variables involved in the design of Table 2-3, two *RV*s and one independent variable. More generally, if an experimental design consists of *n* manipulated variables, an appropriate statistical design, provided certain statistical assumptions are met, is the *n-way analysis of variance*.]

Equating subject RVs with an unselected group of Ss. In the matching methods described so far, certain subject requirements were established in advance, and then **E** set out to find Ss who met these qualifications. Actually, it is more frequently the case that **E** wants to match a subject *RV* in an *unselected* group of Ss, such as a group of volunteers, a group of Ss chosen at random from a larger group of individuals or, in animal research, a batch of experimental animals received from a supplier. In all of these cases, if **E** wishes to match a particular subject *RV*, he can do so only by equating the *RV* with the Ss at hand. One useful, general method follows.

Suppose we wish to perform the present *RT* experiment with 12 individuals who have volunteered as Ss. Let us stipulate that the age variable should be controlled by equating it over the three values of the independent variable

Table 2-3 Equating Both Sex and Age over All Values of the Independent Variable (Percents)

SUBJECTS	GROUP I_1	GROUP I_2	GROUP I_3
21- to 22-year-old males	25	25	25
41- to 42-year-old males	25	25	25
21- to 22-year-old females	25	25	25
41- to 42-year-old females	25	25	25

Table 2-4 Subjects of Reaction-time Experiment Arranged in Order of Increasing Age (Years)

SUBJECT	AGE	SUBJECT	AGE
1	17	7	21
2	17	8	22
3	18	9	22
4	19	10	23
5	20	11	25
6	21	12	26

(i.e., over the three groups). Let the subjects' ages be as indicated in Table 2-4, where they have been arranged in an increasing order. There are several ways in which three groups of four Ss each could be constructed from this list with age equated over the three groups. The one to be described, the "randomized blocks method," has many advantages and has general application.

After the Ss are arranged in increasing (or decreasing) values of the age variable, they are next divided into successive "blocks," three Ss per block. Thus, Ss 1, 2, 3 form the first block, and Ss 4, 5, 6 form the second; Ss 7, 8, 9 form the third, and Ss 10, 11, 12 form the fourth. The final step is to have each block contribute one S to each of the three groups of the experiment, assignment of Ss being by randomization. For example, if a table of random digits is used, the first S might be assigned to Group I_2 and the second to Group I_1; it then follows that the third S goes into Group I_3. Similarly, one S is randomly assigned to each of the three groups from the next block (Ss 4, 5, 6), and the same process is repeated for the third and fourth blocks. When this process is finished, each group will contain four Ss (Table 2-5). Because the Ss within a given block are randomly assigned to Groups I_1, I_2, and I_3, the mean ages of the Ss of these three groups will generally differ somewhat, though the organization of Ss into blocks ensures small differences.

[An appropriate statistical design for this equating method is called the "randomized-blocks analysis of variance" design (cf. Edwards, 1968; Hays, 1963). This design is particularly applicable when the equated RV does *not* interact with the independent variable. When the groups of the experiment

Table 2-5 Equating Age by the Method of Randomized Blocks

\ GROUP I_1		\ GROUP I_2		\ GROUP I_3	
S	AGE	S	AGE	S	AGE
2	17	1	17	3	18
4	19	6	21	5	20
8	22	7	21	9	22
10	23	11	25	12	26
Mean age: 20.25		Mean age: 21.00		Mean age: 21.50	

number two, i.e., two values of the independent variable are involved, the randomized-blocks analysis of variance is closely related to the t test for matched groups.]

The randomized-blocks method is often useful in experiments where learning or related processes are under study. Very frequently in such experiments, two tasks—A and B—are involved, and the tasks are sufficiently related that performance on A may be considered a reasonable predictor of performance on B. In these experiments, the randomized-blocks method can be used to equate Ss' performance level on task A over all values of the independent variable. Suppose, for example, E wished to investigate how *overtraining*, defined as training beyond a specified criterion of learning, affects reversal learning of a finger-maze pattern. His plan is to train a group of 30 Ss on a finger-maze pattern (task A) until each S achieves the criterion of one errorless run through the maze. All Ss return on the next day and are assigned to one of three groups. The 10 Ss of Group I are immediately trained on a maze pattern (task B) that is the reverse of the one learned the previous day. If the sequence of correct responses were RRLRL on the initial pattern, the reverse pattern would be LLRLR. The 10 Ss of Group II first receive 20 overtraining trials on the initial maze pattern before they are switched to the reverse pattern; and the 10 Ss of Group III receive 40 overtraining trials before learning the reverse pattern. Because speed of learning the initial pattern (task A) may reasonably be expected to be related to speed of learning the reverse pattern (task B), E may wish to equate performance on the former over the three values of the independent variable (0, 20, or 40 overtraining trials), and this he could do easily by using the randomized-blocks method in much the same way as illustrated in Table 2-5.

The method of randomized blocks may be applied to qualitative as well as to quantitative RVs. As an illustration of the former, suppose young rats are exposed to five different types of experiences in infancy, and the effects of these experiences are evaluated when the rats reach maturity. It is reasonable to view the litter to which a rat belongs, a qualitative subject RV, as a potentially important RV. One could equate this variable by the randomized-blocks method by using the litter as the block. From each available litter of five or more members, one animal would be randomly assigned to each of the five groups corresponding to the five values of the independent variable (five different types of early experience). Hence, only five Ss would be taken from each litter, unless a litter had 10 or more animals, in which case two rats could be assigned to each of the five groups. It may be apparent that this procedure (exactly) equates the litter variable over the five values of the independent variable.[3]

It turns out that the randomized-blocks method is used often to equate subject RVs, and variants of the basic method exist which further extend its

---

[3] The nature of this illustration prompts the observation that Solomon and Lessac (1968) have pointed out an important deficiency in the experimental designs customarily employed in studies of behavioral development and have proposed the adoption of a design which, though it requires more research effort, may increase greatly the information yield of an experiment.

range of application. Hence, this technique should be remembered when equating subject RVs in unselected groups of Ss is required.

In conclusion, the major purpose of all such equating methods is the equalization of the effects of the controlled RV (on the dependent variable) for all values of the independent variable. In terms of the illustrative RT experiment, for example, the mean RTs of Groups I_1, I_2, and I_3 cannot be influenced to any important extent by a subject RV that has been equated. The student should not feel that the equating designs which were discussed are only useful when employment of the corresponding statistical designs is anticipated. It is true that the appropriate statistical designs are most efficient and extract maximum information from the data, but simpler statistical techniques may be used in piecemeal fashion by the beginner, for example, the comparisons of pairs of group means by the t test. The important consideration at this point is that all comparisons which are based on group means and on certain other group measures will be free of confounding effects from subject RVs that have been controlled by an equating procedure.

2. RANDOMIZED GROUPS

Residual randomization. It might clarify matters to distinguish two uses of randomization. In virtually every experiment performed in psychology, randomization enters, or should enter, into the assignment of Ss to groups. Even in experiments where certain subject RVs are controlled by equating (cf. Tables 2-2 and 2-3), assignment of Ss to each subgroup is by randomization. Thus referring to Table 2-3, which of the 21- to 22-year-old male Ss go into Group I_1, which go into Group I_2, and which into Group I_3, must be determined by random assignment. In the randomized-blocks method (Table 2-5), assignment of Ss from blocks to groups was also by randomization. In short, after E has controlled all the subject RVs he wishes, final assignment of Ss to groups must be accomplished by randomization. This use of randomization we have termed *residual* randomization, which may be loosely defined as the random assignment of Ss to groups after subject RVs have been controlled by matching. Residual randomization is an indispensable requirement of an experiment if one hopes to evaluate the experimental results statistically, and, as suggested by the following illustration, statistical evaluation of experimental results is commonly a necessity.

Imagine that our familiar reaction-time experiment had been performed and that the resulting mean RTs turned out to be 198 milliseconds (msec) for Group I_1, 182 msec for Group I_2, and 171 msec for Group I_3; thus we assume that the expected relationship between tonal-stimulus intensity and RT was realized. The question arises: What is the possibility that the obtained results could have occurred even though tonal-stimulus intensity has no effect on RT? Or, put somewhat differently, how confident can we be that our results are not due to "chance" fluctuations in the mean RTs of the three groups but, rather, reflect a "true" effect of the independent variable on the dependent variable? This is an exceedingly important question, and it is fortunate that appropriate statistical analyses can provide precise answers. However, every single statistical design that is applicable to this problem has been developed from the initial assumption that the observations or scores obtained in the experiment were *randomly* selected from some larger population of scores. In actual practice, this assumption can be accommodated by residual randomization.

Another closely related reason for the importance of residual randomization is that it provides a means of controlling *unknown* subject *RV*s. Even if it were possible to hold constant every known and suspected subject *RV* in an experiment, variation in the performance of individual Ss still would occur because of the operation of completely unknown subject *RV*s. The only way in which one can gain control over the latter is to adopt a procedure that will equalize their effects on the dependent variable in the *long run*. Residual randomization is that procedure. Through its use, one stands a good chance, particularly if the number of Ss in each group of the experiment is large, of having unknown subject *RV*s well equated within the single experiment. Further, when very large numbers of Ss are involved, either in a single experiment or over a series of experiments, good equating of such variables is practically certain. Nevertheless, unlike the matching methods, which assure equalization of the effects of a subject *RV* within the single experiment, residual randomization can guarantee only long-run control, and there always exists the possibility, especially with few Ss, that a given subject *RV* will be poorly equated within a particular experiment.

Although the preceding two features of residual randomization are closely connected, they are not identical. It sometimes happens that residual randomization is used when there is no intention of evaluating the experimental results statistically. For example, suppose that in the reaction-time experiment we were undecided as to which of two response keys to use but preferred the one that was likely to produce the faster *RT*s. To settle this question, we would run a small preliminary (pilot) experiment with two groups of Ss, one group tested with each of the response keys, obtaining *RT*s under conditions similar to those planned for the main experiment. Now, in order to control unknown subject *RV*s, we would use residual randomization in assigning the Ss to the two groups. Yet because we must use one of the response keys in the main experiment, statistical evaluation of the experimental results has little meaning, for we doubtlessly would choose the key that produced the lower mean *RT* without taking the trouble to determine whether or not the obtained difference between the mean *RT*s could be attributed to chance fluctuations.

In summary, then, residual randomization should always be practiced because it fulfills a basic assumption of statistical analyses that are used to evaluate experimental results and because it provides a method of controlling unknown subject *RV*s.

We are now in a position to consider the control of subject *RV*s by the method of randomized groups, a topic which will require little discussion. The method consists of the random assignment of Ss to groups with no matching of subject RVs. Thus, if 60 Ss were available for the reaction-time experiment, 20 Ss would be randomly assigned to each of the three groups with no consideration given to sex, age, or other subject variables. This commonly encountered method is no more than residual randomization with no subject RVs matched, and it is used primarily when no potent subject RVs are known or when matching of known subject RVs is impossible or impracticable.

There are several reasons why it might not be feasible to match significant subject RVs. For example, it would not be possible to match the litter variable if the number of values of the independent variable in an experiment generally exceeded the number of animals contained in a litter. In experiments employing two related tasks, A and B, it would not prove practicable, although it would perhaps be desirable, to equate Ss with respect to performance on task A if Ss performed both tasks in succession within a single experimental session. In all cases such as these, E has no alternative but to randomize subject variables of known relevance.

[As with matched groups in which subject RVs have been controlled by being held constant, randomized groups are composed of undifferentiated (unclassified) Ss; hence, the same statistical design appropriate for the former applies to the latter. This, it might be recalled, was the one-way analysis of variance.]

Randomization of known subject RVs that could be matched. It is altogether another matter, however, when randomization is employed on known, potent, subject RVs that are capable of being matched. This is the second use of randomization mentioned earlier, and a use which should be looked upon with skepticism. No doubt randomization will provide equalization of the effects of an RV in the long run, and doubtless appropriate statistical analyses will "take account" of randomized RVs in revealing the probabilities that obtained results might be due to chance fluctuations. But as experimentalists, we wish to make our *individual* experiments as accurate as possible, and for this reason we wish to equalize as many significant RVs within the single experiment as we can.

Why, then, is it suggested that variables (subject or situational) of known relevance are sometimes better randomized than matched? The answer is statistical in nature and perhaps too advanced for the student's present grasp. Nevertheless the suggestion rests on the fact that if E matches a relevant variable and subsequently evaluates his results with a statistical design that does not take the matching into consideration, he will believe too often that chance fluctuation, rather than a genuine effect of the independent variable, is responsible for his experimental results. That is, E will too often overlook real effects of the independent variable. The solution to this problem is not to randomize known RVs, but rather to match them and use appropriate statistical designs.

To summarize, randomized groups is a method of control in which Ss are assigned to values of the independent variable by complete randomization;

i.e., no subject *RV*s are matched. The method is primarily applicable when no subject *RV*s are known or when, if known, their control by matching procedures is infeasible. Residual randomization, which should always be employed in the assignment of Ss to groups, was distinguished from randomization of known relevant variables, and two important features of the former were discussed.

Control of Subject *RV*s in Single-group Designs

A single-group design, as mentioned earlier, is also applicable to our illustrative *RT* experiment. In employing this design, each S would be tested under all three values of the independent variable, a single group of Ss thus replacing the three groups required in the separate-groups design. A major virtue of the single-group design alluded to in Chap. 1 may now be more explicitly stated. As indicated in Table 2-1, *all subject RVs are automatically equated within such designs.* Because every S serves under all values of the independent variable, subject *RV*s—known or unknown—cannot have differential effects on the dependent variable. In the *RT* experiment, if a subject has generally fast *RT*s because of exceptional reflexes, this subject *RV* is automatically equated because each S is tested under all three values of the independent variable. The same holds true for all other subject *RV*s, e.g., age, sex, and vocation. This conclusion assumes, of course, that the experiment is completed within a reasonable period of time, so that subject *RV*s, all comparatively stable, change little during the course of the experiment.

On the other hand, single-group designs contribute a control problem that was nonexistent with separate-groups designs, a problem concerning the independent variable of the study. Since in single-group designs all Ss serve under all values of the independent variable, problems arise relating to the order or sequence in which the different values of the independent variable are administered to the Ss. The relevant variables that are the concern of such problems are, it will be recalled, sequence *RV*s, which will be discussed later under that heading.

CONTROL OF SITUATIONAL RELEVANT VARIABLES

The second major class of relevant variables requiring control is, as indicated in Table 2-1, composed of situational *RV*s. This class of *RV*s includes all environmental variables operating in the experimental situation, most variables related to the task presented to S, and all type-E subject variables. We consider first their control in separate-groups designs.

Control of Situational *RV*s in Separate-groups Designs

As with subject *RV*s, situational *RV*s are controlled by matching and by randomizing techniques. However, with subject *RV*s, matching and randomization are applied to the Ss or characteristics of the Ss of the experiment; with situational *RV*s, on the other hand, matching and randomization is usually applied to the *conditions* of the experiment. Hence the slightly different terminology in corresponding parts of Table 2-1, e.g., *matched conditions* versus *matched groups*.

1. MATCHED CONDITIONS

(a) *Hold the RV Constant over All Values of the Independent Variable.* By far the most common means of controlling situational *RV*s is by holding them constant over all values of the independent variable. Thus, temperature, lighting, and other such environmental variables are likely to be kept essentially constant in an experiment, as are the many potentially relevant features of the experimental apparatus employed. Situational *RV*s that relate to the experimental task—for example, intertrial interval, number of items in a list of words to be learned, instructions given the *S*s, number of training trials per day, and criteria used to evaluate *S*'s performance—are also likely to be controlled by being held constant over all values of the independent variable. Similarly, the type-E subject variables of this class are normally controlled by being held constant.

Although the technique of holding situational *RV*s constant over all values of the independent variable provides flawless control of these *RV*s, it entails the same potential limitation here as in its application to subject *RV*s, namely, that important interactions between the independent variable of the study and one or more controlled situational *RV*s might go undetected. This point may be illustrated by the familiar *RT* experiment. The experimenter himself is a situational variable of possible, but usually neglected, relevance (McGuigan, 1963; Rosenthal, 1966). Although unlikely, the type of relationship obtained between *RT* and intensity of the tonal stimulus might be determined in part by characteristics of the experimenter, e.g., *E*'s sex. If such were actually the case and the experimenter variable were controlled by being held constant, there would be little chance of detecting the interaction between the latter variable and tonal-stimulus intensity.

As a somewhat more realistic example, suppose we wished to investigate the general question of how motivational level affects rate of learning. We initiate an experiment in which rate of learning is to be determined for two groups of *S*s, one group of high motivation and one of low motivation. The particular task employed in the experiment doubtless would be controlled by being held constant over the two groups of *S*s. If it turned out that the more highly motivated *S*s learned the experimental task faster, we probably would surmise that high motivation generally facilitates learning. According to the consensus of actual research on this question, however, such a generalization would be unwarranted, for it appears that although high motivation usually facilitates the learning of relatively simple tasks, the reverse is likely for complex tasks. Thus, task complexity interacts with motivational level in determining rate of learning. Such interactions are not at all uncommon in psychological research, and the conflicting, perplexing results to which they often give rise frequently remain unresolved until some insightful individual notices the interacting situational RV that lies at the root of the divergence.

There is, unfortunately, no easy way of knowing in advance which situational RVs will interact with the independent variable of an experiment. And, of course, it is impossible to vary systematically (equate) all situational RVs that might do so, hoping thereby to achieve maximum generality for the obtained experimental results. What actually occurs is that one holds constant as many of the situational variables as is practicable, and if discordant results are obtained in different experiments, one searches for, among other things, an interacting situational RV that might account for the difficulty. If one is located, a further experiment is performed in which the possibly interacting RV is manipulated, usually at the values that produced the conflicting results, and if the latter are reproduced by the experiment, the problem is solved. An important implication from this discussion is that if one hopes to replicate (duplicate in essential aspects) the results of a previous experiment, great care must be exercised in reproducing as many of the conditions of the original study as possible. Conversely, failure to replicate previous results should immediately suggest that one examine the RVs held constant at different levels in the two experiments, seeking among them one or more explicating interactions.

(**b**) *Equate the RV over All Values of the Independent Variable.* In general, control of a situational RV through equating is not employed unless E is unable to hold it constant. In the RT experiment, for example, if E were forced by circumstances to run the experiment at two different locations, he would undoubtedly see to it that equal proportions of Ss from the three groups of the experiment were tested at one of the locations and equal proportions at the other, thus controlling this situational RV by equating it over all values of the independent variable. Similarly, in an animal experiment where duplicate experimental chambers (e.g., Skinner boxes) are used, the careful E would equate the latter situational RV by having equal proportions of Ss from the various groups of the study tested in one of the chambers and equal proportions tested in the other. Although examples such as these could be multiplied, most often situational RVs can be held constant, and this is the control procedure adopted.

Equating situational RVs by "yoking." "Yoking" is often employed as a method of equating a situational RV which arises from S's behavior and therefore is not under E's direct control. Consider the following illustration.

It has been established that the classical conditioning paradigm (unconditioned stimulus presented on every trial) results in eyelid conditioning superior to that produced by instrumental (avoidance) conditioning (unconditioned stimulus omitted when S makes a conditioned response—CR). Does this result indicate that certain response systems, eyelid closure among them, are more sensitive to classical conditioning than to instrumental procedures? Or can the obtained difference between instrumental and classical conditioning be due to other circumstances, such as the fact that in classical conditioning the unconditioned stimulus (*UCS*) is presented on every trial whereas with the avoidance paradigm the pattern is irregular; or that in classical conditioning the *UCS* occurs more often and may hence maintain *S*'s motivation at a higher level? Clearly, the number and pattern of occurrences of the *UCS* will have to be controlled before a meaningful comparison can be made as to the relative efficiency of the classical and instrumental procedures themselves.

Yoking appears to provide the answer. An experimental *S* trained with the avoidance procedure is yoked to a classically conditioned *S* who receives the *UCS* only on those trials that the experimental *S* fails to avoid. Thus, although both *S*s receive the *UCS* on precisely the same trials, in the case of the experimental *S*, the *UCS* is response-contingent (that is, it occurs only when *S* fails to make a *CR*), whereas in the case of the control *S*, it is response-noncontingent. With the number and pattern of appearances of the *UCS* thus controlled, the instrumental procedure turns out to be superior to classical conditioning (e.g., Gormezano, 1965).

Though the yoked control design is a rather neat and efficient means of controlling *RV*s generated by *S*s' behavior, it is not without danger. Church (1964) pointed out that in many situations its use may seriously bias the experimental results in subtle ways. As an illustration, suppose *E* wished to evaluate the notion that visual-recognition thresholds can be sharpened by having *S* perform a response to produce the stimulus to be recognized rather than having him be the passive recipient of the same stimulus. Thus *E* has an experimental *S* produce an unfamiliar word, for example, by pressing a button, which he tries to recognize as quickly as possible. (With the emphasis on speed, presumably *S* will make some errors.) A control *S*, yoked to the experimental *S*, experiences the same exposure durations as the latter, only they are presented to him by *E*. Assume that appropriate precautions are taken so that both *S*s are equally attentive before each stimulus exposure.

Although both *S*s might have identical recognition thresholds, the probable result of this procedure—assuming both *S*s vary from trial to trial in their thresholds—is that the experimental *S* will make fewer errors than the control *S*. The reason for this expected result is that the experimental *S*, because he controls the duration of the stimulus exposure, can take advantage of his momentary changes in threshold. On trials when it is low he will present himself with only brief exposures of the stimulus, whereas on trials when his threshold is high, the exposures will be longer. The yoked control *S*, on the other hand, is likely to have the exposure durations out of phase with his threshold changes, so that a relatively brief exposure may come at a time when his threshold is relatively high. As a consequence he would be bound to make an error. On the other hand, long exposures would not be of value to him if they happen to occur at a time when his own threshold is relatively low. In a word, the source of the bias is simply that because the distribution of exposures is produced by the experimental *S*, he profits from the fact that it is geared to his distribution of thresholds and not to that of the yoked control *S*.

When this interpretation is applied to the eyelid conditioning illustration, the superiority of the experimental Ss trained with the avoidance procedure over their classically conditioned yoked controls might have nothing to do with the fact that the UCS was response-contingent in the first case and not in the second. Even if the only effective factor in eyelid conditioning were the pairing of CS and UCS, the experimental Ss could have done better because, once again, the distribution of presentations of the UCS would maximize conditioning for them but not for the yoked controls. With the instrumental procedure, the UCS is presented to the experimental S only on those trials where he fails to make a CR, that is, precisely at the time when he needs such reinforcement. The yoked controls, on the other hand, receive the same number of UCSs independently of their behavior, and it is therefore extremely unlikely that they are applied as efficiently.

The lesson from these illustrations is clear. Before employing the yoking method, which in many cases is extremely valuable, one must examine the situation to assess whether this method of control will operate to facilitate performance of the experimental Ss at the expense of the yoked controls. If there is danger of such a confound, yoking should not be employed; instead it may be possible to manipulate the equated RV as an independent variable (see Church, 1964). Or one may be able to utilize a variant of yoking, called a "reciprocal" yoked design, recently developed for the purpose of circumventing the objections raised by Church (Kimmel & Terrant, 1968).

(The statistical designs applicable here are similar to those appropriate when matching subject RVs. Situational RVs that are held constant, or equated by yoking, have no effect on the required statistical design. If the control of subject RVs were such that a one-way analysis of variance was appropriate, the latter would still apply. However, when a situational RV is equated, it usually adds another "dimension" to the statistical design. Using a method of randomized groups in the RT experiment, three groups of undifferentiated Ss result, requiring a one-way analysis of variance. But if a situational variable, such as the location at which the experiment was conducted, were equated in the manner discussed earlier, each of the three groups would then be differentiated into two subgroups, classified on the basis of the location at which the experiment took place. A one-way analysis of variance is no longer adequate, and a two-way analysis of variance is required.)

It sometimes happens that a situational RV is equated in each S separately; that is, every subject serves under all the values of the RV that occur in the experiment. When this procedure is employed, S serves under more than one condition of the experiment, and therefore the problem of controlling sequence RVs, discussed later, arises.

2. RANDOMIZED CONDITIONS. Randomization is not as important a control technique for situational RVs as it is for subject RVs. When applied to situational RVs, randomization has two uses, the first of which is illustrated by the following example.

Consider an experiment in which S is taught to discriminate between two stimulus objects presented simultaneously. One of the stimulus objects is positive: choice of it leads to reward. The other stimulus object is negative: choice of it does not lead to reward and may result in punishment. Because both the positive and negative stimuli are presented on each trial, a question arises as to their spatial arrangement—which stimulus is to be on the right and which on the left? One obviously would not consent to having the positive stimulus on the right on every trial, because S could then "solve" the discrimination problem merely by always choosing the stimulus positioned on the right. For the same reason one would not simply alternate the spatial positions of the stimuli from trial to trial. A procedure of assignment is needed that provides no useful position cues (information) on which S can base a correct choice. Randomization, of course, is the answer; E simply assigns the position of the positive stimulus on each trial by tossing a coin or, better, by using a table of random digits. However, for a variety of reasons including the desire to avoid long series of trials with the same spatial arrangement, strict randomization is rarely used in practice. A "quasi-randomization" procedure, incorporating one or more well-defined restrictions on randomization, is employed instead. Such restrictions should be few in number and as weak as possible, or else the purpose of randomization will be defeated. If, for example, E stipulated that no more than two trials in succession could occur with the same spatial arrangement, S would eventually discriminate this positional cue and make good use of it in his choices, shifting his responses from left to right or vice versa after any two successive correct trials. Pigeons have been known to take advantage of far less restricted randomization, and so have chimpanzees (Ferster & Hammer, 1966). Hence, in all cases where randomization is used to remove a source of information from S, which by the way characterizes the present application of randomization, one should be on guard that the quasi-randomization employed actually succeeds in its purpose. Fellows (1967) has presented quasi-randomized series that are useful in this connection.

The second application of randomization to situational RVs is more conventional, involving activities such as random selection of task materials for an experiment (e.g., words to be learned, stimuli to be discriminated) and random assignment of such materials to individuals participating in the experiment. Although these activities and others like them are legitimate, a note of caution should be sounded against needless randomization of significant situational RVs.

As an illustration of the basis of the concern just expressed, suppose we wished to determine whether thirsty rats prefer a slightly saline solution to pure water as a reward object. There are many ways to pursue this question, but imagine that we have decided to use a simple T maze, and we consistently bait one side of the maze with saline solution and the other with a like amount of water. We shall permit each rat to make 10 choices on the T maze, assuming that if an animal has a preference for one of the fluids, it will be revealed by more frequent choice of one side of the T maze. It is known that rats generally have position preferences; that is, other things equal, some rats tend to make more right turns in a T maze than left turns or vice versa. Further, the rat's first choice is frequently a good indicator of its position preference, if one exists. In our experiment it is clear that if in most cases we happened to bait the preferred side of the T maze with the saline solution, a preponderance of choices of the latter could be ascribed to the rats' position preferences as well as to a preference for a slightly salty solution. Plainly, the side of the T maze baited with saline solution is a situational variable that will have to be controlled.

One could control the latter by randomization: for each rat we toss a coin and if heads turns up, the saline solution is assigned to the right side of the maze on all 10 trials; if tails, the solution is assigned to the left side, and the same procedure is repeated for each animal. Actually this method of control, an instance of randomizing a known revelant variable, has been widely used in situations similar to our hypothetical experiment. Yet if the number of Ss involved is small, there is a substantial chance that the position preferences of the rats will be poorly equated; that is, many more than 50 percent of the rats might have the saline solution assigned to their preferred (or unpreferred) side. Randomization could therefore introduce a serious inaccuracy into our experiment. Such a possibility can be precluded by *equating* the situational *RV*, perhaps as follows.

Assuming the rat's choice on the first trial to be a reasonable indicator of its position preference, one may equate this *RV* by arranging things so that 50 percent of the Ss choose saline solution on the first 10 trials and 50 percent choose pure water. This is accomplished by baiting *both* sides of the T maze on Trial 1 with saline solution for the first subgroup of rats and by baiting both sides with pure water for the second subgroup. Thereafter the saline solution (or the water) appears *only* on the side of the T maze chosen on Trial 1, and the fluid not chosen on Trial 1 appears on the other side. We have by this procedure equated the position-preference variable to the extent that it is guaranteed that 50 percent of the Ss will choose the saline solution on Trial 1 and that 50 percent will choose pure water. The point to be emphasized here is that one should not randomize a situational variable of known relevance if means exist to equate the variable, particularly if the variable is likely to have a strong influence on the behavior under study.

(Randomized situational *RV*s, like situational *RV*s that have been held constant, do not influence the choice of an appropriate statistical design.)

Control of Situational *RV*s in Single-group Designs

As may be seen in Table 2-1, situational *RV*s are subject to the same techniques of control in single-group designs as were already discussed for separate-groups designs. However, there is this difference. Because each S serves under all values of the independent variable, many situational *RV*s are easier to control with the single-group design. For example, as long as S is tested at the same location or in the same experimental chamber, these situational *RV*s are automatically matched in single-group designs, regardless of the numbers of Ss tested in one or the other location or in one or the other experimental chamber. It will be recalled that **E** had to take special measures to equate these same variables when a separate-groups design was employed. Similarly, if in an experiment with a single set of instructions something in the instructions should motivate some **S**s more than others, this situational *RV* would be effectively equated in a single-group design, assuming that the motivation induced by instructions remained fairly constant during the experiment. It turns out, then, that many situational *RV*s are also automatically controlled in single-group designs.

CONTROL OF SEQUENCE RELEVANT VARIABLES

Sequence *RV*s arise when **S**s of an experiment serve under two or more conditions in single or separate experimental sessions. In most important cases, the multiple conditions are different values of the independent variable; i.e., they arise in experiments employing single-group designs. It is less frequently the case that **S**s serve under multiple conditions in experiments utilizing separate-groups designs, but such instances, to be described later, are not uncommon. Nevertheless, it is true that the control of sequence *RV*s is of particular consequence when different values of the independent variable are concerned. Therefore we shall reverse the procedure previously followed and first discuss their control in single-group designs.

Control of Sequence *RV*s in Single-group Designs

ORDER EFFECTS. There are two different kinds of effects that should be distinguished when one is dealing with sequences of conditions (including different values of the independent variable) in an experiment. The first is related solely to the ordinal position of the condition in the sequence and is referred to as "order effects." As an illustration, suppose that in a single-group design involving three values of the independent variable, the **S**s were tested in the morning under the value of the independent variable that was first in the sequence, in the afternoon under the value that was second in the sequence, and in the evening under the last value. It seems likely that order effects would occur in such an experiment because the ordinal positions in the sequence are associated with widely different times of the day. If, for example, the task required considerable alertness and attention from **S**, performance might generally be better during the morning session than during either the afternoon or the evening session. Thus, where order effects operate, performance under a given condition depends in part on the ordinal position (first, second, third, etc.) in the sequence occupied by the condition.

CARRY-OVER EFFECTS. Contrasted with order effects are "carry-over" effects. These occur when performance under a given condition, with a fixed ordinal position in the sequence, turns out to depend on what conditions preceded it in the sequence. This statement requires clarification; consider, then, the following example. A single group of Ss is tested under three experimental conditions, A, B, and C, and each is a different problem-solving task. Suppose that task B happens to contain clues that are helpful for the solution of A. It is quite likely that, because of the information provided by B, performance on A will generally be better for Ss tested on the sequence BAC than for Ss tested on CAB. Thus, even though A occupies the same ordinal position in both sequences, a difference in performance on A can be expected as the result of carry-over effects from the preceding condition. Carry-over effects can occur in the absence of order effects and vice versa, though it is not uncommon for the two to occur together.

We shall have occasion to dwell further on this topic. For the present it is sufficient to remember that order effects are the sole result of the ordinal position that a condition occupies in a sequence; carry-over effects, on the other hand, are attributable to influences stemming from one or more of the earlier conditions of the sequence.

Observe that in Table 2-1 the sequence RVs are controlled by counterbalancing techniques. It is sometimes possible to control sequence RVs within each individual subject, a procedure that is often referred to as "intrasubject" counterbalancing. Where the latter is infeasible or impossible, control of such RVs can be secured only over groups of subjects; the appropriate methods are collectively termed "intragroup" counterbalancing.

1. INTRASUBJECT COUNTERBALANCING. Probably the best-known method of intrasubject counterbalancing is the *abba* sequence (pronounced exactly the way it is spelled), of use primarily when only two values of the independent variable are under study. Two values of the independent variable, *a* and *b*, are administered to each S in the order specified by the *abba* sequence. For example, suppose E is interested in whether lists of nouns are learned faster than lists of verbs, so that the two values of the independent variable are nouns (*a*) and verbs (*b*); the independent variable itself may be described as "types of words," or "parts of speech." To employ the *abba* sequence, E would construct two lists of nouns and two lists of comparable verbs. Each S would then learn in succession a noun list, a verb list, the second verb list, and the second noun list. If the identifications of *a* and *b* were reversed, the order would be verb list, noun list, second noun list, and second verb list.

Under the assumption that order effects will have an influence on the dependent variable by the addition of a *constant* increment (or decrement) to each successive position in the sequence, the virtue of the *abba* sequence is that it guarantees that order effects will be equalized over the two values of the independent variable. When order effects have the property of producing constant increments (or decrements), they are said to be "linear." If, for example, the influence of order effects were to add an increment of 4 units to successive positions in the sequence, the order effects at the first position would be 4 units,

8 units at the second position, and 12 and 16 units at the third and fourth positions, respectively. It is easy to see from these figures that order effects will be equalized over the two values of an independent variable, *a* and *b*, if the sequence *abba* is employed. This would not be true if, for example, the sequence *abab* were used. Note further that if order effects are linear, they are equated for each S separately, and the constant additive increment (or decrement) may differ from subject to subject. Although the *abba* sequence is usually discussed in connection with the control of such sequence *RV*s as practice, fatigue, and boredom, its range of application is more general; that is, it applies to all sequence *RV*s that produce linear order effects.

It is difficult, however, to know in actual practice whether order effects will have the prescribed form; they could, for example, be greatest in the *bb* portion of the *abba* sequence. As a guard against such possibilities, it is common for the total group of Ss to be divided into two equal subgroups, the Ss of one receiving the sequence *abba* and the Ss of the other receiving the sequence *baab*. As a concrete illustration, suppose the actual order effects in the previous example were 2, 6, 7, and 8 units for the first, second, third, and fourth positions, respectively. For the subgroup tested with the sequence *abba*, it is clear that the *b* condition is favored more than the *a* condition, 13 units to 10; for the subgroup tested with sequence *baab*, this advantage is reversed. Consequently, when the dependent variable is averaged over the two subgroups, order effects are equalized over *a* and *b*. A further advantage of using both sequences is that, because *a* occurs first for half of the Ss and *b* occurs first for the other half, it is possible to evaluate the influence of *a* and *b* uncontaminated by sequence effects (see Poulton & Freeman, 1966). In view of these advantages, it is usually preferable, if possible, to utilize both sequences, relieving oneself of the assumption of linear order effects. Where this is done, one is actually combining intrasubject counterbalancing with intragroup counterbalancing.

As for the problem of carry-over effects, the *abba* sequence affords some control in the case where these effects are rather simple. For example, in certain situations shifting from one task to another might be expected to cause a temporary, and approximately equal, decrement in performance, and we would therefore wish to have such shifts occur an equal number of times for each value of the independent variable. It will be noticed that in the *abba* sequence, S shifts once from *a* to *b* and once from *b* to *a*. This is not true for the sequence *abab*. However, as we shall emphasize later, carry-over effects are apt to be much more complicated, in many cases defying complete control. This points to one of the major limitations of the single-group design: because of the difficulties posed by carry-over effects, single-group designs should be restricted to situations where such sequence effects are unimportant or else are of a nature that allows for their control.

Single-subject designs. There is a wide area of application of intrasubject counterbalancing that deserves special mention. In many experimental situations, particularly when animal Ss are employed, it is possible to maintain training on an experimental task over relatively long periods of time, during the course of which S's behavior comes to be very stable and predictable. For example, if a monkey is subjected to an experimental situation in which he must press a lever every 10 sec or sooner to avoid a shock to his feet, his lever-pressing behavior after many daily sessions in this situation will become quite stabilized and predictable from one day to another. His avoidance behavior has achieved a "steady state" (an instance of "baseline" behavior—Sidman, 1960).

If one wishes to determine the effect of a drug, say a tranquilizer, on avoidance behavior in the present situation, it is easy to do so against the background of the steady-state behavior. All one need do is administer the drug, observe the changes in avoidance behavior, withdraw the drug, and—assuming that the steady state is reversible—allow the avoidance behavior to return to its baseline. After behavior returns to the steady state, the cycle may be repeated—the drug readministered for one or more sessions, then withdrawn, and the avoidance behavior allowed again to return to its steady state. One can thus follow the effects of the independent variable, in this case presence or absence of the drug, in the *single* organism; and there is no more convincing demonstration of the influence of an independent variable than to see an individual's behavior manipulated at will by E's manipulation of the variable through several of the preceding cycles. For this reason the single-subject design is probably the most powerful form of single-group designs, achieving maximum control over the three classes of RVs, while requiring a minimum number of Ss to reveal real effects of the independent variable. As mentioned in Chap. 1, it is ovbious that this very efficient design is impossible with most type-S independent variables.

A more explicit definition of a single-subject design is that it is a form of single-group design in which each subject constitutes a separate experiment; i.e., the effects of the independent variable on the dependent variable can be evaluated for each subject separately.

2. INTRAGROUP COUNTERBALANCING. Intrasubject counterbalancing is not often feasible when more than two values of the independent variable are under study, so that some sort of intragroup counterbalancing must be used. With the latter, control of sequence RVs (if achievable) is obtained over a group of Ss and not for each S separately. We will distinguish three types of intragroup counterbalancing techniques: *complete, incomplete,* and *randomized.*

(a) *Complete Counterbalancing.* Suppose three values of an independent variable, A, B, and C, are to be administered to every S of an experiment. By enumeration one finds that six different sequences of the three values are possible: ABC, ACB, BAC, BCA, CAB, and CBA. In complete counterbalancing, *every possible sequence is used an equal number of times,* each S receiving a single sequence. Hence when three values of an independent variable are involved, the number of Ss employed must be some multiple of 6, i.e., 6, 12, 18, 48.

An important feature of complete counterbalancing is that it always controls for order effects, because, considering all Ss together, every value of the independent variable must occur equally often at each ordinal position of the sequence. For example, with the six preceding sequences, *A*, *B*, and *C* will occur twice at each ordinal position if six Ss are employed in the experiment, and four times if 12 Ss are used.

As for the contribution that complete counterbalancing makes in controlling carry-over effects, we face a much more complex, and less satisfactory, state of affairs. The basic difficulty is that the carry-over effects encountered in psychological experimentation are often such that their control in the sense of *equalizing their effects over all values of the independent variable* is impossible. Consider the following illustration.

Suppose that we are interested in studying how amount of monetary reward (5, 10, or 15 cents) influences the performance of children on a simple repetitive task, for example, pulling a plunger 20 times to obtain their reward. Assume that we decide to use a single-group design, with every S serving once under each of the values of the independent variable. Letting the letters *A*, *B*, and *C* stand for the three (increasing) values of the independent variable, the six sequences listed above are possible. Now it is entirely likely that carry-over effects will occur if the experiment is completed within a single session. For example, performance under the 10-cent reward might well be more inspired when the 5-cent reward, rather than the 15-cent reward, is the immediately preceding condition. Similarly, performance under the 5-cent reward may be expected to be somewhat better when this value of the independent variable comes first in the sequence rather than when it follows the 15-cent reward. (Rats sometimes produce analogous effects for different amounts of food reward—see Chap. 7.)

Let us simplify the analysis by assuming that the carry-over effects from one condition to another will be directly proportional to the difference in the monetary rewards of the two conditions. We will assume that going from *A* to *B* or from *B* to *C* results in a positive carry-over effect (increment in performance) of two units, whereas traveling in the reverse direction results in the same amount of carry-over effect but negative in sign, i.e., leads to a decrement in performance of two units. Transitions from *A* to *C* and from *C* to *A* both result in four units of carry-over effects, positive and negative, respectively.

In Table 2-6 the carry-over effects which occur under the above assumptions have been calculated for each of the six possible sequences. It is clear from the table that carry-over effects are not equalized for the three values of the independent variable in spite of the fact that all possible sequences are used an equal number of times. Moreover, the carry-over effects assumed in this illustration are by no means the most complicated encountered in actual research. And as Poulton and Freeman (1966) have shown with numerous illustrations, a variety of asymmetrical carry-over effects can occur even when the values of the independent variable number only two. The lesson is plain: one must be wary about using a single-group design when important carry-over effects are likely to occur, because the latter cannot often be equalized over all values of the independent variable.

Table 2-6 Calculation of Assumed Carry-over Effects in Six Sequences

	VALUE OF THE INDEPENDENT VARIABLE		
SEQUENCE	*A* (5 CENTS)	*B* (10 CENTS)	*C* (15 CENTS)
ABC	0	2	2
ACB	0	−2	4
BAC	−2	0	4
BCA	−4	0	2
CAB	−4	2	0
CBA	−2	−2	0
Total	−12	0	12

Fortunately, however, the situation is not so dismal. If a fair number of Ss are run under each sequence, asymmetrical carry-over effects, if present, can be circumvented by evaluating the data for only the first condition of the experiment; i.e., by treating the experiment as a separate-groups design. Also, there are statistical techniques that enable one to take into account certain types of carry-over effects. These techniques remove statistically the differential carry-over effects from the experimental results, providing a kind of "statistical control." Not so fortunately, the appropriate techniques are rather advanced. The beginning student is well advised to avoid single-group designs when more than two values of the independent variable are involved and when significant carry-over effects may be expected. If a single-group design must be used under these circumstances, then it is best to employ complete counterbalancing, which, apart from controlling order effects, prevents the worst imbalances of carry-over effects from occurring. Thus with reference to Table 2-6, if all Ss were tested on any one of the four sequences, *ACB, BAC, BCA,* or *CAB,* the average imbalance of carry-over effects would be greater than when all six sequences are used an equal number of times.

Complete counterbalancing has two disadvantages which limit its use: (1) The fact that the number of Ss employed must be some multiple of the total number of possible sequences is often a burdensome restriction; and (2) when a large number of values of an independent variable are involved, it may prove too costly to use sufficient Ss to assign even only one S to each of the different sequences. With four values of an independent variable, the number of different sequences increases to 24; with five values, to 120. More generally, if n refers to the number of values of the independent variable, the number of different sequences that can be formed is the number of *permutations* possible with n objects and is very simply obtained. For n equal to 3, the number of different sequences is $3 \times 2 \times 1 = 6$, as was verified above. For $n = 4$, the number of different sequences is $4 \times 3 \times 2 \times 1 = 24$. In general, for n values of the independent variable the total number of different sequences is $n!$ (pronounced "factorial n"), which is equal to

$$n \times (n - 1) \times (n - 2) \times \cdots \times 1$$

(b) *Incomplete Counterbalancing.* When complete counterbalancing is not practicable, one may resort to incomplete counterbalancing, a technique which retains some desirable features of the former. Thus, it is possible to reduce drastically the required number of sequences and still retain the following properties: (1) every value of the independent variable occurs the same number of times at each ordinal position, and (2) every value of the independent variable precedes every other value an equal number of times. Property 1 assures that order effects will be controlled. Property 2 makes it possible, *whenever carry-over effects from any given condition influence only the immediately succeeding condition*, to obtain the same degree of control over such effects as that achieved by complete counterbalancing. A set of sequences possessing the preceding two properties is called a "balanced square."

As an illustration, suppose four values of an independent variable are to be studied. Of the 24 different sequences that exist, we choose the following four:

SEQUENCE NUMBER	SEQUENCE
1	$A\,B\,D\,C$
2	$B\,C\,A\,D$
3	$C\,D\,B\,A$
4	$D\,A\,C\,B$

Note that each of the four values of the independent variable occurs once at each ordinal position. And observe that A precedes B, C, and D exactly once, and the corresponding situation exists for C and D. If carry-over effects, say from B, are such that they have an influence only on the immediately following condition, then the distribution of these effects, as from B to A, C, and D, will be the same in the balanced-square design as in complete counterbalancing. Thus, whatever degree of control is obtained over such carry-over effects by the latter may also be obtained by the less costly balanced-square design.

When the number of values of the independent variable is five or greater, it is difficult to assemble the sequences necessary for balanced squares, so that rules of formation are helpful. In the following, it will simplify matters to use numbers rather than letters to denote the values of the independent variable.

RULE 1. Whenever n, the number of values of the independent variable, is an even number, balanced squares will require n sequences obtained in the following manner. The first sequence required is: 1, 2, n, 3, $(n - 1)$, 4, $(n - 2)$, 5, and so on until all n values are accounted for. If, for example, $n = 6$, the first sequence would be 126354. For $n = 4$, the initial sequence is 1243, and it will be observed that, substituting letters for numbers, this corresponds to the first sequence of the earlier illustration. For $n = 8$, the required initial sequence is 12837465. The remaining required sequences are then easily obtained from the first one by the procedure illustrated for the case of $n = 4$.

SEQUENCE DESIGNATION	SEQUENCE
A	1 2 4 3
B	2 3 1 4
C	3 4 2 1
D	4 1 3 2

Notice the values that occur in the first position of sequences B, C, and D. These values were obtained by simply adding the number 1 to the value in the first position of the preceding sequence. Thus the value which occurs in the first position in sequence B, namely 2, was obtained by adding 1 to the value in the first position in sequence A. By adding 1 to 2, the value for the first position in the next sequence, sequence C, was obtained. By the very same procedure, the values for the other positions of the four sequences were obtained. Of course, where 1 is added to 4, we do not take the result to be 5, because only four different values of the independent variable exist. We simply start all over again with the value 1, as, for example, in the fourth position of sequence C.

RULE 2.   Now let us observe what happens when we generate, by the preceding method, the five sequences which result for the case of $n = 5$. These are:

SEQUENCE DESIGNATION	SEQUENCE
A	1 2 5 3 4
B	2 3 1 4 5
C	3 4 2 5 1
D	4 5 3 1 2
E	5 1 4 2 3

Although each of the five values of the independent variable is represented once at each position, the second property of balanced squares, namely, that each value precedes every other value an equal number of times, is unfulfilled. For example, 4 is preceded by 1 twice, but never by 2. This situation can be remedied by calling upon five additional sequences, which are formed in the usual manner except that the first sequence of the five is simply the reverse of sequence A, i.e., 43521. If the student will generate the remaining four sequences from the latter, he will verify that the 10 sequences taken together satisfy the two requirements of balanced squares. Thus when n is an odd number, $2n$ sequences are required for balanced squares, a cogent reason for restricting n to an even number where possible.

From the preceding examples it follows that given n values of an independent variable, if one wishes to control order effects only, it can always be done with n sequences, whether n is even or odd. A set of n sequences chosen (usually quasi-randomly) so that each value of the independent variable occurs once and only once at each position in the sequence is called a "Latin square." The Latin square, then, is another form of incomplete counterbalancing, and although it controls order effects, it generally makes little contribution to the control of carry-over effects.

(c) *Randomized Counterbalancing*. In randomized counterbalancing, the sequences employed are selected from the set of all $n!$ sequences by a random process. This may be done by actually constructing the required sequences from a table of random digits. For example, suppose seven values of an independent variable are to be investigated. The table of random digits is entered in the usual manner, and the columns (or rows) of digits are scanned until an appropriate sequence is obtained, e.g., 4362175. This sequence may be considered to have been randomly selected from the 7! different sequences that are possible when $n = 7$. If the process is continued, any number of random sequences may be generated. There is, of course, no assurance that the sequences obtained will contain either of the controls that are provided by incomplete counterbalancing. For this reason randomized counterbalancing is most often used when incomplete counterbalancing is unachievable, as, for example, when the number of Ss employed is smaller than the number of sequences required for the latter. [For a statistical treatment of the Latin square and other counterbalancing methods, see Edwards (1968).]

Control of Sequence *RV*s in Separate-groups Designs

Because in separate-groups designs S is tested under only one value of the independent variable, the problem of controlling sequence *RV*s does not arise insofar as the independent variable is concerned. However, this problem can come up in connection with other aspects of the experiment.

A clear example of the latter is furnished by experiments in the area of stimulus generalization (Chap. 10). The student may have learned in introductory psychology that a response conditioned to a particular stimulus will occur in some measure to stimuli that resemble the original conditioned stimulus. For example, if the salivary response is conditioned to a 1,000-Hz (cycles per second) tone, it will occur, though decreased in strength, to tones of 500 and 1,500 Hz. This phenomenon is called "stimulus generalization." Suppose now we wished, with reference to the preceding context, to study how amount of stimulus generalization is affected by S's motivational level, defined in terms of numbers of hours of food deprivation. Using a separate-groups design, we would test one group of Ss for amount of stimulus generalization while under high motivation and a second group while under low motivation. If it were further required that stimulus generalization be measured at both the 500- and 1,500-Hz tones, in the interest of economy we very likely would test each S in both groups twice, once with each of the two preceding tones. Thus, although the experiment is conducted within a separate-groups design, each S is tested under more than one condition of the experiment, raising the problem of controlling sequence RVs.

Sequence RVs are also encountered in separate-groups designs in those cases where a situational RV is controlled by equating it within each individual S. As pointed out earlier, controlling a situational RV by this method requires that each S serve under two or more conditions of the experiment, thereby generating sequence RVs. Concrete illustrations of this source of sequence RVs will be furnished later in our discussion of psychophysical methods (Chap. 5).

It may be apparent that, with respect to the control of sequence RVs, it matters little whether a sequence is constructed of different values of an independent variable or of different experimental conditions that do not include values of the independent variable. Order and carry-over effects are sequence effects that must be contended with irrespective of the nature of the components that make up the sequence. Hence, the appropriate control techniques that apply to sequences of experimental conditions are precisely those already discussed for single-group designs. Nothing new is involved.

COMMENTS ON THE MULTIPLE-INDEPENDENT-VARIABLE STUDY

In our discussion of control techniques it was assumed throughout that a single independent variable was under study. Because, as already discussed, experiments involving two or more independent variables are the rule rather than the exception in psychological research, we should now enlarge our frame of reference. One of the most widely employed designs for investigating two or more independent variables simultaneously is the "factorial" design, a topic to which we now turn.

Factorial Designs

Table 2-7 depicts a factorial design for an experiment involving two independent variables or, more generally, two "factors." The first independent variable takes on the two values a and b, and the second assumes the values A, B, and C. To be more concrete, let the two values of the first independent variable be low motivation and high motivation, respectively, and let the three values of the second independent variable stand for low, moderate, and high reward, in that order. The essence of a factorial design is that *different subgroups of Ss serve under every possible combination of the factors of the design*. In the present example, the two independent variables give rise to six possible combinations, and these are indicated in the six "cells" of the table. Thus, for example, one subgroup serves under combination aA, i.e., under low motivation and low reward; a second subgroup serves under aB, i.e., low motivation and moderate reward; and a third serves under aC, low motivation and high reward, etc. If n refers to the total number of Ss used in the experiment, then $(1/6)n$ of the Ss serve under each

Table 2-7 A Factorial Design for Two Independent Variables

VALUES OF THE FIRST INDEPENDENT VARIABLE	VALUES OF THE SECOND INDEPENDENT VARIABLE		
	A	B	C
a	aA $(1/6)n$	aB $(1/6)n$	aC $(1/6)n$
b	bA $(1/6)n$	bB $(1/6)n$	bC $(1/6)n$

of the six combinations of conditions. Plainly, if one of the factors assumes r values and a second assumes c values, the total number of combinations of the two factors is $r \times c$, and each subgroup consists of $[1/(r \times c)]n$ Ss.[4]

Referring again to Table 2-7, assume that the dependent variable involved is the number of errors S commits in learning an experimental task, and let $n = 24$. The data of such a hypothetical experiment are presented in Table 2-8, where the numbers in the cells of the table indicate the error scores of the four Ss in each of the six conditions of the experiment. The means for the different values of the two independent variables are presented on the periphery of the table. $\bar{A}$ stands for the value of the dependent variable, number of errors, averaged over the eight Ss serving under value A (Ss of combinations aA and bA); $\bar{B}$ and $\bar{C}$ have the same meaning for the Ss serving under values B and C (Ss of combinations aB and bB, and aC and bC, respectively). $\bar{a}$ is defined as the value of the dependent variable averaged over the 12 Ss serving under value a (Ss of combinations aA, aB, and aC), and $\bar{b}$ is defined as the corresponding quantity averaged over the Ss serving under value b (Ss of combinations bA, bB, and bC). *Note that the first independent variable, motivational level, cannot differentially affect $\bar{A}$, $\bar{B}$, or $\bar{C}$ because it is equated across the values of the second independent variable. For the same reason the second independent variable, amount of reward, cannot differentially affect $\bar{a}$ or $\bar{b}$.*

By appropriate statistical analysis of the data of Table 2-8, one can determine separately whether the first independent variable, motivational level, has an effect on the dependent variable; whether the second independent variable, amount of reward, affects the dependent variable; and whether the two independent variables interact—i.e., determine if amount of reward has the same effect on the dependent variable whether Ss are under low or high motivation.

(Assuming that certain statistical assumptions are met, the appropriate statistical technique by which these evaluations are made is the *two-way analysis of variance applied to factorial designs*.)

[4] Although equal numbers of Ss in all subgroups are not essential for factorial designs, such a distribution is most commonly encountered because it greatly facilitates appropriate statistical analyses.

Table 2-8 Results from a Fictitious Factorial Experiment

VALUES OF THE FIRST INDEPENDENT VARIABLE	VALUES OF THE SECOND INDEPENDENT VARIABLE			
	A	B	C	
a	10, 15 17, 18	9, 9 12, 13	9, 10 10, 12	$\bar{a} = 12$
b	12, 17 19, 20	9, 13 14, 17	10, 11 11, 15	$\bar{b} = 14$
	$\bar{A} = 16$	$\bar{B} = 12$	$\bar{C} = 11$	

It may occur to the student that factorial designs have already been encountered in this chapter. Refer, for example, to Table 2-2. By analogy to Table 2-7, the first factor in the former table, an equated subject RV, assumes the two values male and female; the second factor, an independent variable, assumes the three values I_1, I_2, and I_3, which, it will be recalled, were different intensities of the tonal stimulus.

To go one step further, Table 2-3 may be interpreted as a factorial design with three factors, one independent variable and two equated subject RVs, inasmuch as a different subgroup serves under each of the 12 different combinations of the three factors. One subgroup serves under the combination 21- to 22-year-old males; a second serves under the combination 21- to 22-year-old males, and so forth. More generally in a factorial design with three factors—the third factor assuming k values—the total number of combinations possible is $r \times c \times k$, and $[1/(r \times c \times k)]n$ Ss serve under each of the combinations. The effect of each of the three factors on the dependent variable can be evaluated separately in much the same manner as described for the two-factor design, and the interactions, which when three factors are involved number four, can also be individually assessed.

Clearly, then, a factorial design can be employed whenever two or more variables are simultaneously manipulated in an experiment. The manipulated variables may all be independent variables, or they may include one or more equated relevant variables. For a design to be factorial, however, separate groups of Ss must serve under each combination of conditions generated by the manipulated variables.

It is apparent that separate-groups designs and factorial designs are not unrelated, for a factorial design may be considered a separate-groups design generalized to more than one manipulated variable. With reference again to the factorial design in Table 2-7, since different groups of Ss serve under the two values of the first independent variable, a and b, it is fair to say that with respect to this variable a separate-groups design is being employed; obviously, the same conclusion holds true for the second independent variable because each S serves under only one of the three values A, B, and C.

Nonfactorial Designs

Of course it is not necessary when simultaneously manipulating more than one variable that each S serve under only one of the combinations of conditions occurring in the experiment. For example, suppose that in the illustration of Table 2-7, the second independent variable—assumed to be amount of reward— were manipulated in a single-group fashion, each S serving under all three values of the variable. The two independent variables, amount of reward and motivational level, would still generate six combinations of conditions, but only two separate groups of Ss would be involved, one serving under each of the three conditions aA, aB, and aC, and the other under bA, bB, and bC. Considering each independent variable separately, one would say that the experiment was a separate-groups design with respect to the first independent variable and a single-group design with respect to the second. Such experimental designs may be referred to as "mixed" designs, since they mix single-group and separate-groups designs within the same experiment. Mixed designs, then, are nonfactorial designs.

Another source of nonfactorial designs is obtained by generalizing the single-group design to more than one manipulated variable, thus achieving a design in which only one group of Ss is employed, with each S serving under *all* combinations of the conditions of the experiment. The use of such experimental designs, which may be referred to as "multifactor" single-group designs, will obviously be limited to situations where very few manipulated variables are involved and where it is reasonable to assume that sequence effects are relatively unimportant.

There are numerous other variants of nonfactorial designs, many of which are constructed around "incomplete" single-group designs, that is, designs in which each S serves under more than one but less than all values of an independent variable. Quite a few of these designs are treated in detail from the statistical point of view by Winer (1962).

A CAUTION ABOUT GROUP AVERAGES

In most experiments not employing a single-subject design, results are analyzed in terms of averages taken over the entire group of subjects—for example, the group mean, median, and learning curve. Frequently this approach is perfectly justified. At times, however, measures based on averaging group data are so unrepresentative of the performance of the individuals composing the group that they are entirely misleading (e.g., Sidman, 1952). To take a simple example, suppose a certain drug had the effect of enhancing the performance of fast learners while impeding slow learners. Comparison of drug and no-drug groups would probably show little difference between their mean performances, perhaps leading to the erroneous conclusion that the drug was totally without effect. In this case the effect of the drug could probably be determined by considering a different group statistic, the variance (a measure of variability—see Chap. 4); in other cases, however, a more detailed analysis may be required.

A good illustration comes from mathematical models of learning. For a long time there have been two opposing assumptions concerning the basic nature of the learning process. The first assumption is that it is a gradual process, the amount learned increasing by a small magnitude with each practice trial. The second assumption is that the learning process is an all-or-none situation; on any one trial the association is formed completely or not at all. Strange as it might seem, rigorous mathematical models based on these two antithetical interpretations make precisely the same prediction with respect to the group learning curve, namely, that it will be a gradually increasing curve having an exponential form. In order to distinguish between the two points of view, a detailed analysis of the distribution of errors made by individual Ss is required (Atkinson, Bower, & Crothers, 1965, pp. 75–120).

Perhaps the point being made is obvious. Simple group averages may give a distorted picture of what is going on in the individual S. Aware that this possibility exists, one should, wherever possible, examine individual data to evaluate the representativeness of the group measures; certain modified group measures, such as the "backward" learning curve (Hayes, 1953), sometimes prove useful. This caveat applies as well to single-subject designs, where averaging could also have the effect of obscuring S's typical behavior patterns (e.g., Migler, 1964).

SUMMARY

This chapter has been rather long and, in places, perhaps a little difficult. However, since many of the concepts and methods treated are basic to much of what follows, this first acquaintance with them is by no means the last. Let us now briefly identify some of the major features of the chapter. Relevant variables were subdivided into three classes: subject RVs, situational RVs, and sequence RVs (three s's). Three major types of control techniques were distinguished: matching, randomization, and counterbalancing. And as shown in Table 2-1, which may be considered a summary outline of the chapter, classes of RVs and types of control techniques were mated for separate-groups and single-group designs separately.

1. Control of subject RVs in separate-groups designs involves two types of control techniques:

2. Two methods of matching subject RVs are:
    (a) The advantages of the first are:
    (b) The two disadvantages of the first are:
    (c) The important feature of the second method is:
    (d) The randomized-blocks method may be described as:

3. A fundamental difference between controlling subject RVs by matching and by the second control technique is:

4. Residual randomization may be distinguished from randomization of known relevant variables by:

5. In single-group designs, control of subject RVs is:

6. (a) Control of situational RVs in separate-groups designs differs from control of subject RVs in the following ways:
(b) The danger of the yoking control method is:
(c) Control of situational RVs in single-group designs requires more effort than control of subject RVs because:

7. Sequence RVs are of primary importance for single-group designs because:

8. (a) Order effects and carry-over effects both result from sequence RVs, but they differ as follows:
(b) Control of carry-over effects, in the sense of their equalization over all values of the independent variable, is often quite difficult because:

9. The difference between intrasubject and intragroup counterbalancing is:

10. A widely used method of obtaining intrasubject counterbalancing when two values of an independent variable are under study is:
(a) It is used primarily to control:
(b) A basic assumption behind its use is:
(c) If this assumption is untenable, one may:

11. The single-subject design, a special case of the single-group design, is a design in which:

12. (a) Three types of intragroup counterbalancing may be distinguished, namely:
(b) In the first type, the procedure is to:
i Its advantages are:
ii Its disadvantages are:
(c) A balanced square is an instance of the second type of counterbalancing. Its two useful properties are:
(d) A description of the third type of counterbalancing is:
(e) The third type is used primarily when:

13. A factorial design may be defined as:

(a) By its use, and with appropriate statistical analysis, one may determine the following about the factors or variables involved in the experiment:

(b) If a factorial experiment involves three independent variables, the first of which assumes three values, the second assumes four values, and the third, six values, the total number of possible combinations of the three variables will be:

(c) In the preceding example, if n subjects are used in the experiment, the number of Ss serving under each combination is:

14. Two types of nonfactorial designs are:

15. (a) If we say that variables X and Y *interact* in their effects on the dependent variable, we mean:

(b) The concept of interaction is important in psychological research because:

3 DESCRIPTIVE STATISTICS I

The main purpose of Chaps. 3 and 4 is to introduce from descriptive statistics a number of basic concepts and techniques, many of which will be used in Chaps. 5 and 6. The student who has had a course in statistics will already be familiar with a good deal of the material covered in Chaps. 3 and 4; nevertheless a quick reading of these chapters is desirable, if only because the terminology and symbolism used here might differ from those previously encountered.

Statistics consists of two distinct types of activities: *descriptive statistics* and *inference*. Descriptive statistics is concerned with the *description*, usually in mathematical terms, of various properties of data obtained from a *sample*. The aim is to describe meaningful properties of the sample data in terms of mathematical indices or other means, e.g., the arithmetic mean, the median, and frequency distributions. This is the statistical activity known to most people, and it is sometimes wrongly thought to be the whole of statistics. In inference, the more engaging activity, one attempts to go beyond the sample data and infer properties of the *population* from which the sample was drawn.

A simplified but instructive illustration of the difference between the two activities is furnished by the following example. Imagine a jar filled with a large number of red balls and black balls from which 10 balls are drawn, 7 of which are red. The proportion of red balls in the sample, 0.70, describes a property of the sample and is therefore a descriptive or sample statistic. Suppose, however, that interest lies in the corresponding property of the population, namely, in the proportion of red balls in the entire jar. By applying certain well-defined methods of inference to the sample proportion, one can make precise estimates of the *population* proportion of red balls.

All the statistical designs mentioned parenthetically in the previous chapter are additional examples of statistical inference; the aim of these designs is to enable *E* to make precise inferences about characteristics of the populations from which the experimental data constitute a sample.

The descriptive statistics treated in the present chapter fall under the headings *Measures of Central Tendency* and *Graphic Presentation of Data*. Prefacing these topics is a discussion of a simple but important mathematical concept, the *linear function*.

LINEAR FUNCTIONS

It is common for psychologists to make such statements as, "Performance on an IQ test is a *function* of age," or, "The rate of learning a list of words is a *function* of the meaningfulness of the words," or, "Reaction time is a *function* of the intensity of the stimulus employed." Looked at abstractly, all the preceding may be considered special cases of the general statement, "Variable *Y* is a *function* of variable *X*," meaning that variable *Y* *depends* on variable *X*.

Mathematicians have a convenient way of expressing this abstract, general statement. They write, "$Y = f(X)$," which means that variable *Y* equals (is) a function of variable *X*. Sometimes other letters are used to denote the functional relationship between the two variables, e.g., $Y = g(X)$ or $Y = h(X)$, but the interpretation is the same. The variable on the left standing alone, in this case *Y*, is a function of (depends on) the variable enclosed in parentheses on the right and preceded by the letter designating the function (f, g, etc.). Because in these functional equations *Y* depends on *X*—that is, the value of variable *Y* is determined by the value of variable *X* that appears in the equation—mathematicians call *Y* the *dependent* variable and *X* the *independent* variable. As the student may surmise, psychologists borrowed these terms long ago from mathematicians, adapting them to their own purposes yet maintaining a reasonable correspondence with their original meaning.

One specific type of functional equation fundamental and of wide significance in psychology is the linear function. As a rather trivial example of the

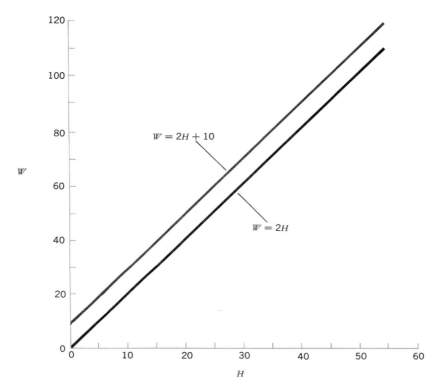

Fig. 3-1. Two linear functions relating H (number of hours worked in week) to W (week's wages in dollars).

latter, if an individual is paid at the rate of $2 per hour, his weekly wages in dollars (call this W) is, of course, a function of the number of hours worked during the week (H), that is, $W = f(H)$. But in this case we can be more explicit and specify the functional equation to be the linear function $W = 2(H)$ or, more simply, $W = 2H$. Thus, if an employee works 30 hours, his pay will be $60 $[W = 2(30) = 60]$; if he works 41.5 hours, his pay will be $83 $[W = 2(41.5) = 83]$, and so on. Should a more generous employer agree to pay him $10 per week more than the $2 hourly rate, the equation relating wages to number of hours worked would be $W = 2H + 10$; this too is a linear function.

Visual representation of the preceding two linear functions may be obtained by plotting their graphs, as in Fig. 3-1. In the figure, values of H are plotted on the horizontal axis (the *abscissa*), and values of W are plotted on the vertical axis (the *ordinate*). More generally, *the independent variable is always plotted on the abscissa and the dependent variable on the ordinate*. The graphs of the two functions quite clearly are straight lines; for this reason the functions are called "straight-line" or "linear" functions. Thus, *any function whose graph is a straight line is a linear function*. Other linear functions have been plotted in Fig. 3-2 where the

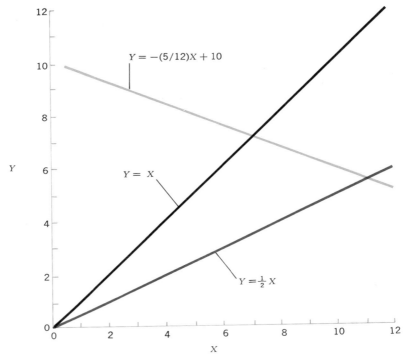

Fig. 3-2. The graphs of three linear functions (see text).

axes have been labeled X and Y, the two letters conventionally used to represent the independent and dependent variables, respectively.

Any function of the form $Y = cX + k$, where c and k are constants (i.e., numbers that remain fixed as variable X assumes different values), will yield a graph that is a straight line. Hence all such functions are linear functions. The constant k is called the "Y intercept" because it determines where the straight line will cross the Y axis. The function $W = 2H + 10$ intersects the Y axis at $Y = 10$, as is evident in Fig. 3-1. The function $W = 2H$ belongs to a special class of linear functions for which $k = 0$. As illustrated by the functions $Y = X$ and $Y = 0.5$ in Fig. 3-2, all such functions go through the "origin," i.e., the point where $X = 0$ and $Y = 0$.

The constant c is called the *slope* of the line (or of the linear function); it determines how steep the line will be. When c is a negative number, the graph of the function points downward (Fig. 3-2). More precisely, the slope of a linear function tells us how much variable Y increases for each unit that variable X increases. Thus in the function $Y = 3X + 2$, we know that for each unit that X increases, the value of Y increases by three units. For example, when $X = 7$,

$Y = 23$; when $X = 8$, $Y = 26$. If X is increased by four units, Y will be increased by 12 units, and so on. In more general terms, if $X_2 > X_1$ ($>$ means "greater than"), the slope of a linear function is defined as

$$c = \frac{Y_2 - Y_1}{X_2 - X_1}$$

where Y_2 is the value of Y when X is equal to X_2 (i.e., $Y_2 = cX_2 + k$) and Y_1 is the value of Y when X is equal to X_1. Applied to the preceding function, if $X_2 = 5$ and $X_1 = 1$, $Y_2 = 17$ and $Y_1 = 5$. Hence, $c = (17 - 5)/(5 - 1) = 3$, which, as we know, is the slope of the function.

EXERCISES

3-1. Suppose we know that a linear function is such that when $X = 6.5$, $Y = 12$, and when $X = 8$, $Y = 18$. What must the slope c be? The answer will be found at the end of the chapter.

It is apparent that two linear functions could have the same slope but be different because the Y intercepts differ. Conversely, two linear functions may have identical Y intercepts but different slopes. In the former case the graph of the two functions will produce a pair of parallel lines (Fig. 3-1); in the latter case, the straight lines will differ in their steepness, but they will meet at the Y axis (Fig. 3-2).

Linear Order Effects

Recall that in Chap. 2 we spoke of *linear order effects*. In the example of linear order effects cited in that chapter, order effects were assumed to be 4, 8, 12, and 16 units for ordinal positions 1, 2, 3, and 4, respectively, in a sequence of four conditions. If we let OE stand for the amount of order effects occurring at any ordinal position of the sequence and OP stand for ordinal position in the sequence, then we say that order effects are linear if they can be described by a linear function—i.e., by a function of the form $OE = cOP + k$ where, as usual, c and k are constants. In the previous example, the relationship between order effects and ordinal position may be expressed as $OE = 4(OP)$, clearly a linear function; hence, these order effects are linear.

Before continuing, the student should test his grasp of linear functions by completing the following exercises, the answers to which may be found at the end of the chapter. Appropriate graph paper, for example, paper with 10 lines per inch, can be purchased in most campus bookstores.

3-2. Plot the functions $Y = X$ and $Y = 2X$ for values of X ranging between 0 and 5, i.e., for $0 \leq X \leq 5$ ($\leq$ means "less than or equal to").

3-3. Plot the function $Y = X^2$ for $0 \leq X \leq 4$, and $Y = 1/X + 2$ for $0.5 \leq X \leq 5$. These are examples of *nonlinear* functions.

3-4. Plot the function $Y = 2$ for $0 \leq X \leq 5$. This function is an instance of the special case where $c = 0$. In all such functions, variable Y does not depend on variable X, because the value of Y is not influenced by the value of X.

3-5. A linear function is such that when $X = 2$, $Y = 9$ and when $X = 4$, $Y = 13$. Determine the constants c and k.

3-6. Given the linear function $Y = cX + k$, express X as a function of Y.

Hints on Constructing and Interpreting Graphs

There are a few details about graph construction that might be commented on here. In plotting graphs the student must choose units for the abscissa and ordinate that will accommodate the range of values which the independent and dependent variables take on, and often it is required that these units differ in size. For example, in plotting the function $Y = 10X$ for $0 \leq X \leq 5$, if units of the same size were used for both axes, the graphed function would occupy 10 times more vertical space than horizontal space, producing an ungainly figure. To bring this graph into more pleasing proportions, one would use a smaller-size unit for the Y axis than for the X axis, so that the height of the graph might be reduced to perhaps twice its width.

Another modification arises when all of the plotted function lies considerably above the abscissa, as in the function $Y = 10X + 100$. Because for positive values of X the Y values of this function never go below 100, the graphed function would appear awkward if the Y axis were numbered in the usual way. To eliminate much of the empty space beween the abscissa and the lowest part of the graph of the function, numbering of the Y axis is started at a value greater than zero, perhaps at 90. In Fig. 3-3 both of these points are illustrated in the graph of the function $Y = 10X + 100$ for $0 \leq X \leq 10$.

Because the visual appearance of the slope of a graphed function can be manipulated by the choice of units for the abscissa and ordinate, one can get a false impression of the slope of the *function* from the apparent slope of its graph. In the function $Y = 0.01X$, Y changes little with relatively large changes in X. This fact would be revealed in a nearly horizontal line if, in the graph of the function, the units used on the X and Y axes were of the same size. However, the apparent steepness of the line can be increased by manipulating the relative size of the units used for the abscissa and ordinate. If in the previous function, 1 Y unit occupied 0.1 in. on the ordinate and 1 X unit extended 1.0 in. on the abscissa, the graphed function would appear visually as steep as the function

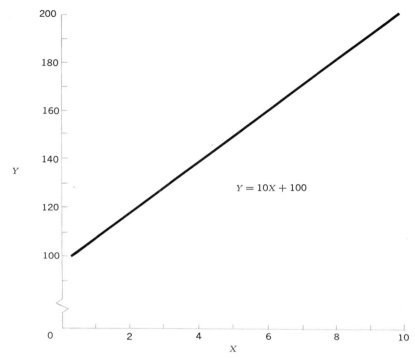

Fig. 3-3. The initial part of the Y axis has been omitted. Units of different size have been used on the X and Y axes to improve the appearance of the graph.

$Y = X$ graphed with equal units on the abscissa and ordinate. This is a point to be remembered when interpreting any graph relating a dependent variable to an independent variable.

Similarly, one can be misled as to the overall change in Y brought about by changes in X when numbering of the Y axis starts at values greater than zero. In the function $Y = X + 100$, $Y = 100$ when $X = 0$ and 110 when $X = 10$, an increase in Y of 10 percent. If, however, in a plot of the function for $0 \leq X \leq 10$ numbering of the Y axis were to start at 100, one might easily gain the impression that X exerts a much greater effect on Y than actually is the case. To guard against such false impressions, attention is called to the missing Y values by a device that signifies a break in the axis, as, for example, that shown in the ordinate of Fig. 3-3.

MEASURES OF CENTRAL TENDENCY

In this section three descriptive statistics, the *mode*, the *median*, and the *mean*, are introduced. These statistics all describe the "central tendency" of a group of numbers, that is, all yield a single (usually different) number which is in some sense "representative" of the group (or distribution) of numbers.

The Mode

Suppose we toss a die seven times and on each toss observe the number of dots present on the face of the die that turns up. The "number of dots on the face of the die that turns up" is, of course, a discrete quantitative variable. Assume that the outcomes of the seven tosses were as follows: 1, 1, 1, 2, 3, 4, 6. Thus, one dot was observed on three of the tosses (not necessarily the first three), and two, three, four, and six dots were each observed on one of the seven tosses of the die. These seven *values* (or *scores, observations,* or *outcomes*) constitute a distribution of values (or scores, observations, outcomes) or, more simply, a distribution.

One measure of the central tendency of a distribution that is always defined but rarely used is the mode (m_0), usually defined as *the most frequently occurring value in a distribution.* In the preceding distribution, therefore, $m_0 = 1$. Suppose, however, the distribution were as follows: 1, 1, 1, 2, 3, 3, 3. Strictly speaking this distribution has no mode because there is no *single* most frequently occurring value. Nevertheless, such distributions are often referred to as "bimodal" distributions, i.e., having two modes. One even hears the term "multimodal" applied to distributions that have several "modes." Because the mode never enters calculations in the statistical analyses that will be our concern—it is used solely for description—there seems little harm in the use of such descriptive terms as bimodal.

The Median

The definition of the median (m) as a measure of central tendency is that it is *the point above and below which lie 50 percent of the observations in the distribution.* In the previously encountered distribution 1, 1, 1, 2, 3, 4, 6, $m = 2$, because we may imagine that "$3\frac{1}{2}$" observations lie above and below this point. In a distribution consisting of the six values—1, 2, 2, 3, 5, 6—the median is the point that is midway between the third and fourth scores; that is, $m = 2.5$. The following procedure may be used in finding the median of a distribution. Arrange the scores of the distribution in increasing order of magnitude, and (1) if there is an odd number of observations in the distribution, the median is equal to the value of the middlemost score; (2) if the number of observations is even, it is the midpoint between the two middle scores. Hence in the following two distributions—1, 3, 2, 4, 6, 5, 5, 4, 3, 2, 6 and 1, 2, 4, 2—the medians are 4 and 2, respectively. There is a more refined method of calculating the median that will be discussed later in this chapter, but it need not concern us here.

The Arithmetic Mean

The (arithmetic) mean is by far the most useful of the measures of central tendency. Unlike the mode and median, the magnitude of every score in a distribution is taken into account in calculating the mean, which verbally is defined as *the sum of all the scores in the distribution, divided by the number of observations*. The mean of the distribution of seven tosses of a die—1, 1, 1, 2, 3, 4, 6—is therefore

$$\frac{1 + 1 + 1 + 2 + 3 + 4 + 6}{7} = \frac{4}{7}$$

It is helpful to introduce certain symbols that make for economy and precision of expression. If a distribution contains five observations, the mean of the distribution is defined as the sum of the five scores divided by 5. Let us, however, refer to the five observations as follows: X_1, X_2, X_3, X_4, X_5, where X_1 is *any one* of the five scores, X_2 may be any one of the remaining four observations, X_3 is any of the remaining three, and so on. Then the definition of the mean of this distribution may be written as

$$\frac{X_1 + X_2 + X_3 + X_4 + X_5}{5} = \bar{X}$$

where $\bar{X}$ is the symbol used to denote the mean of a group of Xs. This formula for obtaining the mean is still cumbersome, but it can be improved by introducing a symbol, Σ, which means "add together." (The symbol Σ is the capital letter "sigma" of the Greek alphabet.) Thus ΣX simply means add together all the Xs; we may therefore define the mean of the preceding distribution as $\Sigma X/5$. To go one step further, because a distribution can consist of any number of observations, that number of observations, whatever it might be, may simply be designated as n. In the general case, then, given any distribution of scores, which we shall write as $X_1, X_2, \ldots, X_n$, the mean of the distribution may be defined as $\bar{X} = \Sigma X/n$.

EFFECT OF A LINEAR TRANSFORMATION ON THE MEAN OF A DISTRIBUTION.   Let the distribution $X_1, X_2, \ldots, X_n$ have the mean $\bar{X}$. Suppose now that each score of the distribution is transformed by the linear function $Y_i = cX_i + k$ so that the values of the transformed distribution are $Y_1 = cX_1 + k$, $Y_2 = cX_2 + k, \ldots, Y_n = cX_n + k$. It involves simple algebra to show that the mean of the transformed distribution, $\bar{Y}$, may be expressed in terms of the mean of the original distribution, $\bar{X}$, as follows: $\bar{Y} = c\bar{X} + k$. The transformation of X scores to Y scores, because it is performed by a linear function, is called a "linear transformation."

The Geometric Mean

For some purposes, instances of which arise in Chap. 6, the *geometric mean* is preferable to the arithmetic mean as a measure of central tendency. The geometric mean (GM) is obtained by multiplying together the n scores of a distribution and then taking the nth root of the product, symbolically

$$GM = (X_1 \cdot X_2 \cdots X_n)^{1/n}$$

As an illustration, given the scores 2, 2, 4, and 16, $GM = (2 \times 2 \times 4 \times 16)^{\frac{1}{4}} = 4$.

The answers to the following exercises will be found at the end of the chapter.

EXERCISES

3-7. Suppose that the mean of a given distribution is 5 and that a new distribution is formed by squaring all the scores of the original distribution. Will the mean of the new distribution be $5^2 = 25$? Why or why not? If not, what information is required to calculate the mean of the new distribution?

3-8. Suppose that the mode of a distribution of 11 scores is 4 and that the median is 7. State, if you can, what the mode and median will be in new distributions obtained by the following transformations: (a) multiplying every score by 10 and subtracting 3 from every score (i.e., $Y_1 = 10X_1 - 3$, $Y_2 = 10X_2 - 3$, etc.) and (b) squaring every score of the old distribution.

TABULAR AND GRAPHIC PRESENTATION OF DATA

At the end of almost every psychological experiment, **E** finds himself with a mass of data obtained from his subjects which he must organize and distill before he can make sense of them. Often one of the first things **E** does is to arrange the data into a *frequency distribution*, which may be defined as *any listing of the values that a variable takes on along with the frequency with which each of the values occurs*. Frequency distributions may be tabular, i.e., presented as a table, in which case they are called "frequency tables," or they may be graphic and are then referred to as "frequency graphs." There are a number of different kinds of frequency graphs, for example, *bar graphs, line graphs, histograms,* and *frequency polygons*. In this section we shall discuss frequency graphs that are appropriate for both qualitative and quantitative variables. The student should be advised that some of the terminology employed in this section is not yet standardized; thus, variations in usage from one text to another should be anticipated.

Bar Graphs

Suppose we toss a coin eight times and observe the following occurrences of heads (H) and tails (T): HHTHTHTH. The outcome of a toss of a coin, heads or tails, is of course a qualitative variable. A *frequency table* of these data is constructed as follows:

VALUE OF THE VARIABLE (H or T)	FREQUENCY f
H	5
T	3

As previously indicated, a frequency table is a tabular listing of the values that a variable takes on—in this case H or T—along with the number of occurrences of each value.

It is often advantageous to present the frequency distribution in graphic rather than tabular form, i.e., in the form of a frequency graph. In Fig. 3-4 a bar graph of the preceding frequency distribution is presented. The values of the variable are listed on the abscissa, and frequency, f, is plotted on the ordinate. Although H precedes T on the abscissa, the reverse order is just as valid. The heights of the bars correspond to the frequencies with which the different values of the variable occur. Finally, to emphasize the fact that one is dealing with a qualitative variable, the bars of the graph are separated from each other.

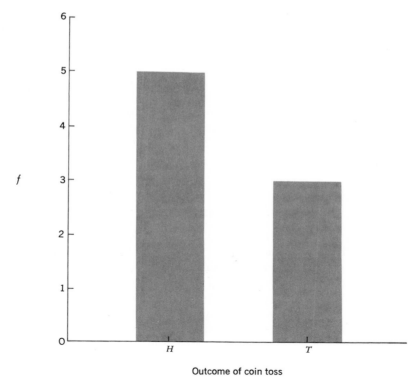

Outcome of coin toss

Fig. 3-4. A bar graph of the frequency distribution of a qualitative variable.

Thus, when one is dealing with a collection of observations on a qualitative variable (having any number of values or categories), the data can be condensed and visually portrayed by a bar graph. The ordering of the values of the variable along the abscissa is arbitrary, and the bars of the graph are not contiguous with each other.

Line Graphs

Suppose we toss a die 90 times, noting on each toss the number of dots on the face that turns up. The latter is a discrete quantitative variable, one with which we are already familiar. Let us suppose that the 90 outcomes were as shown in the following frequency table:

NUMBER OF DOTS OBSERVED	f
1	13
2	14
3	13
4	17
5	15
6	18

A graphic representation of this frequency distribution is given in the line graph of Fig. 3-5. As is usual with frequency graphs, the values of the variable under observation are plotted on the abscissa and frequency on the ordinate. In a line graph, however, lines rather than bars are used to indicate frequencies, because lines portray a discrete variable more accurately than bars. Thus, in the present illustration all values on the abscissa other than the integers 1, 2, 3, 4, 5, and 6 should be assigned zero frequency, inasmuch as observation of such values is impossible (e.g., 1.75 dots cannot possibly occur). It is plain that lines depict this situation more faithfully than bars; nevertheless, the use of bars in frequency graphs of discrete variables is not rare.

Histograms and Frequency Polygons

Imagine that in the following situation we are studying the timing behavior of monkeys. A hungry monkey is placed into a cage containing a bar. Depression of the bar under the proper conditions results in the delivery of a food pellet, the "reinforcement." The proper conditions are that the monkey space his bar-pressing responses by at least 10 sec. If a bar-pressing response occurs less than 10 sec after the immediately preceding response, the monkey does not get his food pellet, and he must now wait 10 additional sec from this last response before a bar press will pay off. This kind of training program, because it encourages low rates of responding, is called a "differential reinforcement of low rates" reinforcement schedule (standardly abbreviated *DRL*). To the extent that the monkey can judge elapsed time, he will tend to space his responses about 10 sec

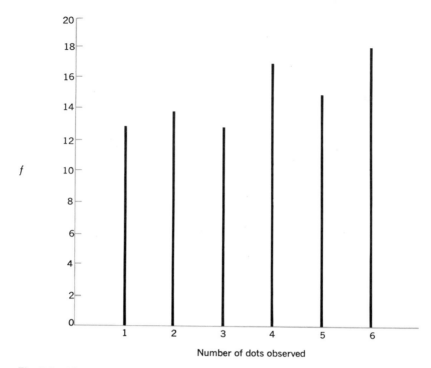

Fig. 3-5. Line graph of a discrete variable.

apart, because postponing his responses much longer than 10 sec unnecessarily delays receipt of the food pellets. With sufficient training in this situation, monkeys, and even rats, can judge a 10-sec interval with surprising accuracy.

The basic dependent variable in studies of this sort is the length of time that elapses between successive bar-pressing responses, called the "interresponse time" (*IRT*). Assume, for example, that S makes four responses spaced as follows: 11.3 sec between the first and second responses, 2.1 sec between the second and third responses, and 11.7 sec between the third and the fourth. The three *IRT*s are then 11.3, 2.1, and 11.7 sec. Because the *IRT* is a time measure, it is obviously a *continuous* dependent variable.

Now suppose that in one daily session our monkey produced a total of 112 bar-pressing responses, yielding 111 *IRT*s recorded to the nearest $\frac{1}{10}$ sec. The first thing we would want to do with these data is to organize them into a frequency distribution. This is accomplished as follows. We first look over the 111 *IRT*s to determine their range of values. Let us assume that none is below 2 sec or above 18 sec; hence, the frequency distribution will have to accommodate *IRT*s ranging between 2 and 18 sec. Although the *IRT*s have been recorded to the nearest $\frac{1}{10}$ sec, we would not want our frequency distribution to be divided into such fine units, because the 111 *IRT*s would then be distributed among 160 intervals each $\frac{1}{10}$ sec in length (i.e., this is the number of successive $\frac{1}{10}$-sec intervals contained between 2 and 18 sec). With such a large number of intervals, it is unlikely that any interval would contain more than a very few of the *IRT*s.

The solution to the present difficulty is to group the data into larger intervals or "classes." If 2.0 sec is chosen as the size of the class, the intervals of the frequency distribution become 0.0 to 2.0 sec, 2.0 to 4.0 sec, 4.0 to 6.0 sec, etc., with the understanding that if an *IRT* falls exactly on the boundary of two classes (e.g., an *IRT* of 4.0 sec), it is to be included in the upper interval (in this case, 4.0 to 6.0 sec). More generally, the size of the intervals used in a frequency distribution depends on the range of values that must be encompassed and the number of observations that are at hand. Other considerations that enter relate to the type of data with which one is dealing and the purpose which the frequency distribution is to serve. Because of the multiplicity of relevant factors involved in the choice of an appropriate class size, it is not feasible to state general rules of formation. However, it may be said that one should strive for the largest number of intervals (hence for intervals of the smallest possible size) consistent with the requirements and purposes of the frequency distribution.

Let us assume that, using the intervals specified above, the 111 *IRT*s produce the frequency distribution shown in the first three columns of Table 3-1 (ignore for the present the last three columns). Interresponse times are grouped into intervals of 2.0 sec in the first column of the table, and the number of *IRT*s falling in each interval (f) is shown in the third column. The value of the midpoint or the "class mark" of each interval is recorded in the second column.

THE HISTOGRAM. The preceding frequency distribution may be graphed in the form of a *histogram* (Fig. 3-6), which we shall define as a *bar graph of a continuous variable*. Note that in a histogram, adjacent bars are contiguous. When the

Table 3-1 Frequency and Cumulative Frequency Distributions of Hypothetical *DRL* Data

(1)	(2)	(3)	(4)	(5)	(6)
IRT (SEC)	MIDPOINT OF INTERVAL	FREQUENCY f	PERCENT f %f	CUMULATIVE f cf	PERCENT cf %cf
0.0–2.0	1.0	0	0.0	0	0.0
2.0–4.0	3.0	3	2.7	3	2.7
4.0–6.0	5.0	4	3.6	7	6.3
6.0–8.0	7.0	6	5.4	13	11.7
8.0–10.0	9.0	10	9.0	23	20.7
10.0–12.0	11.0	30	27.0	53	47.8
12.0–14.0	13.0	40	36.0	93	83.8
14.0–16.0	15.0	15	13.5	108	97.3
16.0–18.0	17.0	3	2.7	111	100.0
18.0–20.0	19.0	0	0.0	111	100.0

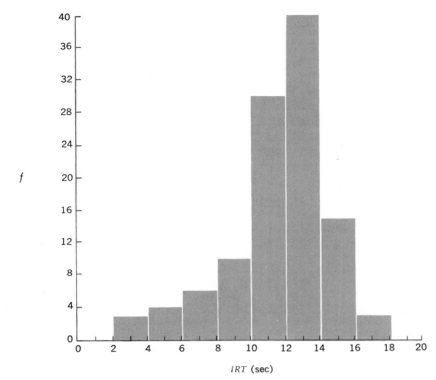

Fig. 3-6. A histogram of the DRL data.

histogram is composed of bars of equal width, the frequency of scores in any interval is, as in the bar graph, indicated by the height of the corresponding column or bar.

THE FREQUENCY POLYGON.   A second kind of frequency graph often used with continuous variables is the *frequency polygon*. Here the frequency in each interval is plotted at the midpoint of the interval with straight lines connecting all of the points. The frequency distribution of Table 3-1 has been graphed as a frequency polygon in Fig. 3-7.

EXERCISES

3-9. Superimpose with pencil the frequency polygon of Fig. 3-7 on the histogram of Fig. 3-6. Note how much area of each bar of the histogram is included within the frequency polygon. Is the area included within the entire histogram the same as included within the frequency polygon?

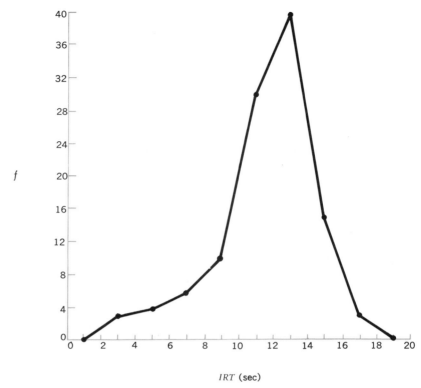

IRT (sec)

Fig. 3-7. Frequency polygon of *DRL* data.

HISTOGRAMS AND FREQUENCY POLYGONS BASED ON PERCENTAGES. It is often useful to graph histograms and frequency polygons in terms of "percent frequency" (%f) rather than to use actual frequencies. That is, rather than indicating the *number* of cases occurring in each interval, the *percentage* of cases is shown instead. In Table 3-1 the percentage of *IRT*s falling in each interval of the frequency distribution is shown in column 4. These values were obtained by dividing each frequency (f) by the total number of *IRT*s and multiplying by 100, i.e., $\%f = 100(f/n)$, where n stands for the total number of observations. The usefulness of histograms and frequency polygons plotted in terms of percent frequency stems from the fact that they make possible direct comparisons of histograms (or frequency polygons) based on different numbers of observations. For example, with the use of such histograms, it would be a simple matter to follow the day-by-day development of timing behavior in our monkey even though the number of bar presses, and hence the number of *IRT*s, varied considerably from day to day.

As an instructive exercise, use the data in columns 1 and 4 of Table 3-1 to construct a percent frequency histogram and compare it with the histogram of Fig. 3-6.

AREA AND FREQUENCY RELATIONS IN A HISTOGRAM. Because of the way histograms are constructed, there is a close relationship between the area of the histogram contained between any two points on the abscissa and the number of observations falling in the interval between the given points. Refer, for example, to Fig. 3-6. The bars of the histogram are identical in width (w); their heights (h), however, are directly proportional to the number of cases falling in the interval they subtend. Thus the area (a) of a bar, which is given by $a = h \times w$, is also directly proportional to the number of cases falling in the interval subtended by the bar. This relationship between frequency and area is not restricted to the intervals which coincide with the endpoints of the bars of the histogram; it applies to any arbitrary interval. Hence, the number of *IRTs* falling between 3.0 and 6.0 sec is proportional to the area of the histogram included between these two values. The number of observations falling above 12.0 sec is, in like manner, directly proportional to the area of the histogram situated above 12.0 sec.

The *relative* area between any two points of a histogram provides even more information: it reveals the *relative frequency* ($rf = f/n$) or *proportion* of cases falling between the given points. The relative area between two points is obtained by dividing the area contained between the points by the total area of the histogram. For example, neglecting units of measurement, the area contained between 8.0 and 10.0 in Fig. 3-6 is 20 units, because $a = h \times w = 10 \times 2$. The total area ($A$) of the histogram is given by

$$A = (h_1 \times w) + (h_2 \times w) + \cdots + (h_8 \times w)$$

where h_1 is the height of the first bar, h_2 is the height of the second bar, and so on; the widths (w) of all the bars are equal. If the student will now form the ratio a/A, he will find after simplification that $a/A = 10/111$, which is simply the proportion of cases or the *rf* in the 8.0- to 10.0-sec interval. With slight elaboration, the same argument holds for *any* interval of the frequency histogram. Accordingly, *the proportion of cases falling in any interval of a histogram is given by the relative area of the histogram contained within the given interval.*

HISTOGRAMS WITH UNEQUAL CLASS INTERVALS. There are cases where it is preferable to group data into intervals that are not all the same length. Suppose, for example, that one of the three observations in the 16.0- to 18.0-sec interval occurred instead in the 18.0- to 20.0-sec interval. Wishing not to present an interval containing only one observation, we would increase the size of the last interval of the frequency distribution to 16.0 to 20.0 sec; this interval, then, would contain three cases. In the construction of the corresponding frequency histogram, all bars would be as they appear in Fig. 3-6 with the exception of the last one, which, because it spans the interval 16.0 to 20.0 sec, must be twice the width of the others. What, however, should the height of this bar be? If the height were set at a value of 3, the relationship between area and frequency just described would be destroyed. (Why?) To maintain the relationship, a frequency of 1.5 must be assigned to the 16.0- to 20.0-sec interval. This assignment may be interpreted as indicating that 1.5 observations lie in the interval 16.0 to 18.0 sec and 1.5 in the interval 18.0 to 20.0 sec, totaling 3.0 cases in the entire interval. The point is that in constructing histograms one must assign frequencies in such a way that the area contained in each bar of the histogram is proportional to the number of cases occurring in the interval subtended by the bar.

AREA AND FREQUENCY RELATIONS IN A FREQUENCY POLYGON.   We have already noted that a frequency polygon contains the same area as its associated histogram, although the distribution of the area is not precisely the same as in the histogram. Despite the latter discrepancy—which is usually small—we may accept that a similar relationship holds for area and frequency in a frequency polygon: the proportion of cases falling in any interval is given by the relative area of the polygon contained within the interval.

Suppose, then, that given the frequency polygon of Fig. 3-7, one wished to know the relative frequency with which *IRTs* of 13.0 sec occurred. Would this value be 40/111? If so, then *IRTs* of 13.1, 13.2, and 13.3 sec must have occurred with relative frequencies of at least 36/111. (Why?) Accepting this premise, we face the embarrassing conclusion that the relative frequencies of these four values alone add up to more than 1.0—an impossible situation. The initial premise obviously must be false.

The solution is, of course, that the frequency of 40 on the ordinate refers to the *total* frequency in the interval 12.0 to 14.0 sec. Hence, because the score of 13.0 sec actually occupies the interval 13.0 to 13.1 sec, or one-twentieth of the entire 12.0- to 14.0-sec interval, one-twentieth of the total frequency in the latter interval (or two cases) may be assumed to have scores of 13.0 sec; therefore the latter value may be said to have occurred with relative frequency equal to 2/111. In terms of area, the same relative frequency may be obtained by taking the ratio of the area located within the interval 13.0 to 13.1 sec to the total area of the polygon.

Consequently, in reading a frequency polygon one must not take the frequency, relative frequency, or percent frequency labeled on the ordinate too seriously; exact information concerning the frequencies with which scores on the abscissa occur is not given by corresponding values on the ordinate but rather by the areas associated with the scores of interest. It would be safer if the ordinate of frequency polygons were labeled with a neutral "*Y*," as they are in mathematically defined distributions (discussed in the following chapter).

EXERCISES

3-10. Draw a histogram of the following *relative* frequency distribution: 3.0 to 4.0, 0.10; 4.0 to 5.0, 0.24; 5.0 to 6.0, 0.30; 6.0 to 7.0, 0.22; 7.0 to 8.0, 0.14. What is the total area of the histogram? What does the area of the histogram contained within any interval of the histogram indicate about the *rf* in that interval? Do *all rf* histograms have the last property?

Cumulative Frequency Distributions

Column 5 in Table 3-1 gives the cumulative frequencies (*cf*) for each successive interval. For example, 7 of the *IRT*s had a duration of 6.0 sec or less; 23 *IRT*s were equal to or less than 10.0 sec; and all 111 *IRT*s were 18.0 sec or less. The cumulative frequencies of column 5 taken in conjunction with the intervals of column 1 constitute a *cumulative frequency distribution*.

In the last column of Table 3-1 the cumulative frequencies have been converted into percent cumulative frequencies (*%cf*) in the same way that frequencies were converted into percent frequencies: $\%cf = 100(cf/n)$. Thus, 6.3 percent of the *IRT*s were 6.0 sec or less in duration, 47.8 percent were 12.0 sec or less, and so forth. Column 6 of Table 3-1 together with column 1 constitutes a *percent cumulative frequency distribution*.

Cumulative frequency distributions and percent cumulative frequency distributions may, of course, be graphed; they are then called "cumulative frequency ogives" and "percent cumulative frequency ogives." In Fig. 3-8 the *DRL* data have been plotted as a percent cumulative frequency ogive. Note that the *%cf* of each interval is plotted not at the midpoint of the interval, but rather at the upper limit. This procedure is correct because an interval's *%cf* indicates the percentage of cases having values *at or below* the upper limit of the interval.

The *%cf* distribution is useful in calculating the median and related quantities from grouped data. It will be recalled from an earlier section that the median was defined as the point above and below which lie 50 percent of the observations of the distribution. The method suggested for calculating the median of an odd number of observations was to rank the observations in order of increasing value and then designate the median to be the value of the middle-most observation. However, as may be illustrated by the *DRL* data of Table 3-1, this method is often too coarse to be useful for data that have been grouped into frequency distributions. The fifty-sixth observation is the median of the *IRT* distribution, and it lies, along with 39 other observations, in the 12.0- to 14.0-sec interval (column 5 of Table 3-1). If all observations in an interval are assigned the value of the class mark of the interval, then the fifty-sixth observation, and hence the median, would be equal to 13.0 sec. But this is hardly an appropriate procedure. Of the 40 observations in the 12.0- to 14.0-sec interval, only 2 were below but 37 were above the fifty-sixth observation, a fact that should be taken account of in calculating the value of the median.

A more refined procedure for calculating the median starts with the assumption that the 40 observations in the 12.0- to 14.0-sec interval are equally distributed throughout the interval, each observation occupying an interval of 0.05 sec. Thus, the fifty-fourth observation occupies the interval 12.00 to 12.05 sec; the fifty-fifth observation occupies the interval 12.05 to 12.10 sec, and so on. It is then reasonable to assume the median is the midpoint of the interval occupied

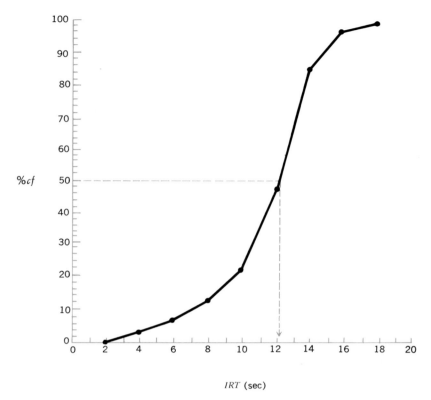

Fig. 3-8. Percent cumulative frequency ogive of *DRL* data.

by the fifty-sixth observation (12.10 to 12.15 sec). Hence, $m = 12.125$ and rounding to one decimal place, $m = 12.1$ sec, a value considerably different from 13.0 sec.

The same result can be obtained more directly through use of the %*cf* distribution. As already described, each entry in column 6 of Table 3-1 reveals the percentage of cases that fall at or below the upper limit of the corresponding interval. Thus 47.8 percent of the 111 *IRTs* had values of 12.0 sec or less in duration and 83.8 percent of the 111 *IRTs* were 14.0 sec or less. The value corresponding to the 50 percent point of the %*cf* distribution is none other than the median, because 50 percent of the observations lie below and above this point. The median is obviously located in the lower part of the 12.0- to 14.0-sec interval, and it may be found as follows.

First we determine what proportion of the 47.8- to 83.8-percent interval lies below the 50 percent point. This is given by

$$\frac{50.0\% - 47.8\%}{83.8\% - 47.8\%} = 0.061$$

It follows that 0.061 is also the proportion of the 12.0- to 14.0-sec interval that falls below the median. Consequently,

$$\frac{m - 12.0 \text{ sec}}{14.0 \text{ sec} - 12.0 \text{ sec}} = 0.061$$

or $m = 0.061(14.0 \text{ sec} - 12.0 \text{ sec}) + 12.0 \text{ sec}$. The median works out to be 12.122 sec, which, apart from rounding errors, is the result obtained earlier.

LINEAR INTERPOLATION.   The method just used to find m is called "*linear interpolation*"; because it is a very useful procedure, we shall describe it in general terms.

We have at hand three values of X, X_1 and X_2 ($X_1 < X_2$), and X_i ($X_1 < X_i < X_2$). On the assumption that X and Y are linearly related in the interval between X_1 and X_2—with Y_1 and Y_2 as the values of Y corresponding to X_1 and X_2, respectively—we wish to find the value of Y, Y_i, that corresponds to X_i. It follows from the given assumptions that

$$Y_i = \frac{Y_2 - Y_1}{X_2 - X_1}(X_i - X_1) + Y_1$$

EXERCISES

3-11. Derive the formula for linear interpolation just presented from the initial assumptions, reviewing Exercise 3-5 if you have difficulty.

Applying the linear-interpolation formula to the problem of finding the median of the *IRT* distribution, we first observe that in assuming that the 40 observations are distributed equally over the 12.0- to 14.0-sec interval, we are also assuming that %cf and interresponse time are linearly related in this interval. In other words, a graph relating %cf to *IRT*s between 12.0 and 14.0 sec would describe a straight line, a situation depicted by the appropriate segment of Fig. 3-8. Next, X_1, X_2, and X_i are taken to be 47.8 percent, 83.8 percent, and 50.0 percent, respectively; it follows that Y_1, Y_2, and Y_i are 12.0 sec, 14.0 sec, and m, in that order. Therefore, as given by the linear interpolation formula, the median is

$$m = \frac{(14.0 \text{ sec} - 12.0 \text{ sec})}{(83.8\% - 47.8\%)}(50.0\% - 47.8\%) + 12.0 \text{ sec}$$

As the student may verify, this is the same equation for m that was obtained earlier; consequently, as already determined, $m = 12.1$ sec.

Linear interpolation can also be performed graphically by interpolating on the %cf ogive. To illustrate, the median may be secured simply by projecting a line at right angles from the 50 percent point on the ordinate to where it intersects the curve, dropping a perpendicular from the point of intersection to the abscissa. The dashed line in Fig. 3-8 shows that the median obtained by this method, which is somewhat less accurate than arithmetical interpolation, is about 12 sec.

LINEAR INTERPOLATION OF THE MEDIAN IN UNGROUPED DATA. The calculation of the median of ungrouped data is also subject to the refinement afforded by linear interpolation. Consider the distribution 1, 2, 2, which by the method described in our earlier discussion of the median would be considered to have $m = 2$. If, however, the variable involved is a *continuous* variable, we may consider that the second and third observations of the distribution are equally distributed over the interval 1.5 to 2.5. Taking the median to be the midpoint of the interval occupied by the second observation, namely, the midpoint of 1.5 to 2.0, the refined median is equal to 1.75. In the event that the variable being dealt with is discrete, this refinement probably should not be employed because the values of the distribution do not then occupy intervals; rather they are concentrated at isolated points (Fig. 3-5). Actually, the median is a concept that, though frequently useful with discrete variables, applies primarily to continuous variables.

PERCENTILES AND RELATED QUANTITIES. The %cf distribution is very useful for calculating various quantities that are related to the median. Suppose, for example, we wished to identify a point on the IRT scale such that 25 percent of the 111 IRT observations fall below it (hence 75 percent above). Finding this value, which is commonly referred to as the "first quartile" (Q_1), poses precisely the same problem as finding the median. Hence linear interpolation into the 10.0- to 12.0-sec interval (Table 3-1), either arithmetically or graphically, will produce Q_1. The second quartile, Q_2, is the point below and above which 50 percent of the observations lie; it is therefore identical to m. Q_3, the third quartile, is defined as the point below which 75 percent of the observations lie, and in the case of the IRT distribution it, like the median, falls into the 12.0- to 14.0-sec interval.

The division of the %cf distribution into *percentiles* is very common and probably is a procedure already familiar to the student. Thus, the point below which 36 percent of the observations of a distribution fall is called the thirty-sixth percentile (P_{36}); the point below which 12 percent of the observations lie is called the twelfth percentile (P_{12}), and so on. Obviously, $P_{25} = Q_1$, and $P_{50} = Q_2 = m$. Like quartiles, any given percentile may be obtained by linear interpolation into the appropriate interval of the %cf distribution, either arithmetically or graphically.

One more point. Take a pencil and ruler and in Fig. 3-8 draw a dashed line perpendicular to the abscissa at the value of 13 sec and extend it until it intersects the curve; from the point of intersection, project the line at right angles to the ordinate. It should meet the ordinate at a value of about 66 (%cf). The significance of this line lies in its pointing out that approximately 66 percent of the 111 IRTs are below 13 sec. Using precisely the same operation one is able to ascertain what percentage of the distribution falls below any point on the IRT scale: we merely need to construct a perpendicular at the point in question and carry it to the point of intersection with the curve and from there carry it at right angles to the ordinate. This procedure, which is the reverse of that employed to obtain percentiles, enables us to find *percentile ranks* (PR). The percentile rank of a score is simply the percentage of the distribution which falls below that score. Thus the percentile rank of 13 sec, referred to as PR_{13}, is 66 because, as we know, 66 percent of the IRT distribution falls below 13 sec. We know that the median of the IRT distribution is 12.1 sec; therefore, $PR_{12.1} = 50$. Conversely, $P_{50} = 12.1$ sec. *A percentile, P_X, is the point or score on the scale of the dependent variable which has the property that X percent of the distribution lies below that point; the percentile rank of a point or score, PR_Y, is the percentage of the distribution that lies below the given score (Y).*

It should be apparent that percentile ranks can be found by linear interpolation in the %cf distribution. Thus, the percentile rank of 13 sec may be calculated from the linear-interpolation formula; the appropriate substitutions are

$$PR_{13} = \frac{83.8 - 47.8}{14.0 - 12.0}(13.0 - 12.0) + 47.8$$

The answer to the previous equation, $PR_{13} = 65.8$, is in close agreement with the answer obtained by graphic interpolation. Note that because the sought-after Y_i is on the %cf scale, the Xs and Ys of the linear-interpolation formula now refer to interresponse time and percent cumulative frequency, respectively.

EXERCISES

3-12. Calculate the following quantities for the IRT distribution: P_{36}, $PR_{13.2}$, and Q_3.

3-13. Is there only one P_{100}?

3-14. Given only a %cf distribution, can one obtain the %f distribution; if so, how?

3-15. Construct a %cf ogive for the frequency distribution graphed in Fig. 3-5. Find m, P_{45}, and P_{60} by graphic interpolation.

3-16. Suppose that X and Y are related by the function $Y = X^3$ so that when $X = 3$, $Y = 27$ and when $X = 5$, $Y = 125$. Find by linear interpolation the value of Y when $X = 4$. Why does this differ from the actual value, i.e., 64?

SUMMARY

1. A linear function may be defined as:

2. The mode, median, and arithmetic and geometric means are measures of central tendency. Their definitions are:

3. A linear transformation refers to:

4. If a distribution of scores has a mean of $\bar{X}$ and all of the scores are transformed by the multiplication of a constant (b) and the addition of a different constant (a), the mean of the transformed scores will be:

5. (a) A frequency distribution is:
   (b) Frequency distributions take two general forms, namely:

6. The appropriate graphs for frequency distributions of qualitative and discrete variables are, respectively:

7. The frequency distributions of continuous variables, on the other hand, may be graphed as either:

8. In the previous two types of graphs, the relative frequency or proportion of cases occurring between any two values of the measured variable is given by the relative area under the curve contained between the given two values. The reason for this is:

9. In the event that the widths of the bars of a histogram are unequal, the heights of the bars should be determined in such a way that:

10. (a) Cumulative frequency (cf) distributions and percent cumulative frequency ($\%cf$) distributions differ in that:
   (b) Their graphs are called:

11. Define percentile, quartile, and percentile rank and explain the methods by which they may be secured from the $\%cf$ table or graph.

ANSWERS TO EXERCISES

3-1. $c = (18 - 12)/(8 - 6.5) = 4$.

3-2, 3-3, and **3-4.** See Fig. 3-9.

3-5. The slope of the function is 2 because $c = (13 - 9)/(4 - 2) = 2$. Hence, the function must be of the form $Y = 2X + k$. But because we know that when $X = 2$, $Y = 9$, we can write $9 = 2(2) + k$ or $k = 5$. Thus, $Y = 2X + 5$.

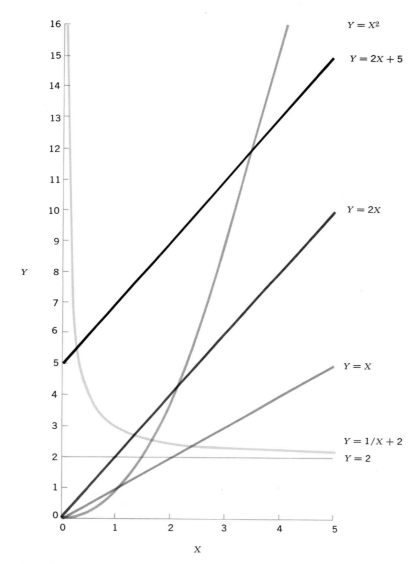

Fig. 3-9. Several linear and nonlinear functions.

3-6. $X = (1/c)Y - k/c$, i.e., X is a linear function of Y. A plot of this function, with X on the ordinate and Y on the abscissa, would yield a straight line with the slope equal to $1/c$ and ordinate intercept equal to $-k/c$.

3-7. No. Consider the distribution, 1, 5, 9, for which $\bar{X} = 5$. If this distribution is transformed to a new one by squaring every score, we obtain 1, 25, 81. The mean of the new distribution is certainly not 25. The reason why $\bar{Y}$ cannot be predicted from $\bar{X}$ in this case is because

$$\bar{Y} = \frac{Y_1 + Y_2 + \cdots + Y_n}{n} \quad \text{and by substitution}$$

$$\bar{Y} = \frac{X_1^2 + X_2^2 + \cdots + X_n^2}{n}$$

Because we cannot factor anything out of the last expression, it cannot be reduced to a quantity involving $\bar{X}$. Thus in order to obtain $\bar{Y}$, all the X values must be known so that the corresponding Y values may be calculated.

3-8. (a) As with the mean, whatever the distribution of the 11 scores might be, the mode of the new distribution will be $10 \times 4 - 3 = 37$, and the median will be $10 \times 7 - 3 = 67$. That is, the same principle that applies to the mean for transformations involving multiplication and addition of constants applies to the mode and median as well.

(b) Unlike the mean, the mode and median of the transformed scores will, if all the original scores are positive, be equal to the squared mode (16) and squared median (49) of the original distribution. The fundamental reason for this difference is that the mean, unlike the mode and median, takes into account the exact magnitude of all the scores of the distribution. However, difficulty can arise if there are negative values in the original distribution. Consider the following distribution of 11 scores, 10, -10, 4, 4, 4, 7, 8, 9, 10, 10, 11, in which, like our earlier distribution, $m_0 = 4$ and $m = 7$. Squaring each value to obtain the new distribution, the following scores result: 100, 100, 16, 16, 16, 49, 64, 81, 100, 100, 121. Thus in the new distribution, $m_0 = 100$ and $m = 81$.

(If the original distribution contained an even number of scores, the median of the squared distribution would not equal exactly the square of the median of the original distribution. See Exercise 3-16.)

3-9. If you superimposed the frequency polygon carefully on the histogram, the total area included within the histogram should be the same as that included under the polygon, although the distribution of the area will differ somewhat from that of the histogram.

3-10. $A = 0.10 + 0.24 + 0.30 + 0.22 + 0.14 = 1.00$. Therefore, $a/A = a$, and it follows that the area contained within any interval in the histogram gives directly the rf in that interval. No; if, for example, the intervals of an rf distribution are 2 units in width, $A = 2$.

3-11. This result is gotten as follows. Given X_i $(X_1 < X_i < X_2)$, Y_i can be obtained from the relation $Y_i = cX_i + k$, because X and Y are presumed to be linearly related in the interval between X_1 and X_2; but we need to know the values of c and k. Because we are given that $Y = Y_1$ when $X = X_1$ and $Y = Y_2$ when $X = X_2$, the slope of the function, c, is expressed as $(Y_2 - Y_1)/(X_2 - X_1)$. Next, we can find the Y intercept by noting that

$$Y_1 = \frac{(Y_2 - Y_1)}{(X_2 - X_1)} X_1 + k, \text{ so that } k = -\frac{(Y_2 - Y_1)}{(X_2 - X_1)} X_1 + Y_1$$

Substituting the values obtained for c and k in the equation $Y_i = cX_i + k$, we obtain

$$Y_i = \frac{(Y_2 - Y_1)}{(X_2 - X_1)} X_i - \frac{(Y_2 - Y_1)}{(X_2 - X_1)} X_1 + Y_1$$

And after simplification we obtain the linear-transformation equation

$$Y_i = \frac{Y_2 - Y_1}{X_2 - X_1} (X_i - X_1) + Y_1$$

3-12. $P_{36} = 11.1$ sec; $Q_3 = 13.5$ sec; $PR_{13.2} = 69.4$.

3-13. No. In Table 3-1, for example, all values above 18.0 sec qualify as P_{100}, though one could define P_{100} to be the smallest of all such values.

3-14. Yes. The method is obvious from Table 3-1. To obtain percent frequencies, subtract successive entries in the %cf column (see columns 4 and 6 of Table 3-1).

3-15. A %cf ogive of a discrete variable yields a graph that looks like a staircase. Strictly speaking, there is no P_{45}, m, or P_{60}, because there is no value such that 45 percent of the distribution lies below it and 55 percent above, and the same holds true for m and P_{60}. If, however, you attempted to obtain these three quantities by graphic interpolation, the results were $P_{45} = m = P_{60} = 4$, which is simply an indication that a large proportion of the distribution is concentrated at the value of 4. This example shows that percentiles and related quantities are not much use with discrete variables that have only a few values. However, if a discrete variable has a relatively large number of values, the individual "steps" in its %cf distribution become rather small, and the range of percentiles having the same value is reduced. Such variables are often treated as continuous variables, and full use is made of percentiles, quartiles, etc.

3-16. The value of Y produced by linear interpolation is 76 and differs from the actual value of Y, 64, because X and Y are *not* linearly related. If the student will graph the function $Y = X^3$, he will see that the curve is far from linear in the region with which the problem deals.

4 DESCRIPTIVE STATISTICS II

In the present chapter the important concept of the *variability* of a distribution is introduced and several measures of variability are discussed. In addition, the *normal distribution*, a cornerstone concept in statistics, is treated in some detail.

MEASURES OF VARIABILITY

Consider the following two distributions: 7, 8, 12 and 1, 8, 18. We shall refer to them as distributions *A* and *B*, respectively. The two distributions have the same means and medians, but they are quite different in another respect. The values of the first distribution are much closer to each other, and therefore to their mean and median, than those of distribution *B*. We say that distribution *A* has less *variability* than *B*. The variability of a distribution is one of its most important characteristics, and as shown by the following illustration, differences in variability can be as illuminating as differences in measures of central tendency in revealing effects of an independent variable.

Suppose **E**, wishing to study the effects of anxiety level—manipulated by means of shock threat—on verbal learning, has a control group and an experimental group learn a list of words in serial order. For simplicity let there be only six **S**s in each group, and let the numbers of training trials required to learn the list of words be 5, 5, 6, 6, 6, 8 in the control group and 2, 2, 3, 9, 10, 10 in the experimental group. Note that the means of the two groups are identical, as are the medians. The variability of the two groups, on the other hand, is quite different. Although the scores in the control group are rather homogeneous, those in the experimental group are either very low or very high. Apparently, although shock threat had no effect on the experimental group as a whole, it facilitated learning in some **S**s and had the opposite effect on others. This result suggests the hypothesis that the effect of shock threat on learning depends on certain characteristics, perhaps personality characteristics, of **S**. In terms already familiar to us, the substantially larger variability in the experimental group points to the possibility of an interaction between the shock-threat variable and one or more subject relevant variables. Had **E** attended only to the means of the two groups, he would have concluded erroneously that his independent variable did not affect the dependent variable.

The problem now is to develop a definition of variability that will enable us to measure exactly the variability of any distribution. As it turns out, however, there are several useful ways of defining variability. In the following paragraphs we shall describe the *range*, the *semi-interquartile range (Q)*, the *average deviation (AD)*, and finally, the *standard deviation (SD)*, which for us will be by far the most important of the group.

The Range

The range of a distribution is simply the difference between its highest and lowest scores. The first of the above two distributions has a range of 5, but the range of distribution *B*, 17, is more than three times greater. As indicated by their respective ranges, the scores of distribution *B* are more "spread out" than those of distribution *A*.

The Semi-interquartile Range

We already know what Q_1 and Q_3 are. It follows from their definitions that the middle 50 percent of a distribution falls between Q_1 and Q_3. To illustrate, in the *DRL* data of Table 3-1, Q_3 is 13.5 sec; Q_1, as calculation will show, is 10.3 sec. Hence, the middle 50 percent of the distribution consists of *IRT*s varying between 10.3 and 13.5 sec. The semi-interquartile range (Q) is a measure of variability based on the range of the middle 50 percent of the distribution:

$$Q = \frac{Q_3 - Q_1}{2}$$

Thus, the semi-interquartile range for the *DRL* data is $(13.5 - 10.3)/2 = 1.6$ sec. It is apparent that the semi-interquartile range has little relevance for distributions consisting of relatively few observations, as, for example, distributions *A* and *B*, or for discrete variables that assume relatively few values.

The relationship between the range and *Q* is instructive. The range is the distance separating the two most extreme scores of the entire distribution; *Q* is one-half the distance separating the two most extreme scores in the middle 50 percent of the distribution. Thus *Q*, as its name indicates, is merely the range of a particular portion of a distribution.

The Average Deviation

Neither the range nor *Q* makes use of all the data of the distribution. The range is based on the two extreme scores, and *Q* depends only on P_{25} and P_{75}. The average deviation (*AD*), in contrast, depends on every score of the distribution. The average deviation is obtained by subtracting the distribution mean from every score of the distribution; these "deviations" from the mean, all taken as positive, are then summed and divided by *n*. Symbolically,

$$AD = \frac{\Sigma|X - \bar{X}|}{n}$$

where the vertical bars signify that "absolute" values are required; i.e., all differences are taken to be positive. Why absolute rather than algebraic differences are needed will be made clear in a future exercise. The average deviation of distribution *A* is equal to $(|7 - 9| + |8 - 9| + |12 - 9|)/3 = 2$.

A word about notation. It will be recalled from Chap. 3 that the mean of a distribution is defined as $\bar{X} = \Sigma X/n$, where ΣX means that all the *n* scores of the distribution are added. When working with more complicated quantities than the mean, one can avoid confusion as to what the summation sign refers to by tagging the variable to be summed with a subscript. For example, the formula for the mean is often written as $\Sigma X_i/n$. In like manner we may write the *AD* as $(\Sigma|X_i - \bar{X}|)/n$. When the meaning of the summation sign is clear, we often drop the subscript(s) from our equations.

While we are on the subject of notation, it should be pointed out that the quantity $(X_i - \bar{X})$ is often written as x_i, which, because it expresses the original score X_i in terms of the number of units by which the latter deviates from the distribution mean, is referred to as a "deviation score." Expressed in terms of deviation scores, then, $AD = \Sigma|x_i|/n$.

The average deviation is not often encountered in psychological research for many reasons. The *AD* can be tedious to calculate when, as is usually the case, $\bar{X}$ is not an even number; its determination in such cases is not facilitated much by use of an automatic calculator. More important, the *AD* does not, in contrast to the standard deviation, enter into the customary statistical evaluations of research data. Hence, it tends to be ignored in favor of the standard deviation.

The *AD*, nevertheless, is occasionally useful when one requires for purely descriptive purposes a measure of variability that takes all scores of a distribution into consideration.

The Standard Deviation

The standard deviation (*SD*) is by far the most important and most utilized of the measures of variability. Its definition is not complex:

$$SD = \sqrt{\frac{\Sigma(X - \bar{X})^2}{n}}$$

Like the *AD*, the *SD* involves forming the deviation of each score from the distribution mean; the squaring operation then converts all the deviations to positive quantities, and after the summing and dividing by n is done, the square root is taken. Expressed in terms of deviation scores, $SD = \sqrt{\Sigma x_i^2/n}$.

The quantity $\Sigma x_i^2/n$, which is the standard deviation squared, is important in its own right and is known as the "variance"; it shall be designated as SD^2.

Before we continue, let us calculate the variance and standard deviation of distribution *A*. First we obtain the variance:

$$SD^2 = \frac{\Sigma x_i^2}{n} = \frac{(7 - 9)^2 + (8 - 9)^2 + (12 - 9)^2}{3} = \frac{(4 + 1 + 9)}{3} = 4.67$$

The standard deviation is the square root of the variance. Thus:

$$SD = \sqrt{SD^2} = \sqrt{4.67} = 2.16$$

It may be apparent that the calculation of the *SD* could be very tedious when, as usually happens, the mean of the distribution is not a whole number or when the observations themselves are largely nonintegers. A little later we shall provide a formula for calculating *SD* which avoids having to work with deviations from the distribution mean. But now, however, let us inquire into some of the more important properties of *SD* and *SD²*.

UNITS OF MEASUREMENT. Suppose distribution *A* were a distribution of weights, i.e., the distribution consisted of the values 7, 8, and 12 lb. The pound, then, is the unit of measurement of the distribution. The variance of the distribution, however, has as its unit of measurement the "square pound" (or lb²) because each deviation score, initially expressed in pounds, is squared to obtain *SD²*. For example, expressing the first score of the distribution as a deviation from the mean with unit of measurement attached, we have (7 lb − 9 lb) = −2 lb. After it is squared, this quantity becomes 4 lb², that is, the unit of measurement as well as the numerical quantity is squared. Hence, the variance of the distribution of weights is 4.67 lb². Because $SD = \sqrt{SD^2}$, however, the standard deviation reverts to the more sensible unit of the plain pound. Thus simply as a measure of variability, the standard deviation, because it is expressed in the original unit of measurement, has more intuitive appeal than the variance.

EFFECT OF A LINEAR TRANSFORMATION ON SD² AND SD. The student will recall that if a distribution of X scores is converted to Y scores by a linear transformation, i.e., by the linear function $Y = cX + k$, the mean of the Y distribution is given by $\bar{Y} = c\bar{X} + k$. Now we wish to inquire what happens to SD^2 and SD when a distribution is subjected to a linear transformation—i.e., what is the relationship between the variance and standard deviation of the X scores, call these $SD_X{}^2$ and SD_X, respectively, and the variance and standard deviation of the transformed scores, namely, $SD_Y{}^2$ and SD_Y? First let us see what the effect is on SD^2 and SD when a constant is added to every score of a distribution.

Effect on SD² and SD of adding a constant to (or subtracting a constant from) the scores of a distribution. Refer to distribution A again. If a constant k were added to every score of the distribution, the range of the new distribution would be the same as the range of the original distribution. Similarly, the AD of the new distribution would be precisely the same as the AD of the initial distribution. (Prove this to your satisfaction.) And it is not difficult to see that if a constant were added to every score of the IRT distribution, the Q of the transformed scores would be equal to the Q of the original distribution. The reason is plain: adding a constant to each score of a distribution results in a new distribution in which the scores are separated from each other by precisely the same distances as separated the scores of the original distribution. Accordingly, such an operation does not affect the preceding measures of variability.

Exactly the same situation prevails for SD^2 and SD; they are unaffected by the addition of a constant to every score. This is easily proved by referring again to distribution A. After the addition of the constant k to every score of this distribution, the first score becomes $(7 + k)$, and the mean of the new distribution is $(9 + k)$. Expressing the initial score as a deviation from its distribution's mean, we obtain $(7 + k) - (9 + k) = -2$, which is precisely the deviation score of the corresponding untransformed score. Because this result holds for all scores of the distribution, both the standard deviation and the variance will be unchanged in the new distribution.

Inasmuch as subtraction of k is equivalent to addition of $-k$, the same conclusion applies when a constant is subtracted from every score of a distribution.

Effect on SD² and SD of multiplying (or dividing) every score of a distribution by a constant. Multiplying each of the three observations of distribution A by the positive constant c, we obtain a new distribution: $7c, 8c, 12c$. The range of the transformed distribution is $12c - 7c = 5c$. Because the range of the original distribution was 5, the range of the new distribution is c times larger.

4-1. How is the range of distribution A affected if all scores are multiplied by a negative constant, $-c$, where c itself is assumed to be positive? How is the AD of the transformed A distribution related to the AD of the original distribution? The answers will be found at the end of the chapter.

Exactly the same result applies to Q and SD if every score is multiplied by a constant c; the Q and SD of the transformed distribution will be equal to the Q and SD of the initial distribution multiplied by the absolute value of the constant.

However, let us see what happens to the variance. Refer once more to our well-used distribution A. Having multiplied each score by the constant c, the variance of the transformed distribution is given by

$$\frac{(7c - 9c)^2 + (8c - 9c)^2 + (12c - 9c)^2}{3} = \frac{(2c)^2 + c^2 + (3c)^2}{3}$$

$$= c^2(4 + 1 + 9)/3 = c^2 4.67$$

In other words, the variance of the transformed distribution is equal to the variance of the original distribution multiplied by the constant c squared. However, because $SD = \sqrt{4.67c^2} = \sqrt{4.67} \times \sqrt{c^2} = 2.16c$, the standard deviation of the transformed distribution is equal to the SD of the original distribution multiplied by the absolute value of the constant c itself.

Because division by a constant is equivalent to multiplication by the reciprocal of the constant, the preceding results are applicable when every score of a distribution is divided by a constant.

The results obtained thus far may be summarized as follows. If a distribution of X scores is converted to a distribution of Y scores by a linear transformation, i.e., by $Y = cX + k$, the standard deviation of the transformed scores, SD_Y, is related to the standard deviation of the original scores, SD_X, by $SD_Y = cSD_X$, where c is always taken to be positive, and the relationship between the two variances is given by $SD_Y^2 = c^2 SD_X^2$. Accordingly, if the standard deviation of a distribution of scores expressed in inches is 6 in. and the variance is 36 in.^{2}, the SD and SD^2 of these scores expressed in feet are 0.5 ft and 0.25 ft^2, respectively.

It should be pointed out that if a distribution of Y scores is obtained from a distribution of X scores by the linear transformation $Y = cX + k$, then the X distribution may be derived from the Y distribution by the linear function $X = (1/c)Y - k/c$. Hence, if the variance and standard deviation of the Y distribution, but not of the X distribution, are known, the latter may be obtained from the former by the relations $SD_X^2 = (1/c)^2 \cdot SD_Y^2$ and $SD_X = (1/c)SD_Y$.

It follows from the above results that, by an appropriate linear transformation, one can convert the mean and standard deviation of a distribution to any value he chooses. For example, if the distribution mean, which is itself a constant, is subtracted from every score, the result will always be a distribution whose mean is zero. Similarly the standard deviation, assuming it is not zero, can be altered to any positive value whatsoever through multiplication of every score by the appropriate constant.

A widely used transformation converts the mean of the distribution to zero and the standard deviation to 1; it may be called the "z" transformation. In order to achieve the specified values with any distribution, one first subtracts the distribution mean from every score and then divides by the distribution standard deviation, which is merely a particular constant. Hence, the transformation called for is $z_i = (X_i - \bar{X})/SD_X = (1/SD_X)X_i - \bar{X}/SD_X$. Note that $1/SD_X$ and $\bar{X}/SD_X$ are merely numbers determined by the mean and standard deviation of the X distribution; therefore the z transformation is a special type of linear transformation. The mean of the z distribution, $\bar{z}$, is obtained from $\bar{z} = (1/SD_X)\bar{X} - \bar{X}/SD_X$—and is obviously equal to zero. The standard deviation of z, SD_z, is gotten from $SD_z = (1/SD_X)SD_X$ and is clearly equal to 1. In order, therefore, to change the mean of any distribution to zero and the standard deviation to 1, all one need do is calculate the numbers $\bar{X}$ and SD_X, subtract $\bar{X}$ from every score and divide by SD_X.

EXERCISES

4-2. Convert the following distribution to a z distribution and check that the transformed distribution has a mean of zero and standard deviation of 1: 2, 8, 8, 8, 11, 11.

CALCULATION OF SD FROM RAW SCORES. We return now to the problem of calculating SD without recourse to taking deviations from the mean, i.e., using the "raw scores" alone.

The really important factor in the definition of SD is $\Sigma(X_i - \bar{X})^2$, a quantity called the "sum of squares of the deviations around the distribution mean," or more briefly, the "sum of squares." We shall first convert this quantity to a different form, once again using distribution A as a model for our calculations. Let us express the sum of squares of distribution A as follows, making use of the symbol $\bar{X}$ rather than the actual distribution mean:

$$\Sigma x_i^2 = (7 - \bar{X})^2 + (8 - \bar{X})^2 + (12 - \bar{X})^2$$

Squaring each of the terms on the right side of the equation we obtain

$$\Sigma x_i^2 = [7^2 + \bar{X}^2 - 2(7\bar{X})] + [8^2 + \bar{X}^2 - 2(8\bar{X})] + [12^2 + \bar{X}^2 - 2(12\bar{X})]$$

Rearranging terms in the following way we arrive at

$$\Sigma x_i^2 = (7^2 + 8^2 + 12^2) + 3\bar{X}^2 - 2\bar{X}(7 + 8 + 12)$$

The first term on the right is simply the sum of the squared scores of the distribution, which we may symbolize as ΣX_i^2. The second term on the right, $3\bar{X}^2$, is—in the general case—$n\bar{X}^2$ because one $\bar{X}^2$ goes with each of the scores of the distribution. Within the parentheses of the last term occurs the sum of all the scores of the distribution, i.e., ΣX_i, in general. Substituting these more general terms into the last equation, we obtain

$$\Sigma x_i^2 = \Sigma X_i^2 + n\bar{X}^2 - 2\bar{X}\Sigma X_i$$

The student should contribute the steps from which the latter equation is reduced to

$$\Sigma x_i^2 = \Sigma X_i^2 - \frac{(\Sigma X_i)^2}{n}$$

Do not confuse the symbols ΣX_i^2 and $(\Sigma X_i)^2$: the former instructs one to square each score of the distribution first and then add them together; the latter requires that the scores be added together first and the resultant sum then squared.

Dividing the new form of the sum of squares by n and taking the square root, we arrive at the raw-score formula for the standard deviation:

$$SD = \sqrt{\frac{\Sigma X_i^2 - (\Sigma X_i)^2/n}{n}} \tag{4-1}$$

If an automatic desk calculator is available, the SD of even a large distribution can be readily obtained by the raw-score formula. In the case of smaller distributions and numbers of moderate size, the SD can be calculated with the help of a table of squares and square roots.

USE OF A LINEAR TRANSFORMATION IN CALCULATING SD. Let us now illustrate the use of equation 4-1 in calculating SD. At the same time we shall see how the calculation of SD can be considerably simplified by the use of an appropriate linear transformation.

The lowest frequency in cycles per second (Hz) that an individual could hear was determined on 10 separate trials, producing the following trial-by-trial results: 26.5, 25.5, 21.5, 22.5, 25.5, 25.5, 21.5, 25.5, 24.5, and 21.5. In order to obtain a measure of the variability of the individual's ability to hear low frequencies, the SD of the preceding scores is to be calculated. It is clear, however, that considerable arithmetic labor will be necessary to calculate SD from the original scores. On the other hand, inspection of the individual values shows that it is possible to convert them to more manageable numbers by subtracting the constant 21.5 from each score. This conversion represents a transformation of the form $Y = X - k$ or, expressing the transformation in terms of obtaining X from Y, $X = Y + k$. Thus, because $SD_X = SD_Y$, we need only calculate the SD of the simpler Y scores in order to obtain the SD of the original scores.

Table 4-1 Employment of the Linear Transformation
$Y = X - 21.5$ in the Calculation of SD_X

(1) X	(2) Y	(3) Y^2	(4) CALCULATION OF SD_Y
26.5	5	25	$\Sigma Y = 25 \qquad \Sigma Y^2 = 99$
25.5	4	16	
21.5	0	0	
22.5	1	1	$SD_Y = \sqrt{\dfrac{99 - \dfrac{25^2}{10}}{10}} = \sqrt{\dfrac{99 - 62.5}{10}}$
25.5	4	16	
25.5	4	16	
21.5	0	0	$= \sqrt{3.65} = 1.91$
25.5	4	16	$SD_X = SD_Y = 1.91$ Hz
24.5	3	9	
21.5	0	0	
	25	99	

In the first two columns of Table 4-1 this transformation has been made; the original values are designated as X, and the transformed values as Y. The third column presents values of Y^2. The calculation of SD_Y by equation 4-1 is shown at the side of the table, and as indicated there, because $SD_X = SD_Y$, the former is equal to 1.91 Hz.

EXERCISES

The following exercises review and extend some of the material covered in this section.

4-3. Must the range always be greater than SD?

4-4. In distribution A the sum of squares was 14. Calculate the sum of the squares of the deviations around 10, i.e., find $\Sigma(X_i - 10)^2$. Do the same for 8, find $\Sigma(X_i - 8)^2$. In $\Sigma(X_i - a)^2$ what value of a makes that quantity as small as possible?

4-5. Using equation 4-1 and an appropriate linear transformation, find the variance and the standard deviation of the following distribution: 6, 36, 36, 96, 126, 156, 156, 186, 276, 276. Make a graph of the original and transformed scores, plotting the former on the abscissa and the latter on the ordinate. The points of the graph should lie on a straight line. Why?

4-6. In finding the mean or standard deviation of a grouped frequency distribution, such as that in Table 3-1, all the observations in an interval are assigned the value of the class mark of that interval. Find $\bar{X}$ and SD for the DRL data in Table 3-1. Hint: Use a linear transformation that reduces the difference between successive class marks to 1 sec and assigns a value of zero sec to the midpoint of the interval containing the maximum number of observations.

4-7. If we *first* divided every score of a distribution by its standard deviation and *then* subtracted its mean, would the resulting distribution have a mean of zero and a standard deviation of 1?

THE NORMAL DISTRIBUTION

We require one more statistical concept before returning to experimental psychology proper, namely, the *normal distribution*. The normal, or Gaussian, distribution is one of the most pervasive concepts in statistics. Most techniques of statistical inference, for example, make use of the normal distribution at one point or another. In psychology, the normal distribution constantly arises in theoretical analyses of many psychological processes; as we shall see in the next chapter, one cannot go far into psychophysics without encountering this ubiquitous concept.

We begin the discussion with a distinction between *sample statistics* and *population parameters*.

Sample Statistics and Population Parameters

It may be recalled that the terms "sample" and "population" were introduced in Chap. 3 in our discussion of descriptive statistics and inference. We now wish to define these terms more exactly and to establish a distinction between corresponding properties of samples and populations, i.e., between sample statistics and population parameters.

Let us consider the following artificial, but instructive, example. We have a container filled with a large number of balls on each of which is inscribed a number from 0 to 9. Ten of the balls are drawn from the container by a random process, e.g., shaking the container between drawings and drawing when blindfolded. The collection consisting of all the balls in the container is called the population; the 10 balls are a sample from this population. To define these terms more generally, *a population is any complete collection of objects or things; a sample is any subtotal portion of a population.*

The individual units of a population have many *characteristics* which could be the subject of measurement and investigation. In the present example our interest lies in the number inscribed on each ball, though every ball has other characteristics, such as weight, diameter, and color, any one or more of which could serve as the focus of interest.

Suppose the 10 balls were numbered as follows: 0, 0, 1, 1, 1, 2, 3, 5, 7, 8. These numbers constitute a distribution, one that we shall refer to as a "sample distribution." A large number of different quantities, or statistics, can be calculated from the sample distribution, such as the sample mean, standard deviation, and range. All such quantities are called "sample statistics"; hence, a sample statistic is any statistic calculated from a sample distribution. The mean of the previous sample is 2.8; its standard deviation is 2.75. If the 10 balls were returned to the container and another sample of 10 chosen, it is likely that the mean and standard deviation of the second sample would differ from the corresponding values of the first sample. Thus sample statistics, such as the mean and standard deviation, differ in general from sample to sample drawn from the same population.

One may of course consider properties of the population, called population "parameters," that correspond to sample statistics, for example, the population mean, standard deviation, and semi-interquartile range. In our illustration, the population mean would be obtained by taking the arithmetic average of *all* the balls in the container; the standard deviation of the population would be secured in the same manner. It is clear, however, that unlike the sample mean and standard deviation, the values of which fluctuate from sample to sample, the population mean and standard deviation do not change in the course of taking different samples. The general principle is that although sample statistics may be expected to fluctuate from sample to sample, parameters remain as fixed properties of the population.

It is important to maintain this distinction between sample statistics and population parameters, and toward this end different symbols are often used to identify corresponding quantities in the sample and in the population. For example, $\bar{X}$ is reserved for the sample mean, and μ, the Greek letter "mu," is assigned to the population mean. In this book SD will always refer to the sample standard deviation and σ, the lowercase form of the Greek letter "sigma," to the standard deviation of the population. As a general rule, population parameters are designated by Greek letters while roman letters denote sample statistics.

All the illustrative distributions cited in previous statistical sections may be thought of as sample distributions arising from unspecified parent populations. The *DRL* data of Table 3-1, for example, may be considered a sample of *IRT*s taken from the population of all possible *IRT*s arising from the fixed conditions under which the sample *IRT*s were collected. Hence, the use of the symbols characterizing sample statistics, e.g., $\bar{X}$ and SD, was appropriate.

Definition and Properties of the Normal Distribution

We have already seen how the shape of a sample distribution can be portrayed by a frequency distribution, e.g., the histogram and the frequency polygon. In the case of a population, however, exact information of the shape of the distribution is usually lacking. In such cases a theoretical distribution, one which is mathematically defined, can serve as a "model" for the population distribution. But even if the exact population distribution were known, it is likely that an approximate theoretical distribution would, for many purposes, prove more useful than the actual distribution. The reason is that mathematically defined distributions are much more susceptible of mathematical manipulation than are actual distributions, with all their irregularities. In point of fact, mathematically defined distributions find very wide use as models for population distributions.

The normal distribution is probably the best known of the model distributions. There are reasons which support its application to a wide range of populations, but these will not concern us here. Our present purposes are to define the normal distribution and discuss some of its important properties.

DEFINITION OF THE NORMAL DISTRIBUTION. Essentially, the normal distribution is a relative frequency distribution where the relative frequency (Y) corresponding to any value of the variable under observation (X) is given by the equation

$$Y = \frac{1}{\sigma \sqrt{2\pi}} e^{-\frac{(X - \mu)^2}{2\sigma^2}}$$

(4-2)

A graph of the function produces the curve in Fig. 4-1.

A normal distribution, then, is any relative frequency distribution that is defined by equation 4-2. In actuality, however, the quantity on the ordinate of Fig. 4-1 is not relative frequency, and this is why it has been labeled "Y" in both the figure and in the corresponding part of equation 4-2. Obviously the curve does not present the proportion of cases that occurs at each specific value of X, for if it did, the sum of the proportions would be infinite rather than unity, because an infinite number of X values occur with proportions greater than zero. Rather, the proportion of cases occurring between any two values of X is obtained from the area included between the values in question.

If, however, one wishes to know the proportion of cases in which a score of, for example, precisely 10 (i.e., 10.000 · · ·) occurred, the answer must be *zero* for two reasons. Mathematically, a score of 10.000 · · · is a point on the abscissa without width; it generates a line above it but no area. Because the area is zero, the proportion of cases having such a value is zero. Empirically,

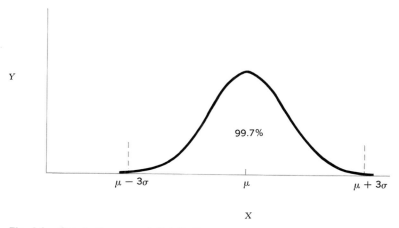

Fig. 4-1. Graph of a normal distribution.

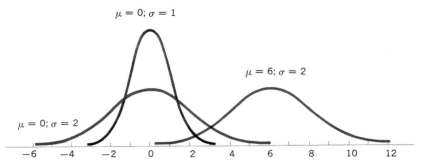

Fig. 4-2. Graphs of several normal distributions.

it is impossible to measure any continuous variable with infinite precision, so that the relative frequency with which a value of precisely 10 occurs must be zero. It will be recalled that a similar situation was encountered with frequency polygons and that, as remarked there, the ordinate of these would be better labeled "Y" than f, $\%f$, or rf. In any event, it should be remembered that the ordinate of a mathematically defined distribution of a continuous variable is labeled "Y" and is called "density" rather than relative frequency.

Let us compare the function which defines the normal distribution with the general linear function, $Y = cX + k$, as to the matter of constants. As we know, the constants c and k control the slope and Y intercept of the linear function. Somewhat similarly, μ and σ are constants in the equation of the normal distribution that control, respectively, the value at which the distribution is centered and the dispersion of the distribution, i.e., the spread of the distribution. In Fig. 4-2 the effects on the normal distribution of varying μ and σ are depicted. As the student may surmise, μ is actually the mean of the normal distribution, and σ is its standard deviation. Note that because we are dealing with a theoretical distribution, we employ the symbols appropriate for population parameters. The remaining two symbols in equation 4-2, π and e, are important mathematical quantities, generally approximated as 3.1416 and 2.7183, respectively.

Because μ and σ are the only two quantities that can vary from one normal distribution to another, it follows that if two normal distributions have equal means and equal standard deviations, they must be identical. Conversely, two normal distributions may differ because their means differ, their standard deviations differ, or both parameters differ. These relations are shown in Fig. 4-2.

Some Properties of the Normal Distribution

Certain properties of the normal distribution are obvious from the graph in Fig. 4-1. It is clear that the normal distribution is unimodal and symmetrical. A distribution is said to be symmetrical if, when divided in two at its mean, the right half of the distribution is the mirror image of the left half. The mean and median of symmetrical distributions are always identical; if in addition the distribution is unimodal, the mean, median, and mode coincide. This, of course, is true for the normal distribution.

Observe that the normal curve does not touch the abscissa at the points of its termination in Fig. 4-1. The mathematical properties of the normal distribution are such that area exists under the curve at all distances on either side of the mean; in other words, the curve extends indefinitely in both directions. However, there is little practical significance to this aspect of the normal distribution because, as shown in Fig. 4-1, more than 99 percent of the area is included within three standard deviations on either side of the mean.

We shall now describe a few more technical properties of the normal distribution. The phrase "X is a normally distributed variable" will often be used in what follows, meaning X is a variable whose distribution is given by equation 4-2.

LINEAR TRANSFORMATIONS. Suppose X is a normally distributed variable with its mean equal to 100 and its standard deviation equal to 10. Hence, the distribution of X is given by the formula

$$Y = \frac{1}{10\sqrt{2\pi}}\, e^{-\frac{(X-100)^2}{2(10)^2}}$$

and the graph of the distribution is shown in Fig. 4-3.

Now let X be subjected to the following linear transformation: $X' = 0.5X + 40$. The question is: What is the distribution of X'? We learned what the effect of a linear transformation is on the mean and standard deviation of a sample distribution, and exactly the same results hold for population or theoretical distributions. Consequently, $\mu_{X'} = 0.5\mu_X + 40 = 90$. The standard deviation of X', $\sigma_{X'}$, is equal to 5.0, because $\sigma_{X'} = 0.5\sigma_X = 0.5(10)$. But what about the form of the distribution; is it still "normal"? The answer is yes. *A linear transformation of a normally distributed variable results in a variable that also is normally distributed.* Accordingly, X' is normally distributed with a mean of 90 and standard deviation of 5 (Fig. 4-3).

It is useful to introduce the symbol $N(\mu, \sigma)$ to refer to normal distributions. Thus, if a variable is normally distributed with a mean of 85 and a standard deviation of 8, these facts are indicated by the notation $N(85, 8)$. A variable that has the distribution $N(0, 1)$ is normally distributed with a mean of zero and a standard deviation of 1; it will be referred to as a "unit" normal distribution.

A useful linear transformation of the normal distribution is one that converts μ to zero and σ to 1, i.e., one that converts the distribution $N(\mu, \sigma)$ to the unit normal distribution. It will be recalled that in sample distributions zero mean and standard deviation of unity can always be achieved by the transformation $z = (X - \bar{X})/SD_X$. Because we are dealing with parameters rather than

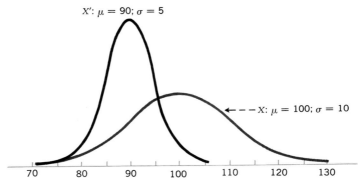

Fig. 4-3. The variable X is normally distributed with $\mu = 100$ and $\sigma = 10$. The variable X', obtained from X by the linear transformation $X' = 0.5X + 40$, is also normally distributed with $\mu = 90$ and $\sigma = 5$.

sample statistics, the analogous transformation for the normal distribution is $z_i = (X_i - \mu_X)/\sigma_X$ or, more simply, $z = (X - \mu)/\sigma$. Therefore, if the distribution of X is $N(6, 2)$, it may be converted to $N(0, 1)$ by the transformation $z = (X - 6)/2$ (Fig. 4-2).

One way of looking at the z transformation is that it expresses each X score in terms of the number of standard deviations that separate the score from the distribution mean, a fact that is evident from its definition. For example, in the distribution of X, with $\mu = 100$ and $\sigma = 5$, an X score of 95 is 1.0 standard deviation below the mean of the distribution; expressed as a z score, its value will be $(95 - 100)/5 = -1.0$. Conversely, if a transformed score has a z value of 0.5, we know that the original score was one-half of a standard deviation above the distribution mean; hence if $\mu = 20$ and $\sigma = 6$, the value of the original score must be 23.

Another, perhaps less obvious, fact about z scores is that they are dimensionless, as illustrated in the following. Suppose X is a variable expressed in pounds, with $\mu = 60$ lb and $\sigma = 10$ lb. Consider a particular value of X, say 65 lb. Expressing the latter as a z score, $z = (65 \text{ lb} - 60 \text{ lb})/10 \text{ lb} = 0.5$. As pointed out earlier in this chapter, when quantities carry dimensions, mathematical operations must be performed on the dimensions as well as on the quantities themselves. In the present illustration this has the consequence of canceling out the dimension of pounds. Accordingly, z scores arising from different distributions are comparable in that (1) they are dimensionless and (2) they express the original scores in terms of the number of standard deviations that separate the scores from the distribution mean. These two properties make z scores and related measures very valuable in the field of psychological measurement, inasmuch as they provide a means of combining scores obtained by the same individuals on different types of tests. For present purposes, z scores are important because of their relation to the area under the normal curve, a topic to which we now turn.

AREA RELATIONS UNDER THE NORMAL CURVE. The first important fact about the area under a normal curve is that *in every normal distribution, the area under the curve is equal to 1*. If you did Exercise 3-10, you will realize that this means the proportion of cases falling in any interval is given by the area under the curve that lies within that interval.

The second important fact is that area relations under the normal curve depend only on the z scores of the values under consideration. For example, 34.13 percent of the area (hence 34.13 percent of the cases) of a normal distribution is located between the mean of the distribution and a score that lies 1σ above the mean, i.e., between values whose z scores are 0 and 1. This is true whether we are dealing with the distribution $N(100, 10)$, in which event we are considering the area lying between the two scores 100 and 110, or with the distribution $N(25, 2)$, where the area of concern lies between the values 25 and 27. Therefore, regardless of the parameters of the distribution, one may assert that 34.13 percent of the area of a normal distribution lies between the two values corresponding to z scores of 0 and 1. Because of the symmetry of the normal distribution, we may state that 68.26 percent of the area of any normal distribution lies between $\mu + 1\sigma$ and $\mu - 1\sigma$ or, in terms of the corresponding z scores, between z values of $+1$ and -1. Similarly, 47.72 percent of the area of any normal distribution lies between the mean and a score that is 2σ above the mean or, equivalently, between values having z scores of 0 and 2, respectively. Hence, 13.59 percent of the area lies between scores that are 1σ and 2σ above the distribution mean, or between z scores of 1 and 2. These and other relations are presented in Fig. 4-4; it should be noted again that all but a small portion of a normal distribution is included between the values $\mu + 3\sigma$ and $\mu - 3\sigma$.

It may be apparent, then, that if the area relations are known for the unit normal distribution, that is, for z scores, one can determine required area rela-

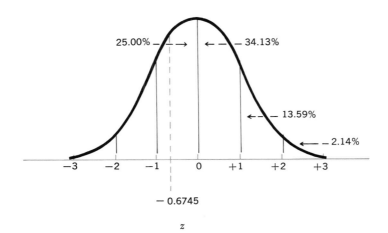

Fig. 4-4. Area relations in a unit normal distribution.

tions for any normal distribution merely by converting appropriate values to z scores and securing the area relations of the latter. If, for example, one is dealing with the distribution $N(16, 4)$ and one requires the percentage of cases having scores between 24 and 28, which is to say the area between these values is desired, he need only convert the two values to z scores and determine the area contained between the latter. Figure 4-4 will provide the required area (2.14 percent).

Table B in the Appendix presents a detailed listing of the areas of a unit normal distribution that lie between the mean ($z = 0$) and a wide range of z scores. The z scores are indicated in the extreme left and top row of the table, and the areas, expressed as proportions, are in the body of the table. A few examples should suffice for an understanding of the uses of the table. It is wise at the beginning to draw an appropriate normal distribution, locating on it the desired areas and other pertinent information. When the relevant procedures are well learned, this aid may be dispensed with, but initially it is valuable.

EXAMPLE 1.   The distribution of X is $N(100, 10)$. Find the percentage of scores in the distribution having values less than 95.

The value of 95 corresponds to a z score of -0.5, so that we require the area of a unit normal distribution lying to the left of this value. Table B tells us that the proportion of area located between z scores of 0.0 and $+0.5$ is 0.1915; thus the same proportion must lie between z scores of 0.0 and -0.5. Because the total area to the left of a z score of 0.0 is 0.5000, it follows that $0.3085 = 0.5000 - 0.1915$ is the area to the left of a z score of -0.5. The correct answer, then, is that 30.85 percent of the scores of the distribution $N(100, 10)$ have values less than 95.

EXAMPLE 2.   The variable X has the distribution $N(7, 4)$. What proportion of the area lies between the values 6 and 11?

If the student will sketch a normal distribution, indicating on it the relevant values, he will see that the sum of two areas is required. The first is situated between the mean and the value 6, and the second area lies between the mean and the value 11. Converting these values to z scores, we obtain the z values -0.25 and 1.00, respectively. The proportion of area lying between the mean and a z score of 0.25 (hence between the mean and a z score of -0.25) is shown by Table B to be 0.0987; the area situated between the mean and a z score of 1.00 is 0.3413. It follows that the area lying between the preceding two z scores, and therefore between the scores 6 and 11 of the original distribution, is

$$0.0987 + 0.3413 = 0.4400$$

EXAMPLE 3.   In the distribution $N(10, 2)$, the percentile rank of a score X_i is 50, i.e., $PR_{X_i} = 50$; what is the value of X_i?

Because X_i has a percentile rank of 50, this means that 50 percent of the cases or 50 percent of the area of the distribution lies below it. Hence it must have a z score of zero, which is to say $X_i = \mu = 10$.

EXAMPLE 4. This one is more difficult. In the distribution $N(10, 2)$, let $PR_{X_i} = 90$; find the value of X_i. Notice that we do not have a z score with which to work; instead we have an area, the corresponding z score of which must be obtained. Once we are in possession of this score, X_i itself is easily calculated.

It is given that 90 percent of the distribution lies below X_i or, equivalently, 40 percent of the area lies between the mean of the distribution and X_i. Thus, we require the z score for which 40 percent of the area occurs between itself and a z score of zero, i.e., the mean. This is the problem of, given the area, finding the corresponding z score. Searching in the body of Table B, we discover that an area of exactly 0.4000 does not occur. However, the value 0.3997 does occur, a value which we shall accept as being close enough to the required area so as to involve only a negligible error. The corresponding z score is $1.2 + 0.08 = 1.28$. This z score, then, includes approximately 40 percent of the area between itself and the mean, a total of almost 90 percent of the distribution's area lying to its left; it is therefore the z score of X_i. The actual value of X_i is obtained from $z = (X - \mu)/\sigma$, or $1.28 = (X_i - 10)/2$; thus, $X_i = 10 + 2(1.28) = 12.56$.

It must be stressed that the area relations discussed above refer only to a normal distribution. Between the mean of a distribution and a value whose z score is 1, almost any proportion of area can occur, depending on the shape of the distribution. The z transformation may be applied to any type of distribution whatever, and it will always be true that the mean of the z scores will be zero and their standard deviation will equal 1. However, the area relations described above and listed in Table B apply exactly only to a normal distribution. The magnitude of the errors involved in using Table B to calculate areas of a non-normal distribution depends, of course, on the extent to which the distribution diverges from normality. Thus, although no actual sample or population can be precisely normally distributed, there are many occasions where the departure from normality is sufficiently small to make the employment of the area relations of Table B quite useful.

Completion of the following exercises will help to consolidate the material just presented.

EXERCISES

4-8. The variable X has the distribution $N(10, 4)$. What percentage of cases fall between the following scores: 9 and 12; 11 and 14; 5 and 7?

4-9. The variable X has the distribution $N(100, 10)$. Find the scores having the following percentile ranks: 15.87; 95.00; 99.00.

4-10. Given a unit normal distribution, i.e., a distribution of the form $N(0, 1)$, find the following percentiles: $P_{97.5}$; $P_{95.0}$; $P_{75.0} = Q_3$; $P_{25.0} = Q_1$. Now express these quantities for an arbitrary normal distribution, i.e., a distribution $N(\mu, \sigma)$.

4-11. Making use of the results of the previous question, express Q, the semi-interquartile range, in terms of σ so that the expression applies to any normal distribution.

4-12. Assume that the distribution of weights (in pounds) of American males between the ages of 20 to 25 is $N(160, 10)$. What percentage of such males weigh 150.000 $\cdot$ $\cdot$ $\cdot$ lb? What percentage weigh 150 lb (i.e., their weight to the nearest pound)?

The Cumulative Normal Distribution

Like any other distribution, the normal distribution can be cumulated. Figure 4-5 presents the graph of a cumulative percentage distribution of a normally distributed variable, X.[1] Note that the curve is S-shaped or "sigmoid," but also observe that it is fairly linear in its middle region, a fact that will be made use of in the next chapter.

As we learned in Chap. 3, any percentile may be obtained from the graph of a %cf distribution by projecting a perpendicular from the appropriate percentage on the ordinate to the point of intersection with the curve, directing the line from here to the abscissa at right angles. Percentiles of a normal distribution may be obtained in precisely the same way from the graph of the cumulative percentage distribution. Thus, in Fig. 4-5 the mean (P_{50}) and $P_{15.87}$ have been located on the graph within the accuracy possible with this method. As shown in the figure, the distance between these two percentiles yields the standard deviation of X, i.e., $P_{50} - P_{15.87} = \sigma$. (Why?) It follows that, as with

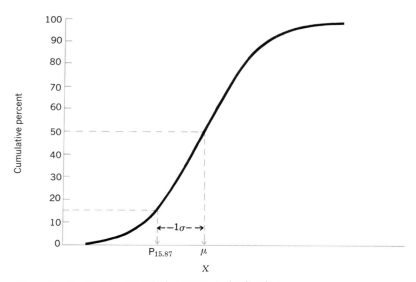

Fig. 4-5. Graph of a cumulative normal distribution.

[1] For a sample distribution, the cumulative distribution in percentages was referred to as a "percent cumulative frequency" (%cf) distribution. The corresponding distribution for a population or a theoretical distribution is called a "cumulative percentage distribution."

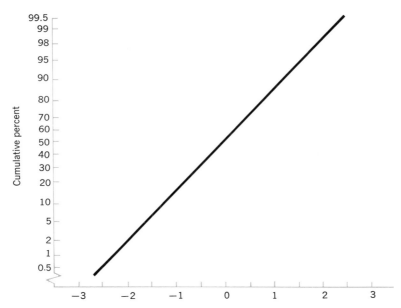

Fig. 4-6. Graph of a cumulative unit normal distribution on probability paper.

%cf distributions, the reverse operation enables one to find the percentile rank of any *X* score.

For many purposes it would be convenient if the normal ogive were graphed in such a way that the resulting curve was a straight line rather than sigmoid. This transformation can be accomplished by the use of special graph paper called "normal-probability" or, more simply, "probability" paper. One axis of probability paper is divided into units of equal size, but the other axis, expressed in cumulative percentages, is divided into units the size of which is systematically adjusted so as to transform the normal ogive into a straight line. The use of probability paper in the graphing of the ogive of a variable having the distribution $N(0, 1)$ is shown in Fig. 4-6.

The transformation that converts the normal ogive to a straight line is simple: the cumulative percentages are plotted as if they were *z* values. We already know that if we transform a distribution of *X* scores to *z* scores and then plot *X* against *z* on ordinary graph paper, the resulting curve must be a straight line. (Why?) Usually, *X* scores are converted to *z* scores by subtracting from each *X* score the mean of the *X*s and dividing through by their standard deviation. If, however, neither the mean nor standard deviation of *X* is known, it is still possible to obtain the *z* values if (1) the percentile ranks (cumulative percentages) of the *X*s are known and (2) the variable *X* is assumed to be normally distributed. For, given these two conditions, we need only refer to Table B to find the *z* score corresponding to any percentile rank. Thus, if *X* is normally distributed and an X score of 25 has a percentile rank of 67, its z score must be 0.44.

On normal-probability paper the distances separating adjacent cumulative percentages are those that are appropriate for the corresponding z values. If the student will convert a few of the cumulative percentages of Fig. 4-6 to z scores, he will observe that with respect to this measure the units on the ordinate are of equal size. Accordingly, on probability paper, a plot of X values against values of cumulative percentages is—if X is normally distributed—essentially a graph of X against z; like all such graphs, it will yield a straight line.

Further insight into the normal ogive will be obtained by completing the following exercises.

EXERCISES

4-13. The variable X has the distribution $N(20, 4)$. On ordinary graph paper, draw the cumulative percentage distribution of X. Hint: Obtain about four points of the graph ranging from values of X that are 3σ below the mean to values that are 3σ above the mean; draw a smooth ogive through the plotted points. It should be apparent that the required values can be calculated with the help of Table B.

Calculate μ and σ from the graph, and observe how close they are to the actual parameters.

4-14. The following values specify several points of the cumulative distribution of X: 2.28, 70; 6.68, 80; 15.87, 90; 30.85, 100; 50.00, 110; 69.15, 120; 84.13, 130; 93.32, 140; 97.72, 150. The first figure between semicolons gives the cumulative percentage, and the second gives the corresponding value of X. Plot these points on probability paper, obtainable in most campus bookstores. Does X appear to be normally distributed? What is the mean and standard deviation of X as calculated from the graph?

4-15. The variable X is normally distributed with $PR_{84.0} = 10$ and $PR_{102.1} = 99$. Convert these X scores to z scores, and plot X against z on ordinary graph paper. Find the mean and standard deviation of X from the graph. (Note: Start labeling the ordinate a bit above the abscissa with a value of z equal to -3; include values of z up to $+3$.)

4-16. Suppose variables A, B, and C, all normally distributed, have their cumulative percentage distributions plotted on the same probability paper graph. Variables A and B have the same standard deviation, but the mean of A is greater than the mean of B. Variable C has the same mean as variable A, but its standard deviation is smaller than A's. What will the curves of the three cumulative percentage distributions look like?

Summarizing this section briefly, we have observed that the normal distribution is important in psychology because it frequently serves as a model for population distributions and because it enters into the theoretical analyses of many psychological processes. Furthermore, the normal distribution plays a vital role in statistics, particularly in statistical inference.

Area relations under the normal curve are identical for all normal distributions if the scores involved are first transformed to z scores. Hence, to obtain the proportion of cases occurring between any two values of a normally distributed variable, one need only express these values as z scores and find the area under the unit normal curve falling between the transformed scores.

We have also seen that the cumulative percentage distribution of a normally distributed variable produces a typical S-shaped curve when plotted on ordinary graph paper but a straight line on probability paper. Because fitting a straight line to a set of points is much simpler than fitting a sigmoid curve, the latter type of graph is very useful for judging whether a given variable is normally distributed and estimating its mean and standard deviation.

SUMMARY

We have now completed the descriptive statistics required in this book. In the discussion of psychophysical methods that follows in the next chapter, many of the topics covered in the present chapter will be put to immediate use.

1. The measures of variability discussed in this chapter were the range, the semi-interquartile range, the average deviation, and the standard deviation.
    (a) Their definitions are:
    (b) The first two are similar in that:
    (c) The last two differ from the first two in that:
    (d) The raw-score formula for the *SD* is:
    (e) If a constant (positive or negative) is added to every score of a distribution, the effect on each of the four measures of variability will be:
    (f) If each score is multiplied by a constant, the effect on the four measures of variability is:

2. We may define sample statistics and population parameters and distinguish between them as follows:

3. The normal distribution is defined as:

4. If X has the distribution $N(\mu, \sigma)$, it may be converted to $N(0, 1)$ by:

5. It is true only in a normal distribution that 34.13 percent of the area of the distribution lies between the distribution's mean and a score that is 1 standard deviation above the mean because:

6. The graph of the cumulative normal distribution may be either a straight line or a sigmoid curve depending on:

7. The significance of the normal distribution for psychology is:

4-1. The range of distribution A (more exactly, the transformed distribution A) is now $-7c - (-12c) = 5c$. Thus, the range is multiplied by the absolute value of the multiplicative constant. The same result holds true for the AD, as may be seen by forming the deviation of the first member of the distribution: $|-7c - (-9c)| = c|9 - 7| = c|7 - 9|$.

4-2. The transformed distribution is obtained by $z_i = (X_i - 8)/3$. It is clear that the transformed distribution, $-2, 0, 0, 0, 1, 1$, has a mean of zero and a standard deviation of 1.

4-3. Yes. Even in a distribution consisting of only two scores, say 10 and 30, the range, 20, is greater than the standard deviation, which in the present example is 10.

4-4. $\Sigma(X_i - 10)^2 = \Sigma(X_i - 8)^2 = 17$. It turns out that the sum of squares of the deviations is a minimum when the deviations are taken around the distribution mean. This may be seen as follows: $\Sigma(X_i - a)^2 = \Sigma X_i^2 + na^2 - 2a\Sigma X_i$. Letting $C = na^2 - 2a\Sigma X_i$, it is clear that $\Sigma(X_i - a)^2$ is a minimum when C is as large a negative number as possible. Now $C = na(a - 2\bar{X})$, and letting $a = \bar{X} + e$, we see that

$$C = n(\bar{X} + e)(\bar{X} + e - 2\bar{X}) = (n\bar{X} + ne)(e - \bar{X})$$
$$= en\bar{X} + ne^2 - n\bar{X}^2 - ne\bar{X} = ne^2 - n\bar{X}^2$$

Thus C is as large a negative number as possible when $e = 0$; consequently, when $a = \bar{X}$.

Accordingly, *the mean of a distribution is the point about which the sum of the squares of the deviations is a minimum.* You have already found that $\Sigma(X_i - \bar{X}) = 0$, showing that *the mean is also the point around which the algebraic sum of the deviations is zero.* The mean is a very gifted quantity indeed. You might be wondering whether, in addition, the mean is the point around which the sum of the absolute deviations is a minimum. Actually, the median is that point, a fact which accounts for still another measure of variability: $AD_m = (\Sigma|X_i - m|)/n$, called the average deviation around the median.

4-5. The transformation $Y = (\frac{1}{30})X - \frac{1}{5}$ converts the original distribution of scores to $0, 1, 1, 3, 4, 5, 5, 6, 9, 9$, the latter having variance of 9.01 and a standard deviation of 3.00. Because X is obtained from Y by the linear function $X = 30Y + 6$, $SD_X^2 = 900SD_Y^2$ and $SD_X = 30SD_Y$. Thus, $SD_X^2 = 8109$ and $SD_X = 90$.

The plotted points should lie on a straight line because they are obtained from a linear function.

4-6. The linear transformation used is $Y = -(\frac{1}{2})X + \frac{13}{2}$. Note that X is therefore obtained from Y by the linear function $X = -2Y + 13$. The midpoints of the eight intervals with frequencies greater than zero are, then, $5, 4, 3, 2, 1, 0, -1, -2$ (reading from top to bottom in Table 3-1). $\bar{Y}$ is 0.70; thus $\bar{X} = -2\bar{Y} + 13 = 11.6$ sec. SD_Y turns out to be 1.46; consequently, $SD_X = 2SD_Y = 2.92$ sec.

4-7. No. The transformation described is $Y = (1/SD_X)X - \bar{X}$. It follows that $\bar{Y} = (1/SD_X)\bar{X} - \bar{X} = \bar{X}(1/SD_X - 1)$, which equals zero only if $1/SD_X$ happens to equal 1. On the other hand, $SD_Y = (1/SD_X)SD_X = 1$.

4-8. 29.02 percent; 24.26 percent; 12.10 percent. To obtain the area of the distribution between scores of 5 and 7 (the last part of the question), we first convert the values to z scores, namely, -1.25 and -0.75, respectively. Table B shows that between the mean and a z score of plus or minus 1.25, there is included 0.3944 of the area of a normal distribution. The proportion of area between the mean and a z score of plus or minus 0.75 is 0.2734. Because both z scores are negative, the area between them is given by $0.3944 - 0.2734 = 0.1210$.

4-9. 90.00; 116.45; 123.27. We will do the last part of the problem. Given $PR_{X_i} = 99$, find X_i. First we find the z score corresponding to X_i. Because 99 percent of the distribution (or area) is below X_i, 49 percent of the area must lie between it and the distribution mean. Table B shows that 49.01 percent of the area of a normal distribution lies between the mean and a z score of 2.33, and 48.98 percent is included between the mean and a z score of 2.32. By linear interpolation we find that a z score of 2.327 locates 49.00 percent of the area between itself and the mean. The latter, then, is the z score of X_i. Because $z_i = (X_i - 100)/10 = 2.327$, $X_i = 123.27$.

4-10. 1.96; 1.645; 0.6745; -0.6745. Let's do the last one. Finding $P_{25.0}$ is exactly the same problem as finding the score whose percentile rank is 25.0, for if $P_{25.0} = X$, then $PR_X = 25.0$. Therefore, we wish to find the z score for which 25 percent of the area of the normal distribution lies to its left, i.e., lies below it; equivalently, 25 percent of the area will lie between it and a z score of zero. We find in Table B that a z score of 0.68 includes 25.17 percent of the area between itself and a z score of 0, but a z score of 0.67 cuts off only 24.86 percent of the area between the mean and itself. We interpolate and obtain the result that 25.00 percent of the area is contained between the mean and a z score of 0.6745. Because we are interested in the z value on the left side of the mean, our required z score is -0.6745, and because we are dealing with a unit normal distribution, no further transformation is necessary. Hence, $P_{25.0} = -0.6745$ in a unit normal distribution.

However, assuming the distribution is $N(\mu, \sigma)$, we must obtain the z score corresponding to the obtained z score of -0.6745, as we did in the previous problem. Because $z = (X - \mu)/\sigma = -0.6745$, $X = \mu - 0.6745\sigma$; in words, in a normal distribution $P_{25.0}$ is always the score that is 0.6745 standard deviation units below the mean. The required answers are, therefore: $\mu + 1.96\sigma$, $\mu + 1.645\sigma$, and $\mu - 0.6745\sigma$. The reason for the greater precision exercised in calculating $P_{25.0}$ is that it enters into the calculation of Q.

4-11. In a normal distribution it is always true that $Q_1 = \mu - 0.6745\sigma$ and $Q_3 = \mu + 0.6745\sigma$. The semi-interquartile range is therefore

$$Q = \frac{(\mu + 0.6745\sigma) - (\mu - 0.6745\sigma)}{2} = 0.6745\sigma$$

Thus, irrespective of the values of the parameters of a normal distribution, 50 percent of the area (hence 50 percent of the cases) will be found within $\pm 0.6745\sigma$ of the mean.

4-12. Zero percent weigh 150.000 $\cdots$ lb for the reasons given in our discussion of the definition of the normal distribution. The percentage of males weighing 150 lb, to the nearest pound, is another matter. We require the percentage of cases falling in the interval 149.5–150.5 lb, and all we need find is the area under the normal curve above this interval. As usual, we first convert the original values to z scores, namely, to -0.95 and -1.05, respectively. The area in a unit normal curve between the mean and each of these values is, in order, 0.3289 and 0.3531. The difference between these areas, 0.0242, is the area contained within the interval defined by the two z scores. Hence, 2.42 percent of males between 20 and 25 years of age weigh 150 lb.

4-13. As suggested in the question, we must first obtain the cumulative percentages, or the percentile ranks, corresponding to various values of X. Because X has the distribution $N(20, 4)$, a value of X equal to 8 lies 3 standard deviations below the mean. Its cumulative percentage is obtained from Table B of the Appendix. Since 49.87 percent of the area lies between the mean and a z score of 3, 0.13 percent of the area must lie below an X score that is 3 standard deviations below the mean; stated in other terms, $PR_8 = 0.13$. It follows that $PR_{32} = 99.87$. If we proceed in this way, the percentile ranks of several other values of X between 8 and 32 may be obtained, the points plotted on graph paper and connected by a smooth sigmoid curve.

4-14. If you plotted the points carefully, they should lie on a straight line; hence, X is normally distributed. However, if the distribution of X differed to a significant extent from normality, the graph of cumulative percentages on probability paper, as well as the graph of X against z derived from the cumulative percentages, would yield a curve different from a straight line.

It is plain both from the graph and from the data provided that the mean of X is 110. The standard deviation of X—which may be obtained from the graph in a number of ways, e.g., $P_{84.13} - P_{50}$—should be close to 20, its actual value.

4-15. First we convert the given X scores to z values with the help of Table B. Because 10 percent of the area of the distribution of X lies to the left of a score of 84.0, its z score is -1.28. In like manner, the z score of 102.1 is 2.33. Next we plot these two points ($X = 84.0$, $z = -1.28$ and $X = 102.1$, $z = 2.33$) on the graph, and because two points completely determine a straight line, we need only connect the given points with a straight line to obtain the graph of the function relating z to X. By graphic interpolation at a z value equal to zero, the mean of X may be obtained. Interpolating at $z = 1$, we then secure a value of X that is 1 standard deviation above the mean. Consequently, the difference between this value of X and the mean of X yields the standard deviation of X. The mean of X is 90.4, and the standard deviation of X is 5; if you drew your line carefully, the values of μ and σ obtained graphically should be close to the true values.

Of course, it is also possible to find μ and σ algebraically. Because $P_{10} = 84.0$, it follows that $84.0 = \mu - 1.28\sigma$; and because $P_{99} = 102.1$, it is true that $102.1 = \mu + 2.33\sigma$. From the first equation, $\mu = 1.28\sigma + 84.0$; after this value of μ is substituted in the second equation, σ is 5.0. Hence, $\mu = 1.28(5) + 84.0 = 90.4$.

4-16. The cumulative percentage curves of variables A and B will be parallel straight lines, with the ogive of variable A located below the ogive of variable B. The ogives of variables A and C will be straight lines that intersect at their common mean, the slope of variable C's ogive being steeper than that of variable A. Essentially the same picture would emerge from a graph of the three variables plotted against z on ordinary graph paper.

5 CLASSICAL PSYCHOPHYSICS AND SIGNAL DETECTION THEORY

In tracing the family tree of experimental psychology, one soon discovers its major roots among a group of measuring techniques called the "psychophysical methods." Psychophysics, as the area of application of psychophysical methods is called, was founded during the middle of the last century by Gustav Fechner, an accomplished physicist of his time, in his classic *Elemente der Psychophysik* (1860).[1] At that time the domain of psychology was largely limited to the events of conscious experience; behavior, considered to be the product of conscious experience, counted little. Given the premise that experimental psychology must start with the study of conscious experience, it is not surprising that its origin was found in psychophysics. A sensation that depends directly

[1] See Boring's *Sensation and Perception in the History of Experimental Psychology* (1942, pp. 34–45) for a description of Fechner's epochal book, and see his *A History of Experimental Psychology* (1950, pp. 275–283) for an account of the man himself. Oddly enough, more than 100 years elapsed before an English translation of Fechner's book appeared (1966).

on a manipulable physical stimulus, as loudness depends on the intensity of the auditory stimulus, is a reliable, reproducible, and relatively simple experience. Hence the study of such sensations—how their magnitudes are related to the intensities of the initiating physical stimuli—seems a natural starting place for a nascent experimental psychology. The psychophysics of the last century consisted largely of such inquiries.

The psychophysical methods, then, were developed for the general purpose of investigating the laws relating sensory experience to properties of the initiating stimulus. Although a number of different psychophysical methods were eventually developed, three methods, explored in detail by Fechner, gained particular prominence. These three—the *method of limits*, the *method of constant stimuli*, and the *method of average error*—exist in one form or another to this day; a good part of the present chapter is devoted to them. One important feature of the three methods is that they call upon the subject to make the simplest possible judgments: to detect the presence or absence of a sensation or to decide whether two sensations are equal in magnitude or different. These discriminations are among the most reliable judgments of which organisms are capable.

ABSOLUTE AND DIFFERENCE LIMENS

One of the central problems with which early psychophysicists were concerned was the determination of thresholds, or as they were more commonly designated, "limens." Two types of limens were of particular interest. The first was the *absolute limen* (*AL*), which may be roughly defined as the minimum value of a physical stimulus that will evoke a sensation. What, for example, is the lowest intensity at which a tonal stimulus can still give rise to an auditory sensation? The *difference limen* (*DL*), the minimum amount of stimulus change required to produce a sensation difference, was the second threshold of interest and was of far greater theoretical significance. To illustrate, a tonal stimulus of 1,000 cycles per second (Hz) gives rise to an auditory sensation, a characteristic of which is *pitch*. How much must the frequency of the tone be increased before one notices the pitch is higher? An enormous amount of time and energy was devoted to the determination of *AL*s and *DL*s for a wide range of sensory dimensions: pitch, apparent brightness, heaviness of hefted objects, cutaneous pressure, and so on. The motivating force behind much of this labor was provided by an important and challenging theoretical issue that, kindled by Fechner, raged through most of the second half of the nineteenth century and beyond. We shall have more to say about this later in the chapter.

After quantities like the *AL* and *DL* are conceptualized, a problem arises as to their definitions. Consider, for example, the *AL* for apparent brightness. Is there really one specific intensity of a visual stimulus which is the lowest intensity that can give rise to a visual sensation? Obviously not, for surely one would admit to different *AL*s among different people, or even in the same person under different conditions of measurement. But even granting that the person and circumstances are held constant, momentary variations in S's receptor system, in his attention, and so forth, are bound to cause variations in the value of the minimum stimulus required to evoke a sensation. For this reason both the *AL* and the *DL* are defined in statistical terms; a favorite definition of the *AL* is *the stimulus value that evokes a sensation 50 percent of the time*. However, the problem is not yet solved. It is difficult to formulate a single statistical definition that is appropriate for all methods of determining a given threshold. The definition of the *AL* just given, for example, is not uniformly applicable to the different methods used to obtain *ALs*; it applies to the method of constant stimuli but is poorly suited to the method of limits. A different definition of the *AL* is assigned to the latter method, one that is also statistical in nature. The point to be remembered is that, though the particular statistical definition may vary from one psychophysical method to another, the *AL* and *DL* are *statistically defined concepts*. Corso (1963) may be consulted for a detailed discussion of the threshold concept and its role in classical psychophysics.

For almost a century the "classical" approach toward the measurement of sensory functions represented by the Fechnerian psychophysical methods managed to stave off serious challenge. In the middle 1950s, however, stimulated by developments in engineering on related problems, a small group of psychologists took sharp issue with traditional psychophysics and formulated an alternative approach that has come to be known as "signal detection theory." A brief description of this contemporary development will be given at the end of the chapter.

PHYSICAL VERSUS PSYCHOLOGICAL CONTINUA

Before we proceed to a discussion of the psychophysical methods, a few points should be made clear.

In psychophysical determinations, such as finding *ALs* and *DLs*, two dimensions—continua really—belonging to entirely different worlds are always involved: the psychological continuum and the physical continuum. (Hence the term "psychophysics.") As depicted in Fig. 5-1, where the two continua are represented by straight lines, a stimulus from the physical continuum, S_1, evokes a corresponding sensory response (sensation) on the psychological continuum, R_1. Also indicated on the stimulus continuum is the *AL*, represented as giving rise to the threshold sensory response, R_0. The latter may be considered to be the zero point or origin of the sensory continuum (cf. Corso, 1963). To avoid confusion in the developments which follow, keep in mind the distinction between the physical continuum (the stimulus) and the psychological continuum (the sensation or sensory response). Different names are commonly assigned to the physical and the psychological dimensions; thus one distinguishes between the "frequency" of an auditory stimulus, usually expressed in cycles per second, and the sensation which is evoked by this property of auditory stimuli, "pitch." In a similar vein, the "intensity" of a tone, most often expressed as decibels

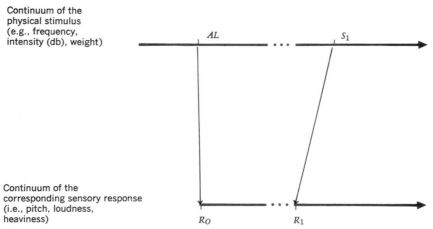

Continuum of the
physical stimulus
(e.g., frequency,
intensity (db), weight)

AL S_1

Continuum of the
corresponding sensory response
(i.e., pitch, loudness,
heaviness)

R_O R_1

Fig. 5-1. A representation of the physical-stimulus continuum and the continuum formed by the corresponding sensations. The absolute limen, AL, evokes the threshold sensation, RO, which is considered the zero point or origin of the sensory continuum. The dots signify that the distances between AL and S_1 and between RO and R_1 are not necessarily as shown.

(db) from some reference point, is a physical property of all auditory stimuli and should always be distinguished from "loudness," which is the corresponding sensory experience. "Weight" (or mass) is a property of lifted objects; "heaviness" refers to the corresponding sensory response. And so on. Hence the continua of the foregoing physical stimuli are called frequency, intensity, and weight, and the corresponding sensory continua are called pitch, loudness, and heaviness (Fig. 5-1).

Actually, however, a third process is involved. It is plain that E cannot directly observe the subject's sensory response (R_s) which is evoked by the presented stimulus (S). This response is private, accessible only to S himself. Thus the subject must communicate information about R_s, his sensation, with an overt, observable response, a judgment of some sort, which we may symbolize as R_j (a judgmental response). The complete sequence of events in any psychophysical determination is therefore stimulus → sensation → judgmental response, or $S \rightarrow R_s \rightarrow R_j$. Traditional psychophysics, concerned mainly with the relationship $S \rightarrow R_s$, that is, the relationship between the stimulus and the resulting sensation, was vitally interested in establishing experimental conditions which to the greatest possible extent maintained a close correspondence between R_s and R_j. Thus highly trained observers were used as subjects, constantly on guard to make their judgments (R_j) wholly dependent on their sensations (R_s) and not on extraneous factors, such as on information they might possess about the stimulus employed. When a subject based his judgment in whole or in part on S rather than entirely on R_s, he was said to have committed a "stimulus error."

Although for traditional psychophysics the $R_s \rightarrow R_j$ link was bothersome but necessary, one that was to be kept as short and direct as possible, more recently the relationship between R_j and R_s has come under study in its own right. Indeed, it is in giving explicit recognition to the $R_s \rightarrow R_j$ link that signal detection theory departs most from classical psychophysics. Provision is made in the theory for assessing the contribution to R_j not only of R_s, but also of such factors as the subject's expectations with respect to S and the value or "costs" to him of correct and incorrect decisions.

However, because we are presently interested in the psychophysical methods themselves, we shall assume a perfect correspondence between R_j and R_s and deal only with S and R_s, that is, only with the stimulus and the corresponding sensory response. Accordingly, we shall employ such terms as "sensation," "sensory response," "judgment," and "judgmental response" without distinction.

One more fact. It is not true that frequency alone determines the pitch of a tone nor that loudness depends only on intensity. To some extent intensity influences pitch, and frequency affects loudness. It is not even true that color depends solely on the wavelength of the visual stimulus. The intensity of a visual stimulus can in some degree influence its perceived color. These interactions, discussed in some detail by Geldard (1953, pp. 40, 121–123), make it important that when one aspect of a physical stimulus is manipulated for psychophysical determinations, other possibly relevant aspects be held constant.

THE METHOD OF LIMITS

The first psychophysical method to be described is the method of limits, which also goes by the following names: "method of minimal changes"; "method of serial exploration"; and "method of just noticeable differences." The method of limits, and its modifications, are applicable to the determination of both ALs and DLs. We first consider its use in the determination of absolute limens.

Determination of the AL by the Method of Limits

The discussion proceeds best by way of an example, and we shall take as our illustration the determination of an individual's AL for *pitch*, the sensation or sensory response determined largely by the *frequency* of a tonal stimulus.

It is apparent that an instrument must be employed which will permit the variation of frequency while holding the intensity of the tone constant. An audio-frequency oscillator of special design performs this function. After the intensity level to be used is decided, S's AL is roughly located by rapid initial testing. Let us assume that it lies somewhere in the region of 25 Hz. A range of stimuli is then chosen on either side of this value, such that the higher frequencies are clearly above threshold and the lower values are well below threshold. Further, the stimuli are chosen so that they are separated by a constant and relatively small difference in frequency. A set of frequencies covering the range of 17 to 33 Hz, in steps of 1 Hz, fulfills these criteria (Table 5-1, column 1).

The stimuli are then presented to S in a decreasing or an increasing order, starting from a point where the stimulus is well above (or below) the pitch threshold. For example, suppose the stimulus presented first is the 33-Hz tone and S responds that the tonal character of the stimulus, its pitch, is present. A plus sign is entered on the data sheet in the appropriate column (Table 5-1, column 2). The next stimulus in the series, 32 Hz, is then presented, and S's response is secured. The response, assumed to be positive, is also entered on the data sheet. This procedure is repeated until S finally reports that the stimulus has lost its tonal quality, a result which is entered on the data sheet as a minus sign (at 26 Hz in the present series). At this transition point the series is terminated. The absolute threshold on any series is assumed to lie midway between the two values of the stimuli over which the response reversal occurred. In the present illustration these values are 26 and 27 Hz; the absolute threshold (T) for the series is therefore taken to be 26.5 Hz and is entered as such at the bottom of the table.

Table 5-1 Determining the AL for Pitch by the Method of Limits

(1) STIMULUS (Hz)	(2) D	(3) A	(4) D	(5) A	(6) D	(7) A	(8) D	(9) A	(10) D	(11) A
			ASCENDING OR DESCENDING SERIES							
33	+		+							
32	+		+							
31	+		+						+	
30	+		+		+				+	
29	+		+		+				+	
28	+		+		+		+		+	
27	+		+		+		+		+	
26	−	+	+		+	+	+	+	+	
25		−	+		−	−	+	−	+	
24		−	+			−	+	−	−	
23		−	+	+		−	+	−		
22		−	+	−		−	+	−		+
21		−	−	−		−	−	−		−
20		−		−		−		−		−
19		−		−		−		−		
18				−				−		
17				−						−
$T =$	26.5	25.5	21.5	22.5	25.5	25.5	21.5	25.5	24.5	21.5

$$AL = \bar{T} = 24.0 \text{ Hz} \qquad \bar{T}_D = 23.9 \text{ Hz} \qquad \bar{T}_A = 24.1 \text{ Hz}$$

In order to distinguish the threshold obtained on a single series from the statistical threshold that is based on a number of such series, we shall continue to refer to the latter as the AL and reserve the letter T for the former. More generally, "thresholds" shall refer to determinations made on single series, and "limens" shall designate statistical thresholds based on a number of determinations.

The same procedure outlined above is repeated for several different series, and on each series a value of T is obtained and recorded, as shown at the bottom of Table 5-1. Note that half of the series is descending (D) and that half is ascending (A). Also observe that the starting point of a series varies among the D series and among the A series. These are control measures which will be discussed at a later point. After completing a total of n series (usually 4 to 20), S's AL is taken to be the mean of the Ts, i.e., $AL = \bar{T}$. In the present illustration $AL = \frac{240}{10} = 24.0$ Hz.

VARIABILITY OF THRESHOLDS. Another feature of interest in the threshold data of Table 5-1 is their variability. It is apparent that two individuals could have exactly the same ALs, which is to say, exactly the same $\bar{T}$s, but differ widely with respect to the variability of their thresholds. It is not difficult to think of situations, particularly in military applications, where in addition to low ALs, low threshold variability, i.e., high threshold reliability, would be greatly desirable.

The range, Q, AD, and SD are all applicable to the threshold data of Table 5-1, but the SD is the measure of variability most commonly employed with psychophysical data. Calculation of the SD of the threshold data is facilitated by subtraction of the constant 21.5 from each of the 10 values. The standard deviation, SD_T, works out to be 1.91 Hz (see Table 4-1).

CONTROL OF RELEVANT VARIABLES. Now that we know something about how the method of limits is applied, let us examine the situation more closely for possible relevant variables and for the kinds of control techniques that may be necessary. To anchor the discussion somewhat, let us assume that ALs are measured in connection with a separate-groups-design experiment involving an experimental and a control group.

Quite distinctly, series direction is a situational relevant variable (RV) that will have to be controlled in the determination of ALs for the experimental and control groups. Conceivably it could be controlled by holding it constant, that is, by using only descending or ascending series in both groups. Or it could be equated across the experimental and control groups, perhaps 50 percent of the Ss in each group serving under descending series only and 50 percent under ascending series. Both methods would prevent the RV from differentially affecting the dependent variable in the experimental and control groups. However, neither of these methods is ever used. Because apart from evaluating the effects of the independent variable E is usually interested in obtaining *for each* S as unbiased an estimate of his AL as possible, it is standard procedure to test all Ss under both types of series—meaning that this RV is equated within each individual S. As pointed out in Chap. 2, control of a situational RV by this method generates sequence RVs requiring control. Of the two kinds of sequence effects distinguished in Chap. 2, i.e., order effects and carry-over effects, the former is of major concern in the present instance because practice effects, fatigue, and boredom are likely to be operating in repeated psychophysical determinations. However, carry-over effects are not of much concern inasmuch as the two conditions involved, D and A series, are very similar in nature and are unlikely to interact.

Sequence RVs, it may be recalled, are controlled in both single-group and separate-groups designs by counterbalancing techniques. The method employed in the present case (Table 5-1) qualifies as a form of intrasubject counterbalancing. If, however, a total of four or eight series was employed with each S, the *abba* sequence would normally be preferable to simple alternation of D and A series.

Psychophysicists have always been particularly concerned with the series-direction variable, pointing out that two opposed tendencies could come into play during any series of judgments. On the one hand, because S makes the same response a number of times before arriving at the threshold, he might become accustomed to making the response and carry it somewhat beyond the point where a reversal in sensation actually occurs. This they called the "error of habituation." On the other hand, because S is usually aware that sooner or later the direction of his sensation must change, he might anticipate the change. This error was appropriately called the "error of anticipation." These errors were referred to as "constant errors" because, if unchecked, they were apt to bias the AL, i.e., produce too large or too small an absolute limen.

Analyzing these constant errors more closely, we find that on a descending series the error of habituation tends to produce too small a value of T, because S continues giving positive responses beyond the point where he fails to perceive the stimulus. On ascending series, contrarily, the error of habituation yields too high a value of T. Accordingly, equal numbers of D and A series tend to cancel this error out, though if S's responses are being influenced by habituation, the mean of the descending series ($\bar{T}_D$) will be lower than the mean of the ascending series ($\bar{T}_A$). For the error of anticipation, the pattern is just the reverse; the value of T is overestimated on descending series and underestimated on ascending series. An indication of the difference in strength between habituation and anticipation can be obtained for any individual from the difference $\bar{T}_D - \bar{T}_A$, positive differences implying dominance of anticipation and negative differences implying habituation. As for our own hypothetical S (Table 5-1), $\bar{T}_D = 23.9$ Hz and $\bar{T}_A = 24.1$ Hz, so presumably "habit" balanced "hope."

A second situational variable requiring control in the method of limits is the starting point of each series (cf. Nachmias & Steinman, 1965). It is perhaps apparent that if the same stimulus were always used to begin D series, S might be influenced by the fact that on all such series approximately the same number of positive responses intervene between the series beginning and the threshold and unwittingly employ this cue to estimate the threshold location. This is a situational RV that provides unwanted information to S; as pointed out in Chap. 2, control over such variables is provided by randomization. Hence, the starting point of each series should be randomized, subject to the restriction that the series origin is not a stimulus too close to threshold.

These then are the important RVs usually associated with the method of limits. There are, of course, many others, such as stimulus duration, time between trials of a series, and interseries interval. Practically all these, however, are controlled by being held constant, thus providing little difficulty apart from their identification.

Determination of the DL by the Method of Limits

The major procedural difference in determining ALs and DLs by the method of limits is that in finding DLs, two stimuli are presented to S on every trial—a standard stimulus (S_t) and a variable stimulus (S_v)—and S's task is to judge whether the magnitude of the sensation evoked by S_v is greater than, less than, or equal to that elicited by S_t. This difference in procedure is a consequence of the fact that unlike the AL, which is an indicator of *absolute* sensitivity, the DL is a measure of *differential* sensitivity, i.e., the ability to discriminate *differences* between stimuli. The determination of DLs by the method of limits will be illustrated in a setting requiring a minimum of materials.

We all know from common experience that, visual cues excluded, it is possible to estimate the size of an object, e.g., its width, by spanning it with the thumb and forefinger. We can learn something about the accuracy of this method of judging size by finding the DL for a stimulus card 50 millimeters (mm) wide. The object of our determinations is to ascertain the minimum increase or decrease in width necessary for a second card to be judged wider or narrower than the 50-mm card. This value—actually the mean of several threshold determinations—is the DL. The two continua always present in psychophysical determinations are, in the present instance, the *actual* width of the stimulus cards (the continuum of the physical stimulus) and the *apparent* or experienced width of these same cards (the continuum of the corresponding sensory response).

The 50-mm card, about 5 in. long, is cut from thin cardboard or even from a 3- by 5-in. index card; this is the standard stimulus. A set of 13 variable stimuli covering the range from 36 to 64 mm in intervals of 2 mm are also cut from cardboard or from 3- by 5-in. index cards (Table 5-2, column 1). These stimuli should meet the criteria that (1) the difference in width of adjacent stimuli be "minimal," i.e., not easily discriminable, and that (2) the S_v include cards that are clearly wider and narrower than S_t.

On each trial S_t and one of the S_v are presented to the subject who, blindfolded, judges their relative width by feeling one card and then the other. A plus, minus, or equal sign is entered by E on the data sheet (Table 5-2) in accordance with whether the subject judges S_v to be wider than, narrower than, or equal to S_t. This procedure is repeated until S registers a reversal in response,

Table 5-2 Determining the *DL* for Apparent Width by the Method of Limits

(1)	(2)	(3)	(4)	(5)	(6)	(7)	(8)	(9)
				STIMULUS PRESENTED FIRST				
SERIES	S_t		S_v		S_v		S_t	
DIRECTION	D	A	A	D	D	A	A	D
S_v (mm)								
64	+							
62	+				+			+
60	+			+	+			+
58	+			+	+			+
56	+			+	+			+
54	=			=	=		+	=
52	=		+	=	=	+	=	=
$S_t = 50$	=	+	=	=	=	=	=	=
48	−	−	=	=	−	=	=	−
46		−	−	−		−	−	
44		−	−			−	−	
42		−	−			−	−	
40		−	−			−	−	
38		−					−	
36		−						
UT	55	49	51	55	55	51	53	55
LT	49	49	47	47	49	47	47	49
$IU = 2DT$	6	0	4	8	6	4	6	6
PSE	52	49	49	51	52	49	50	52

$DL = \overline{DT}$ $\overline{IU}/2 = 2.50$ mm

$DL_D = 3.25$ mm $DL_A = 1.75$ mm $DL_t = 2.25$ mm $DL_v = 2.75$ mm

$\overline{PSE} = 50.50$ mm $\overline{PSE_t} = 50.75$ mm $\overline{PSE_v} = 50.25$ mm

which, if the difference between adjacent stimuli is sufficiently small, will be preceded by one or more "equal" judgments (Table 5-2, column 2).

CONTROL OF RVS.   Because on every trial **S** evaluates two stimuli, S_t and S_v, the temporal arrangement of these stimuli is a situational *RV* with which one must contend. It is possible, of course, to control this *RV* by holding it constant, for example, always presenting S_t first and S_v second. If this procedure were adopted, temporal arrangement of S_t and S_v could not differentially affect the dependent variable in any experiment. As with series direction, however, it is customary with situational *RV*s of this nature to equate them over each **S** individually. Such a control procedure requires that **S** serve under more than one condition of the experiment, obliging **E** to consider the control of sequence *RV*s.

In Table 5-2 a method of counterbalancing both series direction and the temporal arrangement of S_t and S_v is illustrated. There is a total of eight series, four descending and four ascending, with the D and A series arranged in a double *abba* sequence. For four of the eight series S_t is the stimulus presented first on each trial, and for the other four series, S_v is the initial stimulus, this variable arranged in a single *abba* sequence. If, therefore, the order effects operating during the determinations are approximately linear, they should be distributed equally over the D and A series and over the two temporal arrangements of S_t and S_v.

CALCULATING THE DL.   On each series two thresholds, called the "upper threshold" (UT) and the "lower threshold" (LT), are calculated. The UT is the midpoint between the two stimuli where the response changes from "greater than" to "equal" (or vice versa); symmetrically, the LT is the midpoint between the adjacent stimuli where the response of "equal" changes to "less than." For the first series these two values, indicated at the bottom of Table 5-2 (column 2), are 55 mm and 49 mm, respectively. In an inconsistent series, such as that shown in the fifth and seventh columns of Table 5-2, the UT or LT is usually chosen so as to maximize the interval separating the upper and lower thresholds. If a reversal in response occurs without an intervening equality judgment, then obviously $UT = LT$ (column 3). This is a result that falsely implies that the difference threshold is zero for the series in question. The difference $UT - LT$ is often called the "interval of uncertainty" (IU), because in this interval S does not distinguish between S_t and S_v.

Observe that as the interval between UT and LT is traversed, S's response changes from "greater than" to "equal" and then from "equal" to "less than." Hence, this interval spans not one but two difference thresholds (DT). The first, the *upper difference threshold* (UDT), is the threshold located between S_t and stimuli of greater magnitude; its value on any series may be obtained from the relationship $UDT = UT - S_t$. The second, the *lower difference threshold* (LDT), is the corresponding threshold when stimuli below or less than S_t are considered; its value is calculated from the relationship $LDT = S_t - LT$. We shall not at this time distinguish between the two difference thresholds, noting only that in every series $UT - LT$ spans two difference thresholds, i.e.,

$$UT - LT = (UDT + S_t) - (S_t - LDT) = UDT + LDT = 2\ DT$$

Hence on any single series $DT = (UT - LT)/2 = IU/2$. In accordance with the distinction between thresholds and limens introduced earlier—namely, that thresholds refer to determinations made on single series but limens are statistical quantities such as means of thresholds—the DL is defined as the mean of the difference thresholds, or $DL = \overline{DT}$. It follows that $DL = \overline{IU}/2$.

The DL for the data of Table 5-2 is 2.50 mm. When appropriate subgroups of series are considered, the DL can be separately calculated for descending series alone (DL_D), for ascending series alone (DL_A), and for series in which S_t or S_v

was the stimulus presented first (DL_t and DL_v, respectively). These quantities appear in the bottom of Table 5-2. It is important to observe that because of the manner in which the eight series are organized, the temporal arrangement (of S_t and S_v) variable is equated across the series direction variable and vice versa.

THE POINT OF SUBJECTIVE EQUALITY.   There is another quantity of interest that may be calculated from the data of Table 5-2. It is apparent from the table that **S** does not always judge S_t and S_v to be equal when and only when they are in fact equal. The question therefore arises as to the value of S_v that **S** perceives as equal to S_t, a value that carries the suggestive name, "the point of subjective equality." On each series a point of subjective equality (PSE) is determined, its value taken as the midpoint between UT and LT. The PSE for the first series in Table 5-2 is, for example, 52 mm. It is then natural to take the mean of the individual PSE values ($\overline{PSE}$) as the measure of **S**'s point of subjective equality.

THE TIME ERROR.   It is often of interest to calculate the point of subjective equality separately for the series in which S_t is presented first ($\overline{PSE_t}$) and for the series in which S_v is the initial stimulus ($\overline{PSE_v}$). As may be observed from Table 5-2, in the present case these values differ little. Often, however, when $\overline{PSE}$s are calculated separately for the different temporal orders of presentation, they differ markedly. In the determination of the DL for the loudness of tones or the heaviness of hefted weights, for example, $\overline{PSE_t}$ will usually be considerably smaller than $\overline{PSE_v}$. This means that when the standard stimulus is the first of the presented stimuli, a value of S_v which is actually less than S_t appears equal to the standard stimulus. Thus, if in such situations S_t were always presented first, the point of subjective equality would be smaller in magnitude than S_t. This type of constant error has long been recognized by workers in the area and is customarily referred to as the "negative time error": "negative" because the error, taken as the difference $\overline{PSE} - S_t$, yields a negative value; "time" error because the error or bias arises from the temporal arrangement of S_t and S_v, the former always presented first and the latter second. If $\overline{PSE} - S_t > 0$, the time error is said to be positive.

The time error has been the subject of a considerable amount of ingenious research and theorizing, discussed in some detail by Woodworth and Schlosberg (1954, pp. 226–229) and by Koffka (1935, pp. 465–474). Returning to our hypothetical **S**, there is little evidence for the operation of a time error since $\overline{PSE_t} - S_t$ is about equal to zero.

Modifications of the Method of Limits

In actual practice the method of limits is usually subjected to procedural modifications of one sort or another. For example, each stimulus may be presented twice or more before the next stimulus in the series is presented. In the determination of the AL, "check" trials, in which the stimulus is omitted, may be introduced to evaluate S's tendency to guess. Often the nature of the determinations is such that only ascending series may be used, as in obtaining "recognition" thresholds for words and forms. More radical variations on the basic method are discussed by Guilford (1954, pp. 113–115), one of which, the "staircase" method (cf. Cornsweet, 1962), has been employed to obtain thresholds in pigeons (Blough, 1958) and rats (Moskowitz & Kitzes, 1966).

EXERCISES

5-1. Calculate SD_{DT} and SD_{PSE} for the data of Table 5-2.

5-2. Suppose that, after S's DL was determined, S were repeatedly presented with the same two stimuli, S_t and a stimulus (S_1) that was 1 DL greater than S_t, i.e., $S_1 = S_t + 1$ DL. Would S, if required on every trial to judge whether S_1 was greater than, less than, or equal to S_t, always judge S_1 to be greater than the standard stimulus?

5-3. By means of the procedure described in the text, a DL is determined for standard stimuli 25, 50, and 75 mm in width. Would you expect the three DLs (calculated on the same S) to be about the same size? If not, why not?

METHOD OF CONSTANT STIMULI

The method of constant stimuli is the second of the three traditional psychophysical methods treated in this chapter. Like the method of limits, it is particularly suited to the determination of ALs and DLs, though the method has been put to other uses. The fundamental difference between the method of constant stimuli and the method of limits is that the stimuli which S judges are presented, not in serial order, but in a random or quasi-random fashion. Such a procedure eliminates the errors of habituation and anticipation, i.e., the series-direction variable, the absence of which represents one of the major advantages of the method of constant stimuli.

Determination of the AL by the Method of Constant Stimuli

We shall describe the application of the method of constant stimuli to the determination of the AL for pain, an application relevant to a subsequent illustration.

Procedures for working with pain-producing stimuli in the laboratory have been well worked out by Wolff and Wolf (1948) for thermal stimulation with radiant energy. Their method briefly is this. Intense focused light (radiation) from an incandescent lamp is applied for 3 sec on a circumscribed area of the skin which has been blackened with india ink. At low intensities the radiation stimulus gives rise to a sensation of warmth. At higher intensities the feeling of warmth gives way, during the 3-sec period of stimulation, to a sensation of pricking pain. A painful stimulus is defined as one in which the pricking pain becomes barely perceptible at the end of the 3-sec stimulation period. The physical intensity of the thermal stimulus may be expressed as the number of millicalories applied to each square centimeter of skin during each second of stimulation, abbreviated mc/sec/cm^2 (read "millicalories per second per square centimeter"). Pain thresholds obtained by this technique are remarkably stable within the same individual from day to day and vary little from individual to individual tested under comparable conditions. Yet they are quite sensitive to analgesics; in fact, ordinary aspirin in normal doses increases the thermal-pain *AL* by almost 35 percent (Wolff & Wolf, 1948).

The first step in applying the method of constant stimuli is to choose a number of stimuli (four to eight) that bracket the likely value of the *AL* as estimated by prior results. But unlike the requirements imposed by the method of limits, the stimuli should not include values that are clearly superthreshold and subthreshold. Rather, they should encompass values ranging from those that will be perceived on a little more than zero percent of the trials up to magnitudes that will be perceived somewhat less than 100 percent of the trials. Hence, the range of stimuli employed with the method of constant stimuli is more restricted than the range required by the method of limits.

The method of constant stimuli consists in presenting S with *each stimulus a relatively large number of times* and securing after each stimulus presentation S's response as to whether the stimulus elicited the appropriate sensation on that trial. The stimulus presented to S on any trial is randomly determined, subject to the restriction that each of the stimuli occur an equal number of times. The *AL* is the stimulus value that elicits, or would elicit, the appropriate sensation on 50 percent of its presentations to S.

Table 5-3 Summary Data Obtained from the Method of Constant Stimuli in the Determination of the Thermal-pain *AL* for One Subject

STIMULUS (mc/sec/cm²)	PERCENT OF TRIALS JUDGED PAINFUL
225	95
210	90
195	75
180	55
165	40
150	25
135	15
120	5

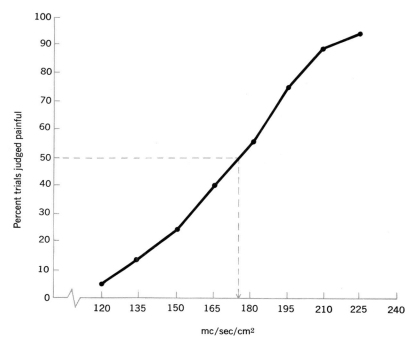

Fig. 5-2. Determination of the *AL* by graphic interpolation. The dashed line indicates the stimulus value that would be perceived on 50 percent of the trials. A graph which relates percentage of "yes" or, more generally, detection responses to stimulus intensity is called a "psychometric function."

Suppose, for example, that in the determination of *S*'s *AL* for pain, each of eight stimuli were presented 20 times, yielding the data of Table 5-3. None of the stimuli produced a report of pain on exactly 50 percent of the trials. The 165-mc/sec/cm² stimulus elicited pain on 40 percent of the trials, and the 180-mc/sec/cm² stimulus elicited pain on 55 percent of the trials. The *AL* must, therefore, lie between these two stimulus values. If we assume that the percentage of trials on which pain is perceived is linearly related to stimulus intensity for stimuli between 165 and 180 mc/sec/cm², we can obtain the stimulus value that will evoke pain on 50 percent of the trials by linear interpolation (see Chap. 3). This value turns out to be 175 mc/sec/cm². If the data of Table 5-3 are graphed, as in Fig. 5-2, the interpolation may be done graphically, as shown by the dashed line in the figure.

As a means of illustrating some of the advantages and limitations of the method of constant stimuli, we now apply the method to an actual experimental problem.

The unpleasantness and pain associated with many dental therapeutic procedures are well known to everyone. The only remedy available has been the application of an anesthetic of one sort or another. Several years ago it was demonstrated that it is possible, in many people at least, to reduce markedly the discomfort and need for anesthesia during such dental operations as drilling and extraction by presenting stereophonic music to the patient simultaneously with intense "white noise."[2] The white noise is the effective agent in the auditory stimulation, the music superimposed to make the noise more palatable and to provide a source of distraction. The patient, outfitted with earphones, controls the intensity of the white noise reaching him by turning a volume control that is always in his possession. When he begins to feel pain or anticipates feeling pain, he increases the volume of the noise until he obtains relief. Such sound stimulation has been reported to have been the only analgesic required in about 90 percent of more than 5,000 dental operations, including extractions (Gardner, Licklider, & Weisz, 1960).

Apart from obvious practical implications of this finding, an important theoretical question arises. Is the intense white noise effective because it actually reduces or suppresses pain, or does it merely provide a source of distraction which, although not altering the sensation of pain itself, serves to affect favorably the more complicated reactions that are usually associated with painful situations, such as anxiety and threat (Camp, Martin, & Chapman, 1962)?

This is a problem that can be attacked experimentally. If it can be shown that the AL for pain is reduced in the presence of intense white noise, one would be inclined to accept the first interpretation, namely, that intense white noise suppresses pain. Conversely, if white noise were found to be without effect on the AL for pain, such a result, though by no means disproving the first hypothesis, would tend to discredit it and render the second interpretation more plausible. Accordingly, Camp, Martin, and Chapman (1962), employing the method of constant stimuli, set out to obtain ALs for thermal pain with and without accompanying intense white noise.

The investigators adopted a single-group design. Each of the 8 stimuli of Table 5-3 were presented to every S 10 times in a random order; 40 of the 80 stimulus presentations were made in the absence of white noise, and the other 40 presentations were accompanied by intense noise (120 db). Rather than calculating ALs separately for each of the 10 Ss of the experiment, they pooled the Ss' responses and plotted group curves for the noise and no-noise conditions. These psychometric functions appear in Fig. 5-3, and from their appearance it seems apparent that, under the conditions of the present experiment, the perception of pain is uninfluenced by accompanying white noise. Graphic interpolation estimates that the group AL is 175 mc/sec/cm^2 with noise present and 180 mc/sec/cm^2 with noise absent. Hence, the results of the Camp, Martin, and Chapman experiment do not support the interpretation that white noise directly

[2] *White noise* is the name given to an auditory stimulus composed of a broad band of frequencies, say 20 to 10,000 Hz, all at about the same intensity level. It produces a "hissing" sound, something like what one hears when an FM-radio receiver is tuned between stations. The noise is called "white" through an analogy with light: white light from most sources is composed of all the visible wavelengths in approximately equal intensities.

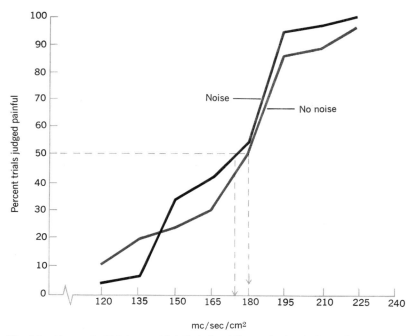

Fig. 5-3. Percent of trials on which Ss judged thermal stimulation, with and with-out accompanying intense white noise, to be painful. The dashed lines indicate the ALs for the two conditions. (SOURCE: W. Camp, R. Martin, and L. F. Chap-man. Pain threshold and discrimination of pain intensity during brief exposure to intense noise. *Science,* 1962, **135,** 788–789. Used by permission.)

suppresses pain, at least not in the sense of raising the *AL* for pain (cf. Carlin, Ward, Gershon, & Ingraham, 1962).

COMPARISONS BETWEEN THE METHOD OF LIMITS AND THE METHO ᵢ OF CONSTANT STIMULI.   Although the method of limits could have been employed to obtain the pain *AL*s, in unmodified form this method would entail serious disadvan-tages. One disadvantage is that on descending series Ss would be subjected to a number of painful stimuli in succession, perhaps causing discomfort to some Ss. A modified method of limits, in which descending series are omitted, elimi-nates this difficulty inasmuch as each series then terminates with a single painful stimulus of threshold value. However, this modification of the method of limits is not without its own shortcomings. For example, the anticipation of pain that results from the knowledge that each series ends with a painful stimulus could, owing to the fact that people differ widely in their reactions to anticipation of pain, prove bothersome in certain experiments.

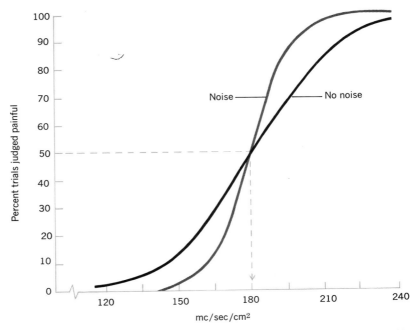

Fig. 5-4. Hypothetical effects of intense white noise on pain perception. Although the noise affects pain perception for most stimulus values, the pain *AL* is identical under the two conditions.

Another potential disadvantage of the method of limits, modified or unmodified, is that it does not yield as much information of the threshold process as the method of constant stimuli. Suppose, for example, that the effect of white noise on pain sensation was complex in that it decreased the likelihood that relatively weak stimuli would be perceived as painful but increased this same probability for stronger stimuli, a situation seen in the psychometric functions of Fig. 5-4. Although, as shown by graphic interpolation, the group *AL*s are identical for the two conditions, the graph clearly depicts that white noise differentially affects pain perception at most stimulus intensities. Effects such as these are not as directly observable in the data provided by the method of limits; rather they must be inferred from such measures as the standard deviation of the individual threshold determinations.

The method of constant stimuli, on the other hand, is free of the above limitations because (1) the stimuli are presented to S in a random order and (2) the most intense stimulus employed is superthreshold on somewhat less than 100 percent of the trials presumably, and therefore cannot be particularly painful. Still, the method has one important disadvantage. In order for an individual's *AL* to be calculated with any degree of accuracy, every stimulus must be presented a large number of times. This is a requirement that often makes threshold determinations by the method of constant stimuli rather tedious.

5-4. Because the *AL* as determined by the method of constant stimuli most commonly falls between two adjacent stimuli, why bother using six or eight stimuli in its determination? Why not simply use two stimuli, one that is sure to elicit the appropriate sensation on less than 50 percent of the trials and one that is just as certain to elicit a sensation on more than 50 percent of the trials, and find the *AL* by linear interpolation?

5-5. Consider the hypothetical curves of Fig. 5-4. If the pain *AL* were defined as the stimulus value that evokes an appropriate sensation on 25 (or 75) percent of the trials, what conclusion(s) would you draw as to the effects of intense white noise on pain *AL*s?

The Normal Distribution as a Model for Distributions of Thresholds

As mentioned in Exercise 5-4, basing *S*'s *AL* on only two data points is a procedure that wastes data. Here we shall develop a method which utilizes all of the data made available by the method of constant stimuli. The method is based on certain assumptions about how *S*'s absolute threshold varies from trial to trial. We proceed to these assumptions, drawing heavily from the material of the last chapter.

It has already been agreed that the absolute threshold is not a fixed quantity but rather one that varies from moment to moment, its particular value on any single trial determined by a large number of known and unknown variables. Recall from the method of limits that the absolute threshold obtained from a single *series*, consisting of several individual trials, was referred to as *T*. We now want an expression for the value of the absolute threshold on a single *trial* (of either the method of limits or the method of constant stimuli). We conceive that during the few seconds required for a single trial, *S*'s absolute threshold exists at a specific value; this absolute threshold we refer to as the "momentary absolute threshold" ($\dot{T}$).

Suppose that it were possible to measure the momentary absolute threshold. To make things specific, refer to the hypothetical *S* of Table 5-3 and imagine that on each of the 160 trials conducted with this *S*, we obtained not only a judgment as to whether the presented stimulus was painful, but, in addition, we measured the precise value of his absolute threshold ($\dot{T}$). Presumably we would find that on any trial during which the value of $\dot{T}$ was *less* than the value of the stimulus presented *S*, the subject would judge the stimulus as painful. Conversely, on trials in which $\dot{T}$ was measured to be *greater* than the presented stimulus, the latter would not be judged painful.

At the termination of the 160 trials, we would possess 160 values of $\dot{T}$, and it would be simple to draw up a relative frequency histogram of the distribution of $\dot{T}$. There are certain things that we know in advance must be true about the distribution of $\dot{T}$. In the first place, relatively few of the $\dot{T}$s will have values of 120 mc/sec/cm² or less; i.e., the momentary absolute threshold will rarely be this low. (Why?) On the other hand, few of the $\dot{T}$s will be 225 mc/sec/cm² or greater. Let us suppose that the distribution of the $\dot{T}$s is as given by the histogram of Fig. 5-5. As indicated by the superimposed curve, the assumed distribution of $\dot{T}$ is reasonably approximated by a normal distribution.

Now, although distributions of $\dot{T}$ are unattainable, their existence is a reasonable postulation. And going one step further, the hypothesis that momentary absolute thresholds are normally distributed—apart from being methodologically useful—often squares with available facts. Consequently, we shall assume for our hypothetical S that the distribution of $\dot{T}$ is $N(\mu, \sigma)$. It is then natural to view μ as the "true" AL, a value which we estimate in various ways by the different psychophysical methods.

This model of momentary absolute thresholds is related to the determination of the AL by the method of constant stimuli in the following way. Suppose that the distribution of the momentary thermal-pain absolute thresholds for our hypothetical S is as indicated in Fig. 5-6. Our job is to estimate μ, the true AL; if we wish an indication of the variability of S's absolute threshold, we will have to estimate σ as well. Imagine that we present to S a large number of times each of the eight stimuli numbered on the abscissa of Fig. 5-6. What information will be provided by the *percentage of trials on which each stimulus is judged by S to be painful?* Consider, for example, the 150-mc/sec/cm² stimulus. Assuming that 20 percent of the distribution of $\dot{T}$ lies to the left of 150 mc/sec/cm², we should expect that on 20 percent of the trials in which the presented stimulus is 150 mc/sec/cm², the value of $\dot{T}$ will be of lesser magnitude, i.e., be less than 150 mc/sec/cm². This is tantamount to saying that on 20 percent of its presentations, the 150-mc/sec/cm² stimulus will be *above* threshold; hence, on 20 percent of its trials, this stimulus should be judged "painful." Similarly,

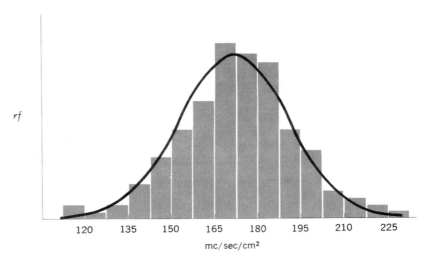

rf

120   135   150   165   180   195   210   225

mc/sec/cm²

Fig. 5-5. Distribution of the hypothetical 160 momentary absolute thresholds ($\dot{T}$).

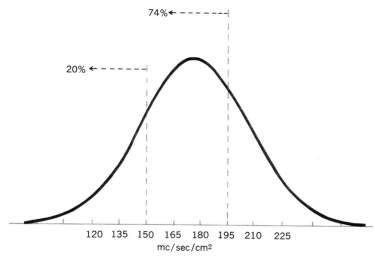

Fig. 5-6. Assumed distribution of $\dot{T}$: $N(\mu, \sigma)$.

let us grant that 74 percent of the distribution of $\dot{T}$ lies below 195 mc/sec/cm². If the number of presentations of a stimulus of this value is very large, 74 percent of them will be judged "painful," because on 74 percent of such trials the value of $\dot{T}$ will be less than 195 mc/sec/cm². In other words, if each of the eight numbered stimuli of Fig. 5-6 is presented to S a large number of times, the resulting percentage of trials on which each stimulus is judged "painful" is the *percentile rank of each stimulus in the cumulative distribution of $\dot{T}$*. Because we already know how to obtain the mean and standard deviation of a normal distribution given the percentile ranks of a few of the scores, the task of estimating μ and σ from the preceding percentages is not a new one.

However, our problem is slightly more complicated because the number of presentations of each stimulus is not large enough to ensure that the percentile ranks of the employed stimuli are accurately reflected in the obtained judgments. The percentages of Table 5-3, for example, are based on only 20 presentations of each stimulus; a percentile rank of 13, for example, could not possibly find accurate representation in the percentages of the table. The obtained percentages are, therefore, *estimates* of the percentile ranks of the stimuli. They may be used, in turn, to estimate the distribution of $\dot{T}$.

ESTIMATING THE DISTRIBUTION OF $\dot{T}$ WITH A PROBABILITY PAPER GRAPH. We learned in the last chapter that a graph of the normal ogive describes a straight line on probability paper. Hence if $\dot{T}$ is normally distributed, the percentages associated with the eight stimuli of Table 5-3 should fall reasonably close to a straight line when plotted on probability paper. We say "reasonably close" because as already pointed out, these percentages are not the actual percentile

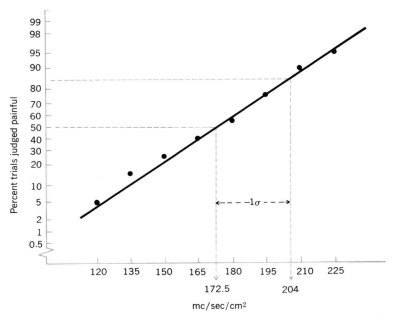

Fig. 5-7. The psychometric function based on the data of Table 5-3 plotted on probability paper.

ranks of the stimuli but only estimates. In Fig. 5-7 the eight points have been plotted on probability paper, and they are reasonably close to the straight line that has been fitted to them by "eye," i.e., by visual inspection. Hence the assumption that T is normally distributed is not contradicted by the data.

The normal distribution represented by the straight line of Fig. 5-7 estimates the distribution of T; therefore, its mean and standard deviation are estimates of the mean and standard deviation of T. These quantities, obtained graphically in Fig. 5-7, are approximately 172.5 mc/sec/cm² for the mean and 31.5 mc/sec/cm² for the standard deviation. The value of the AL (172.5 mc/sec/cm²) calculated by this method is in general agreement with the value obtained earlier by simple linear interpolation (175.0 mc/sec/cm²). The fundamental reason for this correspondence is that the normal ogive is very nearly linear in the region of μ.

ESTIMATING THE DISTRIBUTION OF T WITH Z VALUES. We also saw in the last chapter that given the percentile ranks of a set of scores, the corresponding z values could be obtained from Table B of the Appendix, *on the assumption that the scores are drawn from a normally distributed variable.* A plot on ordinary graph paper of the scores against their z values then describes a straight line. If, however, the variable involved is not normally distributed, a straight line will not

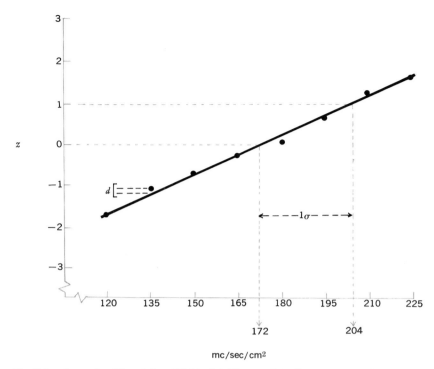

Fig. 5-8. A graph of the data of Table 5-4. The straight line has been fitted to the data points by the method of least squares (see text).

be obtained, because the z values secured from the area relations under the normal curve are not then the actual z values of the scores.

Using this principle, the data of Table 5-3 have been converted to z scores (Table 5-4) and the resulting points plotted in Fig. 5-8. We see again that a straight line (fitted this time by the method of least squares, discussed below)

Table 5-4 Conversion of the Data of Table 5-3 to z Scores

STIMULUS (mc/sec/cm²)	PERCENT OF TRIALS JUDGED PAINFUL	z SCORE
225	95	1.65
210	90	1.28
195	75	0.67
180	55	0.13
165	40	−0.25
150	25	−0.67
135	15	−1.04
120	5	−1.65

reasonably describes the data points. Actually, because a straight line was a reasonable fit for the data points plotted on probability paper, it must be the same for the plot of S against z. (Why?)

The AL is taken to be the stimulus value corresponding to $z = 0$ because this value (171.9 mc/sec/cm^2) estimates the mean of $\hat{T}$. The standard deviation, 32.3 mc/sec/cm^2, estimates the standard deviation of $\hat{T}$ and is thus a measure of the variability of S's absolute threshold. Both of these quantities, it will be noted, are close to the corresponding values obtained from the probability paper graph.

Fitting a Straight Line to the Data Points

The question may occur to the student as to how one goes about fitting a straight line to the set of points in Figs. 5-7 and 5-8. Fitting by eye, the method used in Fig. 5-7, seems somewhat subjective. There are many objective methods by which a straight line may be fitted to a set of points, several of which are described by Guilford (1954, pp. 59–65) and in greater detail by D. Lewis (1960, pp. 10–27). We will discuss in detail only the *method of averages*.

THE METHOD OF LEAST SQUARES.   A technique having a very wide range of application is the *method of least squares*. We shall describe the method only briefly here, but a full discussion may be found in either of the two sources mentioned above. With reference to Fig. 5-8, it is clear that any straight line which we decide fits the eight data points must be of the form $z = cS + k$, i.e., a linear function. In the method of least squares, the constants c and k are chosen so that the *sum of the squared deviations of the observed points from the fitted line is a minimum*. In Fig. 5-8 a deviation (d) of one of the points from the straight line, which was fitted by the least-squares method, is shown. The constants c and k of the linear function relating z to S were chosen so that the following is true. Measure the deviation of each of the eight points from the straight line of Fig. 5-8; square each deviation separately; then sum the eight squared deviations: this sum is smallest for the straight line shown in the figure than for any other possible straight line. In the present illustration c and k are equal to 0.031 and -5.33, respectively. Hence, the function relating z to S is $z = 0.031S - 5.33$.

The mean of the distribution represented by the straight line of Fig. 5-8 is the value of S that yields a z score of zero, i.e., $0 = c\mu + k$, or $\mu = -k/c$. By substitution, $\mu = 5.33/0.031 = 171.9$. Therefore 171.9 mc/sec/cm^2 is the mean of the preceding distribution and the value that estimates the mean of $\hat{T}$; accordingly, it is the value taken to be S's AL.

The standard deviation of the distribution represented by the straight line of Fig. 5-8 is obtained from the relation $1.0 = c(\mu + \sigma) + k$; i.e., the z score corresponding to an S value of $\mu + \sigma$ is 1.0. Then $\sigma = 1/c - k/c - \mu = 1/c$. In the present example $1/c = 1/0.031 = 32.3$. Hence the required standard deviation is 32.3 mc/sec/cm^2.

THE METHOD OF AVERAGES. A much simpler method of fitting a straight line to a set of points is called the *method of averages*. Essentially, this method reduces the total number of data points to two, the latter defining the required straight line. The reduction proceeds as follows.

Each of the employed stimuli in conjunction with its associated z score contains a basis on which to determine the constants c and k of the required linear function, $z = cS + k$. For example, because the 210-mc/sec/cm^2 stimulus was judged "painful" on 90 percent of the trials, its associated z score is 1.28 (Table 5-4). The equation $1.28 = c(210) + k$ may therefore be used in the determination of c and k. If the four such equations arising from the upper four of the employed stimuli are averaged and if the same operation is performed on the four equations resulting from the four lower stimuli, the eight equations are reduced to two. With two equations both containing c and k, it is a simple matter to solve for the two unknowns. The required calculations are

$$
\begin{array}{ll}
1.65 = c(225) + k & -0.25 = c(165) + k \\
1.28 = c(210) + k & -0.67 = c(150) + k \\
0.67 = c(195) + k & -1.04 = c(135) + k \\
0.13 = c(180) + k & -1.65 = c(120) + k \\
\hline
\end{array}
$$

$$(1) \quad 3.73/4 = c(810/4) + k \qquad\qquad -3.61/4 = c(570/4) + k \quad (2)$$

First we obtain c by subtracting (2) from (1):

$$
\begin{array}{l}
 3.73/4 = c(810/4) + k \\
-[-3.61/4 = c(570/4) + k] \\
\hline
 7.34/4 = c(240/4) \\
 c = 0.031
\end{array}
$$

Next we obtain k by substituting 0.031 in (1) and (2), then adding (2) to (1):

$$
\begin{array}{l}
 3.73/4 = (0.031)(810/4) + k \\
-3.61/4 = (0.031)(570/4) + k \\
\hline
 0.12/4 = (0.031)(1380/4) + 2k \\
 8k = 0.12 - 42.78 \\
 k = -5.53
\end{array}
$$

Hence, the linear function relating z to S as obtained by the method of averages is $z = 0.031S - 5.53$. It is only by coincidence that this is precisely the function obtained with the method of least squares. The mean and standard deviation of the distribution represented by this linear function can be found either graphically or arithmetically. [Should an odd number of stimuli be involved, the middle stimulus is included in the calculation of both (1) and (2).]

Summarizing briefly the developments in this section, we set out to make full use of the threshold data obtained by the method of constant stimuli, developing the concept of the momentary absolute threshold, $\dot{T}$, which was defined as the value of the absolute threshold on a single trial. Because the value of $\dot{T}$

may be presumed to vary from trial to trial, it has a distribution, and we postulated that this distribution was $N(\mu, \sigma)$. The next step was to construct a "best-fitting" normal distribution for the obtained threshold data. Because this normal distribution approximates the distribution of $\dot{T}$, its mean and standard deviation are estimates of the mean and standard deviation of the latter. Accordingly, the mean was taken to be S's AL and the standard deviation to be a measure of the variability of S's thresholds. The assumption that $\dot{T}$ is normally distributed is subject to verification in that if the assumption is reasonable, the psychometric function plotted from the original threshold data on probability paper (Fig. 5-7), or from the percentages converted to z scores on ordinary paper (Fig. 5-8), should not deviate unduly from a straight line. If need be, this assumption can be put to more rigorous evaluation by means of appropriate statistical tests (e.g., Guilford, 1954, pp. 133–134).

COMMENTS ON THE VARIABILITY OF THE ABSOLUTE THRESHOLD. We return now to the problem posed by Exercise 5-5 of the last section. It will be recalled that according to the hypothetical data presented in Fig. 5-4, white noise affected pain perception for most stimulus values, but nevertheless the thermal-pain AL was identical under the noise and no-noise conditions. We will now show that the results of Fig. 5-4 may be attributed to an effect of white noise on the *variability* of the absolute threshold, rather than on the AL itself.

Suppose that for a given S, the distribution of the momentary absolute threshold ($\dot{T}$) is $N(180, 30)$ for the no-noise condition. Suppose further that the effect of white noise is to decrease the variability of the absolute threshold so that with accompanying noise the distribution of the momentary thresholds, designated as $\dot{T}_n$, becomes $N(180, 15)$. According to these assumptions, white noise does not affect the AL, because the mean of distribution $\dot{T}_n$ is identical to the mean of distribution $\dot{T}$. These distributions are shown in Fig. 5-9.

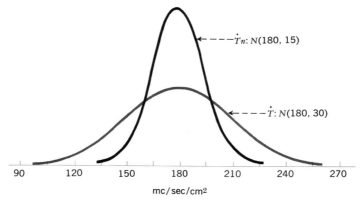

Fig. 5-9. Assumed distribution of S's momentary pain threshold, with and without accompanying white noise ($\dot{T}_n$ and $\dot{T}$, respectively).

Observe that in the presence of white noise, the absolute threshold rarely takes on values less than 150 mc/sec/cm² (on only 2.28 percent of the trials, to be exact, because this stimulus value is 2σ below the mean of $\dot{T}_n$). Without accompanying white noise, however, the absolute threshold will measure less than 150 mc/sec/cm² on 15.87 percent of the trials. Consequently, if the 150-mc/sec/cm² stimulus is presented to S a large number of times with and without accompanying noise, it should be judged as painful on about 2 percent of the "noise" trials but on 16 percent of the "no-noise" trials. The difference in sensitivity is just the reverse for the 210-mc/sec/cm² stimulus: about 98 percent of the presentations of this stimulus should be judged to be painful in the presence of white noise, but only 84 percent with noise absent.

The stimulus value judged "painful" on 25 percent of its presentations will be 159.8 mc/sec/cm² in the absence of white noise and 166.5 mc/sec/cm² in its presence, because these values are the twenty-fifth percentiles of distributions $\dot{T}$ and $\dot{T}_n$, respectively. On the other hand, the stimulus value perceived as painful on 75 percent of the trials will be 200.2 mc/sec/cm² without noise and 193.5 mc/sec/cm² with accompanying white noise. Thus if the AL were defined as the stimulus that evokes a sensation on 25 percent of the trials, white noise would be considered to increase the thermal-pain threshold, but, on the other hand, a definition of the AL as the stimulus eliciting a sensation on 75 percent of the trials would necessitate the opposite conclusion. We see, therefore, that the definition of the AL as the 50 percent point is not entirely an arbitrary decision. If an experimental variable influences the variability of the absolute threshold without affecting its mean, the 50 percent point and, therefore, the AL, will be uninfluenced by the variable, though sizable effects may be observed at other points.[3]

A graph of the ogives of $\dot{T}$ and $\dot{T}_n$ directly portrays the relative effects of noise on pain perception at all stimulus values, and, in fact, these ogives are the same curves that appear in Fig. 5-4.

EXERCISES

5-6. The curves of Fig. 5-3 were plotted from the following percentage points: no-noise condition, 12, 20, 24, 30, 50, 86, 88, 96; noise condition, 4, 6, 34, 42, 54, 94, 96, 100. With the use of Table B of the Appendix, convert these percentages to z scores and plot the two sets of points on the same graph. Use a z score of 3.00 for the 100 percent value.

(a) Considering each condition separately, do the points appear to fall on a straight line?

(b) Fit a straight line to each set of points by the method of averages, and calculate μ and σ. What do these values suggest about the effect of white noise on the perception of thermal pain?

[3] Strictly speaking, the value of $\dot{T}$ that will be perceived 50 percent of the time, i.e., the AL, is the median and not the mean of the distribution of $\dot{T}$; however, in a symmetrical distribution, such as the normal distribution, the mean and median coincide.

(c) Calculate the *AL* for each condition directly from the given percentages. To what do you ascribe the relatively large discrepancy between these values and those obtained from the best-fitting straight line?

Determination of the *DL* by the Method of Constant Stimuli

As with the method of limits, the determination of the *DL* by the method of constant stimuli requires the addition of a standard stimulus (S_t). On each trial a pair of stimuli, S_t and one of the variable stimuli (S_v), are presented to **S**, who judges whether one member of the pair is "greater than" or "less than" the other. The problem of whether **S** should be permitted to give a judgment of "equal" (or "doubtful") is a rather complicated one. Because there seem to be good reasons for excluding the equality judgment when **E**'s task is determining thresholds (Thurstone, 1948) and considering that the data analysis is much simplified by exclusion of the "equal" category, we will treat only the two-category case. The student is referred to Guilford (1954, pp. 135–142) for a discussion of the issues involved.

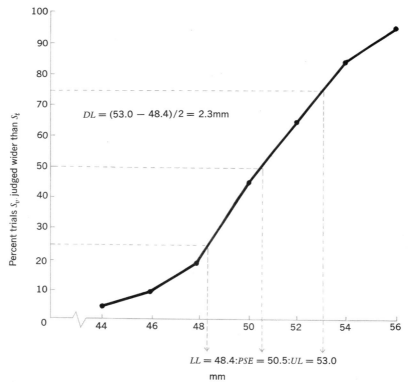

Fig. 5-10. Calculations of the *PSE* and the *DL* by graphic interpolation on the psychometric function.

As an illustration let us return to the problem of determining the *DL* for apparent width. The standard stimulus will again be a 50-mm card; the variable stimuli will consist of seven cards ranging in width from 44 to 56 mm, in steps of 2 mm.

Imagine that each of the seven S_v is presented to S 20 times, making 140 trials in all. The ordering of the S_v over the 140 trials is arranged by means of a table of random numbers. The problem of the temporal order in which S_t and S_v are to be administered can be solved in one of two ways. The temporal order of S_t and S_v can be held constant, for example, S_t being presented first on all 140 trials. Or S_t may be presented first on half of the trials (on 10 presentations with each of the seven S_v) and second on the other half. It has already been mentioned that this variable primarily influences the point of subjective equality and should affect the size of the *DL* little, if at all. Although our interest is in the *DL*, we will adopt the second procedure. Accordingly, each trial has a second random assignment, namely, whether S_t is to be the first or the second member of the pair of stimuli presented S. The conduct of each trial is essentially the same as was described for the method of limits.

Let us assume that the determination of the *DL* for a single S yields the results shown in Table 5-5. The data have been recorded in terms of the percent of trials on which each S_v was judged to be wider than S_t. (Ignore for the present the column of z scores.) The psychometric function appears in Fig. 5-10.

CALCULATION OF THE POINT OF SUBJECTIVE EQUALITY AND THE DL FROM THE UNTRANSFORMED PERCENTAGES. Reasonably enough, the point of subjective equality (*PSE*) is that value of S_v expected to be judged wider than S_t on 50 percent of its presentations. Working with the untransformed percentages (Table 5-5, column 2) either arithmetic or graphic (Fig. 5-10) linear interpolation shows the *PSE* is 50.5 mm.

Table 5-5 Summary Data Obtained by the Method of Constant Stimuli in the Determination of the *DL* for Apparent Width for One Subject

(1) S_v (mm)	(2) PERCENT OF TRIALS S_v JUDGED WIDER THAN S_t	(3) z SCORE
56	95	1.65
54	85	1.04
52	65	0.39
50	45	−0.13
48	20	−0.84
46	10	−1.28
44	5	−1.65

The definition of the DL is more involved than that of the AL and is based on the following reasoning. Variable stimuli judged wider than S_t on more than 50 percent of the trials are, to some degree, discriminated by S as being different from the standard stimulus. Conceivably therefore, the upper limen (UL) could be defined as the value of S_v that is judged wider than S_t on 60, 70, or perhaps 90 percent of the trials, because all these percentages reveal in S some ability to discriminate S_v from S_t. Actually, however, the UL is often defined as that value of S_v judged wider than S_t on 75 percent of the trials, and the lower limen (LL) is symmetrically defined to be the value of S_v judged wider than S_t on 25 percent of the trials. These are reasonable definitions because 75 percent and 25 percent both lie midway between zero discrimination (the 50 percent point) and perfect discrimination (the 100 percent point and 0 percent point, respectively).

As in the method of limits, the difference limen is taken to be one-half the difference between the UL and LL, i.e., $DL = (UL - LL)/2$. The difference between the UL and LL is, as before, known as the interval of uncertainty, IU. Linear interpolation into Table 5-5 shows the UL (the 75 percent point) to be 53.00 mm, and the LL (the 25 percent point) to be 48.40 mm. Consequently, $DL = (53.00 - 48.40)/2 = 2.30$ mm. As may be seen in Fig. 5-10, the same result is obtained by graphic interpolation.

USE OF THE NORMAL OGIVE IN CALCULATING THE PSE AND DL.   If we are willing to assume that the normal ogive is the function relating percent of trials on which S_v is judged wider than S_t to values of S_v (Fig. 5-10), we can then obtain the PSE and DL by interpolating on the normal ogive that best fits the obtained data points.[4] Accepting this premise, we make use of Table B of the Appendix to convert the obtained percentages to z scores (Table 5-5, column 3). A straight line is then fitted (by the method of averages) to the transformed data points, producing the graph shown in Fig. 5-11. The linear function relating z to S_v turns out to be $z = 0.285S_v - 14.37$. Because the PSE is the stimulus that is judged wider than S_t on 50 percent of its presentations, it is the value of S_v corresponding to a z score of zero. Accordingly, $0 = 0.285PSE - 14.37$ and $PSE = 14.37/0.285 = 50.4$ mm, a value very close to that obtained previously by linear interpolation into the untransformed data.

The UL is the value of S_v judged wider than S_t 75 percent of the time. However, another way of looking at the UL is that it is P_{75} of the normal distribution

[4] Note that this hypothesis differs from that made when the AL was under consideration. In the latter case the basic assumption was that the momentary absolute threshold ($\dot{T}$) was normally distributed. From this it *followed* that the normal ogive was the function relating percent of trials on which the presented stimulus was judged "painful" to values of S. We now *assume* the appropriateness of the normal ogive rather than deriving it. This assumption, which is called the "phi gamma hypothesis," has been attacked on the basis that its validity requires that the size of the DL remain independent of the magnitude of S_t (Thurstone, 1928), which is in conflict with Weber's law (discussed below) and the data on which that generalization is based. Nevertheless, there are many situations where the phi gamma hypothesis provides a good "fit" to the psychometric function.

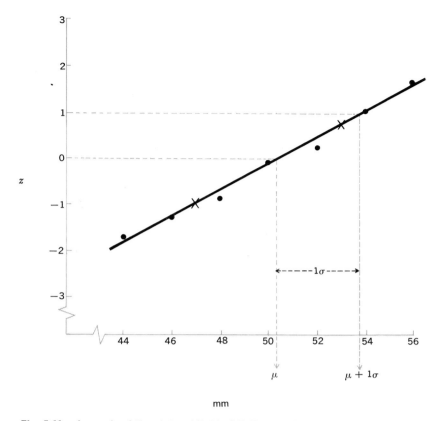

Fig. 5-11. A graph of the data of Table 5-5. The straight line was fitted by the method of averages.

whose cumulative distribution is represented by the graph of Fig. 5-11; the LL may be thought of as P_{25} of that same distribution. Therefore $DL = (UL - LL)/2 = (P_{75} - P_{25})/2 = Q$. In other words, the DL as it has been defined here is simply the semi-interquartile range of the normal distribution whose cumulative distribution is estimated by the transformed data points (Table 5-5, column 3). Recalling that in a normal distribution $Q = 0.6745\sigma$, we may obtain our required DL from $DL = 0.6745\sigma = 0.6745(1/c) = 0.6745(3.51) = 2.37$ mm.

To summarize the procedure followed in determining a DL by the method of constant stimuli, (1) values of S_v are chosen around S_t such that the smallest value is only occasionally judged greater than S_t but the largest value is almost always judged greater. Care must be exercised in choosing the S_v, as it has been shown recently (Levison & Restle, 1968) that the location of the *PSE* is influenced by this decision (cf. Helson, 1964). (2) Each S_v, along with S_t, is presented to **S** a relatively large number of times, the temporal arrangement of S_t and S_v held constant or equalized for each S_v, depending on E's purposes. (3) The PSE is the value of S_v that may be expected to be judged greater than S_t on 50 percent of its presentations, and the DL is one-half the distance between the value of S_v judged to be greater than S_t on 75 percent of its trials and the value of S_v judged greater on 25 percent of its presentations. (4) On the assumption that the normal ogive adequately describes the relation between S's judgments and values of S_v (the phi gamma hypothesis), the obtained percentages are converted to z scores appropriate for a normal distribution, and a straight line, $z = cS_v + k$, is fitted to the transformed data. (5) The PSE is the value of S_v corresponding to a z score of zero, and the DL—which is actually the semi-interquartile range of the normal distribution whose ogive is represented by the preceding linear function—is equal to $0.6745(1/c)$.

As with the method of limits, numerous modifications of the method of constant stimuli exist, some procedural and some calculational. For a discussion of a number of these, the student is referred to Guilford (1954, pp. 142–147).

EXERCISES

5-7. Suppose that the DLs for apparent width ($S_t = 50$ mm) were obtained with both the method of limits and the method of constant stimuli on the same Ss (single-group design). Would you expect the DLs obtained with the former method to be larger, smaller, or about the same size as the DLs obtained with the latter method? Why?

5-8. We saw that in the function which related z to S ($z = cS + k$), $1/c = \sigma$, where σ was the standard deviation of the normal distribution whose cumulative distribution was represented by the preceding linear function. Show that this is a property of *any* distribution; that is, given a distribution of X scores, the linear function relating z to X (i.e., $z = cX + k$) is always such that $c = 1/\sigma$ (or $1/SD$ in the event that we are dealing with sample distributions).

THE METHOD OF AVERAGE ERROR

The third of the classical psychophysical methods to be discussed in this chapter is the *method of average error*, also known as the *method of adjustment*, and the *method of reproduction*. The distinguishing feature of the method of average error is that the terminal judgment obtained from S is always one of equality. The S is presented with a standard stimulus and a variable stimulus, and the latter is adjusted until S judges that S_t and S_v are equal. Most often S does the adjusting of S_v, and though this is the preferable procedure, E may himself provide the adjustments which are called for by S. The method of average error currently finds its widest employment in perceptual experiments; its use in psychophysical determinations, such as obtaining a DL, is relatively infrequent.

Our description of the method of average error may be brief, because both the procedures involved and the treatment of the data are quite simple. To frame the discussion within a specific context, let us apply the method to the problem of quantitatively measuring the vertical-horizontal illusion in a single S.

A curious fact of visual perception is that a vertical line will ordinarily appear longer than a horizontal line of precisely the same length. To study the relevant variables that affect this illusion, it is necessary to devise a method of quantitatively measuring its magnitude in the individual S. This can be accomplished by presenting S with a vertical line of fixed length (S_t) and allowing him to vary an adjustable horizontal line (S_v) until he is satisfied that the two lines appear equal in length. After S has been allowed to make a number of such settings, the mean of the settings is calculated; the difference between this value and S_t reveals both the size and the direction of the illusion. In psychophysical terminology, the mean of the settings is the point of subjective equality; therefore the constant error, $PSE - S_t$, gives both the direction and magnitude of the illusion. Thus, if a 50.0-centimeter (cm) line were used as S_t (the vertical line) and the mean of S's settings were 54.5 cm, the constant error, and therefore the size of the illusion, is obtained from $54.5 - 50.0 = 4.5$ cm. Because the constant error is positive, it indicates that the vertical line appeared longer than the horizontal line. The standard deviation of S's settings provides a measure of the reliability of S's judgments. The basis of the horizontal-vertical illusion, it may be noted, is still under active investigation (Avery & Day, 1969).

Determination of the *DL* by the Method of Average Error

It is always pointed out that the method of average error may be used in the determination of the *DL*, but, in fact, it is rarely used for that purpose. The rationale advanced for this application of the method of average error is that S's settings, because they terminate at points at which S_v appears equal to S_t, may all be considered to lie within the interval of uncertainty, very much like "equal" judgments lie within the *IU* in the method of limits. Accordingly, a reasonable definition of the *DL* is one-half the range of S's settings, which corresponds to the $\overline{IU}/2$ that defined the *DL* in the method of limits.

The more usual suggestion, however, is that the *DL* be defined as the *SD* or *Q* of S's settings. Although this procedure has the merit of basing the *DL* on all S's settings rather than on just two, it does not correspond as closely to the other definitions of the *DL* and is likely to yield values of the *DL* that are considerably smaller than would be obtained by either the method of limits or the method of constant stimuli. However, the definition of the *DL* aside, it would appear that if E is interested in the *DL* itself, the method of limits and the method of constant stimuli are preferable techniques, because both of these measure the threshold process more directly than the method of average error.

In summary, the method of average error is characterized by the requirement that S render a terminal judgment of equality on each trial, based on his (sometimes E's) adjustment of S_v to the point at which it appears equal to S_t. In perceptual experiments the quantity of interest is the constant error, $PSE - S_t$, the PSE being the mean of S's settings. When this method is applied to the determination of DLs, because all S's settings are by definition within the interval of uncertainty, the DL is defined as one-half the range of S's settings; other possible definitions of the DL are the SD and Q of S's settings. Finally, as with the method of limits, series direction and starting point are variables with which E must be concerned when employing the method of average error. It has been shown, for example, that the diminution of the Müller-Lyer illusion which frequently occurs with repeated observations greatly depends on the series direction variable. If a trial always begins with $S_v > S_t$ or $S_v < S_t$ (or even with $S_v = S_t$), reduction of the illusion is much less than if both types of trials are presented to S (Parker & Newbigging, 1965).

CONTEMPORARY RELEVANCE OF THE PSYCHOPHYSICAL METHODS

The psychophysical methods still command study in psychology because, apart from their continuing relevance for the study of sensory processes, the techniques and concepts of which they consist contribute to many areas of psychology (e.g., perception and neuropsychology). Another reason for their continuing prominence is that developments in mathematical psychology (e.g., Luce, 1959; Restle, 1961) have turned up interesting relationships between certain aspects of classical psychophysics and other areas of psychology, such as learning theory, and the psychology of choice and judgment. Although it is perhaps too early to judge the significance of these interrelationships, they provide illuminating bridges across several domains of psychology that have for too long remained isolated from one another.

In recent years various modifications of the classical psychophysical methods have been applied increasingly to the study of sensory and perceptual capacities of animals with remarkable success. Later (Chap. 9) we shall describe in some detail one of these applications which permits continuous monitoring of thresholds (Blough, 1958). For the moment we shall list a few of the recent applications: differential brightness thresholds in rats as a function of the psychophysical method employed (Moskowitz & Kitzes, 1966) and type of reward, food or brain stimulation (Terman & Kling, 1968); comparison of differential thresholds in pigeons as a function of three variants of the method of constant stimuli (Mentzer, 1966); and discrimination of the minimum separable visual acuity in rhesus monkeys (Cowey & Ellis, 1967). The resurgence of interest in threshold phenomena in animals is largely a result of certain conceptual and technical developments which have emerged from operant conditioning (see Chap. 9). By conjoining operant techniques with modifications of classical psychophysical methods, contemporary investigators can obtain far more information than was previously available about the sensory and perceptual capacities of nonverbal organisms (cf. Blough, 1966).

The concept of the just noticeable difference (JND) is closely related to the DL. We saw in the discussion of the method of constant stimuli that the ability of S to discriminate between two stimuli can vary from zero to perfect discrimination. Thus if stimulus S_2 is only slightly greater than stimulus S_1, S will judge the former to be greater than S_1 on somewhat more than 50 percent, but less than 100 percent, of the trials in which they are compared.

This fact has the effect of complicating the relationship between a physical stimulus and the corresponding sensory response which it elicits. In Fig. 5-1 a stimulus, S_1, was represented as always eliciting the same sensory response, R_1. Were this the true state of affairs, however, all stimuli would be perfectly discriminable or perfectly nondiscriminable. For given that S_2 is greater than S_1, the magnitude of the sensory response R_2 is either greater than or equal to the magnitude of R_1. If the latter, by our original representation, R_2 will *always* be equal to R_1, and hence S will be unable to discriminate between S_2 and S_1. If the former, R_2 will *always* be greater in magnitude than R_1 and consequently S_2 may always be expected to be judged greater than S_1.

But, of course, we know that less than perfect discrimination is possible for stimuli that are relatively close to each other. Apparently, then, the same physical stimulus does not always evoke in S a sensation of precisely the same magnitude; rather the sensory response varies in magnitude somewhat from presentation to presentation.

This more realistic formulation is depicted in Fig. 5-12. Stimulus S_1 in repeated presentations elicits a range of sensory responses, with R_1 the average or "modal" sensory response. Similarly, in repeated trials stimulus S_2 evokes in S a range of sensations which, though it overlaps the range elicited by S_1, has a modal sensory response, R_2, that is of greater magnitude than R_1. If, therefore, S_1 and S_2 are presented to S repeatedly, S_1 will on occasion be judged to be greater than S_2, by assumption, on those presentations when the sensation evoked by S_1 happens to be of greater magnitude than the sensory response

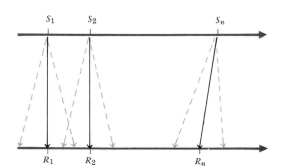

Continuum of the
physical stimulus

Continuum of the
corresponding sensory response

Fig. 5-12. A more realistic representation of the relationship between a physical stimulus and the sensory responses it evokes in repeated presentations (see text).

elicited by S_2. On the other hand, a stimulus, S_n, that elicits a range of sensations that does not overlap the range elicited by S_2 will, as suggested by Fig. 5-12, always be judged to be greater than S_2 (or S_1).

Hence we may say that any stimulus, say S_x, that lies on a reasonably defined physical continuum elicits in S on repeated presentations a *distribution of sensory responses* on the corresponding psychological continuum, with the representative or modal sensory response, R_x, simply being the mean of the distribution. It is but a short leap, as the student may surmise, to the assumption that the distribution of sensory responses elicited by S_x may be described by the normal distribution.

It was Thurstone (1927b) who first developed in detail the notion that repeated presentations of a stimulus, whether from a well-defined physical continuum or not, produces in S a distribution of sensory responses or, as he called them, "discriminal processes." Coupling this assumption with the hypothesis that the distribution of discriminal processes was normal, Thurstone (1927a) devised a scaling model—from which he derived his "law of comparative judgment"—that had a lasting impact on psychometrics.

It is not our intention to pursue further the preceding theoretical development at this point. The important facts are: (1) a stimulus is considered in successive presentations to evoke in S a distribution of sensations rather than a sensory response of constant magnitude; the mean of this distribution is taken to be the modal or representative sensory response. (2) If the distributions of sensory responses to two stimuli overlap, discrimination between the stimuli will not be perfect; further, the more alike the stimuli, the more the associated distributions of sensory responses will overlap and, hence, the more imperfect the discrimination between them.

Let us now return to the concept of the just noticeable difference. Suppose that, using S_1 as a standard stimulus, we obtain by the method of limits the difference limen (DL_1) for a given subject. Let S_2 be the stimulus that is one difference limen above S_1, i.e., $S_2 = S_1 + DL_1$. In Fig. 5-13 these quantities are represented along the continuum of the physical stimulus.

Now let R_1 and R_2, respectively, be the modal sensory responses evoked by S_1 and S_2; for the sake of simplicity we have not indicated in Fig. 5-13 the range of sensations elicited by these stimuli. Modal sensory response R_2 is of somewhat greater magnitude than R_1, but the difference between them is slight because the initiating stimuli, S_2 and S_1, are separated by only 1 DL.

Because it is relatively small, this difference in sensation between R_1 and R_2 is called a "just noticeable difference" (JND). Thus, $JND_1 = R_2 - R_1$ and $R_2 = R_1 + JND_1$.

It should be pointed out that in conformity with the formulation of Fig. 5-12, the magnitude of the sensory response to S_2 could on occasion be less than the magnitude of the sensation elicited by S_1. More generally, the difference in the magnitudes of the sensations elicited by stimuli S_1 and S_2 will vary from presentation to presentation. The JND, as we have defined it, refers not to the difference between sensations that exists on a single trial but rather to the mean

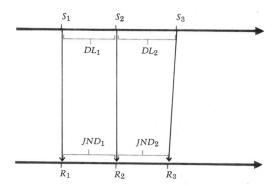

Continuum of the
physical stimulus

Continuum of the
corresponding sensory response

Fig. 5-13. A representation of the relationship between DLs and the corresponding JNDs (see text).

of such differences taken over a large number of presentations of S_1 and S_2. Thus the JND is an *average difference*, or a *difference in averages*, as is evident from the definition of JND_1 (i.e., $JND_1 = R_2 - R_1$), in which R_1 and R_2 are average sensory responses.

Developing things one step further, suppose we now use stimulus S_2 as a standard stimulus and find DL_2, again by the method of limits. Let S_3 be the stimulus that is 1 DL above S_2, i.e., $S_3 = S_2 + DL_2$, or referred to stimulus S_1, $S_3 = S_1 + DL_1 + DL_2$. As shown in Fig. 5-13, S_3 elicits a modal sensory response, R_3, which is 1 JND above R_2, namely, $R_3 = R_2 + JND_2$; JND_2 is the average sensation difference evoked by stimuli S_2 and S_3: $JND_2 = R_3 - R_2$. Finally, R_3 may be said to be 2 JNDs above R_1 because $R_3 = R_1 + JND_1 + JND_2$.

It is clear from Fig. 5-13 that the JND does not refer to a difference between physical stimuli or, indeed, to any aspect of the physical stimulus continuum. Rather, the JND pertains to a difference between *sensations* and belongs entirely to the domain of the psychological continuum. One nevertheless often hears such statements as, "Stimuli S_1 and S_2 are 1 JND apart." Statements of this sort are inaccurate; they are contractions of the more complete statement, "Stimuli S_1 and S_2 *elicit sensations* that (on the average) are 1 JND apart." Should one wish to restrict himself entirely to the stimulus dimension, the correct statement is, "Stimuli S_1 and S_2 are 1 DL apart." Similarly, stimuli S_1 and S_3 of Fig. 5-13 are not 2 JNDs apart; they give rise to *sensations* that are 2 JNDs apart, or, remaining entirely on the stimulus continuum, they are 2 DLs apart ($DL_1 + DL_2$). Because of certain conveniences of expression, however, the less accurate phrases are often encountered.

THE JND AND THE DL.   Although the method of limits was perhaps the favorite way of obtaining two stimuli separated by 1 JND (i.e., DL), the JND, like the DL, is not unique. Hence if S_1 and S_2 are separated by 1 DL as determined by the method of constant stimuli, the difference $R_2 - R_1$ is also designated as a *JND*. In a word, the *JND* is *the (average) difference in sensation elicited by two stimuli that are separated by 1 DL*, the method of determining the *DL* notwithstanding. If under a fixed set of conditions, the *DL*s obtained under one method tend to be smaller than the *DL*s obtained under a second method, there will of course exist a similar disparity between the corresponding *JND*s. But there is little consequence to the mere fact that the size of the *DL*, and therefore the size of the *JND*, may vary from one method of determination to another. The important consideration is that if lawful relationships should be discovered between any of the quantities concerned, e.g., between the size of the *DL* and the magnitude of the standard stimulus, such relationships ought to hold for all accepted methods of determining the *DL*. We turn now to one of the most renown of these relationships.

Weber's Law

That the size of the *DL*, other things constant, depends on the magnitude of the standard stimulus employed is not surprising. As already pointed out in Exercise 5-3, it is reasonable to suppose that the size of the *DL* increases as the magnitude of S_t increases. Is there, however, a simple and general law that describes the relationship between the magnitude of S_t and the size of the *DL*? This problem was of keen interest to the early psychophysicists.

On the basis of his experimental results, E. H. Weber, a psychophysicist of Fechner's time, became convinced that the size of the *DL* was indeed simply related to the magnitude of S_t. He proposed that *the DL is a constant fraction of the standard stimulus*. Stated in mathematical terms, this assertion becomes $DL = cS_t$, or, equivalently, $DL/S_t = c$, where c is a constant. The relation $DL = cS_t$ is, of course, a linear function in which the additive constant k is zero. To provide a numerical illustration, if $c = \frac{1}{10}$ and $S_t = 120$ units, the *DL* will be 12 units, but if S_t is increased to 150 units, the *DL*, still $\frac{1}{10}$ of S_t, is increased to 15 units.

Granting the truth of "Weber's law," as this generalization came to be known, it follows from the relation $DL = cS_t$ that a plot of *DL*s against corresponding values of S_t ought to produce a straight line with slope equal to c and Y intercept equal to zero. A plot of DL/S_t (called the "Weber fraction") against values of S_t should, on the other hand, produce a straight horizontal line (zero slope) that intersects the ordinate at the value c, since according to Weber's law, $DL/S_t = c$.

WEBER'S LAW AND THE JND. Weber's law is most commonly written as $\Delta S/S = c$ (or $\Delta I/I = c$). The quantity ΔS is identified with the increment in S (the standard stimulus) necessary to obtain a stimulus that is 1 *JND* away from S as ordinarily determined by procedures related to the method of limits. Because, however, there is no unique *JND* and because if Weber's law holds for *DL*s obtained by the method of limits, it ought also to hold for *DL*s determined by other means, the formulation of Weber's law as $DL/S_t = c$ seems a legitimate generalization. In addition, the latter formulation specifies more exactly the quantities that the law relates.

THE VALIDITY OF WEBER'S LAW. Because Weber's law states that $DL/S_t = c$, if the DL is obtained at a number of different values of S_t, the graph relating DL/S_t to S_t should, as we have already stated, produce a straight line with zero slope and Y intercept equal to c. Actually, however, with conventional psychophysical techniques, a constant Weber fraction has never been observed throughout any stimulus dimension. Invariably DL/S_t is relatively large for small values of S_t, decreasing rapidly as the magnitude of S_t increases. For some stimulus dimensions, after a rapid decrease in size, the Weber fraction remains fairly constant throughout the stimulus range examined (e.g., intensity of visual and auditory stimuli—Steinhardt, 1936, and Riesz, 1928, respectively). For others, after a shorter or longer period of relative constancy, the Weber fraction increases at the higher stimulus values (e.g., frequency of auditory stimuli, Harris, 1952; and salinity of a tasted solution, Holway & Hurvich, 1937); however, DL/S_t does not normally again reach the values observed at very low magnitudes of S_t.

In Figs. 5-14 and 5-15 both of these patterns are illustrated. In Fig. 5-14 a graph of the Weber function is shown for intensity discrimination of an auditory stimulus. It is plain that DL/S_t is fairly constant for the higher stimulus intensities. A similar pattern is seen in Fig. 5-15, which is a graph of the Weber function for discrimination of the frequency of an auditory stimulus. It may be seen, however, that in the latter figure there is a tendency for DL/S_t to increase at the higher values of S_t. Moreover, in other stimulus dimensions the increasing Weber fraction at the terminal portions of the curve is much more marked.

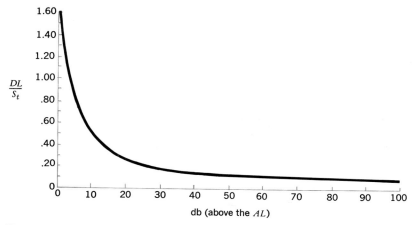

Fig. 5-14. A graph of the Weber ratio for intensity discrimination of a 4,000-Hz tone based on 12 Ss. (SOURCE: R. R. Riesz. Differential intensity sensitivity of the ear for pure tones. *Physical Review*, 1928, **31**, 867–875. Used by permission.)

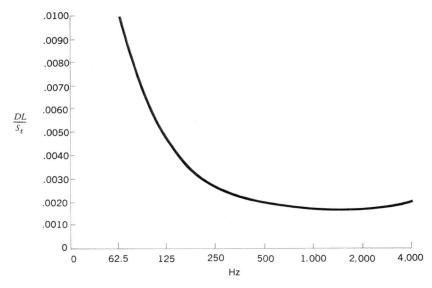

Fig. 5-15. A graph of the Weber ratio for discrimination of the frequency of a tone based on 3 Ss. (SOURCE: J. D. Harris. Pitch discrimination. *Journal of the Acoustical Society of America*, 1952, **24**, 750–755. Used by permission.)

Thus, Weber's "law" fares badly for low values of S_t and sometimes for high values as well. Nevertheless, for large segments of a number of stimulus dimensions, it is a reasonable statement of how the magnitude of the DL is related to the magnitude of S_t. It is, in sum, a generalization of some usefulness, but perhaps not broad enough to be called a law. Various generalized forms of Weber's law exist which often apply better to the relation between S_t and the size of the difference limen. The "linear" generalization is the subject of Exercise 5-9, and a broader version, which includes the linear generalization as a special case, takes the form $DL = c(S_t + k)^r$.

One last point. Presenting brief flashes of light (less than 5 msec) to a dark retina, Cornsweet and Pinsker (1965) obtained a perfectly constant Weber fraction for values of S_t ranging from S's AL to some 5 logarithmic units beyond. Their unorthodox technique also allowed S feedback concerning the correctness of his responses. It is too early to tell what the impact of their finding will be on presently accepted notions concerning Weber's law and its implications (cf. also McGill & Goldberg, 1968).

EXERCISES

5-9. If Weber's law were $DL = cS_t + k$, would it apply better to the data in Figs. 5-14 and 5-15 than Weber's law itself?

FECHNER'S LAW. It was actually Fechner who advertised and promoted Weber's law, seeing in it a means of quantitatively measuring sensation. Starting with Weber's law, Fechner derived a mathematical equation which presumably described the relationship between the intensity of a physical stimulus and the magnitude of the corresponding sensory response (R_s). The equation, known as Fechner's law, stated that *the magnitude of a sensation grows with the logarithm of the initiating stimulus*, i.e., $R_s = c(\log S)$.

We shall return to Fechner's law in the next chapter, after the necessary mathematical groundwork has been established. For now it is sufficient to be aware of what Fechner was attempting. His claim was that it was possible to measure *sensations* quantitatively, even though an individual's sensation, a private affair, would have to be measured indirectly. He maintained, furthermore, that the magnitude of a sensation elicited by a stimulus could be calculated from his law, which he claimed applicable to a large number of stimulus dimensions. No wonder that his law raised so much controversy for so long. Even now there is by no means universal agreement that sensations are measurable on any scale "stronger" than an ordinal scale (e.g., Warren & Warren, 1963).

SIGNAL DETECTION THEORY

In the few years since its first application (Tanner & Swets, 1954), signal detection theory or, as it is often called, the "theory of signal detectability" (*TSD*), has developed into one of the most dominant influences in psychophysics. Moreover, because of the generality of its basic assumptions, certain aspects of *TSD* are increasingly applied to diverse problems in perception, learning, and other areas. Radical theoretical innovation does not lie behind this wide acceptance, however, the accomplishment of *TSD* being more a matter of bringing together already available ingredients in new ways.

Perhaps the single most important feature of signal detection theory is that it provides a means of evaluating the separate contributions to discriminative behavior of an individual's *sensitivity* and his *response criterion*. Virtually every discriminative performance may be considered to be the outcome of two classes of information. First there is the information about the to-be-discriminated stimuli themselves, which is mainly a function of the stimulus parameters in the situation and the individual's sensory apparatus; sensitivity is a measure of this contribution. Then there are numerous variables—such as S's motivation, his knowledge about the likelihood that certain stimuli will appear, the gains and penalties associated with certain responses—which, though independent of sensitivity, nevertheless influence discriminative behavior; collectively they are thought to affect S's response criterion.

Recall that in our discussion of the psychophysical methods, we pointed out that they did not yield "pure" measures of sensitivity, because S's discriminative response was determined not only by his sensory response (R_s) but by other variables as well. The errors of habituation and anticipation, which we discussed in connection with the method of limits, are two such factors; they affect S's discriminative behavior by altering his response criterion. Of course psychophysicists were always aware that factors other than S's sensory response were likely to be involved in discriminative judgments. But without the conceptual means with which to measure independently these "nonsensory" influences, their only recourse was to hold the latter as constant as possible. In some cases "check" trials were administered as a means of adjusting S's threshold for his tendency to "guess." All these efforts, however, fell far short of the goal of obtaining a measure of sensitivity which is largely uncontaminated by other factors.

Sensitivity versus Response Criterion

Signal detection theory distinguishes between sensitivity and response criterion in the following way. The problem is to detect a signal, say a sine wave embedded in a white-noise background. This is the type of problem from which, as its name suggests, signal detection theory originated. Consider, then, a subject whose task is to respond "signal" or "no signal" to indicate whether, during a well-defined interval, a signal was present in addition to the noise background. The first major assumption is that, although the physical stimuli in the situation, the noise (N) and the signal plus noise (SN) are nominally constant, their sensory effects vary from presentation to presentation in a way that is adequately represented by the normal (Gaussian) distribution. This assumption is not new to us, and as was pointed out earlier, Thurstone (1927a, b) was one of the first to pursue such a hypothesis and work out its implications for psychometric measurement. It is also assumed by TSD that the distribution of the noise stimulus (E_N) can be represented on the same continuum as that occupied by the distribution of signal plus noise (E_{SN}), as shown in Fig. 5-16. Granted that N and SN are fundamentally multidimensional in character, the suggestion that both generate distributions on the same unidimensional continuum does not appear to be a fatal simplification. It is not difficult to imagine that the sensory effects of the two stimuli converge somewhere in the central nervous system, where for purposes of decision-making, their various properties are summarized by a single quantity. If, however, one chooses to maintain the multidimensional nature of the stimuli, it is still possible, by employing a measure known as "likelihood ratio," to represent the detection problem in terms of a unidimensional variable (see Green & Swets, 1966). For our own part let us assume that N and SN generate central neural effects which take the form of normal distributions, E_N and E_{SN}, on the same dimension, which we refer to as the "decision axis" (cf. Treisman & Watts, 1966). We will also assume that the two distributions have equal variances. It should be stressed, however, that TSD is much more general than this. Although certain complications arise, the theory is applicable to the case where the normal distributions have different variances and where the distributions are nonnormal, for example, exponential (Green & Swets, Chap. 3). Still, very many applications rely on the hypothesis of normality

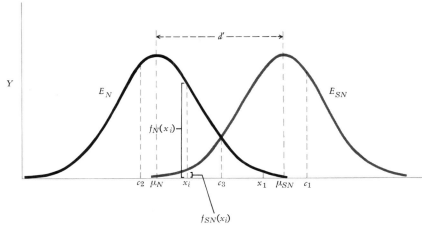

Central neural effect (decision axis)

Fig. 5-16. Representation of a model of signal detection theory. It is assumed that the noise and signal-plus-noise stimuli generate distributions of central neural effects (E_N and E_{SN}) that may be represented on the same continuum (the decision axis); the form of the distributions are normal with equal variance (see text).

and, very frequently, on the equal variance assumption as well. Both of these assumptions are subject to some degree of verification.

Given the model of signal detection represented in Fig. 5-16, it is quite natural to employ as a measure of the discriminability, or detectability, of a signal the difference between the means of the two distributions, d' as shown in the figure. With increasing signal strength, the E_{SN} distribution should be displaced further from the E_N distribution, producing a larger value of d'. Similarly, for a fixed signal intensity, the value of d' ought to vary with the keenness of one's sensory apparatus. In short we take d' to be a measure of **S**'s sensitivity dependent only on the signal and **S**'s sensory acuity.

RESPONSE CRITERION. Let us turn now to the question of evaluating **S**'s response criterion. Given the previous assumptions of *TSD*, the detection task may be stated as follows. The outcome of a trial produces a central neural effect of some magnitude, say x_1 as shown in Fig. 5-16. On the basis of this information as well as other information which we shall discuss later, **S** is to decide whether it was N or SN that generated the central neural effect. *TSD* approaches this problem as a decision-making task, using the concepts of contemporary statistical decision theory (e.g., Wald, 1950). In particular it is assumed that a criterion—a particular magnitude of central neural effect—is selected by **S**, who then responds "signal" whenever the central neural effect equals or exceeds the criterion and "no signal" whenever it is less. Referring to Fig. 5-16, suppose that S set his criterion at c_1. Whenever a central neural effect of magnitude x_1 is experienced, S would respond "no signal," even though this large a value is much more likely to have come from the E_{SN} than from the E_N distribution. Clearly c_1 is a strict criterion, and though S will rarely commit the error of falsely reporting a signal ("false alarms" in the terminology of TSD), he nevertheless will detect only a small proportion of the signals ("hits"). It should be clear from Chap. 4 that given the present criterion, the probability of a false alarm is equal to the area of the E_N distribution lying to the right of c_1, which is negligible, and the probability of a hit is simply the area of the E_{SN} distribution which falls to the right of this same value.

Because for a fixed value of d' the criterion can take on any value whatever, the question naturally arises as to whether there is a "best" criterion. It turns out that for a rather large range of decision-making goals, an optimal criterion does exist and is expressed in terms of a quantity known as "likelihood ratio."

Optimal Criteria

CONDITIONAL AND A PRIORI PROBABILITIES. Before we pursue this question, however, a few definitions must be given. Table 5-6 lists the two possible stimuli, signal plus noise or noise alone; the two possible responses or decisions, "signal" (s) or "no signal" (n); and the four possible outcomes of a trial of the detection experiment. In addition the conditional probabilities associated with the four possible outcomes are shown along with their definitions. We first take note that, considering only trials where the signal is presented, if S scored 0.85 hits, he must have been guilty of 0.15 false rejections, because $P(s|SN) + P(n|SN) = 1$. Similarly the proportion of false alarms and the proportion of correct rejections must sum to 1. Thus if we know the proportion of hits and the proportion of false alarms, we can complete a table such as Table 5-6. In terms of Fig. 5-16, $P(s|SN)$

Table 5-6 The Four Possible Outcomes of the Detection Experiment

		RESPONSE	
		s	n
STIMULUS	SN	"hit" $$P(s|SN) = \frac{\text{no. hits}}{\text{no. } SN \text{ trials}}$$	"false rejection" $$P(n|SN) = \frac{\text{no. false rejections}}{\text{no. } SN \text{ trials}}$$
	N	"false alarm" $$P(s|N) = \frac{\text{no. false alarms}}{\text{no. } N \text{ trials}}$$	"correct rejection" $$P(n|N) = \frac{\text{no. correct rejections}}{\text{no. } N \text{ trials}}$$

is the area of the E_{SN} distribution that lies to the right of S's criterion, while $P(s|N)$ is the area of the E_N distribution lying to the right of this same point.

Another important quantity is the proportion of trials on which the signal is presented, referred to as the "a priori" probability of SN and symbolized as $P(SN)$. Obviously $P(SN) + P(N) = 1$. The proportion of hits achieved over *all* trials is given by $P(s|SN)P(SN)$, as simple numerical illustration will show. The overall proportion of the other outcomes is obtained by multiplying together the appropriate conditional and a priori probabilities. It follows that the proportion of *correct* responses (hits plus correct rejections) is given by $P(s|SN)P(SN) + P(n|N)P(N)$.

LIKELIHOOD RATIO AND OPTIMAL CRITERIA. The statistical concept of likelihood ratio plays a central role in signal detection theory. As an illustration of this concept, suppose a person has a fair coin and one that is so biased that the probability of a head is 0.8. Let $P(H|F)$ and $P(H|B)$ stand for the probability of a head for the fair and biased coins, respectively. Suppose that one of the coins is chosen at random and is tossed, and a head turns up. Clearly the chances are greater that it was the biased coin that had been tossed; likelihood ratio, which is *the ratio of the probabilities of an event under two hypotheses*, provides us with a precise measure. Symbolically, $l(H) = P(H|B)/P(H|F) = 0.8/0.5 = 1.6$, which in words means the likelihood ratio of observing a head from the biased compared to the fair coin is 1.6. With continuous distributions, likelihood ratios are formed by ratios of densities rather than of probabilities. Thus in Fig. 5-16 the likelihood of observing a magnitude of central neural effect equal to x_i from the E_{SN} compared to the E_N distribution is given by the ratio of densities at that point, i.e., $l(x_i) = f_{SN}(x_i)/f_N(x_i)$. In brief, likelihood ratio provides us with information concerning the chances that an observed central neural effect came from the E_{SN} rather than the E_N distribution.

One reason behind the importance of likelihood ratio for TSD is that for a variety of decision aims, the optimal criterion can be stated in terms of this ratio. Referring to Fig. 5-16 once again, suppose that the E_{SN} and E_N distributions are as given, that an equal number of SN and N trials are administered, and, finally, that correct decisions (hits and correct rejections) are of equal value to S, whereas both types of errors are equally unattractive. Whether S's goal is to maximize the number of correct responses or to maximize his overall gain, he can do no better than use as his criterion the magnitude of central neural effect corresponding to a likelihood ratio of 1.0. In other words S should establish his criterion at c_3, the point at which the two distributions intersect, adopting the "decision rule" of responding s for values of central neural effect that equal or exceed c_3 and n for lesser magnitudes. Clearly, magnitudes of central neural effect that are greater than c_3 yield likelihood ratios greater than 1, whereas magnitudes less than c_3 are associated with likelihood ratios less than unity.

It is customary to refer to the criterion, expressed as a likelihood ratio, by the Greek letter β. Let us therefore use β to indicate S's actual (likelihood ratio) criterion and β_0 as the optimal criterion. With the distributions portrayed in Fig. 5-16, it matters little whether the criterion is stated in terms of likelihood ratio or central neural effect inasmuch as these two variables are monotonically related. With other distributions, however, this correspondence may be lost, and the optimal criterion usually must be stated in terms of likelihood ratio. Such would be the case, for example, if the variances of the distributions of Fig. 5-16 were unequal.

EXERCISES

5-10. Granted that the E_N and E_{SN} distributions are normal with equal variance and that S adopts a decision rule of the form previously described, one can estimate S's sensitivity (d') and his criterion from the obtained proportion of hits and false alarms. The problem is only slightly more involved than those encountered in Chap. 4. Assume, then, that over a large number of trials, S's proportion of hits over SN trials is 0.841 [i.e., $P(s|SN) = 0.841$], and his false alarm rate is 0.023 [i.e., $P(s|N) = 0.023$].

(a) What is the value of d' expressed in terms of standard deviation (σ) units?

(b) What is the value of S's criterion expressed as likelihood ratio, i.e., β?

(c) If you assume that $P(SN) = 0.5$ and S's objective is to maximize the proportion of correct responses, is his criterion optimal? If not, how much could S improve his performance by employing an optimal criterion?

OPTIMAL CRITERIA WHEN A PRIORI PROBABILITIES OF N AND SN ARE UNEQUAL. If the a priori probability of SN is a value other than 0.5, the optimal criterion for maximizing the proportion of correct responses is no longer unity, even though both correct responses are equally valued by S and both types of errors are equally disliked. To take a simple illustration, assume that the E_N and E_{SN} distributions are such that 10 percent of the E_N distribution lies above the point on the decision axis where the two distributions intersect, i.e., above the value of central neural effect for which the likelihood ratio is 1. If S employs this value of likelihood ratio as his criterion and $P(SN) = 0.01$, it is apparent from Exercise 5-10 that the proportion of correct responses achieved by him will be $(0.9)(0.01) + (0.9)(0.99) = 0.90$. However, his performance would be far better if he ignored altogether the stimulus information and responded n on every trial, in which case he would be correct on 99 percent of the trials. A priori probabilities must, therefore, enter into the determination of the optimal criterion, and they do so in the following way: $\beta_0 = P(N)/P(SN)$. Applied to the present, rather unrealistic illustration, the proportion of correct responses is maximized for a criterion set at likelihood ratio equal to 99. With equal a priori probabilities, of course, $\beta_0 = 1$, as previously stated.

OPTIMAL CRITERIA FOR MAXIMIZING EXPECTED GAIN. It is not difficult to think of situations in which maximizing the proportion of correct responses might not be the most sensible strategy. Consider, for example, a situation in which S receives 10 cents for every hit and correct rejection, loses nothing if he fails to detect a signal, but is penalized 1 dollar for each false alarm. Because of the asymmetry in the "payoff" structure, maximizing the proportion of correct responses no longer means that S's "gain" will also be maximized. With the latter objective as S's goal, the optimal criterion is

$$\beta_0 = \frac{(G_{CR} + L_{FA})P(N)}{(G_H + L_{FR})P(SN)}$$

where G_{CR} and G_H are the gains associated with correct rejections and hits, respectively, and L_{FA} and L_{FR} are the losses associated with false alarms and false rejections.

The β_0 calculated by the previous equation is said to maximize the "expected value," or the expected gain, which, if the sum of gain and loss in the numerator equals the same sum in the denominator, is equivalent to maximizing the proportion of correct responses. A special case of this equality, which we made use of earlier, occurs when $G_{CR} = G_H$ and $L_{FA} = L_{FR}$.

The expected gain obtainable from a particular decision rule is obtained by multiplying the proportion of each of the four possible outcomes by their associated gain or loss and summing the result. Letting EG stand for expected gain:

$$EG = G_{CR}P(n|N)P(N) + G_H P(s|SN)P(SN) - L_{FA}P(s|N)P(N) \\ - L_{FR}P(n|SN)P(SN)$$

It should be pointed out that even in tasks where explicit gains and losses are not assigned to the four different outcomes, implicit values are usually to be found, such as S's feeling that false alarms are inherently more culpable than false rejections and are to be maintained at as low a level as possible. The effect of such self-instructions is to increase the numerator of the equation defining β_0, raising what S considers to be his optimal criterion.

EXERCISES

5-11. (a) Assuming the gains and losses given in the previous illustration and assuming that the SN and N frequencies are equal, what is the value of likelihood ratio that maximizes expected gain?

(b) Assume further, as we did in an earlier illustration, that the E_N and E_{SN} distributions are normal with equal variance and intersect at a point on the decision axis above which lies 10 percent of the E_N distribution. If S employs as his criterion $\beta = 1$, what is his expected gain?

NEYMAN-PEARSON OBJECTIVE. There is another aim which is a reasonable objective in a signal detection experiment. The subject could decide to maximize the proportion of hits while holding the proportion of false alarms fixed at some small value. For example, S might require that $P(s|N) = 0.05$, working within this limitation to maximize $P(s|SN)$. This goal is called the "Neyman-Pearson objective," and as some will recognize, it is the rationale that underlies many familiar statistical tests.

Perhaps it is fairly obvious how one would go about choosing a criterion to satisfy the Neyman-Pearson objective. With reference to Fig. 5-16, if S had decided that $P(s|N) = 0.05$, his criterion would be set at a value of central neural effect which cuts off 5 percent of the right side of the E_N distribution, with S responding n for values of central neural effect less than this criterion and s for magnitudes which are equal or greater. With the distributions shown in the figure, this criterion maximizes $P(s|SN)$ while holding $P(s|N)$ at 0.05. The criterion satisfying the Neyman-Pearson objective may also be stated in terms of likelihood ratio, which is more general in that it applies to all distributions (cf. Green & Swets, 1966, Chap. 1). In the present illustration, β corresponds to the likelihood ratio calculated at the central neural effect which cuts off 0.05 of the right side of the E_N distribution.

THE CONCEPT OF THE "IDEAL OBSERVER." In order for a subject to perform in accordance with the assumptions of signal detection theory, he must have full knowledge of the E_N and E_{SN} distributions, the a priori probability of SN, and the payoff structure. Information concerning the two distributions is necessary for accurate computation of likelihood ratios, and determination of β_0 requires in addition that $P(SN)$ and the payoff structure be known. To some investigators these requirements appear to be unrealistic in a number of situations in which signal detection theory might be applicable. Treisman and Watts (1966), for example, have proposed that the Neyman-Pearson objective be considered S's proper goal rather than the maximum-expected-gain objective. They prefer the Neyman-Pearson objective because in certain cases it requires only that the subject keep track of his false-alarm rate, setting his criterion at the highest value (on the decision axis) which holds the false-alarm rate at its predetermined value. Precise knowledge concerning the E_N and E_{SN} distributions is not required. In applying decision theory to discrimination performance in the pigeon, Boneau and Cole (1967) developed a theoretical approach which allows S to extract sufficient information from a discrimination situation to establish a criterion that maximizes expected gain, without, however, assuming knowledge of $P(SN)$ or the separate E_N and E_{SN} distributions. They assume instead that the subject learns the form of the *combined* distribution arising from signal and signal plus noise, which requires only that S keep track of the frequency with which each magnitude of central neural effect occurs. It is also assumed that S learns for each specific value of central neural effect the probability of either a gain or a loss being incurred. It would appear that relaxing the assumption that the subject knows the E_N and E_{SN} distributions should serve to enlarge the range of situations to which signal detection theory can be comfortably applied.

The previous discussion relates directly to a central concept of *TSD*, namely the concept of the ideal observer. The general idea is that given exact specification of what is known about N and SN, *TSD* can specify the detectability of the signal on the assumption that the "detector" operates in an optimal manner. As an illustration, suppose the task is one of detecting in a noise background a signal that is "specified exactly," which means essentially that the form of the signal as it occurs during the observation interval is known completely. It turns out that under the assumptions of *TSD*, this problem resolves itself into deciding whether an "observed" quantity derives from one of two normal distributions having equal variance (i.e., the model shown in Fig. 5-16). However, because the distributions are derived from physical properties of the N and SN stimuli, the two can be related. In particular it is possible to specify the separation of the E_N and E_{SN} distributions as follows, $d' = \sqrt{2E_S/N_0}$, where E_S is the signal energy and N_0 is the noise power density. Given the latter two values, then, *TSD* states what the inherent detectability of the signal is, setting a performance standard against which an actual observer's behavior can be compared.

The concept of the ideal observer, discussed in detail by Green and Swets (1966), is particularly useful in psychophysics, where the physical properties of N and SN are often specified precisely. There are, however, a host of situations in which the general approach of signal detection theory is of value, but where it is not currently possible to describe N and SN in the physical detail that would allow derivation of the inherent detectability of the signal, i.e., derivation of the performance of an ideal observer. The appeal of signal detection theory in these cases is that it clearly separates sensitivity from S's response criterion. To take advantage of this feature of *TSD*, one merely assumes that N and SN generate distributions of events on a decision axis, which may be thought of in terms of central neural effects, as we have done earlier, or in related quantities. The analysis proceeds from there, and although obtained measures of sensitivity may not be compared to the performance of an ideal observer, there is a great deal of use to which they can be put.

The difference in emphasis just described is expressed by a distinction that is sometimes made between the theory of signal detectability and signal detection. As Egan and Clarke (1966) recently put it, "The theory of signal detectability is so called because the emphasis is upon the inherent *detectability* of a signal and noise. When the concepts are applied to the study of a real observer, rather than an ideal observer, we speak of *signal detection* [p. 220]." Framed in these terms, what we have been discussing in this chapter is a theory of signal detection rather than of signal detectability, and it seems doubtful that many applications of *TSD* outside of psychophysics proper are likely to make contact with the concepts of signal detectability.

Receiver-operating-characteristic Curves

If a subject is run in a signal detection task of the sort we have been discussing with all parameters held constant, the outcome of the experiment may be de-

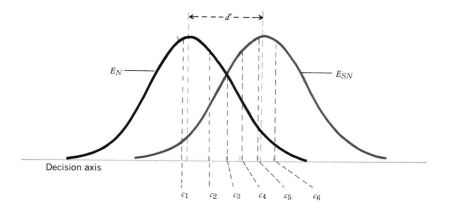

$P(s\|SN)$	0.98	0.90	0.80	0.70	0.52	0.35

$P(s\|N)$	0.65	0.35	0.20	0.13	0.05	0.02

Fig. 5-17. The assumed E_N and E_{SN} distributions for a subject in a signal detection task. It is assumed that either by the manipulation of the a priori probability of *SN* or by other methods the subject is induced to alter his criterion from one block of trials to another as shown by the vertical lines in the figure. The proportion of hits and false alarms associated with each criterion is also shown.

scribed by a pair of numbers, one giving the proportion of hits and the other the proportion of false alarms. Taken in conjunction with the assumptions that the E_N and E_{SN} distributions are normal and of equal variance, these proportions are sufficient, as we have already seen, to allow us to infer both S's sensitivity, d', and his criterion, β. We would like, however, to obtain independent evidence bearing on the distribution assumptions, and this can be done in the following way.

Suppose for fixed stimulus parameters, the E_N and E_{SN} distributions are as shown in Fig. 5-17. Assume also that by varying either the a priori probability of *SN* or by altering the gains and losses associated with the four outcomes of the detection experiment, we induce S to alter his criterion from one block of (say 500) trials to another. Let us imagine that the various criteria employed by S are as shown in Fig. 5-17 (c_1-c_6). Also shown in the figure is the proportion of hits and false alarms that would be obtained (assuming no experimental error) with each criterion. These latter values are plotted in Fig. 5-18 in what is known as a "receiver-operating-characteristic" curve (*ROC*). Note that the curve is symmetrical about the negative diagonal (the line running from the upper left to the lower right corner). Figure 5-19 shows *ROC* curves for varying values of d', again under the assumption that the E_N and E_{SN} distributions are normal with equal variance, which is arbitrarily set at unity. *ROC* functions are also

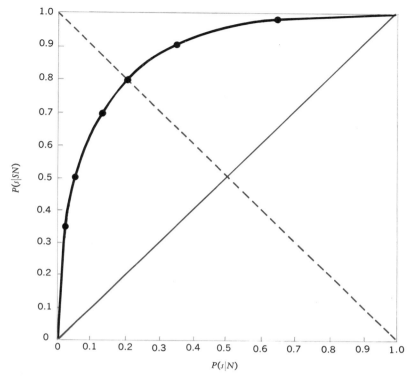

Fig. 5-18. The proportion of hits and false alarms of Fig. 5-17 plotted on linear coordinates to form an *ROC* curve.

referred to as "isosensitivity" curves because every point on a given *ROC* curve arises from precisely the same value of d' as every other point.

The same curves of Fig. 5-19 are plotted in Fig. 5-20 on double-probability (or "normal-normal") graph paper. We have had ample experience with single-probability graph paper, which converts the sigmoid curve of a cumulative normal distribution into a straight line. Double-probability paper performs the same service when both variables, X and Y, arise from cumulative normal distributions. Note that as **S**'s criterion in Fig. 5-17 moves from the extreme right to the extreme left of the decision axis, the proportion of hits and false alarms varies from 0 to 1 in accordance with the cumulative normal distribution. Thus, a sequence of such values will describe a straight line on double-probability paper. Moreover, the slope of the straight line will be equal to 1 only if the two normal distributions have equal variance.

Another virtue of plotting the *ROC* curve on double-probability paper is that d' is easily obtained. Each *ROC* curve may be considered to be displaced vertically a distance in z units equal to the difference between the means of the E_N and E_{SN} distributions. Thus in Fig. 5-20, for example, the lowest of the

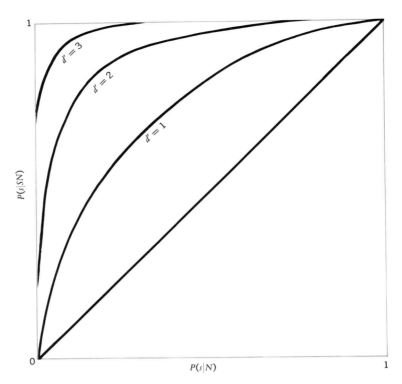

Fig. 5-19. Three *ROC* curves generated from the assumption that the underlying distributions are normal with equal variance. As the separation between the E_N and E_{SN} distributions (d') increases, the *ROC* curve moves toward the upper left-hand corner of the graph. (SOURCE: D. M. Green and J. A. Swets. *Signal detection theory and psychophysics.* New York: Wiley, 1966. Copyright 1966 by Wiley and used by permission.)

ROC curves is displaced upward on the $z = 0$ vertical axis by 1 z unit. The value of d' for a curve such as the uppermost *ROC* curve is obtained by subtracting its lateral displacement (-1) from its vertical displacement $(+2)$, as shown in the graph.

Returning now to the illustration of Fig. 5-17, it should be stressed that whether or not **S** employs optimal criteria, *ROC* curves plotted on double-probability paper will describe straight lines with a slope of unity if the underlying distributions are normal with equal variance and if **S** adopts a decision rule of the sort we have been discussing, namely, responding "signal" if his criterion is equaled or exceeded and "no signal" otherwise. If normality holds but the variances of the E_N and E_{SN} distributions are unequal, the resulting straight-line *ROC* curve will have a slope different from unity. Inappropriateness of the normality assumption will be indicated by a departure from linearity. Thus, as

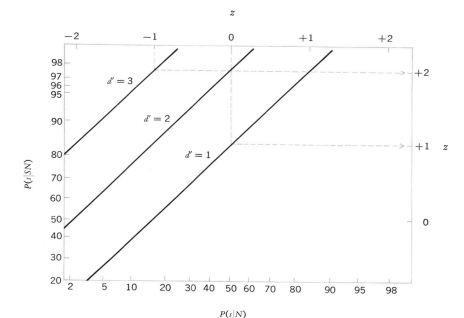

Fig. 5-20. The same *ROC* curves of Fig. 5-19 plotted on double-probability (normal-normal) paper. Two of the axes are marked off in z scores (see text). (SOURCE: D. M. Green and J. A. Swets. *Signal detection theory and psychophysics.* New York: Wiley, 1966. Copyright 1966 by Wiley and used by permission.)

previously noted, assumptions concerning the shape of the distributions that noise and signal plus noise generate on the decision axis are subject to empirical evaluation.

EMPIRICAL ROC CURVES. In our first illustration of an empirical *ROC* curve, S performed in a detection experiment where the signal was a tone embedded in a background of white noise. Changes in S's criterion were induced by manipulating the a priori probability of *SN*; the values employed were 0.10, 0.30, 0.50, 0.70, and 0.90. Each a priori probability was in effect for a block of 600 trials. Figure 5-21 presents the *ROC* curve for this subject plotted on linear coordinates. The data points fall very close to the theoretical *ROC* curve (solid line) generated by the assumptions of normal E_N and E_{SN} distributions, with equal variance and a separation between their means of 0.85σ units. The assumed normal distributions are shown in the insert, where the five dashed vertical lines indicate the position of the various decision criteria adopted by S.

This same subject was run with the a priori probability of signal fixed at 0.50 but with the values of the four decision outcomes manipulated to cause

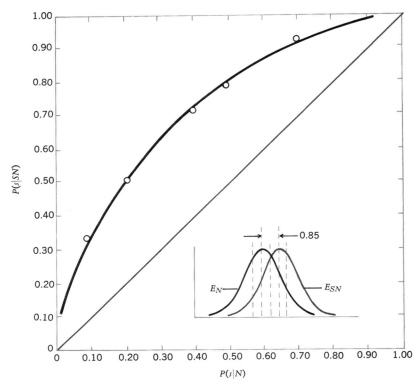

Fig. 5-21. The data points were obtained from a subject who was induced to vary his hit and false-alarm rate by manipulation of the a priori probability of signal plus noise. The *ROC* curve fitted through the data points was generated by the two distributions shown in the insert, where the positions of S's criteria are indicated by the vertical dashed lines. (SOURCE: D. M. Green and J. A. Swets. *Signal detection theory and psychophysics.* New York: Wiley, 1966. Copyright 1966 by Wiley and used by permission.)

the optimal criterion, β_0, to vary between 0.11 and 9.00. Figure 5-22 presents the results of this experiment along with the isosensitivity curve based on the preceding distribution assumptions and $d' = 0.85$. As shown in the insert, the experimental manipulations were successful in inducing S to alter his criterion markedly.

Optimal versus actual criteria. The data of Figs. 5-21 and 5-22 are reasonably fitted by signal detection theory, incorporating the special assumptions of normality of the E_N and E_{SN} distributions and equal variance. The next question concerns the degree of correspondence between the optimal criteria as calculated from the maximized-expected-gain objective and the criteria employed by S as determined empirically. In Fig. 5-23 the obtained β are plotted against optimal β (β_0). If S employed optimal criteria throughout, $\beta = \beta_0$, and hence the points would fall along the diagonal. Although there is a general ordinal correspondence between the obtained and optimal criteria, it is clear that the quantitative disparity is large, particularly for extreme values of β_0. It appears as though S is reluctant to employ very large βs, which require him almost always to say "no signal," or very small βs, which demand a heavy proportion of "signal" responses. As Green and Swets put it, the subject "probably finds it difficult to believe that he would be performing responsibly if the sensory distinctions he makes are exactly those that he could make by removing the earphones in an auditory experiment or by turning his back on a visual signal [1966, p. 92]."

It is clear from these data, as well as from many others gathered in signal detection experiments, that subjects do not generally choose criteria that are optimal in the sense of maximizing expected gain. Nevertheless, although there

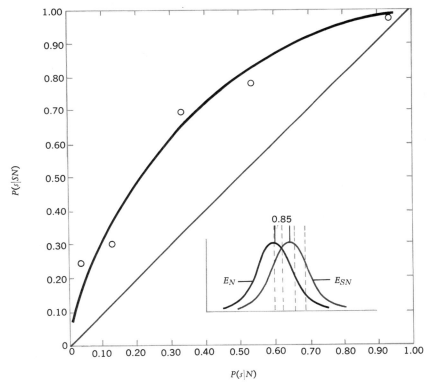

Fig. 5-22. The data points in this graph were obtained from the same subject whose *ROC* curve appears in Fig. 5-21. The experimental conditions were the same in both experiments, except that in the present case the values of the four decision outcomes were different for each of the five points shown in the graph. The theoretical *ROC* curve is the same as that which appears in Fig. 5-21. The insert shows the underlying distributions from which the theoretical *ROC* curve was generated, as well as the position of S's criteria as determined from the data points. (SOURCE: D. M. Green and J. A. Swets. *Signal detection theory and psychophysics.* New York: Wiley, 1966. Copyright 1966 by Wiley and used by permission.)

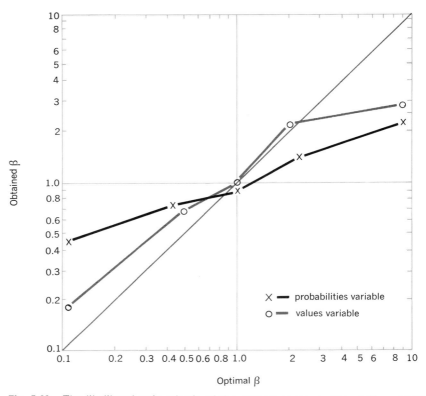

Fig. 5-23. The likelihood-ratio criteria of the subject shown in Figs. 5-21 and 5-22 are plotted against the optimal criteria for the same sets of experimental conditions. If the subject always adopted optimal criteria, the data points would fall along the diagonal shown in the figure. Although there is a perfect ordinal relationship between obtained and optimal β, the discrepancy at extreme values of optimal β is considerable. (SOURCE: D. M. Green and J. A. Swets. *Signal detection theory and psychophysics.* New York: Wiley, 1966. Copyright 1966 by Wiley and used by permission.)

is considerable quantitative disparity, it should be stressed that the ordering of the obtained β often coincides perfectly with that of the optimal β. The subject does move his criterion in the appropriate direction with changes in the parameters of the experiment.

Another circumstance that operates against close quantitative correspondence between β and β_0 is that under many sets of conditions, expected gain does not differ very greatly from the *maximum* expected gain even though S's criterion differs rather widely from β_0. We got a hint of this in Exercise 5-10, where we saw that the proportion of correct responses varied little though there was considerable difference between β_0 and the criterion assumed in that problem.

ROC CURVES BASED ON UNEQUAL VARIANCES. If the E_N and E_{SN} distributions are assumed to be normal but unequal in variance, the *ROC* curve will not be symmetrical about the negative diagonal; and though a plot of the *ROC* curve on double-probability paper will describe a straight line, its slope will not be equal to unity. Figure 5-24 presents the results from a second subject run in the signal detection experiment already described. The *ROC* function fitted to the data points was generated by the two normal distributions shown in the insert, from which it is clear that the variance of the E_{SN} distribution is greater than that of the E_N distribution. Although the factors which determine whether symmetrical or asymmetrical *ROC* curves will be obtained are not yet clearly known, it appears that the detection of visual signals almost always produces asymmetrical functions. Symmetrical isosensitivity curves are much more often seen with auditory signals.

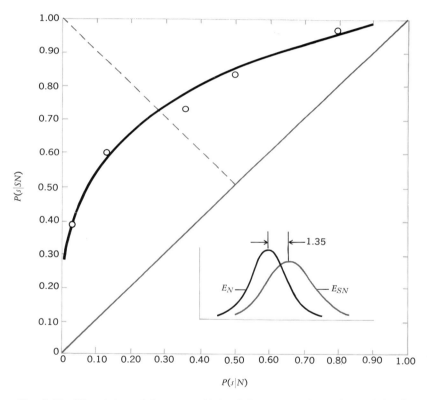

Fig. 5-24. The data points were obtained from a subject whose detection behavior was manipulated by varying the a priori probability of *SN*. The fitted *ROC* curve was obtained from the normal distributions shown in the insert. Note that when the E_N and E_{SN} distributions are normal but of unequal variance, the *ROC* curve is no longer symmetrical around the negative diagonal. (SOURCE: D. M. Green and J. A. Swets. *Signal detection theory and psychophysics.* New York: Wiley, 1966. Copyright 1966 by Wiley and used by permission.)

When the variances of E_N and E_{SN} are unequal, d', based as it is on the assumption of equal variances, can no longer be used as the measure of sensitivity. A closely related measure is d_e', the difference between the means of the E_N and E_{SN} distributions expressed in units of the average of the two standard deviations. Unfortunately for elegance and parsimony, there is no single measure of sensitivity that is equally appropriate for all signal detection models. The various measures in use and their interrelations are discussed by Green and Swets (1966, pp. 404–408). Mention should also be made of performance measures which, while taking different false-alarm rates into account, manage to avoid strong assumptions concerning underlying distributions (e.g., Norman, 1964; Pollack & Norman, 1964).

INVARIANCE OF ROC CURVES.   According to *TSD*, all nonsensory variables which influence S's discriminative behavior do so by influencing the same process, namely, S's criterion. In terms of *ROC* curves, the implication is that such variables merely move S's performance along a fixed *ROC*, or isosensitivity, curve so that the criterion but not the sensitivity changes. In an experiment devoted to the question of the invariance of isosensitivity functions, Galanter and Holman (1967) varied the a priori probability of signal, payoff functions, and instructions in such a manner as to bias S's responses. The task of S was to detect whether the second of two auditory stimuli was equal to or louder than the first. We may conceptualize that E_N is the distribution of central neural effects generated when both stimuli are equal in intensity, and the E_{SN} distribution is that which results when they are unequal. The outcome of the experiment is shown for a single subject in Fig. 5-25, which employs double-probability coordinates. The data points appear to fall on a straight line parallel to the reference line which has a slope of 1. This result supports the assumption of underlying normal E_N and E_{SN} distributions having equal variance. More important, however, is the fact that although the subject was induced to alter his discriminative behavior markedly by manipulation of the three independent variables, his sensitivity, d', remained unaffected. Results of this nature support the contention of *TSD* that a host of nonsensory variables converge on a single mechanism, response criterion, through which discriminative behavior is influenced.

Psychophysical Procedures in Signal Detection

The signal detection paradigm encountered in the previous discussion, often called the "yes-no" procedure, is only one of a number of methods that have evolved in the development of *TSD*. Although effective as a means of obtaining separate measures of sensitivity and response criterion, the yes-no detection task is costly in time and effort. In most applications an *ROC* curve must be generated by inducing S to alter his detection behavior through one means or another. The resulting data points are then fitted by an *ROC* curve, which yields the

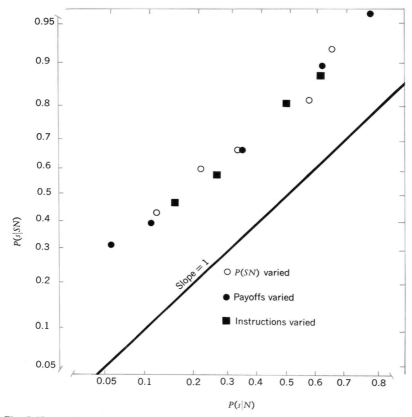

Fig. 5-25. *ROC* or isosensitivity functions for a subject whose detection behavior was altered by manipulation of the three variables shown. (SOURCE: E. Galanter and G. L. Holman. Some invariances of the isosensitivity function and their implications for the utility function of money. *Journal of Experimental Psychology,* 1967, **73**, 333–339. Copyright 1967 by the American Psychological Association and used by permission.)

required sensitivity and criterion measures. Accurate determination of these values requires a fair number of data points, each of which must be based on a relatively large number of trials. When *E*'s interest is in determining the effect of certain independent variables on the *ROC* curve, the experimental task quickly becomes formidable.

RATING PROCEDURE. A more economical method, the rating procedure, is based on the assumption that *S* can maintain several criteria simultaneously and consistently (cf. Pollack & Decker, 1958). The actual experimental details are quite similar to those of the yes-no procedure, except that the subject provides information concerning the confidence of his judgments. For example, *S* might respond on a trial that he was "almost certain," "fairly certain," or "somewhat doubtful" that the signal occurred, using the same kind of confidence categories for his "no signal" responses. Experienced Ss might simply be advised to adopt criteria of varying strictness. It is assumed that S's ratings correspond to the establishment of different criteria and that these criteria are maintained consistently throughout the experiment. Granting the validity of these assumptions, the investigator can obtain information concerning a whole set of criteria from a single set of experimental conditions. In different terms, E obtains from one block of trials several points on the ROC curve rather than just one.

To illustrate the analysis, assume that S was allowed four responses— 1, 2, 3, and 4—by which to indicate his confidence as to whether the signal almost certainly occurred—4—to the other extreme—1—that it almost certainly did not occur. Imagine that the proportion of N and SN trials on which these various responses were recorded is as given in the first two rows of Table 5-7. Based on the assumption that S maintained consistent criteria, the assumed hit rate for each of the criteria represented by the four responses is given in the third row. For the very strict criterion (response 4), the hit rate is 0.15 because this is the proportion of "4" responses which occurred on SN trials (see row 1). The criterion corresponding to response 3 should include not only the responses of this category but those of response 4 as well, because if a central neural effect was strong enough to elicit response 4, it certainly would constitute a detection with the criterion established at a level corresponding to response 3. Thus the proportion of hits assigned to response 3 is 0.58. In this manner one continues to accumulate the hits of the various response categories, assigning a hit rate for each of the possible responses. False-alarm rates are calculated in precisely the same fashion (fourth row). Each pair of hit and false-alarm proportions provides a point on the ROC curve. Because the weakest criterion must have a

Table 5-7 Assumed Data of a Rating-procedure Experiment

		RESPONSE			
		1	2	3	4
(1)	STIMULUS SN	0.18	0.24	0.43	0.15
(2)	STIMULUS N	0.54	0.26	0.17	0.03
(3)	Assumed hit rate	1.00	0.82	0.58	0.15
(4)	Assumed false-alarm rate	1.00	0.46	0.20	0.03

hit and false-alarm rate of 1.0, r responses of a rating experiment yield $r - 1$ ROC data points.

The question arises about the appropriateness of the assumptions underlying the rating procedure, an issue which is illuminated by experiments comparing sensitivity measures obtained from the rating and yes-no procedures. Much of the available evidence shows that comparable values of d' or of related sensitivity measures are obtained from these two detection methods (Green & Swets, 1966, pp. 110–114; Markowitz & Swets, 1967).

FORCED-CHOICE PROCEDURES.   A third procedure that is often used in detection experiments consists of presenting the subject with more than one observation interval, S knowing in advance that the signal is present in one and only one of the intervals. Because SN is presented on every trial and because S is "forced" to make a judgment as to the location of the signal, response criterion plays a far less important role in interpreting results obtained from the forced-choice procedure. The proportion of obtained correct responses is the usual measure of sensitivity utilized in such experiments (cf. Green & Swets, 1966, Chap. 2).

With this brief description, we take leave of the signal detection paradigms. Further discussion of the topic and illuminating insights into matters of experimental technique are available in Green and Swets (1966, Chap. 2 & Appendix III).

Relationship of *TSD* to Classical Psychophysics

The preceding three methods are the most widely used detection procedures. They are quite different from the classical psychophysical methods, which of course are also aimed at obtaining measures of sensitivity (thresholds). Recently, however, certain of the classical psychophysical methods have been put in close congruence with a model based on *TSD* (Treisman & Watts, 1966). Let us take as an illustration of this development a signal detection interpretation of the measurement of the incremental threshold by the method of constant stimuli.

An incremental threshold is merely an upper threshold or, in earlier terminology, an upper limen (UL). To apply the method of constant stimuli to the detection yes-no setting, E merely presents S with signals of various strengths and observes the percentage of trials in which each signal is detected. In this setting the noise stimulus plays the role of the standard stimulus in conventional applications of the method of constant stimuli, and SNs of different intensities serve as the comparison stimuli. The lower portion of Fig. 5-26 presents the psychometric function expected in this situation. The percentage of positive or detection responses appears on the ordinate, and signal magnitude is presented on the abscissa. In correspondence with earlier definitions, the stimulus which elicits a detection (s) response on 50 percent of the trials is defined as the incremental or upper limen; hence, $UL = SN_1$. (The 50-percent criterion, it should be noted, agrees exactly with the 75-percent definition of the UL given

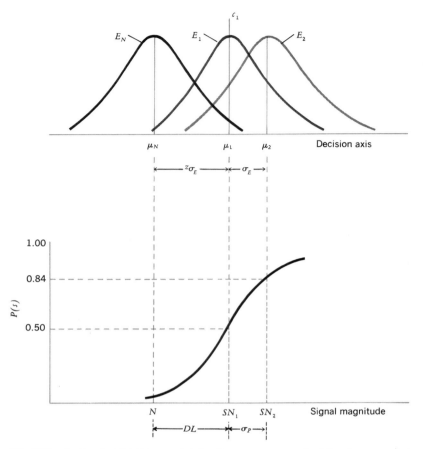

Fig. 5-26. A signal detection model for the measurement of the incremental (upper) limen by the method of constant stimuli. Each of the stimuli presented to the subject is assumed to generate distributions on the decision axis which are normal with equal variance. Only three stimuli and their corresponding distributions of central neural effects are shown in the figure (see text). (SOURCE: M. Treisman and T. R. Watts. Relation between signal detectability theory and the traditional procedures for measuring sensory thresholds: Estimating d' from results given by the method of constant stimuli. *Psychological Bulletin*, 1966, **66**, 438–454. Copyright 1966 by the American Psychological Association and used by permission.)

earlier, because then both upper and lower *DL*s were obtained.) Obviously, $SN_1 - N = DL$. Clearly, then, such familiar quantities of classical psychophysics as the *DL* and *UL* are obtainable in this hybrid detection-constant stimuli procedure.

One signal detection model of the previous paradigm takes the following form. It is assumed that each of the signals presented to the subject, as well as the noise stimulus, generates central neural effects that are normally distributed and of approximately equal variance. As before, these distributions (shown in the upper part of Fig. 5-26) are assumed to lie on the same decision axis. The distances separating the physical stimuli are assumed to be linearly related to the distances separating corresponding mean values on the decision axis. Finally, the objective of S in this task is assumed to be to maximize the proportion of hits while holding the proportion of false alarms at a fixed low rate, i.e., the Neyman-Pearson objective. With the distributions given, this objective is achieved by placing the criterion (in terms of likelihood ratio or magnitude of the central neural effect) at a point of the E_N distribution such that an area equal to the required false-alarm rate lies to the right of the criterion (c_1 in Fig. 5-26).

The criterion now located, the upper limen turns out to be that stimulus value which generates a distribution on the decision axis whose mean is identical with the criterion, because the subject will respond "s" on 50 percent of the occasions that such a stimulus is presented. Thus in Fig. 5-26, SN_1 is shown to generate distribution E_1, whose mean μ_1 coincides with S's criterion. By similar reasoning, a signal of strength SN_2 generates a distribution on the decision axis (E_2) whose mean is $1\sigma_E$ (the common standard deviation of the distributions of the decision axis) away from the criterion. This follows because the subject responds "s" to SN_2 on 84 percent of the trials. (Recall that in a normal distribution 34 percent of the area lies between the mean and a score 1σ to its right.) The difference $SN_2 - SN_1$ is often referred to as the "standard deviation of the psychometric function," σ_P.

Now that the method of constant stimuli has been placed in correspondence with a signal detection model, we may ask whether any of the measures arising from the former are relevant for quantities that are important to signal detection theory. According to Treisman and Watts, if their model is reasonably correct, it should be possible to predict S's false-alarm rate, $P(s|N)$, given certain quantities calculated from the psychometric function. They reason that (as shown in Fig. 5-26) the criterion is separated from the mean of the noise distribution (μ_N) by a distance equal to $z\sigma_E$, where z is the value of the normal deviate that places an area equal to the false-alarm rate in the right tail of the E_N distribution. Under the assumption that the decision axis is linearly related to the dimension of the physical stimulus, an estimate of z can be obtained as follows:

$$z = \frac{z\sigma_E}{\sigma_E} = \frac{SN_1 - N}{SN_2 - SN_1} = \frac{DL}{\sigma_P}$$

Thus, dividing the DL by the standard deviation of the psychometric function provides a normal deviate value (z score) from which one should be able to predict S's false-alarm rate.

Treisman and Watts (1966) checked this implication of the signal detection model by employing the method of constant stimuli in a detection situation to obtain an incremental threshold. Their "noise" stimulus was a 500-Hz tone of fixed intensity to which an increment ranging from 0.3 to 1.3 db was added to form the various signal-plus-noise stimuli. From the empirical psychometric functions they determined for each S his DL and σ_P. The ratio of the two yielded a z score from which S's false-alarm rate (the proportion of the 40 N trials in which S reported the presence of a signal) was predicted. In spite of a considerable amount of variability, Treisman and Watts found a good correspondence between the predicted and the obtained false-alarm rates (Fig. 5-27).

A second, and perhaps more interesting, deduction from the decision theory model is that it should be possible to deduce the sensitivity measure d' from the psychometric function. We have seen that the psychometric function

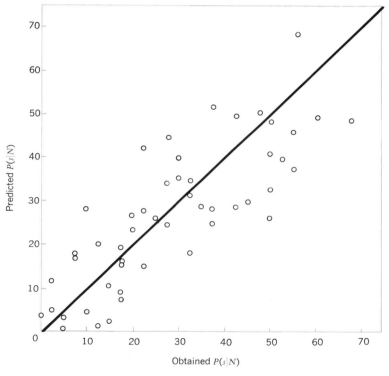

Fig. 5-27. The predicted and obtained false-alarm rates, $P(s|N)$, for each of 51 subjects. The predicted false-alarm rate was obtained from the psychometric function which resulted from determination of an auditory-intensity increment limen by the method of constant stimuli. The obtained false-alarm rate was based on the number of positive responses made on nonsignal trials. (SOURCE: M. Treisman and T. R. Watts. Relation between signal detectability theory and the traditional procedures for measuring sensory thresholds: Estimating d' from results given by the method of constant stimuli. *Psychological Bulletin*, 1966, **66**, 438–454. Copyright 1966 by the American Psychological Association and used by permission.)

provides an estimate, z, of the distance that separates S's criterion from the mean of the noise distribution, μ_N. From Fig. 5-26 it is plain that z also estimates, in units of σ_E, the separation of the means of the E_N and E_1 distributions. Consequently if N and SN_1 were presented in a simple yes-no detection task, z ought also provide an estimate of d'. Indeed an estimate of d' is obtainable from the psychometric function for any stimulus in the neighborhood of the upper limen. If, for example, SN_2 of Fig. 5-26 were employed as the signal-plus-noise stimulus of the detection task, d' is estimated to be $(SN_2 - N)/\sigma_P$.

Exploring this implication, Treisman and Watts (1966) ran 16 subjects in an experiment where estimates of d' were obtained from psychometric functions in the manner just described. These estimates were compared to actual values of d' measured in a detection setting using the rating procedure discussed earlier. Because of such factors as fatigue, it was not possible to obtain the psychometric function first and then use the upper limen as SN in a subsequent detection task. Rather, trials of both tasks were intermixed, the value of the stimulus used as SN in the detection trials of the experiment determined from preliminary threshold measurements. The results of the experiment showed that d's calculated from the rating procedure could be reasonably well predicted from appropriate values of the psychometric function, particularly if the unequal variances of the E_N and E_{SN} distributions were taken into account.

These experiments, along with the finding that Weber's law is derivable from the previous signal detection model (M. Treisman, 1964a), are important developments in herding together under the same theoretical roof many of the concepts of classical psychophysics and contemporary *TSD*.

SENSORY VERSUS RESPONSE THRESHOLDS. An issue alive in psychophysics for a long time but brought into sharp focus by *TSD* concerns the validity of perhaps the most central concept of classical psychophysics, namely, the threshold concept. The history of this controversy has been recounted (Corso, 1963); our purpose is to point out briefly some of the contemporary implications of the concept. By "sensory" threshold we refer to the threshold concept as it was understood by Fechner, Weber, and other psychophysicists of their tradition. According to this view, a physical stimulus less than some specific value (the threshold) evokes in an individual no sensory experience whatever; once the stimulus transcends the threshold value, some conscious sensation, however small, occurs. Within this formulation, the stimulus continuum is divided into those stimuli which elicit a sensation in S (supraliminal stimuli) and those that do not (subliminal). Accordingly, the sensory threshold serves as a reasonable zero point for the sensory continuum.

An alternative view is that no such sensory threshold exists. Rather, sensation is a *continuously* varying quantity which trails off to zero only when the stimulus intensity itself is zero. Signal detection theory provides a clear model of this interpretation. A stimulus dimension is not dichotomized into subliminal and supraliminal stimuli; instead every stimulus generates a distribution of sensations (or central neural effects), including stimuli as close to the zero point of the physical dimension as one would care to choose. In this formulation a subject fails to report a "subthreshold" stimulus, not because the stimulus fails to elicit a sensory response, but because the likelihood ratio associated with the sensory response (central neural effect) is too small to transgress S's response criterion. Signal detection theory dichotomizes the sensory continuum, but it does so on the basis of a response threshold—the response criterion—rather than appealing to a sensory threshold.

Early in this chapter we stressed that the concepts of the absolute and difference thresholds were statistical in nature, a fact that was brought out further by the model of momentary absolute thresholds developed subsequently. These "operational" definitions of threshold raise problems for the consistent use of the sensory-threshold concept in theoretical endeavors. Because a stimulus defined as the AL is perceived, or at least reported, on 50 percent of the occasions that it is presented to S, it can hardly, other than by mere definition, constitute the origin or zero point of a sensory scale. The reason, of course, is that stimuli below the AL so defined elicit positive responses—and are therefore apparently supraliminal—a significant portion of the time. For many applications the disparity between the AL defined statistically and the stimulus value which might better serve as the "true" zero point of the sensation scale probably matters little, particularly if the range of sensations considered is very large. Clearly the latter value cannot be far from the AL. The issue of whether sensation is to be thought of as a continuous or a discontinuous quantity is more important because of the theoretical implications associated with the two positions. To name one that is relevant for developments in the next chapter, Fechner, in his efforts to scale sensation, assumed that the zero point of a sensation scale could be identified with the AL.

At the present time neither side appears clearly to have the upper hand, although increasing sympathy is developing for continuous sensitivity (cf. Green & Swets, 1966, Chap. 5; Swets, 1961). For an illustration of how a sensory-threshold model can handle data from detection experiments, see Luce (1963).

Applications of Signal Detection Theory

As noted earlier, signal detection theory has wide application. The "depth" of application, however, varies greatly. In some cases, such as animal research, little more has been achieved than demonstrations of the potential applicability of certain concepts of signal detection theory. Other uses of signal detection theory have been more substantive as, for example, in the decision-theory analysis of recognition memory. The major motivational thread running through all these applications, however superficial they might be, is the desire to enlist a means of separating a process analogous to the subject's sensitivity, on the one hand, from a response-criterion process, on the other. (The sought-after distinction is perhaps not unlike that often made between learning and performance or, in more general terms, between ability and performance.)

A detailed discussion of a number of applications of *TSD* is provided by Green and Swets (1966, Chap. 12), ranging from animal psychophysics to subliminal perception. To their list one can now add a demonstration that stimulus generalization gradients in animals may be interpreted as a problem of signal detection (Blough, 1967, 1969), as well as a detailed decision-theory analysis of discrimination learning in pigeons (Boneau & Cole, 1967). The relevance of signal detection methods for the analysis of classical conditioning experiments (Grice, 1968; Suboski, 1967) and personality and perception research (Price, 1966) has been stressed recently. A concrete demonstration of the superiority of such methods over classical psychophysical techniques in detecting perceptual differences between normals and schizophrenics has been presented by Price and Eriksen (1966). In Chap. 11 we discuss in some detail a recent application of signal detection theory to the problem of selective attention. To anticipate, it has been concluded from a signal detection analysis that focusing one's attention on one set of stimuli serves to decrease the discriminability (d') of other stimuli, with the response criterion, β, remaining unchanged. One area of application that has recently attracted a great deal of interest is recognition memory (cf. Bernbach, 1967; Parks, 1966; Wickelgren & Norman, 1966); let us conclude this section with a brief description of this development.

In many recognition experiments the subject is confronted with a task not unlike that which faces S in a typical psychophysical detection experiment. Consider the following situation. A group of 100 words is read to the subject, after which a group of 200 words is presented one at a time, and for each word S is to respond whether the word was on the earlier list of items (an "old" item) or whether it was not (a "new" item). Clearly, the subject is confronted with a decision task in arriving at a response for each item. For some items there might be little doubt in his mind that they were part of the original list, and similarly some items might clearly be new; for many items, however, some uncertainty of their status exists. That something like a response criterion is involved in S's decisions immediately suggests itself. If, for example, S were very cautious, he might respond "old" only to those items which he was certain were part of the initial list. This kind of behavior is analogous to employing a strict criterion. Moreover, there is little doubt that S's behavior in this situation can be manipulated by varying the gains and losses associated with "hits" (correct detection of old items), false alarms, and so on.

Traditional analyses of recognition behavior attempted to account for S's criterion by applying a correction for guessing, which consisted of an adjustment of the hit rate downward for false alarms. Such a procedure is equivalent to assuming that recognition is an all-or-none process and that, consequently, S's hits consist of those items which he truly does recognize and those which he gets correct simply by guessing. Signal detection analysis, on the other hand, approaches the problem in a different fashion, by assuming that the subject makes his decision on the basis of mediating processes which are continuous rather than discrete. [It is possible to apply a decision-theory analysis to recognition memory while maintaining that the nature of the basic memory process is discrete rather than continuous. In effect, the memory process is separated from the decision process, and only the latter is considered continuous (cf. Bernbach, 1967).]

One way of applying the concepts of signal detection theory to recognition memory follows. We assume that each item presented during the test phase elicits in the subject a certain magnitude of "familiarity" (Parks, 1966), which then plays a role similar to the central neural effect posited in the case of detection experiments. New and old items elicit familiarity effects that are represented on the same, decision, axis. Adding the special assumption that the distribution of familiarity effects of the old and new items are normal with equal variance yields a model which is identical to that portrayed in Fig. 5-16. The new items correspond to the noise stimulus and the old items to signal plus noise. Similarly, in the recognition model, E_N and E_{SN} are the distributions of familiarity which are generated by new and old items, respectively. The subject adopts a criterion value of familiarity effect (or likelihood ratio), and if a test item produces a familiarity effect equal to or greater than this criterion, S responds "old"; otherwise he responds "new." The separation of the means of the two distributions, represented as d', is a measure of the basic discriminability of the two sets of items and presumably is a function of learning and retention variables. The criterion and, consequently, S's recognition behavior will be affected by the a priori probability of new items and factors that influence the payoff structure. Finally, it is a relatively simple task to obtain ROC curves with which to assess the distribution assumptions and to obtain an empirical value of d'. The rating procedure is particularly useful in this connection (cf. Murdock, 1965).

SUMMARY

Although signal detection theory has had a remarkable impact on psychophysics, it is unlikely that signal detection procedures will displace entirely the methods of classical psychophysics. One can no longer think of a threshold—even if only in the operational sense of that term—without taking note that the measurement is a composite of S's sensitivity and his criterion. In many situations independent specification of the criterion is unnecessary, and hence a threshold measure by itself is satisfactory. In other situations, particularly where inferences concerning changes in S's sensitivity are at stake, independent measures of sensitivity and criterion may be required, in which case the classical methods are no longer sufficient.

It may turn out that signal detection theory will have even a greater impact on areas removed from psychophysics proper, such as perception and recognition, where the need for controlling for response criteria has only dimly been recognized and where decision-theory concepts provide a fresh theoretical approach.

1. The method of limits is also called:
   (a) Two defining characteristics of this method are:
   (b) Two relevant variables requiring control that are peculiar to the method

of limits are:

(c) In the method of limits the definitions of T, $\bar{T}$, UT, LT, UL, LL, UDT, LDT, UDL, LDL, IU, and PSE are:

2. The "constant errors" associated with the method of limits are:

(a) In the determination of ALs, the preceding constant errors affect T on D and A series as follows:

(b) In the determination of DLs, the effects of these constant errors on D and A series are:

3. The method of constant stimuli is characterized by:

(a) The definitions of AL, DL, UL, LL, UDL, LDL, IU, and PSE for this method are:

4. The assumption that the momentary absolute threshold ($\dot{T}$) is normally distributed means:

(a) Granting the validity of this assumption, if a series of stimuli is presented to S a large number of times in the determination of S's AL, the percentage of trials on which each stimulus is perceived will be the percentile rank of the stimulus in the distribution of $\dot{T}$ because:

(b) The mean of $\dot{T}$ is taken to be S's "true" AL; the standard deviation of $\dot{T}$ provides a measure of:

(c) If the percentile ranks referred to in 4(a) are plotted against values of S, the points should fall on a straight line because:

(d) If the percentile ranks are converted to z scores in accordance with the area relations under the normal curve and the z scores are plotted against the corresponding values of S, the points should again fall on a straight line because:

(e) In the latter case the mean and standard deviation of $\dot{T}$ could be obtained from:

(f) The assumption that $\dot{T}$ is normally distributed can be checked by:

5. On the assumption that the psychometric function is adequately described by the phi gamma hypothesis, the PSE and DL may be obtained from the function relating z to S_v as follows:

6. The relationship between the DL and the JND is:

7. Weber's law states:

(a) The significance of the Weber fraction is:

(b) The linear generalization of Weber's law is:

8. The method of average error is also called:

(a) The essential characteristics of this psychophysical method are:

(b) The rationale behind its use in determining DLs is:

9. The connection between *TSD* and Thurstone's view of the sensory effects of individual stimuli is:

10. Define d' and β.

11. The definition of optimal β (β_0) for the objective of maximizing expected gain is:

12. Suppose that S employs a likelihood ratio as his criterion but not necessarily β_0. Does this affect the measured value of d'?

13. Distinguish between sensory and response thresholds, and indicate the opposing theoretical views to which these two concepts are attached.

14. The assumptions of *TSD* that lead to the prediction of an *ROC* curve that is symmetrical about the negative diagonal are:

15. Show how a signal detection analysis can be applied to the task of obtaining an increment threshold by the method of constant stimuli, and indicate how estimates of S's false-alarm rate and d' can be gotten from the psychometric function.

16. Think of a problem area, other than one given in the text, to which a signal detection analysis can be applied, and describe the application; that is, what corresponds to N and SN, what are the E_N and E_{SN} distributions, and what aspects of the behavioral process correspond to d' and the response criterion?

ANSWERS TO EXERCISES

5-1. $SD_{DT} = 1.12$ mm; if you forgot to halve the threshold values given in the table, which correspond to 2 *DTs*, then your answer should be $2(1.12) = 2.24$ mm.

The calculation of SD_{PSE} is facilitated by subtracting 49 from each of the appropriate values given in Table 5-2; this standard deviation turns out to be 1.32 mm.

5-2. No. With reference to Table 5-2, for example, $S_v = 54$ mm is a stimulus that is more than 1 *DL* away from S_t, and yet it was judged equal to S_t on half of the series. If one stimulus is always judged greater than another, it undoubtedly is more than 1 *DL* away from the latter.

5-3. No. Clearly a larger stimulus increment is necessary for one to notice differences between relatively wide cards than is required for the same discrimination between narrow cards. Hence, we may expect the *DL* for $S_t = 75$ mm to be larger than the *DL* for $S_t = 25$ mm. Weber's law, to be discussed later, is a statement of what the relationship between the size of the *DL* and the magnitude of S_t ought to be.

5-4. The use of only two stimuli has actually been suggested as a means of eliminating wasted data in the determination of the *AL*, and under certain circumstances, such a modification may be warranted. However, E would have to know in advance much more accurately the location of S's *AL* than he is likely to know. If the interval between the two stimuli is too small, it may fail to contain the *AL* (the 50 percent point); on the other hand, if the interval between the stimuli is too large, the use of linear interpolation to obtain the *AL* becomes a questionable procedure. Further, the use of only two stimuli may preclude obtaining a reasonable estimate of the variability of S's threshold (a topic discussed in the next section).

A better solution is to employ a method of calculating the *DL* which makes use of all the available data. The next section of the chapter is devoted to this topic.

5-5. From the curves presented in Fig. 5-4, it is clear that if the pain *AL* were defined as the stimulus which evoked a painful sensation on 25 percent of the trials, one would have to conclude that white noise *increases* the thermal-pain threshold, whereas the opposite would be concluded if the pain *AL* were defined as the stimulus that elicited a pain sensation on 75 percent of the trials. According to the accepted definition of the *AL*, however, noise has no effect on the pain *AL*. At the end of the next section, we shall return to this problem with a formulation that will account for these apparent discrepancies and at the same time provide some justification for the accepted definition of the *AL*.

5-6. (a) It is apparent that the points depart rather widely from a straight line in both the noise and the no-noise condition. This suggests that the underlying distribution of momentary thresholds is not very close to a normal distribution; consequently, the method of this section ordinarily should not be employed. It is still possible to make use of all the available data in the calculation of the *AL* by employing a procedure, developed by Spearman, which does not assume that $\hat{T}$ is normally distributed. Spearman's method, which is not difficult, is described by Guilford (1954, pp. 120–122) and Woodworth and Schlosberg (1954, pp. 207–208). However, to demonstrate the size of the errors that are possible when the data depart from the underlying assumption of normality, we shall fit straight lines to the data points.

(b) The value of μ is 169.2 and 165.3 mc/sec/cm² for the no-noise and noise conditions, respectively. The standard deviations are 33.11 and 23.30 mc/sec/cm², in the same order. It would appear from these values that white noise, although having little effect on the *AL*, might have increased the variability of the absolute threshold, because the standard deviation obtained without noise is 42 percent greater than the standard deviation obtained with noise. This is a hypothesis that could be checked by further experimentation.

(c) Linear interpolation into the percentages shows the *AL* to be 175.0 and 180.0 mc/sec/cm² for the no-noise and noise conditions, respectively. These values are much larger than the corresponding values calculated from the best-fitting straight line, though the *difference* between the noise and no-noise *AL* is affected much less by the method of determination. The reason for the discrepancy is, of course, that the obtained percentage points do not adequately approximate a normal distribution. Their conversion to z scores appropriate for a normal distribution and the subsequent fitting of a straight line to the transformed data points introduce errors in the calculation of the *AL*.

5-7. In the method of limits, the interval of uncertainty is in a sense the largest possible, inasmuch as on every trial S traverses the entire range from "less than" to "equal" to "greater than." In the method of constant stimuli, on the other hand, the lower boundary of the IU is the 25 percent point and the upper boundary is the 75 percent point, both boundaries situated well within the IU. Because in both cases the DL is defined as half the interval of uncertainty, the method of limits ought to produce the larger DLs.

5-8. Suppose that we convert a sample distribution of X scores, $X_1, X_2, \ldots, X_n$, to a distribution of z scores by the usual z transformation: $z_i = (X_i - \bar{X})/SD$. The z transformation may be written as $z_i = (1/SD)X_i - (\bar{X}/SD)$, in which it may be seen that $c = 1/SD$ or $SD = 1/c$. In the event that we are dealing with a population or a theoretical distribution, $z_i = (X_i - \mu)\sigma = (1/\sigma)X_i - (\mu/\sigma)$, so that $c = 1/\sigma$ and $\sigma = 1/c$.

5-9. If Weber's law were $DL = cS_t + k$, the function relating the Weber fraction to S_t would take the following form: $DL/S_t = c + k/S_t$. It follows from the latter function that DL/S_t will be relatively large for small values of S_t, decreasing rapidly as S_t is increased. For relatively large values of S_t, DL/S_t remains fairly constant at the value of c. It is apparent that this form of Weber's law, which is a linear generalization of the original formulation, can provide a better fit to the curve in Fig. 5-14 than Weber's original formulation. However, it cannot account for increases in DL/S_t at higher values of S_t (e.g., Fig. 5-15).

5-10. To get a pictorial view of the problem, first sketch a normal distribution to represent the E_N distribution and erect a vertical line that cuts off approximately 2.3 percent of the right side of the distribution. Now add the E_{SN} distribution showing that 84.1 percent of the latter falls to the right of the vertical line. It should be clear that the vertical line represents **S**'s criterion (c_1 in Fig. 5-28) expressed as central neural effect.

(a) To find d' in σ units, we first find the distance in standard deviations separating the criterion from the mean of the E_{SN} distribution. A table of the unit normal distribution tells us that for a z score of -1 close to 84.1 percent of the dis-

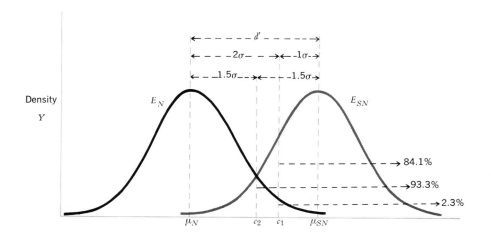

Fig. 5-28. Assumed distribution of noise and signal plus noise for Exercise 5-10 (see text).

tribution lies to its right so that the criterion is 1σ below the mean of the E_{SN} distribution. Similarly, we find that the criterion is 2σ above the mean of the E_N distribution. When these two values are summed, $d' = 3\sigma$. Convention has it that the value 1 is assigned to the common σ; thus, $d' = 3$.

(b) To calculate β we must find the density or ordinate of the E_{SN} and E_N distributions at S's criterion. A table of values of the ordinates of the normal distribution can be found in many statistics texts. The ordinate of a normal distribution at a point 1σ from the mean is 0.2420, whereas the ordinate at 2σ is 0.0540. Hence $\beta = 0.2420/0.0540 = 4.48$.

(c) We have already seen that under the present circumstances the optimal criterion β_0 is equal to unity, so S's criterion is clearly not optimal. The proportion of correct responses obtained by S with his criterion is $(0.841)(0.5) + (0.977)(0.5) = 0.909$ [i.e., $P(s|SN)P(SN) + P(n|N)P(N)$]. To calculate the proportion of correct responses obtainable with $\beta_0 = 1$, we note that this value of likelihood ratio occurs where the two distributions intersect, which is midway between the means of the two distributions. Hence the optimal criterion expressed as central neural effect (c_2 in Fig. 5-28) lies 1.5σ from the means of the E_N and E_{SN} distributions. Because 93.3 percent of the area lies above a score located 1.5σ below the mean, $P(s|SN) = 0.933$, and by similar reasoning, $P(n|N) = 0.933$ also. Thus the proportion of correct responses which would be obtained with the optimal criterion is 0.933. Although this figure is not greatly different from that resulting when $\beta = 4.48$, under different circumstances the disparity could be much larger.

5-11. (a) Expressing gains and losses as dollars, $\beta_0 = \dfrac{(0.1 + 1.0)(0.5)}{(0.1 + 0.0)(0.5)} = 11.$

(b) Under the assumptions given, $P(n|N) = 0.9 = P(s|SN)$ and $P(s|N) = 0.1 = P(n|SN)$. Thus,

$$EG = (0.1)(0.9)(0.5) + (0.1)(0.9)(0.5) - (1.0)(0.1)(0.5) - 0 = 0.04$$

With his likelihood criterion set at unity, S will gain on the average 4 cents on each trial, or in 100 trials he can expect to gain 4 dollars. If, however, S employed the optimal criterion, 11, his expected gain would almost double, increasing to 7.4 cents per trial.

6 PSYCHOPHYSICAL SCALING

The psychophysical methods discussed in the last chapter are applied primarily to the determination of thresholds. They require the simplest possible judgments from the subject, and their modest demands earn them a high degree of reliability. In the present chapter we shall deal with psychophysical problems that are much more challenging than the determination of thresholds, namely, the construction of scales relating the magnitude of a sensory response to the magnitude of the initiating physical stimulus. For example, we would like to determine for two tones of different intensity *how much louder* one tone is than the other. Even more, we would like to develop a scale with which, given a tone of arbitrary intensity, we could predict what intensity a second tone must be in order for it to be judged *twice as loud* as the first. Our ambitious goal is, in short, to achieve a degree of measurability for sensations comparable to that existing for such physical quantities as temperature, length, and weight. The "rulers" of sensation required for this task are provided by the *psychophysical scaling methods*, a group of scaling techniques which will later occupy our attention. However, our first task is to examine some features of the measurement process itself and, following this, to acquire a few notions about nonlinear functions.

THE MEASUREMENT OF VARIABLES: TYPES OF SCALES

Measuring is a commonplace activity to all of us, so common that a discussion of the fundamental features of measurement may seem superfluous. Nevertheless, it is not generally recognized that different types or classes of measurement exist. Scientists, mathematicians, and philosophers, however, have studied in some detail the theory—usually taken for granted—that underlies measurement and have analyzed the various classes of measurement that are in use or are theoretically possible (e.g., Suppes & Zinnes, 1963). The theory of measurement is a topic of special relevance for psychology because many of its significant variables are not measurable in the customary ways of the natural sciences.

In this section four classes of measurement will be discussed: *nominal*, *ordinal*, *interval*, and *ratio* scales. For present purposes a *scale* may be defined as a class of measurement having certain well-defined properties. A more detailed description of these four scales is provided by Stevens (1951), and an alternative scheme of classifying scales will be found in Torgerson (1958, Chap. 3).

The Nominal Scale

The nominal scale, the only type of measurement possible with qualitative variables, is the most primitive of the four scales. The characteristics of a nominal scale are simple. To every separate category of the qualitative variable one assigns a different numeral. "Numeral" is a general term for such systems of symbols as numbers, letters of the alphabet, and Roman numerals. Objects that are identified as belonging to the same category of the qualitative variable receive the same numeral; objects that are identified as belonging to different categories are assigned different numerals (the numerals of their respective categories). In simplest terms, the numerals serve as *names* for the separate categories and may be any symbols whatever. For example, the two categories of the qualitative variable, sex, may have the numerals M and F assigned to them, or 0 and 1, or A and X, or in fact any two discriminably different symbols. The only requirement is that all males be designated by one of the symbols of the pair and all females be designated by the other member of the pair. A similar principle holds for qualitative variables composed of several categories, such as religion and occupation. As may be seen, the nominal (naming) scale is indeed a primitive type of measurement, requiring only the ability to determine whether the measured objects belong to the same or to different categories of the qualitative variable.

The Ordinal Scale

With quantitative variables we arrive at a more familiar type of measurement, that which deals with questions of "how much." Of the three scales that involve quantitative measurement (ordinal, interval, and ratio), the ordinal is the "weakest" in the sense that with ordinal measurement, one merely knows, for example, that object A possesses more of the measured quantitative variable than object B with no knowledge of how much more.

To illustrate, a group of objects no two of which are closely similar in weight could be rank ordered with respect to weight simply by hefting. Suppose that as a result of such an operation, we ranked six objects $(O_1, O_2, \ldots, O_6)$ as follows: $O_1 = 1$ (i.e., O_1 is the lightest); $O_3 = 2$ (O_3 is heavier than O_1); $O_6 = 3$; $O_5 = 4$; $O_2 = 5$; and $O_4 = 6$ (O_4 is the heaviest). The weights of the objects have been measured only with respect to order; we know nothing about their absolute weights nor even about the differences in weight that separate each of the objects. Consequently, the objects have been measured on an ordinal (ordering) scale.

Perhaps it is obvious that, in terms of the information imparted by the numbers employed (1 through 6), the letters A through F could have been assigned to the six objects just as well, or the Roman numerals I, II, III, IV, V, VI, or indeed the numbers 3, 10, 34, 35, 40, 100, because the only property of the numerals used was their relative order. If the last group of numerals were used, then $O_2 = 40$, and $O_4 = 100$, but the significance of these numbers would be only that O_4 is heavier than O_2, not that it is $2\frac{1}{2}$ times heavier. Similarly, the original assignment $O_1 = 1$, $O_3 = 2$, $O_6 = 3$ does not carry the implication that O_6 is as much heavier than O_3 as the latter is heavier than O_1.

There is an important connection between the class of scale employed and the type of measure of central tendency that may be used with complete legitimacy. In terms of the ranks assigned to the six objects, O_1, O_4, and O_6 have a lower average than objects O_2, O_3, O_5—10/3 versus 11/3. It would be incorrect, however, to jump to the conclusion that the mean weights of the second group of objects must be greater than the mean of the first. For if the actual weights in pounds were $O_1 = 1.0$, $O_4 = 10.0$, $O_6 = 2.0$, and $O_2 = 5.0$, $O_3 = 1.5$, $O_5 = 4.0$, it is clear that the mean of the first three objects would exceed the mean of the second. The general point is that because nothing is known about the distances separating objects measured on ordinal scales, strictly speaking, the calculation of means is inappropriate. The median, on the other hand, is a completely legitimate measure of central tendency on ordinal scales. The reader should convince himself that with the given ranking of the six objects, the median of the second group of three objects (O_2, O_3, O_5) will always be greater than the median of the first three, so long, of course, as the original ordering is maintained.

Although the interdiction against the use of means on ordinal scales plainly follows from the properties of ordinal measurement, practical considerations often intervene to require their usage. For example, many rating scales are at best ordinal scales. Yet if everyone took the stricture against the use of means with such scales seriously, a considerable amount of important and fruitful research would have been impossible, or, at the very least, seriously impeded. The successful use of means with rating scales is attributable in part to the awareness of most investigators of the difficulties involved and to their consequent efforts to make successive intervals on the rating scales roughly equivalent. Also of help is the fact that most experiments which find use for manipulating means of rating scales employ a fair number of Ss, which tends to average out the effects of unequal intervals.

The Interval Scale

The usefulness of measurement is considerably augmented if, in addition to ordering objects with respect to a quantitative attribute, one can state exactly what the magnitudes of the differences are that separate them. The extra ingredient required to elevate an ordinal scale to an internal scale is the all-important *unit of measurement*. With a unit of measurement available, it becomes possible to measure the actual magnitudes of the differences separating the measured objects.

We are all familiar with a large number of units of measurement. The yard and the meter, for example, are units of measurement for the quantitative variable *length*, as are the inch and the centimeter. The pound, the ounce, the kilogram, the gram—these familiar quantities are all units of measurement for weight (or mass). However, not all quantitative variables permit the establishment of such simple units of measurement. For example, a unit of penicillin was historically defined as the minimum amount of the antibiotic which, under specified conditions, would just inhibit the growth of a prescribed strain of the bacteria *Staphylococcus aureus*. And many other examples may be cited from pharmacology where the unit of measurement is defined in terms of biological effects which occur on test organisms (or organs) under closely specified conditions. Such units of measurement, quite obviously, are much more complex than the units of measurement first described. Still, before interval measurement of a quantitative variable becomes possible, a reasonable unit of measurement, however complicated, must be created. Some of the oldest and most perplexing problems attending attempts to measure psychological variables have to do with the critical issue of establishing units of measurement. Fechner's law, to be discussed later, is a case in point.

Returning to our earlier example for an illustration of an interval scale, suppose that a weighing scale becomes available to us which we are aware is miscalibrated by an unknown but constant amount, say x pounds, so that an object which by the scale weighs 10 lb actually weighs $10 + x$ lb. Assume that by use of the scale we find the weights of the six objects in pounds to be as follows: $O_1 = 1.0 + x$; $O_3 = 2.0 + x$; $O_6 = 4.0 + x$; $O_5 = 4.5 + x$; $O_2 = 5.5 + x$; $O_4 = 10.0 + x$. Although we still do not know the precise weights of the six objects, we now know more than their rank order; we now know how many pounds separate any pair of objects. Because the magnitudes of the intervals separating the measured objects are known, the objects are said to be measured on an interval scale.

Our ignorance of x, the "correction" factor, can be expressed in more general terms. Essentially, we do not know the location of the "true" zero point, or point of origin, of the attribute under measurement (weight). In essence, our measurements begin at an *arbitrary* zero point, namely, at x lb. It is as though we measured the above-water heights of a group of children standing in a wading pool. The arbitrary zero point in this case is determined by the depth of the water in the pool. And like the previous illustration, although these measurements reveal little about the absolute heights of the individuals, they are sufficient to specify precisely the differences in height separating the members of the group. There are instances in psychology, however, where the difficulty lies not so much with an *unknown* true zero point, but rather with the very *conceptualization* of a true or nonarbitrary zero point. For example, how one is to conceptualize zero intelligence, zero musical aptitude, or even zero pitch is not at all clear.

There are many useful relations between objects measured on an interval scale that are independent of (invariant with respect to) the location of the zero point. One important relation is the ratio of the magnitudes of the differences separating the measured objects. Consider, for example, the differences separating objects O_1, O_3, and O_6. The ratio

$$\frac{O_6 - O_3}{O_3 - O_1} = \frac{(x + 4.0) - (x + 2.0)}{(x + 2.0) - (x + 1.0)} = \frac{4.0 - 2.0}{2.0 - 1.0} = 2$$

Thus, irrespective of the value of x, O_6 is twice as far away from O_3 as O_3 is from O_1. This result is generalized in the statement that *with measurement on an interval scale, ratios of differences are independent of the zero point of the scale.*

A second important invariance of interval scales relates to permissible measures of central tendency. Knowledge of the differences in weight separating the six objects enables us to specify that the average weight of objects O_1, O_4, and O_6, call this $\bar{A}$, will be 1.0 lb greater than the average weight of O_2, O_3, O_5 ($\bar{B}$), *whatever the value of x might be.* The reason for this is that

$$\bar{A} = \frac{O_1 + O_4 + O_6}{3} = \frac{(x + 1.0) + (x + 10.0) + (x + 4.0)}{3}$$

$$= \frac{3x + 15.0}{3} = x + 5.0$$

$$\bar{B} = \frac{O_2 + O_3 + O_5}{3} = \frac{(x + 5.5) + (x + 2.0) + (x + 4.5)}{3}$$

$$= \frac{3x + 12.0}{3} = x + 4.0$$

Thus, $\bar{A} - \bar{B} = (x + 5.0) - (x + 4.0) = 1.0$, for any value of x. We may conclude, therefore, that with objects measured on an interval scale, comparisons of means are always permissible, and *differences between means are independent of the location of the zero point of the scale.*

It is not permissible, on the other hand, to make comparisons of the absolute magnitudes of objects. The ratio O_5/O_1, for example, will vary depending on the value of x, i.e., on the location of the zero point, as may be seen from its definition

$$\frac{O_5}{O_1} = \frac{x + 4.5}{x + 1.0}$$

If the magnitude of x happened to be $\frac{1}{6}$ lb, O_5 would weigh four times O_1; if on the other hand, x were $2\frac{1}{2}$ lb, O_5 would weigh only twice O_1.

An example of an interval scale in common use is the centigrade temperature scale. Although a true zero point of temperature can be conceptualized and is actually in use (the Kelvin scale), the zero point of the centigrade scale is quite arbitrarily set at the point at which water freezes. The arbitrariness of the location of the zero point in the centigrade scale, and in the Fahrenheit scale as well, has the usual consequences. Statements concerning ratios of absolute magnitude (e.g., solution A is twice as hot as solution B) are inadmissible with these scales because they depend on the location of the zero point. But as before, ratios of differences and differences between means are entirely appropriate calculations because they yield the same results wherever the zero point is arbitrarily assigned.

The preceding points may be summarized as follows: (1) To measure objects on an interval scale, it is necessary, in addition to ordering the objects with respect to magnitude, to measure the differences in magnitude that separate the objects from one another; to accomplish this, a unit of measurement is essential. (2) Interval scales do not possess a true (nonarbitrary) zero point either because a true zero point exists but is unknown or because conceptual problems have not yet allowed its establishment (e.g., zero intelligence). (3) Ratios of differences and differences between means are admissible calculations with interval measurement because they are independent of the location of the zero point.

The Ratio Scale

When in addition to a unit of measurement a true or nonarbitrary zero point exists, a level of measurement is achieved which is referred to as the "ratio scale." Over and above the calculations that are permissible with interval measurement, the ratio scale makes calculations based on the absolute magnitudes of the measured objects allowable. Thus, such statements as "A is twice as heavy as B," "twice as long," etc., are perfectly legitimate when they refer to measurements made on a ratio scale. It is evident that the geometric mean (Chap. 3) is based on absolute magnitudes; consequently, it is an appropriate measure of central tendency only on ratio scales. Ratio scales, then, provide maximum flexibility in permissible calculations and are for this reason the preferred class of measurement.

The measurement of our six objects would achieve the level of a ratio scale if the value of x were known, because then the weight measurements would start at the true, rather than at an arbitrary, zero point. This example, by the way, serves to point up the necessity of distinguishing between the measurability of a quantitative variable and the type of scale by which it is actually measured. Although the quantitative variable "weight" is quite obviously capable of ratio measurement, there are situations where, because of the exigencies of the moment, it may be measured on an interval, or even on an ordinal, scale. Similarly, some variables are capable of interval measurement, but current needs may be satisfied by measurement on an ordinal scale. If the ordinal, interval, and ratio scales are listed in order of increasing "strength," we may say that a quantitative variable can be measured on any scale with strength equal to or less than its measurability. The *measurability* of a quantitative variable may, in turn, be defined as the strongest scale of measurement currently feasible with the variable.

Discrete variables, as they were defined in Chap. 1, are always able to be measured by the ratio scale, because the unit of measurement is always specified (i.e., the object or thing to be counted) and the location of the zero point is nonarbitrary (i.e., zero of the objects or things counted). Hence number of siblings, number of digits immediately recalled, and number of heads that turn up in 10 tosses of a coin are all ratio measurable, because the units of measurement are well defined (a sibling, a recalled digit, the occurrence of a head) and the zero points are nonarbitrary (no siblings, no digits recalled, zero heads).

NONLINEAR FUNCTIONS

Linear functions, that is, functions of the form $Y = cX + k$, where c and k are constants, have been encountered repeatedly in previous chapters. In this section two *nonlinear* functions which play an important role in later developments are introduced—the *logarithmic* and the *power* functions. Readers wishing a more detailed treatment of the topics discussed in this section are referred to D. Lewis (1960).

Logarithmic Functions

First we define logarithms. Let X, any positive number whatever, be expressed as some arbitrary positive number, say b, raised to an appropriate power, i.e., $X = b^Y$. To illustrate, $100 = 10^2$. We express the relationship between X and Y by saying that Y *is the logarithm (or log) of X to the base b.* In mathematical terms,

$Y = \log_b X$. Thus, when 10 is used as the base, $2 = \log_{10} 100$; when 100 is used as the base, however, $1 = \log_{100} 100$, because $100 = 100^1$. Logarithms to the base 10 are in wide use and are called "common logs." Specification of the base is seldom included in common logs; thus, $\log 1000 = 3$. Other bases often used are 2 and e (approximated by 2.7183), but these need not concern us.

There are three operations with logs that we will soon encounter: (1) $\log_b (X \cdot Z) = \log_b X + \log_b Z$, (2) $\log_b (X/Z) = \log_b X - \log_b Z$, and (3) $\log_b X^n = n(\log_b X)$, or more simply $n \log_b X$.

The first rule of operation is based on the following. Let $X = b^Y$ and $Z = b^W$, where b is the logarithm base; consequently, $\log_b X = Y$ and $\log_b Z = W$. Now $X \cdot Z = (b^Y)(b^W)$ which, by the rules of exponents, becomes b^{Y+W}. It follows as a matter of definition, then, that $\log_b (X \cdot Z) = \log_b b^{Y+W} = Y + W = \log_b X + \log_b Z$.

The second rule is based on the consideration that $\log_b (X \cdot 1/X) = \log_b 1 = \log_b b^0 = 0$ (note: $b^0 = 1$). Then by rule 1, $\log_b (X \cdot 1/X) = \log_b X + \log_b 1/X = 0$; consequently, $\log_b 1/X = -\log_b X$. And it therefore follows that $\log_b (X/Z) = \log_b (X \cdot 1/Z) = \log_b X - \log_b Z$.

As a special case of the first rule, $\log_b X^2 = \log_b (X \cdot X) = \log_b X + \log_b X = 2(\log_b X)$. It is easy to see that rule 3 is obtained by generalizing on the preceding; for example, $\log_b X^3 = \log_b (X^2 \cdot X) = \log_b X^2 + \log_b X = 3(\log_b X)$, and so on.

GRAPHS OF LOG FUNCTIONS. If Y is a logarithmic function of X, the relationship between the two variables may be expressed as $Y = c \log X + k$, where, as in the equation of the linear function, c and k are constants. The graphs of several log functions are presented in Fig. 6-1. Only positive values of Y are considered.

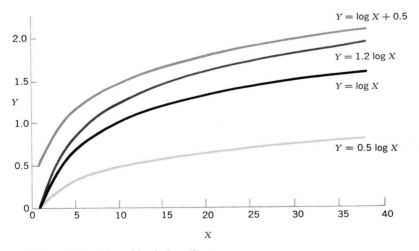

Fig. 6-1. Several logarithmic functions.

If one were given a set of X values and corresponding Y values, it would be difficult to determine from a plot of points on ordinary graph paper, that is, graph paper with "linear-linear" coordinates, whether X and Y were logarithmically related or not. This much is plain from Fig. 6-1. A convenient method of dealing with such questions is to plot Y against log X, rather than against X itself. For if Y is actually a logarithmic function of X, it is a *linear* function of log X. Hence a graph of Y against log X will produce a straight line. In Fig. 6-2 the functions of Fig. 6-1 have been plotted with log X, rather than X, serving as the independent variable. These straight lines have the form $Y = c(\log X) + k$, and it is easy to determine the constants c and k, thus specifying the log function completely.

As an illustration, suppose an experiment yielded the following data:

Y	X	Y	X
1.50	5	3.19	35
2.45	15	3.41	45
2.90	25	3.58	55

A plot of the preceding data points produces the graph of Fig. 6-3 and reveals a clearly nonlinear relationship between X and Y. To ascertain whether the relationship is logarithmic, we first transform X to log X (to the base 10):

X	LOG X	X	LOG X
5	0.699	35	1.544
15	1.176	45	1.653
25	1.398	55	1.740

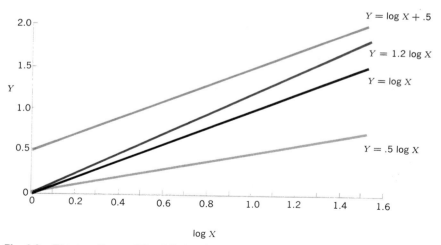

Fig. 6-2. The functions of Fig. 6-1 plotted in terms of log X rather than of X itself.

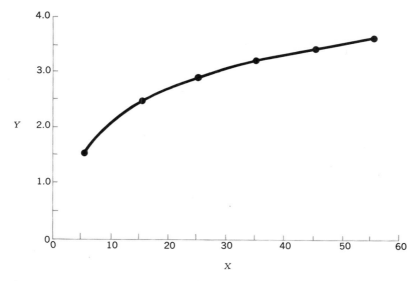

Fig. 6-3. A plot of six data points showing a nonlinear relationship between X and Y.

Next, Y is plotted against $\log X$, and as is apparent from Fig. 6-4, these points tend to fall on a straight line. We conclude, therefore, that the relationship between X and Y is reasonably described by the function $Y = c \log X + k$.

The final task is to determine the constants c and k, which may be accomplished by the method of averages (Chap. 5). First we obtain c.

$$1.50 = c(0.699) + k \qquad\qquad 3.19 = c(1.544) + k$$
$$2.45 = c(1.176) + k \qquad\qquad 3.41 = c(1.653) + k$$
$$\underline{2.90 = c(1.398) + k} \qquad\qquad \underline{3.58 = c(1.740) + k}$$
$$6.85/3 = c(3.273/3) + k \qquad 10.18/3 = c(4.937/3) + k$$

$$10.18/3 = c(4.937/3) + k$$
$$\underline{-\ [6.85/3 = c(3.273/3) + k]}$$
$$3.33/3 = c(1.664/3)$$
$$c = 3.33/1.664$$
$$c = 2.00$$

The constant k is found in the usual manner.

$$10.18/3 = 2(4.937/3) + k$$
$$\underline{6.85/3 = 2(3.273/3) + k}$$
$$17.03/3 = 2(8.210/3) + 2k$$
$$6k = 17.03 - 16.42$$
$$k = 0.10$$

The equation relating X and Y is, therefore, $Y = 2 \log X + 0.10$.

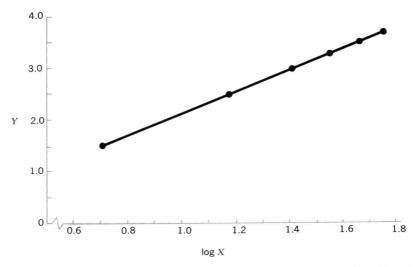

Fig. 6-4. The data of Fig. 6-3 are plotted with Y expressed as a function of log X rather than of X itself. Because the points fall on a straight line, X and Y are logarithmically related.

Use of semilogarithmic graph paper. A more rapid means of determining whether a nonlinear function is logarithmic is available through the use of semilogarithmic graph paper, which is graph paper having one axis marked off in equal (linear) units and the other in logarithmic units. As may be seen in Fig. 6-5, a logarithmic function plotted on "semilog" coordinates describes a straight line. The logarithmic scale on the abscissa is a pretransformation of the X variable to logs and saves us the trouble of this labor. Consequently, if a set of data points falls approximately on a straight line when plotted on semilog coordinates, a logarithmic function is a reasonable description of the relationship between the two variables involved.

Where one's purpose is also to determine the constants c and k of the logarithmic function which best fits the obtained data points, one may nevertheless first plot the data on semilog coordinates to determine quickly whether a logarithmic function is a reasonable description of the data. If so, one would then proceed to the logarithmic transformations, calculating the constants c and k by the method of averages, as illustrated above, or perhaps by the method of least squares.

Power Functions

In the function $Y = X^2$, the independent variable X is raised to a power, namely 2, to obtain the corresponding value of Y. Hence, this function is called a "power function." A more general equation for power functions is $Y = kX^c$, where k is a multiplicative constant. In the special case where $c = 1$, note that the power function reduces to a linear function. Several power functions are presented in Fig. 6-6. Observe that all functions having the same multiplicative constant intersect at the same point.

As with logarithmic functions, it would prove very difficult indeed to evaluate visually from a graph of data points on linear-linear coordinates whether the obtained data are adequately described by a power function. This task can be simplified in the following way. Let $Y = kX^c$. Taking logs on both sides of the equation, we obtain

$$\begin{aligned}
\log Y &= \log kX^c \\
&= \log k + \log X^c \\
&= c \log X + \log k
\end{aligned}$$

Consequently, $\log Y$ (not Y alone) is a linear function of $\log X$ (not X alone), with c the slope of the function and $\log k$ the Y intercept.

As an illustration, consider the following set of points derived from the function $Y = 0.2X^2$, which is one of the power functions graphed in Fig. 6-6.

Y	X	Y	X
0.2	1	3.2	4
0.8	2	5.0	5
1.8	3	7.2	6

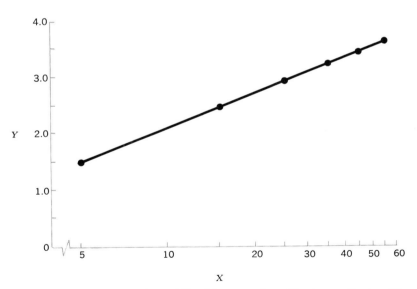

Fig. 6-5. A graph of the data of Fig. 6-3 on semilogarithmic coordinates. The logarithmic scale on the abscissa enables Y to be plotted as a function of $\log X$ without the actual transformation of X values to logarithms. Compare this figure with Fig. 6-4.

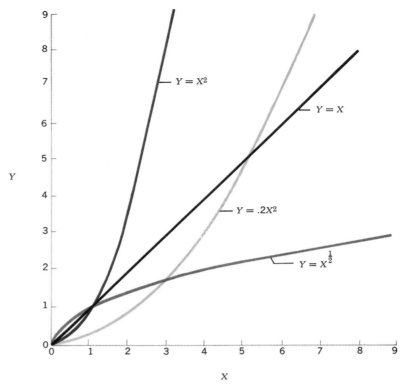

$Y = X^2$

$Y = X$

$Y = .2X^2$

$Y = X^{\frac{1}{2}}$

Fig. 6-6. Graphs of several power functions.

A plot of these points on linear-linear coordinates may be visualized by referring to the appropriate curve in Fig. 6-6.

Converting the X and Y values to logs, we obtain the following quantities:

LOG Y	LOG X	LOG Y	LOG X
−0.699	0.000	0.505	0.602
−0.087	0.301	0.699	0.699
0.255	0.477	0.857	0.778

The transformed points are plotted in Fig. 6-7, and it may be seen that they fall on a straight line. The slope of the line, as the student may verify, is 2, and the Y intercept is approximately −0.7. Recalling that the Y intercept gives log k, rather than k itself, the latter value may be obtained by finding the number whose logarithm is −0.7, which is to say we require the antilogarithm of −0.7. This quantity rounds off to 0.20. Thus, as we already know, the straight line in Fig. 6-7 derives from the power function $Y = 0.2X^2$.

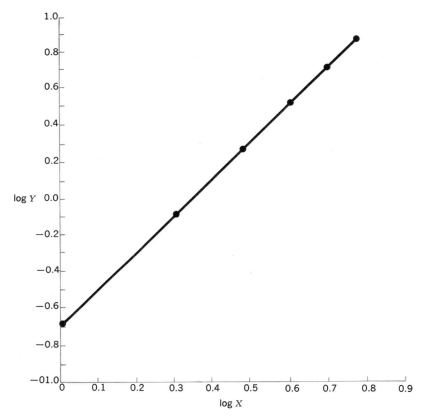

Fig. 6-7. A graph of six points derived from the function $Y = 0.2X^2$ plotted in terms of log X and log Y.

A set of empirical data points (plotted as logs) ordinarily will not fall on a perfectly straight line, even granting that the relationship between the two variables under study is some sort of power function. In actual practice, therefore, after converting the obtained data points to logs and noting whether the transformed values approximate a straight line, one obtains the constant c and k from a best-fitting straight line.

USE OF LOGARITHMIC GRAPH PAPER.   Logarithmic, or "log-log" paper, is graph paper with both axes ruled off in logarithmic units. Because logarithmically scaled axes automatically transform the plotted variables into log values, a graph of a power function on log-log paper will yield a straight line. One may take advantage of this fact to determine quickly and conveniently whether a power function reasonably describes a set of empirical data merely by plotting the data points on log-log coordinates and noting whether they tend to fall on

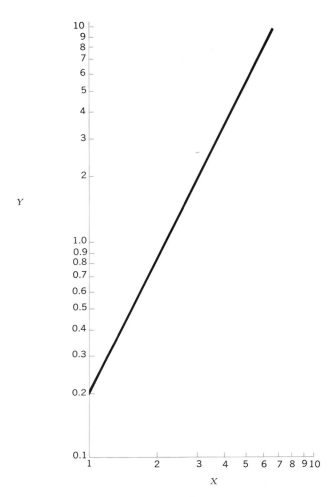

Fig. 6-8. A graph of the function $Y = 0.2X^2$ on log-log coordinates.

a straight line. The graph in Fig. 6-8 illustrates this point for the function $Y = 0.2X^2$.

EXERCISES

Graph paper with semilog or log-log coordinates is usually available in campus bookstores. The log scale is specified in terms of the number of "cycles" occurring along the logarithmically scaled axis, a cycle consisting of nine major subdivisions, logarithmically spaced and numbered from 1 to 10. The graph of Fig. 6-8 incorporates one cycle on the abscissa and two on the ordinate.

6-1. By employing both a semilog and a log-log plot, determine whether the following points were derived from a logarithmic or a power function:

Y	X	Y	X
4.2	2	16.4	30
6.7	5	19.0	40
9.5	10	21.2	50
13.4	20	23.3	60

Use 2-cycle semilogarithmic graph paper and logarithmic paper with 2 cycles on both axes.

6-2. Can the exponent of a power function be obtained from a graph of the function on log-log coordinates? If so, how?

6-3. Use the information obtained from Exercise 6-2 to find the equation of the function described in Exercise 6-1.

FECHNER'S LOGARITHMIC LAW

Having discussed the necessary preliminaries, we turn now to the major topic of this chapter, the measurement of sensation. The measurement of sensation presents a problem which separates into two issues. The first is: Can sensations be coaxed into measurement on anything stronger than ordinal scales? Everyone concedes that a set of tones of differing intensities, if sufficiently spaced, can be ordinally measured with respect to loudness, and the same degree of measurability would be allowed to such sensory experiences as brightness, heaviness, sweetness, and saltiness. But concession ends here; any claim that sensory experience is capable of being measured with greater exactness is frequently met with skepticism. That a set of sucrose solutions, for example, can be selected in such a way that the sensation of sweetness increases in equal increments with each solution, that solutions can be judged such that solution C is twice as sweet as solution B and B twice as sweet as solution A—these are possibilities which are often discounted out of hand. Hence our first problem concerns whether, and by what means, sensory experience can be measured on scales having the properties of interval and ratio measurement.

If we grant that such measurement is possible, a second, more theoretical, question arises. Is there a single "law" that adequately describes how the magnitudes of sensations are related to the intensities of the initiating stimuli? The pressure (P) of a fixed quantity of gas is proportional to the volume (V) within which it is contained, other things being constant. Within limits, this relationship, which may be expressed as $P = cV$, holds for a very wide range of gases. Is there, analogously, a law that relates the magnitudes of sensations (R_s) to the magnitudes of the initiating stimuli (S), a law that applies to a wide range of sensory dimensions?

Fechner decided both questions in the affirmative—and with a single stroke. The general law he proposed was that the magnitude of a sensation grows in proportion to the logarithm of the initiating stimulus, i.e., $R_s = c \log S$.

Derivation of Fechner's Law

It will be recalled from Chap. 5 that, according to Weber's law, the size of a difference limen (DL) is proportional to the magnitude of the standard stimulus (S_t) employed in its determination; symbolically, $DL = cS_t$, or $DL/S_t = c$. Recall also that two stimuli separated by 1 DL give rise to sensations that, on the average, are 1 JND apart (cf. Fig. 5-13). With these two notions as a starting point, Fechner arrived at the conclusion that the law relating sensation and stimulus was $R_s = c \log S$. The manner by which Fechner arrived at this interesting result is sketched in the following simplified version of Fechner's reasoning.

If the validity of Weber's law is assumed, the magnitudes of stimuli located 1, 2, and 3 DLs above the absolute limen (AL) can be calculated easily. The task is diagramed in Fig. 6-9, where the corresponding JNDs are also indicated. Stimulus S_0 is the AL and elicits the threshold sensory response R_0; S_1 is a stimulus 1 DL above S_0 and evokes a modal sensory response, R_1, which is 1 JND above R_0; stimulus S_2 is 2 DLs above S_0, and so on.

According to Weber's law, $DL = CS_t$, where, for convenience, we let C rather than c indicate the multiplicative constant. It therefore follows that

$$S_1 = S_0 + CS_0$$
$$= S_0(1 + C)$$

By the same reasoning,

$$S_2 = S_1 + CS_1 = S_0(1 + C) + C \cdot S_0(1 + C)$$
$$= S_0(1 + C)(1 + C) = S_0(1 + C)^2$$

Continuum of the physical stimulus

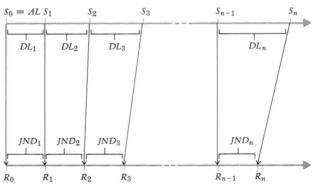

Continuum of the corresponding sensory response

Fig. 6-9. A representation of the relationship between DLs and their associated JNDs (see text).

and

$$S_3 = S_2 + CS_2 = S_0(1 + C)^2 + C \cdot S_0(1 + C)^2$$
$$= S_0(1 + C)^2(1 + C)$$
$$= S_0(1 + C)^3$$

Consequently, the stimulus that is 3 DLs above threshold, or the stimulus that evokes a modal sensory response that is 3 JNDs above threshold, has the value $S_0(1 + C)^3$. Generalizing this result, we can state that, assuming that Weber's law is true, a stimulus that is n DLs above threshold has the value $S_0(1 + C)^n$, i.e., $S_n = S_0(1 + C)^n$. Conversely, given an arbitrary stimulus S_i, we can determine the number of DLs occurring between it and S_0 by calculating the number r that satisfies the equation $S_i = S_0(1 + C)^r$.

We are free to express the last equation in terms of logarithms:

$$\log S_i = \log [S_0(1 + C)^r]$$
$$= \log S_0 + \log (1 + C)^r$$
$$= \log S_0 + r \log (1 + C)$$

from which it follows that

$$r = [1/\log (1 + C)] \cdot (\log S_i - \log S_0)$$
$$= [1/\log (1 + C)] \cdot \log (S_i/S_0)$$

and

$$r = c \log (S_i/S_0) \tag{6-1}$$

where c is a constant defined as $1/\log (1 + C)$.

Equation 6-1 enables us to determine how many DLs any stimulus lies above threshold by solving the equation for the given stimulus. As a concrete illustration, suppose it were established for a group of Ss that the AL for the loudness of a 1,000-Hz tone was 100 stimulus units, and suppose $C = 0.10$. The constant c then turns out to be 24.15 (i.e., $1/\log 1.10 = 24.15$). With a stimulus of 121 units, equation 6-1 tells us that this stimulus lies 2 DLs above threshold, because $24.15(\log 121/100) = 24.15(0.0828) = 2.00$. The same result may be obtained without the use of the equation, of course, simply by noting that $0.10(100) = 110$ and $0.10(110) = 121$.

The importance of equation 6-1 lies not in its use as a simplifying calculational device, however; rather, it lies in the fact that, granting certain assumptions, this equation may be interpreted as a means of measuring sensations on ratio scales. As we have just seen, solving equation 6-1 for a particular stimulus, say S_i, yields a number which, assuming the validity of Weber's law, indicates the number of DLs that separate S_i from S_0, the absolute limen. But because of the conception that there is a corresponding JND on the continuum of the sensory response associated with each *DL*, the number produced by equation 6-1 also indicates the number of *JND*s intervening between the threshold response, R_O, and the modal sensory response evoked by S_i. Now if all *JND*s along a specific sensory dimension *evoke equal increments in sensation*, this number should be an accurate reflection of the magnitude of the sensation elicited by S_i. This is the situation depicted in Fig. 6-9, where the *JND*s (but not the *DL*s) are represented as equal. On this assumption we should expect that if one stimulus were 10 *JND*s above threshold and another were superliminal by only 5 *JND*s, the first stimulus would evoke a sensation twice the magnitude of that elicited by the second. Thus, the assumption that a *JND* added anywhere along a sensory dimension adds an equal increment to sensation provides us with a unit of measurement, namely the *JND*, with which to mark off the magnitude of sensations. Further, R_O, the sensory response evoked by the absolute limen, S_O, is assumed to be a close approximation to the absolute zero point of a sensory dimension. As we recently learned, a unit of measurement and an absolute zero point are the essential requirements of ratio measurement. Consequently, granting the previous assumptions, equation 6-1 provides a "ruler" by which the magnitude of sensations, in *JND*s, may be measured along any sensory dimension for which Weber's law holds.

Altering equation 6-1 so as to make this interpretation explicit, we finally arrive at Fechner's law: $R_s = c \log S$, where R_s is the magnitude of the sensation in *JND* units and S is the eliciting stimulus expressed in units of the absolute limen, i.e., $S = S_i/S_O$.

To recapitulate briefly, as a ratio scale of sensory magnitude, Fechner's law involves at least three important assumptions: (1) that the *JND* may legitimately be used as a unit of measurement, (2) that R_O is a valid sensory absolute zero point, and (3) that Weber's law is an accurate generalization of how the size of the *DL* is related to the magnitude of S_i. It is quite possible for Weber's law to be valid and Fechner's law to be false, as would be the case if 3, but not 1, held true. On the other hand, Weber's law could be totally false and yet it would be possible to measure sensations on ratio scales if 1 and 2 were tenable. In this event, however, R_s could not be calculated from equation 6-1; rather its evaluation would have to be by empirical determination, that is, by experimentally counting off the number of *JND*s located between S_O and the initiating stimulus.

EXERCISES

6-4. An experimenter wishes to determine for a group of Ss the values of six tones that lie at 5, 10, 15, 20, 25, and 30 *JND*s above the loudness threshold. To accomplish this he first locates the *AL*. Then, employing the method of constant stimuli, he finds successive *DL*s and ultimately establishes that the values of the six stimuli are 31.7, 50.2, 79.6, 126.2, 200.0, and 317.0 units, respectively.

(a) Does Weber's law hold over the stimulus values explored? (Hint: Equation 6-1 may be expressed as $r = c \log S_i - c \log S_o$.)

(b) What is the value of the $AL(S_o)$?

(c) Find the value of C, the Weber ratio.

(d) Do the present data support Fechner's law?

Evaluation of Fechner's Law

Fechner's law has been found wanting on at least two counts. In the first place, support is lacking for its foundation, Weber's law. We saw in Chap. 5 that Weber's law has limited generality, and particularly for weak and strong stimuli it can be grossly in error. Consequently, even if the *JND* were a legitimate unit of measurement, summating *JND*s by means of Fechner's law may incur serious error.

The second weakness is in the assumption that a *JND* added anywhere along a sensory continuum adds a constant increment to sensation magnitude. This is an assumption that, at first thought, might not appear capable of empirical test. And yet it is. As already mentioned in the answer to Exercise 6-4d, a stimulus evoking a sensory response 10 *JND*s above threshold should, if each *JND* contributes an equal increment to sensation, be judged twice the apparent magnitude of a stimulus whose corresponding modal sensory response is only 5 *JND*s beyond threshold. Or, conversely, the second stimulus ought to be judged half as loud as the first. Unfortunately for Fechner's law, however, there is a wide range of sensory modalities for which correspondence between numbers of *JND*s and perceived sensory magnitude does not occur, disconfirming the central assumption that the *JND* adds a constant increment to sensation. To describe these modalities further requires a distinction between *prothetic* and *metathetic* sensory continua.

PROTHETIC VERSUS METATHETIC CONTINUA. "Perceptual continua divide themselves into two general classes. . . . The nature of this division is suggested in a general way by the traditional dichotomy between quantity and quality. Continua having to do with *how much* belong to . . . Class I, or prothetic; continua having to do with *what kind* and *where* (position) belong to Class II, or metathetic. Class I seems to include, among other things, those continua on which discrimination is mediated by an additive or prothetic process at the physiological level. . . . Class II includes continua on which discrimination is mediated by a physiological process that is substitutive, or metathetic. An example is pitch, where we progress along the continuum by substituting excitation for excitation, i.e., by changing the locus of excitation [Stevens, 1957, p. 154]."

In a general way, then, prothetic continua are modalities in which the sensory experience retains a rather constant quality while changing in intensity with changes in the magnitude of the applied stimulus. Examples of such dimensions are loudness, brightness, cold, warmth, sweetness, saltiness, apparent time duration, apparent length, smoothness, and perceived electric shock. On metathetic dimensions, on the other hand, changes in the magnitude of the initiating stimulus—if indeed the term "magnitude" applies to either the stimulus or the sensory aspects of these continua—often alters the basic quality of the experience. Thus the pitch of two tones differing in frequency may be experienced as different in kind rather than simply in the magnitude of the "pitchness." The apparent inclination of lines is another instance of metathetic continua, and quite plainly the sensations evoked by lines of varying angles of inclination differ more with respect to quality of sensation than magnitude.

Still, the distinction between the two types of sensory continua is not always easy to make on the basis of the previous criterion. If the distinction is at all important, there will be functional differences between the two classes of continua, and in the final analysis whether a sensory dimension falls into Class I or Class II will depend on how it squares with these functional criteria.

According to Stevens (1957), one such functional criterion is the "size" of the *JND*. On prothetic continua, the *JND* does *not* add a constant increment to sensation. Contrary to Fechner's assumption, the increment in the magnitude of a sensation provided by an added *JND* increases systematically with each successive *JND*. As illustrated by Exercise 6-4d, if S were required to compare the difference in loudness produced by the first pair of stimuli (31.7 and 50.2 units) and the last pair (200.0 and 317.0 units), he would judge the latter difference to be greater although *both* pairs are separated by 5 *JND*s. On metathetic continua, however, the *JND* is thought to behave more in accordance with Fechner's assumption. The evidence of this, however, is scanty and conflicting (cf. Warren & Warren, 1963). Perhaps the best that can be said is that if a dimension yields roughly equal *JND*s, it is likely to be metathetic.

Although not relevant for our immediate purposes, it is of interest that another functional criterion offered by Stevens centers on the time error (Chap. 5), whose occurrence is thought to be restricted to prothetic continua. However, this generalization too has been challenged (Warren & Warren, 1963).

The conclusion that seems warranted from the foregoing is that sensory scales based on summated *JND*s achieve their greatest validity when *JND*s (by means of *DL*s) are summated *empirically* on metathetic continua. The shortcomings of Fechner's law are that (1) *JND*s, however the associated *DL*s are determined, do not add an equal increment to sensation along prothetic continua; (2) on metathetic continua, where the assumption of equality of the *JND* is more likely to hold, Weber's law may be an inaccurate means of determining successive *JND*s (by means of *DL*s); and (3) the assignment of the *AL* as the origin of the sensory scale is, as we saw in the last chapter, an assumption of dubious merit.

As a final observation, our discussion of Fechner's law has been tied to the simplest version of Weber's law, i.e., $DL = cS_t$. A more general treatment of Fechner's law, particularly as it relates to an expanded class of Weber "functions," is provided by Luce and Edwards (1958).

PSYCHOPHYSICAL SCALING METHODS

Because summating *JND*s is not a generally adequate method of producing interval and ratio scales of sensation, we should now consider alternative scaling procedures. There are a considerable number of diverse scaling methods in existence, accompanied by an even greater diversity of nomenclature. We shall restrict ourselves to the "direct" methods and adjust nomenclature when necessary for the sake of uniformity. Later in the chapter we will deal with the distinction between direct and indirect methods and describe two of the latter in brief. A more complete listing of scaling methods may be found in Stevens (1958). Guilford (1954) and Torgerson (1958) are detailed sources which approach our topic at a more advanced level, and a thoroughly mathematical treatment has been presented by Luce and Galanter (1963). Finally, an account of many of the topics of this chapter in terms of adaptation-level theory is provided by Helson (1964).

Two classes of "response procedures" are generally possible in psychophysical scaling experiments. The first consists of *estimation* procedures: S is presented with one or more stimuli and gives an estimate, verbally or otherwise, of the magnitude of the sensation(s) elicited by the stimulus or stimuli. One characteristic of scaling methods that employ estimation procedures is that the stimuli presented to S remain fixed throughout the experimental session.

In the second class of response procedures, S, by varying stimuli at his disposal, is required to produce in himself a sensation or sensations which fulfill certain criteria specified by E. They are therefore termed "production procedures." In some instances E actually adjusts the variable stimuli on S's instructions. Obviously, production procedures require stimuli that can be easily varied along the relevant physical dimension.

A second important aspect of psychophysical scaling procedures is the type of judgment secured from S. He may be required to judge the difference between sensations, their absolute magnitudes, their relative magnitudes, or other aspects. Many of the psychophysical scaling methods can be classified in terms of the response procedure employed and the judgment required of S; this is the method of classification we shall adopt.

We will not be concerned in what follows with ordinal scaling methods, that is, with psychophysical scaling methods that yield sensory scales with only the properties of ordinal measurement. Because sensation is most often monotonically related to its relevant stimulus dimension, the construction of ordinal scales of sensation presents no problems. We address ourselves to the more difficult task of devising sensory scales that achieve the level of interval or ratio measurement.

Direct Methods for Constructing Interval Scales of Sensation

Four important methods of constructing sensory scales with interval properties are obtained by pairing estimation and production procedures with either *category* or *interval judgments*. Interval judgments are judgments about the magnitude of the intervals separating two or more sensations. In a category judgment, on the other hand, S places a sensation in one or more categories (classifications) previously specified by E. The resulting four methods are *category estimation, category production, interval estimation,* and *interval production*.

CATEGORY ESTIMATION. In category estimation, or category "rating," as this method is often called, S is given a set of equally spaced categories labeled by numbers, or less often by adjectives, and required to place each of a series of stimuli, presented singly, into one of the available categories. So that S will have an idea of the range of stimuli which he will encounter, often he is initially presented with an example of a stimulus that should fall in the first category and one that should fall in the last.

This is how Ss were instructed in a representative scaling experiment employing the method of category estimation:

> They were told that this was an experiment to find out how people judged the loudness of noise, and that they were to make 60 judgments using an 11-point scale. They were then given the softest stimulus and told that it should be called "1"; then they heard the loudest stimulus and were told that it should be called "11." They were instructed to assign to each stimulus that number from 1 to 11 that best matched the apparent loudness. . . . (Galanter & Messick, 1961, pp. 364–365.)

A scale relating the psychological continuum to the physical continuum is derived from Ss' estimates by calculating the mean category rating of each stimulus value. Normally, the mean category ratings are plotted on a graph and connected by a smooth curve, as in Fig. 6-10, which depicts an 11-category scale of apparent length obtained by Stevens and Galanter (1957).

A word about terminology. It will be recalled that a plot of percentage of detection responses ("yes," "greater than," etc.) against stimulus magnitude was termed a "psychometric function," a term which is attributed to Urban (1908). A graph relating sensation *magnitude* to stimulus magnitude is usually called a "psychophysical function." This is something of an anomaly because the psychometric function is far less appropriate for the task of measuring psychological quantities than the psychophysical function. Attempting to reverse the referents of these two terms would probably cause too much confusion. Stevens (1965) has suggested that the term "poikilitic" (meaning scatter or variation) function replace psychometric function, as a more accurate label. To avoid complications, we will stay with the common terminology.

Returning to the psychophysical function shown in Fig. 6-10, note that apparent length is not linearly related to physical length; that is, equal increases in physical length do not necessarily result in equal increments in perceived length. Later we shall see that it is questionable whether a dimension such as

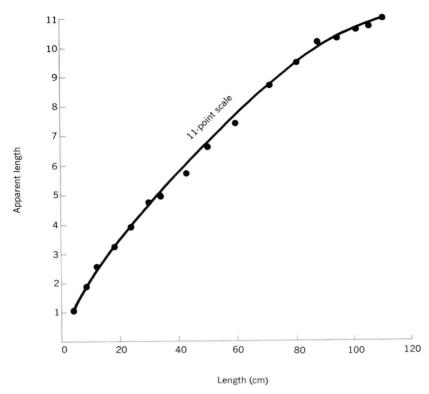

Fig. 6-10. An 11-category scale of apparent length obtained by the method of category estimation. (SOURCE: S. S. Stevens and E. H. Galanter. Ratio scales and category scales for a dozen perceptual continua. *Journal of Experimental Psychology,* 1957, **54,** 377–411. Copyright 1957 by the American Psychological Association and used by permission.)

apparent length is scaled most appropriately by the four methods described in this section, but for the present we will avoid this issue.

CATEGORY PRODUCTION. Category production requires that S adjust a stimulus until he perceives it to fall into a category called for by E. Consider the following illustration. E presents S with a white-noise stimulus of low intensity and informs him that the loudness of this stimulus is to be assigned the number 1; a much more intense stimulus is then presented, and its loudness is assigned the number 7. The range of loudness to be employed thus defined, S is then instructed to vary the intensity of the white noise until its loudness corresponds to an integer in the interval 1 through 7. The seven categories (1, 2, . . . , 7) are called for in a quasi-random order, and S makes several judgments for each category. Labels other than numbers may be used to designate the various categories.

One advantage of category production over category estimation is that with the former method S is free to adjust the stimulus until it appears to correspond closely to the category called for by E. With category estimation, on the other hand, a given stimulus might be perceived by S to fall between two categories, but he is nevertheless constrained to place it in one category or the other. An obvious disadvantage of the production method is that the stimulus dimension which is scaled must be capable of easy manipulation by S (or E). Furthermore, when S adjusts the variable stimulus, the method of manipulation itself may introduce a bias into S's judgments (Stevens & Poulton, 1956).

Data obtained with the method of category production are arranged into an interval scale of sensation in much the same way as described for the method of category estimation. Because in a sense the independent and dependent variables are now reversed—the category rating in the present method is the independent rather than the dependent variable—average values are calculated for the various stimuli judged by Ss to have the same category ratings. The resulting data points are plotted on a graph much like that which appears in Fig. 6-10.

INTERVAL ESTIMATION. The method of interval estimation requires S to render judgments about the sensory intervals separating groups of stimuli presented to him by E. As an illustration, suppose S is required to lift three weights (one at a time) and estimate the perceived differences in heaviness of the three weights. He could accomplish this by giving numerical estimates of the differences in perceived heaviness or by nonnumerical means, such as adjusting a movable slider between two fixed points until the two intervals on the linear scale correspond to the differences in the perceived heaviness of the three weights (Stevens, 1957).

In a word, the essential characteristic of interval estimation is that S makes judgments about the magnitude of *differences* between sensations. He is called upon to judge *directly* the magnitude of a sensation difference or, perhaps more exactly, a difference between sensations. Consequently, if one obtains a set of such judgments for a group of Ss exposed to a number of different weights, it should be possible to construct an interval scale on the psychological dimension of heaviness because, presumably, the differences in perceived heaviness separating adjacent weights are known.

As a concrete example, suppose that 10 Ss are presented with four weights, call these A, B, C, and D in increasing order of heaviness, and two movable sliders on a bar 50 in. long. The Ss are instructed to heft the weights and adjust the two sliders until the three intervals on the linear scale, defined by the two movable sliders and the two end points, correspond to the differences in heaviness experienced among the four weights.

The size of the intervals marked out on the bar constitute the basic data. Suppose that the mean length of the interval representing the difference between weights A and B is 12 in. Suppose further that 14 in. is the size of the mean interval representing the difference between weights B and C, and that, finally, this same quantity is 24 in. for the distance between weights C and D. Armed with these results, we could conclude with some justification that, on the average, the difference in heaviness experienced between weights C and D (represented by 24 in.) was twice that experienced between weights A and B (represented by 12 in.). Beyond statements of this nature, however, we could not go. It is obvious, for example, that we could not legitimately conclude that weight B was perceived as 12 times heavier than weight A. As with the category procedures, the interval methods are most appropriate for constructing sensory scales having the properties of interval measurement.

INTERVAL PRODUCTION. Interval production is better known by the terms "equisection" and "bisection," which are actually special cases of the present scaling method. As the name suggests, interval production is a procedure in which S is called upon to separate a set of variable stimuli into intervals specified by E. Because E commonly requires that the intervals be equal, the more specific term equisection is often employed in place of interval production; in the still more special case where only two equal intervals are to be produced by S—by adjusting a single variable stimulus between two fixed stimuli—the term bisection applies.

The construction of a scale from data obtained by interval production closely follows the procedure employed with the method of interval estimation. Imagine, for example, that a group of Ss has divided a sensory segment into five equal parts, adjusting four variable stimuli between two fixed stimuli until the five sensory intervals separating the six stimuli appear to be equal. Let us suppose that the arithmetic means of the settings of the variable stimuli are 35.1, 42.0, 50.2, and 60.5 units; let the lower and the upper stimuli be 30.0 and 75.0 units, respectively. A plot of these points, connected by a smooth curve, appears in Fig. 6-11.

The psychophysical function presented in Fig. 6-11 was constructed in the following way. The lower fixed point, the 30.0-unit stimulus, was arbitrarily plotted opposite a major divisional marking of the ordinate. The second value, 35.1 units, was plotted against the next major divisional marking, an assignment that also was arbitrary except for the constraint that the position on the ordinate assigned the present stimulus be higher than that assigned the 30.0-unit stimulus. It then follows that the remaining four stimuli must be assigned positions on the ordinate at successive major divisional markings, because we require that equal linear distances on the ordinate—which represents the psychological continuum—correspond to the presumably equal sense distances separating the six scaled stimuli.

To complete the sensory interval scale, one need only affix a numerical scale to the ordinate of Fig. 6-11. Any arrangement is appropriate that assigns equal numerical increments to equal linear increments. For example, the numbers assigned to the major divisional markings might be, reading from the bottom up, 10, 20, 30, 40, 50, and 60; or 10, 11, 12, 13, 14, and 15; or any other arithmetic progression.

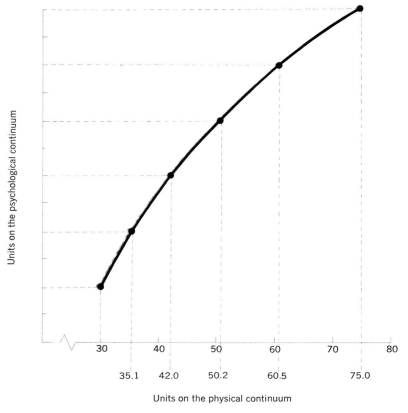

Fig. 6-11. A hypothetical sensory scale constructed by the method of equisection. The numerical scale on the ordinate may be any arithmetic progression (see text).

SOME COMMON FEATURES OF THE "PARTITION" METHODS. Let us now look at some of the common features of the preceding four methods. One property shared by the two category and the two interval methods is that S is required, directly or indirectly, to provide judgments about sensory *intervals*. The task of S is to "partition" a portion of a sensory continuum into equal segments, either by placing stimuli into categories separated by equal sense distances or, more directly, by rendering judgments about the sensory intervals themselves which separate the members of a set of stimuli. Because the final goal in both cases is the partitioning of the sensory continuum into equal sense distances, the scales elaborated by the four methods are often referred to collectively as "partition scales." For convenience the methods themselves will be called "partition methods."

Despite the close similarity between the category and the interval methods, there are notable differences. One difference is in the focus of S's judgments.

In the category methods S makes evaluations based on the perceived (relative) magnitude of the stimuli that are presented to him; in the interval methods S attends more directly to the *differences* between perceived magnitudes than to the magnitudes themselves. There are functional differences too. Sensory scales having ratio properties often find themselves in better agreement with interval scales of sensation that have been constructed from the interval methods than with like scales derived from category estimation or category production (e.g., Stevens & Guirao, 1962).

Another common feature of the category and interval methods is that, because of the lack of a zero point as a fixed point of reference and because in both classes of methods S is not called upon to make judgments concerning ratios of apparent magnitudes, these methods are largely limited to the production of interval scales of sensation. By altering S's assigned task so that his judgments take into account a "true" zero point or by having S judge *ratios* of sensations rather than differences, one obtains data better suited to the construction of sensory scales having the properties of ratio measurement. We turn now to these direct methods, which also number four.

Direct Methods for Constructing Ratio Scales of Sensation

As with the partition methods, two response procedures, estimation and production, are employed in the scaling methods treated below. The judgments required of S are, however, more demanding than those encountered in the partition methods. One class of methods, the *ratio* methods, requires that S render judgments about the apparent ratios holding between two or more presented stimuli. A second class of methods, the *magnitude* methods, requires that S make judgments which are proportional to the magnitudes of the sensations evoked by a set of test stimuli. Because both classes of methods adopt either the estimation or the production mode of response, four types of procedures result: *ratio estimation, ratio production, magnitude estimation*, and *magnitude production*.

Although they are often referred to collectively as the magnitude methods, to avoid confusion we shall employ the term "proportionality methods" to refer to the four preceding psychophysical scaling methods. This term seems appropriate, because the aim of these methods is to construct scales whose numerical values are proportional to the sensations to which they refer. Correspondingly, the sensory scales which they produce will be called "proportionality scales." Magnitude methods shall be reserved as a collective term for the last two methods, and ratio methods for the first two. So much for terminology.

RATIO ESTIMATION. In ratio estimation, as the name implies, S's job is to judge the apparent ratios holding between two or more stimuli presented to him. For example, after hearing two tones differing in intensity, S reports what ratio the louder tone bears to the softer tone. In one variation, the *constant sum method*,

S is required to divide a fixed number of points, typically 100, between the two stimuli. The perceived ratio of the two stimuli is reflected in S's distribution of the 100 points; for example, a distribution of 25:75 implies that the more intense stimulus was perceived to have three times the magnitude of the less intense stimulus.

The direct estimate of ratios and the constant sum method were both employed by Baker and Dudek (1955), who were concerned with the consistency of the sensory scales produced by the two procedures. In one experiment, a series of nine test weights ranging from 108.5 to 919.8 g was presented to Ss in all possible pairings. The Ss divided 100 points between the members of each pair in a way that reflected the perceived ratio of the weights. In a second experiment Ss directly reported the apparent ratio of the two weights of a pair by stating what multiple the heavier weight was of the lighter. By converting these direct estimates of ratios to 100-point assignments—a ratio estimate of 3:1, for example, would be transformed to a point assignment of 75:25—the data obtained from the two experiments were made closely comparable.

The scales relating physical weight to apparent weight were constructed by obtaining estimates of the ratios separating the nine stimuli. To simplify matters, suppose that only three weights were employed; call these A, B, and C in increasing order of physical magnitude. Suppose that on the average the ratios B/A, C/B, and C/A were judged to be 2.10, 3.00, and 5.80, respectively. If stimulus A were assigned the value 1.00 on the *psychological* dimension, then, because $B/A = 2.10$, stimulus B would receive the value 2.10. Similarly, because $C/B = 3.00$, it follows that on the sensory scale, $C = 6.30$. However, we have not made use of the third ratio C/A, which, on the assumption that Ss are relatively consistent in their ratio estimates, can be made to yield an additional estimate of B/A and C/B.

The reasoning is simple. If you (C) have six times as much money as your friend (A), and your brother (B) has twice as much as A, clearly your money equals three times that of your brother. Algebraically, $(C/A)/(B/A) = C/B$, or what is the same thing, $C/A \cdot A/B = C/B$. The ratio C/A provides us, therefore, with an additional estimate of B/A and C/B. Performing the required calculations, we find $C/A \cdot B/C = B/A = 5.80/3.00 = 1.93$; and $C/A \cdot A/B = 5.80/2.10 = 2.76$. Averaging the two estimates of B/A and C/B, we obtain 2.02 and 2.88, respectively. If, then, in our sensory scale we assign the number 1.00 to represent the perceived magnitude of weight A, a value of 2.02 would have to be assigned to stimulus B, and 5.82 (i.e., 2.02×2.88) to weight C. More generally, because our scale has been derived from ratio judgments and thus presumably has the properties of ratio measurement, if the number r is assigned to stimulus A, the numbers $2.02r$ and $5.82r$ must be assigned to B and C, respectively.

With nine test stimuli, the number employed by Baker and Dudek, there are eight estimates available for every ratio of adjacent weights. In general, with n test stimuli, the presentation of all possible pairs produces $n - 1$ estimates of each ratio of adjacent stimuli. The calculation of these ratios is not difficult, and detailed examples may be found in Guilford (1954, pp. 214–220) and Torgerson (1958, pp. 104–112).

Baker and Dudek found that although the scales of apparent heaviness constructed from the direct estimates of ratios and the constant sum method were of the same general form, there were considerable discrepancies among Ss' judgments of the heavier stimuli. When using the direct estimation procedure, Ss tended to overestimate the heavier weights much more than when the constant sum method was employed.

RATIO PRODUCTION.   Some of the earliest attempts to develop ratio scales of sensation made use of ratio production methods—in particular, the method of *fractionation* (e.g., Stevens & Volkmann, 1940). In fractionation S is presented with one of a set of standard stimuli and is required to adjust a variable stimulus until its apparent magnitude is some fraction, usually one-half, of the standard. From such judgments, secured for a number of different standard stimuli, a "halving" function is obtained, and from this a sensory scale is constructed which has ratio measurement properties.

As an illustration we shall consider an investigation performed by Guilford and Dingman (1954), who also worked with weights, a favorite stimulus dimension in psychophysical experiments because of the simplicity with which the physical stimulus dimension may be graded in intensity. Guilford and Dingman's primary interest was in comparing sensory scales of apparent heaviness obtained from ratio estimation—in particular the constant sum method—with like scales constructed from ratio production, more specifically, the method of fractionation.

In the fractionation experiment Ss were presented with one of several standard weights and were required to choose the stimulus which seemed half as heavy as the standard from a set of comparison weights. There were a total of nine different stimuli, ranging from 40 to 2,000 g, but because the range of stimuli was too extensive for all the weights to be housed within identical containers—a necessary control—the standard stimuli were divided into two sets of five stimuli each, one standard stimulus being represented in both sets. A different range of comparison weights accompanied the two sets of standard stimuli.

After each of the standards had been presented to the Ss and their "half" judgments obtained, the first step in processing the results was to find the medians of the half judgments for both sets of standard stimuli. A plot of these medians on log-log coordinates appears in Fig. 6-12. Observe how closely the points are approximated by the straight line. It will be recalled from an earlier section of this chapter that a set of points falling on a straight line on log-log coordinates may be described by a power function. In the present case, however, it is more convenient to express the relationship between the standard stimulus (S_t) and the stimulus judged to be half the magnitude of the standard (S_h) in terms of logarithms rather than in terms of S_t and S_h themselves. As determined by the method of least squares, the function relating S_t and S_h, the so-called "halving" function, turns out to be log $S_h = 1.0105$ log $S_t - 0.2699$.

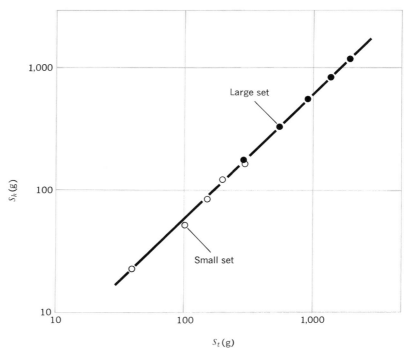

Fig. 6-12. A plot of the medians of the half judgments (S_h) on log-log coordinates. (SOURCE: J. P. Guilford and H. F. Dingman. A validation study of ratio-judgment metho ds. *American Journal of Psychology*, 1954, **67**, 395–410. Used by permission.)

Before proceeding to the construction of a sensory scale of apparent weight from the halving function, we must define the unit by which the psychological dimension is measured. One unit of apparent weight that has general acceptance is the *veg*, defined as the magnitude of apparent heaviness produced by lifting a 100-g weight (Harper & Stevens, 1948). Utilizing this unit of apparent weight, a first point on the sensory scale is immediately established: 1.0 veg corresponds to 100 g.

Further points are derivable from the halving function in the following way. The stimulus value corresponding to 2.0 vegs is that weight for which the 100-g weight is the half judgment. This value is easily obtained from Fig. 6-12 by graphic interpolation, or, more exactly, from the halving function itself. Employing the latter to determine the required stimulus value, we find: $\log 100 = 1.0105 \log S_t - 0.2699$. Consequently

$$\log S_t = \frac{2.0000 + 0.2699}{1.0105} = 2.2463$$

If we take the antilogarithm of the last quantity, $S_t = 176.3$, and therefore the standard weight of which 100 g would be judged to be one-half is 176.3 g.

It may be apparent how, by the very same procedure, values of the physical stimulus corresponding to 4, 8, 16, 32, and 64 vegs are derived. Carrying the calculation one step further, because 176.3 g corresponds to 2.0 vegs, the stimulus value for which 176.3 g constitutes the half judgment is the weight which is assigned the value of 4.0 vegs. The precise value of this weight is derived from the halving function by making the appropriate substitutions: $\log 176.3 = 1.0105 \log S_t - 0.2699$; $\log S_t = (2.24625 + 0.2699)/1.0105 = 2.4900$. Because the antilog of the last quantity is 309.0, the stimulus value of 309.0 g corresponds to 4.0 vegs.

By an inverse process one can find the weights corresponding to fractional parts of a veg. For example, by appropriate substitution in the halving function, one finds that a stimulus of 56.4 g (1.7511 in logs) is the stimulus judged to be half as heavy as a 100-g weight; consequently, 56.4 g is the stimulus value corresponding to 0.50 vegs.

When we have deduced a number of scale points by the preceding method —taking care not to extrapolate injudiciously from the range of test stimuli— a plot of these points connected by a smooth line defines the scale itself. Ten such points were calculated by Guilford and Dingman and are presented in Table 6-1.

As the student will later be asked to verify, a plot of the 10 points shows that the relationship between physical weight and apparent weight obtained by Guilford and Dingman with the method of fractionation is nicely described by

Table 6-1 10 Points of a (Veg) Scale of Apparent Weight Obtained from the Halving Function

VEGS	S_t (g)	LOG S_t
0.125	17.6	1.2454
0.25	31.6	1.4996
0.5	56.4	1.7511
1	100.0	2.0000
2	176.3	2.2463
4	309.0	2.4900
8	538.5	2.7312
16	933.1	2.9699
32	1607	3.2061
64	2754	3.4399

*SOURCE: J. P. Guilford and H. F. Dingman. A validation study of ratio-judgment methods. *American Journal of Psychology*, 1954, **67**, 395–410. Used by permission.

a power function. More specifically, if V represents the perceived heaviness of a lifted weight in vegs and S stands for the physical weight of the stimulus in grams, the function relating the first quantity to the second is $V = kS^c$, where k and c are constants.

In the same article, Guilford and Dingman presented four other scales of apparent weight, all constructed by the constant sum method. In every case the relationship between physical weight and apparent weight was adequately described by a power function, though there was some variation from scale to scale in the constants k and c. The significance of this finding will be discussed later.

Turning now to other features of the ratio production method, it may be apparent that fractionation need not be restricted to judgments of one-half. Other fractions, such as one-third and one-quarter, may be employed, though half judgments are probably easiest for most Ss. Also, the ratio estimate required of S need not be fractional; ratios greater than unity, such as two or three, may be employed. The name "multiplication" applies in such cases. But whether fractionation or multiplication is utilized in the method of ratio production, the construction of the final sensory scale follows much the same procedure as demonstrated above in detail. Such scales are presumed to have the properties of ratio measurement because the basic judgments from which they are derived are themselves ratio judgments.

MAGNITUDE ESTIMATION. Magnitude estimation is the simplest, the most direct, and currently the most widely used method of constructing sensory scales having ratio properties. The disarming simplicity of the method is probably the reason that its utilization, which could have come at any time at all after man learned to use numbers, was delayed until the last decade or so (Stevens, 1956).

To describe the essentials of this method in a sentence, Ss are presented with a series of test stimuli, one at a time, and are required to render *numerical* estimates which are *proportional* to the magnitudes of the sensations evoked by each stimulus; these numerical estimates are averaged, by medians or geometric means, to provide the points of the required sensory scale.

Our illustration of the method comes from a study by Stevens and Guirao (1962). A number of sensory scales were constructed by these investigators, but the one which will concern us here is a scale of apparent loudness of a 1,000-Hz tone developed by means of magnitude estimation. The instructions given the 10 Ss of the experiment follow:

> I am going to present a series of tones. Your task is to tell how loud these tones sound by assigning numbers to them. Call the first tone any number that seems to you appropriate.
> Your task is to assign numbers proportional to your subjective impression. For example, if a tone sounds 3 times as loud assign a number 3 times as large as the first. If it sounds $\frac{1}{5}$ as loud assign a number $\frac{1}{5}$ as large, and so forth. . . . (Stevens & Guirao, 1962, pp. 1466–1467.)

Seven tones, all 1,000 Hz but varying in intensity, were presented twice to each S in an irregular order. Hence, every S made a total of 14 judgments, a very brief task as psychophysical experiments go. The geometric mean (Chap. 3) of the 20 judgments available for each stimulus was calculated for the seven tones, and the resulting scale points were plotted on log-log coordinates. Before we present the data, however, it is necessary to digress momentarily for a brief description of the *decibel*, the conventional unit of auditory measurement. A detailed discussion of the decibel may be found in Stevens (1955).

Stated quite simply, the decibel is a dimensionless unit which expresses the ratio between two values of energy flow, or power, in logarithmic units. Algebraically $db_1 = 10 \log (S_1/S_0)$, where db_1 is the number of decibels that stimulus S_1 lies above the reference level S_0, with both S_1 and S_0 expressed in terms of energy flow or power. For example, in acoustical measurements, a standard reference level is 10^{-10} microwatt per cm^2, a value close to the threshold of hearing. Hence, an auditory stimulus having 0.001 microwatt of power per cm^2 is equal to 70 db, because $10 \log (10^{-3}$ microwatt per cm$^2/10^{-10}$ microwatt per cm$^2) = 10 \log (1/10^{-7}) = 70$.

The resemblance between the formula for calculating decibels and Fechner's law is apparent. Fechner's law asserts that the magnitude of the sensation elicited by a stimulus, say S_1, is given by the quantity $c \log (S_1/S_0)$, with S_0 as the absolute limen of the sensory modality in question. The formal similarity between the two expressions has caused needless confusion. The most important difference between the two is that the decibel has no psychological import whatever; it is simply a ratio between two quantities of energy flow expressed as a logarithm. Fechner's law, on the other hand, purports to show how sensation grows as a function of stimulus intensity; furthermore, the relevant stimuli need not be, and usually are not, expressed as energy flow.

Because decibels are logarithmic units, a plot of decibels on linear coordinates is equivalent to a plot of the original quantities on logarithmic coordinates. This point may be illustrated by noting that the logarithmically spaced quantities 100, 1,000, and 10,000 (dimension omitted), when expressed as decibels from the reference level of 10, become the arithmetically (equally) spaced quantities 10, 20, and 30.

This returns us to the magnitude estimation scale of apparent loudness constructed by Stevens and Guirao. The seven scale points previously described are plotted as open circles in Fig. 6-13. The logarithmic scaling of the psychological dimension, apparent loudness, is obvious, and because the unit employed on the abscissa is the decibel, the auditory stimulus dimension also is logarithmically scaled. It follows, therefore, that because the obtained scale points fall on a straight line, the function relating loudness to the intensity of the 1,000-Hz tone is, insofar as the present data are concerned, a power function. Thus, once again we find that a function of the form $R_s = kS^c$ adequately describes how the magnitude of a sensation grows with increasing intensity of the initiating stimulus.

Magnitude estimation may also incorporate an anchoring standard stimulus

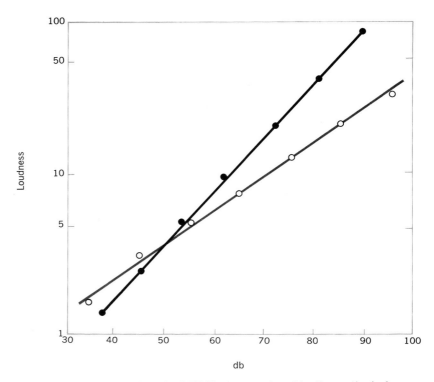

Fig. 6-13. Loudness scales of a 1,000-Hz tone produced by the method of magnitude estimation (open circles) and the method of magnitude production (filled circles). Since the linearly spaced units on the abscissa refer to decibels, in terms of the physical stimulus itself they correspond to log coordinates. Consequently, in both scales loudness is a power function of stimulus intensity. (SOURCE: S. S. Stevens and M. Guirao. Loudness, reciprocality, and partition scales. *Journal of the Acoustical Society of America,* 1962, **34,** 1466–1471. Used by permission.)

referred to as a "modulus." For example, in an experiment aimed at scaling the magnitude of the sensation evoked by electric shock in the form of a 60-Hz current passed through the fingers, the following instructions were given to the somewhat unfortunate Ss:

> I am going to present you with a series of currents of different intensities. Your task is to tell me how intense they feel by assigning numbers to them. The first intensity we will call "10." Your task will be to estimate the intensity of each stimulus in the series. Try to assign numbers proportional to your subjective impression of each stimulus. . . . (Stevens, Carton, & Shickman, 1958, p. 328.)

The modulus was then presented, followed in an irregular order by two presentations of each of the nine stimuli.

Among the advantages of using a modulus is that, in effect, it equates the size of the psychological unit used by the Ss, and therefore averaging may always be performed on the obtained data directly. On the negative side, certain biases in the use of numbers, such as "rounding" tendencies, are more likely to be averaged out if a stated modulus is omitted. The consensus now appears to be that its use should be avoided.

When the modulus accompanies each presentation of a test stimulus (e.g., Stevens, 1956), the method of magnitude estimation comes almost indistinguishably close to the method of ratio estimation. Indeed, in the special case that the modulus is assigned the number "1," the methods are identical. It may be justified, therefore, to limit the term "magnitude estimation" to those procedures in which the modulus, if it exists, does not accompany every test stimulus presentation, for the likelihood is greatest in these cases that S is basing his judgment on the magnitude of the sensation evoked by the test stimulus rather than on the ratio it forms with a second sensation.

We conclude our discussion of magnitude estimation with two points. First, we take note that in two of three relevant experiments reported by Stevens, Carton, and Shickman, apparent intensity of electric shock grew as a power function of the stimulating current. And second, we provide a partial listing of the sensory attributes that have been scaled by means of magnitude estimation: loudness of white noise (Stevens & Guirao, 1962); tonal volume (Terrace & Stevens, 1962); apparent brightness of visual stimuli (J. C. Stevens & Stevens, 1963); warmth and cold (J. C. Stevens & Stevens, 1960; J. C. Stevens & Marks, 1967); coffee (Reese & Stevens, 1960) and alcohol (Engen, 1965) odor; finger span (Stevens & Stone, 1959); apparent roughness of sandpaper (Stevens & Harris, 1962); apparent length of lines, apparent time duration, and apparent weight (Stevens & Galanter, 1957); intensity of salt solutions (McBurney, 1966).

In recent years magnitude estimation has been applied increasingly to the scaling of attributes for which no corresponding physical dimension is known, for example, musical preferences (Koh, 1965), occupational prestige (Perloe, 1963), and attitudes, which have ranged from the rated importance of Swedish monarchs to the seriousness of criminal offenses (cf. Stevens, 1966a). Later we shall have something to say about these last applications.

MAGNITUDE PRODUCTION. Magnitude production, the most recently invented scaling method of those treated in this chapter, has not seen a great deal of service as yet. In principle the use of a modulus with magnitude production is optional though its absence may entail certain practical disadvantages peculiar to the method. Specifically, without a modulus S may place his first adjustment too near the limits of the available stimulus range to allow sufficient freedom for later judgments. Our illustrative experiment includes a modulus.

Among other objectives, Stevens and Guirao (1962) wished to evaluate the consistency of sensory scales produced by magnitude estimation and magnitude production. We have already described how magnitude estimation was employed to construct a scale of loudness of a 1,000-Hz tone. We shall now describe how a similar scale was developed from magnitude production.

Ten Ss were instructed as follows:

> I am going to present a tone whose loudness will be called 10. Then I will present a series of numbers, one at a time. Your task is to adjust the tone until its loudness seems to you proportionate to the numbers I give you, remembering that the first stimulus was called 10. . . . (Stevens & Guirao, 1962, p. 1467.)

The tone presented first and assigned the number 10 had an intensity of 65 db. Following this, the numbers 1.25, 2.5, 5, 10, 20, 40, and 80 were given twice to each S in an irregular order. For each of the seven numbers the arithmetic average was computed. Note that because the decibel is a logarithmic unit, an arithmetic average of decibels is equivalent to performing a geometric average on the stimulus values from which the decibels were derived. It would take us too far astray to discuss the reasons why the geometric mean is the preferred method of averaging in some scaling construction and not in others. It is sufficient to state that where the variability of Ss' judgments (measured in *subjective* units) is relatively constant from one portion of the scale to another, ordinarily the arithmetic mean is the averaging method of choice. But where Ss' variability tends to be proportional to the magnitude of the sensations being judged, then the geometric mean, and sometimes the median, is a more appropriate measure of central tendency.

The seven scale points are plotted as filled circles in Fig. 6-13, and it is quite obvious that they too are well described by a straight line. Thus, the apparent loudness of a 1,000-Hz tone is a power function of the intensity of the auditory stimulus even when the sensory scale arises from magnitude production.

There is, however, an important difference between the loudness scales produced by magnitude estimation and magnitude production. As is quite plain from Fig. 6-13, the magnitude production scale is steeper than the corresponding magnitude estimation scale. It will be recalled from an earlier discussion of power functions that in a log-log plot, the slope of the straight line defining the power function is identical to the exponent c in the power function equation $Y = kX^c$. Consequently, though the relationship between loudness and stimulus intensity is a power function for both methods, magnitude production yields a somewhat larger exponent than magnitude estimation, the actual values being 0.7 and 0.5, respectively.

This disparity is an illustration of what has been called the "regression effect" in psychophysical judgments (Stevens & Greenbaum, 1966). When S attempts to match one variable to another, he tends to restrict the range of the variable that is under his control. The effect of this bias in the magnitude production method is to increase the slope of the psychophysical function, because the fixed range of numbers presented by E are spanned by a restricted range of S's settings. Magnitude estimation is less subject to this sort of bias and may even yield slopes that are flatter than they should perhaps be. It has been suggested by Stevens and Greenbaum that both methods be employed in an effort to obtain estimates of the lower and upper bounds of the exponent of the fitted power function.

The scales produced by magnitude estimation and magnitude production are held to have properties of ratio measurement because S provides estimates that are *proportional* to the magnitude of his sensations. The basic assumption of these methods is that S can faithfully report the magnitude of his sensations by means of numbers, and although there may be many subtleties and nuances to be observed, granting this assumption the construction of ratio scales of sensation becomes a simple and painless business. Though the validity and generality of the assumption that S can quantify his sensations with numbers have not yet been thoroughly assessed, some of the evidence now available is promising. We shall shortly consider this issue.

Summary of the Psychophysical Scaling Methods

A brief summary of the psychophysical methods discussed in this section follows. The four partition methods, category estimation, category production, interval estimation, and interval production, allow for the construction of scales of sensation with properties of interval measurement. The general accomplishment of these methods is that they partition sensory intervals into a series of equal sense distances. The category methods achieve this end by having S classify a set of stimuli into a sequence of categories separated by equal sense distances. The interval methods usually manage the partitioning by requiring S to produce stimuli that have the property that the differences between the sensations elicited by adjacent stimuli are equal (equisection) or less often by having S estimate the differences in the magnitudes of sensations produced by a set of test stimuli (interval estimation). Because judgments are not based on the ratios of sensations nor on their "absolute" magnitudes, partition scales are generally conceded to be interval scales of sensation at best.

The proportionality methods were devised to permit the construction of ratio scales of sensation. In the ratio methods—ratio estimation and ratio production—S literally judges the ratios holding between the sensations elicited by two or more stimuli. More simple and more direct are the magnitude methods— magnitude estimation and magnitude production—which require S to establish a relationship of proportionality between the magnitude of his sensations and ordinary numbers. Both classes of judgments produce proportionality scales which, under appropriate circumstances, appear to possess the characteristics of ratio measurement.

The degree of consistency obtainable among sensory scales constructed from the different scaling methods is a critical problem in psychophysical scaling. Stated from a somewhat less general point of view, what properties of a sensory scale, if any, are independent of the method from which the scale was constructed? We turn to this important problem next.

6-5. Imagine an experiment in which Ss are given the following instructions:
"In this experiment you will adjust stimuli to produce a scale of equal-appearing intervals. I will first present two tones. The loudness of the first will be called '1.' The loudness of the second will be called '7.'

"Then I will present a series of numbers from 1 to 7 in irregular order. You should regard these numbers as representing equal spacings along the scale, and your task is to adjust the tone so that its loudness corresponds to the number I have given you."

What is the scaling method being employed? Explain why it is not one of the other methods discussed in this section.

6-6. Plot the scale points obtained by Guilford and Dingman (Table 6-1) on semilog and log-log coordinates. To simplify matters, use only the six points ranging from 1 through 32 vegs. Observe that the semilog plot may either be a plot of the actual stimulus values on semilog paper or a plot of log S—obtainable from the table—on linear-linear coordinates. A similar option holds for the log-log plot, though if ordinary graph paper is used, the logarithm of the veg values will have to be looked up.

6-7. Using the method of averages, calculate the power function that best fits the six scale points plotted in Exercise 6-6.

6-8. Suppose that a set of five test weights, $W_1, W_2, \ldots, W_5$, receive the following scale values when measured by the method of magnitude estimation: 5, 10, 20, 35, and 50, respectively. Suppose also that the same stimuli are scaled by the method of category estimation—employing the categories 1, 2, . . . , 7—and let the mean category ratings of W_1 and W_2 turn out to be, in order, 1.5 and 2.0. If the category estimation scale is actually an interval scale of sensation and the magnitude estimation scale is in fact a ratio scale of sensation, what should the mean category ratings of the three remaining test stimuli be?

Consistency of Sensory Scales

Inevitably one must face the question of the degree to which sensory scales devised from different techniques or under somewhat different experimental conditions are consistent. Like other psychologists, psychophysicists must concern themselves with interactions, in their case interactions of sensory scales across scaling methods and other variables. To indicate some of the issues involved, consider the scale portrayed in Fig. 6-11. If we assert that the psychophysical function in that figure defines an interval scale relating the physical continuum to the corresponding psychological continuum, there are a number of implications which devolve upon us. In the first place, restricting ourselves to verification by means of the same method by which the presumed interval scale of sensation was constructed, in this case interval production, we should be prepared to accept the implication that if a number of Ss were asked to bisect the interval defined by the fixed stimuli 35.1 and 50.2 units, on the average they would adjust the variable stimulus to a value close to 42.0 units. Furthermore, if ours is an interval scale of reasonable generality, we would hope that if the same stimulus segment, i.e., from 30.0 to 75.0 units, were equisected by three rather than four variable stimuli, or by six or eight variable stimuli for that matter, substantially the same function as depicted in Fig. 6-11 would be obtained.

If the sort of checks just described verified our original scale, our confidence in the latter and in its "interval" properties would be bolstered. But are such checks sufficient? For some purposes they may very well constitute sufficient verification of the original scale. A more universal acceptance, however, would seem to require a more comprehensive validation.

Suppose, for example, that the method of magnitude estimation were used to construct a scale over the same stimulus segment scaled in Fig. 6-11. If the resulting scale departed significantly from the one obtained by interval production, which would be the "true" scale? If the same desk measured by two rulers had different lengths, surely one would resolve the discrepancy by discarding the inaccurate ruler. Unfortunately, however, the corresponding task is far more complex when dealing with the measurement of sensory quantities: there is no true ruler.

Perhaps the notion that any acceptable set of scaling methods ought to lead to similar, if not identical, scales is a naive expectation. Unlike a cash register, a human being does not ring up appropriate numbers in response to stimulus input. We saw (Chap. 5) that in the far simpler detection situation, S's performance was usually an amalgam of sensitivity and response criterion. Surely we must be prepared for at least this much "contamination" in the input-output relations from which sensory scales are devised. The important, and very difficult, problem lies in the discovery of the psychological processes that contribute to this contamination or "noise" and in the invention of means for their elimination or evaluation.

In the last few years efforts to solve this problem have been many. Several studies have been devoted to comparing sensory scales, or scale parameters, obtained with different scaling methods (e.g., Beck & Shaw, 1967; Donnelly & Rimoldi, 1967; Stevens & Greenbaum, 1966; Stewart, Fagot, & Eskildsen, 1967). Independent variables other than the scaling method have also come under intensive analysis (e.g., Eyman, 1967; Fagot, Eskildsen, & Stewart, 1966; Ross & DiLollo, 1968), particularly in the case of magnitude estimation (see Poulton, 1968, for a summary of the latter).

It is hoped that the outcome of these investigations will be a better understanding of how various factors operate to introduce biases into the different scaling methods, followed by the invention of techniques by which such biases might be eliminated or neutralized. To cite one illustration of how problems of this nature might be solved, it was long known that category scales can be heavily biased by the particular set of stimuli employed in the rating task. Pollack (1965) has shown that by employing what is known as "iterative" techniques, much of this bias can be eliminated. Also, we noted earlier that in the case of the magnitude methods, the regression effect so common in psychophysical judgments could be compensated for in part by employing both estimation and production procedures.

Though the problems standing in the way of the development of consistent sensory scales are formidable, there seems little doubt that continuing research will in some measure rescue us from the prospect of "local" scales that have little relevance outside the particular conditions under which they were constructed. Whether we will eventually have sensory scales that enjoy something of the exactness and universality of physical scales is another, and perhaps irrelevant, issue. Useful measurement by no means demands the precision of a micrometer. Knowledge concerning the general form of sensory scales can often be of value, even though a scale's parameter values may be closely coupled to particular experimental conditions. The next section illustrates this point.

STEVENS' POWER LAW

For almost 100 years the only noteworthy hypothesis relating magnitude of sensation to stimulus intensity was Fechner's law. Always mentioned in textbooks and discussed at length in most classrooms where psychophysics came under consideration, it was nevertheless known to have only limited application in a few situations and to be grossly in error in most. But as is usually true of the reign of theoretical ideas in science, no theory or hypothesis, however inadequate, is deposed unless there is a superior formulation to take its place.

During the last decade and a half, however, led by the efforts of S. S. Stevens of Harvard University, evidence has been accumulating at an increasing rate in support of a promising contender, and the demise of Fechner's logarithmic law as it applies to prothetic continua appears certain. The long overdue challenger is Stevens' power law—in a remarkably large number of modalities, sensation is related to stimulus intensity by a power function.

We have already noted that apparent weight, loudness of a 1,000-Hz tone, and apparent intensity of electric shock were all power functions of their respective stimulus dimensions. In Table 6-2 20 sensory continua are listed in which the relationship between the psychological continuum and the corresponding physical continuum is a power function. Note that all the continua listed in Table 6-2 are prothetic. Observe also the wide range of exponents in the table, from a low of 0.33 for the brightness of a 5° target to a high of 3.5 for subjective electric shock. With the help of Fig. 6-6, imagine the enormous differences which must exist in the curves that describe how the intensities of apparent brightness and subjective shock grow as a function of their respective stimulus dimensions. Obviously, only if a mathematical function possesses the flexibility of the power function can it hope to encompass the wide range of behavior shown by the various sensory continua of Table 6-2.

THE GENERALIZED POWER LAW.   Actually far more prothetic dimensions have been scaled and found to follow the power law than are indicated in Table 6-2.

Table 6-2 Representative Exponents of the Power Functions Relating Psychological Magnitude to Stimulus Magnitude on Prothetic Continua

CONTINUUM	EXPONENT	STIMULUS CONDITIONS
Loudness	0.6	Binaural
Brightness	0.33	5° target—dark–adapted eye
Lightness	1.2	Reflectance of gray papers
Smell	0.55	Coffee odor
Smell	0.6	Heptane
Taste	0.8	Saccharine
Taste	1.3	Sucrose
Taste	1.3	Salt
Temperature	1.0	Cold—on arm
Temperature	1.6	Warmth—on arm
Vibration	0.95	60 Hz—on finger
Duration	1.1	White-noise stimulus
Repetition rate	1.0	Light, sound, touch, and shocks
Finger span	1.3	Thickness of wood blocks
Pressure on palm	1.1	Static force on skin
Heaviness	1.45	Lifted weights
Force of handgrip	1.7	Precision hand dynamometer
Autophonic level	1.1	Sound pressure of vocalization
Electric shock	3.5	60 Hz—through fingers
Roughness	1.5	Emery cloth

SOURCE: S. S. Stevens. The psychophysics of sensory function. *American Scientist*, 1960, **48**, 226–253. Used by permission.

In some cases, however, a log-log plot of the psychophysical function deviates from the straight line required by the power law in that at low stimulus values the function turns concave downwards. The scaling of apparent-vibration intensity (60 Hz applied to the arm) by the method of magnitude estimation provides an illustration. It is clear from Fig. 6-14 (lower curve) that the resulting psychophysical function plotted on log-log coordinates is not linear; hence the curve does not describe a power function.

Faced with these data and others like them, Stevens (1959) suggested that the difficulty lay in taking as the origin of the physical continuum the zero point of the physical dimension, rather than a value related to the absolute limen. He proposed the adoption of a more general form of the power law, i.e.,

$$R_s = k(S - S_O)^c$$

where S_O is a constant presumably related to the absolute threshold of the subject. By using an appropriate value for S_O ("roughly equal to the threshold value"),

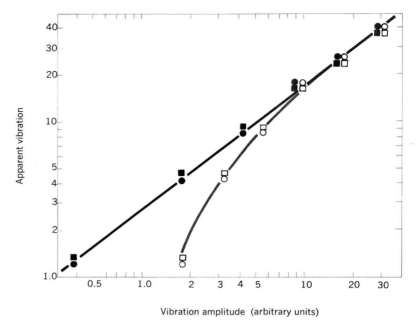

Fig. 6-14. The lower psychophysical function relating apparent intensity of vibration to physical amplitude employed the absolute values of the physical stimuli. In the upper function a constant, S_O, was subtracted from each stimulus value, effectively shifting the origin of the physical scale from zero to S_O. The squares and circles refer to two separate experiments. (SOURCE: S. S. Stevens. Tactile vibration: Dynamics of sensory intensity. *Journal of Experimental Psychology*, 1959, **57**, 210–218. Copyright 1959 by the American Psychological Association and used by permission.)

Stevens found that the previous curvilinear function could be transformed into a power function (upper curve in Fig. 6-14).

Note that when the value of S_O (or the presumed corresponding absolute limen) is small relative to the range of stimuli being scaled, a satisfactory power function may be obtained without taking this constant into account, which explains why in many cases the "simple" power law is supported by the experimental data.

Inclusion of S_O into the power law was not without its complications. It turned out that sometimes the value of S_O required to remove curvature from the function relating sensation to stimulus intensity was not comfortably close to the value of the absolute limen as determined by conventional means. Stevens' (1961) interpretation was that S_O was an "effective" threshold, a view for which Corso (1963) with some justification took him to task. Corso was objecting to the practice of merely adjusting the value of S_O to any number that might be required to obtain a straight line on the log-log plot of the psychophysical function. As he put it, "Psychophysical laws are matters of fact, not expediency."

Although Corso's demand that S_0 be tied to some kind of empirical operation is sound, the appropriate threshold value to be entered into the generalized power-law equation must be chosen judiciously. We have already seen that the concept of the absolute threshold is relative in that its value may vary as a function of a number of factors. An absolute limen obtained after prolonged adaptation to dark might not be an appropriate threshold for a brightness scale generated from relatively intense visual stimuli. The point simply is that a critical test of the hypothesis that S_0 is closely related to the absolute limen requires that the latter be measured under conditions which are as close as possible to those prevailing during determination of the sensory scale.

In this connection Ekman and Gustafsson (1968) showed that the absolute brightness limen determined under conventional procedures was significantly different from that obtained while S was in the process of scaling a set of brightnesses; moreover there was variation in the absolute limen depending upon the intensity of the set of stimuli which S was required to judge. In another recent study Gescheider and Wright (1968) were able to use empirically determined absolute limens to rectify psychophysical functions with curvature in their lower portions (Fig. 6-15).

It would appear, then, that if threshold determinations are made under conditions very close to those under which the scaling judgments are secured, one may very well find a correspondence between the empirically determined absolute limen and the value of S_0 needed to rectify the psychophysical function plotted on log-log coordinates. Of course the requirement that measurement of the physical dimension begin at the absolute limen is subject to the same sort of criticism that was addressed to a similar feature of Fechner's law. Those who disavow a sensory threshold are not likely to look kindly upon this manipulation.

Validation of Stevens' Law

The evidence for the power law is impressive. Still, because a great deal of the support comes from scales derived from the magnitude methods, the necessity for verification is obvious. The methods of magnitude estimation and magnitude production rely heavily on S's sophistication with numbers, and one would be more convinced of the validity of the power law if it were confirmed in a setting in which sensations were estimated without the mediation of numbers. Confirmation of this sort is available in experiments on *cross-modality matching*.

CROSS-MODALITY MATCHING. Comparison of sensory magnitudes across modalities is something we all are familiar with. The rumble of a subway train is more akin in intensity to the brightness of midday than to the twilight of evening, and there is more than poetic similarity between a whisper and a gentle breeze. To some extent intensity can be abstracted from the qualitative aspects of a sensation in much the same way as the weight of an object is abstracted from its more unique properties. Equal-loudness contours, long known in sensory psychology,

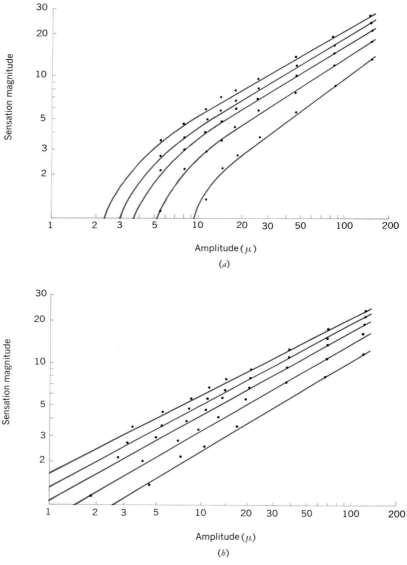

Fig. 6-15. Sensation magnitude as a function of vibrator amplitude (microns) on the right index finger. The five psychophysical functions arise from the different periods—which ranged from 5 sec to 6 min—that intervened after the termination of an adapting stimulus. The curvilinear functions of (a) were recti- fied, as shown in (b), by the subtraction from each stimulus value of an empiri- cally determined absolute threshold. Thus, the generalized power law provides a reasonable fit to the data. (SOURCE: G. A. Gescheider and J. H. Wright. Effects of sensory adaptation on the form of the psychophysical magnitude function for cutaneous vibration. *Journal of Experimental Psychology*, 1968, **77**, 308–313. Copyright 1968 by the American Psychological Association and used by permission.)

testify to the ability of human observers to match the loudness of tones whose pitch may differ widely. One step removed are cross-modality matches, in which S equates the intensity of a sensation in one modality, e.g., brightness, with the intensity of a sensation in another, e.g., loudness. By means of such matches, a bold and rather strong test of the power law becomes possible.

The rationale behind the cross-modality approach is illustrated by a fanciful example. Suppose that by applying pressure by means of an air pump, we are able to lift a column of mercury in a glass tube, and suppose further that the function which relates the height of the column of mercury in inches (H) to the number of strokes per second (sps) applied to the pump is claimed to be $H = 6sps$. Let us also have at hand an electro-chemical means of raising the mercury; passing an electric current (I) through a chemical generates a gas which in turn raises the mercury, presumably in accordance with the function $H = 2I$. Now suppose that five heights are marked off on the tube that contains the mercury, call these $H_1, \ldots , H_5$, and imagine that the number of strokes per second and the amount of current required to raise the mercury to each of the five heights are determined. We now have five pairs of values in our possession, (sps_1, I_1), (sps_2, I_2), $\ldots$, (sps_5, I_5), where sps_1 and I_1 are the number of strokes per second and the amount of current, respectively, required to raise the mercury to the same height, namely H_1, the other points having a similar interpretation.

The question that now arises is: Could we verify with these five "equal-height" points whether the functions relating strokes per second and electric current to height of the mercury column are actually as were given? Indeed we could. For if $H = 6sps$ and $H = 2I$, then the equal-height function—the function that specifies what values of sps and I will raise the mercury to the same heights—is $6sps = 2I$, or expressing strokes per second in terms of current, $sps = I/3$. Consequently, if the five equal-height points are plotted on a graph having strokes per second on the ordinate and current on the abscissa, these points should, if the original functions are correct, fall on a straight line whose slope is $\frac{1}{3}$ and whose Y intercept is zero. Note, however, that functions other than $H = 6sps$ and $H = 2I$ can generate the straight line just described. Were the original functions $H = 1.5sps - 2.0$ and $H = 0.5I - 2.0$, obviously the equal-height function would again be $sps = I/3$. Consequently such evidence can be supportive of the original functions, but not always conclusive.

A similar line of reasoning lies behind the use of cross-modality matching as a method of confirming functions relating sensation magnitude to stimulus intensity. If in one sensory modality sensation is related to stimulus intensity by the power function $R_{s_1} = k_1 S_1^{c_1}$, and if in a second, the corresponding function is $R_{s_2} = k_2 S_2^{c_2}$, then the equal-sensation function—the function specifying what values of S_1 and S_2 will produce sensations of equal intensity—is $k_1 S_1^{c_1} = k_2 S_2^{c_2}$. Solving for S_1, we find that the equal-sensation function becomes $S_1 = k S_2^{c_2/c_1}$, where $k = (k_2/k_1)^{1/c_1}$. In other words, given that the original sensory scales are power functions, the *equal-sensation function will itself be a power function with exponent equal to the ratios of the exponents of the power functions from which it was derived.* Let us now consider a few concrete illustrations.

A dynamometer is an instrument—sometimes seen at amusement galleries—for measuring the force exerted by one's handgrip. A reasonable question that arises is: How is the handgrip force experienced by S (apparent hand-grip force) related to the actual force transmitted to the dynamometer, measured, say, in pounds? Employing three different proportionality methods, namely, the methods of ratio production, magnitude production, and magnitude estimation, J. C. Stevens and Mack (1959) found that apparent force grows as a power function of physical force, the average value of the exponent being about 1.7.

Turning to a second modality, Stevens and Galanter (1957), reviewing a number of scales relating apparent heaviness to physical weight, found that heaviness grows as a power function of physical weight with an average exponent of approximately 1.45.

Now suppose that by having Ss equate apparent force of handgrip to the apparent heaviness of a series of test weights, a number of equal-sensation points are obtained for these two modalities. Because the ratio of the exponents of the two power functions is $1.45/1.7 = .85$, a graph of the equal-sensation points on log-log coordinates, in which physical force is plotted on the ordinate and physical weight on the abscissa, should describe a straight line with slope equal to 0.85. In other words, the equal-sensation function should also be a power function with exponent equal to the ratio of the exponents of the original power functions.

J. C. Stevens and Mack (1959) actually performed this experiment. Ten Ss served in the study. Six test weights, ranging from 28 to 480 g, were used, each weight presented to S three times. While hefting the test weight in his left hand, S squeezed a dynamometer with his right hand until he judged that the apparent force of his handgrip was equal in intensity to the apparent heaviness of the test weight. The median forces exerted on the dynamometer were calculated for each of the test weights, and the resulting equal-sensation points were plotted on log-log coordinates. As may be seen in Fig. 6-16, a straight line describes the data points nicely. Moreover, the slope of the straight line shown in the figure was reported by the authors to be 0.8, a value remarkably close to the theoretical value, 0.85.

Apparent force of handgrip has been paired with a number of different sensory modalities to test further by means of cross-modality matching the validity of the power law. In all cases the apparent force of handgrip has been adjusted to the apparent intensity of the test stimuli, and cross-modality matches have been obtained for apparent electric shock, apparent pressure on the palm, cold, vibration, loudness of white noise and of a 1,000-Hz tone, and brightness. In Fig. 6-17 the equal-sensation functions obtained from these cross-modality matches are graphed in a log-log plot which employs a common abscissa expressed in terms of the relative intensities of the test stimuli. The dashed line shows what a slope of 1.0 looks like in the present coordinates.

A straight line is a good fit for most, if not all, of the equal-sensation functions shown in Fig. 6-17; this fact constitutes formidable evidence for Stevens' law. Much more impressive, however, is the fact that the maximum

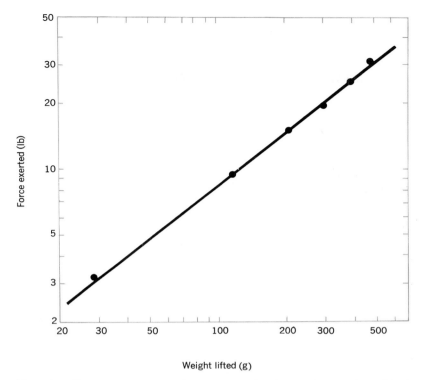

Fig. 6-16. Equal-sensation function for matching force of handgrip to lifted weights. Each point stands for the median of 30 matches by 10 Ss. (SOURCE: J. C. Stevens and J. D. Mack. Scales of apparent force. *Journal of Experimental Psychology,* 1959, **58,** 405–413. Copyright 1959 by the American Psychological Association and used by permission.)

deviation between the exponents calculated directly for the nine modalities represented in the figure (*A* through *I*) and those deduced from the equal-sensation functions has been reported to be only 0.07 (Stevens, 1962, p. 33). Such close agreement between theoretical expectations and empirical observations over so wide a range of sensory modalities is remarkable.

Nor does the stream of evidence end here. Many other combinations of cross-modality matches have been investigated, in most cases with favorable results. Figure 6-18 presents, in log-log coordinates, 10 equal-sensation functions based on cross-modality matching of loudness (of a tone or noise) to various sensory modalities (cf. Stevens, 1966b). In all cases a straight line provides a reasonable description of the data points, indicating the appropriateness of the power function analysis. Moreover, dividing the slope of the equal-sensation function into the exponent of the power function of each of the modalities (achieved by magnitude estimation) yielded, in all but one case, values in the range 0.55–0.75. This range straddles what is considered to be the value of the loudness exponent, i.e., 0.6.

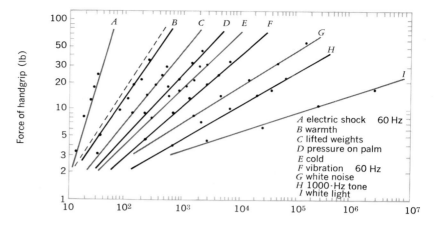

Relative intensity of criterion stimulus

Fig. 6-17. Equal-sensation functions obtained from cross-modality matching of force of handgrip to various sensory modalities. Each point stands for the median force exerted by 10 or more subjects to match the apparent intensity of the corresponding criterion (test) stimulus. (SOURCE: S. S. Stevens. The surprising simplicity of sensory metrics. *American Psychologist,* 1962, **17,** 29–39. Copyright 1962 by the American Psychological Association and used by permission.)

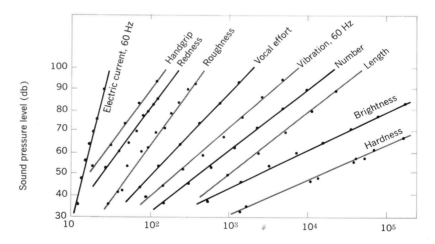

Relative intensity of criterion stimulus

Fig. 6-18. Equal-sensation functions obtained from matching loudness (of a tone or a noise) to stimuli of various sensory modalities. The relative positions of the functions are arbitrary, but the slopes are as determined by the data (see text). (SOURCE: S. S. Stevens. Matching functions between loudness and ten other continua. *Perception & Psychophysics,* 1966, **1,** 5–8. Used by permission.)

Before leaving the topic of cross-modality matching, we should point out that this technique is itself a psychophysical scaling method, one which could be recruited to replace methods that require numerical estimates from S. For example, apparent length of lines has been found to be proportional to physical length. One could scale a modality simply by having S adjust the length of a line until its apparent magnitude was proportional to the apparent magnitude of a test stimulus taken from the modality being scaled. Using precisely this procedure, Stevens and Guirao (1963) scaled the brightness of a transilluminated target and found the resulting scale to be in close agreement with those obtained by magnitude estimation and other methods. Consequently, cross-modality matching may be considered the fifth method of obtaining ratio scales of sensation, a method requiring neither numerical estimates (as in the magnitude methods) nor judgments based on numerical concepts (as in the ratio methods).

THE POWER LAW FOR INDIVIDUAL SUBJECTS.   All the power functions reported thus far are based on averages taken over groups of subjects. If the power law is to be regarded as having significance for sensory functioning, it should apply to individuals as well. Psychologists have long been wary of drawing the implication that a group function necessarily reflects properties of the individual functions of which it is composed (e.g., Estes, 1956).

Addressing themselves to this important issue, Pradhan and Hoffman (1963) found that of six Ss tested with different ranges and spacings of stimuli, only one consistently produced a power function relating apparent heaviness to physical weight. More often than not, the individual sensory scales of the remaining five Ss departed significantly from a power function. And yet a group curve, averaged over the six Ss, yielded the usual power relationship. These investigators suggested that the power law is an "artifact of grouping."

There is now abundant evidence, however, that power functions can frequently be obtained from individual subjects. Marks and J. C. Stevens (1966) have surveyed earlier illustrations of individual power functions and added 34 new instances to the list, which at their writing numbered about 150. As for their own contribution, Marks and Stevens produced individual power functions by cross-modality matching and by a technique which is a composition of magnitude estimation and magnitude production. Let us describe the latter because it is a very useful variation.

As in magnitude estimation, a subject in the Marks and Stevens experiment was given the task of assigning numbers in proportion to the subjective brightness of a light. Unlike that method, however, the intensity of the light was controlled by the subject rather than by E. The period during which the light was available for adjustment and judgment was relatively brief. In this task, by moving the stimulus intensity to some value and then choosing a number which seems to reflect its magnitude, the subject can adopt a strategy that is close to pure magnitude estimation. At the other extreme, S might first choose a number and then repeatedly adjust the stimulus until it corresponds to the

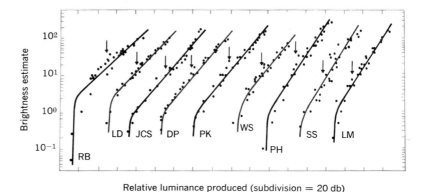

Fig. 6-19. Individual psychophysical functions obtained by the "estimation-production" method. The position of the arrow indicates for each curve the location of 70 db (see text). (SOURCE: L. E. Marks and J. C. Stevens. Individual brightness functions. *Perception & Psychophysics*, 1966, **1**, 17–24. Used by permission.)

number, which is very close to the technique employed in magnitude production. One of the virtues of the magnitude production method is that it places minimal constraints upon S's judgments and therefore presumably mitigates or eliminates some of the response biases which arise from this quarter.

Returning to the experimental data, a sample of the obtained individual functions is presented in Fig. 6-19. Special note should be taken of the fact that every single judgment obtained from S is plotted in the figure; that is, there is no averaging of experimental data whatever. Observe that all functions approximate a straight line in their upper portions with curvature appearing in the lower portions. Subtracting an appropriate value of S_0 from the physical stimuli renders each of the psychophysical functions linear throughout their entire length. Although absolute thresholds were not independently obtained, the values of S_0 which removed curvature were reasonable threshold magnitudes. A stronger case would have been made if the values of S_0 had been determined empirically, but as Marks and Stevens point out, S's absolute threshold probably shifted continually in the course of the experiment as the eye was exposed to various levels of visual stimulation. Similar results were obtained for cross-modality matching of brightness and loudness. Moreover, the slope of the cross-modality function was close to what one would expect from the exponents most often obtained for the loudness and brightness power functions.

There seems little reason to doubt any longer that power functions can be obtained in a large proportion of individual subjects. The value of the exponents calculated for individual Ss varies from one subject to another and even from one determination to another made on the same subject. But it appears that exponents calculated from groups of subjects as small as 10 are relatively stable, as though individual psychophysical functions are prone to a certain degree of noise which is averaged out over the group data.

RECIPROCALITY BETWEEN AN ATTRIBUTE AND ITS INVERSE.   There is another line of evidence bearing on the power law which is of interest. If the loudness of a 1,000-Hz tone is a power function of sound pressure level with exponent equal to 0.6, what kind of function will result if the inverse attribute, *softness* of the tone, is scaled? Granting that judgments of softness are proportional to the reciprocal of judgments of loudness—which is what one would like to believe—softness should also be a power function of intensity with exponent equal in magnitude to the exponent of the loudness function but opposite in sign. The rationale for this consequence is simply that if loudness (L) is related to intensity by the power function $L = kS^c$ and softness (F) is reciprocally related to loudness, i.e., $F = k'/L$ (k' is a constant), it follows as a matter of substitution that $F = k'/(kS^c)$. Consequently, $F = KS^{-c}$, where $K = k'/k$.

The first question of this nature was put forward by Torgerson (1960), who found that judgments of lightness and darkness of patches of grey paper were reciprocally related. More specifically, lightness was found to be a power function of reflectance (a measure of the physical brightness of the stimuli) with exponent approximately equal to 1.2, and darkness of the same set of test stimuli, also a power function of reflectance, came out with an exponent of -1.2.

Stevens and Guirao (1962) subsequently found loudness and softness to be reciprocally related, and soon thereafter these same investigators showed that shortness and longness of lines and smallness and largeness of squares also produced scales standing in a reciprocal relationship (Stevens & Guirao, 1963). The reciprocality between smallness and largeness of squares is shown in Fig. 6-20. Both the scale of largeness and the scale of smallness were obtained by the method of magnitude production, with exponents of 0.67 and -0.72, respectively.

Although the results from tests of reciprocality are generally supportive of the power law, and quantitatively at that, it turns out that often the inverse of an attribute is less precisely a power function of stimulus intensity than the attribute itself. Scale points plotted on log-log coordinates tend in the former case to fall concave downwards rather than along a straight line (e.g., Stevens & Guirao, 1963, pp. 178–179).

To sum up the evidence in favor of Stevens' law, we have seen that when scaled by the proportionality methods a very large number of sensory continua turn out to be power functions of their respective stimulus dimensions, both for groups of Ss and for individuals. Preliminary evidence suggests that even in the pigeon, apparent brightness is a power function of stimulus intensity (Herrnstein & van Sommers, 1962). Quantitative verification of the power law has been achieved for a substantial sample of sensory continua through the technique of cross-modality matching. Finally, the predicted reciprocality between an attribute and its inverse has been satisfactorily approximated for several modalities.

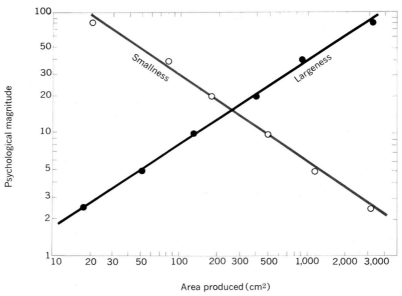

Fig. 6-20. Reciprocality between largeness and smallness judgments of squares. The exponents of the fitted power functions are 0.67 and −0.72, respectively. (SOURCE: S. S. Stevens and M. Guirao. Subjective scaling of length and area and the matching of length to loudness and brightness. *Journal of Experimental Psychology*, 1963, **66**, 177–186. Copyright 1963 by the American Psychological Association and used by permission.)

THE PERVASIVENESS OF THE POWER LAW.   It turns out that the power function is applicable to a wide range of behavioral situations and, moreover, it has been something of a canon in biological measurements for many years. J. C. Stevens and Savin (1962) reported that in a wide variety of learning experiments cumulative performance could be described by a power function of practice time or number of trials, with exponents usually in the range 1–2. Subsequently J. C. Stevens (1964) showed that very orderly power functions resulted when the data from a perceptual-motor task were presented on log-log coordinates with cumulative time-on-target plotted as a function of practice time. Many other behavioral situations could be cited where the power function is a good description of a behavioral measure of performance plotted against one or another independent variable.

Extensive as its use has been in psychology, the power law has seen far more service in biology. Recognition that the relative brain size of anthropoids was best evaluated by the parameters of a power function (deduced from a log-log plot of brain weight against body weight) goes back to the end of the last century (Stahl, 1965). The analysis of the relationship between organ weight and body weight—or more generally between the growth rates of two different biological processes—in terms of power functions became so prevalent it earned the name of "allometry." The sweep of biological relationships to which the power function has been applied is remarkable (cf. Brody, 1945; Huxley, 1932). For example, the power function provides a very good description of the relationship between the mass of certain body organs and total body mass when these values are calculated for subprimate mammals ranging from mice to steers and for primates ranging from the tree shrew to humans. The organs studied include the heart, lungs, liver, kidneys, adrenals, thyroid, pituitary, spleen, and brain. Interestingly, the constants of the power functions fitted to the various organs differ little when mammals and primates are compared, except in the case of the brain, where the k constant is much larger for primates (Stahl, 1965). The similarity of the parameters of the power functions over this vast range of organisms suggested to Stahl that all mammals have in common a basic kind of "physiological design."

One wonders what lies behind this remarkable ubiquitousness of the power function in biological and behavioral spheres. Does it point to some profound and pervasive organizational property of living tissue, or are the diverse manifestations of the power law only a coincidence of that function's inclusiveness?

Some Criticisms of the Power Law

It would be unfair to conclude this section without mention of some reservations that have been voiced concerning the power law and its interpretations. In the first place, the power function does not always closely fit the observed scale points. Apparent roughness and smoothness (Stevens & Harris, 1962) and apparent electric shock (Stevens, Carton, & Shickman, 1958) are instances where correspondence between data and theory leaves something to be desired. Furthermore in these instances as in many others, it is not possible to determine objectively how good or how bad a fit the power function may be to a given set of points because statistical measures of goodness of fit are rarely given. The straight lines of best fit are, moreover, usually fitted by "eye" rather than by objective mathematical means, so that the values of the exponents reported have an unspecified amount of "play" from this source.

This is not to say that the potential value of the power law requires that it fit the data perfectly every time. The "law" would still be valuable if it only provided a first approximation of reasonable generality. "The scientific leverage that accrues from having an equation adequate to the first-order sensory transductions is . . . [that] once the first-order effect is reduced to a formula, the second-order departures from the basic law may conceivably lead to new and deeper understanding [Stevens, 1962, p. 37]."

Still, the generalized power law has three constants, most often all three being estimated from the data. This allows a good deal of freedom to the curve fitter, and as pointed out by Poulton (1968), it would be interesting to know whether the power law provides better fits generally than other reasonable three-constant functions.

Actually, apart from occasional protests (e.g., M. Treisman, 1964b), there is now little quarrel with the power law insofar as it provides a description of how S's judgments are related to the physical-stimulus continuum. The arena of conflict has shifted to matters of interpretation, to the significance that is to be attached to the power law. Stevens' view has been that the power law reflects the relationship that holds between sensation (rather than merely judgment) and stimulus. A mirror of input-output relations, it should tell us something about sensory "transducers." In somewhat oversimplified terms, Stevens sees the exponent c of the power function as determined by basic biophysical properties of the sense organs.

The major argument against this "simple transducer" interpretation is that S's scaling judgments, like the far simpler judgments of classical psychophysics, appear to be determined by many more variables than the sensations associated with the judged stimuli. As Poulton (1968) recently put it, "Central processes involving judgment cannot be understood entirely in terms of the behavior of the sense organs. The mechanisms of response learning and response bias must be included in any adequate description [p. 17]." He then concludes that for himself, the latter presents the more interesting problems. Poulton's conclusion is based on a thorough analysis of six variables which can have important effects on judgments obtained with the method of magnitude estimation, particularly the slope of the power function. In his view the influence of these variables is so permeating that it is doubtful whether any significance concerning the operation of sense organs can be attached to the particular exponents which emerge from the power function relating sensation to stimulus intensity. The particular size of the exponents associated with different modalities he assigns primarily to an uncontrolled relevant variable, namely, the range of stimuli employed in the scaling task (Poulton, 1967). A similar interpretation is offered for the consistency found between exponents determined by magnitude estimation and recovered by cross-modality matching (Poulton, 1968).

Taking a somewhat similar position, Ross and DiLollo (1968) adopt the view that psychophysical judgments in a scaling situation are not determined solely by one aspect of the presented stimuli; rather they are the result of a number of features of the stimuli and the context in which they occur. Accordingly, one must conceive of the determinants of a psychophysical judgment as multidimensional rather than unidimensional. From this point of view it is meaningless to search for a single representative psychophysical function, because the issue is no longer one of relating one unidimensional variable to another.

That S's judgment is based on more than the sensory input arising from a particular stimulus can hardly be doubted; that it interacts with the range of stimuli employed, the type of judgments called for, the past tasks to which S has been exposed, and other variables as well surely must be the case. But bowing to these complexities it may still be possible, by means of "standardized" conditions and remedial procedures, to devise scales of sensation that find significant applications, even to the point of drawing inferences concerning underlying sensory processes. This difficult task is simply another manifestation of the pervasive problem of attempting to discover, or perhaps construct, relationships between independent variables and behavior that are invariant over reasonably wide ranges of experimental conditions. We discussed this issue in Chap. 2.

Stevens' belief that the power law rests on characteristics of the underlying sensory processes can claim some hard neurophysiological evidence. In a careful and detailed study Werner and Mountcastle (1965), working with single afferent nerve fibers in cats and monkeys, counted the number of impulses that resulted from stimulation of the peripheral receptor organ. Under magnification they positioned a 1-mm probe stimulator on the skin in direct line with an Iggo corpuscle, a receptor which responds to compression force with "metronome-like regularity." Varying the compression force by manipulating the distance of skin indentation in microns, they counted the number of impulses that stimulation produced in the single nerve fiber attached to an Iggo corpuscle. Figure 6-21, scaled in log-log coordinates, shows the resulting relationship for a single nerve fiber. Impulses were counted for periods of stimulation varying from 50 to 1,000 milliseconds, accounting for the five curves in the figure. Note that in every case a straight line provides a good fit to the data points; moreover, the fitted functions are very nearly parallel. Thus the input-output relation of this mechanoreceptor is a power function whose exponent remains nearly constant over a stimulation interval varying by a factor of 20. It is of interest that psychophysical functions obtained by magnitude estimation in related sensory modalities are power functions with exponents of the same order of magnitude as found by Werner and Mountcastle for single mechanoreceptor units (cf. Poulton, 1968, p. 13). However, these investigators feel that "it is perhaps unwise to attach great significance to the near identity of the exponents for the psychophysical results and for our study of the fibers ending in Iggo corpuscles. Significance may be attached, however, to the identity of the formal relation between stimulus and response, measured as a subjective magnitude in the one case and as neural activity in afferent fibers in the other. The implication is, we believe, that the neural transforms intervening between input and the final verbal description of an introspective magnitude estimation must be linear for the intensive continuum. This does not imply, of course, that the intervening neural transforms must all be linear, but that the sum of their serial superposition must be so [p. 391]."

The results of the present study, as well as those of related investigations (e.g., Keidel & Spreng, 1965), offer promise for inferring something about sensory transducers from quantitative aspects of the psychophysical function. Although subtle processes intervene between sensation and verbal report, as suggested by Werner and Mountcastle, the sum of these processes may often serve only to transform linearly the primary sensory input.

At times opposition to Stevens' law runs much deeper than even matters of interpretation. It rests on a basic conviction that "sensation by its very nature cannot be quantified—one sensation cannot be considered double another

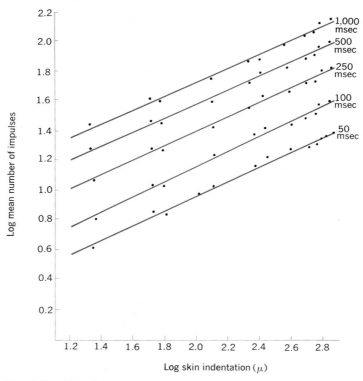

Fig. 6-21. Stimulus-response relations obtained from a mechano-receptor fiber isolated from the saphenous nerve of the thigh of a monkey. Afferent impulses were counted over the periods of time indicated in the separate curves. The data are plotted on log-log coordinates. (SOURCE: G. Werner and V. B. Mountcastle. Neural activity in mechanoreceptive cutaneous afferents: Stimulus-response relations, Weber functions, and information transmission. *Journal of Neurophysiology*, 1965, **28**, 359–397. Used by permission.)

[Warren & Warren, 1963, p. 798]." From this point of view, psychophysical scales do not measure sensation but "merely represent the experimental Ss' estimates of stimulus intensities." When placed in a scaling task, the subject, reaching into past experience, tries to estimate *stimulus*, not sensation, intensity. Warren and Warren propose a "physical-correlate" theory which holds that "the scales of Stevens' New Psychophysics are based upon estimates of physical magnitudes associated with changes in sensory stimulation."

If, of course, we believe that "sensation by its very nature cannot be quantified," there is little point of further discussion. But there seems good reason to contest this view. Simply because "one sensation cannot be considered double another," it does not follow that sensation cannot be quantified. The ordinary temperature scale is a clear case of quantification without one temperature being properly considered the double of another. Nevertheless the admonition is probably directed at ratio scales of sensation, where some such process as doubling must be allowed; indeed it frequently is the very basis upon which ratio scales of sensation are constructed.

Still, sensations surely come in different sizes or else such terms as louder, brighter, and heavier would not be such a prevalent part of our verbal discourse. And if it is granted that sensation B can be greater than sensation A, why can it not be double A? Unlike the case with certain ordinal scales, such as hardness, we are also able to make judgments concerning sensation intervals. It does not seem apparent, therefore, that the possibility of quantitative measurement of sensation should be dismissed purely on a priori grounds. A point that cannot be stressed too strongly is that frequently there is much usefulness in measurement that falls far short of that obtainable with the ideal "extensive" dimensions of physics—mass, length, and time. Perhaps this emphasis would be unnecessary had we looked to biology, rather than to physics, for our models of measurement.

In a rather detailed philosophical critique of the "new" psychophysics, including the power law, Savage (1966) discredits all efforts, new or old, to measure psychological magnitudes. The nub of his argument is that in psychophysical scaling one is attempting to measure psychological events which are private affairs of the individual and consequently not amenable to measurement in the ordinary sense of that term. He draws the conclusion from his argument that "the concept of psychological magnitude ought to be abandoned." A rebuttal by Stevens is appended to Savage's paper (1966, pp. 33–38), and one can do no better than allow Stevens to speak for himself. It would appear to the writer, however, that the futility of purging empirical enterprises purely on philosophical grounds has been shown repeatedly in the history of psychology— as in the dismissal of such concepts as attention, thought, and consciousness by strict behaviorism and their later resurgence as legitimate topics of study. Regardless of philosophical prohibition, scientific study of empirical phenomena will continue so long as there is hope of obtaining fruitful information. And this is as it should be, for philosophical arguments based on rational considerations have a way of underestimating the ingenuity of nature and the investigator.

To conclude this discussion, doubtless there is more involved in the construction of a sensory scale than measurement of sensory responses to scaled stimuli. A number of relevant variables have been isolated and, in some cases, their effects have been eliminated or neutralized. Far more work is necessary, however, before scales of sensation generally secure the degree of invariance required for widespread application and for the drawing of inferences concerning properties of the sensory scale—such as the exponent of the power function— and corresponding properties of underlying sensory mechanisms.

Applications of Stevens' Law

One may agree that the evidence for Stevens' law is impressive yet nevertheless wonder whether its significance was only academic. In particular, does the law have any practical applications? Although it is perhaps too early in the development of the power law for startling applications, it does have its uses. Some notable examples arise from the sone scale of loudness. This scale, in which loudness is a power function of stimulus intensity with exponent equal to 0.6, has been put to good use for some time by acoustical engineers. Moreover, it plays an essential part in an analytic procedure by which it is possible to calculate the loudness of complex sounds (e.g., Stevens, 1961). One version of the latter procedure has been suggested to the International Standards Organization for general adoption (Stevens, 1961, p. 86). For engineering purposes this organization has already accepted the value of 0.6 as the exponent of the loudness function itself (Stevens, 1963).

Unanticipated applications of the methodology surrounding the power law, if not of the law itself, lie in areas outside sensation, in attitude and preference measurement, where no known metrics exist. For 30 years, the major measurement techniques in these areas were based on Thurstone's "indirect" methods, which took advantage of the confusability of stimuli. With the success of the direct methods in psychophysical scaling, it occurred to a number of investigators that these same methods might be of use where an underlying metric was not available. However, before describing these developments, we wish to return to a topic whose discussion was deferred, namely comparison of direct and indirect scaling methods. Following this we shall remark on an interesting relationship that exists between partition and proportionality scales, a discussion that will return us directly to the topic of this paragraph.

DIRECT VERSUS INDIRECT SCALING METHODS

In the direct methods Ss contribute judgments of the test stimuli which are at the same quantitative level as the scales that they, more or less directly, produce. Thus in the partition methods, from which interval scales of sensation are constructed, S's judgments are in one way or another themselves estimates of sensory intervals, and partition scales—through means, medians, etc.—are obtained directly from them. Similarly the proportionality methods are dependent on estimates of ratios of apparent magnitudes, or on estimates of absolute apparent magnitudes within a proportionality factor, and again little elaboration of the basic judgments is normally required to arrive at the final ratio scale of sensation. To their profit, the direct methods usually require little in the way of mathematical manipulation, ordinarily no more than the computation of measures of central tendency. The relatively few judgments required of S is also a point in their favor. On the debit side, the direct methods, apart from cross-modality matching, require subjective estimates of some quantitative sophistication.

The indirect methods distribute their burden differently. Frequently only the simplest judgments are required from Ss, estimates no more quantitative than "A is greater than B." But in order to obtain sufficient aggregate information from judgments which, individually, are not very informative, Ss must often submit to extended series of judgments, which can prove quite tedious. Coupling large numbers of such judgments with appropriate mathematical and psychological assumptions—and frequently with substantial mathematical calculations—interval and ratio scales of psychological attributes are elaborated. The summation of *JND*s to obtain a ratio scale of sensation is one indirect method with which we are already familiar. Determination of the *JND*, whether by the method of limits or by the method of constant stimuli, requires judgments no more quantitative than "greater than," "less than," and "equal." But the derivation of a sensory scale from these quantitatively simple judgments requires either a considerable amount of labor on S's part plus certain psychological assumptions, or, if the empirical summation of *JND*s is to be avoided by means of some such device as Fechner's law, less experimental labor but added psychological and mathematical assumptions.

Another important difference between the direct and indirect methods is the use to which they put S's limited ability to discriminate. The indirect methods capitalize on the fact that if test stimuli are sufficiently close to each other, S will not discriminate among them perfectly. In essence these methods employ the error involved in S's judgments, or the "confusability" of the stimuli, to define the unit by which subjective magnitude is measured. For this reason they are often referred to as "confusion measures" (e.g., Stevens, 1966a). Specific assumptions are made about the distribution of errors, for example, that they are normally distributed, and by virtue of such assumptions, judgments having only ordinal properties are processed into interval scales of apparent magnitude. The direct methods, on the other hand, have no stake in S's errors except to eliminate them. These methods would still be applicable if discrimination among a set of test stimuli were perfect; probably none of the indirect methods could function under such conditions.

A certain amount of partisanship has developed among proponents of each class of methods. Stevens has been the most outspoken opponent of the indirect methods, which he feels are completely inappropriate for the scaling of prothetic continua and an unnecessary inconvenience as well. However, the indirect methods are not without their own supporters (e.g., Garner, 1959; Jones, 1960).

Two of the most prominent indirect scaling techniques are the methods of *paired comparisons* and *successive intervals*. In the first, the stimuli to be scaled are presented to Ss in all possible pairings. The scale value of a stimulus, say *A*, is derived from the proportions of times that *A* is judged to have more of the criterion property than each of the other stimuli with which it is paired. Under certain conditions the procedure is not unlike that by which the sensitivity measure d' is derived in a detection experiment, although there is the added complication that more than two stimuli are involved, and, of course, E is not concerned with a measure of response criterion.

In the method of successive intervals, S is required to make a judgment concerning the magnitude of each stimulus by placing it into an appropriate category, or perhaps by rank-ordering the set of stimuli. Unlike in category estimation, it is not assumed that successive categories are equally spaced; indeed it is the purpose of this method to obtain measures of these spacings. Once again certain assumptions are made concerning the dispersion of S's judgments, on the basis of which an interval scale is derived. Let us note that data arising from a standard category estimation experiment can be used to generate an interval scale directly or they can be processed into an "indirect" interval scale by the successive intervals method (e.g., Galanter & Messick, 1961). Stevens (1966a) has suggested that the name "category confusion scale" be applied to the latter. Further information concerning the indirect methods may be obtained from Guilford (1954) and Torgerson (1958).

Developed primarily by Thurstone (e.g., 1927a,b), the indirect methods were not elaborated for the purpose of measuring sensation. Rather their major aim was the measurement of subjective attributes for which there is no known underlying metric, for example, excellence of handwriting, pleasantness of colors and other stimuli, food preferences, and various attitudes. Such attributes are measurable on the physical side only on a nominal scale. We saw in the last chapter that signal detection theory put certain aspects of Thurstone's approach to use in measuring psychophysical quantities, but for the most part, the indirect methods were found where an underlying metric was absent. The direct methods, particularly magnitude estimation, are now providing serious competition in this area, and though the scales which result from these two quite different approaches are themselves different, it turns out that they are frequently related in a simple way.

PARTITION AND PROPORTIONALITY
SCALES ON PROTHETIC CONTINUA

We learned in Exercise 6-8 that if a partition scale is an interval scale of sensation and a proportionality scale over the same stimuli is a ratio sensation scale, the two scales will be linearly related, and a plot of the partition and proportionality scale values assigned to a set of stimuli will describe a straight line (see Fig. 6-24). Actually, however, such a relationship is rarely obtained on prothetic continua. A partition scale plotted against its corresponding proportionality scale almost always produces a curve that is concave downward. This relationship has been verified to the point that it too might be considered a "law" (cf. Stevens, 1966a; Stevens & Galanter, 1957; Stevens & Guirao, 1963). In Fig. 6-22 two instances of such curves are presented, based on the methods of category and magnitude production. Not only are the functions concave downward, but the amount of curvature differs for the attribute (largeness) and its inverse (smallness). If a proportionality scale is plotted against a confusion scale, as, for example, a category scale obtained by the method of successive intervals, the curvature is likely to be more marked. Frequently the two types of scales are related by a logarithmic function (Galanter & Messick, 1961; Stevens, 1966a).

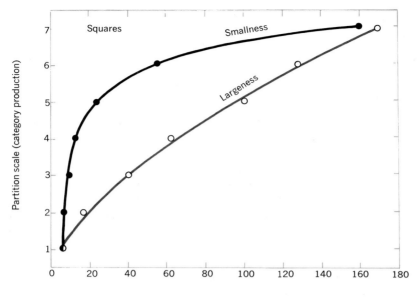

Proportionality scale (magnitude production)

Fig. 6-22. An obtained nonlinear relationship between a partition scale of largeness of squares and a corresponding proportionality scale of the same attribute. Nonlinearity exists to an even greater extent for the inverse attribute, smallness of squares. (SOURCE: S. S. Stevens and M. Guirao. Subjective scaling of length and area and the matching of length to loudness and brightness. *Journal of Experimental Psychology,* 1963, **66,** 177–186. Copyright 1963 by the American Psychological Association and used by permission.)

The failure to find a linear relationship between partition and proportionality scales on prothetic continua is a pointed reminder of the problem of obtaining consistency among sensory scales. Three stimuli shown to be separated by equal subjective distances by a proportionality scale may not appear so if measured along a partition scale. Which scale, then, are we to accept?

Stevens feels that proportionality scales are the appropriate measuring sticks of sensation on prothetic continua. He assigns the discrepancy between partition and proportionality scales to a systematic decrease in discriminability (increase in variability) that occurs as one progresses from lower to higher stimulus values along a prothetic continuum. Because discriminability is better for relatively low intensities, Ss tend to place less subjective distance between categories at the low end of a category scale than at the upper end; consequently, the sensory distance between categories 6 and 7 in a 7-point category scale is likely to be greater than the subjective distance between categories 1 and 2, for example. If we assume that proportionality scales measure sensory intervals accurately, it follows that a concave downward curve will result when partition scales are plotted against proportionality scales. In somewhat different terms, the difference between partition and proportionality scales is attributed by Stevens to the circumstance that subjective variability is roughly proportional to subjective magnitude. Though there is considerable support for this position, theoretical and empirical (e.g., Eisler, 1963; Stevens, 1966a), acceptance is far from uniform (e.g., Torgerson, 1960).

The lack of harmony between partition and proportionality scales has a brighter side. As already pointed out, the concave downward relation between partition and proportionality scales, often closely approximating a logarithmic function, is firmly established by numerous experimental studies. Will a similar relationship be found for attributes which lack a simple metric? If so, such attributes might properly be considered prothetic and as such are perhaps better suited, for purposes of measurement, to direct scaling techniques than to the more commonplace indirect or confusion methods.

There is now a considerable amount of evidence which bears on this issue, much of which is summarized by Stevens (1966a). The conclusion is inescapable that for a large number of nonmetric continua, partition and proportionality scales are related by a concave downward function, often logarithmic. The attributes which display this relationship include occupational prestige (Perloe, 1963), esthetic judgment of music (Koh, 1965), strength of religious attitude expressed by various statements concerning the church, preference for wrist-watches among Japanese students, esthetic value of handwriting, judged political importance of eleven Swedish monarchs, and seriousness of offenses ranging from hit-and-run by a drunken driver to stopping in a no-parking zone (cf. Stevens, 1966a). Figure 6-23 shows for the last attribute how a confusion scale, based on paired comparisons, is related to a proportionality scale derived from ratio estimation.

It appears, then, that useful measurement of complex attributes need not enlist the involved methodology characteristic of the indirect methods. Despite their simplicity, the proportionality methods, particularly magnitude estimation, appear to be as suitable for the measurement of complex attributes as they have proven to be for numerous sensory modalities. The opportunities that this development presents to the social sciences should not be underestimated. Wanting the means to measure adequately their basic independent and dependent variables, many areas of social science have languished for years.

Recognizing this need in connection with the pressing problem of stemming the tide of juvenile delinquency, Sellin and Wolfgang write: "No matter what forms these efforts take . . . we have not yet discovered any reliable way of gauging their effectiveness. Therefore, in order to expend most purposefully and usefully the time, thought, energy, and public and private funds required for the organization and operation of programs that are expected to prevent or reduce delinquency, there is an obvious need of some instrument or device that, alone or in conjunction with other devices, can be used to test the effectiveness of these programs [1964, p. 1]." They devoted a 3-year program to the problem, of which one result was the development of an index of delinquency based on magnitude estimation scales. Their work, briefly

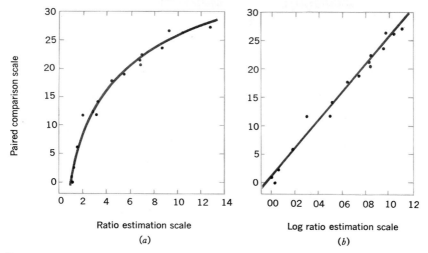

Fig. 6-23. A group of 80 Ss, most of them Swedish students, evaluated 17 immoral actions of varying seriousness by the methods of paired comparisons and ratio estimation. In (a) the scale values obtained from the first method are shown plotted against the scale values gotten from the second, producing the concave downward relation normally observed when a partition scale is plotted against a corresponding proportionality scale. As shown in (b), the relationship becomes linear when plotted against the logarithm of the proportionality scale. (SOURCE: G. Ekman. Measurement of moral judgment: A comparison of scaling methods. *Perceptual and Motor Skills*, 1962, **15**, 3–9. Used by permission.)

reviewed by Stevens (1966a), is a forceful illustration of how the methods and relationships developed in the psychophysical scaling of sensation—and more particularly, in the pursuit of the power law—can be put to productive use far afield in the attack on urgent social problems.

SUMMARY

Psychophysical scaling has made more progress in the last decade or so than in the preceding 100 years. Fechner's logarithmic law, the century-old prototype of measuring sticks of sensation, finally has given way to a new model, Stevens' power law. The extent to which the power law can be pushed as a description of how subjective magnitude grows in response to stimulus intensity, its implications for the physiological mechanisms that underlie sensation, and finally, its generalization to areas outside of sensation proper—these are important issues whose outcomes will play a critical role in determining the fruitfulness and utility of the power law.

1. As a ratio scale of sensory magnitude, Fechner's law involves three important assumptions:

2. Prothetic and metathetic continua may be distinguished in the following way:

3. On prothetic continua the increment in sensation magnitude added by a *JND* is:

4. The judgment required of S in the partition methods is essentially one of estimating:
   (a) The four partition methods are:
   (b) These scales at best produce interval scales of sensation because:

5. In the proportionality methods, S's judgment may be characterized as:
   (a) The four proportionality methods are:
   (b) The constant sum method is a form of:
   (c) Fractionation is one type of:
   (d) A modulus may be used with:

6. A ratio scale of sensation is obtained from the "halving function" in the following way:

7. The *general* form of the power function relating sensation and stimulus intensity is $R_s = ?$.

8. The value of the exponent of a power function relating sensation to stimulus intensity is determined by:

9. The essential characteristics of cross-modality matching are:

10. If the power function of one modality has an exponent of 1.2 and the power function of a second modality has the exponent of 0.6, a plot of the equal-sensation function on log-log coordinates should yield a straight line with a slope equal to 2.0. The reasoning behind this deduction is:

11. If the inverse of an attribute is scaled, the resulting scale would support Stevens' law if:

12. (a) The major lines of evidence supporting the power law are:
   (b) The major counterevidence consists of:

13. On prothetic continua, a plot of a partition scale against a corresponding proportionality scale produces a curve which is usually:

14. Two differences between direct and indirect scaling methods are:

ANSWERS TO EXERCISES

6-1. The points derive from a power function.

6-2. When the power function is of the form $Y = kX^c$, both c and k can be estimated from the log-log graph. The latter is gotten by finding the value of Y corresponding to an X value of 1, because when $X = 1$, $Y = k$.

The exponent c is obtained from the slope of the straight line. In calculating the slope, however, we do not make use of the X and Y values that occur on the abscissa and ordinate. Rather, we must employ their logarithms because it is log X and log Y that are actually plotted when log-log coordinates are used. As an illustration, the function $Y = 0.2X^2$, graphed in Fig. 6-8, has Y values of 0.2 and 5 associated with X values of 1 and 5, respectively. Accordingly, $c = (\log 5 - \log 0.2)/(\log 5 - \log 1) = (0.70 + 0.70)/(0.70 - 0.0) = 2$. Thus, the slope of the straight line corresponds to the exponent of X.

6-3. As a log-log plot shows, the eight points presented in Exercise 6-1 are derived from a power function. The slope of the function may be derived from any pair of points. Taking the first and seventh pair of points,

$$c = \frac{\log 21.2 - \log 4.2}{\log 50 - \log 2}$$
$$= \frac{1.326 - 0.623}{1.699 - 0.301}$$
$$= 0.50$$

By extrapolation on the log-log plot to $X = 1$, we find $k = 3$. The required equation is therefore $Y = 3X^{\frac{1}{2}}$.

6-4. (a) As implied in the description of the problem, although E's interest lies in JNDs, the only quantities that he can directly manipulate are DLs, so that empirically his task is to determine the stimuli that are located 5, 10, 15, 20, 25, and 30 DLs above the absolute threshold. Granting the truth of Weber's law, these stimuli are related to their respective DLs by equation 6-1, which in its restated form shows that the number of DLs (r) between a given stimulus and threshold is a linear function of the logarithm of the initiating stimulus (S_i). Therefore, transformation of the six stimuli to logs followed by a plot of the transformed points on linear-linear coordinates should show that the six points fall on a straight line. Or more expediently, the six untransformed points ought to describe a straight line when plotted on semilogarithmic coordinates. As the student should verify, the latter is indeed the case; accordingly, Weber's law holds.

(b) The value of the absolute limen (S_0) is the stimulus value that is zero DLs (or JNDs) above threshold. Extrapolation of the straight line of the semilog plot to a value of zero DLs (or JNDs) shows that $AL = 20$ units.

(c) It will be recalled that the Weber ratio, symbolized as C, is related to c, the slope of equation 6-1 by $c = 1/\log (1 + C)$. When Y is a linear function of log X, the slope of the function may be obtained from $(Y_2 - Y_1)/(\log X_2 - \log X_1)$. Because the data points deviate little if at all from a straight line, we may calculate the slope from any pair of points. Choosing the first and the last of the six points and taking logs to three decimal places, we obtain $c = (30 - 5)/(2.501 - 1.501) = 25.00$. Consequently $25.00 = 1/(\log 1 + C)$, and log $(1 + C) = 0.04$. Because the antilog of 0.04—the number whose logarithm to the base 10 is 0.04—is 1.096, it follows that $(1 + C) = 1.096$ and $C = 0.096$, a value which may be rounded off to 0.10.

(d) It is not possible to decide from the available information whether the six data points support or disconfirm Fechner's law. If Fechner's law is to receive support from the present data, the loudness of each of the six stimuli must be in direct proportion to the associated number of *JND*s. Thus, for example, the stimulus with a magnitude of 50.2 units, 10 *JND*s above threshold, ought to be perceived as twice as loud as the stimulus of 31.7 units, which was determined to be 5 *JND*s above threshold. The answer to this question must, therefore, hinge on further experimentation in which the perceived loudness of each stimulus is evaluated.

6-5. In narrowing the field of possibilities, the four estimation procedures are immediately ruled out by the requirement that **S** produce stimuli having certain properties specified by **E**. Of the four production methods, ratio production is clearly inapplicable, since **S** is not required to make ratio judgments nor could he consistently base his estimates on such judgments if he so chose. The second of the two initially presented tones, though assigned the number "7," may appear very far from seven times as loud as the first. Magnitude production is ruled out for the same reason.

It is obvious that we are dealing with one of the partition methods, and despite the opening sentence of the instructions, the method employed is category production. The **S** is required to produce stimuli which elicit sensations falling in any of the seven categories separated by equal sense distances and labeled 1, 2, 3, . . . , 7, as these are called for by **E**. The task of **S** is not the direct production of specified sensory intervals, so that interval production is inapplicable.

The instructions quoted come from an experiment in a paper by Stevens and Guirao cited earlier (1962, p. 1467).

6-6. If the sensory scale of vegs conformed to Fechner's law, the function describing these points would be of the form $V = c \log S$, and consequently a plot of the six points on semilog coordinates should define a straight line. Rather than a straight line, however, a steeply rising curve is obtained, which is out of harmony with Fechner's law.

On the other hand, when plotted on log-log coordinates, the six points do fall very nearly on a straight line, and accordingly, it is a power function, $V = kS^c$, that relates apparent heaviness to physical heaviness.

6-7. The constants of the power functions are calculated from the method of averages as follows. We have six equations of the form $\log V = c \log S + \log k$, one for each of the six points with which we are concerned. As usual we reduce these equations to two and calculate from the latter the values of the required constants. Converting the veg and gram values to logs,

$$
\begin{array}{ll}
0.0000 = c(2.0000) + \log k & 0.9031 = c(2.7312) + \log k \\
0.3010 = c(2.2463) + \log k & 1.2041 = c(2.9699) + \log k \\
\underline{0.6021 = c(2.4900) + \log k} & \underline{1.5052 = c(3.2061) + \log k} \\
0.9031/3 = c(6.7363/3) + \log k & 3.6124/3 = c(8.9072/3) + \log k
\end{array}
$$

$$
\begin{array}{l}
3.6124/3 = c(8.9072/3) + \log k \\
\underline{-[0.9031/3 = c(6.7363/3) + \log k]} \\
2.7093/3 = c(2.1709/3) \\
\qquad c = 2.7093/2.1709 \\
\qquad c = 1.2480
\end{array}
$$

Next we find k:

$$4.5155/3 = c(15.6435/3) + 2 \log k$$
$$-6 \log k = 1.2480(15.6435) - 4.5155$$
$$\log k = -2.5013$$
$$k = 0.00315$$

Consequently the required power function is $V = 0.00315S^{1.2480}$. Employing the 10 scale points shown in the table and a different method of curve fitting, Guilford and Dingham obtained the function $V = 0.0039S^{1.2346}$. Observe that the exponent of the power function is greater than unity, and note from Fig. 6-6 that such functions, when plotted on linear coordinates, rise increasingly more steeply as values of the independent variable are increased. Having the opposite property, the logarithmic function (Fig. 6-1), and therefore Fechner's law, will diverge widely from data which are adequately described by power functions with exponents greater than or equal to 1.

6-8. The mean category assignments to stimuli W_3, W_4, and W_5 should be such that on the category scale they maintain the same ratio relations among the four sensory intervals that held on the magnitude estimation scale. Therefore, because on the latter scale the interval between W_2 and W_3 (10 units) is twice the interval between W_1 and W_2, the mean category rating of W_3 should maintain this 2:1 relationship in the size of the sensory intervals and must, therefore, be 3.0. Inasmuch as the interval separating W_3 and W_4 on the magnitude scale is three times that separating W_1 and W_2, stimulus W_4 will have to receive a mean category rating of 4.5 in order to maintain the ratio of 3:1 on the category scale. By the same reasoning, W_5 should receive a mean category rating of 6.0.

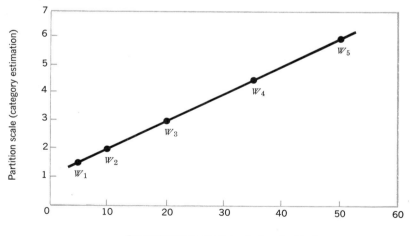

Fig. 6-24. A hypothetical situation in which the category estimations of the five weights, W_1, W_2, . . . , W_5, are linearly related to the magnitude estimation judgments.

Note that the category scale (C) is a linear function of the magnitude scale (M), the specific transformation being $C = 0.1M + 1.0$. If, then, the five weights are plotted on a graph indicating their respective category and magnitude assignments, as demonstrated in Fig. 6-24 the points will fall on a straight line.

More generally, if a partition scale is actually an interval scale of sensation and a proportionality scale of the same modality is a ratio scale of sensation, the two scales will be linearly related, and a plot of the scale values assigned to any set of stimuli from the modality will describe a straight line. We will have occasion to use this result later in the chapter.

PART 2

LEARNING AND BEHAVIOR

INTRODUCTION

The first six chapters have been devoted primarily to "methodological" matters, as distinct from substantive or "content" material. The issues of experimental design and control discussed in Chap. 2 arise wherever experimentation is conducted in psychology, the descriptive statistics presented in Chaps. 3 and 4 are even more ubiquitous, and the psychophysical and scaling methods discussed in some detail in Chaps. 5 and 6 have been adapted to a variety of subject areas in psychology.

The emphasis in Chaps. 7 through 12 switches to one of content. These chapters present a number of research areas—chosen arbitrarily it must be admitted—which enjoy a substantial amount of research interest and which are, in some sense, "important" for experimental psychology. The particular areas chosen bear the stamp of the writer's interests; others would have chosen different topics. Nevertheless, to merit inclusion a topic had to be such as to lend itself to experimentation on the undergraduate level. Recent research into the biochemical basis of memory makes fascinating reading; but the prerequisites, both in equipment and knowledge, required for meaningful research are vastly beyond what one can expect to find at the undergraduate level. Animal facilities, increasingly found in undergraduate laboratories, are probably necessary for research relating to many of the topics presented in Chaps. 7 and 8. However, this is less true for the material covered in subsequent chapters.

The distinction between "method" and "content" is far from absolute; each and every content area is ripe with methodological problems and issues particular to itself. Indeed in many areas methodological problems predominate, and a proper understanding of, or even inquiry into, substantive issues often has to be sidetracked until pressing methodological problems are solved. There is no sign that this is a situation of the past.

It is for this reason that in the chapters which follow a fair amount of emphasis has been placed upon "local" problems of methodology. Nevertheless, an attempt has been made to strike some kind of balance between the methodological problems encountered in a specific research area and the substantive issues involved, which, after all, are the primary concern of experimental psychologists.

7 INSTRUMENTAL APPETITIVE CONDITIONING

Although the term "conditioning" is often used in a much wider context, it is more properly restricted to "simple" forms of learning, in particular, to *classical* and *instrumental conditioning*, two very active areas of research interest. We shall shortly define these terms in a way that delimits their areas of applicability, but for the moment let us observe that classical conditioning has long suffered a measure of neglect in this country. Until recently a disproportionate amount of research effort was devoted to instrumental conditioning. Partly because of this fact, but mainly because classical conditioning procedures frequently require sophisticated apparatus not generally available in undergraduate laboratories, our discussion shall be largely limited to instrumental conditioning. Fortunately, a number of sources are now available which provide a good overview of the methods, procedures, and issues that are germane to classical conditioning (Beecroft, 1966; Gormezano, 1966; Gormezano & Moore, 1969; Prokasy, 1965).

SOME PROPERTIES OF CLASSICAL CONDITIONING

Although we shall not treat classical conditioning in detail, some discussion of its basic terms and concepts will be of value for subsequent portions of this chapter and the following one.

In classical conditioning an association is established by presenting repeatedly a *conditioned stimulus* (*CS*) before the application of the *unconditioned stimulus* (*UCS*). In the beginning the *CS* is presumably a "neutral" stimulus, in the sense that it does not evoke the *unconditioned response* (*UCR*). After sufficient pairings of the *CS* and *UCS* in an appropriate temporal order, the *CS* by itself will evoke the response formerly elicited by the *UCS*; when evoked by the *CS*, the response is called a *conditioned response* (*CR*). The *CR* is not necessarily a replica of the unconditioned response; it may be of lesser intensity or may differ in qualitative aspects. Nevertheless, there is usually little question that it is part of the response complex that makes up the *UCR*.

PAIRING RELATIONS OF CS AND UCS.   Some of the most potent independent variables in classical conditioning relate to the manner in which *CS* and *UCS* are presented to the subject. In the usual classical conditioning paradigm, the *CS* is presented first (*forward conditioning*) and overlaps the onset of the *UCS*, in which case the procedure is called "delay conditioning." In the event that the *CS* terminates before the onset of the *UCS*, the procedure is called "trace conditioning." Generally speaking, conditioning is facilitated by the delay procedure. The interval between onset of *CS* and onset of *UCS* (whether a delay or a trace procedure is employed) is termed the "CS–UCS interval." For many types of responses the optimal interval is about 0.5 sec. At times, especially for control purposes, the *UCS* is made to precede the *CS* in repeated pairings, a procedure known as "backward conditioning"; little, if any, true conditioning occurs under this procedure.

Rescorla (1967a) has recently suggested that the critical relationship in classical conditioning is the *contingency* which exists between *CS* and *UCS* rather than the fact that the stimuli are paired. The difference between the two interpretations is illustrated by the following example. Suppose that food is presented to a dog for brief periods 10 times during an experimental session. Let a tone be paired with half of the food presentations and occur a like number of times separated from that event. Thus the tone is paired with food presentation a number of times, but there is no contingency between it and food because (assuming appropriate durations of tone and no-tone) the probability of food presentation given the tone is the same as given no-tone. In other words, the tone is not a predictor of food. In the usual classical conditioning paradigm, the *CS* is a perfect, or near-perfect, predictor of the *UCS*, inasmuch as the latter occurs only after presentation of the *CS* and never in its absence. As Rescorla points out, this analysis has important implications for what constitutes an appropriate control procedure for the classical conditioning paradigm, which he feels is presentation of *CS* and *UCS* in a random, i.e., noncontingent, relationship. Seligman (1969) has contested this view, citing a number of instances in which the random-control procedure suggested by Rescorla proved inadequate for control purposes.

It may be noted that the notion that the effective property of the *CS* is its predictor value for the *UCS* has a parallel in recent interpretations of "secondary" or conditioned reinforcement. A number of investigators now feel that a neutral stimulus gains conditioned reinforcement strength to the degree that it reliably predicts the advent of "primary" reinforcement (e.g., Egger & Miller, 1962).

DISTINGUISHING CLASSICAL FROM INSTRUMENTAL CONDITIONING. Operationally, classical conditioning is characterized by two sets of conditions. The first is that the response to be conditioned can be produced on demand by **E** simply by presenting the unconditioned stimulus to the subject. Thus, if **E** wishes to condition the salivary response in dogs, salivation may be induced by giving the animals a morsel of food at the appropriate time. The food is the unconditioned stimulus, and the salivary response (when it is elicited by the *UCS*) is the unconditioned response. In instrumental conditioning, on the other hand, **E** does not have at his disposal stimuli which elicit such responses as bar pressing, running down a straight alley, and placing marbles in an aperture. Rather he must "shape" the response to be conditioned, or with human **S**s instruct them in their task. Stated differently, on the response side the raw materials of classical conditioning are *elicited* responses whereas in instrumental conditioning, they are *emitted* (cf. Skinner, 1938, pp. 19 ff).

The second defining property of classical conditioning is that application (or withholding) of the *UCS* is independent of **S**'s behavior. Another way of putting this is that in classical conditioning, reinforcement (the *UCS*) is *not* response-contingent. Quite the contrary in instrumental conditioning. Here whether or not **S** receives the reinforcing stimulus (e.g., food, money) depends entirely on whether the appropriate response is made. Consequently, we say that in instrumental conditioning, reinforcement is *response-contingent*.

A third feature that helps to characterize classical conditioning is the nature of the responses which undergo conditioning. Most often these are responses associated with the autonomic nervous system, for example, salivation, heart rate, and skin conductance (galvanic skin response—GSR). However, the eye-blink response, widely used in this country in classical conditioning studies, is one clear exception. Although it may be true that responses mediated by the autonomic nervous system are more readily conditioned by means of classical conditioning procedures and nonautonomic nervous system responses by instrumental conditioning procedures, the relation is by no means an exclusive one. Nonautonomic nervous system responses (e.g., the eye blink) can be classically conditioned, and a variety of responses mediated by the autonomic nervous system have been reported to be conditionable through instrumental means. These include the *GSR* (e.g., Gavalas, 1967; Kimmel, 1967; Kimmel & Kimmel,

1968), vasoconstriction (Snyder & Noble, 1968), intestinal visceral responses (Miller & Banuazizi, 1968), salivation (Miller & Carmona, 1967), and heart rate (e.g., DiCara & Miller, 1968; Miller & DiCara, 1967; Trowill, 1967).

In one such study, Miller and DiCara (1967) paralyzed the skeletal muscles of rats with a curare drug, maintaining the Ss on artificial respiration. Previously the animals had had electrodes implanted in a region of the brain in which electrical stimulation is positively rewarding. One group of 12 Ss received the rewarding brain stimulation if their heart rates increased over a criterion level, and a second group of 12 Ss was rewarded for heart-rate decreases. As shown in Fig. 7-1, the response-contingent reward was successful in modifying heart rate in both directions.

It is a curious fact that despite a long-standing suspicion that autonomic nervous system responses may be amenable to instrumental conditioning and despite several early attempts to verify this hypothesis, convincing evidence did not appear until recently, when suddenly a large number of experiments producing positive results were published within a period of a few years. Methodological problems notwithstanding (cf. Katkin & Murray, 1968)—perhaps the most nagging of which is the concern that uncontrolled conditioning of skeletal responses may lie behind positive results—it now appears firmly established that a wide range of autonomic responses may be conditioned through instrumental procedures. As Miller has pointed out repeatedly, this result, apart from its significance for learning theory, is extremely important for psychosomatic medicine. The reason is that "if visceral responses can be modified only by classical conditioning, they can be learned and maintained only in situations involving reinforcing stimuli with the unconditioned ability to elicit that particular visceral symptom; whereas if they can be learned as instrumental responses, rewarded by the law of effect, their initial learning and subsequent performance can be reinforced by any one of a wide variety of rewards [Miller & Carmona, 1967, p. 1]." Anger, for example, could be instrumentally acquired if it resulted in some such reinforcement as the individual winning his way. Miller (1969) has recently reviewed much of the data relating to the instrumental learning of visceral and glandular responses.

Among the interesting research problems that face us now is the task of learning something about the importance of instrumental conditioning in shaping the autonomic response patterns of individuals. In pursuing this problem, we shall have to inquire into the relative efficiency of classical and instrumental procedures in the acquisition and maintenance of autonomic responses and their capacity to preserve a conditioned autonomic response against the effects of extinction, a very important point.

To recapitulate, classical and instrumental conditioning differ operationally in terms of the control which E has over the response to be conditioned and the nature of the contingency holding between behavior and reinforcement. The type of response systems involved—autonomic versus nonautonomic or, as sometimes characterized, involuntary versus voluntary—is perhaps a less reliable point of distinction.

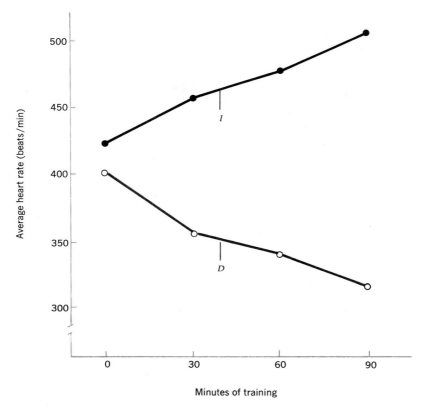

Fig. 7-1. Instrumental conditioning of increases (*I*) and decreases (*D*) in heart rate by response-contingent reward (electrical brain stimulation) of curarized rats. Each point represents the average number of beats per minute during a 5-min observation interval. (SOURCE: N. E. Miller and L. DiCara. Instrumental learning of heart rate changes in curarized rats: Shaping, and specificity to discriminative stimulus. *Journal of Comparative and Physiological Psychology*, 1967, **63**, 12–19. Copyright 1967 by the American Psychological Association and used by permission.)

RESPONSE MAGNITUDE VERSUS RESPONSE DIRECTION

We have now differentiated classical conditioning from instrumental conditioning, but the term "conditioning" itself remains undefined. Without a definition, it is not clear how instrumental conditioning differs from other kinds of learning. The purpose of this section is to introduce an operational criterion that will be of value in separating instrumental conditioning from other forms of learning. The criterion will later be applied to classical conditioning as well.

Like velocities in physics, behavior has *direction* and *magnitude*. If a pigeon pecks one of two keys facing it, we may ask *which* key it pecked (response direction) and *how fast* or with *what force* it pecked (response magnitude). Despite the obviousness of this distinction and its relevance for a variety of experimental results, psychologists have been unaccountably slow in giving it due recognition. Perhaps one factor deferring such recognition is the implicit assumption that laws of learning are independent of the response systems upon which they are formulated. As we shall see later, at this stage of development in psychology at least, this seems not to be the case.

RESPONSE MAGNITUDE.   Of course for a response to have magnitude, it must have direction as well—it must be identified. However, when only a single response class is recorded and reinforced by *E*, response direction is fixed and only response magnitude is subject to variation and measurement. In the straight alley there is only one response class—that of traversing the alley from start to goal box—which is recorded and reinforced by *E*. Variation can occur in response magnitude only, for example, in how fast *S* runs to the goal box. As a second illustration, a monkey given a single lever to press for food reinforcement may engage in all sorts of behavior, but because only his lever-pressing responses are recorded and reinforced, response direction is held constant. It is response magnitude, perhaps response rate or latency, that provides the data of experimental interest.

Magnitude measures may be divided into two classes, those that are *reinforcement-correlated* and those that are *reinforcement-uncorrelated*. In the first class there is a direct relationship between response magnitude and receipt of reinforcement. In the runway, for example, running speed and receipt of reinforcement are perfectly correlated in that the faster *S* runs, the faster it receives access to the reward in the goal box. For many reinforcement schedules, the major dependent variable in the Skinner-box setting, response rate, also is reinforcement-correlated: the higher the rate, the sooner reward is received.

In contrast, most often response force is reinforcement-uncorrelated (or only slightly correlated), inasmuch as a certain minimum force applied to the manipulandum activates the feeder mechanism, and forces of greater magnitude have no effect whatever on receipt of reinforcement. The same is normally true for response duration, a minimum duration of activation of the manipulandum being required and longer durations having no effect on the delivery of reinforcement. It is quite feasible to convert response force and duration into reinforcement-correlated measures, arranging things experimentally so that the greater the force exerted or the longer the duration of response, the faster reward is made available to *S*. But contingencies of this nature are rarely, if ever, used. *DRL* schedules (Chap. 9) are examples where the usual correlation between response rate and reinforcement or between response speed and reinforcement is reversed by requiring that *S* withhold his response for a certain minimum length of time (cf. Logan, 1966).

From among the many existing measures of response magnitude—response rate, latency, force, amplitude, displacement, duration, and so on—

several are often simultaneously available for measurement. It is uncommon, however, that more than one measure of response magnitude is seriously studied within the same experiment, so that our knowledge of how different indicators of response magnitude covary with variations in important independent variables is still very rudimentary (cf. Herrick & Bromberger, 1965; Kobrick, 1956). Quite likely, the clustering of measures of response magnitude will hinge on the nature and extent of the correlation with reinforcement enjoyed by each of the separate indicators. This is an important problem area, one which, because of recent technological advances in response measurement and data processing, ought soon to escape its past neglect.

RESPONSE DIRECTION. When identification of S's response is the important dependent variable, one is dealing with response direction. In principle S chooses between two or more well-defined alternatives, and the basic datum consists of the classification of S's response within the permissible alternatives.

Though also available for measurement, indicators of response magnitude are usually completely ignored when E's first interest is response direction. In verbal learning experiments, for example, where almost always the important datum is the identity of the verbal response given by S, how fast or how loud S responds—measures of response magnitude—are not often considered. Among the few exceptions are certain word-association tests, for which the identification of the verbal response given and its latency are both of importance.

Utilization of both direction and magnitude measures occurs somewhat more frequently in animal studies, where, for example, response speed may be recorded in a T maze as well as S's choice. Not uncommonly in such situations, response direction and response magnitude respond differently to the experimentally manipulated variables.

INSTRUMENTAL CONDITIONING DEFINED

At the outset let us recognize that no definition of instrumental conditioning— or of any other category of learning for that matter—is going to be completely satisfactory. Apart from the problem of capturing closely the thing to be defined, if a definition is to enjoy useful precision, it will have to suffer a certain amount of arbitrariness. These difficulties acknowledged, we take as our definition of instrumental conditioning any learning *based on response-contingent reinforcement that does not involve choice among experimentally defined alternatives.* The requirement that reinforcement be response-contingent qualifies the learning as instrumental, and the specification that the behavior be nonchoice means that only a single response class exists and that the dependent variable must be framed in terms of response magnitude. If the task presented S involves choice among a set of alternatives, we are not dealing with instrumental conditioning. Later we will suggest other categories for simple choice behavior.

Before applying our definition of instrumental conditioning, we should refine it somewhat by making a distinction on the stimulus side. The straight alley, an apparatus in which a rat is given the task of running down a length of runway to obtain reward in the goal box, is a well-used instrumental conditioning situation. Imagine that a light above the alley were turned on during those trials on which food was to be found in the goal box and extinguished on trials when the goal box was unbaited. Soon this (discriminative) cue would come to regulate the rat's running behavior in that S would run to the goal box quickly when the light was illuminated and show little interest in traversing the alley when the light was extinguished. The presence of the discriminative stimulus has a profound influence on S's behavior, though the behavior remains nonchoice, i.e., does not involve a choice among alternatives. We shall choose to consider this situation also one of instrumental conditioning, but to distinguish it from those in which exteroceptive discriminative stimuli are not employed, we will refer to it as an instance of "discriminative" instrumental conditioning. Consequently, we recognize two major subclasses of instrumental conditioning, *nondiscriminative* and *discriminative*. In both the behavior is nonchoice and reinforcement is response-contingent, but in the latter, a discriminative cue is associated with the availability of reinforcement.

It may be objected that, contrary to our dichotomy, there is no such thing as nonchoice behavior, since every response involves a choice among alternatives, no matter how ill-defined the latter may be. A rat not running down the straight alley is doing something else—sitting, sniffing, etc. A child not delivering marbles into the experimental receptacle is engaged in other behavior—looking around him, examining the marbles, and so on. It is only that in some cases we are interested enough in at least some of the alternatives to note and record them, but in others we are not. There is a sense in which this argument is correct, indeed, is logically correct. If S is not performing the instrumental response, he must be engaged in alternative behavior, which may be considered to have been "chosen" over the instrumental response.

But not all sets of alternatives are equivalent. A rat not running a straight alley because, say, the discriminative cue is absent on that trial is engaging in a class of alternatives (sitting, grooming, sniffing, etc.) which bears little similarity to the instrumental response required in the situation, running. At a common sense level, the alternatives to the instrumental response chosen by the rat are not for the purpose of arriving at the reinforcement. It is quite different in the case of a monkey—to mix phylogenetic levels—who must choose between lifting stimulus object A or B for the raisin that is under one of them. Here the alternatives (choosing either A or B), potentially at least, are both routes to reinforcement, and on each trial the animal chooses one or the other of the two alternatives available to him.

It turns out that this analysis applies directly to classical conditioning, which is also restricted to nonchoice behavior. A single response, that elicited by the UCS, comprises the behavior of interest; accordingly, the dependent variables must be framed in terms of response magnitude, as indeed they are. Typical dependent variables are amount of salivation, magnitude of the *GSR*, and other such "intensive" measures. Even occurrence and nonoccurrence of the conditioned response may be considered a magnitude measure because, fundamentally, it is based on response latency. If the present analysis is accepted, it becomes possible to define the entire class of conditioning as *acquisition involving nonchoice behavior*.

CLASSIFICATION OF INSTRUMENTAL CONDITIONING PROCEDURES

A number of different experimental procedures have been conventionally included under the rubric of instrumental conditioning (e.g., Grant, 1964, pp. 8–13; Kimble, 1961, pp. 65–71; cf. also Bitterman, 1962). The purpose of the present section is to describe the more important of these within the context of the definition of instrumental conditioning offered above.

An exceedingly important variable in instrumental conditioning is the nature of the reinforcing stimulus, whether it is "positive" or "negative." Positive reinforcers (S^{R+}) are defined at bottom as stimuli which S will work to attain. Conversely, negative reinforcers (S^{R-}) are stimuli which S will work to avoid; they are often referred to as "aversive" or, when painful, as "noxious" stimuli. The term "appetitive conditioning" is often used to refer to those procedures which employ positive reinforcement, "aversive conditioning" being the corresponding designation for procedures based on negative reinforcement.

In many cases a stimulus can act as both a positive and a negative reinforcer, depending on circumstances. For example, a weak electric shock which ordinarily would serve as a negative reinforcer can be converted to a positive reinforcer by appropriate pairing with a potent S^{R+}, say food. Similarly a very small quantity of food might serve as a positive reinforcement to a hungry animal, but if the animal is accustomed to obtaining a substantially larger reward in the experimental situation, this very same quantity of food may often be shown to develop aversive properties. Thus the reinforcing value of a stimulus object cannot often be determined solely from its physical characteristics. The subject's past experience with the stimulus situation, his current motivational state, and his expectations concerning future rewards all enter to determine the effective reinforcing value of the stimulus object. Of course for some stimuli, for example, strong electric shock, the dependence of reinforcing value on these factors is much attenuated. Even so it has been shown that through appropriate scheduling, response-produced shock can serve to maintain behavior in monkeys for long periods of time (see Chap. 8).

Despite the complexities involved in specifying the "sign" of the reinforcing stimulus, it is useful to classify instrumental conditioning in terms of the nature of the reinforcement employed. By forming the possible pairwise combinations of the two operational criteria—employment of positive or negative reinforcement and presence or absence of a discriminative stimulus—we arrive at four major types of instrumental conditioning. A brief discussion of each follows.

Instrumental Conditioning with Positive Reinforcement

NONDISCRIMINATIVE CONDITIONING. This procedure is often called "reward training." With animal Ss, the reward is usually food or water; with humans (often children), it may be money, a trinket, or a piece of candy. The positive reinforcer may either be primary—that is, presumably unlearned (food, water, etc.)—or it may be secondary or "conditioned"—its rewarding properties traceable to past learning (money, tokens, goal boxes in which food was previously obtained, etc.). There seems to be no compelling reason to distinguish, as is sometimes done, between procedures in terms of whether the reinforcement employed is primary or conditioned, because the effects on behavior of both are closely comparable.

The straight alley has been a favorite setting for research in this type of instrumental conditioning, rivaled only by the Skinner box and related apparatuses. Most of the research employing Skinner boxes has involved "free responding" rather than discrete trials. The first technique leaves S free to make the instrumental response at his own pace, but in the second, each opportunity to respond (a trial) is regulated by E. With children and adults as experimental subjects, instrumental conditioning often occurs within the context of such simple tasks as placing marbles in an aperture, playing a slot machine, and so forth.

DISCRIMINATIVE CONDITIONING. In this variety of instrumental conditioning, a cue signals the availability of reinforcement, and eventually S comes to execute the instrumental response vigorously in the presence of the cue but weakly, if at all, in its absence. In the straight alley situation, the stimulus associated with reward, and hence called the "positive stimulus" (S+), might be a white alley, in which case the stimulus associated with nonreinforcement, the "negative stimulus" (S−), is likely to be a black alley. The S is run on the two alleys in a quasi-random order, usually 50 percent of the trials conducted on each alley; soon S's behavior reveals that it discriminates that reward is available only in the white alley. Goodness of discrimination is generally determined by comparing response speed in S+ with speed in S−.

This type of instrumental conditioning is often referred to as "successive" discrimination conditioning, because S responds to S+ and S− in succession. Successive discrimination is to be contrasted with "simultaneous" discrimination, where S+ and S− are presented simultaneously, as, for example, in a two-choice situation. Because choice between alternatives is always involved, simultaneous discrimination does not qualify as instrumental conditioning.

In the Skinner-box situation, successive discrimination conditioning is arranged in a precisely analogous manner, only here the positive stimulus is usually referred to as the "discriminative" stimulus (S^D), and the counterpart of S− is S^Δ (S-delta). Response rate is usually the dependent variable of interest so that ordinarily goodness of discrimination is assessed by comparing rate of responding in S^D with rate in S^Δ.

A serious complication for our definition of instrumental conditioning arises here and should be acknowledged. The richness of discriminatory behavior which can be developed by appropriate schedules of reinforcement, even when the instrumental behavior is nonchoice, is well known. Simply because choice among alternatives is not involved, must all this behavior be classified as instrumental conditioning? It is possible, though admittedly not likely, that there are functional similarities running through all discrimination learning based on nonchoice behavior, however complex, which argue convincingly for their inclusion within the category of instrumental conditioning. A second possibility is that in order to maintain reasonable homogeneity and cogency for this category, some restrictions will have to be placed on the stimulus side, perhaps that only a single S^D and a single S^Δ be involved. If so, any such cleavage should split off categories which are separated by meaningful functional differences.

A similar problem, though perhaps with fewer ramifications, arises in the case of nondiscriminative conditioning where, though manipulated discriminative stimuli are lacking, the scheduling of reinforcement can take on many and varied forms, some quite complex, as in "mixed" schedules (see Chap. 9). It remains to be seen whether there are important functional similarities running through the behavior generated by all such schedules—due at bottom to the fact that only a single response class is involved—or whether the behavior is too richly varied to be profitably encompassed within the category of instrumental conditioning.

Instrumental Conditioning with Negative Reinforcement

NONDISCRIMINATIVE CONDITIONING. When reinforcement is positive, the contingencies between response and reinforcement are limited in that, almost always, S works under some schedule or another to obtain reinforcement. With negative reinforcement, on the other hand, more possibilities appear, and three in particular have received much attention: punishment, escape, and avoidance conditioning.

If a particular response acts to produce a negative reinforcer, the paradigm is one of *punishment*. More precisely, in punishment the *application* of the aversive stimulus is contingent upon the execution of a member of a specific response class. For example, a pigeon accustomed to pecking a key to obtain food might later be greeted by an electric shock each time that it makes the instrumental response. To cite a more familiar example, children are ordinarily scolded, if not worse, for uttering obscenities in the presence of their parents. Note that the aim of punishment is not the acquisition of an instrumental response but rather the weakening or elimination of a response already in S's repertoire in some strength.

In *escape* conditioning the negative reinforcer is applied independently of S's behavior; execution of a specific response then terminates S^{R-}. The grid floor of an experimental chamber housing a rat might suddenly be electrified, and S must press the bar in order to terminate the noxious stimulus. As a second example, a perceptive child may terminate abruptly his mother's ire by a look of unusually deep remorse or another acquired strategy.

Finally, in *avoidance* conditioning performance of the instrumental response at the appropriate time allows S to prevent or postpone for a time the appearance of the negative reinforcer. A motorist pays a $15 parking fine only to prevent the consequences of not paying it. In laboratory situations, S might press a lever, withdraw a limb, or remove himself to a different location in order to avoid an impending aversive event.

All three conditioning procedures—punishment, escape, and avoidance—are possible in nondiscriminative situations, an obvious point in the case of punishment and escape. In nondiscriminative avoidance conditioning, S^{R-} is applied periodically unless S makes the required instrumental response, which postpones the negative reinforcer for a period of time. Named after the individual who first reported its use, it frequently is referred to as the "Sidman procedure."

All three procedures employ nonchoice behavior; consequently, the dependent variables must be expressed in terms of response magnitude, usually response latency or response rate. Choice among alternatives can be introduced into these conditioning procedures, in which case they would fall beyond the scope of instrumental conditioning.

DISCRIMINATIVE CONDITIONING. In *discriminated* punishment a cue signals when execution of the instrumental response is likely to produce S^{R-}. If the pigeon whose key pecks led to shock as well as to food were afforded a cue which indicated when responding was likely to lead to S^{R-}, S would soon put this information to good advantage and respond only in the absence of the stimulus. In the "real life" example cited above, although punishment for swearing is likely to occur if parents are present, such behavior under different stimulus conditions—say in the presence of peers—provides no such danger.

Discriminated escape conditioning is a completely feasible instrumental conditioning procedure, but it seems to have found little use in the laboratory. In this variant, a cue would signal when escape from the negative reinforcer was possible; performance of the instrumental response in the absence of the cue would have no effect on S^{R-}.

In *discriminated* avoidance conditioning, a cue signals the impending S^{R-}, and performance of the instrumental response soon enough after the appearance of the cue enables S to avoid the aversive stimulus. An apparatus widely used in studies of discriminated avoidance learning is the "shuttle box," so called because S remains in one compartment of this apparatus until the discriminative stimulus appears which, if shock is to be avoided, S takes as the signal to move into the other compartment. After a time the stimulus appears again, and S can again avoid S^{R-} by removing himself within the allotted time to the first compartment. By "shuttling" back and forth between the two compartments in response to the discriminative stimulus, S is able to stay out of harm's way.

The major dependent variable in studies of discriminated avoidance conditioning is the percentage of trials on which S makes an avoidance response, i.e., responds soon enough after the appearance of the discriminative cue to avoid S^{R-}. Actually, this measure is one of response magnitude because it is based directly on response latency. If the latency of a response measured from the onset of the discriminative cue is shorter than the interval separating onset of S^{R-} from onset of the cue, the CS–UCS interval, the response counts as an avoidance response; if it is longer, S fell victim to the aversive stimulus, and the response, an escape response, merely terminated S^{R-}.

EXTINCTION PROCESSES IN INSTRUMENTAL CONDITIONING

Our discussion of instrumental conditioning has been restricted thus far to acquisition processes. However, extinction of an instrumental response is of even greater interest to many investigators, and in this and the subsequent chapter we shall have something to say about this topic.

The operation of extinction as applied to positively reinforced instrumental responses is well defined and unique. It consists simply of the withholding of S^{R+}, which results, of course, in the weakening of the instrumental response. When referred to conditioning with negative reinforcement, this uniqueness is lost, and extinction after escape, punishment, and avoidance conditioning can in each case refer to at least two quite different operations. Extinction of an escape response, for example, may be accomplished either by the complete removal of S^{R-} from the experimental situation or, quite the opposite, by applying the negative reinforcer throughout a trial sequence, S^{R-} no longer being terminated by the instrumental response. The first procedure is much more common than the second. Various options also exist for extinction after punishment and avoidance conditioning. In Chap. 8 we shall deal with these extinction operations in some detail, as well as with their interrelationship.

OTHER FORMS OF INSTRUMENTAL LEARNING

A type of instrumental learning which is not far removed from instrumental conditioning results from simple choice situations based on spatially distinct alternatives, as provided by a T maze or by a pair of manipulanda (bars, levers, etc.). Here again there is an option with respect to the presence or absence of discriminative stimuli (also called "discriminanda"). If these are lacking, the correct and incorrect responses are defined in terms of spatial (or response) characteristics; for example, the left arm of a T maze might be the correct one. Acquisition of a choice response based on alternatives which are differentiated by means of spatial (or response) characteristics only is often called "selective learning" or "spatial discrimination learning." When the alternatives available to S are defined by discriminative cues, one often uses the term "nonspatial discrimination learning," frequently abbreviated as "discrimination learning." In such tasks, of course, S must attend to the discriminanda in order to solve the problem. The topic of discrimination learning is treated in some detail in Chap. 11.

The balance of the present chapter is devoted to appetitive instrumental conditioning. We begin with nondiscriminative conditioning, drawing from our discussion a number of principles that are applicable to discriminative, or, as it is frequently called, "differential," conditioning.

EFFECTS OF SEVERAL VARIABLES ON NONDISCRIMINATIVE INSTRUMENTAL CONDITIONING

Of the large number of variables that have been investigated in nondiscriminative instrumental conditioning, we will focus only on a few—magnitude of reward, drive (motivational) level, delay of reinforcement, schedule of reinforcement, and level of acquisition training. There are some interesting interrelationships among these five variables which, in part, account for their selection; moreover, all have been the target of considerable research effort. In the course of the chapter we shall also become acquainted with some of the theoretical formulations that treat the known influence of these and other variables of importance. We turn our attention first to the acquisition process.

Nondiscriminative Acquisition

RATE OF ACQUISITION VERSUS ASYMPTOTE.   Two processes can be distinguished in the acquisition of a conditioned response, *rate of acquisition* and *asymptote.* "Asymptote" refers to a relatively stable "terminal" level of performance, and "rate" reflects the rapidity with which the asymptote is reached. Figure 7-2 illustrates how acquisition curves can differ in rate, asymptote, or both.

It is difficult, if not impossible, to be sure that acquisition of a response has reached asymptote in the technical sense of that word, that further training would not improve performance. Consequently, the term "asymptote" must be taken with a grain of salt, interpreted to mean a point in acquisition where rate of acquisition has been reduced to a negligibly low value.

Where the data warrant it, we will indicate whether a given relevant variable influences rate of acquisition, asymptote, or possibly both.

MAGNITUDE OF REWARD.   The size of the reward, or incentive, used has an important and somewhat complex effect on instrumental conditioning, both in acquisition and in extinction. Though many questions still remain, we now understand the action of this variable in instrumental conditioning much more fully than we did a few years ago.

Before proceeding, we must comment on the methods by which magnitude of reward is manipulated. With hungry Ss, the commonest procedure is to vary the weight or the volume of solid and liquid nutrients. If E wishes to hold volume constant, perhaps to control for the amount of consummatory activity, the concentration of a liquid nutrient, such as sucrose solution, is manipulated. In

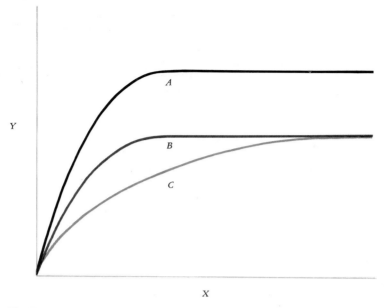

Fig. 7-2. Curves *B* and *C* have the same asymptote but different rates of approach. Curves *A* and *B* have different asymptotes but the same rate. Curves *A* and *C* differ in both rate and asymptote.

recent years a unique and extremely potent reward has become available through the use of direct electrical stimulation of certain centers of the brain. Animals with electrodes implanted in these areas will perform an instrumental response diligently and almost endlessly in order to receive electrical brain stimulation (e.g., Valenstein & Beer, 1964). By manipulating the intensity of the electrical stimulation, as well as other parameters of the stimulating current, precise control may be obtained over the magnitude of this unusual reward.

Simple effects of reward magnitude. Turning now to the effects of reward magnitude on instrumental conditioning, the first generalization of importance is that within wide ranges of amount of reward and training level, asymptotic performance is positively related to reward magnitude: *the greater the magnitude of reward, the higher the acquisition asymptote.*

Representative data are presented in Fig. 7-3. Hungry rats ran down a straight alley to obtain access to 2.5, 5.0, or 10 percent concentration of sucrose solution. It is clear from the figure that despite extensive training (99 trials at one trial per day), the three groups of Ss had different running speeds throughout acquisition. With suitable experimental controls, this result is obtained repeatedly on the animal level (e.g., Hill & Wallace, 1967a; Kintsch, 1962; Spence, 1956, p. 131).

With human subjects, the effect of reward magnitude on instrumental conditioning is less clear. Heber (1959) measured the time required for mentally

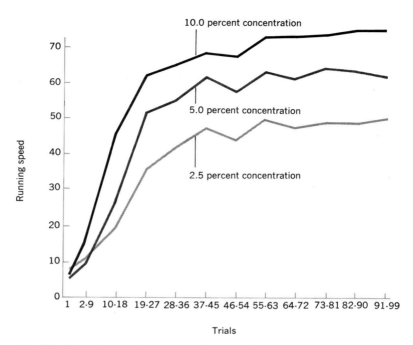

Fig. 7-3. Running speed as a function of magnitude of reward (concentration of sucrose solution). Note that the three curves arrive at different asymptotes. (SOURCE: D. Kraeling. Analysis of amount of reward as a variable in learning. *Journal of Comparative and Physiological Psychology,* 1961, **54,** 560–565. Copyright 1961 by the American Psychological Association and used by permission.)

retarded Ss to complete a motor task, working for either a highly preferred reward or one that was low in preference. There was a clear performance difference in favor of the high-preference reward group (cf. Nakamura & Krudis, 1967). On the other hand, neither Bruning (1964), studying a lever-movement response in kindergarten children, nor Ellis (1962), employing an operant response with mental defectives, found amount of reward to be an effective variable. As we shall soon note again, it is often difficult to translate adequately research problems from the animal to the human level. In the present case, there is a question whether the high-reward conditions were sufficiently differentiated from the low-reward conditions and, perhaps more important, whether satiation for the cumulative rewards did not offset any facilitation that the high-reward conditions might have otherwise produced.

In the studies just cited separate-groups designs were employed (cf. Chap. 2), as each S was exposed to a single reward magnitude. Consequently, experience with different reward magnitudes was eliminated as a factor in these experiments. We have used the term "simple effects" to emphasize this condition. The generalization that in instrumental conditioning, magnitude of reward and asymptotic performance are positively related applies most closely to the simple effects of reward magnitude.

Shifts in reward magnitude. A large number of studies have investigated what happens in instrumental conditioning when reward magnitude is shifted abruptly to higher and lower values. Their results provide a second generalization, namely, that *initial shifts in magnitude of reward will be matched by rapid shifts in performance to conform to the new reward magnitude.* The rapidity of the adjustment in performance depends on a number of factors, among them the type of reward employed. Apparently sucrose solutions, varying in either concentration or quantity, result in more sluggish shifts than either electrical brain stimulation or different quantities of dry food (e.g., Homzie & Ross, 1962; Rosen, 1966). Nevertheless, sooner or later instrumental performance adjusts itself to a level at or near that appropriate for the prevailing reward magnitude.

A question of some interest is, What happens when S is exposed repeatedly to a number of different reward magnitudes? Does performance of the instrumental response continue to adjust itself appropriately to the changing reward magnitudes? The answer is that it usually does.

The data of Fig. 7-4, which were obtained within a single-group design from a rat with electrodes implanted in the median forebrain bundle, illustrate

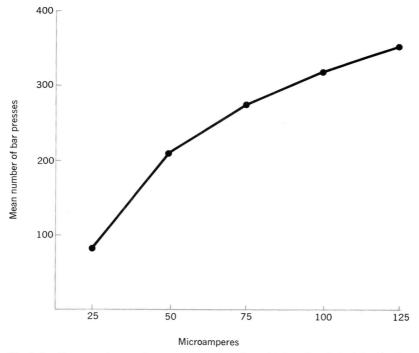

Fig. 7-4. Bar-pressing performance as a function of intensity of electrical brain stimulation. (*Data courtesy of Dr. S. S. Steiner.*)

this point. On each of 4 days, S pressed a lever for electrical brain stimulation, which varied between 25 and 125 microamperes (μa), in steps of 25 μa. Each of the five reward values occurred for 10 min each day, and the order of the five values was randomly determined daily. The number of responses made in the last 5 min of the 10-min periods was recorded for each of the five intensities and averaged over the 4 training days. As shown in the figure, despite the rapidly shifting reward values, there is a perfectly orderly relationship between rate of bar pressing and intensity of brain stimulation (reward magnitude). Comparable results have been obtained with repeated shifts of more conventional rewards (e.g., Capaldi & Lynch, 1967).

When, however, training with the different reward magnitudes is very prolonged and the range of magnitudes sampled is restricted, an appropriate shift in performance may occur only for a brief period with each shift in magnitude (Keesey & Kling, 1961).

Contrast effects. At times, adjustments to new levels of reward magnitude, particularly initial adjustments, tend to overshoot their mark, rising too high with increases in reward and descending too low with reductions. The first effect, much less reliable than the second, has been picturesquely called the "elation" effect and the second, the "depression" effect (Zeaman, 1949). These suggestive names have now succumbed to the more neutral terminology "positive" and "negative contrast effects" (see Fig. 7-5).

Mainly because of their implications for the Hull-Spence theory of conditioning, an unusual research interest has developed in contrast effects during the last decade or so. The topic was recently reviewed in detail (Black, 1968; Dunham, 1968), so we shall limit our discussion to a few highlights. As in so many other research areas, methodological problems abound in this one with the result that unequivocal demonstrations of contrast effects are not as simple to achieve as one might assume (cf. Dunham, 1968). Nevertheless there is a strong consensus that for initial shifts, negative contrast (depression) effects are obtainable over a fairly wide range of experimental conditions, though when sucrose solution rewards are employed, failures are not uncommon (e.g., Homzie & Ross, 1962; Rosen, 1966). Positive contrast (elation) effects are rarely reported, and at least some of the positive instances can be attributed to one confounding condition or another (Black, 1968; Dunham, 1968). White rats, it appears, are much better at expressing disappointment than joy.

There have been a number of theoretical attempts to account for contrast effects, ranging from Helson's (1964) adaptation-level theory, which has been characterized as a perceptual-motivational approach, to Amsel's frustration theory, an emotional-motivational interpretation. The full spectrum of these endeavors may be examined by consulting Bevan (1968), Black (1968), Capaldi and Lynch (1967), Dunham (1968), and Spear (1967). All the theories have trouble digesting some of the currently available results. For example, the failure to obtain positive contrast effects falls hard on perceptual-motivational explanations.

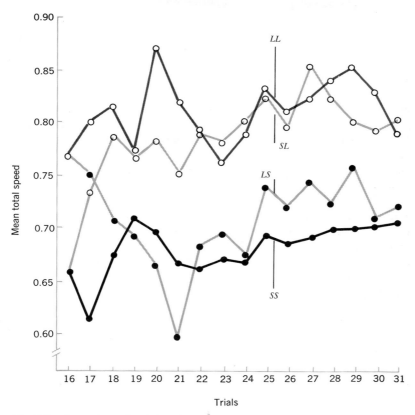

Fig. 7-5. A number of points relating to the effects of reward magnitude on instrumental conditioning are illustrated in the figure. Four groups of rats were run 1 trial per day either to a 2-pellet (*S*) or a 24-pellet (*L*) reward. After the first 16 trials, half of each group was shifted to the reward magnitude it had not yet experienced, and training then continued for another 15 trials. The running speeds during these "postshift" trials are shown in the figure for the four experimental groups. Note first of all that on the last "preshift" trial (Trial 16) the large-reward groups (*LL* and *LS*) show a much higher level of performance than the small-reward groups (*SS* and *SL*). Second, shifts in reward magnitude (Groups *SL* and *LS*) are followed by very rapid adjustments to the levels achieved by the respective nonshift control groups (*SS* and *LL*). Third, Group *LS* shows a negative contrast effect in that its performance temporarily declines below that of its control, Group *SS*. Although the depression effect observed in this study is rather transient, possibly because of the small number of preshift trials (cf. Davis & North, 1968), much more prolonged effects have been reported (e.g., DiLollo, 1964). Finally, there is no sign of a positive contrast effect in the performance of Group *SL*. [SOURCE: E. J. Capaldi and E. J. Lynch. Repeated shifts in reward magnitude: Evidence in favor of an associational and absolute (noncontextual) interpretation. *Journal of Experimental Psychology,* 1967, **75**, 226–235. Copyright 1967 by the American Psychological Association and used by permission.]

One disquieting feature of the research effort devoted to contrast effects is that, even more than in other areas of conditioning, this research is largely based on the laboratory rat. We have little information, for example, as to whether the asymmetrical contrast effects so often found with the laboratory rat are characteristic of other animals or of humans. Without some knowledge of the range of validity of this relationship, it is perhaps premature to dismiss perceptual-motivation interpretations. Moreover, we do not know if the divergent results obtained with sucrose and solid food rewards in the runway are peculiar to the rat or whether they point to a more pervasive interaction between contrast effects and type of reward. Parenthetically, there does not appear to be a single report in which these rewards are compared within the same experimental setting.

Unfortunately the few germane studies using human Ss that do exist employ tasks of questionable relevance. The study of contrast effects developed in the context of instrumental conditioning, and as a consequence, the basic phenomena relate to response magnitude rather than to choice behavior. Indeed the many interpretations of contrast effects in terms of motivational mechanisms arose because of the nature of the dependent variables: the role of motivation in choice behavior is far more complex, empirically and theoretically. In any event, the basic definition of contrast effects has been that S performs a criterion response with greater or lesser vigor depending upon the shift in incentive magnitude.

When the problem was translated to human research, a switch to choice measures somehow occurred. In a recent study, for example, college students were given the task of guessing whether the face of a card contained a dot or a line; a correct response was worth 5 cents in some cases and 1 cent in others (Halpern, Schwartz, & Chapman, 1968). Actually in all conditions either the dot or the line appeared on 60 percent of the trials. The investigators were interested in the percentage of trials that S guessed the more frequent event as a function of shifts in incentive magnitude. If, when Ss were shifted from large to small incentive, this value declined below that maintained by Ss who experienced the small incentive only, a negative contrast effect could presumably be inferred. It is by no means clear, however, that changes in response vigor have anything in common functionally with changes in guessing strategies. From the point of view of frustration theory, for example, why should not a subject, upon encountering the reduced incentive, increase rather than decrease his guesses of the more frequent event? Apart from these considerations, there are features of the results obtained by Halpern et al. that are greatly incongruent with the negative contrast literature. Perhaps this is the place to stress the more general point that when translating a research problem from one area to another, particularly from the animal to the human level, one must establish meaningful functional correspondences if the essence of the problem is not to be lost in the translation.

Our discussion of contrast effects has been brief. However, the topic will come to our attention again in this chapter because it has an important bearing on processes involving extinction, which may be interpreted as a special case of reward shift to zero magnitude.

Varied magnitude of reward. Let us suppose that shifts in reward magnitude are made rapidly and unpredictably; for example, 50 percent of a day's trials are conducted with a relatively large reward and 50 percent with a smaller reward, with the sequence of trials determined by chance. Will Ss' asymptotic performance be representative of the large reward, the small reward, or an intermediate reward magnitude? The answer appears to be that it will most nearly resemble the performance level characteristic of the average of the two reward magnitudes, as though S "averages out" the reward magnitudes (Logan, Beier, & Ellis, 1955; Logan, 1960; but cf. Grimsley & McDonald, 1964).

Summary. One conclusion from the work on magnitude of reward is that behavior in an instrumental conditioning situation can be controlled closely for long periods of time by manipulating reward magnitude. Although this conclusion might seem obvious after the fact, things need not have turned out that way. The Ss of our experiments could have been so constituted that they would run to, or press a lever for, any reasonable reward at just about the same level of performance, or, if small differences in performance did occur early in acquisition, these would rapidly disappear with continued training. That such behavior does not ordinarily occur has implications for the kind of theory that is likely to prove successful in accounting for behavior in the instrumental conditioning situation.

A second, more theoretical, implication of the preceding results drawn by some is that magnitude of reward has its major influence on ongoing behavior and has little, if any, effect on more permanent "habit structures." The rapid shifts in instrumental performance to conform to the prevailing reward magnitude has been interpreted to mean that this variable determines the extent to which a habit is exercised or performed rather than influencing the strength of the habit itself. In more technical terminology, amount of reward is thought to affect *performance* rather than *learning* (see, for example, Kimble, 1961, pp. 4–5). If reward magnitude influenced the learning process itself, presumably its effects on behavior would be more lasting than they have proven to be.

DRIVE (MOTIVATIONAL) LEVEL. The motivational level of S is another variable that has an important influence on instrumental conditioning. Normally drive level is manipulated by some deprivation operation, such as depriving S of food, water, a sexual or social partner. Also available for drive-manipulation purposes are more direct physiological techniques, for example, subcutaneous injection of hypertonic saline solution to instigate the thirst drive or, even more directly, chemical and electrical stimulation of the hypothalamic centers of the brain which regulate thirst and hunger (e.g., Grossman, 1960). One of the important potentialities of the physiological techniques, which have become available only recently, is that they enable E to manipulate S's drive level, say hunger or thirst, extremely rapidly; deprivation operations require considerable time to become effective.

Simple effects of drive level. There is a remarkable similarity between the simple effects of drive level on instrumental conditioning and those of magnitude of reward. Hold magnitude of reward constant and manipulate drive level—for example, by varying the number of hours of food deprivation—and in all probability, a set of acquisition curves will result that is indistinguishable from that obtained when magnitude of reward is varied. The curves in Fig. 7-6, obtained from hungry rats in an elevated platform apparatus, show the same prolonged separation as those in Fig. 7-3. Drive level, then, also exerts a strong influence on asymptotic instrumental performance and, as with reward magnitude, within wide limits, *the more intense the drive, the higher the performance asymptote.*

Shifts in drive level. Rapid shifts in drive level are more difficult to realize by conventional means than are corresponding shifts in reward magnitude; consequently, we have much less information on how well performance in instrumental conditioning tracks shifts in motivation. However, the available evidence suggests that instrumental performance is also highly sensitive to changes in drive level (e.g., Zaretsky, 1966). One possible difference between incentive and drive manipulations is that contrast effects may not occur upon shifts in motivation level. The evidence on this score is very scanty, however.

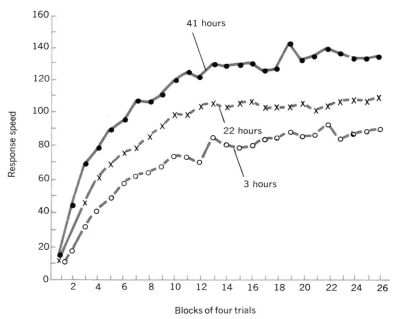

Fig. 7-6. Instrumental performance as a function of hours of food deprivation with magnitude of reward held constant. (*Data from Davenport, 1956.*)

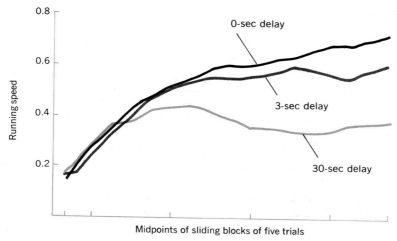

Fig. 7-7. Running performance as a function of delay of reward. (SOURCE: F. A. Logan. *Incentive.* New Haven, Conn.: Yale University Press, 1960. Copyright 1960 by the Yale University Press and reproduced by permission.)

DELAY OF REWARD. The normal procedure in instrumental conditioning is to reward S immediately upon making the required response. If, however, a time delay is interposed between completion of the conditioned response and delivery of reward, acquisition is interfered with, and the extent of the interference is determined by the duration of the delay. Historically, delay of reward has been a significant learning variable, as attested to by the empirical and theoretical attention it has received (cf. Renner, 1964). For the most part our treatment will be limited to its effects on instrumental conditioning.

Simple effects of delay of reward. Figure 7-7 presents the acquisition curves for three groups of rats running to an identical food reward which was delayed for 0, 3, or 30 sec after S reached the goal box. There are three features of these curves that deserve notice. First and most important, a clear separation develops among the three groups, a separation showing no sign of convergence (cf. Sgro, Dyal, & Anastasio, 1967; Wike & McWilliams, 1967). Although the 0-sec-delay group does not appear to have arrived at asymptote, the curves of the figure are demonstrative of the generalization that *asymptotic performance in instrumental conditioning is inversely related to the duration of reward delay*—the longer the delay, the lower the asymptote. Second, unlike the effects of reward magnitude and drive level, the performance differences to which different delays of reward give rise emerge rather slowly. It is as though performance early in training is governed by variables other than reward delay, which takes hold only somewhat later in the acquisition process. Finally, there is evidence in the curves of a drop-off in performance in the 30-sec-delay group—for the first time we encounter *non-monotonicity* in a curve relating performance level to amount of practice.

One possible interpretation of the preceding results is that in initial acquisition, performance is controlled primarily by the prevailing motive-incentive conditions, and because these are constant across groups, the behavior in the three groups is comparable. As learning progresses and S begins to discriminate the reward delay, a measure of aversiveness becomes associated with the latter (perhaps through a mechanism such as frustration, discussed below), which either limits asymptotic behavior to a value below that possible with zero delay or, if the delay is relatively long, actually causes a decline in the level of performance already achieved.

While verifying the nonmonotonicity noted above, recent evidence suggests that a 30-sec delay in the runway produces asymptotic behavior which is no better than no reward at all (Couch & Stanley, 1967). There is no convincing explanation of this result.

Shift effects. Suppose Ss trained with a long delay of reward are suddenly shifted to a short delay. How does instrumental performance adjust itself to the new delay? Unfortunately, the evidence is far from consistent, though one result seems firm: Ss shifted to a shorter delay adjust their performance to conform to the more favorable delay (e.g., Harker, 1956). Moreover, under certain circumstances, such Ss will exceed the performance levels of Ss run consistently with the shorter delay, producing behavior resembling a positive contrast effect (Sgro & Weinstock, 1963). Shifts from a short (1-sec) to a long (10-sec) delay, however, sometimes fail to result in a performance decrement (Harker, 1956).

Varied delay of reward. When delay of reward is shifted abruptly and unpredictably between two values, unlike the results obtained with reward magnitude for the corresponding operation, the usual result is that S's performance arrives asymptotically at the level typical for the *shorter* delay. As may be seen in Fig. 7-8, a group of Ss trained on a straight alley with a 1-sec delay on 50 percent of its trials and a 9-sec delay on the other 50 percent ultimately performed at the same level as achieved by a group run on all trials with the shorter of the two delays. A third group that experienced a delay of 5 sec on all trials turns out to be the slowest of the three groups. Note, again, the nonmonotonicity in the last group.

OTHER VARIABLES. Nondiscriminative instrumental conditioning is, of course, affected by a number of other variables, such as schedules of reinforcement, intertrial interval, and response effort. At least some of these variables are potentially reducible to the three already discussed. For example, a random partial reinforcement schedule could be considered a limiting case of varied magnitude of reward where, on some trials, reward magnitude is reduced to zero. Alternatively, it might be interpreted as a special case of varied delay of reward, composed of

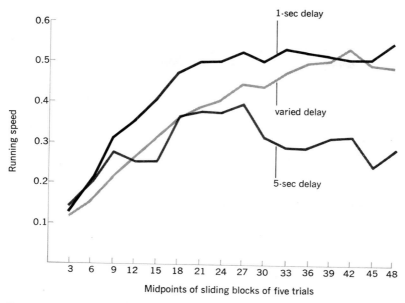

Fig. 7-8. Running speed as a function of constant and varied delay of reward. The varied delay group experienced a 1-sec delay on 50 percent of its trials and a 9-sec delay on the other 50 percent. (SOURCE: F. A. Logan, E. M. Beier, and R. A. Ellis. Effect of varied reinforcement on speed of locomotion. *Journal of Experimental Psychology*, 1955, **49**, 260–266. Copyright 1955 by the American Psychological Association and used by permission.)

zero-reward delay on reinforced trials and "infinite" delay on nonrewarded trials. Inasmuch as randomly rewarded Ss often perform asymptotically at a level comparable to continuously reinforced Ss (Ss rewarded on all trials), it appears that the analogy with varied delay of reward might be the more fitting of the two. It will be recalled that varied delay (between two equally likely values) tends to produce asymptotic performance that is appropriate for the shorter of the two delays, whereas varied magnitude of reward usually leads to asymptotic performance that falls below the level attained by the more favorable of the two magnitudes.

For a discussion of other variables that influence instrumental conditioning, sources such as Kimble (1961) and Logan (1960) may be consulted.

SUMMARY. To summarize briefly the effects of reward magnitude, drive level, and reward delay on the acquisition of a nondiscriminative instrumental response, we have seen that response magnitude is quite sensitive to all three variables. However, compared with magnitude of reward and drive level, delay of reward shows certain clear differences of detail, suggesting that the mechanisms underlying the effects of these variables are themselves different, at least in part.

Nondiscriminative Extinction

Perhaps more attention has been paid to extinction in instrumental conditioning than to acquisition. The factors governing the persistence of a response in the absence of reinforcement is a topic of considerable theoretical and practical significance. In a sense, however, the operation of extinction—by definition the removal of the reinforcing stimulus—is simply a special case of reward-shift effects, in which reward magnitude is reduced from some positive value to zero. And in all probability, the data relating to extinction will dovetail with the results obtained when shifts are between two nonzero reward magnitudes. To illustrate this point, it is often found that performance during the early trials of extinction is poorer than performance on later trials. Recalling our discussion of contrast effects of reward magnitude, this result could be attributed to an initial depression effect from which Ss recover on later extinction trials.

THE CONCEPT OF FRUSTRATION. Before we proceed to the data of extinction, it is convenient to introduce here an explanatory mechanism useful in the interpretation of many aspects of conditioning and extinction in instrumental conditioning—the concept of frustration. To get to this notion, however, we must first become acquainted with a related idea, the fractional anticipatory goal response.

The fractional anticipatory goal response. Suppose that S runs off repeatedly a stimulus-response (S–R) sequence which terminates in reward (S^{R+}), which we symbolize as S_1-R_1, S_2-R_2, . . . , $S_n-R_n \rightarrow S^{R+} \rightarrow R_G$. The S–R sequence may be a chain of stimuli and responses constituting the running response (in a straight alley), the bar-pressing response, or any other instrumental sequence. The terminal response in the sequence, R_G, is the goal response that is appropriate to the reward employed—eating, drinking, etc. Part of the goal response will depend closely on S^{R+}, in the sense that its likelihood of occurring in the absence of the reward object is very slight. For example, the peristaltic movements of the gullet which are a component of the goal response to a food reward are not likely to occur unless food is present and ingested. On the other hand, a portion of R_G is not so directly tied down to the reward. Salivation regularly accompanies eating, but clearly it can occur in the absence of ingesting food, as when one anticipates a preferred food. This part or "fraction" of the total goal response, the "detachable" component of R_G, may be symbolized as r_G.

Because r_G is detachable from R_G, it is available to various stimuli for conditioning in the experimental situation. For example, it is expected that with repeated trials, r_G would become classically conditioned to the cues immediately preceding reward. (The *UCS* for this postulated conditioning is S^{R+}, the *UCR* is R_G, and r_G becomes the *CR*; the *CS* is made up of those apparatus and situational cues which regularly precede the *UCS*.) In terms of our symbolized S–R sequence, S_n would then elicit not only R_n, a link in the instrumental response chain, but also r_G. Moreover, either through further conditioning or through the mechanism of stimulus generalization, stimuli very early in the S–R chain would also evoke r_G. Thus

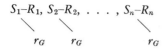

$$S_1–R_1, S_2–R_2, \ldots, S_n–R_n$$

$$r_G \qquad r_G \qquad\qquad r_G$$

Because the r_G response is elicited very early in the S–R sequence and, therefore, "anticipates" S^{R+}, it is called the "fractional anticipatory goal response." Inasmuch as any response made by S may be assumed to have stimulus consequences—e.g., proprioceptive feedback—the fractional anticipatory goal response always appears with an associated stimulus component s_G, i.e., $r_G–s_G$. There are certain special properties assigned to s_G, but these need not concern us now. The important point is that the $r_G–s_G$ mechanism is an objective way of capturing the notion that after a number of rewarded trials S comes to anticipate, or to expect, a reward as a consequence of performing the instrumental response.

The frustration mechanism. It is at this point that the concept of frustration enters. If after the conditioning of r_G to the components of the S–R sequence reward is omitted, it is assumed that a primary frustration response, R_F, occurs. In ordinary terms, frustration is assumed to be an unconditioned response which occurs when an anticipated reward fails to materialize.

One of the important properties of R_F is that it gives rise to a drive state, which, like other "irrelevant" drives (drives not appropriate to the reward object employed), summates with the relevant motivation to produce in S a heightened drive state.

This assumed property of frustration has been supported by evidence of the following sort. Rats are trained on a double runway which has two goal boxes, GB_1 and GB_2, the latter some distance beyond GB_1. On an initial series of trials, S finds reward in both goal boxes. Then comes a series of test trials on some of which S still finds reward in GB_1 (and GB_2), but on others reward is given only in GB_2. The critical datum is the speed with which S runs to GB_2 after failing to find food in GB_1. Is this speed greater than when food is presented in GB_1, as should be the case if the frustration presumably experienced in GB_1 owing to the omission of food there resulted in a drive increment? We must recall here that response magnitude is sensitive to differences in drive level. Most relevant experiments agree in showing a "frustration effect," i.e., S runs faster to GB_2 after experiencing nonreward in GB_1 (e.g., Amsel & Roussel, 1952).

A second property assigned to frustration is a mechanism providing for the *anticipation* of frustration—the fractional anticipatory frustration response. Just as R_G was assumed to have a conditionable component r_G, the primary frustration response R_F is assumed to have a detachable portion, r_F, which is available for classical conditioning to stimuli that occur early in the S–R chain. Thus, after one or more frustrating experiences, r_F may become conditioned to, and elicited by, stimuli occurring relatively early in the response chain, which is to say S would anticipate being frustrated. And in further analogy with the fractional anticipatory goal response, r_F has its distinctive stimulus consequences s_F, so that the complete anticipatory frustration mechanism is $r_F–s_F$.

It is a reasonable assumption—and there are supporting data—that frustration stimuli are aversive, in the sense that normally S will avoid frustrating situations if at all possible. Granting this assumption, it follows that S will ordinarily act to avoid stimuli that produce fractional anticipatory frustration responses, i.e., stimuli which elicit the expectation of frustration.

Because they act in opposite ways, it is important to distinguish between the two effects of frustration just discussed. On the one hand, the *experience* of frustration leads to a motivational increment that serves to *augment* in magnitude immediately following responses. On the other hand, the *anticipation* of frustration, because of its assumed aversiveness, will often *reduce* response magnitude in instrumental conditioning inasmuch as S will tend to avoid or postpone making responses which intensify anticipatory frustration ($r_F–s_F$). In attempting to predict the role of frustration in any specific situation, one must, therefore, assess which of these two processes will be predominant.

The concept of frustration, as defined here, is useful in explaining in an informal way many of the facts of instrumental conditioning and extinction. For example, we have seen that when S is shifted to a smaller reward, one often obtains a depression effect, a drop in performance below that maintained by Ss that have always experienced the smaller reward. Applying the frustration hypothesis to this result, one would assume that on encountering the smaller reward, a "mild" frustration response occurs. Although we defined the frustration hypothesis in terms of a transition to zero reward, it is a reasonable generalization that frustration will also occur, but to a lesser extent, if a significant reduction in reward is imposed, but not necessarily to a zero value. [This assumption is in need of empirical support; see Bower (1962) and McHose and Ludvigson (1965).] Through stimulus generalization, or perhaps rapid conditioning, the anticipatory frustration response is evoked in some measure by the stimuli occurring early in the appropriate S–R chain. Because the nearer S progresses to the goal box, the stronger $r_F–s_F$ becomes, and because *anticipatory* frustration is assumed to be aversive, it seems a fair inference that Ss shifted to smaller rewards will, at least temporarily, run slower than Ss whose speed is regulated by reward magnitude uncomplicated by anticipatory frustration responses. Other deductions are possible in this situation. We know that frustration cannot develop until an appropriate anticipatory goal response has been conditioned to the S–R chain. Accordingly, a depression effect should not occur if the reward shift occurs very early in training (cf. Davis & North, 1968). Later in the chapter, we shall cite further applications of the frustration hypothesis, but now let us discuss some of the variables that significantly affect the extinction process in nondiscriminative conditioning.

DRIVE LEVEL. Variables relating to the nature of the reinforcement employed (e.g., amount, delay, and schedule of reinforcement) can, by definition, be manipulated only during acquisition because in extinction, reward is unavailable. However, variables that are independent of the reinforcement operation (e.g., drive level, intertrial interval, and response effort) may be studied for their effects on extinction separately for manipulations taking place during acquisition and during extinction. In the case of motivational level, the consensus is that drive manipulations restricted to the acquisition period have little effect on later resistance to extinction when proper controls are employed (Barry, 1967; Kimble, 1961, pp. 411–416). This could have been guessed from our discussion of acquisition where we noted that, though nondiscriminative instrumental behavior was sensitive to differences in contemporary drive level, it tended to adjust itself rapidly to motivational shifts. Extinction simply provides the added complication of a concurrent shift of reward magnitude to zero magnitude.

We might also expect from the acquisition data that differences in drive level operating during the extinction process itself would prove effective in influencing resistance to extinction, and indeed this is the case (Barry, 1967; Horenstein, 1951; Singh, 1967). Consequently, the influence of drive level on extinction may be considered to be simply an extension of its effects on acquisition.

AMOUNT OF ACQUISITION TRAINING.   It is an almost universal assumption that the greater the amount of training, the stronger the habit. Instrumental conditioning is no exception, and so it has been generally assumed that the strength of a conditioned response is a monotonic function of the amount of training afforded the conditioned behavior. In many quarters resistance to extinction has been considered a fair measure of the strength of a conditioned response, implying that as the amount of training given to an instrumental response is increased, resistance to extinction also increases. For many years learning theorists rested in the comfort of the knowledge that this putative relationship was actually the case. Recently, however, unmistakable evidence has been obtained showing that in certain experimental situations, resistance to extinction is *reduced* by higher levels of acquisition training (e.g., Ison, 1962; North & Stimmel, 1960). Because it is known that in these situations at very low levels of training resistance to extinction increases with increasing practice, the implication is that the two variables are nonmonotonically related; that is, at relatively low acquisitional levels, both increase together, but at higher levels resistance to extinction decreases with further increases in amount of training.

One complicating aspect of this relationship is that almost without exception, level of acquisition training and resistance to extinction have been found to be *monotonically* related in the free-operant Skinner-box setting. To cite one example, D'Amato, Schiff, and Jagoda (1962) carried training to a maximum of 1600 reinforced bar-press responses distributed over 32 days and, as shown in Fig. 7-9 (lower curve), found an essentially monotonic function between acquisition level and resistance to extinction (cf. Born, 1967; Schiff, 1965). The basis of this striking disparity is not altogether clear, though there is evidence which

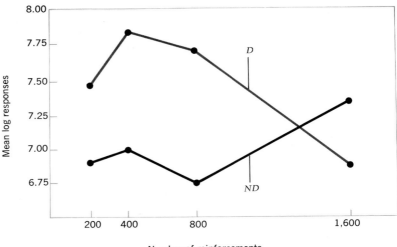

Fig. 7-9. Bar-pressing performance in extinction (expressed as a logarithmic measure) as a function of number of reinforcements and type of instrumental conditioning, discriminative (*D*) versus nondiscriminative (*ND*). (SOURCE: M. R. D'Amato, D. Schiff, and H. Jagoda. Resistance to extinction after varying amounts of discriminative or nondiscriminative instrumental training. *Journal of Experimental Psychology,* 1962, **64,** 526–532. Copyright 1962 by the American Psychological Association and used by permission.)

suggests it might have something to do with the magnitudes of the rewards employed, a variable to which we now turn.

MAGNITUDE OF REWARD. The effect of reward magnitude on resistance to extinction presents a confusing picture until one realizes that it is impossible to consider this variable in isolation of all others. The question "How does reward magnitude affect resistance to extinction?" is simply too open-ended, too unspecific to be adequately answered. In the terminology of Chap. 2, amount of reward interacts importantly with the level of training, with the nature of the dependent variable employed, and possibly with other variables as well, in determining resistance to extinction.

Earlier work suggested that resistance to extinction of the running response was increased by large magnitudes of reward, but then the very opposite result was obtained in similar experimental situations (Armus, 1959; Hulse, 1958). To confuse matters further, Hill and Spear (1962), attempting to resolve the discrepancy, thought that reward magnitude might interact with the intertrial interval in determining resistance to extinction. They found, however, that their larger reward *increased* resistance to extinction for both the intertrial intervals they used.

The results of the studies just cited, as well as those of certain others, can be explained if we assume that in the straight alley, amount of training interacts with reward magnitude in determining resistance to extinction. The nature of the hypothesized interaction is shown in Fig. 7-10 for two reward values. With a small reward, resistance to extinction is assumed to be monotonically related to acquisition level; with larger rewards, on the other hand, the function turns nonmonotonic.

If there is any validity to this hypothesis, it would explain why free-operant Skinner-box studies almost always produce monotonic functions relating resistance to extinction to reward magnitude, because customarily the reward employed in such studies is relatively small. It would also explain why Armus (1959) and Hulse (1958) found large reward to lead to less resistance to extinction than small reward although Hill and Spear (1962) encountered just the opposite. Armus and Hulse used relatively large numbers of acquisition trials (B in Fig. 7-10), but Hill and Spear used relatively few (A). Note from the graph that for some intermediate value of training, there should be no difference between large and small reward. The evidence bearing on the relations postulated in Fig. 7-10 is favorable (Ison & Cook, 1964; Wilton & Strongman, 1967), but not unanimously so (Hill & Wallace, 1967b).

An important lesson from this discussion is that one must be exceedingly careful about extrapolating experimental results beyond the range of values sampled. One must be continually aware that in any experiment a large number of possibly relevant variables (subject and situational) are held constant, usually at arbitrary values. Whether and to what extent the obtained results can be

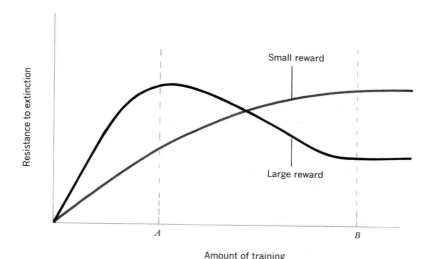

Fig. 7-10. Assumed interaction between reward magnitude and amount of training in determining resistance to extinction. Note that with a relatively small amount of training (A), large reward will lead to more resistance to extinction than a small reward; when training is very substantial, however, this relationship is reversed (B).

generalized beyond these unavoidable boundaries is a question that should always receive close attention.

There is no reason to be discouraged by the complexity confronting us even at the comparatively "simple" level of instrumental conditioning. First, an awareness that such interactions as illustrated in Fig. 7-10 exist should protect us from taking an oversimplified approach toward behavioral analysis and help in tempering appropriately our empirical generalizations. Perhaps more important, as these interactions become clear, they sensitize us to the sort of interactions we should look for in other situations. It seems plain, for example, that before **E** thinks too generally about an interesting finding obtained in an instrumental conditioning setting, he ought to wonder whether his result is bound to the particular training level (or reward magnitude) employed in his study.

We may also hope that, as the level of our analysis deepens, the empirical interactions themselves will become deducible from a limited set of theoretical principles or concepts. It has been suggested, for example, that where non-monotonicity between acquisition level and resistance to extinction occurs, this result can be understood in terms of the interplay between the r_G-s_G and the r_F-s_F mechanisms (e.g., Clifford, 1964). It will be recalled that the development of frustration depended on the earlier establishment of r_G-s_G. Other things being equal, it is reasonable to suppose that the fractional anticipatory goal response will be stronger after high levels of training than after low levels. As a consequence, one might suppose that after intensive acquisition training, Ss will encounter more disruptive frustration upon confronting extinction trials than comparable Ss allowed lesser amounts of acquisition training (cf. Marx & Tombaugh, 1967).

One difficulty with this formulation is, of course, that it does not accommodate the known importance of reward magnitude. However, it is not inconsistent to suppose that the strength of r_G-s_G is positively related to magnitude of reward (Krippner, Endsley, & Tacker, 1967; Peckham & Amsel, 1967), so that other things being equal, nonmonotonicity will be in evidence at lower levels of training when reward magnitude is high. Conceivably, with very small rewards—as used in the Skinner-box studies—an enormous amount of training is necessary to cause substantial differences in the fractional anticipatory goal response and hence in the degree of frustration experienced in extinction.

There are other details for which frustration theory might account. It appears that with sucrose solutions serving as reward the interaction between acquisition level and reward magnitude is less likely to occur, as resistance to extinction is often monotonically related to acquisition level over a wide range of reward magnitudes (Ison & Rosen, 1968; Uhl & Young, 1967). We have already noted that sucrose solutions frequently fail to produce negative contrast effects. These two results fit together in that they both are deducible from the assumption that downward shifts in sucrose rewards generate less frustration than comparable shifts of ordinary dry food. This assumption could be evaluated by obtaining an independent measure of frustration—perhaps in the double-runway situation—for magnitudes of sucrose reward that fail to produce a negative contrast effect and the expected interaction between acquisition level and reward magnitude. Going one step further, the different degrees of frustration generated by downward shifts of dry food and sucrose solutions possibly reside in the different preexperimental experience that the laboratory rat has with these commodities.

The point of this discussion is not to present a favorable prospectus for the frustration hypothesis, but rather to illustrate that even a relatively simple interrelationship between two assumed underlying processes can engineer a plausible explanation of a complicated structure of behavioral data (cf. Theios & Brelsford, 1964).

DELAY OF REWARD.   In any attempt to assess the role of delay of reward on subsequent resistance to extinction two methodological problems arise which, though of considerable importance, can only be mentioned here. Recall that delay of reward had a powerful influence on asymptotic performance in acquisition. Because Ss who experience different reward delays during acquisition are likely, as a consequence, to enter extinction at different performance levels, what one should take as his measure of "resistance to extinction" is not unambiguous. Absolute level of response will not do generally, but corrections for disparities in initial response levels are not always easy to justify. Though the problem has not been completely solved, some practical guidelines have been established (Anderson, 1963). For present purposes, it is sufficient that we be aware of the problem and be on guard that proffered differences in rate of extinction reflect more than differences in response strength at terminal acquisition. Obviously, this caveat applies as well to variables other than delay of reward.

The second methodological problem concerns the manner in which reward delay is manipulated. Actually, there is a whole cluster of methodological problems involved here, but we will cite only one, the time during which S is confined to the goal box during acquisition and during extinction. Where delay of reward has been manipulated by subjecting Ss to different waiting periods in the goal box before receipt of reinforcement, the duration of goal-box confinement to be employed during extinction must be given careful consideration. During extinction the investigator has the option of maintaining the delays employed during acquisition, or he can extinguish all groups with the same goal-box-confinement time. As we shall see shortly, the two procedures do not necessarily lead to the same results.

Varied delay of reward. Although the methodological problems just cited complicate interpretation of the available data, the results arising from *varied* delay of reward seem rather consistent: resistance to extinction is increased when delay of reward is introduced on a portion of the training trials (cf. Renner, 1964; Schoonard & Lawrence, 1962). To be effective, the delay must be substantial, for rats in the neighborhood of 20 to 30 sec (e.g., Logan, 1960, p. 191).

Apparently, the effect holds whether the confinement time during extinction is brief or is maintained for a period of time corresponding to the delay interval.

Constant delay of reward. The results obtained with constant delay of reward, i.e., with all acquisition trials of a given condition conducted under the same reward delay, are less conclusive (e.g., Fehrer, 1956; Logan, 1960). Here the problem of goal-box-confinement time during extinction appears to be more critical, though, unfortunately, the designs of most relevant experiments do not permit direct analysis of the contribution of this variable.

Tombaugh (1966), systematically manipulating this variable, trained four groups of Ss on a runway with reward delays of 0, 5, 10, or 20 sec. In subsequent extinction trials, half of the Ss in the last three groups were confined in the goal box for an interval equal to their reward delay while the other half received 0-sec confinement. With differences in terminal acquisition levels taken into account, it turned out that in the first set of groups delay of reward had no effect whatever on extinction performance. In the groups that were extinguished with 0-sec confinement, however, resistance to extinction was positively related to delay of reward (cf. Capaldi & Bowen, 1964).

Despite the lack of unanimity of results, the clear consensus is that where constant delay of reward does have an effect, it acts to increase resistance to extinction. In a way this is an unexpected result inasmuch as delay of reward interferes, often markedly, with the establishment and maintenance of an instrumental response. Nor is this the first time that we have found resistance to extinction to be at variance with measures of response strength based on acquisition performance. A comparatively large reward raises instrumental asymptotic performance, but in some cases it results in lowered resistance to extinction. Clearly, resistance to extinction and response vigor measured during acquisition cannot both be direct measures of response strength. Lawrence and Festinger (1962), in their extension of the theory of cognitive dissonance to the data of instrumental conditioning, lean heavily for support on this incongruity.

SCHEDULES OF REINFORCEMENT. One of the most potent variables affecting resistance to extinction is the schedule or pattern of reinforcement experienced during acquisition. Reinforcement can be administered according to a number of different schedules, but the one of primary interest here is a random partial reinforcement schedule, or, in operant terminology, a "variable ratio" schedule. In such schedules, reinforcement is presented on a percentage of the trials, often 50 percent, and the reinforced and nonreinforced trials are programmed in a random or a quasi-random sequence. The major point of interest is that resistance to extinction is increased, often remarkably so, with partial reinforcement schedules, a phenomenon often referred to as the "partial reinforcement effect" (*PRE*).

The *PRE* has received much attention from researchers and theorists for the same reason that the nonmonotonicity sometimes found between acquisition level and resistance to extinction has attracted interest: Because of the paradox that in both instances a measure of response strength, resistance to extinction, fails to be in direct correspondence with variables—amount of training in the one case and percentage of reinforcement in the other—naturally thought to be means of manipulating the strength of an instrumentally conditioned response. The theoretical effort expended in trying to bend this result into harmony with conventional learning theory has been considerable (cf. Amsel, 1962; Capaldi, 1966; D. J. Lewis, 1960).

In one form or another, hypotheses arising from the Hullian orientation have ascribed the *PRE* to differential stimulus generalization effects. The argument advanced is that a partial reinforcement schedule better prepares *S* for the stimulus conditions which are to be confronted during extinction than does a continuous reinforcement schedule.

The frustration hypothesis is one such interpretation and has been applied to the *PRE* in detail (Amsel, 1967). The gist of the argument is that, owing to the nonreinforced trials of a partial reinforcement schedule, *S* experiences frustration during acquisition and in some measure becomes accustomed to making the instrumental response in the presence of cues characteristic of frustration (s_F). During extinction, anticipatory frustration responses disrupt partially reinforced *S*s less than they disrupt continuously reinforced *S*s, who in extinction encounter frustration for the first time. This oversimplified presentation does not do justice to Amsel's careful treatment of the topic, and the reader is referred to his previously cited papers for a fuller discussion.

Theoretical accommodation aside, the *PRE* is one of the most robust results in instrumental conditioning. Unlike so many other phenomena in instrumental conditioning in which a number of variables often interact in many and sometimes inexplicable ways, the *PRE* is obtainable with a wide range of conditions and organisms. For a time there was some question whether it occurred in fish (cf. Gonzalez & Bitterman, 1967), but at the mammalian level, it has enjoyed the status of a behavioral law, at least insofar as separate-groups designs are concerned.

The PRE in single-group designs. As pointed out in Chap. 2, the *PRE* may not occur in single-group designs. A partial reinforcement experiment is arranged in such designs by associating a continuous reinforcement schedule with one instrumental task and a partial reinforcement schedule with another, each *S* trained on both tasks. The two tasks are usually differentiated on the basis of exteroceptive cues, for example, a black versus a white alley, with continuous reinforcement associated with one alley and partial reinforcement with the other. Less frequently, different responses are employed, such as running versus climbing (e.g., Rashotte, 1968). It is generally the case that single-group designs lend themselves to two different ways of evaluating extinction performance. The method used most frequently in experiments concerned with the *PRE* is to extinguish each *S* on both tasks; thus extinction too follows a single-group design. However, extinction performance may also be assessed by extinguishing half of the *S*s on one task only and half on the other. This method essentially consists of an acquisition single-group design followed by an extinction separate-groups design.

The usual finding with both methods is that Ss extinguish at approximately the same rate on the two tasks (e.g., Amsel, 1967; Galbraith, Rashotte, & Amsel, 1968). The *PRE* fails to occur because during early extinction trials Ss do not show the precipitous decline in performance on the continuously reinforced task so characteristic of the continuously reinforced subjects of separate-groups designs. Amsel (1967), who has analyzed the problem in detail, attributes this anomalous result to generalization of the frustration-induced persistence that develops in the partially reinforced task. The precise nature of this assumed generalization, i.e., whether it is "primary" or "mediated" (see Chap. 10), remains to be worked out, and alternative interpretations are possible (e.g., Brown & Logan, 1965). The role of some sort of generalization process is suggested by the results of Rashotte (1968), who was able to obtain graded differences in extinction performance, including a *PRE*, as a function of the difference in the stimulus and response characteristics of the two instrumental tasks.

One serious difficulty facing an interpretation based on generalization of "persistence" from the partially reinforced task is that occasionally in single-group designs, resistance to extinction is *superior* in the continuously reinforced task—the so-called "reversed" *PRE* (Pavlik & Carlton, 1965; Pavlik, Carlton, Lehr, & Hendrickson, 1967). Obviously no amount of generalization of persistence could account for *greater* resistance to extinction of the continuously reinforced response.

In a single-group partial reinforcement experiment conducted on a T maze, Spear and Spitzner (1967) found a within-subject *PRE* for speed measures but not for choices. Uniformly, Ss developed a preference for the continuously reinforced alternative which persisted throughout a lengthy extinction session. This is but one of a number of results which point to the necessity of distinguishing between response magnitude and response direction (cf. Mackintosh, 1963).

Clearly it is important to get to the bottom of the interactions just discussed, and doubtless future research and analysis will construct a more coherent picture (cf. Grice, 1968). But in the meanwhile one must keep these interactions in mind when designing and interpreting research to which they may be applicable. Results obtained with a separate-groups design may differ in degree or even in kind from those generated by a comparable single-group paradigm; relationships resulting from measures of response magnitude do not necessarily apply to response direction, even though both dependent variables are based on the same response.

OTHER VARIABLES.　　There are, of course, a number of other variables that affect the extinction process significantly, for example, the length of the response chain and the intertrial interval (cf. Sperling, 1965). But in general, the most important variables determining the rate of extinction of a nondiscriminative instrumental response are those relating to the conditions of reinforcement.

SUMMARY. The facts of extinction, even in the relatively simplified situation of instrumental conditioning, are, as we have seen, rather complex. The frustration hypothesis, including the fractional anticipatory frustration response, is probably one of the most useful explanatory mechanisms available. It is applicable to the negative contrast effect and the *PRE*, to the interaction between magnitude of reward and level of training in determining resistance to extinction, and, possibly, to the influence of delay of reward. Many successful applications have been made to the behavior of children in experimental tasks (cf. Ryan & Watson, 1968). Still, there are difficulties which face this approach, both empirical and theoretical (cf. Hill, 1968; Lawrence & Festinger, 1962, Chap. 5).

EFFECTS OF SEVERAL VARIABLES ON DISCRIMINATIVE INSTRUMENTAL CONDITIONING

Our treatment of discriminative (differential) conditioning will be comparatively brief, because much less data are available in this area and many of the obtained results are deducible from the principles established in nondiscriminative conditioning.

Acquisition

MAGNITUDE OF REWARD. The effects of reward magnitude on discriminative instrumental conditioning are what we would expect from the data obtained in the simpler, nondiscriminative, case. We know, for example, that asymptotic running speed in a straight alley is directly related to reward magnitude. Consequently, if one group of Ss is trained on a discriminative instrumental task (a "successive" discrimination) with relatively small reward and a second with a larger reward, any measure of discrimination that is based on response speed should show better discriminative conditioning in the second group.

The reasoning is simple. Both groups receive zero reward in S— (for example a white alley) and so, apart from contrast effects, running speed in the presence of this stimulus should be comparable in the high- and low-reward groups. However, the former group receives a larger reward in S+ (for example, a black alley) than the latter group and should therefore run faster in this alley. Results confirming this expectation have been obtained in the straight alley (e.g., Bower & Trapold, 1959), and corresponding data based on response rate have been reported in the Skinner-box setting (Stebbins, 1959).

Observe that contrast effects, to the extent that they operate in discriminative instrumental conditioning, serve to increase further the differences in running speeds to S+ and S— in the high- and low-reward groups, thus accentuating the influence of reward magnitude on discriminative instrumental conditioning.

The conclusion, then, is that because response intensity is sensitive to reward magnitude, discriminative instrumental conditioning will be facilitated by increasing magnitudes of reward.

Discrimination between nonzero reward magnitudes. One may generalize discriminative conditioning to include all cases of acquisition in which a randomly presented S— is associated with a reward condition that is less favorable than that which occurs in conjunction with S+, such as a smaller amount of reward, a longer reward delay, and a smaller percentage of rewarded trials. Thus the single-group partial reinforcement experiments considered earlier qualify as discriminative conditioning.

There have been a number of experiments in which discriminative conditioning was based on different reward magnitudes, prompted for the most part by an interest in contrast effects. Although there is an occasional exception (e.g., Goldstein & Spence, 1963), the clear consensus from runway experiments is that performance for a nonzero reward in S— is characterized by a negative contrast effect whose size is determined by the magnitude of reward received in S+ (e.g., Bower, 1961; Ludvigson & Gay, 1967). As one might expect, with a fixed magnitude of reward in S+, discriminative performance is an inverse function of the reward magnitude associated with S—, although there must be a fairly sizable difference between the two rewards before discriminative performance is evident (cf. MacKinnon, 1967).

DRIVE LEVEL.   The role of drive level in discriminative instrumental conditioning is not so easily deduced from its effects in the nondiscriminative case. We have seen that asymptotic performance is positively related to drive level in nondiscriminative conditioning. However, Ss trained on a discriminative conditioning task under relatively high drive will be operating under the higher motivation both when responding to S+ and to S—. As a consequence, the facilitation exerted by the higher drive level will apply in both instances, and it becomes a matter of whether performance is enhanced more when responding to S+ or to S—.

Another way of framing this problem is in terms of the interaction between reward magnitude and drive level in determining response strength. In our discussion of the role of drive level on nondiscriminative conditioning, we pointed out its facilitating effects in the context of a single reward magnitude. If the facilitating effects of this variable were, in some sense, about the same for all magnitudes of reward including zero reward, then motivational level could not affect discriminative conditioning, because S's performance would be augmented (under high drive) as much in S— as in S+.

There is, however, a further complication that is best presented by an example. A frequently used measure of the goodness of an operant discrimination is the "discrimination ratio," namely, the ratio of the rate of responding in S^Δ to the rate in S^D. In instances where discriminative behavior is completely absent, the discrimination ratio will be close to 1, whereas in the case of perfect discrimination, the ratio will be zero. Now suppose that the effect of drive level on response rate were independent of reward magnitude in the sense that for all magnitudes of reward, the effect of drive was to multiply response rate by a certain factor. Thus, for example, if in a specific situation low drive (perhaps 4 hours food deprivation) led to a rate of, say, 100 responses per minute, high drive (24 hours deprivation) would multiply this rate by, let us say, a factor of 1.2. Granting that high drive has this effect for all reward magnitudes including zero reward, it is clear that discrimination performance, as defined by the discrimination ratio, would not be affected by drive manipulations. In terms of the figures just given, if S has a discrimination ratio of 0.6 under low drive, his ratio under high drive would remain 0.6 because response rate in S^Δ as well as rate in S^D would be multiplied by the assumed factor of 1.2. If, however, a measure of discrimination were employed which was based on the *difference* in response rates in S^Δ and S^D, then, according to the above assumed action of drive, this variable would indeed affect the measured discrimination. Consequently, whether or not drive is found to influence discriminative conditioning will depend, in part at least, on one's measure of discrimination performance.

In the operant situation, where the discrimination ratio is usually employed, the evidence bearing on the role of drive in discriminative conditioning is sparse and inconsistent. Dinsmoor (1952) found that response rate in S^D increased more rapidly, proportionally, with increases in drive level than did rate in S^Δ. His results, therefore, imply a facilitating role of this variable on discriminative conditioning. On the other hand, Gray (1965), in a more recent study, obtained the opposite result.

In the straight alley and related apparatuses, discrimination performance must be based on time scores rather than on response rate, e.g., running times and starting latencies. The practice has been to measure goodness of discrimination in terms of *differences* between, say, running time in S+ and in S—. Ratios of such measures are rarely, if ever, used, though they are much more comparable to the discrimination ratio.

We stated above that the problem of the role of drive in successive discrimination can be referred to the nondiscriminative case by considering the question of whether drive level and reward magnitude interact in determining response strength. If in nondiscriminative conditioning, the facilitating effect of increasing drive level were the same—in terms of time-score *differences*—for all values of reward magnitude including zero reward, then we could not reasonably expect motivational level to affect discriminative conditioning in any important way. There has been a large number of experiments addressed to this problem, but, unfortunately, sometimes these two variables have interacted in determining running speed and related measures and sometimes not (cf. Black, 1965; Dyal, 1967). Usually, the basis of the interaction when found is that in terms of performance differences, the facilitatory effect of drive is greater the larger the reward (e.g., Kintsch, 1962). If such a result could be generally anticipated, we would expect performance in discriminative conditioning, when measured in terms of differences in responding to S+ and to S—, to be facilitated by increasing drive levels. There is some evidence that, under certain special conditions at least, this is the case (Spence, Goodrich, & Ross, 1959).

In spite of the sparseness of the relevant data, some conclusions and guesses can be made about the role of drive in instrumental discriminative conditioning. First, because manipulations of drive level encompass both the positive and the negative stimulus, response augmentation occurs with respect to both discriminanda at the higher drive levels, and this tends to reduce the effect of the drive variable irrespective of how goodness of discrimination is measured. Second, measures of discrimination based on differences are much more likely to produce a positive relationship between discriminative conditioning and motivational level than measures based on ratios. Indeed, it is possible for the former to show a positive relationship between the two variables while the latter points toward the opposite conclusion. Third, because drive level and reward magnitude have been often found to interact in determining response strength in nondiscriminative conditioning, it is expected that this variable will frequently be positively related to discriminative conditioning where, as on the straight alley, measures of goodness of discrimination are based on response differences. Finally, there are probably a number of other variables that modulate the relationship between drive and discriminative conditioning, but our knowledge of these is still rudimentary.

OTHER VARIABLES.   Of the many other variables that affect discriminative instrumental conditioning we will discuss only two.

Intensity of the positive stimulus. Intensity of the CS is a relevant variable in classical conditioning. The question thus arises as to whether a comparable effect holds for instrumental conditioning. Recently it has been shown that in an operant discrimination, the intensity of S^D (white noise) is positively related to discriminative performance (Gray, 1965), so that, apparently, this variable does have a similar effect in classical and instrumental conditioning.

Relative exposure to the positive and the negative stimulus. The nature of discriminative instrumental conditioning is such that S+ (or S^D) and S− (S^Δ) are presented to S in serial order, with the relative amount of exposure to each stimulus essentially an arbitrary decision. A natural and, for some purposes, convenient arrangement is to program equal numbers of S+ and S− trials or, in the operant case, equal times in S^D and S^Δ. It is reasonable to inquire, nevertheless, whether a more efficient distribution of training experience can be arranged, whether experience with one of the stimuli is more critical than experience with the other.

It has been shown in both the straight alley (Notterman, 1951) and the Skinner box (Sherman, Hegge, & Pierrel, 1964) that discriminative performance is enhanced by increasing amounts of exposure to the negative stimulus, the amount of training with the positive stimulus held constant. In the second study cited, data were also presented which suggested that a given amount of training on S^Δ had a relatively constant effect on the discrimination ratio over a considerable range of training in S^D. In other words, it appears that performance in conventional successive discrimination situations is governed more importantly by conditioning which takes place in the presence of the negative stimulus than by the reactions associated with the positive stimulus.

One does not have to look far for an explanation of this result. Granting that the instrumental response itself is easily conditioned in most instrumental situations (running down an alley, pressing a bar, etc.), not much training is required to establish the response at a fairly high strength. On the other hand, the other requirement of a successive discrimination, namely, to withhold the instrumental response in the presence of the negative stimulus, will depend on a good bit of training because S "has nothing to lose" in responding also to the negative cue. In more technical terms, the contingency between the instrumental response and reward results in, first, the establishment and strengthening of the instrumental response, which naturally generalizes from the positive stimulus to the negative cue. The complementary process in discriminative conditioning, extinction of the instrumental response in the presence of the negative stimulus, comes later and depends, of course, on experience with nonreinforced responding to $S-$ (S^Δ); the more of such experience, the faster this process is established.

Generalizing from this line of reasoning, it is apparent that variables which encourage extinction in nondiscriminative conditioning will, when operating in association with the negative cue, facilitate discriminative conditioning; similarly, variables which augment performance in nondiscriminative conditioning, when they occur in conjunction with the positive stimulus, will also enhance discriminative conditioning. An interesting conjecture is that, generally speaking, the first class of variables is more powerful than the second.[1]

The method of intermixing $S+$ and $S-$ trials is also an important consideration. Random sequencing is likely to lead to better discrimination than either alternating blocks of $S+$ and $S-$ trials or, in the extreme, having all $S+$ trials occur first followed by all $S-$ trials (Davenport & Hagquist, 1968). Apparently the likelihood that S will attend to the relevant stimuli is increased by larger numbers of $S+:S-$ transitions (cf. Honig, Thomas, & Guttman, 1959).

Extinction

As suggested by our discussion of single-group partial reinforcement experiments, discriminative training presents more options in extinction than exist for nondiscriminative conditioning. During extinction of a discriminative response, S's experience with the discriminanda may be restricted to the former $S+$, to the former $S-$, or to both stimuli, in arrangements that are the same as or are differ-

[1] It should be pointed out that acquisition of a successive discrimination can be accomplished with little or no responding to the negative stimulus. However, as shown in Chap. 11, there are some important and interesting functional differences between such "errorless" discrimination learning and that in which normal responding to the negative cue is permitted.

ent from those which prevailed during acquisition (cf. Senf & Miller, 1967). Apart from the single-group partial reinforcement experiments, comparatively few relevant data are available within this context. Therefore our discussion of this topic will be brief.

EXTINCTION AFTER DISCRIMINATIVE AND NONDISCRIMINATIVE TRAINING. A question of some interest is whether discriminative conditioning leads to greater resistance to extinction of an instrumental response than a comparable amount of nondiscriminative training. As pointed out by Jenkins (1961), early in discriminative training, the reinforcement schedule *with respect to S's response* is effectively one of partial reinforcement, because some responses (those executed in S+) are reinforced and others (those occurring in S−), are not. Accordingly, reasoning from the partial reinforcement effect found in nondiscriminative conditioning, one might suspect that discriminative conditioning would result in augmented resistance to extinction.

Jenkins (1961), working with discrete trials in a Skinner-box setting, got just such a result. Pigeons trained on a successive discrimination problem responded more to the former S+ in later extinction than Ss whose training had been nondiscriminative. A similar result was obtained by D'Amato, Schiff, and Jagoda (1962), in a Skinner-box study employing free responding rather than discrete trials. On the other hand, augmented resistance to extinction was not observed after discriminative conditioning in a straight alley (Birch, Allison, & House, 1963). A possible explanation of this discrepancy is that the discrimination facing S in the last study was learned too soon for the nonreinforced responding on S− trials to generalize to S+ trials. Although successive discrimination training in a straight alley is such that ordinarily S executes the instrumental response on every trial, if S differentiates between the discriminanda at an early point in training, the reinforcement events of S+ and S− trials cannot be expected to coalesce into a quasi-partial reinforcement schedule. The indicated conclusion is that discriminative conditioning is likely to result in augmented resistance to extinction when the discrimination task is not too easily acquired.

AMOUNT OF DISCRIMINATIVE TRAINING. We have seen that within the confines of the Skinner-box setting, characteristically, resistance to extinction is monotonically related to amount of nondiscriminative training. Apart from the possible role that reward magnitude might play in accounting for the observed monotonicity, it appears that even with the usual small rewards employed in such situations, the relation can be altered radically by discriminative training. D'Amato, Schiff, and Jagoda (1962) compared the effects of discriminative and nondiscriminative training on the resistance to extinction of a bar-pressing response. As mentioned earlier, with nondiscriminative training they found resistance to extinction and acquisition level to be monotonically related up to

1600 reinforced responses. With discriminative training, however, the function obtained between the two variables was clearly nonmonotonic (upper curve in Fig. 7-9).

One possible explanation of this result is that at lower acquisition levels, resistance to extinction of a discriminative response is inflated by the partial reinforcement experience associated with discrimination training. However, with prolonged training Ss form a stable discrimination and, as a consequence, experience what is effectively a continuous reinforcement schedule. Conceivably this experience, if extensive, counteracts the effects of the earlier quasi-partial reinforcement schedule. This otherwise promising explanation conflicts with the consistent finding that, in nondiscriminative situations, even a substantial amount of continuous reinforcement following upon partial reinforcement does not eliminate the partial reinforcement effect (e.g., Sutherland, Mackintosh, & Wolfe, 1965; Theios & McGinnis, 1967). Consequently, the result may depend on some aspect of the discriminative behavior itself rather than on a concomitant fortuitous partial reinforcement experience.

SUMMARY. There is a close continuity between the facts of nondiscriminative and discriminative instrumental conditioning. At bottom this confluence is due to the fact that both situations focus upon the same behavioral manifestation, response magnitude, and the variables that affect response magnitude in the one situation influence it in much the same way in the other. In a real sense discriminative instrumental conditioning is simply a generalization of nondiscriminative conditioning. Apart from contrast effects—whose influence can, as we have seen, be worked out in the nondiscriminative case—the relationships established in nondiscriminative conditioning may generally be expected to hold as well for discriminative conditioning.

Moreover, as already noted, what we earlier defined as discriminative conditioning is itself a special case of the more general paradigm in which S is presented serially with two discriminatively different situations which have different "payoffs." The more favorable situation we label S+, and the less favorable S−. The still wider generalization to more than two differentiable situations with varying payoffs is apparent.

There is one immediate pitfall to this increasing generalization. Is zero reward located on the continuum of reward values, as only a "reward" of particularly small magnitude, or does it have unique properties? We have encountered some evidence favoring the former view; namely, a frustration effect may occur upon reduction of a reward to a nonzero value (Bower, 1962). But in the ability of even very small rewards to sustain conditioned behavior apparently indefinitely, we come upon imposing counterevidence. Animals will work for very long periods for the smallest rewards, rewards insufficient to maintain them physically. Yet, as we know, instrumental behavior soon collapses when reward is reduced to zero. Here is a point at which the assumed continuity between zero and nonzero reward values needs to be investigated further.

Effects of Reward Magnitude and Drive Level on Instrumental Learning

It will be useful at this point to pause to inquire into the role played by the familiar variables reward magnitude and drive level in simple instrumental learning. In doing so, we will encounter complications which illustrate the difficulties standing in the way of generalizing the results of instrumental conditioning to choice behavior.

MAGNITUDE OF REWARD. A substantial number of experiments have investigated the role of reward magnitude in simple discrimination learning. The results appear confusing, but some degree of order can be brought out of them.

Several experiments employing rats as Ss failed to produce differences in the learning of a simple visual discrimination task when manipulating amount of reward (e.g., McKelvey, 1956; Reynolds, 1949). It appeared from these studies that if the reward was of sufficient size to motivate S to learn the discrimination problem, S learned independently of reward magnitude. On the other hand, studies appeared in the literature showing that with monkeys as Ss reward magnitude did indeed influence acquisition of a discrimination task, larger rewards facilitating learning (e.g., Schrier & Harlow, 1956).

Apart from the fact that these two sets of studies are obviously correlated with differences in the phylogenetic level of the Ss employed, there was a difference in design that could have accounted for the conflicting results. In the rat studies, a separate-groups design was employed. As monkeys are much more expensive than rats, a single-group design was used in the studies in which they served as experimental Ss; each monkey was tested under each of the reward values investigated. As we already know, these two designs can lead to divergent results when the same independent variable is investigated.

In any event, it appeared that magnitude of reward was more likely to influence simple discrimination learning when a single-group, rather than a separate-groups, design was employed. Schrier (1958) investigated this possibility with monkeys and found that with the former design, amount of reward was directly related to discrimination performance; with a separate-groups design, on the other hand, amount of reward did not show a uniform relationship with discrimination performance, and in general there was less overall influence. Precisely the same kind of interaction between the effect of reward magnitude on discrimination learning and the type of research design employed was reported by Lawson (1957) for rats and by Harley (1965a,b) for college students learning a paired-associates task.

The mechanisms responsible for these differences observed with between- and within-groups designs are not at all clear, though it is apparent that contrast effects might be at work. In Schrier's (1958) study, for example, the greatest divergence between his two design groups occurred at the lowest amount of reward employed; the group experiencing the single-group design was substantially inferior to the corresponding separate-groups Ss. This suggests the operation of a depression effect, and if such were the case, it would help to account for the greater sensitivity shown toward the reward magnitude variable by single-group designs. With human subjects, differential rehearsal of high-reward and low-reward items might also be a factor (cf. Harley, 1965a).

Whatever the interpretation, it is clear that within the separate-groups design—which was the design employed in the instrumental conditioning studies that revealed asymptotic performance to be directly related to reward magnitude—instrumental conditioning is much more sensitive to variations in reward magnitude than is discrimination learning. This fact naturally poses a problem for theorists who hope to derive, as a matter of principle, choice behavior from instrumental conditioning. Furthermore, running-time differences—that is, differences in response magnitude—have been reported in discrimination studies in which reward variations had no effect on choice behavior (e.g., McKelvey, 1956).

Quite recently two reports appeared which revealed that magnitude of reward facilitated discrimination learning in rats trained within a separate-groups design (Mackintosh, 1969; Waller, 1968). The experimental situation of the Waller study was somewhat anomalous in that the brightness discrimination task was learned within only 14 trials on the average, far faster than a corresponding position discrimination. Apparently the brightness cues were extremely salient, possibly attenuating greatly the observing behavior normally required in visual discriminations. It is interesting in this connection that Mackintosh (1969) found that large reward facilitated discrimination acquisition more for an easy discrimination than for a difficult one.

A hypothesis that might be reasonably entertained at this point is that within separate-groups designs, amount of reward will influence discrimination learning only if little is required in the way of observing responses or, put differently, only if the probability of attending to the relevant stimulus dimension is high (see Chap. 11). Some support for this view comes from the well-established result that nonspatial discrimination (selective) learning is reliably facilitated by larger reward magnitudes (e.g., Pubols, 1961; Waller, 1968; Wike & Farrow, 1962). It is frequently suggested that the probability of attending to the relevant cues of a spatial discrimination task is ordinarily quite high (e.g., Lovejoy, 1966; Mackintosh, 1965b).

DRIVE LEVEL. We have seen that drive level also influenced importantly non-discriminative instrumental conditioning. Its effect on discriminative conditioning was not unambiguous, however, perhaps in part because of the different measures of goodness of discrimination that have been employed. Nevertheless, despite occasional exceptions (e.g., Eisman, Asimow, & Maltzman, 1956), the majority of studies which have manipulated drive level within a simple discrimination learning situation have found this variable ineffectual in influencing discriminative performance, irrespective of the type of design employed (e.g., Hillman, Hunter, & Kimble, 1953; Meyer, 1951; Miles, 1959). As with reward magnitude, the failure of drive level to influence choice behavior has occurred in situations where response magnitude has proven sensitive to motivation differences (e.g., Hillman et al., 1953; Lachman, 1961).

True, a mechanism exists within the Hull-Spence theory by means of which one could account for the failure of drive level to influence discrimination learning, at least under certain specified conditions (Spence, Goodrich, & Ross, 1959). It appears, however, that these conditions are not characteristic of many studies which have failed to show drive level to be an effective variable in simple discrimination learning, so we have here another illustration of the difficulties facing the theorist who would derive choice behavior from instrumental conditioning.

On the brighter side, a few studies have shown a *qualitative* correspondence between discriminative conditioning and discrimination learning within what is essentially a single-group design. If two alleys of different brightnesses are used as the discriminanda of a successive discrimination, a closely analogous simultaneous discrimination task is achieved by having S choose between these same alleys. If the trials are appropriately intermixed, S may be trained concurrently on the two tasks. Exploiting such a technique, Spence, Goodrich, and Ross (1959) showed that drive manipulations exerted parallel effects on discriminative conditioning and discrimination learning. More recently, Pennes and Ison (1967) found that, like discrimination learning, discriminative conditioning suffers when the reinforcement schedule associated with S+ is 50 percent rather than continuous. Moreover, Ss' performance in the discriminative conditioning task suggested something about the nature of the deficit which occurs in discrimination learning. The speeds of the partially reinforced Ss were comparable to those of the continuously reinforced subjects for performance in S+; however, the first group responded much faster in S− than the second. This suggests that the deficit shown by partially reinforced Ss in discrimination learning results, not from a deficient approach strength toward S+, but from a lower level of aversion of S−.

The results of the preceding studies are interesting and potentially useful. Nevertheless one must not ignore the points of divergence that occur between the conditioning and learning data. In the Pennes and Ison study, for example, Ss displayed a distinct discrimination in their choice behavior (in the direction of preferring S−) for a number of days, whereas, on the other hand, their response speeds to S+ and S−, if not identical, favored S+. Champion and Smith (1966) used discriminative conditioning performance to predict choice behavior based on different reward magnitudes; they achieved a degree of success for some Ss but not for others, who gave evidence of discriminating the different rewards in their conditioning performance but not in their choice behavior.

Possibly the accuracy of the correspondence between discriminative conditioning and instrumental learning would be enhanced if separate groups of subjects were used in the successive and simultaneous discrimination tasks. Unless within-subject comparisons are required, there are few advantages to offset the added complications that the single-group design may entail. But in any case, this is a research area that merits far more attention than it has received. If choice behavior can indeed be derived from conditioning performance, this would seem the ideal proving ground.

THE HULL–SPENCE THEORY OF INSTRUMENTAL CONDITIONING

Our treatment of instrumental conditioning has largely omitted discussion of formal conditioning theories. The best known and most widely applied of these is the Hull-Spence theory, which after Hull's death in 1952 was carried forward single-handedly by Spence until his own death in 1967. The prominent role of this theory in the area of instrumental (and classical) conditioning requires that we give it some consideration, though a detailed treatment cannot be offered here (cf. Hull, 1943, 1952; Spence, 1956).

MAJOR INTERVENING VARIABLES. We will describe the Hull-Spence theory by showing how it can handle a number of the facts of instrumental conditioning with which we are already familiar. To begin with, the theory is based on a family of theoretical constructs, often referred to as "intervening variables," by means of which manipulated independent variables are ultimately related to observed behavior. These intervening variables are meant to embody, in a relatively precise way, those processes or factors which importantly determine performance in instrumental conditioning. The fact that motivational level—or in a specific case, hunger deprivation—is an important factor in instrumental conditioning is incorporated into the theory by the coordinate intervening variable D (*drive*). The more elementary fact that performance in instrumental conditioning improves with training—that learning occurs—is accommodated by the intervening variable H, or *habit strength*.

A number of theoretical constructs having been postulated—with each construct subsuming a large class of empirical operations which are presumably homogeneous in their effects on the conditioning process—the critical task is to interrelate these constructs in a way that leads to successful prediction of instrumental behavior. As an illustration, let us trace how these constructs are combined to obtain the known result that asymptotic performance in instrumental conditioning is directly related to motivational level.

First, looking closely at the intervening variable habit strength, we find that it is tied down to the conditions of training by the following equation: $H = A(1 - 10^{-iN})$. In this defining equation, N stands for the number of training trials and hence provides the bridge between H and the empirical world. The symbol A, a constant characteristic of the individual learner, determines the limiting value of H, i.e., its asymptote. And i, again a function of the individual, is the rate parameter, specifying the rapidity with which acquisition asymptote is reached. We see, therefore, that the "negative growth" function so often observed in instrumental conditioning curves is built directly into the construct H.

To continue the theoretical development, habit strength and drive are assumed to combine multiplicatively to determine one of the terminal intervening variables in the construct chain, reaction or excitatory potential (E). Thus $E = H \times D$. Such dependent variables as response speed, latency, and amplitude are tied directly to reaction potential and its derivatives.

The fact that variations in drive affect asymptotic performance in instrumental conditioning now follows directly. The higher the motivational level (the longer the period of deprivation), the greater the value of D, and because manipulation of D is essentially equivalent in its effect to manipulation of A, the greater the motivation, the higher the performance asymptote.

This feature of the theory has received a good deal of attention, particularly with respect to human conditioning. Starting from the assumption that emotionality, as measured by the Taylor Manifest Anxiety scale, may be considered a form of motivation and hence a means of manipulating D, Spence was able to predict that eyelid conditioning, nondiscriminative and discriminative, should be augmented in high-anxiety subjects. Although most experiments support the general lines of this deduction (cf. Prokasy, 1967; Spence, 1964), the theory encounters difficulties when more detailed implications are tested. Prokasy (1967) has examined the problem carefully, and his paper is recommended to those who wish to pursue this aspect of the Hull-Spence theory.

Also entailed in the previous theoretical formulation is the implication that *rate* of acquisition will not be influenced by drive manipulations. Although we had little to say about this aspect of acquisition curves in our earlier discussion—mainly because the available evidence is not as unequivocal as the evidence for asymptotic performance—drive level and reward magnitude appear to have little effect on acquisition rate (cf. Fig. 7-3). So this feature of the Hull-Spence theory also seems congruent with the tenor of the available data.

Simple effects of reward magnitude, which it will be recalled closely resembled the corresponding drive-level effects, are handled in a similar fashion. Manipulations of reward magnitude are reflected in a construct called "incentive motivation," K. For example, the larger the amount of reward employed, the higher the value of K. This new construct is joined with the others in the postulated relation $E = H(D + K)$. Consequently, variations in magnitude of reward are reflected by variations in K, and these in turn, just as in the case for D, imply differences in acquisition asymptote but not in rate.

In the case of contrast effects of reward magnitude, additional concepts, such as anticipatory frustration, are necessary to accommodate elationlike and depressionlike manifestations. The fractional anticipatory goal response $r_{G}\text{–}s_{G}$, it might be noted here, is thought by Spence to be the mechanism underlying incentive motivation. That is, the purpose of K is to mirror the strength of $r_{G}\text{–}s_{G}$, and variables which affect K do so because they play a role in determining the strength of the anticipatory goal response.

D $+$ K OR D $\times$ K?   One of the points at which Hull and Spence departed in their theorizing concerns the manner in which drive (D) and incentive motivation (K) combine in the equation determining reaction potential. Hull assumed that the relationship was multiplicative, while Spence took the view that D and K combined additively. It was originally thought that, because they appeared to lend themselves to contrasting predictions, experimental evidence would quickly provide a clear decision between the two alternatives. Under the $D + K$ assumption, manipulations of K result in equal differences in reaction potential for all values of D. This deduction follows from the definition of reaction potential and is easily verified algebraically. Under the multiplicative assumption, however, the difference in reaction potential wrought by different values of K is directly related to drive level.

Translating these deductions to operational terms, according to the $D + K$ hypothesis the difference in response speeds generated by 1 and 5 reward pellets under 12 hours food deprivation ought to be equal to that observed when deprivation is increased to 48 hr. The $D \times K$ assumption predicts that the latter difference will be larger than the former. Cast in statistical concepts (cf. Chap. 2), an observed interaction between drive level and reward magnitude may be taken as evidence that Hull is right whereas the absence of such an interaction presumably supports Spence.

In spite of the comparatively large number of studies devoted to this problem spanning about 10 years, the issue is still in doubt (for reviews of the literature, see Black, 1965; Dyal, 1967). Perhaps the strongest generalization that can be made with confidence is that an interaction between drive and incentive motivation is more likely to occur when a zero value is employed for one of the variables, for example, zero reward. As noted earlier, the form of the interaction, when obtained, is such that manipulations of K exert a greater influence at higher levels of D, which, of course, is the direction predicted by the multiplicative relationship.

Evans (1967) has pointed out a number of objections to the use of the interaction paradigm as a means of deciding between the Hull and Spence formulations. Perhaps, however, the problem is much deeper in that possibly far more variables enter into determining the effects of D and K on instrumental performance than are currently represented in the theory. If so, both interpretations are oversimplifications bound to conflict with some portion of the experimental data.

Recalling the earlier discussion of the effects of drive level on discriminative conditioning, if the sort of interaction predicted by the $D \times K$ hypothesis exists for the nondiscriminative case, performance in discriminative conditioning ought to be positively related to drive level. It would appear, then, that the $D + K$ formulation implies that discriminative conditioning is independent of drive level. Actually, however, this follows only if equal numbers of $S+$ and $S-$ trials are administered. As Spence, Goodrich, and Ross (1959) have shown, under the assumption that only contiguity of stimulus and response is required for learning to occur in appetitive situations, discriminative performance will be independent of drive level if the numbers of $S+$ and $S-$ trials (and hence the values of $H+$ and $H-$) are equal. Unfortunately, the data bearing on this deduction are very few.

AN INHIBITORY MECHANISM. We saw earlier that compared to magnitude of reward and drive level, delay of reward showed some clear differences in its role in instrumental conditioning. For one thing, performance differences emerged more slowly with different delays, and for another, with longer delays performance not uncommonly fell off with increasing training. Clearly, delay of reward must enter the theory in a different way from drive level and reward magnitude if these differences are to be accommodated. Such is the case. Delay of reward is one of the independent variables determining an inhibitory factor I which, in subtracting from excitatory potential, produces what is termed "effective" excitatory potential $(\bar{E})$. Thus, $\bar{E} = E - I = H(D + K) - I$. This inhibitory factor is also presumed to be a function of the number of delay of reward trials encountered. Although the exact way in which these two classes of independent variables determine I has not been specified, it is entirely possible to relate them monotonically to I and still be able to deduce the two effects of reward delay under consideration.

The Hull-Spence theory extends to discriminative instrumental conditioning in the assumption that the theory applies separately to $S+$ and to $S-$. Of course, contrast effects and generalization between $S+$ and $S-$ act to complicate the derivation of the "positive" and "negative" excitatory potentials, but these difficulties are relatively minor.

Perhaps enough has now been said to give the reader some feeling of the general approach of the Hull-Spence theory of instrumental conditioning (cf. Logan, 1959 for further information). The theory, it should be pointed out, has by no means limited its horizons to conditioning. Explicit methods have been proposed by means of which the response magnitude measures of discriminative conditioning can be transformed to derive the choice measures characteristic of simple instrumental learning (e.g., Spence, 1958b; Spence, Goodrich, & Ross, 1959). As yet, however, these attempts toward the solution of what must be acknowledged to be an extremely difficult and complex task have met with only limited success.

SUMMARY

As is evident from even this highly selective treatment of positively reinforced instrumental conditioning, the topic has been of keen interest to many experimental psychologists and has been investigated in considerable detail. Why all this interest in rats running down runways and pressing bars? The answer lies in the scientist's quest to study his phenomena in the simplest possible situations and in the faith of some experimental psychologists in fundamental "laws" of learning having general, if not universal, application. These laws of learning, or laws of behavior as they are often referred to, are the analogue in psychology to fundamental laws in physics and chemistry. And just as the latter have been strikingly successful in permitting the control and prediction of complex physical and chemical events, many psychologists believe that basic laws of behavior, once discovered, will contribute significantly to the understanding and control of more complex behavioral events. Such laws are more likely to be discovered and interrelated, it is assumed, in experimental situations that reduce the studied phenomena to their essentials. Hence the emphasis on instrumental conditioning.

In this chapter the distinction between response magnitude and response direction was emphasized. The term conditioning was restricted to behavioral situations in which response direction, i.e., choice among experimentally defined alternatives, does not arise, and consequently the dependent variables must be framed in terms of response magnitude—such as latency, rate of response, and amplitude.

1. Framed within the preceding distinction, classical and instrumental conditioning may be differentiated in that:

2. (a) Magnitude of reward and drive level have similar "simple" effects on nondiscriminative acquisition. These are:

(b) The effects of delay of reward on nondiscriminative acquisition are different in that:

3. Contrast effects of reward magnitude refer to:

4. (a) The fractional anticipatory goal and frustration responses are assumed to develop in the following way:

(b) The *UCS*s are:

(c) The purpose of these mechanisms is:

5. (a) The nature of the interaction between reward magnitude and level of acquisition training in determining resistance to extinction of a nondiscriminative instrumental response is:

(b) The significance of such interactions for generalization of experimentally obtained relationships is that:

6. The effect of reward magnitude on discriminative conditioning may be deduced from its effects in nondiscriminative conditioning in the following way:

7. On the other hand, the effect of drive level on discriminative conditioning is much more difficult to predict from its effects on nondiscriminative conditioning because:

8. In the Hull-Spence theory of instrumental conditioning, the simple effects of reward magnitude and drive level on rate and asymptote of acquisition are accommodated in the following way:

9. Many theorists, in particular Hull and Spence, have proposed that basic empirical relationships arising from nondiscriminative conditioning situations can be fashioned into a learning theory from which, in turn, more complex behaviors, such as dicriminative conditioning and simple discrimination learning, may be derived. Relate the empirical findings presented in the present chapter to this issue.

8 INSTRUMENTAL AVERSIVE CONDITIONING

In this chapter we shall present at the outset a theoretical account of some of the mechanisms assumed to be implicated in instrumental conditioning with negative reinforcement. This formulation will provide a valuable frame of reference within which to view the empirical facts and principles that later follow.

MOTIVE–INCENTIVE CONDITIONS UNDER NEGATIVE REINFORCEMENT

When positive reward is employed as the reinforcing agent, it is usually a simple matter to designate exactly the motive-incentive conditions operating in the conditioning of a bit of behavior. Motivation most often derives from some sort of deprivation procedure; the incentive, of course, is simply the positive reinforcer employed—food, water, etc. However, in conditioning with negative reinforcement, the reinforcing agent is often not easy to specify. What is the reinforcing event on a trial in which S successfully avoids S^{R-}? This question in particular has spurred the development of a number of theoretical approaches by means of which the motive-incentive mechanisms underlying conditioning with negative reinforcement might be conceptualized. The one described here has proven quite fruitful over the years, during which time it has gained widespread acceptance, explicit and implicit. Although originally proposed to accommodate avoidance conditioning, it has a much wider range of application.

THE FRACTIONAL ANTICIPATORY PAIN RESPONSE—FEAR. In escape conditioning, where S's task is to remove himself from S^{R-}, the source of his motivation is evident. It arises from S^{R-} itself, which is applied until the escape response is made, terminating the aversive stimulation. But in punishment and avoidance conditioning the presence of S^{R-} cannot always be appealed to as providing the motivational or reinforcing basis of S's behavior. A well-punished response may fail to occur for a considerable time even though punishment has been long discontinued; as already noted, by definition S spares himself S^{R-} when he performs an avoidance response. To provide for a motivating and reinforcing mechanism which operates in the absence of S^{R-}, the present formulation enlists an anticipatory mechanism that captures in a relatively objective way the intuitive notion of fear or anxiety.

Aversive stimuli, such as electric shock or intense visual, auditory, and thermal stimulation, arouse in S a state of pain or discomfort which S will ordinarily attempt to alleviate, just as he attempts to alleviate hunger or thirst. Let us refer to the response complex elicited by S^{R-} as R_P, "P" standing for pain or discomfort. Part of R_P is detachable from S^{R-} in that it can occur in the absence of its normal eliciting stimulus, much as we assumed that a portion of the goal and frustration response complexes, r_G and r_F, were detachable from their primary eliciting stimuli. As usual, we refer to this component as r_P and, as before, we assume that r_P is (classically) conditionable to stimuli which precede or signal the onset of S^{R-}. (The UCS in this presumed conditioning is S^{R-}, the UCR is R_P, of which r_P serves as the CR; the CS is composed of stimuli that regularly precede S^{R-}.) In further correspondence with the anticipatory goal and frustration responses, we refer to r_P as the "fractional anticipatory pain (or discomfort) response."

The parallel between the fractional anticipatory pain response and the everyday notions of fear and anxiety may be apparent. Like r_P, these terms are usually employed to refer to the anticipation of a painful event or, more generally, an event capable of producing distress or discomfort. In what follows we shall use the terms "anticipatory pain response," "fear" and "anxiety" interchangeably.

Because r_P is a portion of R_P it is a reasonable assumption that S will attempt to avoid stimuli which elicit r_P, just as S attempts to avoid S^{R-} itself. More exactly, stimuli that evoke in S the anticipatory pain mechanism r_P-s_P

will be responded to as aversive stimuli, avoided by S where possible or terminated or reduced when avoidance is not allowed. Such stimuli may therefore be termed "conditioned" or "secondary aversive stimuli." By way of contrast, stimuli that elicit the anticipatory *goal* response will be sought out or approached by S; they are therefore called "conditioned" or "secondary reinforcing stimuli."

To recapitulate, a primary aversive stimulus S^{R-} elicits in S a primary pain or discomfort response, R_P, which has a detachable and conditionable component, r_P. This response, along with its proprioceptive stimulus concomitant s_P, constitutes the fractional anticipatory pain response or, more simply, fear or anxiety. Cues which signal the onset of primary aversive stimuli become conditioned aversive stimuli because they become conditioned to, and elicit, r_P-s_P.

The extremely close correspondence between r_P and r_F suggests that there should be some points of close similarity in the roles played by anticipatory pain and frustration responses in instrumental conditioning. As we shall later see, there is a fair amount of evidence supporting this expectation.[1]

POSITIVE AND NEGATIVE REINFORCEMENT COMPARED

The terms "positive reinforcement" and "negative reinforcement" suggest a misleading duality of function. If by "reinforcement" we mean a stimulus situation that tends to strengthen behavior sequences upon which it is contingent, then clearly all reinforcement is positive. All reinforcement must consist of stimulus situations that are in some fashion attractive to S. There is, in fact, a very tight correspondence between the origin and function of the motive-incentive events which occur during positively reinforced instrumental conditioning and those that occur during conditioning with negative reinforcement. With positive reinforcement a drive state is induced by some sort of deprivation procedure, whether it be deprivation of food, a social partner, or adequately varied sensory stimulation. The incentive, it follows, is the restoration of the commodity denied S—food, a companion, etc. With negative reinforcement, on the other hand, motivation is instilled by the application of a stimulus that causes S some degree of pain or discomfort. And in this case removal or reduction in the intensity of the unpleasant stimulation constitutes the basis of reinforcement.

[1] The preceding formulation differs in terminology, though probably not in substance, from most accounts of the role played by fear or anxiety in conditioning with negative reinforcement. The terminology employed here serves to highlight the common conceptual status of r_G, r_F, and fear (r_P). Some authors have maintained that the unconditioned reaction to a strong S^{R-} includes not only pain but fear as well, and that the conditioned anticipatory fraction of this total reaction be termed "anxiety" to distinguish it from the unconditioned fear component (e.g., Solomon & Wynne, 1954, p. 354). Because there are at present no operations by which fear and anxiety may be distinguished, and because, as will be pointed out later, negative reinforcers need not evoke a pain reaction, the formulation of fear as an anticipatory pain or discomfort response is preferred by the writer.

But because hunger, thirst, and other such "appetitive" drives implicated in positive reinforcement may be considered to cause S discomfort or distress and because the corresponding reward objects serve to reduce in some measure these unpleasant sensations, it is apparent that the structure of motive-incentive conditions in positive reinforcement is similar, if not identical, to that of negative reinforcement. What then, if any, are the essential differences between the motive-incentive conditions operating in these two types of conditioning situations?

Of the several obvious divergences that come to mind, the one with the most significant consequences relates to differential rates of drive induction. In virtually all applications of negative reinforcement, the drive-inducing stimuli are so managed that drive onset is very abrupt, practically instantaneous. Aversive intensities of, for example, electric shock, light, noise, and cold are applied to S at the outset, causing him immediate pain or discomfort. It should be noted, however, that this is not an inherent feature of negative reinforcement. Any terminally aversive stimulus, including electric shock, can be administered in gradually increasing intensities, reaching aversive levels only after a substantial period of time.

In contrast with the normally abrupt action of aversive stimuli, deprivation procedures require considerable time to achieve effective motivational levels. But here too a reversal of normal events is possible in the use of physiological methods of manipulating appetitive drives, which, as we pointed out in the last chapter, offer the promise of enabling E to induce such motivational states very quickly. Thus, although in practice an extreme contrast exists in the rate of drive induction attained under positive and negative reinforcement, in principle this divergence is subject to manipulation, even to the point of being reversed from its normal order.

One significant consequence that flows from the different rates of drive induction is that certain conditioning procedures, notably punishment and avoidance conditioning, are not feasible with the motive-incentive conditions of positive reinforcement. The reason is that, although appetitive drives may be considered to cause discomfort or distress to S, their rates of induction are so slow by ordinary deprivation procedures that it is difficult to associate a specific stimulus with the onset of these drive states or to arrange for sharply discriminable contingencies between them and a specific bit of behavior. To take avoidance as an illustration, if a strong thirst drive could be instigated (and removed) immediately in S and if a cue were made to signal the onset of this artificially produced thirst, then doubtless S would learn to "avoid" the thirst by making an appropriate instrumental response when the cue appeared. With reference to punishment, a response that produced the artificially induced thirst would doubtlessly be suppressed, just as if it had produced more conventional primary aversive stimuli. Consequently, the implausibility of having deprivation states serve as primary aversive stimuli stems directly from their gradual onset.

There are many other obvious differences between positive and negative reinforcement, but, on analysis, none of them seem to be useful means of differentiating between the two. One might maintain, for example, that with negative reinforcement the source of motivation is confounded with the source of reward. Shock is applied to instigate drive and then removed to produce reward; thus a very large reward is not possible in a mildly shock-motivated S. This argument is not very convincing, however, because it is plain that the upper limit of the reward possible in positive reinforcement is also dictated by the extent of the drive operating in S. It is not possible, for example, to reward an S deprived of food for 2 hr to the same maximal extent as an S deprived of food for 24 hr.

Neither is it useful to differentiate positive and negative reinforcement on the basis that in positive reinforcement a commodity is removed to produce motivation and restored to provide reward, whereas just the opposite order prevails for negative reinforcement. A rat swimming through cold water to get to a warmer goal box is clearly involved in conditioning with negative reinforcement. Yet it is reasonable to maintain that the animal's motivation arises from deprivation of heat, which is restored in the warmer goal box.

Finally, it probably is also largely irrelevant that primary aversive stimuli are often painful. True, strong intensities of visual, auditory, and thermal stimuli, as well as electric shock, are capable of producing pain in S, whereas, in contrast, the usual ranges of hunger, thirst, and other deprivation states achieved by normal deprivation procedures do not trespass upon the pain threshold. Nevertheless, conditioning with negative reinforcement is often conducted with primary aversive stimuli that do not provoke pain, and although the presence of pain undoubtedly accentuates certain aspects of negative reinforcement, its effects appear to be more quantitative than qualitative.

In conclusion, it appears that the single essential feature distinguishing negative from positive motive-incentive conditions is that the onset of drive is instantaneous in the one case and quite prolonged in the other. From this one crucial difference, many divergences appear.

Because of their different motivational structures, the patterns of reward employed with positive and negative reinforcement are quite different. In positively reinforced conditioning, E usually reinforces S on each trial with a reward magnitude that reduces his drive state by a relatively small quantity. (Usually because E wishes to "conserve" S's motivation from trial to trial.) With negative reinforcement, however, reinforcement on each trial is often "complete"; the aversive stimulus is removed (or avoided) entirely. When comparing conditioning under positive and negative reinforcement, this methodological difference must be kept in mind.

ESCAPE CONDITIONING

Reflecting the fact that research in the area of negative reinforcement has centered around escape, punishment, and avoidance conditioning, the organization of this chapter will revolve around these three paradigms, rather than around a few, centrally important, empirical variables. Nevertheless, where possible, parallels will be drawn to the conclusions and principles stated in the preceding chapter.

In a recent compilation of references pertinent to instrumental escape conditioning, fewer than 20 references bear publication dates of 1950 or earlier (Woods, 1965). The number of items in this bibliography increases about sixfold over the next 15 years, with the period 1960 to 1965 producing approximately as many published items as all previous years. Interest in the topic since 1965 has continued unabated (cf. Brush, 1970; Campbell & Church, 1969). Thus, after a long period of neglect, research in escape conditioning has increased in popularity. Despite the recent upsurge, however, our knowledge in this area is spotty; seldom will we find the kind of firm generalizations that were possible with positively reinforced conditioning.

Although the favorite S^{R-} used in escape studies has been electric shock, less noxious negative reinforcers, such as strong auditory and thermal stimuli and force required to execute the instrumental response (e.g., Miller, 1968), appear to be gaining favor. Indeed, in the interest of broadening the empirical base, nonnoxious aversive stimuli are finding increasing employment in aversive conditioning. This trend may gain momentum from the recent demonstrations that stimuli associated with nonreinforcement, such as time-outs, possess aversive properties not unlike those of electric shock (cf. Kaufman & Baron, 1968; McMillan, 1967).

Nevertheless, electric shock is still the most widely used S^{R-}, and a few words about its manipulation are in order. Contrary to what one may expect, close control over a shock stimulus is not easy to achieve. The physical parameters of the electric shock are often readily specified. With a shocker that delivers "constant" current, for example, E may set the output at 5 ma and be confident that approximately that amount of current is delivered to S. However, if shock is administered through a grid floor or by means of a similar arrangement, the distribution of current through S will differ widely in accordance with the area of contact that S makes with the electrified surfaces. And it is likely that the aversiveness of a fixed current level depends on how the current is distributed through S's body. To surmount this difficulty, Azrin (1959) introduced the technique of implanting electrodes directly into the pubis bones of the pigeon. Stationary electrodes have been clamped to the tails of monkeys and rats to achieve the same end. Whenever it is essential to obtain close control over the shock stimulus, some such technique recommends itself.

The intensity of shock delivered to S is specified in different ways. One of the most common is to indicate the current applied to S, expressed as microamperes (μa) or milliamperes (ma). Frequently the parameter given is voltage, which is useless unless one knows something about the impedance of the circuit. Assuming resistance is the major component of impedance, one may calculate the current in the circuit by Ohm's law, $I = V/R$. Thus if the circuit voltage is 400 volts (V) applied through a 400,000-ohm current-limiting resistor (R), approximately 1 ma will be delivered to S, assuming S's resistance is negligible in comparison to the limiting resistor. Campbell and Teghtsoonian (1958) have reported on the electrical and behavioral effects in the rat of different types of shock sources. Basic principles of electricity, along with much information concerning instrumentation, may be found in Cornsweet (1963) and Sidowski and Smith (1966).

Acquisition in Escape Conditioning

MAGNITUDE OF REWARD. Escape conditioning, better than punishment or avoidance training, lends itself to an analysis of the kinds of variables investigated in the case of conditioning with positive reinforcement. To investigate the role of reward (incentive) magnitude on response strength with negative reinforcement, one might, for example, run Ss in a straight alley under a fixed shock level, say 400 volts (applied through an appropriate current-limiting resistor). In analogy with conditioning with S^{R+}, S would be rewarded by a reduction in shock intensity when he arrived in the goal box. Reducing the goal-box shock level to different values provides an operation which bears a close correspondence to manipulations of positive incentives, such as amount of food reward.

Just such an experiment has been performed a number of times with the usual outcome that asymptotic performance is positively related to amount of shock reduction (e.g., Bower, Fowler, & Trapold, 1959; Campbell & Kraeling, 1953). A similar result has been found with thermal aversive stimuli (Woods, Davidson, & Peters, 1964; Woods & Holland, 1966). Consequently, at least with respect to its simple effects, incentive magnitude appears to play similar roles in negatively and positively reinforced instrumental conditioning.

There is much less data available relating to contrast effects arising from incentive shifts in negative reinforcement. From those that do exist, contrast effects appear much less likely to occur with negative reinforcement. Bower, Fowler, and Trapold (1959) shifted Ss from large reward (200-volt reduction) to small (50-volt reduction) and vice versa and found that although Ss adjusted their running speeds quickly to the new reward magnitudes, there was no evidence of the over- or under-shooting that defines elation and depression effects (Fig. 8-1). More recently, Woods (1967) also failed to obtain a positive contrast effect in rats escaping from cold water, but he did observe a moderate depression effect.

The currently indicated conclusion seems to be that although negative reinforcement parallels positive reinforcement in the simple effects of reward magnitude, and perhaps also with respect to rapid adjustments to shifts in magnitude (but cf. Howe, 1961), contrast effects are more difficult to obtain with S^{R-}. It will be recalled, however, that contrast effects, particularly the elation effect, also failed to occur under certain circumstances with positive reward. Conceivably, the same variables that preclude its occurrence with S^{R+} operate more generally in the case of S^{R-}.

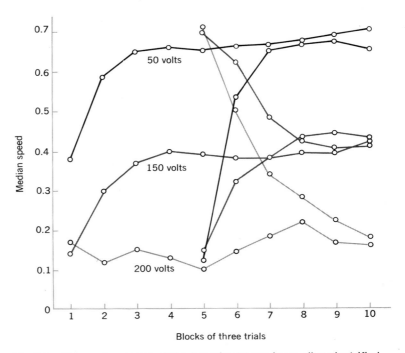

Fig. 8-1. The seven groups of the experiment ran in an alley electrified with 250 volts; the goal-box voltage during Trials 1 to 15 was as indicated in the figure. For two groups of Ss goal-box voltage was shifted from 50 to either 150 or to 200 volts, starting on the sixth block of trials, and for two others the shift was from 200 to 50 or to 150 volts. Note that, as with positive reinforcement, performance level is directly related to the magnitude of shock reduction; moreover, shifts in performance to correspond to the changed reinforcement conditions are relatively rapid. However, there is no sign of either a positive or a negative contrast effect. (SOURCE: G. H. Bower, H. Fowler, and M. A. Trapold. Escape learning as a function of amount of shock reduction. *Journal of Experimental Psychology,* 1959, **58,** 482–484. Copyright 1959 by the American Psychological Association and used by permission.)

Another possibility is that with negative reinforcement contrast effects may be masked by S normally experiencing on each trial two rewards in sequence rather than a single reward, as is the case in positive reinforcement. In the Bower, Fowler, and Trapold study, for example, after receiving its large or small incentive in the goal box, S was removed from the latter and placed in the start box; during this interval S^{R-} was, of course, reduced to zero. Consequently, S experienced on each trial either the reward sequence large-small or small-large. Repeated experience with these contrasting reward magnitudes could have caused Ss to adapt to shifts in incentive magnitude (cf. Capaldi & Lynch, 1967). If so, when the "small" reward Ss were shifted to a large goal-box reward, they would show no elation effect because they had already experienced in the experimental situation many transitions from small to large rewards. And the reverse argument holds for those Ss that were shifted from a large to a small goal-box reward.

It is, of course, quite possible to arrange for more comparable incentive conditions when testing for effects of reward magnitude shifts in positive and negative reinforcement. With positive reinforcement, a second reward might be given to S upon its removal from the goal box, a reward of a size that would sum the goal-box and post-trial incentives to a constant and relatively large magnitude. Conversely, with negative reinforcement, the second reward might be eliminated by maintaining S at the goal-box shock intensity throughout the intertrial interval, until the moment the next trial begins. Whether under such modifications a greater degree of consistency in contrast effects would be obtained from positive and negative reinforcement remains to be seen.

DRIVE LEVEL. With negative reinforcement drive level is usually manipulated by varying the intensity of the primary aversive stimulus. To investigate the role of drive level on instrumental conditioning, one must hold incentive magnitude constant, a precondition achieved by reducing S^{R-} a constant amount. Drive level and constant reward magnitude thus defined, the resulting data are not what we would expect from our knowledge of how variations in appetitive drives affect instrumental conditioning.

Campbell and Kraeling (1953) ran different groups of rats on a straight alley with shock levels varying between 200 and 400 volts. Each group received a constant shock reduction of 100 volts as reward upon entry into the goal box. They found that running speed in their escape situation was *inversely* related to shock (drive) level. One possible explanation of this result is that strong shock might have caused S to engage in responses which reduced the aversive stimulus while competing with the instrumental sequence, responses such as jumping, pressing down on its paws to increase the contact area (thereby reducing current density), and so on. Supporting this view is the fact that Ss in the 400-volt group did not increase their average running speed over their 15 training trials; rather, they showed a slight declining trend.

A more consonant result was obtained by Woods, Davidson, and Peters (1964), who used cold water as the source of drive in their Ss. Although asymptotic speed of swimming to a reward of warmer water was not affected by temperature variations between 15° and 25°C, it increased when the alley-water temperature was reduced to 12°C. In these comparisons incentive magnitude, defined in terms of the difference in temperature between the alley and goal-box water, was held constant (cf. Woods & Holland, 1966).

It appears, therefore, that if the opportunity for S to reduce the severity of S^{R-} by engaging in responses which simultaneously compete with the instrumental response is eliminated, drive level may play a similar role in positive and negative reinforcement. Obviously, however, the relevant data are scanty.

DELAY OF REWARD. Figure 8-2 depicts the running-speed curves of six groups of rats running down a straight alley charged with 250 volts; upon reaching the gal box, S^{R-} was terminated after various delays ranging from 0 to 16 sec. It is apparent from the curves that asymptotic speed is inversely related to reward delay, and in this respect the data are in harmony with the corresponding results from conditioning with positive reinforcement. Delay has a comparable effect on children escaping a loud tone (Penney, 1967). Note, however, that non-monotonicity does not occur to any substantial degree in any of the curves. It will be recalled that nonmonotonicity was commonly encountered with delays

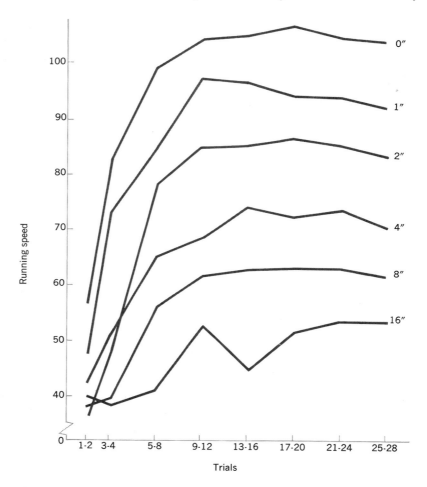

Fig. 8-2. Running speed as a function of the delay (in seconds) of shock termination. (SOURCE: H. Fowler and M. A. Trapold. Escape performance as a function of delay of reinforcement. *Journal of Experimental Psychology*, 1962, **63,** 464–467. Copyright 1962 by the American Psychological Association and used by permission.)

of positive reward. Possibly, nonmonotonicity would have been obtained if training had been continued beyond 28 trials (cf. Fig. 7-8).

A second possibility is that perhaps the critical factor operating again relates to motive-incentive differences. In the Fowler and Trapold study, every trial ended with complete reward, which is to say S^{R-} was ultimately reduced to zero after S reached the goal box. This procedure contrasts with the corresponding operation used in the studies cited earlier, in which a small food reward was given on each trial, reducing the hunger drive by an insignificant degree. In view of this sharp disparity in reinforcement procedures, the question arises as to whether nonmonotonicity would disappear in positively reinforced conditioning if a very large food reward were used. Or conversely, would it appear in escape conditioning if reward were reduced to a relatively small value?

Delay of reward, it might also be noted here, plays an important, if somewhat complex, role in punishment. As we shall see later, depending on circumstances, an immediate punishment can be either more or *less* effective than a delayed punishment.

SUMMARY. Although in their general effects the three variables discussed display important similarities in positively and negatively reinforced conditioning, it is clear that the correspondence is far from perfect. There is far less evidence of contrast effects with shifts in the magnitude of S^{R-}, nonmonotonicity with substantial delays of negative reinforcement has not yet been reported, and, finally, drive-level effects are not as marked nor as reliably obtained as with positive reinforcement. Perhaps all these points of divergence would disappear if the motive-incentive conditions operating in negative reinforcement paralleled more closely those characteristic of the analogous positive-reinforcement paradigms. To achieve this goal a close analysis is required of the motive-incentive patterns operating in the two conditioning situations which are to be placed in correspondence. As yet, however, only the barest beginning has been made in this direction.

INESCAPABLE SHOCK AND "LEARNED HELPLESSNESS." If S is exposed to a series of inescapable shocks, performance of a subsequent escape or avoidance task is often seriously impaired. To take a recent illustration of this interesting phenomenon, Seligman and Maier (1967) gave three groups of dogs 40 conventional escape-avoidance trials in a shuttle box, using a rather strong shock (4.5 ma). On these trials S could, as usual, avoid shock by jumping after the onset of the CS but before the application of the UCS. If S failed to do so, it could escape the UCS by performing the instrumental response within the next 50 sec, after which the trial was terminated.

The important independent variable was the type of associated escape experience received by the three groups. Group 1 was subjected to a series of sixty-four 5-sec inescapable shocks (6.0 ma) 24 hr *before* the 40 escape-avoidance trials. It is important to note that the inescapable shock was *not* administered in the shuttle box but rather in a completely different, hammocklike, apparatus, in which S was restrained while shock was delivered to the footpads of its hind feet. The Ss of Group 2 received precisely the same experience with inescapable shock, except that the shock occurred 24 hr *after* they had first received 10 of the 40 escape-avoidance trials. The last group, Group 3, received no inescapable shock, merely spending the same time in the hammock apparatus as Group 1 before the 40 escape-avoidance trials.

Figure 8-3 shows the percentage of trials on which Ss failed to escape the *UCS* during the 40 escape-avoidance trials, i.e., trials on which S took 50 sec of shock without jumping to the other compartment of the shuttle box. It is perfectly clear that when experience with inescapable shock came first (Group 1),

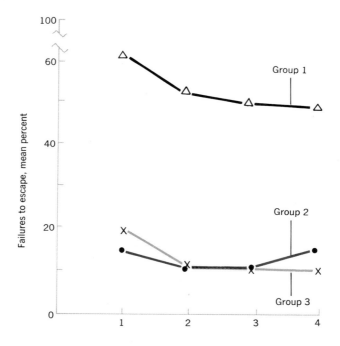

Fig. 8-3. Percentage of trials on which Ss failed to perform the escape response within the allotted 50 sec during which the *UCS*, a 4.5-ma shock, was continuously present. Group 1 was subjected to a series of inescapable shocks before the initiation of the 40 escape-avoidance trials; Group 2 experienced their inescapable shocks after they had first received 10 escape-avoidance trials; Group 3 received no inescapable shocks. (SOURCE: M. E. Seligman and S. F. Maier. Failure to escape traumatic shock. *Journal of Experimental Psychology*, 1967, **74**, 1–9. Copyright 1967 by the American Psychological Association and used by permission.)

subsequent escape behavior was dramatically impaired. Equally interesting is the fact that the detrimental effects of inescapable shock were completely neutralized by the earlier presentation of 10 trials on which S had the opportunity to escape (Group 2). Substantially the same results were obtained for the avoidance behavior of the three groups, though the differences were less pronounced (cf. Overmier, 1968).

The interpretation favored by Seligman, Maier, and their colleagues is that when experience with inescapable shock comes first, S learns that termination of shock is independent of its behavior. Consequently S abandons attempts to terminate the shock, adopting instead an attitude of passivity which, in everyday terms, might be called "helplessness." Presumably the learned helplessness transfers to other situations in which shock is presented, even though they might be quite different in their physical aspects. This interpretation fits with the failure to observe any lasting interference in the Ss of Group 2, inasmuch as they had had previous experience with shock that was escapable—and avoidable. However, it may require modification to handle other related results. For example, Overmier (1968) found that previous inescapable shock interfered with the acquisition of an avoidance response which did *not* involve learning to escape shock; the escape contingency was eliminated by the use of a very brief (inescapable) shock as the UCS. It appears, moreover, that the difference in the pattern of effects generated by inescapable shock in dogs and rats is not presently accommodated by the learned helplessness formulation (cf. Anderson, Cole, & McVaugh, 1968).

Theoretical interpretations aside, there is no question but that previous experience with inescapable shock can have a potent effect on a wide range of subsequent behavior, in many cases impeding the acquisition of adaptive responses, in other cases exerting a facilitating influence. Far more research is required to work out the ramifications of the results which have been obtained thus far, many of which are summarized in the recent papers of Anderson et al. (1968), Seligman, Maier, and Solomon (1970), and Maier, Seligman, and Solomon (1969).

Extinction in Escape Conditioning

Extinction is a concept which has its genesis and major application in the area of positive reinforcement. The motive-incentive conditions implied by the operation of extinction in the latter context are that (1) the magnitude of S^{R+} be reduced to zero and (2) the motivational state (as produced by the deprivational procedure) be unchanged. The second requirement is implicit but nevertheless essential. Parallel conditions are obtained in escape conditioning by no longer having the instrumental response terminate S^{R-}. Primary reinforcement is thereby eliminated while maintaining primary drive. As noted in the previous chapter, however, employment of this extinction procedure is rare. More commonly S^{R-} is eliminated entirely during "extinction" trials, a procedure which abolishes primary drive as well as primary reward. Where one is seeking parallels in the effects of various independent variables upon the extinction of positively and negatively reinforced conditioning, these two different extinction procedures must be distinguished. Elimination of primary reward, but not primary drive, would seem to provide the extinction paradigm more closely analogous to extinction with positive reinforcement. We shall consider briefly both extinction operations.

EXTINCTION AS REMOVAL OF PRIMARY REWARD. One of the most interesting relationships arising from our earlier discussion of extinction with positive reinforcement was the interaction of amount of reward and level of acquisition training in determining resistance to extinction. Does an equivalent interaction hold for negative reinforcement? The answer is that we simply do not know; the relevant literature is extremely meager.

Campbell (1959) trained partially restrained rats in a Skinner-box type apparatus to poke their heads through a hole and depress a lever to turn off shock delivered to their tails. Number of reinforced trials was varied between 0 and 500. During a subsequent 15-min extinction period, throughout which S^{R-} was applied continuously, a *monotonic* relation was obtained between the number of instrumental responses made (resistance to extinction) and amount of previous escape training.

Several comments are in order here. First, inasmuch as during training reinforcement was complete—each escape response terminated S^{R-}—the suggestion is that incentive magnitude was of comparatively large proportions. A possibly mitigating factor, however, is that the shock employed apparently was rather mild. Second, because trials in a Skinner-box setting seem to be less efficacious in obtaining the kinds of effects presently under consideration, it is possible that 500 training trials is an insufficient number to demonstrate non-monotonicity in escape conditioning.

In a more recent study, Fazzaro and D'Amato (1969) varied escape training in a Skinner-box setting between 200 and 1600 trials, distributed 100 trials per day. They used as S^{R-} a pulsating or "discontinuous" shock (0.2 sec on time, 2.0 sec off time) of approximately 0.8 ma. Discontinuous shock, which has been found to facilitate avoidance learning markedly, was used in the present context to provide a strongly aversive, but not overly disorganizing, S^{R-}. Extinction entailed five daily 10-min periods during which the escape response, bar pressing, no longer terminated S^{R-}. In Fig. 8-4 the results, in terms of the total number of responses made during the five extinction sessions, are presented for four groups of the experiment. It is clear that there is no evidence of nonmonotonicity in the data.

From these results it seems unlikely that the monotonicity obtained by Campbell (1959) resulted from either inadequate magnitude of reward or an insufficiently high degree of training. The data also suggest a reinterpretation of the general failure to find nonmonotonicity in Skinner-box settings when reinforcement is positive. Contrary to an earlier conjecture, these failures may

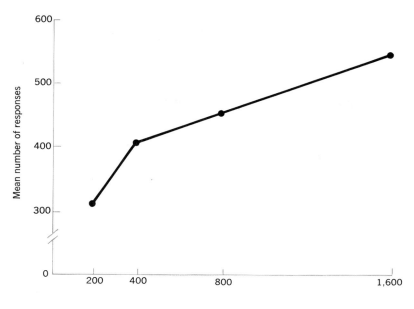

Fig. 8-4. Mean numbers of responses during the five extinction sessions plotted as a function of numbers of acquisition trials (see text). (SOURCE: J. Fazzaro and M. R. D'Amato. Resistance to extinction after varying amounts of nondiscriminative or cue-correlated escape training. *Journal of Comparative and Physiological Psychology,* 1969, **68,** 373–376. Copyright 1969 by the American Psychological Association and used by permission.)

not be the result of the fact that studies utilizing Skinner boxes tend to employ small food rewards; rather, they may point to a fundamental difference between Skinner-box apparatuses and runway devices. Possibly, the relevant variable operating is the amount of effort required in the two situations to execute the instrumental response, or, perhaps, competing responses are more likely to occur in one situation than in the other. (Distracting stimuli are much more prevalent in runway apparatuses, which, in general, maintain poorer environmental control than Skinner-box situations.) Whatever the cause, it is clear that the interactive relationship between level of training and amount of reward in determining resistance to extinction needs to be tested under a much wider range of conditions before it can be safely generalized from the runway to other instrumental conditioning situations or, farther afield, to negatively reinforced conditioning.

EXTINCTION AS REMOVAL OF s^{R-} (REMOVAL OF PRIMARY REWARD AND PRIMARY DRIVE). If, after S has been trained to escape S^{R-}, the negative reinforcer is removed from the experimental situation, eliminating the basis of primary motivation as well as primary reward, will S respond at all during such "extinction" trials? The answer is yes. For an explanation of why the instrumental response continues to occur in the absence of primary drive and primary reward we must recall the fractional anticipatory pain mechanism, r_P–s_P.

The explanation begins with the assumption that during escape training r_P–s_P, or fear, becomes conditioned to the cues of the apparatus in the presence of which S was shocked or endured other negative reinforcers, as, for example, the stimuli occurring in the start box or the alley of a runway apparatus. To carry this illustration further, during a subsequent extinction trial even though S^{R-} is no longer present, fear presumably occurs in some measure in both the start box and the alley, providing the motivational thrust for the escape response.

Moreover, when S arrives in the goal box, S's fear is reduced partly or completely because of the goal box's status, acquired during training, as a cue associated with shock termination. Because fear reduction, like reduction of S^{R-}, is rewarding, the instrumental response should be strengthened during such an "extinction" trial. Thus, we come to a different problem; namely, why should S ever stop responding during this sort of extinction procedure? The answer is that eventually the fear itself extinguishes. Remember that fear, r_P–s_P, is classically conditioned to apparatus cues, the unconditioned stimulus being shock, or more generally, S^{R-}. Because S^{R-}, the *UCS*, never occurs during the extinction procedure under consideration, we have at hand a necessary and sufficient condition for extinction of a classically conditioned response, namely, removal of the unconditioned stimulus. With the eventual extinction of r_P–s_P, the motivating and reinforcing basis of S's responding collapses, and the instrumental response soon follows suit.

This interpretation has a direct bearing on an interesting bit of behavior which some have termed "masochism"; others give it the more neutral appellation "vicious-circle" or "self-punitive" behavior. The usual experimental situation is as follows. Rats are first trained on a simple escape response in a runway. During these trials S is placed in the start box and after a few seconds, shock is applied to the floor of the alley and of the start box. After the establishment of the escape response, a series of extinction trials carried out under one of two different conditions ensues. One group of Ss is extinguished by the removal of S^{R-} procedure; these Ss never again encounter shock in the runway. The second group of Ss is no longer shocked in the start box, but shock is applied in a section of or throughout the alley portion of the runway, for example, in the first 8 in. of the alley (Martin & Melvin, 1964). The remarkable fact is that, contrary to common sense, the Ss that experience shock in the alley take *longer* to extinguish than those that do not. That is, they do not do the sensible thing of staying put in the start box in which they never are shocked during extinction; rather they venture out of the start box, are shocked, then continue on their way to the goal box. We seem faced here with the paradox that punishment serves to strengthen, rather than to weaken, an instrumental response.

Although there are several possible interpretations of this interesting result (cf. Brown, Martin, & Morrow, 1964; Melvin, 1964), the one which appears to enjoy the most support is expressed in terms of the anticipatory pain mechanism (fear). To state this explanation in a few words, it is assumed that the group of Ss for which shock no longer occurs in the runway extinguishes in accordance with the description given above for the removal of S^{R-} procedure. The superior resistance to extinction of the second experimental group of Ss is then ascribed to the fact that the shock which they encounter during their extinction trials serves to maintain the fear response (r_P–s_P) at a relatively high level (cf. Mowrer, 1947).

Let us be more specific. When a rat of the experimental group is placed in the start box on an extinction trial, it experiences the anticipatory pain mechanism, of which the s_P portion during training was associated with running to the goal box (where both S^{R-} and fear were terminated or reduced). Even though during extinction the start box is no longer electrified, fear alone is sufficient to initiate the escape response. When S emerges from the start box and is shocked in the alley, he continues his run to the goal box, terminating again both S^{R-} and fear. In short, the shock experienced by S on these "extinction" trials greatly attenuates extinction of the fear response, which, as we have seen, must be eliminated if the instrumental response is to be extinguished.

If S is shocked during every trial on which it emerges from the start box, thus maintaining the fear response, why should extinction ever occur? The answer is that the fear elicited by the start box, which motivates initiation of the escape response, itself gradually extinguishes inasmuch as shock never occurs there. As the fear begins to extinguish, S takes longer and longer to leave the start box, and consequently the fear generated there is reduced more and more. It has been shown, in fact, that if the electrified portion of the alley is far removed from the start box, rather than adjacent to it, the facilitative effect of shock on resistance to extinction is very much attenuated (Martin & Melvin, 1964).

It has also been shown that the aversive stimulus applied during extinction need not be the same as that under which S initially acquired the escape response. Melvin and Martin (1966) produced vicious-circle behavior in a situation where S^{R-} was shifted from shock to a loud buzzer and vice versa, suggesting that both these aversive stimuli elicit similar fear responses.

We see, then, that the anticipatory pain mechanism provides us with a reasonable and consistent explanation of the foregoing self-punitive behavior, which, possibly because of its significance for certain neurotic behaviors (Mowrer, 1947), is receiving a good deal of attention. Brown (1969) has recently reviewed in detail the available relevant literature, providing an extensive list of factors that contribute to the appearance of this seemingly aberrant behavior.

SUMMARY. We have not discussed all the points of possible parallel between escape conditioning and conditioning with positive reinforcement that have been investigated. For example, the partial reinforcement effect has been obtained with escape conditioning (Bower, 1960). The interaction between drive level and amount of positive reinforcement discussed in the last chapter has been investigated for the case of escape from fear-inducing stimuli, apparently with comparable results (McAllister & McAllister, 1967). Finally, a number of studies have concerned themselves with the question of how well certain behavioral properties characteristic of fixed-ratio schedules under positive reinforcement are retained when reinforcement is negative (e.g., Winograd, 1965). Inasmuch as most of the properties of standard operant reinforcement schedules have been worked out under positive reinforcement, the more general issue arises as to the extent to which these properties are independent of the sign of the reinforcer (cf. Morse & Kelleher, 1966). As already emphasized, however, in making all such comparisons, E must be on guard that the motive-incentive conditions under negative reinforcement correspond as closely as possible to those normally prevailing when reinforcement is positive.

PUNISHMENT

In Chap. 7 we defined punishment as response-contingent aversive stimulation. At times, however, the term is also applied to the application of aversive stimulation without any requirement of response contingency. As an illustration, S might be busy pressing a bar to obtain food when, either unheralded or preceded by an appropriate signal, shock is applied to the grid floor, independently of what S is doing at the moment. Where a stimulus signaling the onset of shock is employed, S soon ceases his instrumental activity upon its onset, adopting a posture of freezing and crouching in anticipation of S^{R-}; apparently, the cue has become a conditioned stimulus for fear. The response suppression elicited by this stimulus has been called, perhaps unfortunately (cf. McAllister & McAllister, 1970), the "conditioned emotional response" (CER), a term which frequently refers as well to the experimental paradigm itself. A good deal of research effort has been devoted to the CER, which has proven a useful behavioral tool in a number of research areas. We shall not discuss the CER (more generally, response-noncontingent aversive stimulation) but will restrict ourselves to the response-contingent case, which, for us, shall define punishment. McAllister and McAllister (1970) have recently examined in detail a number of behavioral indices of fear, among them the CER, and their paper is recommended to the interested reader. It might be noted here, however, that response suppression—the consequence of punishment investigated most—occurs to a greater extent when application of S^{R-} is response contingent than when it is independent of S's behavior (e.g., Camp, Raymond, & Church, 1967; Church, 1969; Rachlin & Herrnstein, 1969). On the other hand, the suppression induced by the CER procedure appears to be more resistant to extinction than that which results from a comparable punishment paradigm (e.g., Hoffman & Fleshler, 1965; Hunt & Brady, 1955). Punishment, it seems, leads to more "adaptive" behavior modification than noncontingent aversive stimulation.

Punishment has a very long history, as long as man himself, who undoubtedly has always used punishment to influence the behavior of others. Law and order, whether local or national, rely heavily on a calculated system of punishments. Nevertheless differences of opinion with respect to the efficacious-ness of punishment have probably always existed. The "spare the rod and spoil the child" school has always had its opposition, though probably never as strong as during the last half-century. In spite of the very important role played by punishment in the affairs of men, only recently has it come under steady research efforts in the laboratory.

Most accounts of punishment start with Thorndike, who was one of the first to give a systematic account of the role of punishment in learning. Thorn-dike has been called a "connectionist," one who views the learning process as the establishment of "connections" or "bonds" between stimuli and responses. Within this orientation, Thorndike (1913) originally maintained that positive reinforcement strengthened stimulus-response connections, whereas punish-ment, or negative reinforcement, weakened such connections.

This symmetry in the effects of positive and negative reinforcement upon learned associations was pleasing but not destined to last uninterrupted. Thorn-dike (e.g., 1932) later modified his view of the role of punishment, holding that it weakened S–R connections little if at all. With this change in view, Thorndike became one of the first of modern psychologists to disparage the usefulness of punishment in behavior control, though it was left for Skinner to develop and stress the point. In any event, for a time the major research question in the investigation of punishment was whether it was an effective agent in the elimina-tion of a conditioned response, a topic of obvious practical consequences. Experi-ments by Estes (1944) and Skinner (1938, p. 154) fortified the view that punish-ment was an ineffective device for the elimination of unwanted behavior and that extinction was by far the better alternative. This attitude prevailed in many quarters for more than a score of years. More recently, however, there has been some shift on both these issues. Symmetry in the effects of punishment and reward has been restored, albeit in a different fashion, by some theorists and investigators (e.g., Estes, 1969; Mowrer, 1960; Schuster & Rachlin, 1968); and it has been recognized that punishment, applied temporarily, can suppress behavior lastingly. We shall say more about this topic later.

The discussion of punishment provided in the present section is neces-sarily selective. The interested reader can fill in by consulting Azrin and Holz (1966), Church (1963), and Solomon (1964). A number of current germane papers are found in two recent edited volumes, one by Brush (1970), *Aversive Conditioning and Learning*, the other by Campbell and Church (1969), *Punish-ment and Aversive Behavior*. An extensive bibliography on punishment is provided by Boe (1969).

Acquisition Processes in Punishment

PUNISHMENT AS PASSIVE AVOIDANCE LEARNING. The paradigm of punishment presupposes the existence of a goal-directed response in some strength. In the laboratory this response is usually a conditioned instrumental response established by positive reinforcement—pressing a bar, running down a runway, etc. If this conditioned response is conceived of as an S–R association and if punishment is conceded to have no effect on the bond or association itself, how then shall we conceptualize the well-established empirical result that punishment suppresses instrumental behavior? How shall we interpret the known fact that, penalized with a sufficiently noxious stimulus, S will no longer lead to R if R in turn leads to S^{R-}?

A number of theoretical approaches have been advanced to handle this problem (cf. Church, 1963; Estes, 1969; Solomon, 1964). We will describe here only one of these, the so-called "avoidance hypothesis" proposed by Mowrer (e.g., Mowrer, 1960). This hypothesis makes use of the fractional anticipatory pain mechanism, or fear, in establishing both the motivation and incentive for the response suppression that normally follows punishment.

Suppose that S has learned in a given situation to make an instrumental response which secures for him some sort of positive reinforcement and suppose that conditions are altered so that the response now also produces an aversive stimulus, S^{R-}. After a few such experiences S will either show hesitancy in making the instrumental response or stop altogether. On an intuitive level the explanation is clear: S simply is afraid to make the response because he "knows" that it will lead to the aversive event. The achievement of the present hypothesis is that it incorporates this common-sense explanation within a systematic objective theoretical approach. Or as Mowrer has put it in a closely related context:

> Our "rediscovery" of phenomena which, it seems, are as old as mammalian life itself may not seem like much of an accomplishment; and certainly there is every reason to be appropriately modest about it. But in one respect, there is real progress here: these phenomena are now being identified in a *systematic conceptual framework* and their definition is in terms of *clear-cut, empirical operations* (Mowrer, 1960, p. 166).

According to the avoidance hypothesis, as a result of punishment, fear in the form of the r_{P}–s_{P} mechanism becomes conditioned to the proprioceptive stimuli characteristic of the instrumental, punished act. Thus, when S begins to perform the instrumental response, the resulting proprioceptive stimulation elicits r_{P}–s_{P}, or fear. Cessation of the instrumental response, on the other hand, results in a cessation of fear because the proprioceptive stimuli to which fear has become conditioned are themselves terminated. Because fear reduction is reinforcing, the act of terminating or diminishing in intensity the instrumental, punished response is thereby reinforced. As fear becomes conditioned to proprioceptive stimuli occurring earlier and earlier in the instrumental response sequence, cessation of the latter will tend to occur at an earlier and earlier point. Eventually, if the conditioned fear is sufficiently antedating, only the merest fragment of the response sequence will occur before fear intervenes and motivates termination of the instrumental response.

Because in deferring from initiating or completing the instrumental response S is acting to avoid S^{R-}, Mowrer has suggested that punishment may be viewed as a form of avoidance conditioning. However, the avoidance response is not an active, explicit response specified by E, but rather the more passive reaction of *not* responding. He has suggested, therefore, that punishment be called "passive" avoidance learning and that the behavior characteristic of the usual avoidance paradigm be termed "active" avoidance conditioning (Mowrer, 1960).

The preceding interpretation squares with a number of facts of punishment conditioning. For example, if application of S^{R-} were delayed too long at the completion of the response to be punished, its effectiveness in suppressing behavior should (under certain conditions) be reduced, because conditioning of fear to the proprioceptive stimuli characteristic of the instrumental act would thereby be impaired. This deduction has been upheld in laboratory experiments on animals (delay of punishment gradient), and it embodies a useful principle of child-rearing discovered independently by many.

On the debit side, it is difficult to see how this account of punishment can handle the response suppression which occurs with *CER* training. In the latter, it will be recalled, S^{R-} is applied independently of S's behavior. Consequently, because termination of the instrumental response does not in any way affect the appearance of S^{R-}, cessation of the instrumental response sequence cannot be reinforced by fear reduction. It would seem that intense fear has the ability to suppress behavior generally, even when S^{R-} is not correlated with a specific bit of behavior. Response suppression, or partial immobility, apparently is a general response to intense fear present at many phylogenetic levels, including man. Perhaps the *CER* data can be reconciled with the avoidance hypothesis of punishment by assuming that strong fear, whether generated from response-contingent aversive stimulation or not, has the initial effect of suppressing behavior generally. When, however, S^{R-} is response-correlated, the fear eventually differentiates out, so to speak, and becomes associated primarily, if not solely, with the proprioceptive consequences of the response which leads to negative reinforcement.

FACTORS AFFECTING EXTENT OF RESPONSE SUPPRESSION. Because response suppression is the major behavioral result of punishment, particularly of strong punishment, let us sample a few of the important variables determining the amount of suppression likely to be obtained. The first variable to be discussed—perhaps the most obviously relevant one—is intensity of S^{R-}.

Intensity of S^{R-}. There are three generalizations relating to the effect of intensity of the aversive stimulus which are well established. First, with mildly aversive stimulation response suppression is likely to be slight; further, as punishment conditioning continues, the instrumental response recovers, often completely (e.g., Azrin, 1960a; Rachlin, 1966). Second, with aversive stimulation of moderate intensity, suppression is greater, and although partial recovery of the response may occur, response strength is not likely to return to its pre-punishment state (e.g., Appel & Peterson, 1965; Camp, Raymond, & Church, 1967). There is a moral here; namely, if mild punishment is to remain effective, it must be used sparingly. The child who reacts with near indifference to his parents' repeated scoldings or slaps is an illustration of how mild punishment becomes ineffective through overuse.

Finally, with severe punishment, response suppression may be complete and of long duration. As an illustration, Appel (1961) punished the bar-pressing response in two squirrel monkeys who had been trained to respond for a food reward during 8-hr training sessions. After a single session in which Ss were shocked for making the instrumental response, their response rates fell almost to zero and stayed there for the following 50 experimental sessions, *even though shock was eliminated during the last 30 sessions.* The monkeys were very highly motivated for food, having been reduced to 60 percent of their normal body weight. Yet they preferred to endure 8 straight hr in the experimental chamber without food rather than perform the instrumental response, which might result in shock. Similar results were obtained with squirrel monkeys by Hake, Azrin, and Oxford (1967), who found that after complete suppression, Ss had to be "reshaped" in order to get them to resume responding. Complete and enduring response suppression has also been obtained with pigeons (Azrin, 1960a) and rats (Storms, Boroczi, & Broen, 1962).

These results from animal investigations have some direct implications for the proper use of punishment in the control of human behavior. First, punishment has the effect of suppressing the punished response, and advantage can be taken of this respite to redirect behavior into more acceptable channels. Mild punishment has the advantage that it does not precipitate intense fear, which is likely to impede attempts toward the rechanneling of behavior. Second, as we have already noted, in order to remain effective, mild and moderate punishment must be used sparingly. Finally, where one is dealing with incorrigible behavior, seemingly immune to normal behavioral control methods, the results obtained with severe punishment are suggestive. It seems possible that strong punishment employed in conjunction with other techniques might be an efficient and effective means of suppressing and eventually eliminating incorrigible and chronic behavioral problems which, at present, are unresponsive to more conservative behavioral control techniques. It is conceivable that alcohol and drug addiction, for example, could be suppressed in addicted individuals if the behavior associated with the attainment and consumption of these substances were associated with intense negative reinforcement.

The goal of a therapeutic program based on negative reinforcement would be to have the fear generated by S^{R-} work back through the instrumental chain to its earliest portions and eventually to the very act of thinking about drugs or alcohol. In response to the objection that even if, under such a program, the addiction itself were cured, one will have treated a symptom only rather than the underlying causes, it need only be pointed out that "symptoms" of this nature could easily become in themselves causes of events and experiences which perpetuate and accentuate the psychological difficulties facing the afflicted individual. Furthermore, elimination of even the symptoms alone is by no means easy to come by, and contributions toward this end are to be welcomed.

There are, of course, a number of important problems facing any attempts to use strong aversive stimuli in the control and treatment of behavioral problems. First of all, the ability of the patient to discriminate the conditions under which negative reinforcement is administered could defeat the whole procedure. The patient might very well come to fear alcohol or drugs in a therapeutic situation, where he knows he will be punished for partaking of them, but be bothered little if at all by fear of such activity when outside the clinic. This problem, really one of inadequate generalization of the fear elicited in the clinic, has its no less important counterpart in the necessity to obtain a degree of differentiation of the experimentally induced fear. We wish the fear or anxiety elicited by S^{R-} to remain associated with the proprioceptive and other stimuli characteristic of the addiction behavior, whether the patient is in or out of the clinic. On the other hand, we must require that the fear be extinguished to other, irrelevant components of the patient's behavior. Appel's monkeys, for example, were generally fearful as a result of their experience with intense punishment. They cowered in one corner of the experimental cages, doing nothing, and showed signs of fear even outside the experimental situation.

In spite of these very real difficulties, the possibility of using strong punishment as a means of eliminating serious behavioral problems should not be dismissed prematurely. As a matter of fact, aversive stimuli have been employed in the treatment of alcohol addiction and other behavioral problems—treatment known as "aversion therapy"—for some time (cf. Bandura, 1961). The use of nauseant drugs as unconditioned stimuli in efforts to classically condition reactions of nausea in alcoholics to the sight, smell, and taste of alcohol dates back at least 30 years. However, there is increasing feeling that for several reasons electric shock is a better aversive stimulus for therapeutic purposes than chemical means, which in general cannot be manipulated with the precision of electric shock (cf. Rachman, 1965). Moreover as Feldman (1966) points out in his review of aversion therapy of sexual deviants, instrumental methods are potentially more powerful than classical conditioning techniques. Apart from punishment, aversion therapy may employ avoidance conditioning and, where possible, combine aversive techniques with the conditioning of appropriate approach reactions. It may be useful to point out that an event may be highly aversive without being physically painful. Anant (1968) describes what he calls "verbal" aversion therapy, in which the "aversive stimulus" consists of the patient vividly imagining very unpleasant or frightening events. He has employed this technique with alcoholics, drug addicts, homosexuals, and a mentally defective promiscuous girl.

A few years ago an interesting series of studies was reported in which electric shock was employed as a means of modifying the behavior of autistic children (Lovaas, Schaeffer, & Simmons, 1965). Painful electric shock was used as punishment in an attempt to suppress such "pathological" behaviors as self-stimulation and temper tantrums and as negative reinforcement in an escape-avoidance situation designed to establish social responsiveness. These investigators met with some success, though they encountered the sort of problems discussed earlier.

To terminate this section with a further digression, we note that virtually all the conditioning paradigms discussed in this and the preceding chapter, as well as certain operant conditioning techniques (Chap. 9), have been translated to the therapeutic situation (cf. Krasner & Ullmann, 1965; Ullmann & Krasner, 1965; Wolpe & Lazarus, 1966; Wolpe, Salter, & Reyna, 1964). This broader area of application has now acquired a rich literature, a name—"behavior therapy"—and a pair of journals—*Behaviour Research and Therapy* (cf. Rachman, 1963) and *Behavior Therapy*. As might be expected, the response to this development has not been uniformly positive (e.g., Breger & McGaugh, 1965; Weitzman, 1967).

Strength of the punished response. Other things constant, it is a reasonable assumption that the degree of response suppression arising from punishment will be a function of the strength of the punished response. This expectation turns out to be justified, but the kind of relationship which apparently holds in conditioning situations is not at all what intuition would suggest. At least two studies have reported that rats given a relatively large amount of reward training before the introduction of S^{R-} are, compared to Ss given smaller amounts of training, *less* resistant to the effects of punishment; the former Ss show, in other words, *more* response suppression (Karsh, 1962; Miller, 1960). In Miller's experiment, for example, rats were trained on a runway to obtain food, and after either 21 or 38 days of such training, shock was introduced in the goal box (in addition to food) on each trial. The effect of the shock was to reduce the running speed in the second group of animals to a much greater degree than in the first.

More recently Born (1967) reported for a free-operant response that resistance to the suppressive effects of punishment was nonmonotonically related to acquisition level, although his experiment was complicated by the simultaneous removal of reward upon introduction of S^{R-}. The interpretation of these unanticipated results is not clear, but if they turn out to hold generally, the outlook for the use of punishment in the control of long-standing habits is more promising than common sense would lead us to suspect.

Delay of punishment. As already mentioned, the effects of delay of punishment are somewhat complex. Generalizing from the data which we discussed in connection with delay of reward in positive reinforcement and in escape conditioning, we might suppose that the effectiveness of S^{R-} in a punishment situation would be reduced as the period of time intervening between execution of the instrumental response and application of S^{R-} increases. If, however, we carefully consider the fractional anticipatory pain mechanism, another possibility comes into view. Given that a period of time, say 30 sec, intervenes between completion of the instrumental response and the appearance of S^{R-}, it is likely that after sufficient training, the anticipatory pain response, fear, will become conditioned to stimuli characteristic of the 30-sec preshock interval. When this occurs, S would come to anticipate shock during the 30-sec delay interval and be fearful. If we grant that this is the case, the aversiveness of S^{R-} might actually be enhanced when it is delayed, because in addition to the shock itself, S must contend with the fear which arises from its anticipation.

As a matter of fact, when given a choice between immediate and delayed punishment, both rats (Knapp, Kause, & Perkins, 1959; but see Renner & Houlihan, 1969) and humans (Badia, McBane, Suter, & Lewis, 1966; Cook & Barnes, 1964; D'Amato & Gumenik, 1960) prefer the immediate punishment (shock). Because all the experiments just cited involved choice between experimentally defined alternatives, the question arises as to their relevance for punishment in instrumental conditioning, where choice is not involved. Will delayed S^{R-} suppress behavior more effectively than immediate negative reinforcement in a punishment paradigm restricted to instrumental conditioning?

The data that are now available uniformly point to a negative answer. Immediate shock has been found to be more effective than delayed shock in nonchoice punishment paradigms involving human subjects (Banks & Vogel-Sprott, 1965), rats (A. Baron, 1965; Camp, Raymond, & Church, 1967), and fish (Myer & Ricci, 1968). In several cases an orderly delay-of-punishment gradient was obtained, one of which is illustrated in Fig. 8-5.

Thus we are faced with something of a paradox. Given a choice between immediate and delayed shock, Ss frequently prefer the former. A reasonable explanation is that delayed shock engenders anxiety during the delay interval, which must be borne by S in addition to S^{R-} itself. Another possible interpretation is that delayed shock is more aversive because it is less predictable than

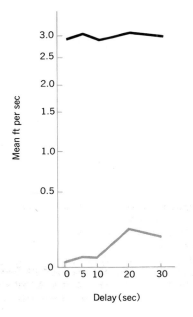

Fig. 8-5. Runway speed as affected by delay of punishment (lower curve). The upper curve shows runway performance for the five delay groups during the prepunishment trials. (SOURCE: A. Baron. Delayed punishment of a runway response. *Journal of Comparative and Physiological Psychology,* 1965, **60,** 131–134. Copyright 1965 by the American Psychological Association and used by permission.)

immediate shock. Indeed, Badia et al. (1966) and D'Amato and Gumenik (1960) used *randomly* delayed shock in their experiments. It is known, moreover, that both rats and humans often prefer signaled (predictable) to unsignaled shock (e.g., Badia, Suter, & Lewis, 1967; Lockard, 1963). However, unpredictability may also exert its effects through the mechanism of anxiety. Seligman (1968), for example, found that rats working for food reinforcement were far more suppressed by unpredictable shock than by the same shock made predictable by a preceding signal. And very interestingly, the unpredictable shock led to extensive stomach ulcers, whereas predictable shock had no such effect. In any event, whether it is the delay itself or the lack of predictability which accompanies delay that is the essential factor, the consistent preference of immediate over delayed shock is not congruent with the effect of delayed punishment in nonchoice paradigms. Why should delayed shock not be experienced as more aversive in such situations and thus suppress responding to a greater extent than immediate shock?

One possible resolution of the conflicting results lies in the amount of punishment training afforded S. If relatively little training is given, conditioning of r_{P-SP} to the cues of the delay interval may not occur to a degree sufficient to elicit intense fear during the preshock interval. Under such circumstances, immediate punishment might prove more effective than delayed punishment in suppressing behavior because the contingency between the instrumental response and S^{R-} will be recognized (discriminated) more quickly. It is of interest that several experiments supporting the notion of a simple delay-of-punishment gradient have employed few punishment trials (e.g., Banks & Vogel-Sprott, 1965; A. Baron, 1965). In other cases, however, punishment training appears to have been carried to reasonable levels (e.g., Camp et al., 1967). Nevertheless, explicit investigation of this variable is desirable.

The disparity between the choice and conditioning data is another instance of the sort of interactions encountered in our discussion of the partial reinforcement effect. We saw in Chap. 7 that the *PRE* is obtained reliably in separate-groups designs, but it frequently fails to occur with single-group designs; moreover, a reversed *PRE* was sometimes obtained in the latter designs. We also noted that although based on the same dependent variable, measures of response magnitude and direction may yield quite different results. In the present case it is not clear whether the apparently inconsistent effects of delay of punishment relate to the different designs employed or to the different response measures. The choice experiments were single-group designs inasmuch as each S experienced both immediate and delayed shock. On the other hand, the conditioning studies have all been separate-groups designs essentially. A single-group-design experiment suggests itself in which S receives immediate shock in one situation and delayed shock in another (e.g., alleys of different brightness). The results of such an experiment might prove illuminating.

Other variables. There are, of course, a number of other variables that influence the extent of response suppression obtained in punishment conditioning. Among these, schedule of punishment employed has been found to be a significant variable (e.g., Camp, Raymond, & Church, 1966; Ferraro, 1967; Kelleher & Morse, 1968), as has S's earlier reward training. It is an interesting finding, the significance of which we shall discuss later, that a partial reinforcement reward schedule results in less suppression when punishment is later introduced than does continuous reinforcement (e.g., Brown & Wagner, 1964; Vogel-Sprott & Thurston, 1968). A repeated finding of some practical importance is that S's tolerance for punishment (electric shock) can be increased, often dramatically, by providing earlier experience with mild aversive stimuli of the same (e.g., Miller, 1960) or even of different (Terris & Wechkin, 1967) modalities. The general references cited earlier may be consulted for further information concerning these and other relevant variables.

OTHER EFFECTS OF PUNISHMENT.   There are a number of situations in which punishment has been found to facilitate rather than suppress instrumental behavior. We have already encountered one such instance in our earlier discussion of vicious-circle behavior, in which, it will be recalled, punishment applied during extinction served to maintain rather than suppress the instrumental (escape) response. Our second illustration comes from a study by Holz and Azrin (1961). Pigeons were stabilized on an intermittent schedule of positive reward, every response punished by a moderate shock. During some sessions neither food nor shock was administered, and, of course, Ss soon came to respond very little at these times.

Figure 8-6 shows the effect of introducing into such extinction sessions a 10-min period during which punishment but not reward was restored. Upon the introduction of punishment, both Ss quickly increased their rate of response, maintaining the augmented rate throughout the punishment period and even a little beyond. It seems apparent that the basis of the observed response facilitation resides in the previous association of punishment with reward, by virtue of which S^{R-} became a discriminative cue for the availability of reinforcement.

Holz and Azrin (1961) also showed that a very mild shock—so mild that it had little suppressive effect by itself—could be made to inhibit responding sharply by being paired with extinction, which makes it a discriminative cue for nonreinforcement. As Holz and Azrin point out, the discriminative properties of punishment may account for certain perplexing features of punishment observed outside of the laboratory. In their words, "one might be *more* disposed to supply reinforcement to an individual following administration of punishment, in a sense to try to 'make up' for the punishment. If so, the punishment would be (inadvertently) paired with reinforcement and it could be expected to acquire a discriminative property. Thus, the severe punishment would be ineffective as a deterrent [p. 231]." Obviously, the opposite effect, rendering a very mild punishment as an effective deterrent, could be accomplished by arranging for the punishment to become a discriminative cue for withdrawal of positive reinforcement.

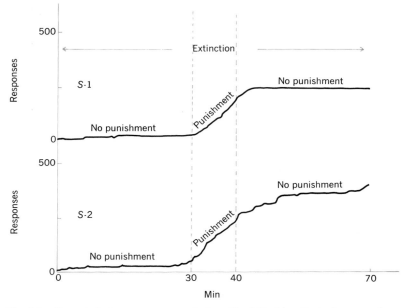

Fig. 8-6. Cumulative response records (see Fig. 9-1) of two Ss during an extinction session in which a 10-min period of punishment was introduced after the first half hour. As the nearly horizontal record of the initial 30 min of extinction indicates, response rate was very low before the introduction of punishment, which led to a rapid and marked increase in rate that persisted throughout the punishment period. The facilitation of instrumental behavior shown in the figure is a manifestation of the discriminative function of punishment (see text). (SOURCE: W. C. Holz and N. H. Azrin. Discriminative properties of punishment. *Journal of the Experimental Analysis of Behavior*, 1961, **4,** 225–232. Copyright 1961 by the Society for the Experimental Analysis of Behavior, Inc. and used by permission.)

Other situations in which punishment, serving as a discriminative cue, has been found to facilitate instrumental behavior include avoidance behavior and simple discrimination learning (cf. Fowler & Wishner, 1969). Fowler (1970) has recently provided a detailed discussion of the cue properties of punishment, which he separates into discriminative, secondary reinforcing, and "distinctive cue" functions.

Long-term maintenance of behavior by punishment. A recent study by Kelleher and Morse (1968) shows in a remarkable way how varied the effects of punishment can be. Kelleher and Morse extensively trained two squirrel monkeys on a series of schedules involving positive reward alone and reward plus punishment. The details of the experiments are somewhat involved, but we shall concentrate on essentials. To begin with, Ss were trained on a variable-interval 2-min food reinforcement schedule for a number of sessions until their performance was relatively stable. In this type of reinforcement schedule, abbreviated as *VI* 2 (see Chap. 9 for a discussion of the topic), reward becomes available every 2 min on the average; characteristically S responds at a rather constant rate. In the part of the investigation described here (Experiments II and III), the *VI* 2 schedule was in effect for 11 min, followed by a 1-min time-out period, during which all responses were nonreinforced. The purpose of the time-outs, which were accompanied by a darkening of the experimental chamber, was to organize the experimental sessions into clearly defined 11-min cycles. Figure 8-7 shows what performance looked like for one S after its behavior on the *VI* 2 had stabilized.

In the next phase a strong shock was introduced in the form of a fixed-interval 10-min punishment schedule (*FI* 10). Thus, the first response which occurred after 10 min of a cycle had elapsed was greeted with a 12.6-ma shock to the tail, lasting for 45 msec. Although the initial effect of the punishment schedule was to suppress responding, eventually performance recovered and even reached higher rates under the punishment condition. At this point a second punishment schedule was added: every response which occurred during the 1-min period that followed completion of the *FI* 10 was shocked.

In summary, a *VI* 2 food schedule was in force throughout each 11-min cycle and, concurrently, an *FI* 10 punishment schedule was in effect followed by approximately 1 min of a continuous punishment schedule. One would suppose that the most sensible behavior in this situation is for S to respond rapidly after a time-out because shocks never occur at this point; as the interval wears on, S should perhaps reduce its responding until, when shock becomes imminent toward the end of the interval, it ought to cease responding altogether. After completion of the time-out, which was adequately signaled by an external cue, S could resume responding in safety. The behavior actually obtained was far different.

Figure 8-8 shows S's performance after a large number of sessions on the preceding schedules. Note first of all that in many of the 11-min cycles, S ran off

150 responses

VI 2 (food)

Fig. 8-7. A cumulative response record of one subject working on a *VI* 2 reward schedule. The experimental session was organized into a series of 11-min cycles, each terminated by a 1-min time-out period, the beginning of which is shown by a vertical line. The short oblique lines mark the delivery of food reward. Note the saw-tooth appearance of the record, which indicates that S was responding at a fairly constant rate during each cycle and from one cycle to another. It is apparent from the scale on the ordinate that S often performed fewer than 150 responses during a single cycle. (SOURCE: R. T. Kelleher and W. H. Morse. Schedules using noxious stimuli. III. Responding maintained with response-produced electric shocks. *Journal of the Experimental Analysis of Behavior*, 1968, **11**, 819–838. Copyright 1968 by the Society for the Experimental Analysis of Behavior, Inc. and used by permission.)

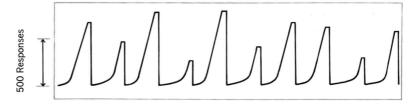

Fig. 8-8. Performance of the same subject as shown in Fig. 8-7 after more than 100 sessions under the *VI* 2 food schedule plus an *FI* 10 punishment schedule followed by a 1-min continuous punishment component. Note the huge increase in the number of responses run off in each cycle (cf. Fig. 8-7). The positive acceleration that occurs in most of the cycles is characteristic of performance under a fixed-interval schedule of positive reinforcement. The horizontal peak of each "spike" results from the response s'·ppression which occurred during the 1-min continuous punishment component. (SOURCE: R. T. Kelleher and W. H. Morse. Schedules using noxious stimuli. III. Responding maintained with response-produced electric shocks. *Journal of the Experimental Analysis of Behavior*, 1968, **11**, 819–838. Copyright 1968 by the Society for the Experimental Analysis of Behavior, Inc. and used by permission.)

a large number of responses, far more than the number executed in the *VI* 2 alone (Fig. 8-7). Moreover, the pattern of responding is just about the reverse of that predicted for a "rational" organism. At the beginning of each cycle, response rate is at its lowest point, increasing gradually through the 11-min interval and reaching its highest value near the completion of the *FI* 10. This pattern produces the positive curvature that is characteristic of fixed-interval schedules of positive reinforcement (cf. Fig. 9-3). It would appear from its performance that *S* was working *for* shock rather than to forestall it. Also observe that very few responses occurred during the 1-min period during which continuous punishment was in effect, which attests to the aversiveness of the shock parameters employed.

Kelleher and Morse checked the possibility that performance was not maintained by food reward solely by eliminating the *VI* 2 schedule, leaving intact the *FI* 10 and continuous punishment components. The remarkable behavior which ensued is shown in Fig. 8-9. The upper and lower panels present *S*'s behavior on sessions 99 and 126, respectively, *after* the *VI* 2 food schedule was deleted. The figure shows plainly the survival of the positive acceleration that is characteristic of the *FI* 10 component and the subsequent suppression during continuous punishment. The animal persisted in this bizarre behavior for 140 sessions spread over a 6-month period, *never obtaining food reward in the experimental situation and never experiencing food deprivation after the first few sessions.*

If one had suspicions that factors other than the response-produced shock were maintaining *S*'s behavior, the data shown in Fig. 8-10 dispel them completely. All punishment was eliminated for two sessions and, as is apparent from the figure, by the end of the second session responding collapsed almost to

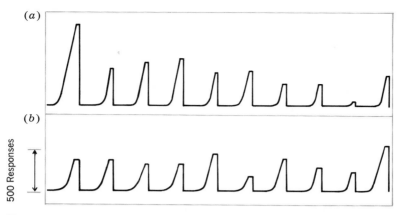

Fig. 8-9. Cumulative response curves obtained with the *VI* 2 food reinforcement schedule deleted and only the *FI* 10 and 1-min continuous punishment schedules in effect. (a) and (b) present sessions 99 and 126, respectively, during which *S* was working for shock alone. Although the number of responses executed in a cycle varies from one cycle to another, positive acceleration is still evident in the records, and, moreover, *S* never failed to produce at least one shock during each cycle of the two sessions. Indeed, during the 170 sessions that the punishment schedules alone were in effect *S* delivered more than 1,900 shocks to itself. (SOURCE: R. T. Kelleher and W. H. Morse. Schedules using noxious stimuli. III. Responding maintained with response-produced electric shocks. *Journal of the Experimental Analysis of Behavior,* 1968, **11,** 819–838. Copyright 1968 by the Society for the Experimental Analysis of Behavior, Inc. and used by permission.)

the zero point. Upon reinstatement of the two punishment schedules, the characteristic positively accelerated pattern reappeared.

Essentially the same overall pattern of results was obtained with the second *S* of the study, and similar, equally striking behavior has been reported under different circumstances. [See Morse and Kelleher (1970) for a review of this work.] Thus, one cannot dismiss this unusual finding as a mere curiosity.

The interpretation of this phenomenon, which we shall refer to as "punishment-maintained behavior," poses an important challenge for conventional theories of punishment. It is hard to understand, for example, why the shock received at the completion of the *FI* 10 schedule, as well as any received subsequently, did not result in the establishment of fear and hence to the sustained suppression of responding during most of the latter portion of each 11-min cycle. The situation cannot be rescued by appealing to the discriminative function of punishment, for it is difficult to fathom for what postive event punishment could have been a discriminative cue. Perhaps punishment served as a discriminative cue for the time-out period, but generally speaking, such periods themselves tend to have aversive properties (Kaufman & Baron, 1968; McMillan, 1967). It must be remembered in this connection that the *FI* 10 punishment component maintained behavior in the absence of the *VI* food schedule and even in the absence of food deprivation and, hence, presumably in the absence

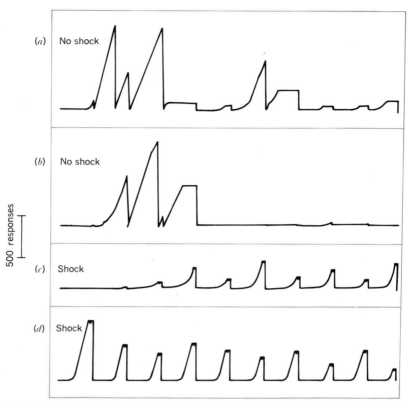

Fig. 8-10. (a) and (b) present S's performance during two sessions in which the punishment schedules were removed. (The *VI* 2 food schedule had long since been deleted.) Performance soon deteriorated, and by the end of the second session S was nearly extinguished. Upon reinstatement of the *FI* 10 and 1-min continuous punishment schedules [panels (c) and (d)], S's behavior quickly recovered, showing the typical positive acceleration during the *FI* component and suppression during the continuous punishment schedule. The oblique marks indicate delivery of shock. (SOURCE: R. T. Kelleher and W. H. Morse. Schedules using noxious stimuli. III. Responding maintained with response-produced electric shocks. *Journal of the Experimental Analysis of Behavior,* 1968, **11,** 819–838. Copyright 1968 by the Society for the Experimental Analysis of Behavior, Inc. and used by permission.)

of hunger motivation. One possible interpretation is that through its long association with a food reinforcement schedule, the shock of the *FI* schedule became an event with positive properties, much as one comes to enjoy the bitterness of certain foods and beverages which initially are experienced as unpleasant-tasting. If so, then given a choice between the *FI* 10 punishment schedule and, say, the same schedule producing a different stimulus—perhaps a light—S should choose the former. Unfortunately, however, this interpretation is not easily applied to other instances of punishment-maintained behavior (cf. McKearney, 1968; Morse, Mead, & Kelleher, 1967).

Whatever the explanation turns out to be, punishment-maintained behavior of the sort reported by Kelleher and Morse is likely to attract a good deal of research interest. Although there are certain resemblances between it and other instances in which punishment has been shown to facilitate performance, for example vicious-circle behavior, there are notable differences. Foremost among these is the extended period over which response-produced shock was able to sustain behavior in Kelleher and Morse's Ss and the absence of experimentally applied motive-incentive conditions that might have been relevant for Ss' behavior.

Although we have some knowledge of the processes that modulate the effects of punishment (cf. Fowler, 1970), there is much to be learned before we gain an adequate understanding of punishment-related phenomena and achieve the means with which to control such behavior in and out of the laboratory.

Extinction Processes in Punishment

Unlike the other negative reinforcement paradigms, punishment does not establish an instrumental response of its own; its primary effect, as we have seen, is to suppress to a greater or lesser degree an instrumental response established and maintained by positive reinforcement. It is the strength of this response which is manipulated during studies of extinction. One interesting question, for example, is whether a positively reinforced instrumental response established in the presence of punishment is more or less resistant to extinction (when both S^{R+} and S^{R-} are eliminated) than a response acquired without negative reinforcement. Another question of practical as well as theoretical significance is whether *extinction* of a positively reinforced response can be facilitated by the use of punishment during the extinction period.

One may also look at the other side of the coin—extinction of the *effects* of punishment. In this case S^{R+} is maintained and S^{R-} is eliminated, with interest focused on the *recovery* of the instrumental response. In terms of our previous analysis, extinction of r_{P-SP} is at issue here. We touched on this question in the last section where we saw that with severe punishment, recovery of the instrumental response may not occur for long periods; extinction of r_{P-SP} apparently is extremely slow when S^{R-} has been intense. The present section will deal only with the question of how punishment affects resistance to extinction.

EFFECT OF PUNISHMENT APPLIED DURING EXTINCTION. If during extinction the instrumental response in addition to no longer leading to S^{R+} is punished, will extinction be facilitated? Clearly, punishment ought to suppress the instrumental response during extinction just as it does during acquisition. But that is not the issue. The question is whether the applied punishment will leave a "residue" of suppression so that, when terminated, a permanent weakening of the instrumental response is left behind. The answer appears to be that, unless S^{R-} is reasonably strong, punishment applied temporarily during extinction will have little effect on the course of extinction (e.g., Estes, 1944, Experiment A; Skinner, 1938, p. 154).

The explanation of this result follows directly from the $r_{P-S P}$ mechanism. When punishment is applied during extinction, the instrumental response suffers weakening from two sources, elimination of S^{R+} and introduction of response-contingent S^{R-}. When S^{R-} is mild, the contribution from the latter source is relatively small. In fact, the response suppression observed upon introduction of mild punishment might not result entirely from the aversive character of S^{R-}; part of such suppression might be attributable to the sudden introduction of a "novel" stimulus. Controls for the evaluation of the "suppression" arising from this source are rare. In any event, during the period that punishment is applied, $r_{P-S P}$ (fear) becomes conditioned in some measure to the proprioceptive consequences of the instrumental response, and whether or not resistance to extinction will suffer upon the removal of S^{R-} depends on the strength of this conditioning. With mild punishment fear conditioning is presumably quite weak and extinguishes rapidly after withdrawal of S^{R-}; hence, overall resistance to extinction is affected little, if at all. With strong or intense punishment, on the other hand, $r_{P-S P}$ is more firmly established, and upon removal of punishment, it extinguishes so slowly that an effect is seen on the customary measures of resistance to extinction.

The importance of shock intensity in determining whether temporary punishment will have permanent effects on extinction was nicely shown by Boe and Church (1967). After a lever-press response under positive reinforcement was established, nine 1-hr extinction sessions ensued, during the first of which an intermittent punishment schedule was introduced for 15 min. There were six groups of Ss differing in shock intensity received during the 15-min punishment period. The rationale behind the experiment was that if the temporarily applied punishment was without permanent effects on the instrumental response, all groups should emit approximately the same number of responses by the end of the nine extinction sessions. As Fig. 8-11 shows, however, this was far from the case. The brief experience with punishment was sufficient to depress the extinction performance of most groups far below that achieved by the nonpunished control group.

In this same report Boe and Church showed that temporary application of *noncontingent* shock was far less effective than punishment in inducing postshock suppression of the instrumental response, pointing to another significant difference between response-contingent and response-noncontingent aversive stimulation.

EFFECT OF PUNISHMENT APPLIED DURING ACQUISITION ON SUBSEQUENT RESISTANCE TO EXTINCTION. We have just seen that if moderate or intense punishment is introduced during extinction, even temporarily, resistance to extinction

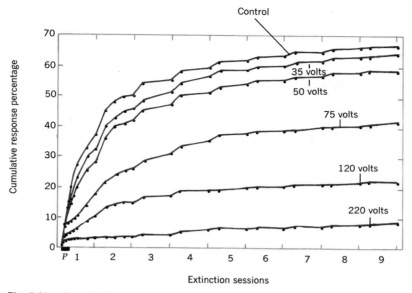

Fig. 8-11. Cumulative response curves expressed as percentages. For each S the total number of responses accumulated at any point during extinction was divided by the number of responses made by the subject during its final acquisition session and then multiplied by 100, producing a cumulative-response percentage curve. The purpose of this transformation was to compensate for performance differences which existed before the introduction of the independent variable. Response-contingent shock of the intensities shown in the figure was applied only during 15 min of the first extinction session (P). Each session lasted 1 hr. It is perfectly clear that the temporarily applied punishment had lasting suppressive effects, which, moreover, were directly related to the level of shock employed. (SOURCE: E. E. Boe and R. M. Church. Permanent effects of punishment during extinction. *Journal of Comparative and Physiological Psychology,* 1967, **63,** 486–492. Copyright 1967 by the American Psychological Association and used by permission.)

is likely to be impaired. Suppose, however, that an instrumental response is *acquired* under the burden of punishment, which is removed during subsequent extinction. Will resistance to extinction be augmented by the punishment which accompanied acquisition of the instrumental response? Does response acquisition in the face of punishment lead to a kind of response "fixation"?

There have been a number of studies which have shown just that: Ss who acquired an instrumental response while being punished were later more resistant to extinction than controls who never experienced punishment (cf. Karsh, 1964; Logan, 1960; Martin, 1963; Rachlin, 1966). As an illustration, Brown and Wagner (1964), in a study to which we shall return later, ran one group of rats on a runway with food reward and a second group with food plus shock, 50 percent of its acquisition trials being punished. During a subsequent extinction series (S^{R-} now eliminated), the formerly punished group turned out to be more resistant to extinction than the nonpunished group.

However, not all acquisition situations in which punishment is applied lead to augmented resistance to extinction. If, for example, partial reinforcement is employed during acquisition and punishment is selectively associated with either rewarded or nonrewarded trials, resistance to extinction may not be enhanced (e.g., Fallon, 1968). It would appear that the discriminative function of punishment must often be taken into account when contemplating the effect on resistance to extinction of punishment applied during acquisition.

In any event it is clear that punishment applied during acquisition of an instrumental response often augments subsequent resistance to extinction, and the question arises as to how this result shall be interpreted. Does punishment applied during acquisition somehow "strengthen" the response over and above the strengthening contributed by S^{R+}, or is the augmented resistance to extinction a result, not so much of the application of punishment, but rather of its removal? To enlarge on the latter possibility, if termination of punishment were generally accompanied by an elationlike effect, the observed enhanced resistance to extinction might simply be due to the fact that punishment is terminated during extinction, rather than to a direct effect of punishment on the acquisition of the instrumental response. Unfortunately, appropriate controls for the evaluation of this factor are not usually included in relevant studies. It is true that in our discussion of incentive shifts in escape conditioning we made the point that elationlike effects were not observed in such conditioning. But it does not necessarily follow that an elationlike effect does not occur in punishment. As a matter of fact there have been several reports of compensatory responding after the termination of punishment (e.g., Azrin, 1960b; Holz, 1968; Rachlin, 1966). Although it is unlikely that all instances of punishment-facilitated extinction can be attributed to this potential artifact, the latter deserves more attention than it has received.

Let us assume for the moment that the enhanced resistance to extinction associated with the application of punishment during the acquisition of an instrumental response is not an artifact resulting from the removal of punishment during extinction, but rather is indicative of a genuine effect of punishment on response acquisition. Although there are a number of mechanisms by means of which punishment could exert such an influence on subsequent resistance to extinction (e.g., Lawrence & Festinger, 1962), one plausible and interesting possibility is that punishment applied during acquisition augments subsequent resistance to extinction simply because there is a degree of commonality between punishment and extinction. As we shall now see, there are several studies which support this view.

SIMILARITIES BETWEEN PUNISHMENT AND EXTINCTION. In our discussion of the anticipatory pain mechanism, $r_{P}-s_{P}$, we noted that it and the anticipatory frustration response, $r_{F}-s_{F}$, had a number of formal properties in common. Both their mode of establishment and their aversive properties were similar. Shifting to the intuitive level, although we can certainly distinguish between the anticipation of frustration and the anticipation of pain, the emotional responses attending both types of experiences have some degree of commonality. Perhaps it is more than terminological convenience that a slap to the backside and the dispatching to bed without supper are both called punishment. Withdrawal of privileges, a frequent form of "punishment," probably would not be effective unless accompanied by feelings of frustration.

The assumption, then, is that punishment and extinction have overlapping behavioral effects because anticipatory frustration (r_F-s_F) and fear (r_P-s_P), the mechanisms assumed to mediate the manifestations of these operations, partially overlap themselves. The laboratory evidence supporting functional similarities between fear and anticipatory frustration takes several different forms. One approach has been to show that certain drugs have a similar effect on behavior mediated by anticipatory frustration and behavior mediated by fear. For example, alcohol and sodium amytal, although depressants, are known to facilitate behavior that has become suppressed through punishment (e.g., Barry & Miller, 1962). Presumably these drugs are effective because they inhibit or reduce the fear which underlies suppression of the instrumental response.

If fear and anticipatory frustration bear fundamental similarities to each other, drugs that reduce fear ought to reduce anticipatory frustration as well. Barry, Wagner, and Miller (1962) put this hypothesis to test by determining whether alcohol and sodium amytal increased resistance to extinction of an instrumental response established under positive reinforcement. In accordance with the assumptions underlying the anticipatory frustration mechanism, Ss extinguished after a continuous reinforcement schedule ought to experience considerable frustration upon encountering nonreward, and in short order the fractional anticipatory frustration response should become conditioned to (in the case of a runway) the cues of the start box and alley. Because anticipatory frustration (s_F) is aversive and because the nearer to the goal box S proceeds the stronger this stimulus component becomes, the effect of anticipatory frustration will be to interfere with the instrumental response. Put differently, S will try to "avoid" anticipatory frustration by avoiding the cues which elicit it. If, therefore, alcohol and sodium amytal administered during extinction actually reduce anticipatory frustration, the treated Ss ought to run faster—be more resistant to extinction—than controls that receive a placebo injection. As shown in Fig. 8-12, exactly this was found. Animals extinguished under either alcohol or sodium amytal extinguished much more slowly than controls.

Moreover, there have been a number of other demonstrations showing that behavior thought to be mediated by anticipatory frustration can be strongly affected by sodium amytal. The depression effect, it will be recalled, has been attributed to the frustration which develops when S is shifted to a relatively small reward. Rosen, Glass, and Ison (1967) have reported that sodium amytal can reduce markedly the decrement in performance exhibited by rats shifted to a small food reward, eliminating entirely the depression effect that would other-

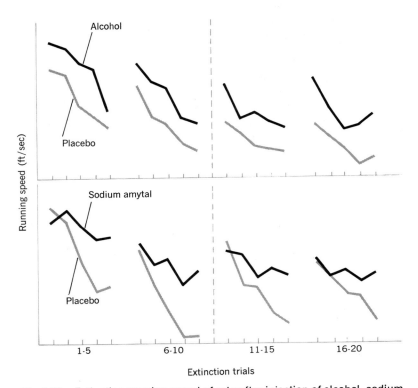

Fig. 8-12. Extinction running speed of rats after injection of alcohol, sodium amytal, or placebo. After Trial 10 the alcohol and placebo groups were divided into two, half of each group receiving alcohol during Trials 11 to 20 and half receiving placebo; the same manipulation occurred for the sodium amytal and placebo groups shown in the lower graph. Observe that extinction performance adjusted itself rapidly to the current drug condition and that both alcohol and sodium amytal resulted in faster running. (SOURCE: H. Barry, III, A. R. Wagner, and N. E. Miller. Effects of alcohol and amobarbital on performance inhibited by experimental extinction. *Journal of Comparative and Physiological Psychology,* 1962, **55,** 464–468. Copyright 1962 by the American Psychological Association and used by permission.)

wise occur. And yet, the drug had no effect on the rate at which rats increased their running speed when reward magnitude was *increased*, showing that the action of sodium amytal was rather specific to emotional responses which exert an inhibitory influence (Ison & Northman, 1968). Sodium amytal has also been shown to increase $S-$ speeds in a successive discrimination task but to have no measurable effect on $S+$ speeds (Ison & Rosen, 1967). Finally, the drug has caused partially reinforced Ss to have slower acquisition runway speeds than comparable continuously reinforced Ss, which is the reverse of the relationship usually obtained with nondrugged Ss and attributed by certain theorists to drive effects arising from anticipatory frustration (Wagner, 1963).

Similar effects have been noted for a related drug, sodium pentobarbital. McMillan (1967) was able to demonstrate that, like electric shock, response-contingent time-out suppressed responding in squirrel monkeys working for food reward. He then showed that administration of pentobarbital resulted in increased responding during both the shock and the time-out punishment components.

If, indeed, there is a significant similarity between the anticipatory frustration and pain responses, can one substitute, in some measure, one for the other? In more operational terms, can punishment and nonreinforcement be used, at least in part, interchangeably? Brown and Wagner (1964), addressing themselves to this question, sought to determine whether punishment applied during the acquisition of an instrumental response would act like nonreinforcement in increasing subsequent resistance to extinction (a point we have already discussed) and conversely, whether nonreinforcement experienced during acquisition would later render Ss more resistant to the suppressive effects of punishment.

In their experiment three groups of rats were trained on a runway under one of three conditions. One group, Group C, received a food reward on each trial and never experienced punishment during acquisition training. A second group, Group N, was a partially reinforced group that encountered food on only 50 percent of its trials; it also never experienced punishment during acquisition training. The last group, Group P, was continuously reinforced with respect to S^{R+}, but on 50 percent of its trials (precisely those trials on which Group N was nonrewarded), this group encountered both food *and* shock in the goal box. After acquisition was completed, each of the three groups was divided into two equated subgroups, and each subgroup was exposed to one of two testing conditions. One of the testing conditions was plain extinction; all three subgroups received neither S^{R+} nor S^{R-} during the extinction trials. Under the second testing condition, all three subgroups received both S^{R+} and S^{R-} (punishment) on every test trial.

If anticipatory frustration and fear are partially equivalent mechanisms and if, as assumed, frustration plays a central role in extinction, the group that was punished during acquisition (Group P) ought to extinguish more slowly than the continuously reinforced Ss (Group C). Of course, Group N ought to be more resistant to extinction than Group C; this is merely the partial reinforcement effect. If r_{F-s_F} and r_{P-s_P} are completely equivalent processes, there should be no difference between Group P and Group N.

As for the second test conducted with S^{R+} and S^{R-} applied on every trial, one would naturally expect the best performance in the group that had been punished during acquisition (Group P). If, however, enduring nonreinforcement during acquisition produced effects similar to those arising from punishment, then the formerly nonreinforced group (Group N) ought to be less suppressed than Group C by the punishment encountered during testing.

As may be seen in Fig. 8-13, these predicted results were obtained. In the extinction test, Group P was superior to Group C. Note, however, that Group P

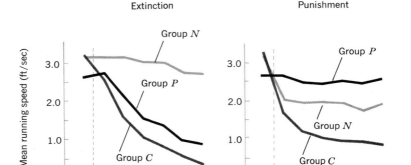

Fig. 8-13. Mean running speeds on the last day of acquisition and subsequent daily blocks of six test trials under conditions of extinction or punishment (see text). (SOURCE: R. T. Brown and A. R. Wagner. Resistance to punishment and extinction following training with shock or nonreinforcement. *Journal of Experimental Psychology,* 1964, **68,** 503–507. Copyright 1964 by the American Psychological Association and used by permission.)

is closer in its performance to Group C than to Group N. In the right half of the figure we see that in the test involving punishment, the ordering of the groups is P, N, and C, with Group N approximately midway between the other two groups.

These results, consistent and attractive as they are, would be somewhat more forceful if certain controls had been employed. We have already alluded to one type of control group that would be desirable in the test conducted under extinction. Because for Group P both S^{R+} *and* S^{R-} are eliminated during extinction, contribution of an elation effect (with respect to S^{R-}) should be ruled out, or at least assessed, as a contributing factor to Group P's superiority over Group C. A related control group would have been desirable for the test conducted under punishment, namely, a group shifted from 50 percent to 100 percent reinforcement on S^{R+} without the accompaniment of punishment. It seems possible that a shift from 50 to 100 percent reward, as occurred in Group N, would by itself be sufficient to augment performance over a group of Ss always experiencing a continuous reinforcement schedule (Group C). The possibility to be ruled out is an elation effect based on an enrichment of the prevailing positive reinforcement schedule.[2]

[2] There are a number of studies germane to this question, but their results are conflicting. Shifting Ss from 50 percent partial reinforcement to 100 percent reinforcement has been reported to lead to an enhancement in performance (Harris, Smith, & Weinstock, 1962; Leung & Jensen, 1968); often, however, such an effect has not been observed (e.g., Badia, 1965; Jenkins, 1962). One difficulty is that, after even a moderate amount of training, partially reinforced Ss respond with considerable vigor, sometimes exceeding the performance of continuously reinforced Ss. Under the circumstances, a "ceiling" effect may attenuate the facilitative effect of shifting from a poor to a richer reinforcement schedule.

Despite the qualifications just mentioned, the pattern of results obtained in the investigations cited points decidedly to a significant and meaningful partial equivalence between the r_F–s_F and r_P–s_P mechanisms, or more operationally, between extinction and punishment (cf. Wagner, 1966).[3] This suggests the interesting possibility of viewing extinction not as a process *sui generis*, but rather as a special case of punishment. The weakening of the instrumental response which attends normal extinction procedures may be considered a form of response suppression in which the "punishment" consists of nonreinforcement, or perhaps more exactly, of the frustration which attends nonreinforcement. Such an interpretation can draw on a few parallels between punishment and extinction for support (in addition to those already cited). Recall that Miller (1960) found that a higher level of acquisition training before the introduction of punishment led to more response suppression than a lesser amount of training. Now recall that in the previous chapter we pointed out that in the runway at least, resistance to extinction seems to be nonmonotonically related to acquisition level. The analogy between these two results from disparate areas is clear and appealing.

A somewhat different interpretation of the partial reinforcement effect also arises from this reorientation. As we have already pointed out, Miller (1960) was able to induce in his Ss a marked resistance to the suppressive effects of punishment by first exposing them to a series of gradually increasing shocks. If we think of a partial reinforcement schedule as a means of exposing S gradually to the punishing experience of frustration, we lay hold of a second interesting parallel between extinction and punishment.

A conceptual advantage is also gained by thinking of extinction as a means of inducing response suppression. Theorists would no longer be obliged to "explain" extinction in terms of some sort of reorganization between stimulus and response. The association may be permitted to remain intact, with weakening of the instrumental response attributed to response suppression arising from the conditioning of anticipatory frustration to the proprioceptive consequences of the instrumental act. Of course, eventually one would have to deal with extinction of the anticipatory mechanisms themselves. One could not forever rely on suppressive mechanisms to account for the decline of once dominant instrumental behavior. However, the anticipatory mechanisms (i.e., r_G–s_G) are assumed to be conditioned by means of classical conditioning procedures, and it may very well be that here "true" conditioning occurs. Associations or bonds are perhaps here established and destroyed by the reinforcement contingencies appropriate to classical conditioning (cf. Mowrer, 1960). Be that as it may, there are a number of interesting and intriguing implications in the view that extinction, or rather the weakening of an instrumental response which occurs as

[3] Although we have not discussed the question of the similarities that may exist between the primary pain and frustration responses themselves, R_P and R_F, it should be noted that there is accumulating evidence that both these states (or on the operational level, shock and extinction, respectively) elicit aggressive (attack) behavior in a variety of organisms, ranging from pigeons to monkeys (e.g., Azrin, Hutchinson, & Hake, 1966; Azrin, Rubin, & Hutchinson, 1968; Hutchinson, Azrin, & Renfrew, 1968).

a result of the extinction operation, is a form of response suppression (cf. Kaufman & Baron, 1968).

AVOIDANCE CONDITIONING

We turn now to the final topic of this chapter, avoidance conditioning. If escape and punishment conditioning have been relatively neglected research areas during the recent past, avoidance learning has had more than its fair share of attention. A bibliography of the number of researches conducted in the last 20 years employing avoidance conditioning paradigms would doubtlessly run to the thousands, and the rate of output shows no sign of declining. After a one-sided emphasis on discriminated avoidance conditioning, nondiscriminated avoidance conditioning came into its own through the invention of the "Sidman" technique. Both types of paradigms have been used extensively in purely behavioral analyses of avoidance learning, as tools in psychophysiological and psychopharmacological research, and in other enterprises. Despite the enormous amount of data compiled, however, our conception of the processes underlying avoidance conditioning has not changed very much during the last couple of decades. The most widely accepted analysis of avoidance learning is the "two-factor" or "two-process" theory, a formulation which is largely responsible for the conceptualization of fear as an anticipatory classically conditioned response.

Two-factor Theory of Avoidance Conditioning

Before proceeding to this interpretation, let us review the essentials of a discriminative avoidance conditioning paradigm. A signal of some sort precedes the aversive stimulus (usually shock) by an interval of time, often about 5 sec. Avoidance conditioning was first investigated in the context of classical conditioning, and the terminology applied to the instrumental case bears the stamp of this origin. Hence, despite the fact that the instrumental response usually cannot be considered to be an unconditioned response to the aversive stimulus applied to S, the latter stimulus is nevertheless most often referred to as an unconditioned stimulus rather than a negative reinforcer. Similarly, the cue which signals the aversive stimulus is not referred to as a discriminative stimulus, as it very well might be, but as a conditioned stimulus. And in further correspondence with the terminology of classical conditioning, the interval separating onset of the discriminative cue from onset of S^{R-} is referred to as the $CS–UCS$ interval.

Although for adherents of two-factor theory, there is a certain justice to the classical conditioning nomenclature, a compromise in terminology might serve their theory more accurately. If the discriminative cue continues to be referred to as the CS but the aversive stimulus has its designation changed to S^{R-}, we perhaps would thereby capture the notion that both classical and instrumental conditioning are involved in avoidance conditioning, as well as indicate that the avoidance response is not necessarily an unconditioned response to the aversive stimulus. We shall, however, leave the promotion of this terminological reform to others.

To return to the avoidance paradigm, the instrumental response, which may be bar pressing, wheel turning, running or jumping from one compartment to another, or any of a variety of other responses, is called an "avoidance response" (often a "conditioned response," CR) if it occurs before the termination of the CS–UCS interval, i.e., before the onset of the UCS. Under usual procedures such a response terminates the CS and results in the omission of the UCS on that trial. When the instrumental response postdates the onset of the UCS, it is termed an "escape response" and by ordinary procedures serves to terminate both the CS and the UCS.

According to two-factor theory, classical conditioning and instrumental conditioning are both involved in the establishment of an avoidance response. Classical conditioning serves the function of associating the anticipatory pain response, fear, to the CS, a process which is accomplished very rapidly, and because it is based on classical conditioning, it requires only the pairing of the CS and UCS in a favorable temporal order. Instrumental conditioning, for its part, is assigned the task of associating the instrumental response to the CS in sufficient strength for it to occur early enough to antedate the UCS. What constitutes the reinforcement for this association has caused a good bit of controversy. Escape trials present no problem because on such trials the instrumental response serves to terminate the UCS; consequently, the association between the CS and the instrumental response may be considered to be reinforced by the latter event. On avoidance trials, however, the UCS cannot provide a source of reinforcement, and so one must assume either that the instrumental response is weakened on such trials or that the reinforcing event lies elsewhere. Some have assumed that avoidance of the UCS is by itself sufficient to constitute a reinforcing event. However, this position has proven unpalatable to many because it appears to require that S have an expectation (not in the objective sense of an anticipatory response) about the occurrence of shock. In other words, failure to be shocked can be reinforcing only if S expects such treatment. Two-factor theory appeared to discover a way of circumventing such expectations by appealing to fear reduction, brought about by CS termination, as the reinforcing event on avoidance trials.

The rationale is simple enough. Fear is presumed to be elicited by the CS; an avoidance response terminates the CS and by eliminating the stimulus which elicited fear results in a reduction, if not total abolishment, of the fear itself. Fear reduction, coming *after* the instrumental response, serves to reinforce the latter in the normal manner of instrumental conditioning.

There is a distinction that needs to be made here between CS termination and the reduction or termination of fear which is assumed by two-factor theorists to follow upon the former. It is completely possible to maintain, as many have, that CS termination (or termination of proprioceptive cues associated with the UCS) is the sole reinforcement for avoidance responses, without any mention of fear arousal or fear reduction (**e.g.**, Schoenfeld, 1950). According to this point of view, any stimulus that comes to signal a primary negative reinforcer becomes a secondary negative reinforcer. And just as a response which escapes S^{R-} is reinforced by termination of the primary negative reinforcer, a response which allows S to escape a secondary negative reinforcer is likewise reinforced by termination of the latter. In other words, proponents of this view are simply accepting the empirical fact that secondary negative reinforcers can strengthen responses which terminate them, without theorizing about the basis of this source of reinforcement.[4] In the context of two-factor theory, however, *CS* termination is reinforcing only if it leads in turn to fear reduction or termination.

The central point, then, is that two-factor theory does not accept avoidance of the *UCS* per se as a reinforcing event; rather, it is *escape* of the anxiety instigated by the *CS* which serves as the reinforcement for the instrumental response on avoidance trials. This is a fascinating conjecture, a feature of two-factor theory which has made it attractive to many. But as we shall see shortly, despite the empirical support that seems to accrue to this position, there is a real question whether the basis of reinforcement on avoidance trials resides solely in the termination of the *CS*.

A Brief Appraisal of Two-factor Theory

Before considering some of the relevant data, a logical point should be made. If one takes two-factor theory completely seriously, there really is no such thing as avoidance learning. A response that serves to avoid an aversive event does so quite accidentally, according to two-factor theory (and related theories which stress termination of secondary aversive stimuli). The motivation for such a response is *escape* from the fear that is generated by the *CS*, and reinforcement is the associated fear reduction. In more intuitive terms, an avoidance response is not made for the "purpose" of avoiding the *UCS*, nor does the latter event have anything to do with the strengthening of an avoidance response. This point has been stressed by proponents of two-factor and related formulations (Mowrer, 1960, p. 30; Schoenfeld, 1950). Logically, then, either two-factor theory is correct, and there is no such thing as "true" avoidance learning, or, alternatively, termination of the *CS* (with attending fear reduction) cannot be the sole basis of reinforcement in avoidance conditioning.

Empirical support for two-factor theory, most of it indirect, converges from a number of different directions. Avoidance learning is frequently more difficult to obtain with trace conditioning than with delay conditioning procedures (e.g., D'Amato, Fazzaro, & Etkin, 1968; Mowrer & Lamoreaux, 1951). The reason is that, presumably, with trace conditioning the opportunity for the instrumental response to terminate the *CS* is either much reduced or elimi-

---

[4] As pointed out earlier (Herrnstein, 1969; Sidman, 1966), this approach is also a two-factor interpretation inasmuch as the stimuli whose termination presumably reinforce the avoidance response come by their aversiveness by means of what is essentially a classical conditioning paradigm. Schoenfeld (1969) has recently taken a different view of avoidance behavior, placing it in closer continuity with positively reinforced behavior.

nated altogether. Avoidance conditioning is also put at a disadvantage when the CS is programmed to be of fixed duration rather than response terminated (Mowrer & Lamoreaux, 1942). Similarly, extinction of an avoidance response has been shown to progress much more slowly when the CR is closely associated with CS termination than when CS termination precedes the instrumental response (Kamin, 1954). A different line of evidence shows that acquisition of an avoidance response is sometimes interfered with by drugs and surgical techniques thought to attenuate anxiety reactions (e.g., Wynne & Solomon, 1955).

But the sum and substance of these studies and of the many others like them which may be interpreted as supporting two-factor theory (cf. Rescorla & Solomon, 1967), is that avoidance conditioning is facilitated, sometimes markedly, by response termination of the CS and by the maintenance of "normal" anxiety or fear reactions (which presumably mediate the reinforcing effect of CS termination). In no case, however, has CS termination been shown to be *necessary* for avoidance learning. And never has avoidance conditioning suffered total abolition by interference with anxiety reactions. These are facts which must be kept in mind when judging the adequacy of two-factor theory and related interpretations of avoidance conditioning.

PRINCIPLES OF ANXIETY CONSERVATION AND PARTIAL IRREVERSIBILITY. In a detailed elaboration of two-factor theory, Solomon and Wynne (1954) proposed two modifications which they felt were necessary to accommodate certain avoidance conditioning data that appeared to them not tractable to two-factor theory as it then stood. The breadth of their analysis and their ingenious extensions of the theory provide another kind of support for the two-process interpretation. They noted that in previous experimental work (e.g., Brush, Brush, & Solomon, 1955) it was observed that when a shock UCS assumed "traumatic" intensities, Ss often failed to extinguish an avoidance response despite prolonged extinction testing. In these studies dogs were trained in a shuttle box to avoid intense shock, a task which they usually mastered in only a few trials. Even though the CS–UCS interval was as long as 10 sec, in short order the latencies of the CRs shrank to about 1.5 sec. Moreover the mean latencies often continued to decrease during subsequent extinction trials, which sometimes numbered 200 or more.

A second observation that seemed at variance with unmodified two-factor theory was that "overt signs of anxiety rapidly disappeared while the dogs were becoming more and more stereotyped in their jumping and their latencies to the CS were shortening [Solomon & Wynne, 1954, p. 359]." They further observed that if "anxiety was being reduced by jumping, the anxiety reduction certainly was not evident at that stage."

Another detail of their data which seemed to require explanation outside of two-factor theory was that if "a dog happened to have an abnormally long latency on a particular trial, he typically acted 'upset' immediately *after* the instrumental response had occurred, and jumped very quickly on the next few trials [p. 359]."

In the light of these apparent strains on two-factor theory, Solomon and Wynne attempted to provide theoretical relief in the form of a "principle of anxiety conservation." According to this principle, fear was not an inevitable response to the CS. If S responded fast enough at the onset of the CS, fear might not have a chance to develop to any significant proportions; in common parlance, S responds before he has a chance to become afraid. Coupling this assumption with the assumption that extinction of a classically conditioned response occurs only if the CR is performed on the trial on which the UCS is omitted, they concluded that weakening of the fear reaction will not take place on extinction trials which stimulate very short response latencies. On such trials, consequently, anxiety is "conserved."

This principle is useful in explaining the fact that few or no overt signs of fear were observed when Ss were jumping rapidly to the CS; it also accommodates the third observation mentioned previously, that Ss did manifest anxiety reactions after jumps having long latencies. Furthermore, because fear presumably occurs on such trials and its reduction serves to reinforce the preceding instrumental response, the shorter latencies observed on subsequent trials are also accommodated.

Although the principle of anxiety conservation provides a mechanism for stretching the extinction phase of avoidance conditioning, it cannot, of course, incorporate the failure of extinction to occur at some point in testing, if indeed traumatic avoidance conditioning is "inextinguishable." True, the fear reaction would not be weakened on trials which elicit fast CRs, but without fear there is no basis for continued reinforcement of the instrumental response; hence, on such trials the CR should undergo weakening. Response latencies will increase to the point that eventually anxiety has time to occur, and at this point some extinction of the fear reaction will take place as well as some strengthening of the instrumental response. With sufficient trials, therefore, the anxiety should be totally extinguished.

Recognizing this fact and convinced that the avoidance response in their Ss was essentially inextinguishable by ordinary extinction procedures, Solomon and Wynne proposed a second principle, the "principle of partial irreversibility of anxiety," as a way out of the problem. The notion is that an anxiety reaction conditioned by a traumatic UCS simply does not extinguish completely; some residue always remains to serve as reinforcement for the instrumental response.

The necessity of the principle of partial irreversibility of anxiety seems doubtful, even for UCSs of traumatic intensity. In the first place, avoidance learning motivated by traumatic UCSs does not always lead to "inextinguishability" or even to excessive resistance to extinction. Kamin (1954), for example, in a study previously cited found that after trace conditioning with a 20-sec CS–UCS interval, extinction was accomplished within a reasonable number of trials. And even considering those conditions of the Kamin study under which some Ss failed to extinguish, others treated in an identical fashion extinguished within the allotted number of test trials.

Furthermore, "inextinguishability" has been found with shock intensities as low as 0.7 ma, a small fraction of the approximately 10 ma that was used in the studies that suggested the principle of partial irreversibility to Solomon and Wynne (Brush, 1957). As Brush points out, this result discredits the plausibility of the partial irreversibility principle, which was based in part on the assumption that extremely intense UCSs produce qualitatively different effects—perhaps at the neurological level—than more moderate intensities. Brush's suggestion is probably correct that the extreme resistance to extinction found in his study and others like it is because the experimental situation during extinction permitted response termination of the CS for all instrumental responses, *whether or not they constituted avoidance responses.* In Brush's study, for example, although the CS–UCS interval during acquisition was only 10 sec, during extinction the CS (lowering the barrier door and extinguishing the light in the compartment occupied by S) remained in force until S responded or until 2 min elapsed (which defined a failure-to-respond). In other words, even when S failed to emit a CR (jumping within 10 sec), his response was reinforced by CS termination. This procedure is quite unlike one in which, during extinction, the CS acts for only the duration of what was the CS–UCS interval during acquisition, which in the present example was 10 sec. Had the door been lowered and the light illuminated when S failed to jump within 10 sec, doubtless many more, and perhaps all, Ss would have extinguished within the 200 trials allowed them. In our laboratory we have found in sharp contrast to the results just described extraordinarily rapid extinction of well-established and long-standing avoidance behavior. We have worked with (discontinuous) shock levels up to 30 ma and have never failed to observe orderly extinction in our Ss.

The magnified resistance to extinction which response termination of the CS can cause is further evidence of the potent reinforcing ability of this variable. But if CS termination can reinforce the instrumental response, it can perform the same function for other responses, responses which may compete with the instrumental behavior. When CS termination is correlated with behavior other than the instrumental response, such behavior will be strengthened and very likely will subsequently compete with the instrumental response. This seems to account for the fact that avoidance behavior extinguishes very rapidly with our extinction procedure, and in all probability this is why the 20-sec CS interval group of Kamin's (1954) trace conditioning study extinguished so fast. Having again granted the potency of CS termination as a reinforcing agent, we should, however, stress once more that this fact does not itself imply that CS termination is *necessary* for avoidance conditioning.

The principle of anxiety conservation, although more appealing than partial irreversibility, also has its difficulties. The supposition that the weakening of a classically conditioned response occurs only on trials in which the CR is evoked is probably incorrect. Many years ago, Pavlov (1927) described a phenomenon of extinction "below zero." Pavlov was referring to the fact that the recovery of an extinguished salivary conditioned response could be inhibited by administering extinction trials beyond the point where S failed to give any response at all to the CS. This would appear to be a clear counterexample to the principle of anxiety conservation. Another difficulty is that if it is assumed that the fear reaction does not occur on trials in which anxiety is "conserved" or that it occurs to a very insignificant extent, one then has the problem of accounting for the motivational basis of such avoidance responses. Unmodified two-factor theory has the attractive property that with a single concept, conditioned fear, it provides both the motivation and the reinforcement for avoidance behavior.

TERMINATION OF THE CS AND AVOIDANCE OF THE UCS AS FACTORS IN AVOIDANCE CONDITIONING. In the standard discriminative avoidance-conditioning paradigm, termination of the CS and avoidance of the UCS are confounded as possible sources of reinforcement. That is, when S's response antedates the UCS, it usually serves both to terminate the CS and to avoid the UCS. Strengthening of the avoidance response could therefore be due to either of these factors or to some combination of the two. If two-factor theory is correct, reinforcement should result solely from response termination of the CS.

Kamin (1956) made the first attempt to untangle these two potential sources of reinforcement in a study that manipulated independently CS termination and UCS avoidance. In his study four groups of rats were trained in a shuttle box on a simple avoidance task. On escape trials (trials on which the instrumental response postdated the UCS) all groups were treated identically: the escape response resulted in the termination of both the CS and the UCS. On avoidance trials (trials on which S made a CR) the treatment given the four groups was quite different. For one group, the "Terminate-CS" group, the CR benefited S only by terminating the CS; the UCS was delivered at its appointed time (5 sec after the onset of the CS), and S had to leave the compartment he occupied in order to terminate the shock. Kamin reasoned that if two-factor theory were completely correct, the Terminate-CS animals ought to be as reinforced on "avoidance" trials as Ss for whom a CR both terminated the CS and avoided the UCS. The latter Ss, called the "Normals," made up the second group of the experiment.

For a third group of Ss, the "Avoid-UCS" group, avoidance responses did not terminate the CS, which continued for the entire 5 sec of the CS–UCS interval; however, such responses did serve to avoid the UCS. If avoidance of the UCS per se is a factor in avoidance learning, then this group ought to show some learning of the avoidance task despite the fact that CRs do not lead immediately to termination of the CS. A fourth group, the "Classical" group, was allowed neither the benefit of CS termination nor UCS avoidance on trials on which a CR was made. In this group, even when the instrumental response antedated the UCS, the CS was maintained; at the end of the CS–UCS interval, shock was delivered, and S had to escape it by running into the unoccupied compartment.

The results of this experiment are shown in Fig. 8-14 for the 100 trials of training. As one would expect, the Normal group shows by far the best avoidance performance and the Classical group, the worst. The Terminate-CS and

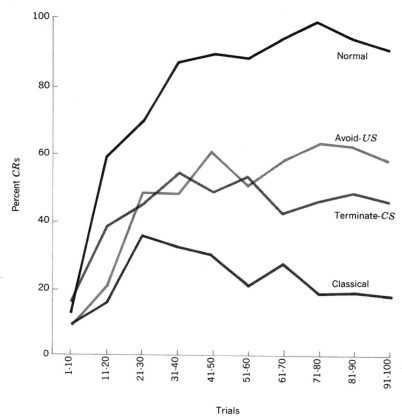

Fig. 8-14. Percent conditioned responses over the 100 avoidance acquisition trials. The four groups differ with respect to the treatment received on *CR* trials, i.e., trials on which the instrumental response was performed before the onset of the *UCS* (see text). (SOURCE: L. J. Kamin. The effects of termination of the CS and avoidance of the US on avoidance learning. *Journal of Comparative and Physiological Psychology*, 1956, **49**, 420–424. Copyright 1956 by the American Psychological Association and used by permission.)

Avoid-*UCS* groups are intermediate, and though the latter group does somewhat better than the former during the last 40 training trials, the difference between the two groups is not statistically significant.

Taken at face value, the results of this experiment imply that both factors, *CS* termination and *UCS* avoidance, contribute to the avoidance performance observed in the Normal group. Kamin points out, however, that it is quite possible to rationalize the failure of *CS* termination to appear as the sole reinforcing agent. Perhaps, he conjectures, the Terminate-*CS* group did not achieve the level of performance attained by the Normals because *CR*s in this group suffered a sort of delayed punishment. If, for example, S performed a *CR* 4 sec after the onset of the *CS*, the *UCS*, delivered 1 sec later, would serve as a punishment for the instrumental response. Clearly, this factor should depress responding in the Terminate-CS group.

A contrasting facilitatory effect, may, according to Kamin, be expected in the Avoid-UCS group. Although the CS does not in this group terminate with the execution of a CR, some benefit should be derived from the fact that often the CS terminated within a second or two after completion of an avoidance response. If, as an illustration, S completed a CR within 3 sec after the onset of the CS, termination of the CS would have followed 2 sec later. Though admittedly the reinforcing effect of delayed CS termination might not be as great as an immediately terminating CS, some strengthening of the CR might nevertheless come from this source (cf. Kamin, 1957).

Another aspect of this study merits mention. Recall that in all groups the CS and UCS both terminated upon execution of an escape response. If CS and UCS termination on escape trials are important factors in determining the *emergence* of avoidance responding (cf. Bolles, Stokes, & Younger, 1966; Kamin et al., 1959), it is not difficult to see that all four groups would have profited equally from these factors (disregarding different numbers of escape trials); as a consequence, any effects arising from manipulations performed on avoidance trials would tend to be masked. In any event, it is perfectly clear that no unambiguous conclusions concerning the respective roles of CS termination and UCS avoidance are possible on the basis of this study. We may conclude, as we already know from other sources, that CS termination is a powerful reinforcing event in avoidance conditioning. But whether UCS avoidance plays a role, indeed perhaps even a *necessary* role, remains an open issue for the present. Later we shall consider more recent data bearing on this important question.

MODIFICATION OF AVOIDANCE BEHAVIOR BY PAVLOVIAN CONDITIONING PROCEDURES.   In recent years two-factor theory has found support in a different line of research. The major point of these studies has been to show that avoidance behavior can be influenced importantly by classical, or Pavlovian, conditioning experience given in different contexts (cf. Rescorla & Solomon, 1967). As a specific example, Rescorla and LoLordo (1965, Experiment 1) trained dogs to jump a hurdle in a shuttle box to avoid shock. They employed a Sidman procedure (see Chap. 9) in which shocks were delivered every 10 sec if S remained in the same compartment of the shuttle box. A response, jumping the hurdle, postponed shock for 30 sec. If S responded sufficiently often—at least once every 30 sec—all shocks were avoided.

After 3 days of acquisition training on the avoidance task, Ss received the following Pavlovian conditioning experience while they were restricted to one side of the shuttle-box apparatus. A stimulus, CS_1, was presented for 5 sec, after which S received an electric shock. On an equal number of trials, however, a second stimulus, CS_2, followed CS_1, and shock was omitted. The authors reasoned that because CS_1 had been a signal for shock, it ought to become an elicitor of fear; on the other hand CS_2, a signal for no-shock, should develop the capacity to *inhibit* fear. Their reasoning was based on Pavlov's (1927) demonstrations of similar excitatory and inhibitory phenomena which he derived from parallel operations performed on an observable conditioned response, e.g., salivation. Rescorla and LoLordo assumed that the fear response, though inferred, ought to follow the same principles as an observable response if the operations relating CS and UCS were alike in both cases.

Five days of such Pavlovian conditioning were alternated with daily sessions of additional avoidance training. Finally, the previous assumptions were tested by presenting CS_1 and CS_2 to the subjects while they were performing on the Sidman schedule. Each CS was presented 60 times during the test session, each presentation lasting 5 sec. If CS_1 functioned as a fear-eliciting stimulus during these test trials, S should be very likely to perform the avoidance response during its presentations; conversely, if CS_2 possessed the capacity to inhibit fear, avoidance responses should be reduced in rate during its presence. The obtained results are shown in Fig. 8-15, which presents the mean number of hurdling responses made during the 5 sec immediately preceding presentation of a CS (providing a "base" response rate) and the mean number of such responses performed during the 5-sec presentations of CS_1 and CS_2. Note that CS_1 did indeed result in a greatly increased rate of response over the base-level of responding, whereas CS_2 had precisely the opposite effect. This basic result has been substantiated and extended in a number of ways (e.g., Bull & Overmier, 1968; Grossen & Bolles, 1968; Rescorla, 1967a, 1968; Solomon & Turner, 1962).

Formally, there is little difference between the assumed conditioning of fear as proposed by Rescorla and LoLordo and the conditioning of anticipatory goal and frustration responses. In view of all that has been said about r_P-s_P, it is perfectly consistent to imagine that this anticipatory response would become conditioned to CS_1 and perhaps function in the avoidance situation as assumed. It is not clear, however, how fear *inhibition* can be accommodated within the r_P-s_P mechanism. Must one speak of a conditioned *reduction* in r_P-s_P, or is perhaps a different kind of anticipatory response conditioned to CS_2? We shall return to this question later, when we consider two-factor theory within the broader context of appetitive as well as aversive conditioning.

In the conventional "fear" version of two-factor theory, anxiety plays three roles. It motivates and reinforces behavior and serves a cue function as well. Thus the theory has little trouble accounting for the increased rate of responding shown by Rescorla and LoLordo's Ss. Fear not only motivates S to respond but, because its stimulus component (s_P) has been associated with the instrumental response, it also contributes to the elicitation of the response. Variants of two-factor theory which do not enlist fear mechanisms in their behalf—relying instead on the conditioned aversiveness of CSs—must strain to account for the activation of avoidance responses. Although CS_1 may be expected to acquire a degree of aversiveness by virtue of its pairing with shock, it is by no means clear that aversiveness alone need result in augmented performance of the instrumental response upon presentation of CS_1. Perhaps the argument can be made that the avoidance response generalizes from one aversive stimulus (the "CS" of the Sidman situation) to the other (CS_1). Be that as it may, CS_2 presents even more of a problem. The aversion theories do not seem to possess the con-

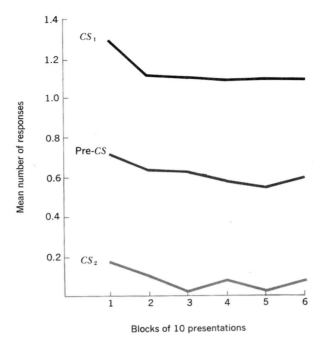

Fig. 8-15. Mean numbers of hurdling (avoidance) responses performed during the 5-sec presentations of CS_1 and CS_2 and during the 5 sec that immediately preceded onset of the two CSs (pre–CS period). Thirty presentations of each CS were given during a single test session. (SOURCE: R. A. Rescorla and V. M. LoLordo. Inhibition of avoidance behavior. *Journal of Comparative and Physiological Psychology,* 1965, **59,** 406–412. Copyright 1965 by the American Psychological Association and used by permission.)

ceptual means to accommodate the reduction in rate of avoidance responding that was brought about by the Pavlovian conditioning in which CS_2 participated.

Despite the success of conventional two-factor theory in accounting for Rescorla and LoLordo's results and related data, it should be pointed out that what has been shown is that Pavlovian conditioning, presumably of fear responses, can modulate already acquired avoidance behavior. The relevance of these data for avoidance *acquisition* is, on the other hand, as yet a matter of inference (cf. Weiss, Krieckhaus, & Conte, 1968).

Some Difficulties Faced by Two-factor Theory

Several pieces of evidence, again all indirect, can be brought to bear against the two-factor interpretation of avoidance conditioning. They take the form of disconfirming both the necessity and the sufficiency of CS termination in avoidance acquisition and denying the central role assigned by two-factor theory to fear reduction as a source of reinforcement. The first line of attack, which implies that *UCS* avoidance is an important reinforcing event in avoidance learning, is equally effective against two-factor theory and related approaches that reduce avoidance learning to escape from secondary aversive stimuli. The second strikes more particularly at two-factor theory.

AVOIDANCE CONDITIONING WITHOUT RESPONSE-PRODUCED CS TERMINATION. One fact is clear. Avoidance conditioning is possible with procedures that preclude the possibility of termination of an exteroceptive *CS* by the avoidance response. Perhaps the clearest example of this is the Sidman procedure (see Chap. 9), a variety of nondiscriminative avoidance conditioning in which an experimentally produced *CS* is not employed. Usually the *UCS* is an inescapable brief pulse of shock, so that the instrumental response does not even serve to escape the *UCS*. Nevertheless, it is beyond question that very respectable levels of avoidance performance can be obtained with this procedure in rats, in monkeys, and in other organisms.

It is quite difficult to see how two-factor theory, or any interpretation that places the burden of avoidance learning on escape from secondary aversive cues, can accommodate Sidman avoidance conditioning in any satisfactory way. It is characteristic of this procedure that shocks are delivered at regular intervals, say every 10 sec, unless **S** makes the instrumental response, which postpones the next shock a fixed interval of time, say 20 sec. Possibly one could assert that the time interval separating shocks serves as the *CS*, and as the interval from the last shock wears on, **S** becomes more and more anxious. Finally he makes the instrumental response, which reduces his anxiety because it terminates the "*CS*." Such an interpretation seems rather contrived, to say the least. Carried to its logical conclusion, it would seem impossible ever to deny the existence of a *CS*, for one could always be postulated within the organism. And having hypothesized the existence of a *CS*, hypothesizing its termination is a natural complement. Much the same argument applies to those interpretations which look to proprioceptive or temporal cues as the source of secondary aversive stimuli (e.g., Anger, 1963; Sidman, 1953).

There appears to be increasing sentiment that the utility of conventional two-factor approaches decreases as the events which must be appealed to as providing the source of reinforcement for avoidance behavior become more and more inferential (cf. Bolles, 1970; Herrnstein, 1969; Sidman, 1966). Perhaps the limit of such efforts may be reached in attempting to account for the results of Herrnstein and Hineline (1966), which showed that rats could acquire an "avoidance" response that served only to reduce the frequency of randomly presented shocks. Thus in this study both exteroceptive stimuli and interoceptive temporal cues were eliminated as potential sources of *CS*s.

Trace conditioning with *CS*s of such short duration that response termination of the *CS* is impossible presents a similar difficulty. An illustration of this point is a study by Taub, Bacon, and Berman (1965) in which monkeys learned a trace avoidance response (arm flexion) although they were disadvantaged by deafferentation of their responding limb, which was kept out of S's sight. These animals could neither see nor, presumably, feel the arm that was performing the instrumental response, and there was no possibility whatever of response-produced CS termination. Though not up to unoperated controls, all the operated Ss reached an 80-percent criterion of avoidance conditioning. The experiment has relevance for more than the two-factor theory of avoidance learning, but it does show that avoidance learning can occur in the absence of response termination of an exteroceptive CS as well as in the presence of total impoverishment of sensation from the response sequence constituting the instrumental response.

FAILURES TO OBTAIN AVOIDANCE CONDITIONING WITH RESPONSE-PRODUCED CS TERMINATION. If the Sidman and related procedures and trace conditioning show that response-produced CS termination is not necessary for avoidance conditioning, numerous failures to acquire an avoidance response despite long training with CS termination procedures suggest that it is not sufficient (e.g., Meyer, Cho, & Wesemann, 1960). In one study rats were trained on a total of more than 7,000 trials distributed over a 4-month period under procedures which appeared to be favorable for avoidance conditioning (D'Amato & Schiff, 1964). Yet half of the rats tested failed to average more than 16 percent of avoidances in any one session, even though they escaped quickly and each instrumental response terminated the CS. As Turner and Solomon (1962) have pointed out, failures to learn are not uncommon in avoidance conditioning and may even occur among human Ss; characteristically, however, such failures are ignored by E. Turner and Solomon attempted to accommodate theoretically this unexpected aspect of avoidance conditioning within a framework consistent with two-factor theory. However, their theory does not appear to provide an appropriate explanation for the learning failures which occur in the discriminated bar-press avoidance situation (cf. D'Amato, Keller, & Biederman, 1965).

INVERSE RELATIONSHIP BETWEEN SHOCK INTENSITY AND AVOIDANCE CONDITIONING. Another circumstantial bit of evidence not congruent with two-factor theory is the repeated finding that rate of avoidance conditioning is *inversely* related to shock intensity. Manipulating shock intensity between the extremes of very mild and quite strong shock, Moyer and Korn (1964), Bolles and Warren (1965), Levine (1966), and D'Amato and Fazzaro (1966a) all found avoidance conditioning to develop most rapidly at the lowest shock intensity employed.[5] This result is embarrassing for two-factor theory, which must concede that fear conditioning is more intense at the higher shock levels. And though the theory

[5] Naturally, this relationship is limited to shock intensities that are sufficient to motivate the escape response; apparently it does not extend to "one-way" avoidance conditioning (Moyer & Korn, 1966).

might not be obliged to predict that avoidance acquisition and shock level be positively related for all intensities—obviously with very strong shock, response disorganization might become a disrupting factor—it nevertheless ought to predict that short of this point stronger shock should facilitate avoidance acquisition.

Results more consonant with two-factor theory have been reported for avoidance *maintenance*, where it has been found that performance of an already established avoidance response is positively related to shock level (Boren, Sidman, & Herrnstein, 1959; D'Amato, Fazzaro, & Etkin, 1967). But the failure to find a similar relationship for acquisition indicates that as it stands, two-factor theory is, at best, incomplete.

DISAPPEARANCE OF FEAR SYMPTOMS WITH WELL-ESTABLISHED AVOIDANCE BE-HAVIOR.　Another set of observations that appears to be inconsistent with two-factor theory relates to avoidance maintenance. To be consistent, two-factor theory must require that the maintenance of even long-established avoidance behavior be based on fear arousal and reduction, though the intensity of the fear reaction may become attenuated to some unspecified irreducible minimum. Turning first to ordinary experience, it does not seem that the vast repertoires of avoidance behaviors maintained in our daily lives require the elicitation of fear for their evocation and fear reduction for their reinforcement. We stop at a red traffic signal not because that stimulus evokes in us fear which is reduced by bringing the automobile to a halt, but rather because we wish to avoid the unpleasant consequences which failing to stop might cause us. It is entirely conceivable that when first learning to drive, something of an anxiety reaction was elicited by a red traffic signal, but all traces of such a reaction appear to be completely extinguished in most experienced drivers. Similarly, because of an anxiety motive instilled by his parents, a child may initially learn to stop before crossing a thoroughfare and look about for approaching automobiles. But what adult approaching an avenue first experiences fear, stops, looks about, crosses the street, and then experiences fear reduction?

The same point can be made in a more objective way by observing animals who have mastered an avoidance conditioning task. After a reasonable amount of experience in the experimental situation, such animals show no outward indication of fear when the *CS* appears and may even make the instrumental response with a degree of deliberation that one is tempted to interpret as non-chalance. The disappearance of fear symptoms in animals well practiced in an avoidance task is an observation that has been made many times (e.g., Wood-worth & Schlosberg, 1954, p. 675). Obviously, without an independent criterion of anxiety—a limitation that two-factor theorists are often reminded of—there is no sure way of determining whether or not fear does extinguish entirely in the course of protracted training. The evidence, little as it is, is that if anxiety is occurring, it is too mild to be reflected in overt symptoms or, in the case of humans, in experience (cf. Kamin, Brimer, & Black, 1963).

Further inferential evidence may be derived from the fact that highly practiced Ss may avoid on 99 percent or more of their trials. We know that instrumentally conditioned responses can be maintained with reinforcement ratios as little as one in one hundred. But usually Ss must be shaped for a time to sustain this behavior on such an impoverished reinforcement schedule. So far as we know, classically conditioned (appetitive) responses differ from their instrumental counterparts in that they do not react well to low reinforcement ratios. Pavlov (1927), for example, observed that it was very difficult to obtain salivary conditioning if the unconditioned stimulus was not applied on every second or third trial. Granted that this last observation does not necessarily hold for fear conditioning and that the anxiety complex may include skeletal as well as autonomic components, from all the available evidence it seems unlikely that anxiety could play a very significant role in the maintenance of highly successful avoidance behavior acquired rapidly and motivated by a mild to moderate *UCS* (cf. Wagner, Siegel, & Fein, 1967).

ALTERNATIVE INTERPRETATION OF THE ROLE OF RESPONSE-PRODUCED CS TERMINATION IN AVOIDANCE CONDITIONING. The fact that response-produced *CS* termination can influence avoidance behavior markedly can be accommodated outside of two-factor theory. D'Amato, Fazzaro, and Etkin (1968) suggested that prompt *CS* termination reinforces the acquisition of an avoidance response because it serves as an excellent discriminative cue for the avoidance contingency operating between the instrumental response and postponement of shock. In their view, avoidance acquisition is impeded by delaying *CS* termination upon performance of the instrumental response or by employing a trace conditioning technique, not because such procedures interfere with the prompt reduction of fear, or analogously the prompt removal of secondary aversive stimuli, but because they remove the important stimulus support for *S*'s discrimination of the avoidance contingency. To test this hypothesis, they provided Ss with a cue other than *CS* termination by means of which the avoidance contingency could be discriminated.

In brief, one group of Ss was trained on a standard discriminated avoidance-conditioning task with prompt *CS* termination attending each escape and avoidance response. A second group also received prompt *CS* termination on escape trials; but on each trial that an avoidance response was made, the *CS* persisted for 8 sec beyond execution of the instrumental response. It was expected from previous results (e.g., Kamin, 1956) that Ss in this group would perform poorly. A third group of Ss was treated in exactly the same fashion as the previous group, except that an "avoidance cue" was presented in conjunction with each avoidance response. Specifically, each time *S* made an avoidance response the *CS* persisted for 8 sec beyond, but in addition, a second stimulus, the avoidance cue, was presented for the same duration.

D'Amato et al. assumed that the avoidance cue would serve the same function as prompt *CS* termination in providing *S* with a means of discriminating the avoidance contingency. The results of two separate experiments were in accord with this expectation. As in Kamin's study (1956), in Experiment 1 the group denied prompt *CS* termination on avoidance trials performed very poorly, but the deficit was eventually eliminated entirely in the group that was given the avoidance cue. The results of Experiment 2, which employed a trace conditioning technique, are shown in Fig. 8-16. It is clear that the avoidance cue dispelled completely the detrimental effects normally observed with a trace avoidance-conditioning paradigm. Note that the effect of the avoidance cue was slow in developing, coming to full force only on the sixth block of 100 trials. This is reasonable, inasmuch as the significance of the avoidance cue could only be learned by *S* on those trials on which an avoidance response occurred, thus requiring a fair amount of acquisition experience. Bolles and Grossen (1969) have recently verified the efficaciousness of the avoidance cue and extended its range of application.

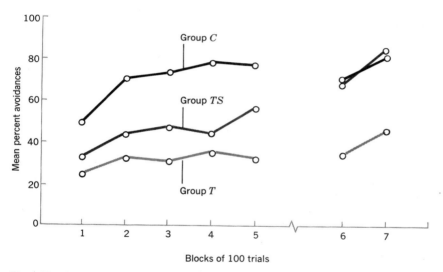

Fig. 8-16. Group *C* was a control group that received standard bar-press avoidance training with "delayed" conditioning and an 8-sec *CS–UCS* interval. Groups *T* and *TS* received "trace" conditioning with the same *CS–UCS* interval, i.e., the *CS* was presented for only 1 sec. However, the latter group had the benefit of an avoidance cue, which was presented for 5 sec each time that *S* performed an avoidance response. Note, first of all, that delayed conditioning led to far better avoidance acquisition than trace conditioning. Second, although the avoidance cue had only a small facilitating effect during the first 500 training trials, the detrimental effects of trace conditioning were completely eliminated by the latter part of training. The break in the curves indicates that 24 hr intervened between the fifth and sixth blocks of trials. (SOURCE: M. R. D'Amato, J. Fazzaro, and M. Etkin. Anticipatory responding and avoidance discrimination as factors in avoidance conditioning. *Journal of Experimental Psychology*, 1968, **77**, 41–47. Copyright 1968 by the American Psychological Association and used by permission.)

Another interpretation of these data is possible, one which pulls them more in line with two-factor theory. Recall the Rescorla and LoLordo (1965) experiment described earlier in which Pavlovian conditioning was interspersed with Sidman avoidance training. There appears to be some similarity between the CS_2 of that study and the avoidance cue of the present experiment, in that both stimuli were selectively associated with periods of nonshock. It is possible, therefore, to conceive of the avoidance cue as a conditioned inhibitor of fear and to attribute its reinforcing properties to this factor rather than to any discriminative function it might have served. Although there are a number of salient differences between the procedures employed in the two experiments which raise some question about the parallel drawn, perhaps the most significant divergence is that the Rescorla and LoLordo study was concerned with the regulation of an already established response, whereas D'Amato et al. dealt with the *acquisition* of avoidance behavior. It is not inconsistent to suppose that fear processes are significant for the motivation and elicitation of avoidance behavior but are of secondary importance for its establishment. A close parallel is that level of hunger is critically important in *activating* appetitive discriminative habits. But no one any longer believes that hunger reduction is necessary for the *acquisition* of discriminative responses. Experiments such as that of Rescorla and LoLordo have as little bearing on the role of fear reduction in avoidance acquisition as studies which show that by momentarily increasing or decreasing hunger drive S can be induced to modulate his performance of discriminative responses have on the role of hunger reduction in the acquisition of discriminative behavior. And in the view of D'Amato et al., avoidance acquisition is simply another discriminative task (cf. Herrnstein, 1969; Keehn, 1966). This is not to deny that as S acquires an avoidance response, his level of fear may subside. But presumably it is because S learns the avoidance response that his fear is reduced, and not vice versa.

Another discriminative—as opposed to a motivational—role of the CS is shown by the following type of experiment. The subject is trained on a Sidman avoidance task, each response postponing shock for 20 sec. A CS which precedes shock by 5 sec is then introduced. The subject has the option of responding before the onset of the CS and hence avoiding both shock and CS, or S can wait until the CS appears, responding then and avoiding shock only. Inasmuch as the CS is paired with shock each time that S fails to make the avoidance response, it should in time become capable of eliciting fear. It appears, therefore, that two-factor theory should predict that S will tend to respond before the onset of the CS, thereby avoiding both shock and fear.

There have been a variety of experiments employing variants of this procedure, including introduction of the CS at the very beginning of training, and the common result is that Ss tend to withhold their responses until the CS makes its appearance (e.g., Keehn, 1959; Shnidman, 1968; Sidman and Boren, 1957; Ulrich, Holz, and Azrin, 1964). Evidently, whatever aversiveness is possessed by the CS is outweighed by its discriminative function. It appears, then, that both the presence of the CS and its termination have discriminative properties which are important in the establishment and control of avoidance behavior, just as they are in appetitive conditioning.

Perhaps we can now see why Kamin (1956) obtained the results he did. The Avoid-*UCS* group performed poorly because it was denied *CS* termination and hence a salient cue with which to discriminate the avoidance contingency. On the other hand, the relatively good performance of the Terminate-*CS* group is probably due to the fact that every trial ended with *S* escaping the *UCS*. Escape responses are known to become anticipatory and, as pointed out below, such responses are not to be confused with bona fide avoidance responses.

AVOIDANCE CONDITIONING AS DISCRIMINATION LEARNING. Two-factor interpretations of avoidance conditioning have tended to set this type of learning apart from other acquisition phenomena. With the emphasis of two-factor theory on the motivational and reinforcing basis of avoidance acquisition, the discriminative requirements have often been overlooked. It is true that in simple one-way avoidance situations there is little discriminative burden placed on *S*, and acquisition is usually very rapid, a matter of a few trials. But there is a question as to whether acquisition in this setting represents "true" avoidance learning or whether it is perhaps better thought of as escape behavior—escape from a physical location associated with an aversive event. The discriminative requirements are far more demanding in the shuttle-box or bar-press situations, where *S* must differentiate a threatening stimulus against a more or less constant background of stimulation and act accordingly.

A number of investigators have made the point that the experimental analysis of avoidance conditioning might proceed faster if it were accepted that avoidance is merely another form of discriminative behavior. Both Keehn (1966) and Herrnstein (1969) have pointed out that the *CS* in an avoidance task may be viewed as a discriminative stimulus, an S^D which sets the occasion for the instrumental response. As for the source of reinforcement for avoidance behavior, Herrnstein notes that there is no reason to suppose that animals, including rats, cannot discriminate differences in shock frequency. Granting the ability of *S* to form such discriminations, perhaps one need only appeal to a simple "law of effect" to account for the strengthening of avoidance responses. As noted previously, D'Amato et al. (1968) have emphasized the discriminative function of response-produced *CS* termination, which presumably provides an important cue for discrimination of the avoidance contingency. Combining these suggestions, we may hypothesize that where a *CS* is employed in avoidance tasks, this stimulus serves two discriminative functions. First, response-contingent *CS* *termination* provides a salient cue with which to discriminate the avoidance contingency; second, as the avoidance response is acquired, *onset* of the *CS* provides a discriminative stimulus for performance of the instrumental response. The evidence cited in the last section is in accord with this interpretation.

Omitted from this account, however, is some mechanism for getting avoidance behavior started. The subject usually has no means of detecting the avoidance contingency until he begins making the avoidance response. In a very real sense, S must avoid before he can learn to avoid. The dilemma is more apparent than real, but it does point to a very potent variable in avoidance conditioning.

There is much evidence to show that where S, failing to avoid, is permitted to escape the UCS, the escape response has a strong tendency to become anticipatory and occur before the onset of the UCS. Thus, even in the absence of an avoidance contingency, substantial numbers of "avoidance" responses—better called "CRs" or "anticipatory" responses—often occur (cf. D'Amato et al., 1968).[6] An illustration of anticipatory responses is available in Fig. 8-14, where it may be seen that the Classical group produced a fair percentage of CRs, particularly during early training, in spite of the fact that these Ss could only escape shock (cf. Bolles, Stokes, & Younger, 1966). From all available evidence it seems a reasonable inference that in escape-avoidance training, early avoidance responses are generated by factors other than the avoidance contingency; possibly the most important of these is escape from the UCS.

Nevertheless, avoidance acquisition is possible when the UCS is inescapable, as, for example, when it consists of a very brief pulse of shock. In many such instances an escape contingency is unnecessary to generate anticipatory responses because the instrumental response is itself highly probable under the experimental conditions employed. The locomotor response in either the running-wheel apparatus or in the one-way avoidance situation is an example of a response which has a high "operant" level even though escape of the UCS is not permitted. Bolles (1970) has stressed the important role played in avoidance conditioning by such responses, among which are what he calls "species-specific defense reactions." Brief inescapable shocks are often used in the Sidman avoidance procedure with bar pressing as the instrumental response, and one may wonder how the instrumental response becomes anticipatory under these circumstances. Apparently, investigators using this technique have learned to use bars or panels that are so situated (e.g., close to the grid floor, Leaf, 1965) that it is likely they are activated by S's unconditioned responses to shock. On the other hand, the not infrequent failures to obtain Sidman avoidance conditioning (e.g., Weissman, 1962) may be related in part to an inadequate "operant" level of responding.

In any event the suggestion is that the first phase of avoidance conditioning consists of the emergence of anticipatory or related responses—instrumental responses that are generated by factors other than the avoidance contingency. The occurrence of such responses in sufficient numbers puts S in a position to discriminate the avoidance contingency if one is in effect. It is apparent that this interpretation implies that factors affecting the rate of anticipatory responding ought to influence the rate of avoidance acquisiton in like manner.

[6] These anticipatory responses are not to be confused with fractional anticipatory "emotional" responses, such as anticipatory goal and frustration responses. The former are observable instrumental responses, whereas the latter are inferred responses which need not be identified with any specific peripheral activity, autonomic or otherwise.

Exploring this implication, D'Amato, Fazzaro, and Etkin (1967) found that anticipatory bar-press responses were severely depressed by strong shock, and they attributed the previously noted inverse relationship between shock intensity and avoidance acquisition to this factor. Similarly, variables which impede discrimination of the avoidance contingency will also interfere with avoidance acquisition. Important among these are the amount of change in the CS produced by the instrumental response (Bower, Starr, & Lazarovitz, 1965) and the alteration in shock frequency brought about by the avoidance response (Leaf, 1965; Sidman, 1962).

The potential value of the present analysis is that, apart from relating avoidance acquisition to the broader issue of discrimination learning (cf. Chap. 11), it seems to promise a more complete analysis of the variables that affect avoidance behavior. Two-factor theory, despite its long reign, has provided surprisingly little illumination as to why failures to acquire avoidance behavior so frequently occur or why certain variables—for example, shock intensity—affect avoidance acquisition as they do. We now know that if experimental parameters are so chosen that the level of anticipatory responding is low, avoidance acquisition will suffer. Or if discrimination of the avoidance contingency is impeded by having the CS terminate either before or after the instrumental response, or in Sidman avoidance by employing a relatively long shock-shock interval, avoidance acquisition will be slow and failures to learn will be frequent. One-way avoidance, if it can be called that, is extremely rapid because normally it encourages a very high rate of anticipatory responding and provides conditions which are highly favorable for discriminating the avoidance contingency. Perhaps the effects of certain drug and surgical manipulations may also be understood in terms of their effects on anticipatory responding and discrimination of the avoidance contingency (cf. Collins & D'Amato, 1968).

The two-factor and "discriminative" accounts of avoidance behavior are perhaps more complementary than competitive. The former stresses the motivational basis of avoidance behavior, while the latter stresses the discriminative aspects. Clearly, contributions from both directions need to be understood. Perhaps the point of major dispute concerns the source of reinforcement. Is the reinforcement for an avoidance response the reduction in fear (or the removal of secondary aversive stimuli) that follows upon the avoidance response, or is it instead the fact that the instrumental response avoids or reduces the frequency of the primary aversive stimulus? Unfortunately, choosing between these alternatives is not entirely an empirical matter. In practice it turns out to be difficult, if not impossible, to design an experiment in which the latter condition is fulfilled but the former is not. Interoceptive CSs or secondary aversive stimuli can be inferred whenever an avoidance contingency is in effect, prompting Herrnstein (1969) to observe that two-factor theory may have crossed the border of refutability.

Quite possibly both sources of reinforcement are involved in avoidance conditioning. Where an exteroceptive CS is employed, response-produced termination of the CS may be reinforcing, particularly early in training before S has had sufficient opportunity to discriminate the avoidance contingency. It will be recalled that the avoidance cue of the D'Amato et al. study (1968) was relatively ineffective on early training trials (cf. Fig. 8-16). As training progresses, however, the major source of reinforcement very likely shifts to the avoidance contingency itself. If so, fear arousal and reduction would come to play a secondary role, which is in keeping with the characteristics of well-established avoidance behavior.

General Two-factor Theory

It is time to enlarge our frame of reference concerning two-factor, or "two-process," theory and to take note that it applies to appetitive as well as to aversive behavior. An excellent historical review and discussion of general two-factor theory has been provided by Rescorla and Solomon (1967), and their paper is recommended to the interested student. Although we cannot dwell on the topic in detail, it should be recognized that classical, or Pavlovian, conditioning processes are intimately involved in appetitive conditioning, as we have seen in a number of instances. The concepts of the anticipatory goal and frustration responses were developed in the last chapter, where it was explicitly stated that these anticipatory responses were considered to be conditioned through classical or Pavlovian paradigms. Moreover, a number of studies have shown that, like avoidance and other aversive behaviors (e.g., the *CER*), instrumental appetitive conditioning can be strongly influenced by Pavlovian conditioning procedures (cf. Rescorla & Solomon, 1967). Thus it has been demonstrated that an instrumental response (bar pressing) will become associated to $S+$ faster if the latter stimulus is first paired with S^{R+} in a Pavlovian conditioning paradigm, and, conversely, that responding to $S+$ will extinguish faster if $S+$ is first associated by Pavlovian means with nonreward (Trapold & Winokur, 1967). It has been shown more than once that differential instrumental conditioning is facilitated if the discriminanda are first appropriately paired with reward and nonreward in a differential classical-conditioning paradigm (e.g., Bower & Grusec, 1964; Trapold, Lawton, Dick, & Gross, 1968).

Indeed, it must be apparent that virtually all cases of instrumental conditioning, discriminative and nondiscriminative, contain the ingredients for concurrent Pavlovian conditioning. Some consequence (the "reinforcer"), positive, negative, or perhaps both, follows as a result of instrumental behavior. There are always stimuli, exteroceptive or interoceptive, that regularly precede the instrumental response and are therefore available to enter into associative relationships with events that follow the instrumental act. For some theorists anticipatory responses, such as r_G, r_F, and r_P, are the vehicles by means of which properties of the reinforcer are transported back to the signaling stimuli, capturing thereby much of what is meant by the ordinary concept of "expectation." Others maintain only that the aversive or positive value of the consequence becomes conditioned to the antedating stimuli, speaking only of conditioned aversive and conditioned positive reinforcers. As pointed out earlier, because both these approaches enlist events which arise from Pavlovian conditioning to account for the facts of instrumental conditioning, both may be considered variations of two-process theory.

Although theorists have found it difficult to account for the facts of instrumental conditioning without resorting to Pavlovian conditioning, there is little agreement on precisely how Pavlovian and instrumental conditioning combine to produce instrumental behavior. According to a "strong" interpretation of two-factor theory, Pavlovian conditioned responses mediate instrumental learning, in the sense of eliciting and reinforcing instrumental behavior. Taking avoidance conditioning as an illustration, assume that an increase in heart rate becomes classically conditioned to the CS. The proprioceptive feedback from this Pavlovian CR is then assumed to elicit, and a decrease in heart rate to reinforce, the avoidance response. This interpretation demands that certain temporal relationships exist between the instrumental behavior and the mediating Pavlovian CR. In the case of the previous illustration, heart-rate conditioning should precede the development of avoidance behavior, and its diminution ought to antedate extinction of the avoidance response; moreover, each avoidance response should be preceded by the conditioned heart-rate response. If salivation is assumed to be the relevant Pavlovian CR mediating appetitive behavior, its time course ought to follow a similar pattern with respect to the development of instrumental appetitive conditioning.

A good deal of research has been devoted to the task of identifying Pavlovian CRs that might plausibly mediate instrumental behavior and to investigating the time relationships between these CRs and relevant instrumental responses. Rescorla and Solomon (1967) have reviewed much of the literature bearing on this issue, arriving at the conclusion that "the simple idea that some peripherally observed CR is essential in the mediation of operant behavior seems implausible [p. 169]." The basic problem is that the time relations required for the "strong" version of two-factor theory simply have not been verified for the peripheral CRs that have been studied to date.

Rejecting this version of two-factor theory, Rescorla and Solomon (1967) suggested that mediation of instrumental responses is not by peripheral CRs but by "states" of the "central nervous system" which are established and modified by Pavlovian conditioning procedures. Thus it is not the peripheral conditioned heart-rate response but the central state of fear that mediates—i.e., motivates and reinforces—avoidance behavior. Presumably the instrumental response and the peripheral CR are both subject to the influence of fear, which accounts for such concomitance as is observed between the two. A corollary of this interpretation is that Pavlovian conditioning paradigms can be employed to alter the "common central states" and hence to manipulate instrumental behavior. We have already discussed some of the data bearing on this implication. A number of other interactions between Pavlovian and instrumental conditioning are theoretically feasible. It is conceivable, for example, that instrumental conditioning paradigms can be employed to affect common central states and thus influence

Pavlovian conditioned behavior. In their paper, Rescorla and Solomon (1967) discuss in detail this and other possible Pavlovian-instrumental interactions which their interpretation of two-factor theory suggests.

GENERAL TWO-FACTOR THEORY AND FRACTIONAL ANTICIPATORY RESPONSES. The central states referred to by Rescorla and Solomon, such as fear, may be conceptualized as fractional anticipatory responses. Although such responses are conceived of as "fractions" of S's response to the reinforcing situation, there is no reason why the fraction must include peripheral responses. Anticipation of food or shock seems possible without the necessity of concomitant peripheral responses such as salivation or change in heart rate, though of course under certain circumstances the latter may indeed occur. Presumably it is these anticipatory states that constitute the "common central states" to which Rescorla and Solomon refer.

Let us speculate as to how fractional anticipatory responses may be fitted to general two-factor theory in such a way as to accommodate both appetitive and aversive conditioning. As pointed out in the last chapter, anticipatory goal responses were thought by Spence to be the mechanism underlying incentive motivation (K). Thus for Spence, acquired appetitive motivation is embodied in the r_G–s_G mechanism. Moreover, some theorists have assigned a reinforcing function to r_G–s_G, thereby accounting for conditioned positive reinforcement. On the other hand, negative or aversive effects in appetitive conditioning are mediated by a separate fractional anticipatory response, r_F–s_F. If r_G–s_G is not subsequently followed by the accustomed goal object, primary frustration is assumed to occur, a fraction of which is conditionable to antedating stimuli as the fractional anticipatory frustration response. Because of its imputed aversiveness, behavior which produces r_F–s_F tends to be suppressed. In instrumental appetitive conditioning, then, r_G–s_G provides a source of acquired drive and, together with the *presence* of appropriate goal objects, constitutes the basis of positive reinforcement. As we saw in the last chapter, many facts of instrumental appetitive conditioning have been thought to be mediated by the fractional anticipatory goal and frustration responses, i.e., interpreted in terms of two-process theory.

When we turn to instrumental aversive conditioning, we find that only one fractional anticipatory response has seen much service—fear or r_P–s_P. It has been widely assumed that the occurrence of fear serves as the mechanism of acquired aversive motivation and its reduction as a source of reinforcement. It seems doubtful, however, that fear reduction is necessarily reinforcing. To cite one apparent counterexample, in most punishment situations S comes to anticipate negative reinforcement, and consequently fear (r_P–s_P) presumably is then elicited before the advent of S^{R-}. After S responds and is punished, it is reasonable to suppose that a reduction in r_P–s_P occurs, inasmuch as S "knows" that he will not be molested until the next instrumental response is performed. Clearly one would not generally want to consider such a reduction in fear to be reinforcing. A similar situation exists for the anticipatory goal response. Aversive properties are not assigned to reductions in $r_G\text{--}s_G$; rather, one makes use of a separate fractional anticipatory response, $r_F\text{--}s_F$. This seems reasonable because a reduction in $r_G\text{--}s_G$ could be the result of either the failure of an expected reward to materialize or, quite the opposite, the occurrence of the anticipated reward, which thereby terminates the expectation.

Perhaps the reinforcing function in aversive conditioning ought to be served by a second fractional anticipatory response. Consider the following possibility. Imagine that S engages in a bit of behavior that terminates in an aversive event; presumably fear, $r_P\text{--}s_P$, soon becomes conditioned to antedating stimuli. If, however, S^{R-} is not administered at the usual time, an unconditioned "relief" response (R_R) occurs, which has positive reinforcing value. Like other such responses, we suppose that it has a detachable component, which through Pavlovian conditioning becomes anticipatory in the form of the *fractional antici-patory relief response*, $r_R\text{--}s_R$.

With $r_R\text{--}s_R$ general two-factor theory achieves a large measure of symmetry (cf. Mowrer, 1960). Instrumental appetitive conditioning has its positive classically conditioned anticipatory component, $r_G\text{--}s_G$, and for instrumental aversive conditioning $r_R\text{--}s_R$ plays the same role; the negative anticipatory components are $r_F\text{--}s_F$ and $r_P\text{--}s_P$, respectively. The major difference is that in appetitive conditioning, the positive anticipatory response develops first; if there is to be a negative anticipatory response, it comes second and is generated by the absence, rather than the presence, of a reinforcing event. In aversive conditioning the order is reversed, and it is the positive component that arises from the failure of an event to occur. We have already seen that there is a substantial amount of evidence showing that anticipatory frustration and fear possess a number of functional similarities. This naturally raises the question whether the positive components, $r_G\text{--}s_G$ and $r_R\text{--}s_R$, also have important properties in common. If they do, perhaps an important theoretical economy can be effected by conceiving of only two anticipatory responses, one positive and one negative.

Associating the reinforcing function of aversive anticipatory responses with $r_R\text{--}s_R$ rather than with a reduction in $r_P\text{--}s_P$ (fear) increases the compatibility of the two-factor and discriminative accounts of avoidance acquisition. With fear reduction as the mechanism of reinforcement, the two-factor explanation becomes an escape interpretation which views the avoidance contingency as essentially irrelevant. We have already given reasons for maintaining reservations about this view. On the other hand, shifting the burden of reinforcement onto an anticipatory relief response requires that for reinforcement to occur, S must first discriminate that the anticipated S^{R-} has failed to occur. In other words, S must detect the avoidance contingency, which is what the discriminative account maintains.

If one is prepared to accept the theoretical device of the anticipatory frustration response, which is also based on the failure of an anticipated event to occur, there seems no reason whatever to reject the notion of an anticipatory relief response. Perhaps it frequently is more difficult to discriminate the absence of an anticipated negative event than the absence of a positive reinforcing event. In principle, however, the two processes differ little.

The anticipatory relief response may also be of value for a consistent two-factor interpretation of the Rescorla and LoLordo (1965) results and related experimental data. Recall the CS_2 of their study, which was paired in a Pavlovian paradigm with the *absence* of shock. Rescorla and LoLordo maintained that the reduction in instrumental responding caused by this stimulus was due to the inhibition of fear which it occasioned. With fear the only anticipatory response available, the implication is that CS_2 directly elicited a reduction in fear, which presents something of a conceptual problem. Usually, when the presentation of a stimulus causes a reduction in some criterion response, it is because the stimulus elicits a response system that is incompatible with the criterion response. Perhaps, then, a more consistent view is that CS_2, because it was associated with the omission of an anticipated shock, became capable of eliciting the anticipatory relief response, $r_R{-}s_R$. The observed result would follow on the assumption that fear and anticipatory relief are incompatible, just as in the case of appetitive conditioning, $r_G{-}s_G$ and $r_F{-}s_F$ are assumed to be incompatible.

SUMMARY

The reason anticipatory mechanisms have received so much attention is that instrumental conditioning appears to require some means of accounting for the fact that such behavior is influenced importantly by S's expectations of future events. There is nothing mysterious or loose-thinking about this; it is no more than recognition that knowledge of past relationships—that certain actions have led to certain consequences—governs present behavior to an important extent. Fractional anticipatory responses constitute one class of mechanism that allows for behavior based on anticipation of future events. Other approaches are possible. Recognizing this need but preferring not to employ fractional anticipatory responses, Estes has observed in a related context, "There appears to be no simpler account . . . than to say that the animal learns to anticipate a specific reward stimulus following a particular stimulus-response combination. In conventional terminology, we appear to be led toward a theory involving stimulus-stimulus, rather than stimulus-response, conditioning . . . [1966, p. 283]." In addition to stimulus-stimulus conditioning, Estes goes on to propose a "scanning" model of response selection to bridge the gap between stimulus and response. Although the exact form that successful anticipatory mechanisms will eventually take is not certain, there seems little doubt that they will find increasing theoretical use.

1. (a) The chief difference between the motive-incentive conditions of positive reinforcement and those of negative reinforcement appears to be:

(b) Such instrumental conditioning paradigms as escape, punishment, and avoidance conditioning are largely limited to conditioning with negative reinforcement because:

2. Fear or anxiety may be conceptualized as a fractional anticipatory pain (or discomfort) response which becomes established in the following way:

3. (a) Viewed as a fractional anticipatory response, fear (r_P–s_P) and anticipatory frustration (r_F–s_F) have the following formal properties in common:

(b) Some of the data which suggest a commonality between fear and anticipatory frustration, or, in terms of operations, between punishment and extinction, are as follows:

4. (a) Reward magnitude, drive level, and reward delay have similar effects on escape conditioning and conditioning with positive reinforcement. These are:

(b) Some differences are:

5. (a) "Learned helplessness" behavior refers to:

(b) One interpretation of this behavior is:

6. (a) "Vicious-circle" behavior refers to:

(b) It may be explained as follows:

7. (a) Thorndike's "early" and "late" views concerning the effects of punishment on S–R "bonds" were:

(b) The "avoidance" interpretation of the effects of punishment assumes, on the other hand, that punishment acts by:

8. The facts of punishment derived from animal studies have a number of implications for the use of punishment in the control of human behavior. These are:

9. Although the primary effect of punishment is response suppression, response-contingent negative reinforcement serves other functions which can result in facilitation rather than suppression of behavior. For example:

10. (a) The presently available data indicate that if punishment is applied temporarily during extinction, resistance to extinction will be:

(b) If punishment is applied during *acquisition*, subsequent resistance to extinction may be:

11. (a) The two processes assumed by two-factor or two-process theory to be involved in avoidance conditioning are:

(b) A number of other interpretations of avoidance conditioning which rely on aversion rather than fear may also be considered two-factor theories because:

(c) Both versions of two-factor theory essentially reduce avoidance learning to:

12. (a) Some of the evidence favoring two-factor theory is:

(b) Some of the opposing evidence is:

13. (a) The "discriminative" account of avoidance acquisition stresses:

(b) Perhaps the two-factor and discriminative interpretations of avoidance behavior can be combined in the following way:

14. (a) The argument against the notion that Pavlovian, peripheral *CR*s mediate instrumental conditioning is:

(b) Perhaps an alternative is mediation by "central states" conceptualized as fractional anticipatory responses. For example:

9 OPERANT CONDITIONING

In our discussion of instrumental appetitive and aversive conditioning (Chaps. 7 and 8), we alluded to a divergence in views that we should now make explicit. Recall that we distinguished between the positive stimulus of discrete-trial discrimination situations ($S+$) and that of operant discrimination studies (S^D), on the side of the negative stimulus, between $S-$ and S^Δ. The basis of these minor terminological distinctions is a formidable conceptual and technological development, spanning the last three decades, that has had a profound influence on experimental psychology. "Operant conditioning," as this development is often referred to, was inaugurated by B. F. Skinner's influential *Behavior of Organisms* (1938). Since that time, the methods, technology, and vocabulary of operant conditioning have so increased in complexity and in range of application (cf. Honig, 1966a; Schoenfeld, 1970; Ulrich, Stachnik, & Mabry, 1966) that the term "conditioning" has lost its original appropriateness. But because a more fitting designation is not easy to come by, we shall continue to use it, capitalizing the expression to avoid ambiguities which would otherwise arise later.

During its early years, Operant Conditioning, like any enthusiastic new-comer, was coolly received by the then entrenched. Ignored and rebuffed, it kept to itself and developed in comparative isolation of even those research areas most closely allied to it, eventually founding in 1958 its own scientific journal, the *Journal of the Experimental Analysis of Behavior*. In time, however, the powerful techniques and methods it developed were adopted and assimilated by experimental psychologists holding a variety of allegiances, and, further afield, by pharmacologists interested in behavior. Despite the diffusion of its wares, Operant Conditioning managed to maintain a fair degree of cohesiveness. Its adherents organized a separate division of the American Psychological Association, the Division of the Experimental Analysis of Behavior, and published their own journals under the auspices of the Society for the Experimental Analysis of Behavior. However, it is a mistake to suppose that psychologists identified with Operant Conditioning fit into a neat mold. Many of them share similar attitudes toward the selection of, and the strategies to be employed in pursuing, research problems and draw from a common pool of experimental techniques and language. But in each of these categories, considerable diversity exists and differences of opinion are probably as sharp as in other areas of psychology.

If history is any guide, we may expect that the processes of diffusion and assimilation will continue, reducing further existing distinctions between Operant Conditioning and related areas of experimental psychology.

SOME IMPORTANT FEATURES OF OPERANT CONDITIONING

The contributions of Operant Conditioning may be found in (1) its conceptualization and analysis of the processes thought to be of prime importance in the acquisition and maintenance of instrumental behavior, (2) its methods of investigating these processes (particularly "schedules of reinforcement"), and (3) the techniques which have been devised to implement its methodology. Because neither methodology nor technology necessarily imposes a particular conceptualization of behavioral processes, many psychologists have adopted aspects of (2) and (3) while rejecting (1) in various degrees.

Central Concepts in Operant Conditioning

OPERANT VERSUS RESPONDENT CONDITIONING. We have already discussed in some detail the distinction between classical and instrumental conditioning (Chap. 7). It will be recalled that in classical conditioning a response is established by pairing a conditioned stimulus with an unconditioned stimulus. Following the lead of Skinner, this paradigm is widely referred to as "respondent" rather than classical conditioning; a response established by such a procedure is termed a "respondent." Respondents are *elicited* by their respective CSs.

Again following the early precedent established by Skinner (e.g., 1938), what we have called "instrumental conditioning" is referred to as "operant conditioning." "An operant is an identifiable part of behavior of which it may be said . . . that no correlated stimulus can be detected upon occasions when it is observed to occur [Skinner, 1938, p. 21]." Because eliciting stimuli are not identifiable in the case of these responses, they are said to be *emitted* rather than elicited. The word "operant" is meant to emphasize the response-contingent nature of reinforcement in operant conditioning, inasmuch as the response serves to "operate" on the environment to produce reinforcement.

It should be clear now why we capitalize "operant conditioning" when referring to the experimental approach based on operant methodology. We wish to distinguish between this application and its use as a referent for what others call "instrumental conditioning."

For all practical purposes, the respondent-operant distinction is coordinate with the classical-instrumental dichotomy. The former nomenclature has the advantage of being somewhat more descriptive than the latter and somewhat more flexible. One may refer to an instance of the two categories as a "respondent" and an "operant," respectively, both terms being more specific in referent and more pleasing to the ear than a "classical" or an "instrumental." For our part we shall use the two distinctions interchangeably.

Often the term operant conditioning or operant behavior is meant to have a narrower significance than that just indicated. It then refers to instrumental situations in which S is free to perform the instrumental response at will, and rate of response becomes the significant dependent variable. To stress this intention the term "free-operant" (conditioning or behavior) is frequently employed, a policy which we also shall adopt.

Very few of the tools and techniques developed by Operant Conditioning are directly applicable to respondent conditioning. Rate of response, for example, is a meaningless dependent variable within the classical conditioning paradigm, and rarely can a schedule of reinforcement devised for operant conditioning be adopted to the respondent case. As a result, the research activities generated within Operant Conditioning have been largely, but by no means solely, confined to instrumental behavior.

REINFORCEMENT. The concept of reinforcement commands a central position in Operant Conditioning. All instrumental behavior, from the modest movements of primitive organisms to man's most complex activities, are in the first place fashioned (shaped) by reinforcement contingencies and subsequently maintained by the very same agent. It is the consequences of behavior that determine its fate. The "law of effect," originally promulgated by Thorndike (e.g., 1911), becomes the keystone of instrumental behavior.

Reinforcement cannot be defined without some measure of circularity. A positive reinforcer is defined as any stimulus situation which, when it follows a bit of behavior, serves to increase the probability that the behavior will occur at a future time (under similar stimulus conditions). Thus, in order to classify a stimulus as a positive reinforcer, one must first show that the stimulus is capable of increasing the probability of the behavior upon which it is contingent. Complete circularity is escaped in that a stimulus situation which displays this property under one set of circumstances often, but not always, can serve as a positive reinforcer under different conditions.

For the most part advocates of Operant Conditioning ("operant conditioners"—cf. Catania, 1968, p. 341) have been indifferent to what ultimately constitutes the basis of reinforcement. Unlike psychologists of the Hullian tradition who looked (without much success) to need reduction or drive reduction for an underlying mechanism of reinforcement, a theory of reinforcement has been of little concern to them. Rather, given a reinforcing stimulus with which to work, their interest has been in how behavior is modified by the particular relationships ("contingencies") which couple behavior and reinforcement. Perhaps it was inevitable that this orientation would change. Intensive study of such contingencies was bound to reflect inquiry back to the nature of the reinforcers themselves. Thus Morse and Kelleher (1970), partly on the basis of the punishment-maintained behavior discussed in the last chapter, go further than most psychologists in denying inherent reinforcing properties to stimulus events. They emphasize the importance of previous behavior and current reinforcement schedules in determining the magnitude and even the sign of a reinforcer. However, inquiries of this nature are still far from prevalent.

Reinforcement accounts not only for the establishment of instrumental behavior but also for its elimination. Removal of all sources of reinforcement is the necessary and sufficient condition for the abolishment of acquired behaviors ranging from the running response of a rat in a straight alley to the bizarre feeding habits sometimes encountered in schizophrenics (Ayllon & Haughton, 1962). Often the sources of reinforcement which serve to maintain a specific bit of behavior may not be entirely obvious, as in the latter case. Social approval and parental attention are as effective reinforcers for some types of behavior as food and water are for others. But the strategy is always clear. Behavior is maintained by reinforcement; to eliminate the behavior, find and eliminate the reinforcement.

RESPONSE DIFFERENTIATION (SHAPING). Virtually any bit of instrumental behavior is actually an assemblage of component parts. Even the bar press of a rat, which when well practiced appears to be a unitary and simple act, is actually composed of an integrated chain of responses. The rat must be taught to approach the bar, press it with a certain minimum force, remove itself from the bar to the food cup when the appropriate cues appear, and so forth. An experimenter who has properly analyzed this behavioral chain can construct it bit by bit by appropriate reinforcement of its component parts. Extinction also comes into play, as when *E* must discourage behaviors that become reinforced adventitiously and interfere with the proper integration of the response sequence.

This process of constructing specific response chains by appropriate reinforcement and differential extinction of component parts is called "response differentiation" or "shaping." By skillful shaping a rat can be taught to do remarkable things, such as the rat who could pull a chain to obtain a marble from a rack, pick the marble up with his forepaws, carry it to a tube projecting 2 in. above the floor of its cage, lift it to the top of the tube and, finally, drop it inside (Skinner, 1966b, p. 1206). But shaping is by no means restricted to animal training. The very same analysis can be applied to such human skills as spelling, reading, and arithmetic. And it constitutes an essential feature of programmed instruction.

The contribution of Operant Conditioning to reinforcement contingencies and shaping is certainly not in their discovery. Long before these concepts were articulated, animal trainers, to say nothing of insightful parents, were using them quite effectively. The noteworthy achievement of Operant Conditioning arises from the detailed extension of these concepts to the full range of acquired behavior, from the willingness and ability to put the principles gleaned from these concepts to work to deal with a variety of problems of the real world (cf. Honig, 1966a) and from the resoluteness of commitment. It takes unshakable faith in the principles of reinforcement and extinction to stand by confidently while, in a program aimed at reshaping the eating behavior of mental patients with severe feeding problems, a recalcitrant patient decides to go without food for 7 or even 15 days (Ayllon & Haughton, 1962). It is in the systematic and intensive use of response differentiation and reinforcement that the contribution of Operant Conditioning is to be found.

STIMULUS CONTROL (DISCRIMINATION). Very often different stimuli are associated with different reinforcement schedules. For example, in a simple discrimination situation, reinforcement is available in S^D but not in S^Δ (i.e., the schedule in S^Δ is one of extinction). When **S** confines his responding to S^D, one says that good "stimulus control" has been achieved or that **S** "discriminates" the stimuli. Programming reinforcement in S^D and extinction in S^Δ by no means guarantees that **S** will cease to respond to the latter. Adventitious reinforcement—presumably the basis of "superstitious" behavior (cf. Herrnstein, 1966; Skinner, 1948a)—can maintain responding in S^Δ for considerable periods of time. If, for example, **S** were responding in S^Δ when the program shifted to S^D and a reinforcement were shortly obtained, responding in S^Δ will have been adventitiously reinforced. The solution to this problem, as well as to others of this nature, is to revise the programming so that a minimum period of delay is guaranteed to intervene between responding in S^Δ and receiving reinforcement while responding in S^D.

Viewed in more general terms, "Stimulus control refers to the extent to which the value of an antecedent stimulus determines the probability of occurrence of a conditioned response. It is measured as a change in response probability that results from a change in stimulus value [Terrace, 1966c, p. 271]." In other words, if by manipulating a stimulus we cause S's behavior to change, that stimulus exerts some control over S's behavior. Moreover, the greater the behavioral change induced for a fixed stimulus change, the greater the control exerted by that stimulus. Thus in a simple successive discrimination task, initially in discrimination learning, changing S^D (say a red-illuminated key) to S^Δ (a green key) is likely to result in little change in S's rate of key pecking, which indicates that key color is exerting little stimulus control. With continued training, however, the same stimulus change (from red to green or vice versa) would be accompanied by a marked change in response rate, attesting to the development of stimulus control by key color.

Unlike many other psychologists who deal with stimulus and response, operant conditioners do not assign an "eliciting" role to discriminative stimuli (cf. Chap. 7). Theirs is not an S–R psychology that has stimuli conditioned to and later eliciting responses. In the very beginning Skinner insisted that discriminative stimuli merely "set the occasion" for the response, a phrase that has yet to be improved upon (cf. Keller & Schoenfeld, 1950). If there is some agreement between Thorndike and Skinner on the efficacy of reinforcement, there is none at all on the nature of the relation holding between S and R, which, for Thorndike, as well as for many others following his tradition, was in the nature of a "connection" or a "bond" (e.g., Thorndike, 1913; cf. Hilgard & Bower, 1966). The implications, behavioral and neurophysiological, of this conception caused widespread controversy for many years. The concept of stimulus control may be viewed as Operant Conditioning's replacement of the notion of associative connections between stimuli and responses, an interpretation that perhaps is more in keeping with contemporary views (cf. Chap. 12).

RESPONSE RATE AS THE BASIC DATUM. Widely influential, though of less systematic importance, is the view that rate of response is the fundamental dependent variable for behavior analysis. One can do no better in describing the importance assigned to this dependent variable than to quote Skinner's analogy between it and the role played by mass in chemistry:

> Rate of responding is one of those aspects of a subject matter which do not attract attention for their own sake and which undergo intensive study only when their usefulness as a dependent variable has been discovered. Other sciences have passed through comparable stages. The elements and compounds studied by the chemist also have fascinating characters—they exist in many colors, textures, and states of aggregation and undergo surprising transmutations when heated, dissolved, combined, and so on. These are the characteristics which naturally first attract attention. They were, for example, the principal concern of the alchemists. In contrast, the mere weight of a given quantity of a substance is of little interest in its own right. Yet it was only when the weights of substances entering into reactions were found to obey certain laws

that chemistry moved into its modern phase. Combining weight became important because of what could be done with it. Rate of responding has emerged as a basic datum in a science of behavior for similar reasons—and, hopefully, with comparable results (Skinner, 1966a, p. 16).

Skinner's commitment to response rate as a dependent variable has not, however, been shared by psychologists outside of Operant Conditioning. One major problem is that entire research areas would be virtually abolished if no other dependent variables were considered. Research in such areas as verbal learning and verbal behavior, concept formation, psychophysics, and perception depends heavily on response direction rather than response magnitude. In some of these areas if the need arose, a dependent variable based on response magnitude (cf. Chap. 7)—perhaps even rate of response—could be substituted for those currently in use; in others, response magnitude simply could not serve in place of choice measures.

But even within Operant Conditioning there have been defections from Skinner's point of view. Aspects of response magnitude other than rate have come under serious consideration repeatedly in recent years (e.g., Herrick & Bromberger, 1965; Jenkins, 1970; Kellicutt, 1967; Notterman & Mintz, 1965). Notterman and Mintz maintain that "there are, indeed, fundamental theoretical and experimental issues bearing upon schedules of reinforcement, drive operations, rate of expenditure of effort, serial effects, differentiation and discrimination, response-induced exteroceptive and proprioceptive feedback, reactive inhibition, and so on that demand more information than is provided by 'time-between-occurrence' measures [i.e., response rate (1965, p. 3)]." Moreover choice behavior—within discrete-trials situations—is increasingly serving as a research setting (e.g., Ray, 1967; Ray & Sidman, 1970; Sidman & Stoddard, 1967). Despite these trends, a substantial portion of research conducted by operant conditioners still employs rate of response as the sole dependent variable.

Schedules of Reinforcement

The contingencies that can be designed to couple behavior and reinforcement are rich in their variety and are known collectively as "schedules of reinforcement." This concept has far more significance than simply referring to the programming of reinforcement in laboratory experiments (cf. Morse, 1966). The establishment and maintenance of virtually all acquired patterns of behavior, whether they arise in animals roaming their wild habitats or in man living in his regulated society, may be viewed as the result of specific—though perhaps at the moment unspecifiable—contingencies which hold between behavior and reinforcement, which is to say, the result of schedules of reinforcement. Skinner (1966b) has even found certain parallels between the ways in which contingencies of reinforcement operate to establish behavioral patterns in the individual organism and the manner by which evolutionary contingencies serve in nature to establish phylogenetic behavioral patterns.

In attempting to account for the behavioral properties generated by schedules of reinforcement, operant conditioners have engaged in their most vigorous theorizing. Ferster and Skinner (1957), in their detailed analysis of reinforcement schedules, adopted the theoretical position that the behavioral phenomena produced by schedules of reinforcement are reducible to the operation of such elementary conditioning processes as reinforcement and extinction, stimulus control (discrimination), and response differentiation. This view has been challenged by Jenkins (1970), who feels that the "basic" principles of conditioning are not yet so well established that they can serve as the reductive elements of the complex behaviors that arise from many reinforcement schedules. On another front, Dews (e.g. 1966, 1970) has attacked conventional interpretations of the processes (e.g., mediation by S's own behavior) assumed by Ferster and Skinner and others to underlie the response scalloping observed in fixed-interval schedules of reinforcement. Dews would lift the level of analysis from separate stimuli, responses, and their consequences to the *pattern* of contingencies which form a schedule; it is "the schedule itself that determines the pattern of responding [1966, p. 578]." The theoretical activity stimulated by schedules of reinforcement is likely to gain momentum from two recent volumes on the subject, Skinner's *Contingencies of Reinforcement: A Theoretical Analysis* (1969),[1] and *Theory of Reinforcement Schedules* (1970), edited by Schoenfeld.

It is neither possible nor necessary to describe all the schedules of reinforcement that have been devised over the last 30 years, nor will it be possible to describe the behavioral characteristics generated by all available schedules. We shall, however, present a sufficient sampling to demonstrate the wide range of behavioral situations that are describable in terms of technically defined schedules of reinforcement. More detailed discussions of various aspects of schedules of reinforcement may be found in the references of the previous paragraph and in papers referred to below.

SIMPLE SCHEDULES. By "simple" schedules we refer to those in which a single type of reinforcement contingency, maintained with constant parameters, is in force throughout an experimental session.

There are two fundamental dimensions upon which reinforcement may be made contingent: time and behavior. A reinforcement may be set up in terms of the period of time that has elapsed from the delivery of the last reinforcement—a procedure which generates "interval" schedules; or it may be based on the number of responses emitted by S since the last reinforcement—the "ratio" schedules.

A reinforcement contingency may also take both time and behavior into account; that is, it may be based on rate of response. Thus a reinforcement is programmed in such schedules only when response rate meets some specified criterion, as in *DRL* 10 (see below) where, in order to be reinforced, a response

---

[1] Skinner's monograph, which I was unable to obtain before publication, appeared too late for inclusion in this chapter.

must be separated from a previous response by at least 10 sec. The criterion of response rate may be specified in terms of a single interresponse time (IRT)—the time interval separating two adjacent responses—or a certain minimum (or maximum) number of responses may be required to be executed during some fixed interval of time (e.g., Verhave, 1959). The first is the usual method of defining response rate.

Continuous or regular reinforcement. One basic reinforcement schedule is *continuous (regular) reinforcement (CRF)*, which is nothing more than reinforcing every response that is emitted.

Extinction. Another basic schedule is *extinction (EXT)*, in which no responses at all are reinforced.

Fixed ratio. The *fixed-ratio (FR)* schedule is one in which reinforcement follows the completion of a constant (or fixed) number of responses counted from the preceding reinforcement. Standard usage specifies a given ratio by adding a number right after the abbreviation for the schedule; e.g., *FR* 10 refers to a fixed ratio of 10 responses. Consistent with this terminology, a *CRF* schedule is a special ratio schedule, i.e., *FR* 1.

Variable ratio. In *variable-ratio (VR)* schedules the number of responses required for reinforcement varies in a random or quasi-random fashion. To specify this schedule exactly, one must provide a frequency distribution of the number of responses required for reinforcement, but this is rarely done. Usually only the mean value is given, as in *VR* 50, which signifies that on the average, S has to perform 50 responses to obtain reinforcement.

Fixed interval. One time-contingent schedule is the *fixed-interval (FI)* schedule. Here the first response which occurs after a given interval of time, measured from the delivery of the preceding reinforcement (or from the onset of an S^D), is reinforced. Usually fixed-interval schedules are indicated in minutes, so that an *FI* 5 refers to a 5-min fixed-interval schedule. Note that in fixed-interval schedules, reinforcements do not necessarily occur at intervals specified by the schedule. The reinforcement is "set up" at those intervals, but S must respond in order to receive the available reinforcement.

Variable interval. In *variable-interval (VI)* schedules reinforcements are scheduled according to a random or quasi-random series of intervals, and, as with *VR* schedules, precise specification requires that the frequency distribution of intervals employed be provided. The convention is to specify the mean in minutes, as in *VI* 5, though sometimes the shortest and longest interval are also given.

Differential reinforcement of low rate. This is a schedule which is based on rate of response. In a *differential reinforcement of low rate (DRL)* schedule an interresponse time must be equal to or exceed a certain value in order for reinforcement to occur. In *DRL* 10, for example, a reinforcement becomes available 10 sec after S's previous response. (Note that in *DRL* schedules the number indicates not minutes but seconds.) If S responds before the 10-sec interval has expired, he "resets the clock," and the availability of reinforcement is delayed 10 sec beyond this last response. Obviously such schedules encourage a very low response rate, which accounts for their designation.

An interesting variation of *DRL* schedules can be arranged by specifying both minimum and maximum *IRT* values. As an illustration, in order for a response to be reinforced, it may be required that the response occur no sooner than 10 sec after the previous response but no later than 12. Such a schedule is referred to as a *DRL* 10 with a "limited hold" of 2 sec. Fundamentally, however, the schedule requires that S's momentary response rate fall within a specified interval.

Differential reinforcement of high rate. In contrast to *DRL* schedules, it is possible to arrange reinforcement contingencies so that *high* response rates are differentially reinforced. Such programs are called *differential reinforcement of high rate (DRH)* schedules. Essentially *DRH* schedules serve to reinforce *IRT*s falling *below* a specified interval (cf. Ferster & Skinner, 1957).

Differential reinforcement of other behavior. The *differential reinforcement of other behavior (DRO)* schedule is unique in that it makes reinforcement contingent on the *failure* of a response to occur for some specified period (Reynolds, 1961b). Thus with bar pressing as the criterion response, a *DRO* 50 schedule presents a reinforcement after each 50-sec period during which no bar presses occur. This schedule is useful where one wishes to analyze separately the effects of reinforcement from the behavior that normally produces reinforcement. By appropriate choice of schedule parameters, it is possible to associate the same frequency of reinforcement with two stimuli which control sharply different rates of response (cf. Yarczower, Gollub, & Dickson, 1968).

Other schedules based on interresponse time have been devised, such as the *reinforcement of least-frequent interresponse time (LF)* schedule introduced by Blough (1966a), which requires the use of an on-line computer. The aim of this schedule is to develop a response pattern in which, unlike other schedules, response emission is essentially a random process. The schedule is of value in producing stable and predictable baseline rates of responding against which the effects of manipulated variables may be measured.

Free-operant avoidance schedules. There are a number of avoidance schedules which, because S is free to make the instrumental response throughout the experimental session, are referred to as *free-operant avoidance schedules* (Sidman, 1953, 1966). In the basic free-operant avoidance schedule (referred to in Chaps. 7 and 8 as the "Sidman schedule") shocks are programmed to occur at fixed intervals, say every 10 sec, if S fails to make the instrumental response. This feature of the schedule is called the "S–S interval," i.e., the "shock-shock interval." The avoidance contingency is introduced by allowing the shock to be postponed for a fixed period of time whenever the instrumental response occurs. For example, each response might serve to postpone shock for a 20-sec interval. This interval is known as the "R–S interval," i.e., the "response-shock interval." Consequently the basic free-operant avoidance schedule is specified by listing the S–S and R–S intervals (in seconds) as in *avoid SS 20 RS 30*, which refers to an avoidance schedule in which the shock-shock interval is 20 sec and the response-shock interval is 30 sec. It should be pointed out that S does not accumulate "safety" time under this schedule. If, for example, S responds twice within 2 sec, he does not accumulate—taking the last avoidance schedule as an illustration—60 sec of freedom from shock; rather, shock is postponed for 30 sec beyond the second response. Optimal behavior under this schedule consists of responding every 29 sec or so.

Note that if the R–S interval is shorter than the S–S interval, S can actually hasten shock by responding inopportunely. With a 10-sec S–S interval and a 5-sec R–S interval, for example, a response made 2 sec after the receipt of shock would, if no further responses were forthcoming, cause shock to be delivered 5 sec later, or only 7 sec after receipt of the earlier shock. Normally, however, R–S intervals are either equal to or greater than S–S intervals.

From this basic avoidance schedule a large number of modifications are possible. For example, S may be allowed to accumulate safety time with each successive instrumental response, so that if S were working on an R–S interval of 5 sec, three responses which occur within a second would earn S approximately 15 sec of freedom from shock (cf. Sidman, 1966 on this and other modifications of the basic avoidance schedule).

Although we discussed free-operant avoidance schedules earlier in the context of nondiscriminative avoidance conditioning, it is obviously possible to introduce a discriminative component into such schedules. For example, one could signal impending shock with a cue that was presented 2 sec before the termination of an S–S or an R–S interval. It may be recalled that we discussed such applications in Chap. 8.

BEHAVIOR GENERATED BY SOME OF THE SIMPLE SCHEDULES. Discussion of the kinds of behavior that are generated by the basic schedules first requires some familiarity with the cumulative recorder, a widely used instrument in operant studies. The cumulative recorder is a device which plots S's responses and other selected aspects of the data, such as occurrences of reinforcement. The recorder advances a paper roll at a slow, continuous rate, and each response made by S pulls a writing pen a fixed distance across the paper. High rates of response trace a path with a steep slope (Fig. 9-1*a*), whereas low response rates result in shallow slopes (Fig. 9-1*b*). With appropriate paper speed, the cumulative recorder provides E with a faithful replica of S's response pattern.

Fixed-ratio schedules tend to generate high response rates, and if the FR is relatively small, pausing after reinforcement is slight (Fig. 9-2*a*). With larger FRs a sizable "postreinforcement pause" develops, with the length of the pause

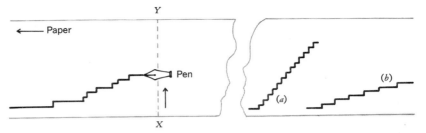

Fig. 9-1. A simplified version of a cumulative recorder. Each time S responds, the pen moves a fixed distance along the dashed line toward Y. If S responds at a relatively high and constant rate, a record such as that in (a) is traced out; a low, steady rate produces a record with a shallow slope, as in (b). In an actual cumulative-recorder record, because the pen moves only a slight distance with each response, individual responses are not easily discernible. (SOURCE: J. G. Holland and B. F. Skinner. *The analysis of behavior.* New York: McGraw-Hill, 1961. Copyright 1961 by McGraw-Hill Book Company and used by permission.)

a function of the size of the *FR* (cf. Felton & Lyon, 1966). These pauses may produce a record that resembles a staircase (Fig. 9-2b).

Variable-ratio schedules, like *FR* schedules, differentially reinforce high rates of response (because reinforcement is contingent on the number of responses emitted). But because the number of responses required for reinforcement varies unpredictably, postreinforcement pauses are not a characteristic of this program. Rather, pausing is much more likely to occur—particularly if the *VR* is large—between reinforcements that are separated by a large response requirement. Behavior has been maintained with fixed-ratio schedules at least as high as 900 in the pigeon (Skinner, 1957) and 4,000 in the chimpanzee (Findley & Brady, 1965); variable-ratio schedules of many hundreds are not uncommon (Ferster & Skinner, 1957).

Fixed-interval schedules produce a characteristic pattern of behavior that is often called "scalloping" (Fig. 9-3). We have already noted that the basis of the scalloping pattern, which reflects an increasing response rate as the end of an interval is approached, has been the subject of much research effort (cf. Dews, 1970).

In variable-interval schedules S cannot make use of temporal discriminations to anticipate the availability of reinforcement. Consequently, as contrasted with *FI* schedules, performance is much more uniform under *VI* schedules (Fig. 9-4). Catania and Reynolds (1968) have provided a detailed quantitative analysis of the performance properties of interval schedules.

Although the various basic schedules give rise to response patterns that are earmarked by certain characteristics, factors outside the schedules themselves, such as motivation variables and adventitious reinforcement, have an effect on the response-rate pattern. Nevertheless, there is often sufficient regularity in the behavioral patterns associated with the different schedules to allow them to

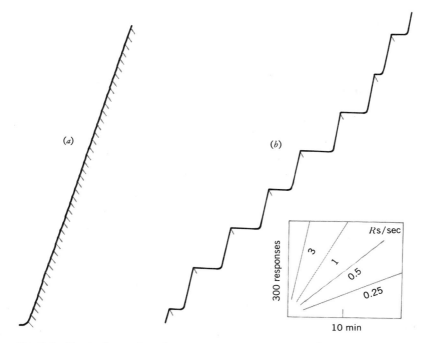

Fig. 9-2. Illustrations of performance under fixed-ratio schedules. Record (a) was obtained from a pigeon on an *FR* 20 schedule and depicts a high and fairly constant rate of responding. The oblique markings indicate receipt of reinforcement; thus 20 responses intervene between two such markings. The insert on the lower right provides a rate-of-response scale from which one may estimate response rate in any part of the obtained records. Record (b) is from a pigeon on an *FR* 120. Note that after each reinforcement a lengthy postreinforcement pause occurs, often lasting for several minutes, at the end of which *S* runs off the required 120 responses at a high, and rather constant, rate. (SOURCE: C. B. Ferster and B. F. Skinner. *Schedules of reinforcement.* New York: Appleton-Century-Crofts, 1957, Figures 19 and 24. Copyright 1957 by Appleton-Century-Crofts, Inc. and used by permission.)

serve as baseline conditions against which the action of a wide range of independent variables can be investigated.

COMPOUND SCHEDULES. It is often useful to combine two or more of the simple schedules into what we shall call a "compound" schedule. Compound schedules can be *sequential*, in which case only a single schedule is in effect at any one time, or they can be *simultaneous*. If two reinforcement schedules operating simultaneously are independent of each other, they are termed "concurrent" schedules (cf. Catania, 1966).

Before turning to a consideration of sequential schedules, we should point out that some compound schedules lend themselves to being viewed as

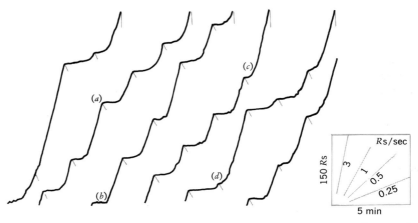

Fig. 9-3. Performance of a pigeon after 66 hr of training on an *FI* 4. The "scalloping" effect arises from a postreinforcement pause followed by responding that increases in rate as the interval wears on. Where, as at (*a*), *S* enters its terminal rate immediately upon completing the postreinforcement pause, scalloping does not appear, and the resulting record is more like one obtained with a large *FR* (cf. Fig. 9-2).

When the pen of a cumulative recorder reaches the top edge of the paper, it resets automatically, producing the vertical marks which appear at the top of each segment of the record. In an original cumulative record the bottom edge of each segment is located directly below the top portion of the previous segment. To conserve space, in published records the segments are brought together as closely as possible. (SOURCE: C. B. Ferster and B. F. Skinner. *Schedules of reinforcement.* New York: Appleton-Century-Crofts, 1957. Copyright 1957 by Appleton-Century-Crofts, Inc. and used by permission.)

"second-order" schedules, that is, as schedules of schedules (cf. Kelleher, 1966). A tandem *FI* 2 *FI* 2 *FI* 2, for example, a schedule (described below) in which *S* must complete 3 *FI* 2 components in succession in order to receive reinforcement, may be interpreted as an *FR* 3 (*FI* 2). In the latter designation the *FR* refers, not to a single response, but to an entire *FI* component.

SEQUENTIAL SCHEDULES. In sequential schedules primary reinforcement is available in one or both components (restricting our consideration to a two-component schedule), or reinforcement is available only upon the completion of the second (more generally, the last) component of the schedule.

Tandem schedules. In a *tandem* schedule two or more component schedules, *not* identified by separate *S*^D s, must be completed in sequence before primary reinforcement is delivered. In *tand FI* 10 *FR* 20, for example, the *FI* 10 component must be satisfied before responses start to count toward the *FR* 20. Upon receipt of reinforcement, the schedule recycles to the *FI* component. In *tand FI* 2 *FI* 2 *FI* 2 reinforcement becomes available only after completion of the third *FI* 2 component. We shall shortly encounter an illustration of tandem schedules.

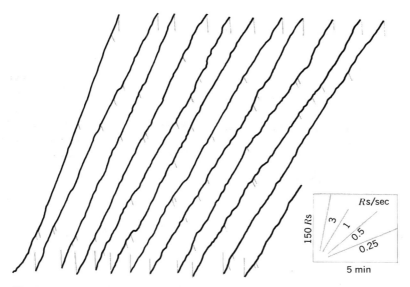

Fig. 9-4. Performance of a pigeon after 45 hr of training on a *VI* 3. Although there are local variations in response rate, the overall rate is fairly constant. In contrast to *FI* schedules there is some tendency in *VI* schedules for response rate to increase immediately after reinforcement. (SOURCE: C. B. Ferster and B. F. Skinner. *Schedules of reinforcement.* New York: Appleton-Century-Crofts, 1957. Copyright 1957 by Appleton-Century-Crofts, Inc. and used by permission.)

Chained schedules. Chained schedules are similar to tandem schedules except that a separate discriminative stimulus is associated with each component of the schedule. In *chain FI* 10 *FR* 10, for example, a visual cue may be present when the *FI* component is in operation but absent during the *FR* component. In *chain FI* 2 *FI* 2 *FI* 2 each component is associated with a different S^D, for example a red-, green-, and yellow-illuminated key, respectively. This schedule is very useful in investigating properties of conditioned (secondary) reinforcers (e.g., Kelleher & Fry, 1962).

Mixed schedules. In a *mixed* schedule, primary reinforcement is available in each component, which is usually presented to *S* in an alternating or quasi-random order. In *mix FI* 10 *FR* 100, for example, the *FI* component may be in force for 20 min, say, followed by the *FR* component for perhaps 15 min, and so forth. Obviously *S* is able to discriminate which schedule is in operation only by discriminating the contingency operating between his behavior and reinforcement. If the components of a mixed schedule are sufficiently different from each other, animals eventually learn to adjust their behavior to the component that is in effect at the moment.

In an interesting application of mixed schedules, Keehn (1965) showed that rats have a remarkable ability to keep track of events that are not differentiable on the basis of exteroceptive or immediately preceding proprioceptive cues. He trained rats on a "repeating" *mix* (*FR* 15 *FR* 45 *FR* 15 *FR* 135), which is a schedule in which each component is in effect for a single reinforcement, with the components continually repeating themselves in the same order. The question asked by Keehn was whether, after completing an *FR* 15 component, S "knew" where he was in the schedule. Keehn felt that this question was relevant for the classical problem concerning the extent to which rats are capable of learning a double-alternation temporal maze (cf. Munn, 1950), for which Keehn thought the mixed schedule was a reasonable operant analogue. In any case, Keehn reasoned that if the rat were capable of making the discrimination described, this fact should be indicated by the duration of the postreinforcement pauses following *FR* 15 components. It will be recalled that the larger the *FR*, the larger the postreinforcement pause. Thus if S were able to anticipate the advent of the *FR* 135 component, pauses after completion of the second *FR* 15 should be longer than after completion of the first. This, indeed, turned out to be the case.

Multiple schedules. A *multiple* schedule is similar to a mixed schedule except for the addition of discriminative cues to set off each of the components. Thus in *mult FI* 10 *FR* 20 a different discriminative cue is associated with the *FI* and the *FR* components. In present terminology, a successive discrimination situation, whether conducted within a discrete-trial or a free-operant setting, may be designated as a multiple schedule. For example, *mult CRF EXT* specifies that S is continuously reinforced in one component ($S+$ or S^D) and nonreinforced in the other ($S-$ or S^Δ).

The components of multiple schedules need not be simple schedules. In the next chapter we shall encounter a *mult* (*tand VI* 30 sec *DRL* 4) (*tand VI* 3 *DRL* 2). Both components of this multiple schedule are tandem schedules, each composed of a variable-interval and a *DRL* component. The purpose of this complex schedule was to achieve comparable response rates in the two discriminative stimuli associated with the schedule while maintaining a significant imbalance in frequency of reinforcement. Note that the *VI* component of each tandem establishes the availability of reinforcement. Thus in the first tandem schedule, reinforcement is "set up" every 30 sec on the average; in the second, every 3 min. But in order to obtain an available reinforcement, S must complete the second component of the tandem, which is a *DRL* 4 (seconds) in the first case and a *DRL* 2 in the second. Of course the function of the *DRL* is to slow down S's rate of responding. Consequently, although the shorter *VI* of the first tandem schedule tends to generate a relatively high rate of response, this is counteracted by the longer *DRL*. The net result is that average response rate remains very comparable in the two components of the multiple schedule but frequency of reinforcement differs considerably, in an actual experiment about 3 to 1 (Yarczower, Dickson, & Gollub, 1966).

SIMULTANEOUS SCHEDULES. It will be recalled that simultaneous schedules may operate independently of each other (concurrent schedules) or they may be coupled together in some fashion. We shall consider the latter type first.

Alternative schedules. In an *alternative* schedule two or more components are programmed simultaneously, and reinforcement is delivered upon completion of any one of the components. At reinforcement all components recycle, and the process begins over again. In *alt FI 5 FR* 100, for example, reinforcement occurs at the completion of 100 responses or, if less than that number has been made before 5 min elapses, at the first response after the termination of the 5-min period. Upon delivery of reinforcement, the two components recycle together.

Conjunctive schedules. In *conjunctive* schedules all components must be completed before reinforcement occurs. In *conj FI 5 FR* 100, to obtain reinforcement S must complete 100 or more responses of which at least one must occur more than 5 min after the last reinforcement. A reinforcement resets all components and the process begins anew.

Concurrent schedules. As already noted, in *concurrent* schedules the component schedules are completely independent of one another. On the response side, however, a number of different possibilities exist. A single response system may be employed, as a bird pecking a single key or a rat pressing a single bar; two different but incompatible response systems may be utilized, as with two keys or two bars so arranged that only one key or one bar can be activated at one time; or, finally, the response systems may be completely compatible, with S provided with two manipulanda which may be activated simultaneously (cf. Catania, 1966). The option chosen by E will depend upon a number of factors, among them the organism employed—it is somewhat difficult to take advantage of the last-described procedure with the pigeon—and the purposes of the research. In any event concurrent schedules are used increasingly because they provide a natural extension of schedules of reinforcement to more complex behaviors. In *conc VI 5 FI 10*, then, both components are in force simultaneously and continuously, with reinforcement available as each component is satisfied.

We have already been introduced to concurrent schedules in the punishment-maintained behavior discussed in the last chapter. Recall that the Ss of the Kelleher and Morse (1968) study worked for food on a *VI 2* schedule, while, concurrently, two shock schedules, an *FI 10* followed by an *FR 1*, were in effect. If the time-out periods are neglected, perhaps this schedule may be described as a *conc* (*VI 2*—food) (*mix FI 10 FR 1*—shock).

A further degree of complexity can be introduced into reinforcement schedules by combining successive and simultaneous schedules as in, for example, *mult FI 10 conc FI 10 avoid RS 30 SS 30* (Ferster & Skinner, 1957). The schedule designated is a multiple schedule, of which one component is an *FI 10*, and the other component is a concurrent schedule composed of an *FI 10* and a Sidman avoidance schedule with response-shock and shock-shock intervals of 30 sec. A buzzer served as the S^D for the first component of the multiple schedule, and its absence was the cue for the concurrent component. Figure 9-5 depicts a response record obtained after this schedule was in effect for some time. The rat in this experiment had a single bar available to him; nevertheless, the effects of the different components of the multiple schedule are clearly evident. In

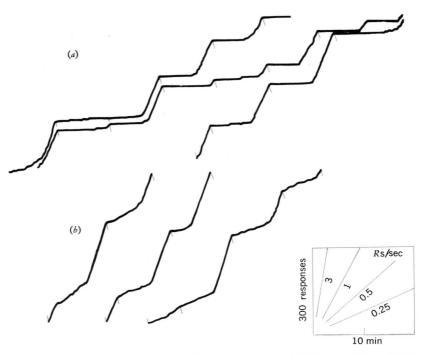

Fig. 9-5. Performance of a rat after 31 sessions on a *mult FI* 10 *conc FI* 10 *avoid RS* 30 *SS* 30. In (*a*) the segments of the *FI* component of the multiple schedule have been brought together, and it can be seen that S's performance is typical of a fixed-interval schedule. In (*b*), which shows segments of the concurrent portion of the schedule, it is evident that postreinforcement pauses do not occur. Rather, a low but steady rate of responding—appropriate to the avoidance portion of the concurrent component—is superimposed on what normally would be a postreinforcement pause. (SOURCE: C. B. Ferster and B. F. Skinner. *Schedules of reinforcement.* New York: Appleton-Century-Crofts, 1957. Copyright 1957 by Appleton-Century-Crofts, Inc. and used by permission.)

(*a*) the *FI* component was in force, and the normal scalloping of fixed-interval schedules is clearly evident. In (*b*) the concurrent component was in operation, and it will be noted that S does not show the prolonged postreinforcement pause that is found with *FI* schedules. Rather a low but steady rate of response is maintained during the postreinforcement interval, behavior which is characteristic of the avoidance component.

Applications of Schedules of Reinforcement

Schedules of reinforcement, particularly compound schedules, have been applied to an enormously wide range of research problems. They have proven extremely valuable in psychopharmacology and physiological psychology, where they have become standard tools in the armamentaria of research techniques. The reasons for their widespread acceptance in these areas are not difficult to find. By appropriate application of reinforcement schedules, a high degree of control over S's behavior can be achieved, often for long periods of time. Thus a variety of baseline behaviors are available against which one may assess the action of drugs and physiological manipulations (cf. Boren, 1966; Teitelbaum, 1966).

Precisely the same advantages accrue to a great deal of research in which the independent variables consist of behavioral manipulations, i.e., manipulations of some aspect of S's past or present experience. It would serve little purpose to enumerate the kinds of behavioral research problems that have been investigated with the aid of schedules of reinforcement. A number of instances have been encountered in previous chapters and more are to come in Chaps. 10 and 11. Instead, let us consider a detailed illustration of an application of operant methodology to the measurement of thresholds in animals. This illustration will draw into focus many of the points discussed thus far in the chapter.

OPERANT METHOD FOR DETERMINING THRESHOLDS IN ANIMALS.   The determination of the sensory capacities of animals by experimental means has a long history in psychology (cf. Munn, 1950), but until recently the techniques available were relatively crude and insensitive. Moreover, thresholds could be obtained only for "points" in time rather than be continuously monitored. Taking his clue from Békésy, who had developed a technique for tracking auditory thresholds in humans, Blough (1958) sought to achieve the same end in animals by using Operant Conditioning techniques. In the Békésy procedure, the subject listens to a soft tone, and when it is audible, S presses a key, which causes the tone to diminish gradually. When the tone is no longer audible, S releases the key, which in turn causes the tone to increase in intensity. When the tone is again audible, the subject once more presses the key, thus reducing its intensity. This process continues, with the tone continuously traversing S's threshold.

Analyzed in terms of the concepts of Operant Conditioning, the task is one of creating a situation in which the tone—or another stimulus of interest—obtains stimulus control over S's responding. The technique devised by Blough employed two keys. The subject (a pigeon) was required to peck response key A when an illuminated stimulus patch was visible and response key B when the patch appeared dark (Fig. 9-6). Pecks on key A reduced the intensity of the stimulus while pecks on B increased it. Assuming that S was responding only in terms of whether or not the stimulus was visible, a plot of the oscillating stimulus intensity should yield a continuous record of S's threshold. However, the pigeon is not as obliging as the human subject. It will peck the keys only for some kind of reinforcement, and the problem is to arrange reinforcement contingencies in such a way as to generate the required behavior.

Getting S to peck key B when the stimulus patch appears dark presents little problem. One simply removes the stimulus by means of the shutter (Fig. 9-6), at the same time making reinforcement available for responding to key B.

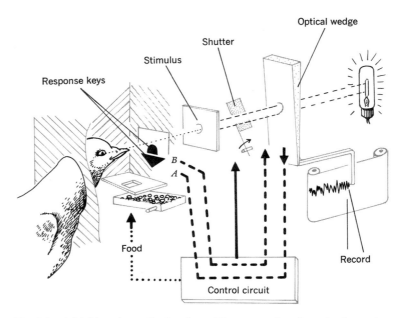

Fig. 9-6. A highly schematic drawing of the apparatus. In order to peck at the response keys, *S* had to reach through the cutout in the front panel. The brightness of the stimulus was manipulated by moving the optical wedge in the vertical axis. (SOURCE: D. S. Blough. A method for obtaining psychophysical thresholds from the pigeon. *Journal of the Experimental Analysis of Behavior*, 1958, **1**, 31–43. Copyright 1958 by the Society for the Experimental Analysis of Behavior, Inc. and used by permission.)

For a variety of reasons continuous reinforcement is inadvisable; a variable-ratio schedule, e.g., *VR* 9, was used instead. Because *S* is reinforced for pecking key *B only* when the stimulus patch is in fact dark, presumably it will peck that key when the patch *appears* dark to *S*, i.e., when the stimulus is below *S*'s threshold.

To maintain responding on key *A*, Blough used a conditioned, rather than a "primary," reinforcement. Because *S* is reinforced on key *B* only when the stimulus patch is dark, any response which causes the patch to go dark will be thereby reinforced; that is, the change from a visible to a dark stimulus patch will serve as a conditioned reinforcer. Consequently having pecks on key *A* lead to activation of the shutter provides sufficient reinforcement for maintaining responding on that key. Again, an intermittent schedule, e.g., *VR* 8, is employed rather than *CRF*.

We are not yet finished, however. If each time *S* completed the *VR* schedule on key *A*, the shutter closed—thus establishing the conditions for reinforcement on key *B*—it is likely that little data of value would be obtained. Most of the time the stimulus patch would be dark because the stimulus was absent rather than because it was below *S*'s threshold. Hence *S* would be reinforced on key *B*, switch to key *A*, then back to key *B* for reinforcement, and so on. To overcome this difficulty, another schedule is imposed on key *A*. A variable-interval component is inserted before the variable-ratio requirement to form a tandem schedule, e.g., *tand VI* 30 sec *VR* 8. The purpose of the *VI* component is to stretch the period during which pecks on key *A* fail to activate the shutter. Because each response on key *A* causes the intensity of the stimulus patch to diminish, *S* now will frequently switch to key *B* because it appears dark rather than because the stimulus has been eliminated by the shutter. When *S* pecks key *B* "erroneously"—that is, during periods when the shutter is *not* activated— each response causes the patch to get brighter. Consequently, after a sufficient number of responses on key *B*, the stimulus will become superthreshold again, and *S* will switch back to key *A*.

The events just described are diagrammed in Fig. 9-7. During the period that the interval timer is activated (line 1), responses on key *A* (line 2) are ineffective in activating the shutter (lines 4 and 5). Because of the changes in stimulus intensity which accompany key pecks (line 8), during this interval *S* will shift between the two keys. Upon the completion of the *VI* portion of the tandem, pecks on *A* start to count toward the *VR* requirement (which in this case is 7—line 4). Note, however, that *S* is penalized if, during this period, it switches to key *B*. Each response on *B* subtracts a count from the responses accumulated toward the *VR* requirement of the tandem schedule. This "punishment" component is superimposed on the tandem to prevent *S* from falling into a pattern of alternating short bursts of responses between the two keys. When *S* has finally completed the *VR* component on key *A*, the shutter closes, and responses on *B* start to count toward the variable-ratio schedule that is required for food reinforcement (line 6). During the period that the shutter is closed, key pecks do not lead to stimulus-intensity changes. Finally, after reinforcement

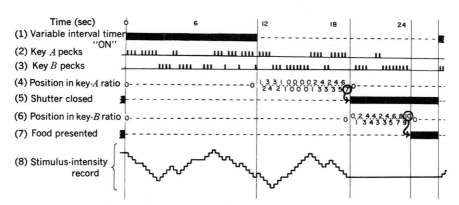

Fig. 9-7. A simplified diagram of the events which occur between two food reinforcements. See text for description. (SOURCE: D. S. Blough. A method for obtaining psychophysical thresholds from the pigeon. *Journal of the Experimental Analysis of Behavior,* 1958, **1,** 31–43. Copyright 1958 by the Society for the Experimental Analysis of Behavior, Inc. and used by permission.)

(line 7) the cycle repeats itself—at least on 80 percent of the occasions. If reinforcement is always followed by opening of the shutter, S will (and in this case did) eventually learn this contingency and shift to key A immediately after receiving reward, whether or not the stimulus patch was visible. To mitigate this tendency, the cycling was itself placed on a schedule. On 20 percent of the occasions, the shutter remained closed for an additional reinforcement before recycling to the VI component of the tandem. This modification eliminated the previous contingency and kept S pecking on key B if, after reinforcement, the key appeared dark.

There are a number of details omitted from this account (cf. Blough, 1958, 1966b), but it demonstrates how, by careful analysis of the behavioral requirements of a situation and appropriate application of operant concepts—including schedules of reinforcement—close control over complex behavior can be attained.

ROLE OF REINFORCEMENT CONTINGENCIES IN "NATURAL" BEHAVIOR.   The belief of some operant conditioners that contingencies between behavior and reinforcement are the key to understanding behavior development and maintenance and that these contingencies can be formalized in precise schedules of reinforcement, poses a challenge that requires substantiation.

One avenue of support takes the form of identifying in our everyday lives significant reinforcement contingencies that are analogous to those operating in technically defined schedules of reinforcement. Skinner has long pointed out in general terms the role of reinforcement contingencies in the control of human behavior (cf. Skinner, 1959, p. 3-36). The following quotations, taken from Ferster (1965), contain a number of explicit analogies.[2]

Shaping of complex behavioral repertoires.

The major process responsible for the development of the progressively more complex forms of behavior that emerge during the growth and development of an individual is the shaping of behavior by reinforcement of successive approximation of a final complex repertoire. . . . The growth and development of the child is a specification of such a shaping procedure by which its immediate environment reinforces its existing behavior and gradually shifts the contingencies of reinforcement toward more complex forms as the child grows older (p. 13).

Self-control as an instance of "chaining."

The development of self-control is another example of a complex behavioral development that requires very specific histories of reinforcement

[2] From L. Krasner & L. P. Ullmann (Eds.), *Research in behavior modification.* New York: Holt, Rinehart & Winston, 1965. Copyright 1965 by Holt, Rinehart & Winston, and reproduced by permission.

contingencies. . . . The behaviors that are required before an individual can manipulate his own behavior so as not to spend money as soon as he receives it, but to retain it to avoid later aversive consequences, form a complex repertoire that can be generated only under a specified range of conditions. Reinforcers that require long chains of responses will maintain the required behavior only if very special development histories are present. The technical analysis of the development of these long chains of behavior reveals that they must be established progressively. The individual's behavior must first be maintained on short chains, and the order of magnitudes must be very gradually increased as the individual's behavior is well sustained at each value (p. 14).

The multiple schedule as a model.

The process is seen most clearly in a pigeon that pecks differentially at a red and green light, because pecking produces food when the light is green and goes unreinforced when the light is red. . . . With such an animal, it becomes possible to weaken the repertoire instantly simply by changing the color from red to green. Similarly many aspects of human behavior are under narrow control of particular aspects of the environment. An extreme case is the classical description of a psychotic depression that results from the death of one of two spinster sisters who have lived together in complete seclusion. The death of the sister is functionally analogous to changing the color of the light from green to red, virtually denuding her repertoire of behavior because of the very narrow control of the behavior of one sister by the other (p. 14).

Instances of fixed-ratio schedules.

The schedule of reinforcement of a performance is one of the major factors that may seriously weaken behavior, even though it has been reliably occurring in the repertoire for a long time. Fixed-ratio schedules, in particular, where a relatively fixed amount of behavior is required per unit of effect upon the environment, may lead to very low dispositions to engage in the behavior, as, for example, the very low disposition of a novelist to begin another book, the student's disinclination to study immediately following an examination, or the procrastination of a scientist in beginning a new project (p. 19).

Ferster's purpose in this article was to suggest a system of classification of behavioral pathology based on "the functional relation between the individual's current repertoire and the existing and potential contingencies in the milieu":

Such a formulation has the advantage that it specifies specific performances and explicit effects of those performances on the environment, which make possible the application of principles of behavioral control derived from an experimental, natural scientific account of behavior formulated in the same terms as any other datum in biology. To the extent that we understand some of the general processes by which new behavior is created in a repertoire, strengthened, weakened, and so forth, such a formulation leads us closer to procedures by which deficient behavioral repertoires may be altered by manipulating the relevant causes in the environment (p. 26).

It is clear, then, that the concepts of Operant Conditioning can be applied to a wide range of human behavior, normal and abnormal. Illustrations—or at least analogies—of shaping, stimulus control, and the operation of many schedules of reinforcement are abundant. There is, of course, some question as to the aptness and relevance of the analogies drawn (cf. Jenkins, 1970). Empirical studies in which reinforcement contingencies are imposed on behavior rather than inferred after the fact are perhaps one way of enhancing their plausibility.

A CONTINUOUSLY PROGRAMMED ENVIRONMENT. A unique experiment in which a human subject was provided with a continuously programmed environment for several months is relevant here (Findley, Migler, & Brady, 1963; described in less detail in Findley, 1966). An adult male volunteer subject was socially isolated in a three-room experimental chamber (Fig. 9-8) for 5 months. During this time virtually every activity that S engaged in, ranging from the use of toilet facilities to sleeping, was explicitly programmed and became available to S only upon completion of appropriate behavioral sequences. An important feature of the overall program was the manner in which certain activities were chained together, which is best illustrated by describing the program in a little detail.

After completing a period of sleep, in order to advance the program to its next component, the subject had to return the bed to its locked position (folded up against the wall), which then permitted S access to toilet facilities. Pressing a button marked T.O. (toilet operations) released an electrical lock on the door to the toilet allowing S to make use of the available facilities, which included a shower, a basin, a separate fresh-water drinking source, a sun lamp, and an electric shaver. Pressing the button also unlocked a drawer (the T.O. drawer) in the main room which allowed S access to fresh clothes and other items. A vacuum cleaner, available in the main room, could also be used during this period. The subject was free to remain in the T.O. activity for as long as he wished; however, he could not proceed to the next component in the chain until he relocked the bathroom door and closed the T.O. drawer.

When the latter requirements were satisfied, S's next task was to express his attitude toward the experiment by pressing one of two buttons, which indicated whether he wished to extend the duration of the experiment or reduce it. In actual fact, however, the duration of the experiment was under the control of the experimenters, and S was aware of this although he was told that his attitude would be considered along with other factors in deciding when to terminate the experiment. It is of interest that when the experiment was initiated, no fixed duration was established.

After recording his attitude toward the experiment, the subject then pressed a weight-temperature button, after which he was required to suspend his

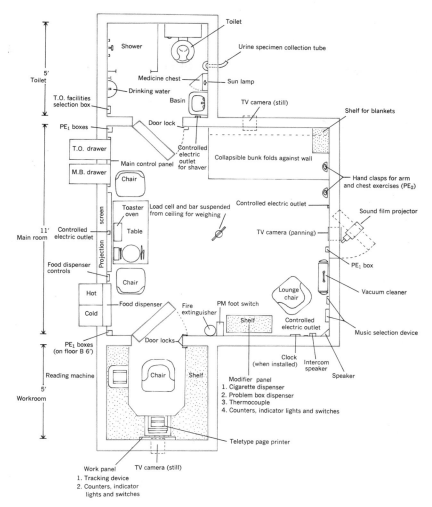

Fig. 9-8. Diagram of experimental chamber showing furnishings and facilities in each room. [SOURCE: J. D. Findley. Programmed environments for the experimental analysis of human behavior. In W. K. Honig (Ed.), *Operant behavior: Areas of research and application.* New York: Appleton-Century-Crofts, 1966. Copyright 1966 by Appleton-Century-Crofts, Inc. and used by permission.]

weight from a bar near the ceiling for approximately 20 sec, so that an accurate measure of his body weight could be obtained. Next, S placed a heat-sensitive probe into his mouth for 20 sec for the purpose of recording his temperature.

When these activities were successfully completed, the next activity, physical exercise, became available. The first phase of physical exercise required S to move about the room extinguishing one of five lights by pressing a related button within certain maximum and minimum time intervals. When S's response fell within the correct time interval (attained the proper *IRT*), he received a 1-sec buzzer stimulus as (conditioned) reinforcement, and this phase continued until S accumulated a certain number of reinforcements, which automatically moved the program into the second physical-exercise activity. This consisted of the use of a weight and cable device for chest and arm exercises. Fifteen-pound weights had to be pulled to their upper limits and released to their lower limits a pre-determined number of times to terminate this activity.

Upon completion of the latter, an optional component in the chain became available. The subject could obtain a light food snack from a food dispenser if he wished, or he could bypass this activity and choose instead from a group of three activities—sleeping, work task 1, or work task 2. If S chose to sleep, he pressed an appropriate button which resulted in the unlocking of the bed, the lowering of the temperature of the room from 75° to 70°, and the availability of electrical power at an outlet near the bed for an electric blanket. Ten minutes later the overhead fluorescent lights were turned off, and the subject was free to sleep for as long as he desired, although a minimum sleep period of 30 min was imposed. At the end of the sleep activity, S, by returning the bed to the locked position, recycled the program to the toilet operations phase.

If, on the other hand, the subject chose work task 1, the door to the work room was unlocked; the subject entered the room and locked the door behind him in order to activate the work task, which consisted of a tracking activity. The subject earned points on this tracking task by performing within certain required limits. In order to terminate this activity, S had to complete a conjunctive schedule: he had to remain at the activity a minimum of 30 min and accumulate a minimum of 150 points. After achieving these criteria, S was free to terminate the task and this phase of the program by leaving the work room and locking the door behind him, which advanced the program to the next set of options.

If S chose work task 2 rather than work task 1, he obtained from a dispenser a box containing a problem, which required intellectual, clerical, and/or manual behaviors. Specific directions were given to the subject with each problem box, and he was required to follow the directions in completing the problem. The subject had to work at this activity a minimum of 30 min, after which he could return the problem box to the dispenser and advance the program to the next set of activities.

Two more classes of options followed in the program. In one group S was provided with the opportunity of working at programmed instruction (using a reading machine in the work room) or engaging in verbal behavior (using a teletype machine in the work room). In the second group of options, by appropriate behaviors the subject could earn record selections, cigarettes, the chance to engage in oral communication, various food selections, and so forth.

An avoidance schedule was superimposed on the entire program. Each time S progressed through the complete program a counter advanced one count, and in order to maintain electrical power in the room, S had to prevent the counter from reaching 25. If he failed to do so, a power failure occurred; all lights in the main room were extinguished and all activities were suspended for a 5-hr period. Power failure could be avoided by pressing a heavy foot switch on an *FR* 25 schedule, which reset the threatening counter.

There were also provisions for obtaining reinforcement (positive and negative) of an unpredictable nature. The subject could choose a "variable consequences" activity, which resulted at some later date in a positive or negative consequence. For example, one variable consequence was the restriction for several days of all food selections to banana-flavored food pellets, milk, and oranges. At other times the variable consequence was positive, such as the delivery of a tape recorder. This activity was not very well maintained in *S*.

The aim of this ambitious experiment was to gain control over most, if not all, of *S*'s normal activities by explicit programming of reinforcement contingencies. Activities which were deemed necessary but of relatively low intrinsic reinforcing value—for example, weight and temperature measurements and, perhaps, the exercises—were chained to the more reinforcing activities of eating and sleeping. Thus, without resorting to aversive techniques it was guaranteed that the former activities would occur.

The importance of chaining to the maintenance of behavior not sufficiently reinforcing in itself is illustrated by the following development. The subject was equipped with devices to measure his activity level and requested to record readings on these devices and transmit the information through the T.O. drawer. However, after the first few weeks of the experiment, he failed to report the readings on a regular basis. Doubtless this behavior would have been maintained had it been included as a component in the initial portion of the schedule. However, because there were no programmed consequences for reporting the readings, this behavior soon dropped out.

Throughout the 5 months of the experiment, the subject was monitored 24 hr a day, and his behavior was recorded automatically. The major accomplishment of the experiment was to demonstrate that an extraordinarily wide range of behavior could be programmed in advance and knit into a tightly woven schedule. By the end of the experiment it became clear, however, that the extended social isolation was placing a serious strain on the subject. An obvious indication was the fact that "the subject frequently questioned the motives of the experimenters, became suspicious of the purposes of the experiment, and generally reflected some loss of confidence and realism concerning those events over which he had no control or information [Findley, Migler, & Brady, 1963, p. 62]." Also, suspicions and verbal aggressions were directed toward the experimenters and toward psychology in general. As a further indication, the subject eventually gave up obtaining his drinking water from the drinking facility, turning to the water available from the basin instead. His reasons were that the water from the drinking source had lost its quality and had become rusty (although this was not detectable by the experimenters, who also obtained their water from the same cooling source), and he expressed "some question about the possible introduction of drugs into the water from the drinking facility" (no drugs were employed at any time).

Interestingly, the percentage of time spent in work tasks and in reading, writing, and creative activities steadily declined over the course of the experiment, with a commensurate increase in the percentage of time spent in toilet operations. When at the end of 152 days the experiment was terminated by mutual consent, these two curves converged, and the subject was spending more time in T.O. than in the former set of activities (Fig. 9-9).

The experimenters suggest that social isolation was primarily responsible for the "behavioral strain" developed during the course of the experiment. For example, they ascribed a decline in certain "creative" activities, such as the use of art supplies, to the absence of social reinforcement, which ordinarily serves to maintain such behavior.

From their experiment the authors conclude that a highly programmed environment can serve a variety of useful purposes, with respect to both research and practical matters. Certainly they have shown the feasibility of establishing an integrated program which covers a great range of activities normally engaged in by human beings. The strain placed on the subject of their experiment by the extended period of social isolation could, in principle, be alleviated by including another individual in the environment. Social interaction could itself be explicitly programmed and made contingent upon specified behaviors, perhaps thereby extending significantly the possibilities of a continuously programmed environment.

To return to the point that initiated consideration of this experiment, it appears that the concept that day-to-day human behavioral activities are governed by a complex set of interwoven reinforcement contingencies is not an unreasonable hypothesis. Properly explored, this concept could have fruitful and far-reaching consequences.

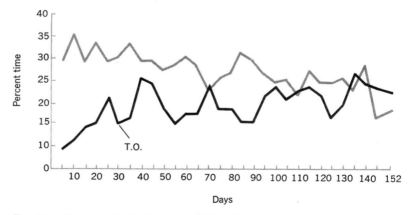

Fig. 9-9. Percent of total time spent in toilet operations (T.O.) compared with total time spent in work tasks, reading, writing, and creative activities. [SOURCE: J. D. Findley. Programmed environments for the experimental analysis of human behavior. In W. K. Honig (Ed.), *Operant behavior: Areas of research and application.* New York: Appleton-Century-Crofts, 1966. Copyright 1966 by Appleton-Century-Crofts, Inc. and used by permission.]

Operant Technology

The third important feature of Operant Conditioning is its impressive technology. The sharp focus placed on schedules of reinforcement—that is, on the contingency between reinforcement and behavior—has had two important consequences for technological and related matters. In the first place it was natural that a wide variety of schedules of reinforcement of varying complexity would be developed, and in order to investigate such schedules, appropriate techniques of programming would have to be devised. Furthermore, the heavy emphasis placed on obtaining and maintaining control over environmental factors pushed the development of laboratory equipment capable of accomplishing this task. Initially much of the required apparatus was devised by the researchers themselves. Very soon a modest industry devoted solely to the development and construction of apparatus devised for experimentation in operant conditioning became established, and it made available sophisticated solid-state programming and recording apparatus on an off-the-shelf basis. More recently computers have been employed, on line, for the programming (and data recording) of schedules that are too complex to be handled by conventional means (e.g., Blough, 1966a).

Emphasis on precisely defined schedules of reinforcement also had the effect of stimulating the development of appropriate language and symbolism. The abbreviated language by means of which the various schedules are designated constitutes more than "jargon." Repetitious expression of some of the more complex schedules on a purely verbal basis would be cumbersome and tedious. But apart from convenience and economy, an efficient and succinct language can serve as a thinking aid in exploring the interrelationships and possible extensions of the various schedules of reinforcement. Skinner (1958) has shown how many schedules can be represented by simple diagrams on response-time coordinates (Fig. 9-10). More comprehensive notational systems have been devised by Findley (1962) and Mechner (1959), by means of which many details of operant procedures may be precisely and succinctly expressed. As yet, however, none of these notational systems has been adopted generally; investigators prefer to refer to reinforcement schedules by means of the abbreviations used above and by filling in procedural details in "long hand." It is to be expected, however, that eventually some such notational system will take hold.

CONTROL OF BEHAVIOR VERSUS PREDICTION

The aim of psychology is often described as the "prediction and control of behavior." Some psychologists have placed heavy stress on the first goal while others have focused their attention on the second. Prediction and control are by no means equivalent pursuits or accomplishments. It will be argued in the following paragraphs that many characteristics of Operant Conditioning which have distinguished it from other developments in psychology—for example,

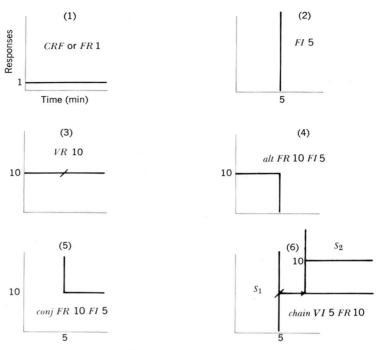

Fig. 9-10. Diagrammatic representation of schedules of reinforcement. Imagine that a cumulative record is traced out on the response-time co-ordinates beginning at the origin (0, 0). Whenever the response curve meets the reinforcement lines shown in the diagrams, reinforcement is presented. Diagram (1) illustrates the case for *CRF* or *FR* 1; a horizontal line at 10 would represent *FR* 10. The oblique line in (3) indicates a variable schedule, in which case the reinforcement line would change from one reinforcement to another. Note that the definitions of alternative and conjunctive schedules are maintained in their respective diagrams, (4) and (5). The chained schedule shown in (6) becomes a tandem schedule if the specification that different stimuli are associated with the two components is omitted. (SOURCE: B. F. Skinner. Diagramming schedules of reinforcement. *Journal of the Experimental Analysis of Behavior,* 1958, **1,** 67–68. Copyright 1958 by the Society for the Experimental Analysis of Behavior, Inc. and used by permission.)

from the Hull-Spence brand of *S–R* behaviorism—stem directly from its long-standing commitment to stringent behavioral control.

Role of Theory in Prediction and in Control

When the major emphasis is on prediction, theory construction is accorded urgent priority. For if prediction means more than merely generalizing from empirical laws, some sort of theory is necessary to prophesy the behavior that ought to be observed under "unique" sets of circumstances. Many psychologists, long envious of the predictive power of theory in the physical sciences, have accepted the ability to predict as a major criterion of scientific accomplishment. And the most direct route to successful prediction appeared to lie in the direction of theory construction.

Of course, in order for the enterprise of theory construction to be pursued at any length, some degree of behavioral control is necessary. However, within the kind of theorizing engaged in by Hull, Tolman, and Guthrie, only the barest essentials of control are necessary, principally the control of manipulated independent variables. The need for precise control over the behavior of individual subjects can be sidestepped by the use of groups of Ss, and the major research issues become expressible in terms of how the manipulation of one or another independent variable affects each group's behavior.

Within this orientation, experimentation initiated and guided by hypothesis testing—the hypotheses devolving from the theory under construction—is the rule. The final goal of this enterprise is the establishment of a theory both sufficiently general and precise to enable one to predict behavior under an interestingly wide range of experimental conditions.

When, on the other hand, one's commitment is to the control of behavior, theory construction tends to play a secondary role, particularly in the early stages in the development of a science such as psychology. It is no accident that the most eloquent detractor of the role of theory in psychology has been Skinner (e.g., 1950), a position from which he has never retreated. The behavioral regularities, relatively invariant across many species and many experimental situations, which are obtainable through some of the schedules of reinforcement are testament that a considerable degree of behavioral control can be obtained without a shred of support from theory of the type engaged in by Hull, Spence, and other learning theorists.

This is not to say that theory in all forms is eschewed by operant conditioners. We have already mentioned that a number of them have attempted to account for the complex behavior generated by various schedules of reinforcement in terms of elementary conditioning principles. Although this might be considered a form of theorizing, it is far more restricted in scope than the efforts of most theorists in psychology. It seems more a matter of analysis than theorizing—analyzing complex behavior, not in terms of "neural, mental, or conceptual" events (Skinner, 1950, p. 194), but in terms of well-founded basic conditioning principles.

Just as successful prediction of behavior implies a certain amount—however minimal—of behavioral control, so does successful control imply a degree of ability to predict behavior. But the sort of prediction required need not be anything more sophisticated than the expectation that a behavioral law formulated in the past will continue to operate in the future under reasonably similar circumstances. For example, allow an operant conditioner to specify the environmental conditions, and he can guarantee (predict) that a subject after sufficient training will respond with a scalloped pattern on an FI schedule. And he can make similar "predictions" about the behavior generated by other schedules, simple and complex. But his predictions reside in previously established behavioral "laws" and not in the implications of a theoretical structure. If required, he may guess as to the kind of behavior one will observe under conditions for which he does not have empirically established laws available. But these are no more than guesses; they are not predictions in the sense of formal deductions from theory. And their confirmation or disconfirmation would be of little significance other than for the individual's personal satisfaction. In a word, the behavioral control which the operant conditioner has at his disposal does not arise from a theory which is in more or less good correspondence with reality and therefore grinds out reasonably accurate predictions; rather, it is the product of a painstaking analysis of the environmental variables which influence behavior and the development of the means with which to control such variables.

Different Implications for Research Approaches

Perhaps nowhere are the implications stemming from emphasis on either control or prediction of behavior more divergent than in the adopted research strategies. With control the primary aim, a detailed analysis of the variables influencing an *individual's* behavior is crucial, and as a consequence, behavioral processes strongly affected by variables which the experimenter cannot easily manipulate receive relatively little attention. Inasmuch as *acquisition* processes—such as the speed with which S acquires a discrimination or the manner in which a scalloped pattern under an *FI* schedule is developed—are importantly influenced by variables over which the experimenter often has extremely little control (variables such as previous experience), these processes are often ignored. On the other hand, "asymptotic" or "steady-state" behavior is less at the mercy of such variables and more closely modulated by manipulations occurring within the experimental situation itself (cf. Sidman, 1960). Consequently, Operant Conditioning emphasizes these processes.

In the usual operant experiment one finds very few subjects, with each S having received the experimental manipulations over long periods of time, perhaps months. Failure to obtain regularities in the behavioral patterns observed in his Ss would suggest to E that their behavior was not under adequate experimental control, and an analysis of the basis of this failure to obtain sufficient control would be forthcoming.

When interest is focused on theory construction and hypothesis testing, the experimental strategy is often quite different. A prediction of some sort or another is at stake. The vast majority of such predictions are related to the acquisition process (at least in classical learning theory) and often take the form that under such and such circumstances learning will be faster than under a different set of circumstances, or that variable X facilitates learning so that the more of X, the faster the learning. Often the only control required to evaluate the hypothesis being tested is to ensure that the independent variable or variables under examination be manipulated in such a way as to avoid confounding factors (cf. Chap. 2). Characteristically only a small sample of each S's behavior—

perhaps no more than an hour or two—is obtained, and *E* is primarily concerned with comparisons that can be made between groups of subjects, perhaps between an experimental and a control group. Variability of results from subject to subject is not only tolerated but expected. Little or no attempt—other than maintaining comparable experimental conditions—is made to force comparable performances by the subjects of a group; the lack of such uniformity is attributed to "individual differences," i.e., to variables over which *E* does not presently have control.

Hand in hand with this divergence in research strategy comes a sharp cleavage in attitude toward the role of statistics in behavioral research. Statistical evaluation of experimental results is rendered a necessity by the variability which research based on theory construction inevitably entails, so much so that graduate training in statistics has long been a requirement in American psychology. According to the operant conditioner, however, resorting to statistics is no more than an admission of inadequate behavioral control. The behavioral processes which they examine are, according to them, evident in the cumulative records of each organism. They are there for the eye to see, and statistics are usually superfluous. They control their relevant variables experimentally, not statistically.

Another way of describing the above differences in experimental strategies is in terms of the types of experimental designs employed (cf. Chap. 2). Research based on the testing of hypotheses derived from theory most often, though of course not necessarily, takes the form of separate-groups designs. Operant conditioners, on the other hand, rarely use such designs; their research fits more naturally into single-group designs. Their preferred design, however, is the single-subject design, in which each subject may be considered a replication of the entire experiment.

One further implication of the control-prediction distinction is the different emphasis placed on equipment development, a topic we have already mentioned. It is no accident that the greatest spur to the development of experimental apparatus and programming equipment has come from Operant Conditioning. If one is to obtain tight behavioral control, he must be able to exert close environmental control over static environmental stimuli, internal stimuli arising from motivational and related states, reinforcement contingencies, and any other source of stimulation which could possibly affect behavior. To achieve such a degree of environmental control requires carefully designed and, at times, sophisticated equipment. In contrast, the modest demands on control which arise from research emanating from hypothesis testing permit the use of much more relaxed experimental situations, and homemade wooden T mazes and straight alleys exist with only minor refinements to this day.

Different Attitudes toward Applied Problems

There is a further divergence that seems to relate to the different emphasis psychologists place on prediction and control. It appears that despite the enormous amount of research stimulated by theoretical notions arising from the classical learning theories, relatively little has filtered down from this body of information to the management of behavioral problems of a practical nature. To be sure, many efforts have been made to demonstrate the applicability of classical learning principles to problems of psychotherapy. But two observations must be made concerning these attempts. First, when made by the learning theorists themselves, they were apt to be little more than a recasting of well-known psychotherapeutic problems into the language of learning theory (e.g., Dollard & Miller, 1950; Mowrer, 1950; cf. Bandura, 1961). And second, such attempts that were made to influence psychotherapeutic practices have come largely from clinicians or from clinically oriented psychologists who borrowed from the learning theorists. This is not to deny the contribution that learning theory has made to the development of "behavior therapy" (cf. Wolpe & Lazarus, 1966; Wolpe, Salter & Reyna, 1964), but merely to point out something of the nature of its contribution.

It also seems to be the case that practical applications of classical learning theory have been restricted, for the most part, to problems relating to psychotherapy. Thorndike, of course, had an enormous impact on educational philosophy, but the same cannot be said about the learning theorists who followed him.

In any event when we evaluate the role that Operant Conditioning has played in applied problems, we encounter a sharp contrast, with respect to both the nature and the scope of their involvement. Skinner has always taken an active interest in applying the behavioral-control principles established in the laboratory to the management of practical problems (cf. Skinner, 1959). Indeed, his *Walden Two* (1948b) was a preliminary blueprint for engineering an entire society from basic behavioral principles. Many years ago, in an effort to ease the lot of mothers, he turned his attention to controlling the environment of infants, developing the so-called "baby box," which because of extraordinary and universal conservativism in such matters never took hold (Skinner, 1959, pp. 419–426). During World War II he worked seriously on the development of a guided missile, the guidance machinery of which was a pigeon whose pecking was so instrumented as to home the missile in on the target. But this effort, too, was destined not to end in success (Skinner, 1960). The teaching machine, or, more exactly, programmed instruction, which is currently revolutionizing instruction in certain areas (cf. Leib et al., 1967), owes much of its development to operant conditioners (e.g., Skinner, 1959, pp. 145–182). To provide a readily available publication outlet for these activities, the *Journal of Applied Behavior Analysis* was launched in 1968, dedicated to "research applying the experimental analysis of behavior to problems of social importance."

Though they did not totally ignore such matters, a comparable concern with applied behavioral problems was never evident in Hull or in many of the other leading learning theorists.

It is also of interest that operant conditioners, not leaving the task to others, have often taken it upon themselves to extend operant principles to areas of practical concern. Thus, for example, it was Ferster who pointed out the applicability of operant methodology to the analysis of behavioral problems of autistic children (Ferster, 1961; Ferster & DeMeyer, 1962) and interpreted obesity as a matter of the control of eating behavior (Ferster, Nurnberger, & Levitt, 1962). Other operant conditioners attacked such problems as stuttering (Goldiamond, 1965b), thumb-sucking in children (Baer, 1962), the management of mental patients (Ayllon & Azrin, 1968; Ayllon & Haughton, 1962), and "self-control" (e.g., Goldiamond, 1965a). The first space-traveling primates were trained by the methods of Operant Conditioning (cf. Rohles, 1966). Applications have even been made to the evaluation of television advertising (Lindsley, 1962) and industrial quality control, where it has been shown that pigeons can very likely supplant humans in such matters as the inspection of electronic components (Cumming, 1966) and drug capsules (Verhave, 1966).

In all instances mentioned above, as well as others which could be cited, researchers trained, or at least knowledgeable, in the ways of Operant Conditioning themselves recognized and promoted extensions of their concepts and techniques to matters of practical concern. It seems likely that this willingness to accept the challenges of practical behavioral problems stems in part from the deep concern that operant conditioners have cultivated for behavioral control in the laboratory and from the availability of a methodology by means of which such control can be pursued.

To summarize these last paragraphs, the emphasis placed on behavioral control by operant conditioners has pointed them in a different direction from psychologists who stress prediction of behavior. Their path has led to a detailed analysis of response-reinforcement contingencies, which for them constitute the most important class of variables controlling instrumental behavior. The quest for behavioral control led to an emphasis on the study of individual organisms, a disinterest in theory construction—which in no case could give them any greater control over behavioral processes than they already possessed in their laboratory techniques—and a disdain for statistics, whose employment was seen as capitulation to inadequate control. Concern with practical matters followed as a matter of course. Some of these endeavors—programmed instruction, for example—have been highly successful, if acceptance is any criterion. For others, such as the treatment of serious behavior disorders (cf. Krasner & Ullmann, 1965; Ullmann & Krasner, 1965), it is perhaps too soon to gauge the measure of their success, although the evidence is promising (e.g., Leff, 1968). However, our purpose has not been to evaluate these efforts but rather to stress the fact that they occurred in the first place and to suggest a plausible interpretation, namely, that they are but one consequence of a thorough commitment to behavioral control.

SUMMARY

In this rather brief survey of Operant Conditioning we have tried to point out the essential features which distinguish the operant approach from others in related areas of experimental psychology. Let it be emphasized that many of the techniques and methods of Operant Conditioning have diffused widely throughout experimental psychology. Nevertheless, many psychologists who are committed to the basic tenants of Operant Conditioning tend to adopt attitudes toward research priorities and strategies that render them—in method and in aim—discriminably different from other experimental psychologists. In view of the ever-increasing acceptance of operant methodology, this distinction is likely to wane in years to come.

1. Reinforcement, response differentiation, stimulus control, and rate of response as a basic datum, are all central concepts in Operant Conditioning. The importance of these concepts is:

2. The methodological and conceptual roles played by schedules of reinforcement in Operant Conditioning are:

3. "Simple" schedules are those in which only a single reinforcement schedule, with constant parameters, is in effect throughout an experimental session.
(a) Simple schedules in which the reinforcement contingency is based on time alone are:
(b) Simple schedules in which the reinforcement contingency is based on behavior alone are:
(c) Simple schedules in which the reinforcement contingency is based on both time and behavior are:

4. Some sequential schedules are:

5. Two nonconcurrent simultaneous schedules are:

6. A concurrent schedule has the following properties:

7. It was hypothesized that the emphasis of Operant Conditioning on behavioral control, rather than on prediction, had the following consequences for its development:

10 GENERALIZATION

Generalization and discrimination are two of the most fundamental behavioral processes known to us, perhaps second only to association itself. Discrimination, the ability to "tell things apart," is the antithesis of generalization, which causes us to react in the same or similar ways to different—perhaps only subtly different—stimulus situations. Much of what we call "learning" can be viewed as the development of discrimination where previously generalization existed. Thus a child labors hard to distinguish between the spoken N and M and between the written P and R or even between W and M. Ornithologists and botanists come by their ability to distinguish between myriads of birds and plants only through detailed study of "what to look for," eventually becoming capable of detecting differences between closely related birds and plants that are all but invisible to the inexpert.

However, generalization is by no means the constant villain. We place ourselves on the side of generalization when, for example, we protest against expressions of racial or religious "discrimination." We do not wish "cues" signifying a man's race or religion to constitute the discriminative stimuli for a wide range of behaviors—hiring practices and social activities among them. We want these classes of activities to generalize completely over the set of stimuli by means of which race and religion are identified. The law, one aphorism has it, should be "color-blind." Generalization is also of value at a conceptual level, as when we suddenly gain deep insight by noticing similarities among objects or situations that outwardly seem different.

Because of their importance and ubiquitousness, the concepts of generalization and discrimination are very widely used in psychology, and, on the empirical level, they have been intensely investigated. In this chapter we shall sketch the range of situations to which the term generalization applies and point out a number of important methodological considerations. We shall not dwell in detail on substantive issues, which the student can find treated amply in such works as Kalish (1969), Mostofsky (1965), and Terrace (1966c). The topic of discrimination learning will be discussed in the next chapter.

BASIC CONCEPTS AND METHODS IN GENERALIZATION

Let us begin by defining a number of central concepts.

Definition of Terms

PRIMARY AND MEDIATED STIMULUS GENERALIZATION.   Suppose that by means of classical conditioning, a dog is made to salivate when presented with a tone of 1,000 Hz (the CS). If a tone of 1,500 Hz is now presented to the animal, salivation will occur to some degree, although strictly speaking this stimulus was never itself paired with the salivary response. We use the phrase *stimulus generalization* to refer to the fact that the CR has been evoked in some measure by a stimulus other than the CS—in the present illustration the 1,500-Hz tone. In more general terms *stimulus generalization refers to the empirical fact that an acquired response is evoked by a stimulus which itself has never been paired with the response under study.* When the CS (or S+) and the "test" or "generalized" stimuli are *physically* similar to each other—as the CS and test stimulus of the above illustration—we speak of *primary* stimulus generalization. Although stimulus generalization applies to both classical and instrumental conditioning (or learning—cf. Chap. 7), to avoid redundancy we shall use the terminology of one or the other.

Primary stimulus generalization is contrasted with *mediated* stimulus generalization. The following illustration is an instance of *semantic* generalization, a type of mediated stimulus generalization. College students conditioned to salivate upon seeing the word "style" (again through classical conditioning), later salivated more to the synonym "fashion" than to the homophone "stile" (Razran, 1939). Because style and stile are physically far more similar—both visually and aurally—than style and fashion, much of the generalized responding to the synonym is presumed to have been mediated by past learning.

The paradigm behind this assumption takes the following form. Let S_1 and S_2 be two stimuli which have little in common physically. Let both stimuli be conditioned to the same response, r_X, which we assume, as we did in the case of anticipatory goal and frustration responses, possesses a characteristic stimulus accompaniment, s_X. If now S_1 is conditioned to a response R, some degree of associative control will devolve to s_X, inasmuch as the occurrence of S_1 elicits r_X–s_X and hence s_X is available for conditioning to R. It then follows that if S_2 is presented, it will tend by means of the common response-stimulus component r_X–s_X to evoke R in some measure.

The generalized responding which occurs to S_2 is mediated by the r_X–s_X mechanism, and r_X is consequently called the "mediating" response. In principle any sort of response—autonomic, skeletal, linguistic—may serve as a mediating response. Moreover the mediating responses conditioned to S_1 and S_2 need not be identical. Similar responses will also support mediated generalization, but of course not to the extent possible with identical mediating responses (and therefore identical mediating stimuli).

Semantic generalization, which is based on similarity in the meaning of words, has been interpreted as a case of mediated generalization in which the mediating mechanism is a "meaning" response (cf. Staats, Staats, & Heard, 1959). Hence a response conditioned to a word tends to be elicited by synonyms because of the mediation of similar meaning responses. The implications of conceptualizing meaning as a mediating response have been subjected to considerable research effort (e.g., Osgood, 1962; Osgood & Suci, 1955; Staats & Staats, 1963, Chap. 4), but it would take us too far afield to consider this interesting literature. It is sufficient that one be aware of the manner in which past learning can serve to enlarge the scope of the generalization process and take note that, because mediated generalization is presumed to rest on the similarity of mediating responses (or more exactly, on the similarity of the stimuli accompanying mediating responses) basically it differs little from primary stimulus generalization. Presumably it is the physical similarity of the s_Xs that lies behind mediated generalization.

Primary stimulus generalization is generally assumed to reside in the physical similarity of the principal stimuli themselves or in the sensory mechanisms that process these stimuli and not to be dependent in any essential way on past experience. In the view of many writers, generalization is a basic property of neural tissue. Actually, however, the role of past experience in primary stimulus generalization has been contested for years. The available evidence now suggests that stimulus generalization gradients can occur in animals totally deprived of differential experience with the relevant stimulus continuum, which implies that the process does not depend critically on past learning. We shall return to this point later in the chapter.

STIMULUS GENERALIZATION AS A PROCESS. We have defined stimulus generalization in terms of an observation or a datum, namely, that a response associated with a particular stimulus will be evoked in greater or lesser measure by other, similar stimuli. Often, however, the term is used in a different sense. It frequently refers to one or another process thought to be the mechanism which gives rise to the *observed* generalization, as, for example, the notion that (observed) generalization is attributable to a "spread" of association from the CS to related stimuli (assumed *process* of generalization).

Although there has been relatively little quarrel about the existence of stimulus generalization as an empirical phenomenon, much controversy has arisen when the discussion has turned to its properties as a process, a topic that shall occupy us during the last pages of the chapter. To maintain a healthy distinction between data and theory, these two different usages of the term generalization should be kept in mind. [See Brown (1965) for a detailed discussion of this point.]

RESPONSE GENERALIZATION. In stimulus generalization the response is fixed, and we focus our attention on the extent to which stimuli other than the CS evoke the CR. In *response generalization*, on the other hand, the paradigm is reversed. Here the CS is held fixed, and we inquire into the range of responses other than the CR that is elicitable by the CS. As an illustration, a dog trained in a classical aversive-conditioning paradigm to flex his left front leg at the appearance of a CS will initially tend to flex his other legs as well; only after much training will this generalized responding subside.

Although response generalization has been used extensively as an explanatory tool, particularly in verbal learning and transfer phenomena, it has not been the subject of a great deal of research—certainly nothing like the amount of research effort devoted to stimulus generalization.

STIMULUS GENERALIZATION GRADIENTS. Another term that needs defining is *stimulus generalization gradient*. This concept applies only where the test stimuli can be ordered with respect to their "distance" from the CS. Most often the ordering is established by simple physical measurement, as, for example, wavelength in the case of color stimuli, the number of square inches in the case of area stimuli, the number of degrees in the angle formed by the line and the horizontal in the case of line tilt, and so on. In other instances psychologically derived units may be employed, for example, the number of JNDs in pitch separating adjacent test stimuli (see Chap. 5) or even rated judgments of similarity. Whatever the means of ordering the various test stimuli along a dimension, a question of interest concerns how the amount of generalized response strength accruing to a test stimulus varies as a function of the distance that separates it from the CS.

Figure 10-1 depicts the amount of generalized responding obtained from a pigeon that was presented the test stimuli shown on the abscissa. The S+

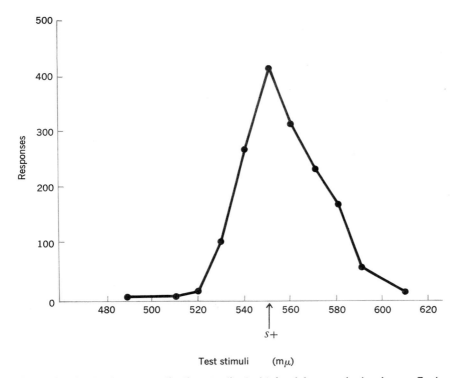

Fig. 10-1. A stimulus generalization gradient obtained from a single pigeon. Each point on the figure shows the number of key-pecking responses made by S when tested with a stimulus of a particular wavelength. The training stimulus (S+) was 550 mμ. (SOURCE: N. Guttman and H. I. Kalish. Discriminability and stimulus generalization. *Journal of Experimental Psychology*, 1956, **51**, 79–88. Copyright 1956 by the American Psychological Association and used by permission.)

was 550 millimicrons (mμ), or more exactly, the illumination of a transparent key with a light of that wavelength.[1] The curve which connects the data points, each showing the amount of responding obtained for a particular test stimulus, defines a stimulus generalization gradient. We shall describe later in more detail the particular techniques employed in obtaining such gradients, but now we wish to observe that many important theoretical and empirical questions revolve around (1) the origin of stimulus generalization gradients and (2) the variables that determine the steepness or shallowness of the gradients.

If S responds to the same degree to all test stimuli, we say that a generalization gradient was *not* obtained or that we observed a *flat* gradient. In such a case it is apparent that the stimulus dimension in question has no relevance for S, or, in other terms, it possesses no stimulus control for S's responding. In still different terms we may say that S is not "attending" to this particular stimulus

[1] A millimicron is equal to one-billionth of a meter; an equivalent unit is the nanometer (nm).

dimension. There now exists substantial evidence that a flat gradient is likely to be obtained unless measures are taken to ensure that during original training S attends to the stimulus dimension along which generalization testing is to take place.

Techniques and Methods for Studying Stimulus Generalization

The area of stimulus generalization provides a salient illustration of how the development of an experimental technique can lead to an explosive development of a research area. Stimulus generalization was first studied in detail by Pavlov and his associates within the classical conditioning paradigm (Pavlov, 1927). Early studies in this country (e.g., Hovland, 1937) employed classical conditioning of the galvanic skin response, though certain shortcomings inherent in this technique remained unresolved (Burstein, Epstein, & Smith, 1967). With the rapid development of instrumental conditioning, it was natural that stimulus generalization would be investigated within that setting. Consequently, a number of investigations were conducted with the rat as subject and the running response in the straight alley as the instrumental response. Frequently, humans were employed as subjects, and in these cases the instrumental response was apt to be the movement of a rod or the pressing of a button, and the stimuli were squares of different areas, rectangles of different heights, or spatial location of electric lights. Although these techniques were adequate to investigate gross generalization phenomena, they had shortcomings which precluded their use in more refined analyses. To appreciate these limitations, one must understand how stimulus generalization is measured and how stimulus generalization gradients are calculated.

When testing for the strength of S's disposition to respond to test stimuli, one must decide whether or not to reinforce responses made to the latter. This immediately raises complications for if, on the one hand, such responses are reinforced, it is clear that stimulus generalization very quickly becomes contaminated with the response strength accruing from the reinforcement itself. If, on the other hand, generalized responding is unreinforced, one suffers, immediately after the first test, the complementary contamination of extinction effects. Ideally, then, the way to generate a "pure" generalization gradient is to test each subject only once, recruiting a large number of Ss for each test stimulus. Such a procedure, however pristine, is prohibitively expensive in time and effort and is rarely employed. But even if it were practicable, there is at least one reason why this method would still not be completely adequate. Although such a technique would provide us with *group* gradients, we would have no information whatever about generalization gradients of individual Ss, and it is quite likely that a very substantial amount of information would be masked by the group data.

In any event, some investigators took the compromise path of testing their Ss on some but usually not all the test stimuli, and even where Ss were exposed to all the test stimuli, this was done in such a way that sequence effects (see Chap. 2) could not be eliminated except by considering group data. Furthermore, because in the then available techniques, extinction progressed rapidly when reinforcement was withheld (by far the predominant testing procedure), E could not afford to prolong the testing session. Indeed, there was even a question for a time whether the generalization gradient itself was not an artifact of the group testing procedure.

In 1956 Guttman and Kalish—anticipated by Brush et al. (1952), who in turn took their cue from a suggestion of Skinner (1950)—showed that by application of operant conditioning techniques it was possible to obtain stimulus generalization gradients for individual Ss. They trained pigeons to peck a key illuminated with monochromatic light (say 550 mμ). During conditioning the birds were on a VI 1 schedule, S+ periods of 60 sec alternating with 10-sec blackout or time-out periods. At the completion of training, each S was presented with 11 test stimuli in 12 different random orders, totaling 132 stimulus presentations (thus controlling sequence effects). Each stimulus presentation was 30 sec in duration (10 sec intervening between any two presentations), and there was no reinforcement during testing for generalization. As Fig. 10-2 shows, orderly generalization gradients were demonstrable for individual subjects.

Since the publication of this study, a very large number of investigations of stimulus generalization have been conducted using substantially the same techniques, which offer the advantages of close control over stimulus variables and a criterion behavior that survives the transition to the extinction conditions of testing with good stability. Although wavelength has often served as the manipulated continuum, other stimulus dimensions, such as brightness and line tilt, have broadened the empirical base. Recently analogous procedures have been extended to research with human Ss.

ABSOLUTE VERSUS RELATIVE GENERALIZATION GRADIENTS. The gradients shown in Fig. 10-2 are *absolute* stimulus generalization gradients inasmuch as the measure of performance is the actual number of responses obtained with each test stimulus. Occasions arise, however, where absolute stimulus generalization gradients do not provide all the information we desire. For example, suppose that E, interested in the relationship between generalization and drive level, obtains stimulus generalization gradients under high and low motivational levels. It is a likely outcome, as we learned in Chap. 7, that responding would be more vigorous under high drive, yielding something like the absolute generalization gradients shown in Fig. 10-3a. It is obvious that, in terms of absolute response strength, more generalization occurred under high than under low drive. But E may also be interested in whether drive level affects the *proportion* of response strength observed at non-CS stimuli. That is, does the amount of generalization obtained under the two drive conditions differ when differences in response strength at the CS are taken into account? Moreover, E is often interested in the related question of whether the shapes of the gradients (their slopes) are the same or different when compensation has been made for different response levels at the CS.

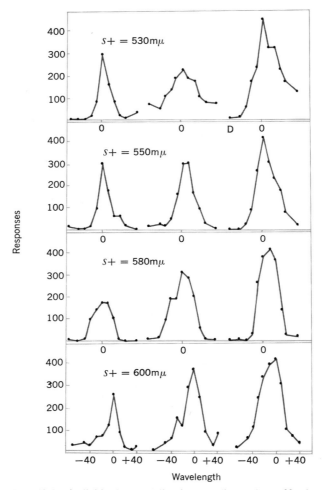

Fig. 10-2. Individual generalization gradients from 12 of the 24 Ss of the experiment. Four different wavelengths served as S+. The abscissa depicts the test stimuli in terms of the numbers of mμ away from S+. (SOURCE: N. Guttman and H. I. Kalish. Discriminability and stimulus generalization. *Journal of Experimental Psychology,* 1956, **51,** 79–88. Copyright 1956 by the American Psychological Association and used by permission.)

    Two transformations are employed to adjust for different response levels, producing what are called "relative" generalization gradients. One method is to express the level of responding (say the number of responses) observed at each test stimulus as a percentage of S's total amount of responding (total number of responses). In Fig. 10-3*b* the absolute gradients have been transformed in

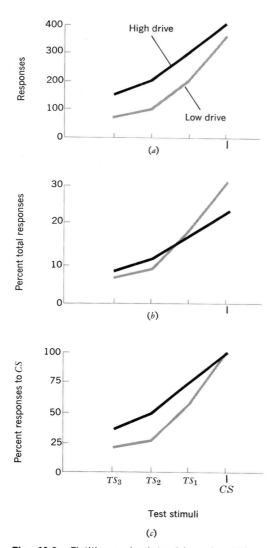

Fig. 10-3. Fictitious absolute (a) and relative (b and c) generalization gradients obtained under high and low drive. Only one "wing" of the gradients is shown; for simplicity, we assume the gradients are symmetrical. The test stimuli are ordered from the least (TS₃) to the most (TS₁) similar to the CS. See text for explanation.

accordance with this technique. Plotted in this fashion the gradients suggest that high drive (1) increases the amount of generalization to non-*CS* stimuli and (2) tends to flatten, or to decrease the slope of, the relative generalization gradient.

An alternative way of presenting relative stimulus generalization gradients is to express performance at each test stimulus as a percentage of the performance observed at the *CS*. The absolute gradients of Fig. 10-3*a* have been transformed in this manner in Fig. 10-3*c*. Note that this technique causes both stimulus generalization gradients to coincide at the *CS*, and for this reason differences in slope are immediately apparent.

Whereas the latter method can be applied to any absolute stimulus generalization gradient, the former method is most appropriate with discrete dependent variables, such as number of responses and number of drops of salivation. For continuous dependent variables the second method seems more natural, although it is possible to use the first as well. In any event, though the two methods do not lead to identical results, they are highly correlated. The first method has the virtue that in "normalizing" the generalization gradient, it makes use of all the data, rather than only those obtained at the *CS*.

EXCITATORY STIMULUS GENERALIZATION GRADIENTS

Stimulus generalization gradients have been obtained under a variety of experimental conditions. A convenient classification is in terms of whether the test stimuli tend to evoke the criterion behavior or to inhibit it. In the first instance we speak of "excitatory" or "positive" stimulus generalization gradients, or analogously, of "excitatory control." Gradients obtained under the second set of circumstances are called "inhibitory" or "negative" stimulus generalization gradients, and one speaks of "inhibitory control." A very large proportion of research in stimulus generalization has concerned itself with excitatory gradients, and although inhibitory gradients have always commanded an important theoretical position, the added complexities often involved in their investigation has limited relevant research efforts.

Excitatory gradients are usually established by positive reinforcement, as in the several examples given earlier in this chapter. However, negative reinforcement may also be used for this purpose. In discriminative avoidance conditioning, for example, an avoidance response might be established with a tone of a certain frequency serving as the *CS* and *S* tested later with tones of different frequencies (e.g., Hoffeld, 1962).

A very large number of variables have been investigated for their effects on excitatory gradients. In this section we shall describe only a few of these: type and amount of acquisition training, drive level, schedules of reinforcement, and the training-test interval.

Type of Acquisition Training—Role of Attention in Generalization

The fact that a stimulus is associated with reinforcement by no means guarantees that a stimulus generalization gradient will be obtained when generalized stimuli are presented to S. For example, suppose a pigeon pecks a key in the presence of a 1,000-Hz tone, and suppose a test for generalization is given later with tones ranging from 300 to 3,500 Hz (equally spaced on a logarithmic scale). From all that has been said, one might expect an orderly stimulus generalization gradient to be generated. But a flat gradient (no gradient) is by far the more likely outcome. However, change the acquisition procedure slightly, by alternating S+ periods with S− periods *in which no tone at all is presented* (and, of course, letting all key pecks go unreinforced), and now a typical gradient will appear (Fig. 10-4).

ORTHOGONAL DISCRIMINATION TRAINING AND STIMULUS CONTROL.   Note that the S− of the above illustration was not a tone of a different frequency from S+; rather, it was merely no tone at all. If S were taught to discriminate between two stimuli lying on the same physical continuum, the resulting stimulus generalization gradient would be contaminated by the inhibitory control developed by S−. That a gradient (between S+ and S−) arises under such conditions is hardly remarkable. The interesting point here, however, is that an "orthogonal" discrimination—a discrimination which is not based on the same physical dimension along which stimulus generalization is evaluated—causes a stimulus generalization gradient to appear which might not otherwise occur. Recall that in the Guttman and Kalish (1956) study periods of S+ (key illuminated by 550-mμ light) alternated with periods during which the key was dark. Thus, they too employed an orthogonal discrimination-training procedure during acquisition. In addition to the Jenkins and Harrison (1960) study, there are a number of other reports in which flat stimulus generalization gradients were obtained after nondiscriminative acquisition training (e.g., Jensen & Cotton, 1961; Schiff, 1965).

Why is orthogonal discrimination training often necessary for a generalization gradient to be obtained? The answer appears to be that such training helps focus S's "attention" on the relevant stimulus. Put differently, orthogonal discrimination training helps to ensure that the relevant stimulus gains control over S's responding; consequently later variations in this stimulus ought to be mirrored in the degree of control it exercises over the instrumental response. It is interesting that the classical conditioning paradigm—which has so often been employed in stimulus generalization studies—inevitably incorporates orthogonal discrimination training, inasmuch as the UCS is presented only when the CS has made an earlier appearance, and never when it has not.

IMPLICIT ORTHOGONAL TRAINING.   Is some sort of explicit orthogonal discrimination training always necessary for a generalization gradient to be obtained?

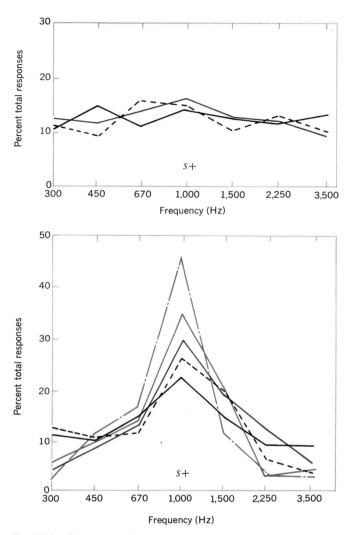

Fig. 10-4. The flat gradients in the upper panel were obtained from three pigeons that received nondiscriminative training. The five orderly individual gradients shown in the lower panel were gotten from Ss that had the benefit of orthogonal discrimination training; a 1,000-Hz tone served as S+, and S− was the absence of this tone. (SOURCE: H. M. Jenkins and R. H. Harrison. Effect of discrimination training on auditory generalization. *Journal of Experimental Psychology,* 1960, **59,** 246–253. Copyright 1960 by the American Psychological Association and used by permission.)

Apparently not. Blough (1959) was able to demonstrate orderly generalization gradients based on the brightness of a red patch of light (on the response key) even though, during acquisition training, S+ was continuously present (see also, Switalski, Lyons, & Thomas, 1966). However, some measure of orthogonal discrimination is involved even here because S, to be rewarded, must peck at that portion of the experimental chamber on which S+ is located. If, for example, the red light were diffused continuously from above, rather than being located on the response key, a flat generalization gradient might have been obtained (see Heinemann & Rudolph, 1963). Possibly a similar argument applies to the Newman and Grice (1965) study where rats literally had to poke their heads through the CS to obtain their reward.

To account for the considerable latitude in the ease with which stimulus generalization gradients are obtained along different stimulus dimensions, some investigators have proposed that "attending-hierarchies" exist, based on either innate factors or previous experience (e.g., M. R. Baron, 1965). Doubtlessly there is merit in this suggestion, but one should also consider the discriminative requirements of the experimental situation, which may promote or inhibit the development of stimulus control on the part of S+.

The conflicting results of Peterson (1962) and Ganz and Riesen (1962) with respect to the important issue of the role of early visual experience on wavelength generalization may be resolved on this basis. Peterson reported that ducks raised in monochromatic light subsequently failed to display a generalization gradient along the wavelength dimension. In contrast, monkeys raised from birth in darkness produced (after the first test series) sharp generalization gradients when trained and tested on this same dimension. From their results Ganz and Riesen concluded that "in some cases [generalization] follows automatically from the physiological properties of the receptor system and does not require previous experience [p. 97]." The two experiments differ procedurally in that there was little opportunity for Peterson's ducks to form an orthogonal discrimination during acquisition training; periods of S+ were separated by brief 3-sec blackout intervals. On the other hand Ganz and Riesen explicitly trained their Ss to discriminate between the presence and absence of S+. It seems possible that the different training procedures employed in the two studies resulted in markedly different degrees of stimulus control on the part of S+. Supporting this interpretation is the fact that more recent studies in which conditions were favorable for the establishment of orthogonal discriminations have reported equally steep gradients for chickens and quail raised normally and for groups raised in the dark or in monochromatic light (e.g., Malott, 1968; Rudolph, Honig, & Gerry, 1969). Previous discriminative experience with the relevant stimulus dimension does not, therefore, seem to be a necessary requirement for the appearance of normal generalization gradients.

We may summarize these paragraphs by saying that even though a stimulus is impinging on S's receptors while he is responding and is being rewarded, it may gain very little control over S's behavior; in other words, such circumstances are no guarantee that S will attend to the relevant stimulus. If the latter fails to gain stimulus control during acquisition training, flat generalization gradients will emerge during subsequent tests for generalization.

STIMULUS CONTROL (OR ATTENTION) VERSUS GENERALIZATION. It is perhaps obvious that there is a certain amount of circularity in the preceding pair of sentences. We say that unless S attends to the relevant stimulus (S+), a flat generalization gradient will be obtained, and then we use the generalization gradient itself as evidence of whether or not S attended to S+. Or, in terms of stimulus control, we maintain that a flat gradient will appear unless during acquisition, S+ gains stimulus control over S's responding. But we have only the generalization gradient itself from which to infer whether or not this control was achieved. The difficulty arises because we have two concepts—stimulus control (or attention) and the concept of a stimulus generalization gradient— and only one indicator of behavior—S's responding during generalization tests. The dilemma may be escaped by using the generalization gradient to *define* stimulus control (or attention), so that if we wish to know whether S is attending to a particular stimulus component present during acquisition, we need only apply generalization tests to get our answer.

Turning to discrimination learning for an illustration, suppose we have S discriminate between a vertical line superimposed on a green background (S+) and a horizontal line superimposed on a red background (S−). After S has achieved a discrimination, we may ask whether it is the color component that has gained stimulus control, the line-orientation component, or perhaps both. There are a number of ways in which this question may be answered (e.g., D'Amato & Fazzaro, 1966b; Reynolds, 1961a; Underwood, Ham, & Ekstrand, 1962), but a simple solution is to provide independent generalization tests for the two stimulus components. If, for example, a gradient were obtained for the color component but not for line orientation, this may be interpreted to mean that S attended to the former and not the latter, i.e., that color but not line tilt had gained stimulus control during discrimination training (cf. Heinemann, Chase, & Mandell, 1968).

As the following experiments show, however, a flat generalization gradient does not always imply failure of attention. Newman and Baron (1965) trained four groups of pigeons with a compound S+ consisting of a white vertical line superimposed on a green background. One of the two groups of interest to us received discrimination training in which S− consisted of the green background only; the other group received nondiscriminative training on S+. During generalization tests all Ss were presented with lines of varying angular orientation superimposed on the green background; i.e., generalization was assessed along the line-tilt dimension. The results were very similar to those of Jenkins and Harrison (1960). The discriminatively trained Ss produced a sharp gradient whereas the gradient of the nondiscriminative Ss was flat. Their results suggested to Newman and Baron that because color was a more "dominant" cue than the vertical line, in the absence of an appropriate discriminative procedure Ss were likely during acquisition training to attend solely to the color background.

Subsequently, however, Freeman and Thomas (1967) showed that if the green background was eliminated *during generalization tests*, a sloping gradient could indeed be obtained. Obviously this outcome would have been impossible if Ss had not attended to the vertical line during acquisition training. The best hypothesis is that in this and in the Newman and Baron study, Ss attended to both the green background and the vertical line during acquisition training, though perhaps not to the same degree. Because color is in some sense a more dominant cue for pigeons or perhaps because color achieved more stimulus control during acquisition, it and not line orientation controlled Ss' behavior during subsequent generalization tests. With the color cue removed during the test phase, the less potent line-orientation cue could express itself.

In the light of these results, which were recently verified by Newman and Benefield (1968), the significance of a flat generalization gradient must be relaxed to indicate either that the dimension in question failed to achieve stimulus control during acquisition or that S's behavior during generalization tests was under the control of a more dominant cue and hence not sensitive to variations in the manipulated dimension. One way of deciding between these alternatives, of course, is to identify the prepotent cues and eliminate or neutralize them during generalization tests.

Without pursuing the suggestion further, it is worth pointing out that the present problem is closely related to the topic of stimulus selection, which is discussed in detail in the next chapter. We shall also discuss there the role of attention in discrimination learning, and we shall be somewhat more precise about what we mean by "attention" and the extent to which this concept is equivalent to "stimulus control."

Amount of Acquisition Training

If a response is conditioned to S+ under appropriate experimental conditions, we know that the response will generalize to related stimuli. An interesting question is whether we can reduce the amount of generalization obtained by increasing the level of acquisition training. In different terms, will increased acquisition training develop a discrimination between S+ and physically similar stimuli? It was Pavlov's view, based on the failure to obtain such a discrimination even after more than 1,000 conditioning trials, that discriminative behavior was not likely to be established by this means. Subsequent research has supported Pavlov's position, at least for excitatory gradients established under positive reinforcement. The usual finding is that higher acquisition levels lead to higher absolute generalization gradients, i.e., to a greater amount of absolute generalization (e.g., Hearst & Koresko, 1968; Hovland, 1937; Margolius, 1955; Spiker, 1956).

There is a question, however, whether raised generalization gradients necessarily imply that discrimination is impaired or not enhanced. Hearst and Koresko (1968) have reported that increased acquisition training serves to increase the *slope* of the absolute generalization gradient. Conceivably, a very steep slope might imply heightened discrimination even though the gradient generated by extensive acquisition training is everywhere higher than the flatter gradient which arises from a lesser amount of training. Kalish and Haber (1965), for example, found that they could accurately predict discriminative performance from absolute generalization gradients by simply extracting from the gradients the ratio of responding to the future $S-$ and $S+$. Thus during generalization tests a highly trained group might very well respond more, in absolute terms, to a pair of stimuli than a lesser trained group; but if the appropriate ratio of responses to the two stimuli were smaller in the former group, it should, generalizing from Kalish and Haber's results, acquire a conventional discrimination based on the same stimuli faster than the latter group.

The lesson of this illustration is plain. In order to make sensible inferences concerning discriminability from stimulus generalization gradients, one needs to know which properties of generalization gradients are relevant for predicting discriminative performance. This is largely an empirical matter, one in which, unfortunately, relatively little headway has been made.

The effect of amount of acquisition training on relative generalization gradients is not at all clear. At times a nonmonotonic (first increasing then decreasing) function is found (e.g., Hovland, 1937) and occasionally a monotonically increasing function is reported (Margolius, 1955); recently the range of possibilities was brought near completion with a report of *decreasing* relative generalization with increased acquisition training (Hearst & Koresko, 1968). According to the Kalish and Haber predictive criterion, this last result clearly implies increasing ability to discriminate with increased acquisition training.

In spite of the somewhat conflicting results, it is apparent that for a response established with positive reinforcement, increasing the level of acquisition training is an ineffective means of developing a discrimination between $S+$ and related stimuli. Explicit discrimination training is far more efficient.

As a final observation, in the case of an "active" avoidance response, higher levels of acquisition training may decrease the amount of observed generalization, absolute as well as relative (e.g., Hoffeld, 1962; Thompson, 1958, 1959). The basis of this disparity is yet to be discovered.

Drive (Motivation) Level

DEDUCTIONS FROM THE HULL-SPENCE CONDITIONING THEORY. According to the conditioning theory of Hull-Spence, excitatory potential (E) is related to drive (D) and habit strength (H) as follows: $E = D \times H$. Although we did not make the point during earlier discussion (Chap. 7), it is apparent that the E in this equation refers to the excitatory potential that is available at $S+$. If a stimulus other than $S+$ is presented to S, the habit strength associated with the generalized stimulus will be less than that associated with the positive stimulus. Indeed Hull (1952) provided an exact equation by means of which one could calculate the "generalized" habit strength given only the distance in

JND units separating *S*+ and the test stimulus. In any event, because generalized habit strength is assumed to vary with the distance of the test stimulus from *S*+ and not with drive level, two "gradients" of excitatory potential generated from the same set of stimuli but under different drive levels will be related to each other by a multiplicative constant. Thus if high drive (D_h) is related to low drive (D_l) by $D_h = cD_l$, the corresponding reaction potentials will be similarly related for all stimuli, i.e., $E_h = cE_l$ (see Fig. 10-5).

In the case of *excitatory potential* gradients, then, the effects of manipulating drive level are apparent. First, the higher the drive level, the higher the gradient of excitatory potential. Second, as illustrated in Fig. 10-5, the slope of the gradient is made steeper by increasing drive level. Finally, gradients of excitatory potential generated by different drive levels are multiplicatively related to each other. Thus the upper gradient in Fig. 10-5 is obtained from the lower by multiplication by the constant 1.2.

When, however, one turns to the relevance of the previous deductions for *empirical* generalization gradients, various complications are encountered. In

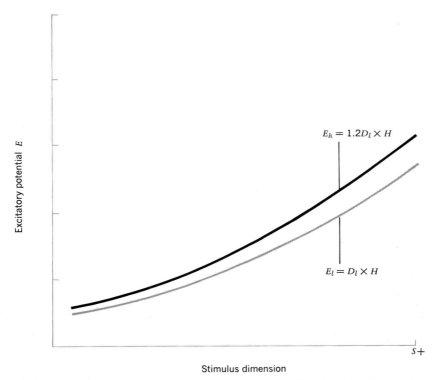

Fig. 10-5. Gradients of excitatory potential generated under high drive (D_h) and low drive (D_l) in accordance with the Hull-Spence theory. It is assumed that $D_h = 1.2 D_l$. Thus for any stimulus value the excitatory potential obtained under high drive is 1.2 times that generated by low drive (see text).

the first place a number of "boundary" conditions, such as response competition, response threshold, and drive stimulus effects, can sharply alter the deductions flowing from the Hull-Spence formulation (Storms & Broen, 1966). But let us neglect these variables, assuming their effects are minimal. Another critical factor is the relationship that is presumed to hold between the empirical dependent variable employed and the theoretical quantity E, which of course is unobservable. On the assumption that the dependent variable is proportional to E, the deductions given in terms of reaction potential stand as well for empirical generalization gradients. That is to say, the absolute generalization gradient will be higher the greater the drive level (i.e., the higher the drive, the greater the amount of generalization); the slope of the absolute generalization gradient will increase with higher drive levels; and, finally, generalization gradients obtained under different levels of drive will be related to each other by multiplicative constants. If the dependent variable and reaction potential are linearly related, as is assumed for a number of behavioral measures (cf. Spence, 1956), the first two implications still hold but the applicability of the third will depend upon the magnitude of the additive constant.

Unfortunately, investigators have not always paid sufficient attention to the contingencies involved in drawing legitimate implications from the Hull-Spence theory (cf. Prokasy, 1967; Storms & Broen, 1966). As a consequence, empirical results obtained from studies of generalization sometimes have a questionable bearing on the theory.

In addition to theoretical expectations concerning the effects of drive level on stimulus generalization gradients, the topic has been of considerable interest to psychologists because of its relevance for a number of related research areas, such as conflict behavior (e.g., Epstein & Fenz, 1965; Miller, 1959), displacement (e.g., Miller & Kraeling, 1952), and the discriminative behavior of schizophrenics (e.g., Broen, Storms, & Goldberg, 1963).

SOME EMPIRICAL RESULTS. Drive level has been manipulated by means of a wide range of operations, including food deprivation, loud auditory stimuli, shock and threat of shock, squeezing a dynamometer, and employment of such selection procedures as diagnostic classification and paper and pencil tests of anxiety level. In spite of this diversity in the operational definition of "drive," the experimental data consistently show that over a wide range of motivational levels, *absolute* generalization increases with increasing drive (e.g., Kalish & Haber, 1965; Newman & Grice, 1965; Rosenbaum, 1953; Thomas & King, 1959). Thus the first of the three implications arising from the Hull-Spence theory has earned a fair amount of confirmation.

The deduction that the slope of the absolute generalization gradient should be positively related to drive level is less well established. Newman and Grice (1965) and Porter (1962), among others, have reported supporting data, but other investigators have obtained results inconsistent with this implication (e.g., Thomas & King, 1959).

As one might expect, the most stringent deduction—that generalization gradients obtained at different motivational levels ought to be related to each other by a multiplicative constant—has been buffeted most by the empirical evidence. Jenkins, Pascal, and Walker (1958) found that high-drive Ss yielded a flatter relative generalization gradient than pigeons tested under low drive, and Thomas and King (1959) reported, again for pigeons, a nonmonotonic relationship between drive level and slope of the relative generalization gradients. The expected multiplicative relationship was found by Coate (1964), but this was for generalization gradients obtained after discrimination training.

Thus it appears that the deduction from the Hull-Spence theory which depends least on one's choice of response measure and boundary conditions—namely, that in a noncompetitive situation amount of absolute generalization is monotonically related to drive level—is well supported by the empirical data. The failure of more refined predictions to find substantiation in empirical data may reflect either a basic deficiency in the theory or incorrect accounting of the effects of boundary conditions and related factors. The difficulty involved in measuring such variables quantitatively has been pointed out by Storms and Broen (1966), and until they have been surmounted, the relevance of generalization data for refined predictions flowing from the Hull-Spence theory remains uncertain.

POSSIBLE PERCEPTUAL EFFECTS OF MOTIVATION LEVEL. Apparently drive manipulations may also have perceptual effects which contribute to the shape of the obtained generalization gradient. For example, Zajonc and Cross (1965) trained two groups of pigeons—one group at 70 percent of its free-feeding body weight and the other at 90 percent—to discriminate a 10-mm circular spot of light from 4- and 16-mm spots. After training was completed, the deprivation states in the two groups were reversed. Generalization gradients (actually, "postdiscrimination" gradients) were then obtained for stimuli ranging from 6 to 14 mm. It was found that in the group which was shifted from low to high drive, there was a displacement of responding toward the larger stimuli; that is, more responses were given to the 12- and 14-mm stimuli than to the 6- and 8-mm stimuli. The reverse was true for the group which was shifted from high to low drive. These results, as well as others like them, have been interpreted to mean that the stimulus component of drive influences S's perception of the eliciting stimulus, so that in a sense a 14-mm spot of light is perceived somewhat differently under high and low drives (Zajonc & Dorfman, 1964).

Schedules of Reinforcement

One of the most powerful determiners of stimulus generalization gradients is the reinforcement schedule employed during acquisition training. Hearst, Koresko, and Poppen (1964) trained pigeons on either a 1-min VI or a 6-sec DRL schedule to peck a vertical line ($S+$). As the relative generalization gradients

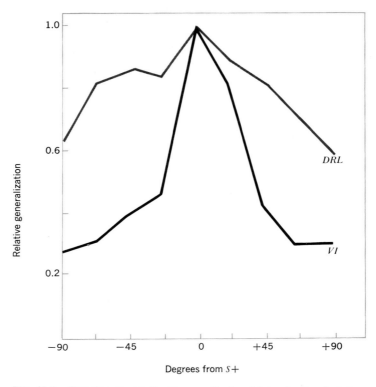

Fig. 10-6. Relative generalization gradients obtained after training on a *DRL* 6 or a *VI* 1 schedule; the stimulus dimension is line tilt. Relative generalization was calculated by dividing the number of responses made at the test stimulus by the number executed at *S+*. (SOURCE: E. Hearst, M. B. Koresko, and R. Poppen. Stimulus generalization and the response-reinforcement contingency. *Journal of the Experimental Analysis of Behavior*, 1964, **7**, 369–380. Copyright 1964 by the Society for the Experimental Analysis of Behavior, Inc. and used by permission.)

of Fig. 10-6 show, the *DRL* group later displayed a much flatter gradient than the group trained on the *VI* schedule. In a second experiment these investigators reported an equally marked effect for different *VI* schedules ranging from *VI* 30 sec to *VI* 4 min (Fig. 10-7). Subsequently Thomas and Switalski (1966) reported that a group of pigeons trained on a *VR* 40 schedule (*S+* was the illumination of the response key with 550-m*μ* illumination) displayed a flatter generalization gradient than a second group trained on a comparable *VI* schedule.

The dramatic change that can be wrought in stimulus generalization gradients by schedules of reinforcement demands that this class of variables be closely scrutinized when interpreting generalization data. It would seem to detract from the plausibility of hypotheses concerning universal properties of

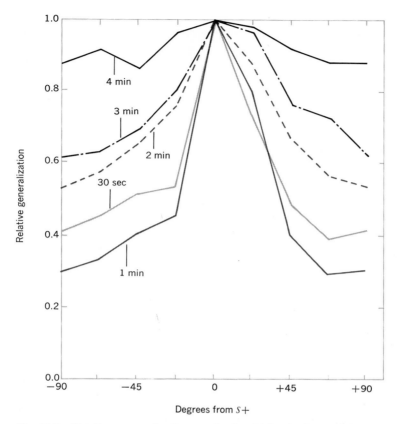

Fig. 10-7. Relative generalization gradients obtained after training on various *VI* schedules. In all cases $S+$ was a vertical line. (SOURCE: E. Hearst, M. B. Koresko, and R. Poppen. Stimulus generalization and the response-reinforcement contingency. *Journal of the Experimental Analysis of Behavior*, 1964, **7**, 369–380. Copyright 1964 by the Society for the Experimental Analysis of Behavior, Inc. and used by permission.)

generalization gradients, for example, that "avoidance" gradients are normally steeper than "approach" gradients (cf. Hearst, 1969).

EXTEROCEPTIVE VERSUS INTEROCEPTIVE STIMULUS CONTROL.   As for the possible reasons why certain schedules produce relatively flat gradients, it has been suggested that the basis might reside in a splitting of behavioral control between exteroceptive and interoceptive stimuli. In a *DRL* schedule, for example, stimulus control of *S*'s responding is exerted not only by $S+$ but also by the temporal cues by means of which *S* discriminates the *DRL* interval. When $S+$ is altered during subsequent generalization tests, a relatively flat gradient results because the other component of the stimulus complex which controls *S*'s responding, the temporal cues, remains undisturbed. A similar argument has been advanced to account for the flatter gradients obtained with ratio schedules, which "make proprioceptive feedback from rapid responding a positive discriminative cue for additional responding [Thomas & Switalski, 1966, p. 236]." To apply this interpretation to the finding that long *VI* schedules result in flat gradients, one must assume that such schedules generate controlling internal stimuli, a possibility supported by the observation of Hearst et al. that stereotype "mediating" response chains were much more likely to develop on long *VI* schedules than on short *VI* schedules.

Another possibility is that the flatter gradients obtained with certain schedules are the result of the fusing of excitatory and inhibitory gradients. There is a fair amount of evidence supporting the notion that certain schedules of positive reinforcement possess aversive properties. For example, under certain conditions S will terminate discriminative stimuli associated with long *FR* schedules (Thompson, 1964; see also Guttman, 1959). In common-sense terms, if a schedule forces S to work very hard for reinforcement or requires uncongenial behavior—such as withholding responding, as in a *DRL* schedule— S may work to obtain the reward which he requires, but he may not like it.

Figure 10-8 (upper panel) presents the theoretical excitatory and inhibitory gradients which could result in a situation where the schedule of positive reinforcement contained an aversive component. Assuming that the behavior observed in generalization tests is generated by the gradient obtained by subtracting the inhibitory from the excitatory gradient (Fig. 10-8, lower panel), one can account for the flatter generalization gradients which appear with such schedules. Interestingly, in the Thomas and Switalski (1966) study, although the *VR* and *VI* schedules were arranged so that the same number of reinforcements were received, the group operating under the *VR* schedule responded on the last day of acquisition training with approximately twice the number of responses produced by the *VI* Ss. Thus for the same amount of reinforcement they expended twice the effort of the *VI* subjects.

If the present hypothesis—which has been suggested before (e.g., Hearst et al., 1964)—is correct, one should be able to obtain a series of increasingly flatter gradients by punishing the instrumental response during acquisition with progressively higher levels of shock intensity.

Training-test Interval

The time interval separating completion of acquisition training and generalization tests has also come under investigation. Perkins and Weyant (1958), working with rats on a straight alley, found an increase in absolute and relative generalization when a period of 1 week intervened between training and generalization tests. This finding was extended by Thomas and Lopez (1962), who reported a flattened relative generalization gradient for pigeons that experienced a training-test delay interval of only 24 hr; extending the delay to 7 days did not, however, flatten the gradient further. Obviously this is a potent relevant variable which must be controlled in stimulus generalization investigations.

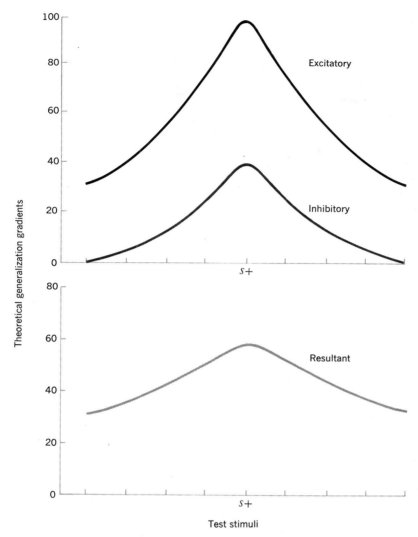

Fig. 10-8. The upper panel presents theoretical excitatory and inhibitory generalization gradients assumed to occur in a schedule of reinforcement incorporating an aversive component. In such a case the observed generalization would presumably be a function of the resultant gradient (lower panel), obtained by subtracting the inhibitory gradient from the excitatory.

Avoidance Gradients

Avoidance gradients have spurred much interest because of their relevance for Miller's analysis of conflict behavior (e.g., Miller, 1944, 1959, 1961). A central assumption in Miller's theory is that ordinarily "approach" generalization gradients are flatter than "avoidance" gradients. By "approach" Miller initially meant the tendency of S to move toward a desired goal. Thus in present terminology, approach gradients correspond closely to excitatory gradients established under positive reinforcement. However, by "avoidance" Miller meant the tendency to go away from a feared or an unpleasant object or situation. It would thus appear that passive avoidance—punishment—is a more congruent conditioning paradigm for this aspect of Miller's theory than active avoidance conditioning.

A study by Miller and Kraeling (1952) illustrates this point and reveals something of Miller's theory as well. Rats were trained to run down an alley to obtain food; next, Ss were shocked each time they touched a shield which contained the reward, until they stopped. A conflict thus established, Ss were finally tested on alleys which differed in the degree of their physical similarity to the training alley. The theoretical deduction under test was that if the "avoidance" gradient is steeper than that of approach, Ss will be increasingly likely to venture down the alley and touch the food shield the more different the test alley is from the training alley; the deduction was confirmed in the present case. The major point being made here, however, is that avoidance gradients, as they enter conflict theory, are perhaps better conceived of as punishment gradients. The Ss in the present illustration were punished for touching the food shield, and the generalization of the induced response suppression was under study.

RELATIVE STEEPNESS OF APPROACH AND AVOIDANCE GRADIENTS.   Studies which have employed an active avoidance response to compare the steepness of approach and avoidance gradients have led to sharply divergent results. Using a Sidman avoidance procedure, Hearst (1962) reported extremely flat avoidance gradients for both monkeys and rats, whereas excitatory gradients based on S^{R+} (approach gradients) were quite steep. Hoffman and Fleshler (1963), wishing to make their acquisition procedures comparable for the approach and avoidance responses, employed a discriminated avoidance response in lieu of the Sidman procedure. Their results were just the opposite of Hearst's; the approach generalization gradient was considerably flatter than the avoidance gradient.

One does not have to search far for possible explanations of this disparity (cf. Hearst, 1969). In the Hearst study there probably was a wide difference in the degree to which the extinction of the test period weakened the approach and avoidance responses, inasmuch as it is much more difficult to discriminate termination of (negative) reinforcement in a Sidman schedule than termination of positive reinforcement in a *VI* schedule of moderate duration. Perhaps more important, recall from our discussion of the effects of schedules of reinforcement on generalization gradients that one interpretation of the flatter gradients obtained with *DRL* schedules was that schedules for which internal cues are an important part of the discriminative complex are likely to show less generalization decrement than those for which the major discriminative cues arise from external sources. Because of the temporal discrimination required in Sidman avoidance, it is reasonable to suppose that internal cues are an important part of the discriminative complex of this schedule. In the Hoffman and Fleshler study, on the other hand, a discriminative avoidance response was employed, which removed the dependence on internal cues.

Our discussion of the profound effects which different schedules of reinforcement can have on generalization gradients makes it apparent that any statement concerning the relative steepness of approach and avoidance gradients must take this variable into account. It is pointless to compare approach and avoidance (passive or active) gradients unless the schedules of reinforcement by means of which the instrumental responses are established are made as equivalent as possible. And, of course, other variables known to influence the shape of generalization gradients must also be controlled. We have seen that drive level can have important effects on the generalization gradient. Thus results obtained from a study comparing approach and avoidance gradients at arbitrary drive levels may simply reflect differences in motivation rather than any fundamental properties of such gradients.

CONFLICT AND ANXIETY INHIBITION. While on the topic of the bearing of approach and avoidance gradients on theories of conflict, we might mention that Epstein and Fenz (1965), in an interesting application of Miller's theory, found it necessary to invoke a third generalization gradient—a gradient of inhibition of fear or anxiety. They studied two groups of individuals who parachuted for sport, one experienced and the other inexperienced. The subjects gave self-ratings of their experienced approach and avoidance tendencies concerning the jump for various periods spanning about a week before the event. Although they found some evidence supporting the notion that the avoidance gradient was steeper than the approach, the most significant result was that the point of maximal avoidance occurred in both groups, not at, but *before* the time of the actual jump. In the case of the experienced parachutists, avoidance reached a maximum on the morning before the jump and decreased to a relatively low level by the time they were waiting in the airplane to parachute. Maximum avoidance was reached by the novices at the time they received the "ready" signal, a short time before the actual jump. These results suggested to Epstein and Fenz that a gradient of inhibition of anxiety, steeper than the avoidance gradient, lopped off part of the latter, thereby shifting the location of maximum avoidance to a point before the goal act. Presumably, in the experienced parachutist, the gradient of inhibition developed faster than in the novice. An interesting research problem is whether such a gradient of inhibition of fear—or at least the evidence on which this concept is based—can be demonstrated in the laboratory.

INHIBITORY STIMULUS GENERALIZATION GRADIENTS

Inhibitory generalization gradients arise from stimuli which exert inhibitory control, the latter established either through nonreinforcement or through negative reinforcers. We may distinguish three types of inhibitory gradients defined in terms of the operations which produce them. *Extinction* gradients are generated by nonreinforcement; *punishment* gradients are established by response-contingent negative reinforcement, and *CER* (conditioned-emotional-response or conditioned-suppression) gradients are established by response-noncontingent negative reinforcement. Because inhibitory gradients reflect the extent of inhibitory control possessed by the various test stimuli, the shape of such gradients bears an inverse relationship to excitatory gradients. A minimum amount of response strength ordinarily occurs at the "training" stimulus, with response strength increasing as the test stimuli become further removed from the CS.

Extinction Gradients

Gradients of extinction have played a central role in the discrimination learning theory of Spence (1937) and Hull (1943), as well as in other theoretical endeavors. It is assumed that when nonreinforcement is associated with a particular stimulus (S—), that stimulus develops a tendency to inhibit the instrumental response (inhibitory control); moreover, the inhibition is assumed to generalize in much the same way as excitatory tendencies generalize, so that the further away physically a stimulus is from S—, the less inhibition it exerts.

Obtaining extinction gradients presents certain problems, however, especially if one wishes to make direct comparisons between extinction and excitatory gradients. In one procedure devised to obtain extinction gradients, Ss are initially trained to respond to a number of different stimuli on the same dimension (S+s). Following this training, Ss are extinguished on one of the S+s; later they are tested for generalization of the extinction experience. As an illustration, Honig (1961) trained pigeons to peck at 13 stimuli ranging from 510 to 630 mμ in steps of 10 mμ. Subsequently Ss were extinguished on 570 mμ and then tested for generalization of extinction across the 13 stimuli. Although Honig obtained reliable extinction gradients, they turned out to be extremely shallow in comparison to comparable gradients of excitation.

EXTINCTION VERSUS EXCITATORY GRADIENTS. The latter result, which was obtained a number of times, raised the general question of whether, as a rule, extinction generalizes more broadly than excitation. Put in terms of gradients, are extinction gradients generally flatter than corresponding excitatory gradients? It is obvious that before this question can be meaningfully answered, one must devise procedures for obtaining excitatory and extinction gradients which are comparable in all important aspects. Although this task is more difficult than one might initially assume (cf. H. M. Jenkins, 1956a), it is not too difficult to devise training conditions for extinction and excitatory gradients that are much more comparable than was the case in the previous illustration.

A number of investigators, independently and at just about the same time, hit upon the idea of using an orthogonal discrimination to obtain relatively pure extinction gradients (Honig, Boneau, Burstein, & Pennypacker, 1963; Jenkins & Harrison, 1962; Schwartzbaum & Kellicutt, 1962). In the Honig et al. experiment, one group of pigeons was trained with a vertical line as $S-$ and a blank response key as $S+$; a second group was trained with these conditions reversed. This, it will be recalled, is what we termed an "orthogonal" discrimination. The strategy was to vary, in both groups, the angle of line tilt in subsequent generalization tests, thus generating a gradient of extinction in the first group and a gradient of excitation in the second. Note that, at least with respect to procedures, the experimental conditions are completely comparable in the two groups. Furthermore, because all test stimuli are lines of different angles of tilt, they must be considered equally "distant" from the blank key. Consequently the extinction gradient should not be influenced by the excitation that was developed to the blank key, nor should the excitatory gradient be affected in any important way by the inhibitory effects accruing to the blank key that served as $S-$ in the second group of Ss.

The results of the two replications of the Honig et al. study are shown in Fig. 10-9 in terms of relative generalization gradients. If the excitatory and extinction gradients were exactly the same form but the inverse of each other, averaging the two gradients would produce a horizontal line. As may be seen from the figure, such averaging does, in the case of the first replication, very nearly produce a horizontal line. This is less so in the second replication, where the departure of the average of the two gradients from a horizontal line signifies that the extinction gradient is shallower than the gradient of excitation. Honig et al. attribute the latter result to a tendency of the extinction gradient to flatten rapidly with successive generalization tests. When the early test periods of the second replication are considered alone, the extinction gradient more nearly resembles the excitatory gradient.

It would appear, then, that when acquisition conditions are closely comparable, excitatory and extinction generalization gradients themselves are comparable in general form, at least for the line-tilt dimension. Unfortunately, however, this conclusion apparently does not generalize easily to other dimensions. Schwartzbaum and Kellicutt (1962) performed a very similar experiment using frequency of a tone in place of line tilt as the dimension along which generalization gradients were obtained. They found the extinction gradient to be substantially flatter than the corresponding excitatory gradient. Extinction gradients were obtained under very similar conditions by Jenkins and Harrison (1962), and though they did not independently obtain excitatory gradients, their gradients of extinction were extremely shallow—much shallower than excitatory gradients obtained under similar conditions by these investigators in an earlier study (1960). It seems that ensuring comparable training conditions by no means guarantees that equivalent excitatory and extinction generalization gradients will be obtained. Possibly extinction does tend to generalize more than excitation, or perhaps the difficulty lies in the methods by which we measure excitatory and inhibitory generalization gradients (H. M. Jenkins, 1965a, pp. 58–59).

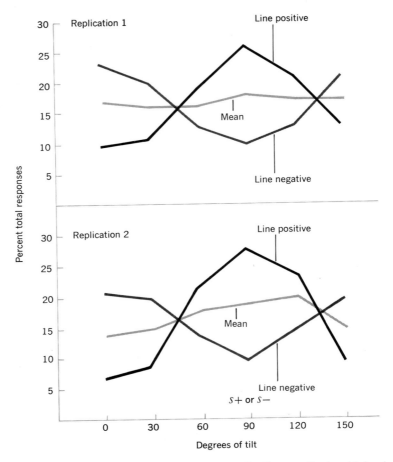

Fig. 10-9. Excitatory and extinction generalization gradients obtained under comparable acquisition procedures (see text). (SOURCE: W. K. Honig, C. A. Boneau, K. R. Burstein, and H. S. Pennypacker. Positive and negative generalization gradients obtained after equivalent training conditions. *Journal of Comparative and Physiological Psychology,* 1963, **56,** 111–116. Copyright 1963 by the American Psychological Association and used by permission.)

Punishment Gradients

In principle, punishment gradients can be obtained in much the same way as Honig et al. (1963) obtained extinction gradients. Using an orthogonal discrimination between a blank key and a vertical line, one group of Ss could be trained with the former as the punished stimulus and the latter as the unpunished cue; the relationship is reversed for a second group of Ss. Subsequent generalization gradients produced by lines of different angles ought to reveal properties of the punishment gradient and be procedurally comparable to the corresponding approach gradient. Apparently this experiment has yet to be performed. In most relevant experiments, Ss are tested in the presence of both the punished and the unpunished stimuli.

As an illustration, Hoffman and Fleshler (1965) sought to obtain comparable punishment and CER gradients by yoking their Ss in such a manner that the frequency and temporal distribution of shock were identical in the two groups during acquisition training. Both groups, pecking for food on a VI 3 schedule, experienced shock in the presence of a 1,000-Hz tone but not in its absence, and, of course, the shock was response-contingent in the first group and noncontingent in the second. By the end of acquisition training, Ss in both groups were responding at a low rate during tone periods. Generalization gradients were then obtained by presenting tones of different frequency (but without shock) as well as periods of no tone. It turned out that the CER gradient was substantially flatter than the punishment gradient; also, response suppression extinguished very rapidly in the punishment group, whereas it showed little decrement in the CER subjects (Fig. 10-10).

PUNISHMENT GRADIENTS AND ORTHOGONAL DISCRIMINATION TRAINING. More recently Honig (1966b) has shown that, like excitatory gradients, some degree of orthogonal discrimination (during the punishment experience) seems to be necessary if a punishment gradient is to be obtained. Like Hoffman and Fleshler (1965), he found extremely rapid recovery from the effects of punishment during the punishment-free generalization tests. There probably are two reasons for the rapid dissipation of the suppressive effects of punishment; one is the relatively low shock level employed. Perhaps more important, during acquisition training punishment was administered on a CRF schedule whereas positive reinforcement was intermittent. Be that as it may, there seems little doubt that the inhibitory effects of punishment generalize in an orderly fashion, provided the punishment cue gains discriminative control during acquisition training.

CER Gradients

CER or conditioned suppression generalization gradients are generated around a discriminative cue which has been associated with noncontingent negative reinforcement. We have already seen that such gradients are much flatter than comparable punishment gradients and that the effects of noncontingent negative reinforcement are slow to extinguish (Hoffman & Fleshler, 1965).

LONG-TERM CER GRADIENTS. Recently Hoffman, Selekman, and Fleshler (1966a) presented a 5-year history of four pigeons that dramatically confirms these observations. The birds, trained to peck for food on a VI 2 schedule, were periodically presented with a 1,000-Hz tone which terminated in shock, until they no longer pecked in the presence of the tone. They were then given generalization tests—with shock discontinued—for 12 sessions. Left undisturbed

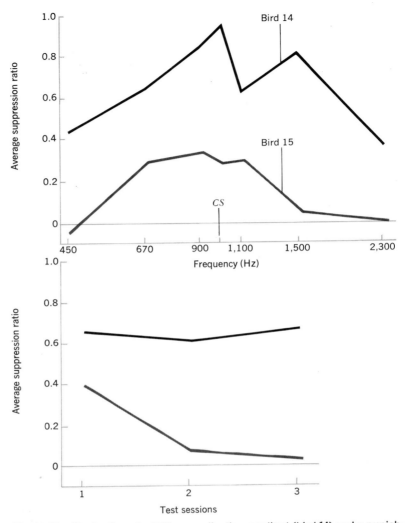

Fig. 10-10. Illustration of a *CER* generalization gradient (bird 14) and a punishment gradient (bird 15) obtained under comparable experimental conditions (upper panel). The dependent variable, average suppression ratio, is a measure of the degree to which the test stimulus suppresses the instrumental response. Complete suppression yields a value of 1.0 and no suppression a value of 0; negative values occur if *S* responds more in the presence of the test stimulus than in the comparable control interval.

The lower panel of the figure shows the course of suppression over the three test sessions. Note that in the punished *S* suppression extinguishes rapidly whereas in the *CER* bird virtually no reduction in suppression occurs during the three sessions. (SOURCE: H. S. Hoffman and M. Fleshler. Stimulus aspects of aversive controls: The effects of response contingent shock. *Journal of the Experimental Analysis of Behavior,* 1965, **8,** 89–96. Copyright 1965 by the Society for the Experimental Analysis of Behavior, Inc. and used by permission.)

for a period of 2.5 years, they were then retested for 20 sessions. There were several noteworthy results. First, even after the 2.5-year interruption, a clear *CER* gradient was obtained. The gradient, initially shallow, gradually sharpened with repeated testing until finally Ss suppressed only to the training tone (1,000 Hz). Apparently, the repeated generalization tests led to improved discrimination between the training and test tones. Second, the ability of the 1,000-Hz tone to suppress responding survived repeated testing and the 2.5-year interruption, extinguishing extremely slowly.

At the termination of this phase, Ss were given "shock stress" in the experimental apparatus, which consisted of shocks delivered during the time-out periods (periods of total darkness). Because for a pigeon shutting off the lights in the experimental chamber is equivalent to shutting off the bird, these shocks were associated with neither the tone stimuli nor S's responding. Nevertheless, the shock stress immediately reinstituted the *CER* generalization gradient, and increased substantially the amount of suppression elicited by the training stimulus. Although response suppression was restricted to the 1,000-Hz tone when shock stress was terminated, the gradient reappeared after a 1.5-year interruption, again showing that *CER* effects dissipate little with the passage of long periods of time.

INTERACTION BETWEEN GENERALIZATION GRADIENTS

Conceptually we can distinguish between an *empirical* generalization gradient which is based on a single underlying gradient and one which is the resultant of two or more such gradients. Empirical excitatory gradients, whether based on positive or negative reinforcement, usually fall into the first category. In both cases only a single type of reinforcement is employed in the training conditions which generate the observed generalization gradient. This is less true for inhibitory gradients.

We have seen that with appropriate orthogonal discrimination training, one can produce relatively pure extinction gradients (Honig et al., 1963). But the punishment and *CER* gradients obtained to date are better considered resultants of interactions between underlying excitatory and inhibitory gradients. The reason for this is that in all the cases we have considered, the training stimulus was associated with both positive and negative reinforcement. Thus the response strength observed during generalization tests was necessarily determined jointly by the amount of excitation and inhibition that generalized to each test stimulus. It is a fair guess that "pure" punishment gradients would be far shallower than those observed thus far.

We may distinguish three kinds of interaction among generalization gradients: summation of like gradients, interaction between excitatory and inhibitory gradients associated with *different* stimuli (e.g., postdiscrimination gradients), and interaction between excitatory and inhibitory gradients associated with the *same* stimulus. We have already pointed out that punishment and *CER* gradients fall into the last category, and we shall have nothing further to say on this score except that such interaction forms a theoretical basis for a good deal of research in conflict behavior.

Summation of Generalization Gradients

The major point of interest here is whether overlapping (underlying) generalization gradients summate to determine response strength at a test stimulus. Suppose, for example, that a pigeon is reinforced for pecking at 540 and 550 mμ. We would expect an underlying generalization gradient to be generated around both these stimuli with the gradients overlapping in the central region. If the response strength of the test stimuli in the region of overlap is determined by some sort of summation of the two underlying gradients, we ought to observe more responding to such stimuli than would be predicted from a single generalization gradient established at either 540 or 550 mμ. Indeed, it might even be possible to observe a higher rate of responding to a stimulus *between* 540 and 550 mμ than at either of the latter two values, a stimulus that never was presented during acquisition training. If, on the other hand, the overlapping gradients do not summate but instead response strength at all test stimuli is determined by the more dominant of the two gradients, neither of the above possibilities would hold true.

Although there are exceptions (e.g., Kalish & Guttman, 1959), most relevant experiments support the idea of some kind of summation of excitatory gradients (e.g., Blough, 1969; Carterette, 1961; Kalish & Guttman, 1957; LaBerge & Martin, 1964). Recently, Hoffman, Selekman, and Fleshler (1966b) reported evidence that inhibitory (*CER*) gradients also show summation. Although we know little about the precise manner in which summation takes place, the evidence favors the view that some sort of summation usually takes place when gradients of like form overlap. [See Blough (1969) for an interpretation of summation in terms of signal detection theory.]

Postdiscrimination Gradients

Of the interactions among gradients that involve excitation and inhibition associated with different stimuli, the *postdiscrimination* gradient (*PDG*) is perhaps the most thoroughly investigated. A postdiscrimination gradient is a generalization gradient obtained after discrimination training. Hence, the interaction in question is usually between an excitatory gradient centering around $S+$ and an extinction gradient centering around $S-$. Less often *PDG*s are obtained after discrimination training in which both stimuli are reinforced but with unequal reward "density."

SPENCE'S THEORY OF DISCRIMINATION LEARNING, PDGS, AND THE "PEAK SHIFT." The discrimination theory of Spence (1937) provided much of the theoretical thrust for studying *PDG*s. According to his formulation, discrimination training (between two stimuli on the same physical continuum) results in the establishment of a gradient of excitation around S+ and an overlapping gradient of inhibition centering on S−. The tendency of S to respond to any stimulus along the relevant stimulus dimension is determined by the "net" excitatory strength, obtained by subtracting the inhibition accruing to that stimulus from the corresponding excitation. One triumph of the theory was that it was able to predict "transposition" behavior, i.e., that a subject trained with, for example, the larger of two stimuli as S+ would, when presented with two test stimuli other than those used in training, continue to choose the larger of the pair though it might be the former S− (see Fig. 10-11). There is now a sizable literature on transposition, which has been recently reviewed in some detail by Riley (1968, Chap. 3) and Reese (1968). Suffice it to say that, while the theory's accomplishments must be acknowledged, the facts of transposition are too complex to be handled fully by Spence's analysis.

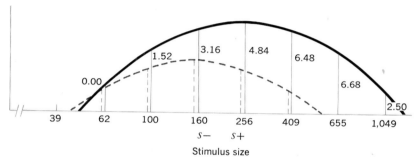

Fig. 10-11. Illustration of Spence's theory of discrimination learning based on algebraic summation of excitatory and extinction generalization gradients. The values on the abscissa indicate stimulus size in square centimeters, scaled in logarithmic units. The solid line represents the gradient of excitation generated around S+, and the dotted line represents the gradient of extinction developed around S−. It is assumed that the excitatory strength accruing to any other stimulus on the dimension is a function of the algebraic sum of the two gradients, i.e., inhibition subtracted from excitation. The numbers which appear near the vertical lines indicate the "net" or "effective" excitatory strength obtained by this operation.

Observe that although S+ is the larger of the two discriminanda, if, after discrimination training had proceeded to the point where the gradients of excitation and extinction achieved the values shown in the figure, S were presented with S+ and the 409 cm² stimulus, he should choose the latter. This follows because the net excitatory strength for the 409 cm² stimulus is 6.48 as compared to 4.84 for S+. Similarly, if S were presented a test pair consisting of the 100 and 160 cm² stimuli, he should choose the latter even though it was the S− of discrimination training. These are instances of "transposition" or "relational" behavior. Note, however, that relational responding would break down if S were presented the test pair 655 and 1,049 cm². (SOURCE: K. W. Spence. The differential response in animals to stimuli varying within a single dimension. *Psychological Review*, 1937, **44**, 430–444. Copyright 1937 by the American Psychological Association and used by permission.)

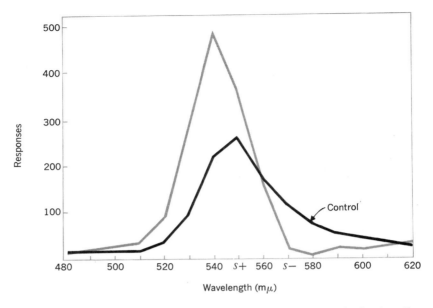

Fig. 10-12. The dark line (Control) is a generalization gradient obtained on the wavelength dimension after training with 550 mμ as $S+$. The light line is a post-discrimination generalization gradient obtained after discrimination training with 550 mμ as $S+$ and 570 mμ as $S-$. (SOURCE: H. M. Hanson. Effects of discrimination training on stimulus generalization. *Journal of Experimental Psychology,* 1959, **58**, 321–334. Copyright 1959 by the American Psychological Association and used by permission.)

Hanson (1959) put the discrimination theory of Spence to direct test by obtaining postdiscrimination gradients from pigeons who had mastered a wavelength discrimination. His results, a portion of which appear in Fig. 10-12, support certain aspects of the theory while disconfirming others. Note, first of all, that in the group receiving discrimination training, the point of maximum generalization (the mode of the generalization gradient) is not at $S+$ but rather is shifted to the left, i.e., away from $S-$. This feature of PDGs, called the "peak shift," has stimulated considerable research interest in recent years.[2] Both the peak shift and the sharper slope of the PDG (compared with a control gradient) in the region of $S-$, are in keeping with Spence's analysis. (This may be checked by constructing a PDG from the net excitatory values given in Fig. 10-11.) On the other hand, Spence's theory does not account for the height of the PDG, which, according to the subtraction hypothesis, should everywhere be equal to or less than the corresponding simple excitatory gradient. In the present study there is the complication that the control Ss received less acquisition training than the experimental group. However, other experiments have verified the last feature of PDGs (e.g., Terrace, 1964).

[2] Another measure of the displacement of the PDG is based on the amount of area in the PDG that lies on either side of $S+$; this is the "area shift" criterion.

Hearst (1968) has suggested that Spence's theory is perhaps better evaluated in terms of relative, rather than absolute, generalization gradients. He was able to show good correspondence between predicted *PDG*s based on empirical relative excitatory and inhibitory gradients and actual (relative) *PDG*s obtained from independent groups of Ss.

The peak shift, which has also been obtained on the line-tilt dimension (Bloomfield, 1967) and with human Ss (Doll & Thomas, 1967; LaBerge, 1961), is an interesting but somewhat puzzling phenomenon. During generalization tests, why should S respond with greatest intensity to a stimulus other than S+? Is it because of the nonreinforced experience with S—? Apparently the underlying cause is more complicated than this, for Honig, Thomas, and Guttman (1959) first trained Ss on S+, followed this training with extinction on S—, and then obtained a "postextinction" gradient. There was no trace of a peak shift, the postextinction gradient having the same form as the control gradient but reduced by a multiplicative constant.

Moreover, the peak shift has been obtained in multiple schedules in which extinction was not one of the components. Recall from Chap. 9 that a successive discrimination in operant terminology is a multiple schedule of which one component is extinction. Guttman (1959) obtained a *PDG* after discrimination training on a *mult VI* 1 *VI* 5. Considering the stimulus which was associated with the *VI* 1 as S+ and the stimulus associated with the *VI* 5 as S—, Guttman observed a peak shift; i.e., the mode of the *PDG* was shifted away from S—. Similar results were obtained by Terrace (1966c, 1968), who employed a *mult VI* 1 *DRL* 7.

FRUSTRATION AND THE PEAK SHIFT. Terrace has suggested that the peak shift is the result of emotional responses (e.g., frustration) which are generated by the contrast in the reinforcement conditions of the components of the multiple schedule, or in somewhat different terms, the peak shift results from the aversiveness developed by S—. Supporting this view is the fact that Ss trained on a discrimination in such a way that few or no responses are made to S— ("errorless" discrimination training—see Chap. 11) display little of the emotional signs that attend normal discrimination training nor do they produce a peak shift in subsequent *PDG*s (Grusec, 1968; Terrace, 1964). Terrace has also shown (1966a) that the peak shift can be eliminated by extensive discrimination training, which apparently extinguishes the emotional responses elicited by the less favorable component of the multiple schedule (see Fig. 10-14).

Further evidence in support of this interpretation comes from a recent experiment by Grusec (1968), who used noncontingent shock to render S— aversive. Grusec trained pigeons to discriminate between 550 mμ (S+) and 570 mμ (S—), employing a technique that produces little or no responding to the negative stimulus. As mentioned in the previous paragraph, subsequent *PDG*s did not reveal a peak shift; in all cases the mode of the generalization gradient was located at S+ (Fig. 10-13). Discrimination training was then

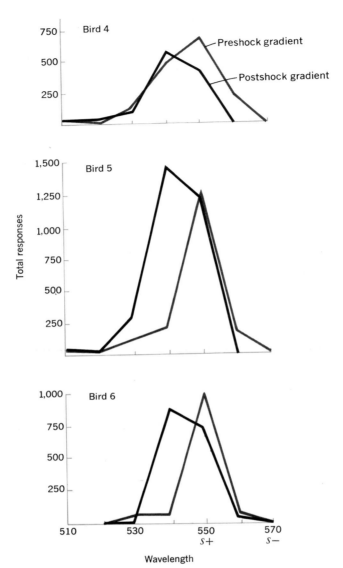

Fig. 10-13. Postdiscrimination gradients generated after "errorless" discrimination training ("preshock" gradients) and after experience with noncontingent shock in $S-$ ("postshock" gradients). (SOURCE: T. Grusec. The peak shift in stimulus generalization: Equivalent effects of errors and noncontingent shock. *Journal of the Experimental Analysis of Behavior,* 1968, **11,** 239–249. Copyright 1968 by the Society for the Experimental Analysis of Behavior, Inc. and used by permission.)

reinstated but with the important modification that noncontingent shock was delivered to S during periods of S—. Finally, a second *PDG* was obtained. As may be seen in Fig. 10-13, a peak shift now appeared in all Ss. An appropriate control group showed that the peak shift was assignable to the noncontingent shock and not to either the second round of discrimination training or generalization testing. Grusec also reported that noncontingent shock increased the extent of the peak shift in Ss that received the same sequence of treatments already described but with conventional discrimination training.

In addition to supporting the contention that emotional reactions to S— lie behind the peak shift, Grusec's results, which have been verified by Terrace (1968), may be viewed as extending the parallel between anticipatory frustration and fear which was developed in Chap. 8. This is another instance where anticipatory frustration and fear, or in terms of operations, extinction and aversive conditioning, lead to similar behavioral effects.

Apparently, however, aversiveness of S— is not the whole story behind the peak-shift phenomenon. We mentioned that extinction on S— (570 mμ) after training on S+ (550 mμ) was not a sufficient condition to produce a peak shift (Honig et al., 1959). Yet if Ss are trained with 550-mμ illumination as S+ and a cross embedded on this same illumination as S—, and then are subsequently extinguished on 570 mμ, a peak shift does occur, although it does not appear in control Ss that do not receive the extinction experience (Friedman & Guttman, 1965). Thus training on an explicit orthogonal discrimination is sufficient to permit the later extinction experience to generate a peak shift. It is difficult to see why extinction should result in a peak shift in the one case and not in the other. Perhaps a greater degree of inhibitory control is achieved by the stimulus associated with extinction when the latter occurs after training on an explicit orthogonal discrimination.

BEHAVIORAL CONTRAST AND THE PEAK SHIFT.   When S is trained on a successive discrimination, rate of responding in S+ increases over what it would have been if no S— periods were presented; simultaneously, rate of response in S— decreases. When one component of a multiple schedule causes the response rate of a second component to change in a direction opposite from its own changing rate, the interaction is called "contrast" or "behavioral contrast" (Reynolds, 1961b). Thus in the previous illustration, response rate in S— decreases while, simultaneously, rate in S+ increases over the level that would have been achieved if there were no S— periods (see Fig. 10-14).

The processes underlying behavioral contrast and the contrast effects discussed in Chap. 7 are basically probably quite similar. Terrace (1966a), for example, attributes behavioral contrast to the "emotional effects of non-reinforced responding," which, when translated to frustration, communicates directly with the frustration-motivation interpretation of negative contrast effects. However, because of the somewhat atheoretical views of some investigators concerned with behavioral contrast (e.g., Reynolds & Limpo, 1968), and because of the

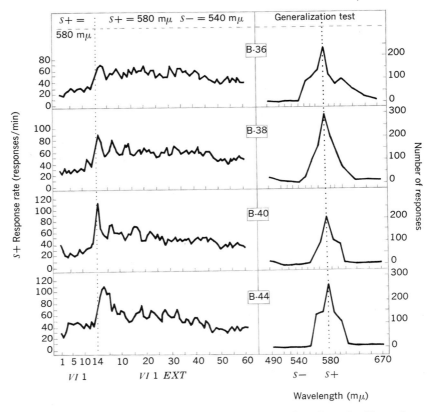

Fig. 10-14. The Ss (4 pigeons) were first trained on S+ alone for 14 sessions (extreme left portion of the figure). Periods of S — were then introduced and discrimination training continued for 60 sessions. Only performance in S+ is shown. It is apparent that upon introduction of discrimination training, rate of responding in S+ increased over its prediscrimination level—an instance of behavioral contrast. By the end of the extended discrimination training phase, however, rate in S+ declined to a level that is close to prediscrimination performance. Hence, behavioral contrast appears to be a temporary characteristic of discrimination performance.

The right panel presents the generalization gradients obtained after the termination of discrimination training. Clearly there is no sign of a peak shift in the gradients. Moreover, in a second experiment generalization gradients were gotten after each successive 15 discrimination training sessions. Although peak shifts were found in the initial gradients, they became reduced in extent with successive tests, and by the fourth and last test they were all but abolished. (SOURCE: H. S. Terrace. Behavioral contrast and the peak shift: Effects of extended discrimination training. *Journal of the Experimental Analysis of Behavior,* 1966, **9,** 613–617. Copyright 1966 by the Society for the Experimental Analysis of Behavior, Inc. and used by permission.)

rather different conditions under which behavioral contrast and contrast effects are studied, there has been surprisingly little contact between the two areas. One hopes that this unfortunate situation will soon change.

To return now to the topic of this section, because by definition *PDG*s are obtained after discrimination training—usually multiple schedules—the peak shift has almost always occurred in close association with behavioral contrast. The question therefore arises as to whether behavioral contrast is a *necessary* accompaniment of the peak shift. Terrace (1968), who apparently leans toward this view, has pointed out a number of cases in which the peak shift and contrast covary with manipulation of an independent variable. Thus, for example, both the peak shift and behavioral contrast disappear with extended discrimination training (Fig. 10-14). In this view presumably a single underlying process, such as the aversiveness of the negative stimulus, accounts for behavioral contrast and the peak shift. There is good evidence, however, that the two phenomena can be disassociated.

In Grusec's (1968) study there was little evidence of behavioral contrast upon introduction of noncontingent shock, although the accompanying variability in performance precluded a firm conclusion on this point. A clearer illustration of the separability of contrast and the peak shift was reported by Yarczower, Dickson, and Gollub (1966), who trained pigeons on a *mult tand VI* 30 sec *DRL* 4—*EXT* schedule. This is a multiple schedule, of which extinction (associated with S—) is one component and the other is a *tand VI DRL* (correlated with S+). Recall from Chap. 9 that in a tandem schedule S must satisfy each of the requirements in sequence. In the present case, when S+ appears, the first response after the *VI* component is satisfied places the subject into the *DRL* portion of the tandem. The *DRL* component ensures that only interresponse times of 4 sec or longer will be reinforced. This, in turn, reduces the possibility of behavioral contrast occurring, because an increase in the rate of responding would defeat the *DRL* component. Possibly only the *DRL* portion of the tandem is sufficient to accomplish this purpose, but the *VI* was included (to form a tandem) because the investigators also wished to manipulate reinforcement frequency without simultaneously manipulating response rate. Yarczower et al. report that behavioral contrast did not occur under the present schedule; nevertheless, a peak shift was obtained. Thus it would appear that contrast is not a necessary condition for the peak-shift phenomenon.

In this same experiment Yarczower et al. showed that even though frequency of reinforcement might be quite different in two components of a multiple schedule, a peak shift need not occur, provided response rates in the components are comparable (recall the Guttman, 1959, study). They achieved these conditions by an interesting multiple schedule, *mult* (*tand VI* 30 sec *DRL* 4) (*tand VI* 3 *DRL* 2). The potentiality for reinforcement is greater in the first component of the multiple schedule than in the second—every 30 sec on the average versus every 3 min (established by the *VI* 30 sec and the *VI* 3, respectively). But the *DRL* 4 requirement of the first component keeps S's rate relatively low, whereas the shorter *DRL* of the second component places less of a brake on response rate. The net result is that although response rate in both components is very comparable, there remains a considerable difference in the frequency of reinforcement associated with each component. As already noted, a peak shift failed to occur under these conditions. The suggestion from this portion of their experiment is that the peak shift obtained by Guttman (1959) with his *mult VI* 1 *VI* 5 schedule was probably attributable to the differences in response rate that existed at the end of discrimination training rather than to a difference in reinforcement density. However, the ratio of reinforcement was only 3 to 1 in the present study as compared to an average of 5 to 1 in Guttman's study.

The pattern of existing results seems too complex to attribute the peak-shift phenomenon entirely to a single underlying process, such as the aversiveness of S—. One would like to know whether the peak shift also disappears with extended training on multiple schedules not involving extinction, for example, schedules where the less favorable component is a *DRL*. Another question of interest is whether, in the complex schedules employed by Yarczower et al., peak shifts would have occurred with very extended training, when the properties of the schedule were fully discriminated. Still, there can be little doubt that the degree of aversiveness of S— is a major factor in the peak-shift phenomenon, even if it cannot account for all instances in which a peak shift occurs.

THEORETICAL ISSUES IN STIMULUS GENERALIZATION

Despite the enormous amount of research devoted to empirical aspects of stimulus generalization and the constant use of the concept of generalization gradients in various theoretical enterprises, the area has never wanted for critics. Pavlov's theoretical interpretations of stimulus generalization, and even some of his findings, were questioned by his contemporaries (Razran, 1949, p. 338). In 1946 Lashley and Wade mounted a determined attack on neo-Pavlovianism in general and on the conceptual basis of stimulus generalization in particular, an attack which reverberated in a more recent critical paper by Prokasy and Hall (1963), who proposed that we abandon the notion of stimulus generalization altogether.

To appreciate the basis of the criticisms leveled at stimulus generalization, we must look a little closer at how this phenomenon is conceptualized by the major theorists. A cardinal assumption of such theorists is that stimulus generalization is a process that develops automatically during conditioning; that through one mechanism or another there is a "spread" of the associative strength developed between the *CS* and the *CR* to stimuli that are in some sense similar to the former. Moreover, the spread is greater the greater the degree of similarity. Pavlov framed the underlying mechanism in physiological terms, conceiving of it as a spread of excitation ("irradiation") from the point on the cortex stimulated by the *CS* to neighboring tissue, which presumably contained the loci for related stimuli. Hull merely accepted the spread of association to similar stimuli as an axiom.

On the other hand many critics, particularly Lashley and Wade (1946) and Prokasy and Hall (1963), vigorously denied the proposition that stimulus generalization develops during acquisition training, maintaining that any gradient that might be obtained under procedures not otherwise suspect must be the result of certain aspects of the testing procedure. In other words, they place the locus of generalization gradients in the testing, rather than in the training phase.

The "Failure-of-association" Hypothesis

As a result of his "stimulus equivalence" studies with rats, Lashley had become convinced that not all stimuli acting at the time an instrumental response is made and reinforced get connected to, or associated with, the response. He was one of the first to emphasize the role of selective attention in animal learning, a view that is now becoming increasingly prominent (see Chap. 11). Applying this notion to generalization, Lashley and Wade took the position that much of what passed for stimulus generalization could be attributed to S's failing to attend to the relevant stimulus dimension—"failure of association," as they put it. In simple terms, if S had not attended to the relevant dimension during acquisition training, variations in this dimension during testing could be expected to have little effect upon S's responding, and consequently "generalization" should occur.

But under this hypothesis one would expect *complete* generalization to all test stimuli, not a stimulus generalization *gradient*. Lashley and Wade's attempts to account for the gradient are not altogether convincing. Their suggestion that somehow generalization gradients might be the result of variations in "discriminative thresholds" does not appear to provide a mechanism for orderly generalization gradients. Their interpretation—as well as that of Razran (1949)—that generalization develops, not during original training, but during subsequent generalization tests, clearly does not cover all instances in which a generalization gradient has been obtained (e.g., Hiss & Thomas, 1963).

The failure-of-association account is, of course, closely related to the view that a flat generalization gradient is likely to occur if "stimulus control" is not achieved by the relevant stimulus during acquisition training. However, whereas more recent investigators have maintained that stimulus control gives rise to a generalization gradient, Lashley and Wade apparently thought that if S did attend to the relevant stimulus dimension during conditioning, in later tests he would respond only to $S+$ and reject other stimuli until his discriminative threshold was approached, at which point differential responding would break down. This of course seems not to be the case, inasmuch as we have seen numerous instances where graded responses occurred during generalization tests to stimuli among which, it must be assumed, S is fully capable of discriminating.

Apart from the fact that the failure-of-association hypothesis is hard put to account for gradients of stimulus generalization, there is a fair amount of empirical evidence that does not square with such an interpretation. We have seen, for example, that absolute generalization *increases* as a function of training level. It would appear that if failure of association formed the basis of stimulus generalization, such failures should be less frequent with increased training levels, so that measured over a group of Ss less stimulus generalization should occur at higher training levels (Mednick & Freedman, 1960). Also, it is difficult under this hypothesis to fathom why certain independent variables, such as the training-test interval and schedules of reinforcement, should affect stimulus generalization gradients as they do.

The finding that the slope of (excitatory) generalization gradients tends to increase with successive generalization tests—often a flat gradient is obtained on the initial test—is frequently cited as indication that the stimulus generalization gradient must in part at least be generated by the testing procedure. This assertion certainly applies to those experiments in which opportunity for discrimination learning was provided during testing, e.g., experiments in which S continued to be reinforced for responding to S+ during a test series. Possibly a certain amount of discrimination occurs even when differential reinforcement is not allowed during generalization tests. But even if there were no contribution from this source whatever, a flatter gradient on initial test trials is likely, for the reason that often S+ and the test stimuli have certain characteristics in common which promote equal responding by S. For example, the onset of a stimulus as against no stimulus at all probably is a feature of S+ that becomes associated to the instrumental response. And this is a property all test stimuli have in common. Presumably, during the extinction trials of generalization testing, this property extinguishes rapidly, permitting other, more differentiable, features of the stimulus series to exert their effect.

Another point made by Lashley and Wade was that a stimulus dimension does not exist for S until established by differential training, i.e., by discriminative experience. This experience might come during the generalization tests themselves, if the CS continued to be reinforced and non-CS stimuli went unrewarded. In the more usual case where generalization tests were conducted under nondifferential reinforcement, the required differential training could have come from past experience with stimuli from the dimension under study. This suggestion was influential in prompting research aimed at determining whether generalization gradients could be obtained in Ss that had been deprived of past differential experience with the relevant stimulus dimension. And as we learned earlier, the answer now appears to be that such experience is *not* a prerequisite for orderly generalization gradients.

On the basis of the evidence which exists today, there seems little reason to doubt the empirical validity of ordered stimulus generalization gradients, gradients that do not depend upon such artifacts as failure to associate. How to conceptualize the mechanisms which give rise to such gradients is entirely another matter. Whether they are best conceived of as a "spread" of excitation from $S+$ to physically similar stimuli, or perhaps as a case of $S+$ having certain "elements" in common with related stimuli, or as the result of S's classification of the relation of the various test stimuli to $S+$, is largely a matter of how fruitful the various approaches turn out to be. There is little question that the first interpretation has stimulated a great deal of experimentation and theoretical application. Naturally experimental and theoretical fruitfulness is not equivalent to validity, but until one theoretical approach can lay more significant claim on the latter than its rivals, the former criterion is bound to be weighed heavily.

Generalization versus Discrimination

Prokasy and Hall (1963), reiterating a number of points made by Lashley and Wade (1946), came to the conclusion that there is no need for a separate "construct" of stimulus generalization. They view stimulus generalization as the result of "failure of discrimination," the failure of S to discriminate between the CS and test stimuli. This interpretation is somewhat different from Lashley and Wade's failure-of-association hypothesis—to which Prokasy and Hall also subscribe—in that even if S had associated the CR to the appropriate relevant stimulus, he might later fail to discriminate between the test and training stimuli and, as a consequence, respond to the latter. Their argument may be summarized in their own words: "That the subject makes the same response to two events may not mean, in two steps, that the events were discriminated and then that the subject generalized. If the events were not discriminated, the conclusion that generalization occurred is unwarranted [p. 319]."

Prokasy and Hall are saying that for the concept of stimulus generalization to be significant, it must be shown that S "discriminates" the test from the training stimulus but responds nevertheless. If the test stimulus appears to him identical to the training stimulus, his response to the former is better ascribed to a failure of discrimination than to an active process of generalization. He may fail to make such a discrimination for several reasons. He may not have associated the relevant aspects of the stimulus with the response (failure-of-association hypothesis); or perhaps conditions of testing discouraged discrimination —for example, if S were required to respond rapidly, he may not have taken proper note of the stimulus which was presented to him (failure-of-discrimination hypothesis).

There are several counterarguments which can be brought to bear against this position. First, as with the failure-of-association hypothesis, it is difficult under the failure-of-discrimination interpretation to account for stimulus generalization *gradients*. Prokasy and Hall recognize this obligation stating, "The question arises as to how such an explanation [theirs] can account for the decreasing response magnitude plotted as a function of the distance between test stimuli and CS sometimes reported in the literature. We know, for example, that changes in the environment may induce altered response levels . . . and that the introduction of different physical events can induce other response characteristics (such as orienting responses). There is no reason why such a change cannot suppress, partially, a response that has been initiated, or why such changes, related to the past history of the organism cannot induce responses where, ordinarily, one might not have been expected [p. 318]."

Prokasy and Hall appear to be saying that when a test stimulus is presented, S might not at first discriminate it from the CS and therefore initiate the conditioned response. Then, however, he apparently notices some difference in the environment, which leads to "orienting" responses, or other competing behaviors, which serve to inhibit the CR. But before such competing responses can occur, S must perceive that a change in the environment has occurred, which seems close to conceding that he has discriminated some aspects of the test stimulus from the CS. Even if we grant that S perceives a change in the environment while failing to perceive a change in the relevant aspects of the CS, their hypothesis does not account for an ordered gradient, unless the further assumption is made that the extent of the perceived change in the environment is directly related to the degree to which the test stimulus differs from the CS. It would appear arbitrary, however, to concede that the amount of environmental change discriminated by S is proportional to the CS–test stimulus difference while at the same time maintaining that S fails totally to discriminate any aspect of the difference itself.

It may also be noted that the failure-of-discrimination hypothesis seems to encounter difficulty with certain aspects of semantic generalization data. Recall the earlier illustration in which a greater degree of generalization was displayed toward a synonym ("style," "fashion") than to a homophone ("stile"). That generalization occurs to semantically related test items is itself not easily related to a failure-of-discrimination hypothesis; moreover, if differences in discriminability exist between synonyms and homophones, probably the latter are usually the less discriminable. Although it must be acknowledged that Prokasy and Hall addressed their arguments against primary stimulus generalization, the question of accommodating mediated generalization within a systematic view of the generalization process is not an irrelevant consideration.

DIFFERENT MEANINGS OF GENERALIZATION AND DISCRIMINATION.　If we mean by generalization the extent to which S responds similarly to the CS and non-CS stimuli, and if we mean by discrimination the degree to which he does not respond similarly, then clearly—though trivially—generalization and discrimination are inversely related, and S generalizes to the extent that he fails to discriminate. It is in this sense that we have occasionally used these terms in apposition, as a matter of convenience and not of enlightenment.

But the discrimination that Lashley and Wade and Prokasy and Hall are talking about is based not on S's responses but rather on his perceptions—on how stimuli "appear" to S and not on how S responds to them. As pointed out by Brown (1965), this duality in the meaning of discrimination has been the source of much difficulty. Theories of "discrimination" learning have concerned themselves with how S learns to *respond* differentially to different stimuli, not with his perceptions. Obviously, the *discriminability* of stimuli enters into such an analysis, but in the overwhelming majority of discrimination studies there is never any question that S can tell the stimuli apart. Spence, in fact, proposed two theories of discrimination learning. In one, S+ and S− were from the same stimulus dimension, so stimulus generalization effects had to be taken into consideration (Spence, 1937). In the other, the stimuli were assumed to be completely discriminable; thus stimulus generalization played no role whatever (Spence, 1936).

It is true that by paying little heed to S's perceptions, particularly to the features of the stimuli to which S attends, theories of discrimination learning left out a good part of the total picture, and it is also true that a great deal more emphasis on this aspect of discrimination learning is evident today. Nevertheless it is equally true that discrimination learning (perhaps more accurately, discrimination *behavior*) is affected by far more variables than S's perceptions. It is powerfully influenced by probability of reinforcement, sequences of stimuli, past experience with the various stimuli, payoff structure, and a number of other variables for which there is no convincing evidence that they exert their effects by altering S's perception of the relevant stimuli.

The same duality of meaning applies to generalization. Obviously, if S perceives different stimuli as identical, he will react to them in a similar way, so that *discriminability* of stimuli influences generalization just as it did discrimination. But it is generalization *behavior* that is of interest to us, which includes more than discriminability. Thus it is doubtful that schedules of reinforcement, shown to have a profound effect on stimulus generalization, exert their influence by altering S's perception. And although drive manipulations possibly do have such an effect where intensive dimensions are concerned (Zajonc & Dorfman, 1964), the same cannot be said for such dimensions as wavelength, line tilt, and other "metathetic" dimensions (Chap. 6).

One might retort that the fact that there is more than discriminability involved in discrimination and generalization does not by itself require the maintenance of the two concepts. This would follow only if one could show that the two processes were affected differently by at least some independent variables. One might also point to such accomplishments as the prediction of discrimination performance from generalization gradients (Haber & Kalish, 1963; Kalish & Haber, 1965; Marsh, 1967) and to the demonstration of an inverse relationship between generalization and discrimination (Kalish, 1958; Marsh, 1967) as evidence of the essential equivalence of the two concepts.

Doubtlessly the meaningful coalescence of discrimination and generalization into a single process would represent an important simplification and integration of psychological concepts, and further efforts in this direction are to be encouraged. But at the present time, there seems little to be gained from what appears to be the premature banishment of an extremely useful concept. The points at which generalization and discrimination, as empirical processes, form two sides of the same coin are still few. As yet we have little reason to believe that the behaviors we call generalization and discrimination are always affected in comparable ways by important independent variables (cf. Hoffman, 1969). Moreover, it is not even clear what aspects of generalization gradients—heights of gradients, absolute slope, or relative slopes—ought to be the criterion behavior with which to explore this question (cf. Brown, 1965). But perhaps the strongest argument against disposing of the concept of generalization is its past empirical and theoretical fruitfulness. It is doubtful that the peak shift, for example, would have been discovered and exploited were the term generalization deleted from our vocabulary. Such topics as transposition, semantic generalization, and conflict behavior are reminders of the contributions of that concept. Finally, there is some very interesting research aimed at uncovering the physiological basis of stimulus generalization that probably would not have been undertaken but for the existence of the concept of generalization (e.g., John & Killam, 1959).

SUMMARY

To return to a point mentioned earlier, the importance of technique for experimental research in psychology is perhaps nowhere seen more clearly than in the area of generalization. Operant methodology has made possible the production of stable generalization gradients for single organisms, and it has permitted the investigation of a wide range of variables under highly controlled conditions—conditions, moreover, which are often deftly sensitive to the independent variables under study. Refinements of technique have permitted the exploration of problems—such as the basis of the peak shift—for which more conventional methods are clumsy and awkward.

As yet, however, we do not agree about the mechanisms which control the generalization phenomenon. That selective attention, or stimulus control, is critically involved few doubt. But there is no consensus about whether generalization arises from "spread of association"—an acquisition phenomenon—or whether it arises primarily during testing, essentially as an artifact of impaired discrimination. Possibly the growing interest in the physiological basis of generalization may produce results which will help provide an answer to this interesting and important question. The concept of generalization permeates behavior theory so deeply that any improvement in our understanding of the process is bound to have wide ramifications.

1. Primary stimulus generalization differs from mediated stimulus generalization in that:

2. Absolute and relative generalization gradients differ as follows:

3. One way of classifying generalization gradients is in terms of excitatory and inhibitory control, namely:

4. Some of the data which support the view that a flat, rather than a graded, generalization gradient is likely to occur if S fails to attend to the relevant stimulus dimension are:

5. The available data which bear on the role of level of acquisition training and amount of generalization in excitatory gradients do not support the notion that increased training (on $S+$) automatically increases discrimination between $S+$ and related stimuli. More specifically:

6. (a) Ignoring certain complications relating to boundary conditions, etc., the Hull-Spence theory of conditioning makes the following deductions concerning generalization and manipulations of drive level:

(b) The theory predicts that relative generalization gradients (calculated by either of the two methods discussed in the chapter) obtained at different drive levels will be identical because:

(c) The congruence between the pattern of deductions and the pattern of available data is:

7. (a) The shape of the generalization gradient can be altered drastically by the schedule of reinforcement employed during acquisition. For example:

(b) One possible basis for the effects of schedules on the shape of generalization gradients is:

8. Generalization gradients play a central role in conflict theory, particularly the assumption that the avoidance gradient is ordinarily steeper than the approach gradient. Some of the difficulties facing this hypothesis are:

9. There are three types of inhibitory gradients, namely:

10. (a) An orthogonal discrimination is:

(b) An orthogonal discrimination can be employed to generate comparable excitatory and extinction gradients by:

11. Punishment gradients are not "pure" gradients because:

12. Summation of like gradients, if firmly established as an empirical phenomenon, would support the spread-of-association interpretation of generalization but not the failure-of-discrimination hypothesis, because:

13. The peak-shift phenomenon is related to Spence's discrimination learning theory in the following way:

14. The evidence for and against the view that the peak shift is the result of emotional responses (such as frustration) occurring during acquisition is:

15. (a) The failure-of-association hypothesis attributes generalization to:

(b) The failure-of-discrimination hypothesis, on the other hand, holds that the major source of generalization is:

(c) Some major shortcomings of these interpretations are:

11 DISCRIMINATION LEARNING AND ATTENTION

INTRODUCTION

In general terms a *discrimination situation* is one in which two or more schedules of reinforcement are in operation (not necessarily simultaneously), each associated with its own distinguishing stimulus. Essentially, S's task is to learn about the reinforcement schedules and associate them with their correlated stimuli, a task which often involves learning about the stimuli themselves. We say that discrimination has occurred when S responds "appropriately" to the stimuli, i.e., in a manner congruent with their associated reinforcement schedules. In a simple simultaneous-discrimination situation in which $S+$ is associated with continuous reinforcement and $S-$ with extinction, S discriminates between the stimuli (discriminanda) when he consistently chooses $S+$. In practice an operational criterion of discrimination learning is often employed, such as 90 percent correct choices over a day's trials.

Defined in this way, discrimination situations include both *discriminative conditioning* and *discrimination learning*. It will be recalled from Chap. 7 that we distinguished between the two on the basis of a distinction between response magnitude and response direction (choice). "Discriminative conditioning" referred to discrimination situations in which response choice is not involved and in which the dependent variable is framed in terms of response magnitude (e.g., rate of response and latency of response). In contrast, discrimination learning always involves choice among experimentally defined alternatives. We had something to say about discriminative conditioning in Chap. 7, and the present chapter will be devoted exclusively to discrimination learning. Though there are notable exceptions (e.g., H. M. Jenkins, 1965b), the vast majority of investigations bearing on discrimination acquisition have employed discrimination learning situations.

It was also pointed out in Chap. 7 that the distinction between conditioning and learning perhaps should not be pushed too far, inasmuch as extremely complex behaviors can be generated by many schedules of reinforcement which, because they do not provide for choice behavior, fall into conditioning paradigms (see Chap. 9). Nevertheless, there appear to be sufficient functional differences between choice and nonchoice behavior to warrant continuing awareness of the distinction.

Perhaps it should be observed that, although the correspondence is by no means complete, discriminative conditioning paradigms fall within the nonconcurrent schedules discussed in Chap. 9, whereas simple discrimination-learning situations may be viewed as special cases of concurrent schedules. For example, a simple two-choice discrimination-learning situation may be considered a concurrent *CRF EXT* schedule with incompatible instrumental responses.

The Role of Nonperceptual Variables in Discrimination Learning

It should be evident from our description of discrimination learning that more than *stimulus discriminability* is involved in discrimination behavior, a point which was made in the previous chapter. Of course, S's discriminative behavior can be influenced strongly by manipulating features of the stimuli to be discriminated. But it can also be affected markedly by such "nonperceptual" variables as delay of reward, reinforcement schedules, trial sequences, and response discriminability. The failure to realize fully that both classes of variables, perceptual and nonperceptual, contribute to discriminative behavior can lead to erroneous conclusions. An investigator interested in perceptual processes may conclude incorrectly that S is discriminating between a pair of stimuli simply because S displays better-than-chance discriminative behavior. Such behavior could, however, be the result of one or more nonperceptual variables. If, for example, the experimental task were a two-choice discrimination situation and training had been very prolonged, S might eventually discriminate certain features of the program, perhaps that reward was never forthcoming more than three times in succession on the same side. This cue alone might be sufficient to increase S's performance above the chance level.

On the other side of the coin, failure to display discriminative behavior may result even though S is capable of distinguishing between the discriminanda. If, for example, the intertrial interval is so brief that S can achieve a substantial density of reward without attending to the stimuli, it is possible that S will fall into position responding and never show discriminative behavior. Munn's (1950) account of the problems encountered in investigating color vision in the rat is an interesting illustration of the problems involved in inferring perceptual discrimination from discriminative behavior.

Perceptual Processes in Discrimination Learning

For the past 30 years or so the major concern of most investigators in this country actively involved in discrimination learning has not been with perceptual problems; rather it has focused on the learning process itself. Questions concerning the manner in which S comes to differentiate features of the discriminanda, whether he attends to some aspects of the stimuli rather than to others, and related problems were largely ignored. Highly discriminable (to E) stimuli were employed in much of the relevant research in an effort to exclude discriminability of the stimuli—and hence perceptual problems—as a central issue. The independent variables manipulated were rarely concerned with the discriminanda themselves, but instead were drawn from the classical variables of learning research—motivational level, amount and delay of reward, intertrial interval, etc.

As a result of this emphasis on the response side, most of the vast body of data and theorizing that has accumulated in the area of discrimination learning since the 1930s has virtually no relevance for problems of a perceptual nature. We can say very little, for example, about how an individual comes to distinguish between stimuli that initially are bewilderingly similar to him. We all know that foods, faces, wines, trees, music, etc., though they may initially appear very similar to us, come to be clearly distinguished with practice. We also know that if we are intently involved with our newspaper, the radio or a familiar voice recedes into the background and apparently fails to be perceived. About the important processes of *stimulus differentiation* and *attention*, conventional theories of discrimination learning unfortunately can tell us little at present.

However, perceptual problems were not always neglected by those employing discrimination learning paradigms. In fact at the outset much of the early work in discrimination learning was motivated by an interest in perceptual and related problems (e.g., Klüver, 1933; Lashley, 1938). Lashley wanted to discover whether the rat organized stimuli in a manner similar to man or whether its perceptual mechanisms were radically different. Both he and Klüver were intimately involved in trying to discover what constituted the effective aspect of the stimulus displays to which their animals responded. For them the response itself was merely an indicator from which to infer perceptual and related processes, not a means of gaining access to general (instrumental) learning mechanisms.

Partly because of the rapid rise and success of the behavioristic systems of Hull and Spence and partly because of the difficulties inherent in the task of inferring perceptual processes from instrumental behavior, there appears to have been a shift of emphasis away from perceptual problems, which, starting in the late thirties, has persisted to quite recently.

The development was not uniform, however, and certain issues concerning perceptual matters managed to survive. The "continuity-noncontinuity" controversy was one such issue, which really arose from this difference in emphasis. Lashley, as well as others (e.g., Krechevsky, 1938), maintained that only those aspects of the stimulus situation to which S attended became associated with the instrumental response and that the other features of the stimulus had no significance whatever (noncontinuity view). The continuity view placed less emphasis on perceptual processes, maintaining that if the stimuli hit the receptor surfaces in a discriminable form, they were utilized effectively in learning. Actually the situation is more complex than this, but the central point of disputation concerns the part played by selective mechanisms in perception and learning. [See Goodrich, Ross, and Wagner (1961) for a review of the controversy and Mackintosh (1965b) for an extension of the noncontinuity view.] The role of attentional processes in discrimination learning, although clearly demonstrated many years ago by Lashley and Klüver, among others, has been increasingly emphasized in recent years (cf. Gilbert & Sutherland, 1969). Later in the chapter we shall examine this general topic more closely.

Concern for the role of perceptual processes in discrimination learning comes from another quarter. According to E. J. and J. J. Gibson, perceptual learning—particularly stimulus differentiation—constitutes a fundamental process in discrimination learning and related activities. Through processes not well understood at present, we somehow are able to learn to distinguish aspects of stimulus arrays which initially do not register on us. Our sensitivity to various facets of a stimulus array increases so that eventually with little effort we are able to distinguish subtle differences between fabrics, handwriting, paintings, etc., differences to which we were originally insensitive. They view this process of stimulus differentiation as a perceptual process sui generis. It is not a matter of amplifying already marginally detectable differences by associating them with highly differentiable responses (the "acquired distinctiveness of cues" position); rather it is a matter of learning to "see" differences that were initially "below threshold." We shall return to this interpretation at a later point, but for the present we are simply noting the different avenues by which the topic of discrimination learning has been approached.

In summary, although research employing discrimination learning paradigms initially had the investigation of perceptual processes as its major aim, a dramatic shift away from such an involvement occurred in this country in the late 1930s. Discrimination learning came to be viewed as an extension of the principles of conditioning. None of the major theoretical efforts since that time, including those of Hull (1943, 1952), Spence (1936, 1937), Harlow (1959) and of various mathematical theorists, took much notice of perceptual processes in discrimination learning. This condition now seems to be reversing itself, with an ever-increasing emphasis being placed on attentional processes and perceptual learning. The recent monographs of Trabasso and Bower (1968) and Lovejoy (1968) are pertinent illustrations of these developments, as is Mackintosh's earlier paper (1965b).

Before turning to a closer examination of the issues just raised, we shall first briefly survey the kinds of experimental situations that are employed in discrimination learning research.

DISCRIMINATION LEARNING PARADIGMS

Actually there are a very large number of discrimination learning paradigms with any number of modifications (e.g., French, 1965). We shall discuss only those which the student is likely to encounter.

Simple Two-choice Discrimination Learning

The simplest paradigm is a two-choice situation with $S+$ and $S-$ spatially distinct from each other. The apparatuses employed range from simple T mazes, where $S+$ might be a black alley and $S-$ a white alley, to sophisticated experimental chambers in which programming of trials and recording of data are completely automatic. The jumping stand, invented by Lashley (1930), still is used today, though not nearly as much as in the past. In this apparatus (Fig. 11-1) the subject—usually a rat—is required to jump to the stimulus of his choice. Because the rat must soon learn to "look before he leaps," learning is often far faster than in many other two-choice situations.

A widely used apparatus is the Wisconsin General Test Apparatus (WGTA), developed primarily for use with primates but also adaptable to humans, cats, and other organisms (see Meyer, Treichler, & Meyer, 1965). In this apparatus the two discriminanda, often common objects, are placed over reinforcement wells (Fig. 11-2) which they hide from view. The instrumental response consists simply of S pushing aside the stimulus of his choice.

In an effort to obtain better environmental control and to attain programming potentialities not possible with manual apparatuses, a number of investigators have adapted operant technology to discrimination learning paradigms. In the case of the rat, for example, the experimental chamber might contain two bars with provision for stimulus presentation above the bars. Discrete trials are usually employed, rather than free-operant responding.

A very elaborate discrimination apparatus has been developed by Pribram, Gardner, Pressman, and Bagshaw (1962), which provides as many as 16 alternatives and incorporates automatic programming of trials and data recording.

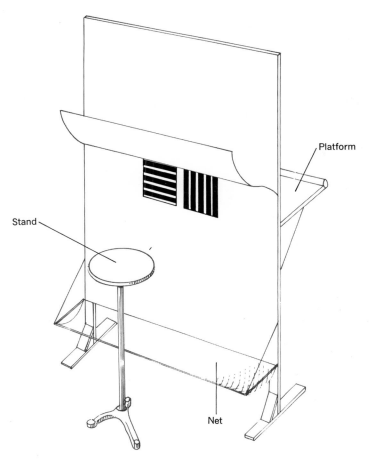

Stand

Platform

Net

Fig. 11-1. The Lashley jumping stand. In the original version the rat jumped from the stand to the discriminanda. If S chose the correct stimulus, the stimulus card fell, allowing the animal access to the platform where food was available. On an incorrect jump S hit the locked stimulus and fell into the net located at the bottom of the apparatus. In later versions S was spared this unpleasantness by being allowed to jump to a ledge in front of the stimulus card. (SOURCE: K. S. Lashley. The mechanism of vision. I. A method for rapid analysis of pattern-vision in the rat. *Pedogogical Seminary and Journal of Genetic Psychology*, 1930, **37,** 453–460. Used by permission.)

A few years ago the author devised an experimental chamber which has proven adaptable to a large number of discrimination paradigms. A brief description of the apparatus will facilitate later exposition of the various discrimination paradigms. The front wall of the chamber (Fig. 11-3) houses an array of five stimulus projectors each faced with a transparent response key. The subject responds to the stimulus of his choice merely by pressing the key on which that

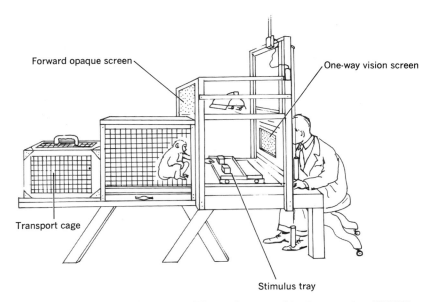

Fig. 11-2. An early version of the Wisconsin general test apparatus (WGTA). (SOURCE: H. F. Harlow. The formation of learning sets. *Psychological Review,* 1949, **56,** 51–65. Copyright 1949 by the American Psychological Association and used by permission.)

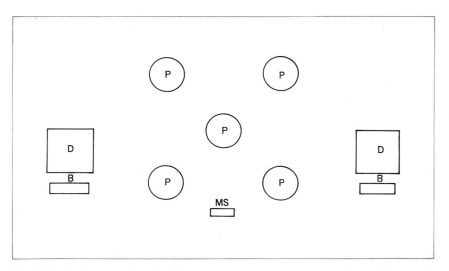

Fig. 11-3. A diagram of a discrimination apparatus for monkeys. In addition to the five stimulus projectors (P) described in the text, there are two stimulus display units (D) capable of presenting various spatial configurations of lights or patterns. A bar mechanism (B) is located beneath each display. The microswitch (MS) is used by S to initiate a trial.

stimulus appears. The projectors employed are a type available commercially at a reasonable cost, and as a consequence they are widely used in discrimination studies. Any one of 12 stimuli, or any combinations thereof, can be displayed simply by powering the appropriate light bulbs directly through holes punched in a paper tape, which serves to program the stimulus presentations (D'Amato, 1965a). In a simple two-choice discrimination problem, $S+$ and $S-$ can be made to appear on any two of the five projectors, thereby reducing considerably the possibility that "position" habits will be established. Obviously, it is a simple matter to program multiple-choice problems with one or more $S+$s and one or more $S-$s. Other applications will be described later.

Conditional Discriminations

A *conditional discrimination* is one in which the reinforcement contingency associated with a specific cue depends upon the status of a second cue. For example, the discriminanda of a two-choice problem might be a circle and a square, with color the conditional cue. Thus, if the circle and square appear against red backgrounds, the square is $S+$ and the circle is $S-$. When the circle and square appear against green backgrounds, however, this relationship is reversed and the circle is now $S+$.

There is a special case of conditional discriminations, which might be called a "spatial" conditional discrimination, that appears to involve only a single stimulus dimension. As an illustration of this paradigm, a rat is trained on a T maze to turn right when both arms of the maze are white and to turn left when both arms are black. When we consider that in turning right, for example, S is responding to a particular stimulus complex (i.e., approaching the cues on the right side of the maze), we see that this arrangement is not very different from that given in the illustration of the previous paragraph. Choosing the right alley when both arms are white is closely analogous to choosing the square when both backgrounds are red. Unfortunately, however, a number of writers still refer to this type of conditional discrimination as a "successive" discrimination, merely because the differential stimuli are presented successively. Some writers attribute this nomenclature to Hunter (1914), but he merely pointed out that in this paradigm the discriminative stimuli are presented successively rather than simultaneously. As our previous illustration indicates, however, it is generally true of conditional discriminations that variation of the conditional cue occurs successively.

The conditional discrimination paradigm seems to be widely relevant inasmuch as our responses to objects and stimuli are often dependent upon the context in which they appear. A husband who at home treats his wife with indifference often will show her a good deal of consideration when dining at his employer's home. His behavior toward his wife is conditional upon the contextual stimuli provided by other people. As a further illustration, negative transfer is a common experience when one purchases a second car. The turn-signal indicator, for example, might be on the right side of the steering column in one automobile and on the left side in the other, with the driver reaching for a lever that does not exist. Eventually, however, one comes to adjust this response, as well as others, in accordance with the vehicle which one is driving. Such responses as turning, braking, etc., become conditional upon the contextual cues of the automobile itself.

Conditional discriminations can be made extremely complex by employing a relatively large number of conditional stimuli. For example, when size characterizes the discriminanda (large or small squares, say), a conditional cue of brightness (white or black) may be introduced to produce two possible pairs of stimuli [large ($S+$) and small ($S-$) white squares and large ($S-$) and small ($S+$) black squares]. Introducing a second conditional cue of form (squares versus triangles) enlarges the number of pairs of stimuli to four, with the small white and large black triangles serving as $S+$s. Eight possible pairs of stimuli are generated by adding a third conditional cue, for example, the absence or presence of a margin around the stimulus object. Now the large black triangle is correct only if the margins are absent. Adding a fourth conditional cue increases the total number of possible stimuli to 32, or 16 two-choice pairs. In order for S to determine whether it is the large or the small form which is correct, he must take account of the color of the forms, the nature of the forms (squares or triangles), the presence or absence of a margin, and finally, the status of the fourth conditional cue, which in an actual experiment was the absence or presence in both stimuli of a wooden peg. A particularly capable chimpanzee was able to solve this very difficult conditional discrimination in some 15,000 trials (Nissen, 1951). And there was no indication that this was the limit of the animal's ability.

In simple conditional problems it is a moot point whether S is responding to the conditional cue as such or whether he merely is learning two separate but concurrent discriminations. For example, in the first illustration, S might simply learn that $S+$ is a square on a red background or a circle on a green background, without any appreciation that the background color determines which form is correct. Although the first approach is probably often the basis for learning a conditional discrimination (cf. North, Maller, & Hughes, 1958), there is little doubt that monkeys can make use of a conditional cue in a more abstract way.

Riopelle and Copelan (1954) trained rhesus monkeys on a number of discrimination reversal problems. The animals were given a series of acquisition trials on a simple object-discrimination problem, a yellow tray bearing the stimulus objects. The reversal trials, on the other hand, were presented with a green stimulus tray. In a sense, then, the acquisition-reversal trials constituted a conditional discrimination problem in which the conditional cue (tray color) was manipulated over blocks of trials rather than being intermixed. After sufficient training, all Ss responded appropriately during the *first* reversal trial. In other words the change in the color of the tray came to signify that $S+$ and $S-$ had been reversed. Moreover, the Ss transferred this behavior to other colors and even showed appropriate reversal responses the first time that a new color change was instituted. It seems clear that the behavior of these animals had become conditional on the color of the tray and, in fact, on the more abstract property of whether the tray color remained the same or changed.

It is an interesting observation that very young children are far less skilled than test-wise adult rhesus monkeys in acquiring simple conditional discriminations (e.g., Gollin, 1966; Warren, 1964). But whether this difference arises from different capacities or from procedural variations remains to be determined.

Matching to Sample

The matching-to-sample paradigm, although simple in its basic form, has many interesting extensions. The task of S is simply to choose from a set of alternatives the stimulus which matches a sample item. In simultaneous matching the sample is available during the time that S must make his choice. With reference to the apparatus of Fig. 11-3, the sample (e.g., a triangle) appears on the center key with the alternatives (e.g., a triangle, a square, and a vertical line) presented on three of the four outer keys. The subject is correct only if he chooses the triangle. On other trials the square and the vertical line serve as the sample stimuli.

By delaying the appearance of the alternatives, one achieves a technique that is useful in studying memory processes. In this application, which is called "delayed" matching-to-sample, the sample appears as usual on the center key. However, S is required to press the center key (to ensure his attending to the sample stimulus), a response which causes the sample to disappear. After an interval of time, the alternatives appear on the outer four keys, and S must remember what the sample had been. It has been shown that if the opportunity for rehearsal is restricted, human adults show substantial forgetting of simple stimulus materials, such as consonants, after periods as short as 3 sec (e.g., Peterson & Peterson, 1959; cf. Chap. 12). Apparently monkeys too may have the ability to rehearse, for we have found in our laboratory that the capuchin monkey can display excellent retention after a delay interval as long as 120 sec.

The matching-to-sample technique can also be extended to study concept formation. In this extension matching is based on conceptual properties rather than on identity. For example, matching might be on the basis of number, on the basis of form versus nonform stimuli, or on other conceptual properties. The paradigm provides a very useful technique by means of which one can gradually shape S from matching based on identity to matching based on more subtle aspects of the stimuli (cf. Wright, French, & Riley, 1968).

Oddity Discrimination Learning

Closely related to matching to sample is oddity learning. Here S learns to choose the different rather than the identical stimulus. In a simple form of oddity learning, S might be faced with triangles on two of the keys (Fig. 11-3) and a square on a third. The square, the odd figure, is S+. Obviously, by making the basis of the difference more subtle, one can employ oddity discrimination in the study of concept-formation behavior.

Delayed-response Discrimination Learning

The delayed-response problem is one of the oldest techniques employed in behavioral research (Hunter, 1913). In the procedure used most often, S observes which of two food wells is baited. The food wells are then covered with identical stimuli, and after a period of delay from 5 to 30 sec, S is permitted to choose between the alternatives. As described, this method, called the "direct" method (Fletcher, 1965), is a nondiscriminative problem. However a somewhat cleaner version, the "indirect" method, introduces discriminative stimuli. Instead of observing the position of the reward, S first learns a simple discrimination problem—for example, responding to the lighted key of a two-choice situation (in Fig. 11-3 assume only the two lower keys are used). After acquisition of the discrimination, the delayed responding phase is entered, during which one of the keys is illuminated for a time and then extinguished. At the termination of the delay interval, S is permitted to choose between the two keys; his task is to remember the one which had been illuminated. Fletcher (1965) gives a detailed description of the problems and results characteristic of the delayed-response paradigm, one of the most reliable of which is the performance decrement suffered by monkeys handicapped by bilateral lesions of their frontal cortex.

At least in its indirect form, the delayed-response paradigm appears closely related to delayed matching-to-sample, with the difference that in the former the information that is to be retained over the delay interval is a spatial location whereas in the latter it is a visual stimulus.

Concurrent Discrimination Learning

A concurrent (or serial) discrimination-learning paradigm is one in which two or more separate discrimination problems are learned simultaneously. For example, Leary (1958) trained rhesus monkeys on nine separate (two-choice) object discrimination problems daily. A "trial" consisted of a single exposure to each of the nine problems, and 10 trials were conducted daily. Each day S was exposed to a new set of nine problems. At the end of 20 days of training, Ss were responding correctly at better than the 85-percent level by the third trial of a day's 10 trials and better than the 90-percent level by the fourth trial.

VERBAL DISCRIMINATION LEARNING. With human Ss, concurrent discriminations often employ verbal materials, constituting what has been called "verbal discrimination learning" (cf. Chap. 12). In one version of this paradigm, S is required to learn which of two (or more) verbal stimuli is the correct one, a number of different pairs (or sets) of stimuli being presented in succession. Clearly, this paradigm closely parallels the concurrent discrimination paradigm employed with animals.

Learning Sets

Learning-set (LS) procedures, rather than constituting a unique paradigm, are extensions of previously described discrimination procedures. They consist merely of presenting S with a large number of problems of the same type but with different discriminanda. On the dependent variable side, the behavior of interest is not S's learning of the individual problem but rather the manner in which his learning changes from problem to problem, i.e., with interproblem rather than intraproblem learning.

Unfortunately, the term "learning set" is often used in two very different ways. First, it is employed simply to refer to the experimental procedures themselves, which is the usage encountered thus far in this chapter. Second, it signifies the changes in learning proficiency that occur as a result of the LS procedures, so that one speaks of an animal developing an object-discrimination LS, or a reversal LS. This duality in meaning should not cause confusion, though it should be kept in mind.

It was Harlow (e.g., 1949) who first saw clearly the implications of learning-set procedures and the behavior modifications which they produce, and we turn to Harlow for a concrete illustration. Eight rhesus monkeys were trained on 344 separate two-choice object discrimination problems in the WGTA; the number of trials on each problem ranged from 6 to 50. The objects which served as discriminanda changed with each problem. In Fig. 11-4, data are presented only for the first six trials averaged over blocks of problems. An astonishing change in learning proficiency occurs over the series of discriminations. Initially learning is quite slow, with very little acquired from the experience of Trial 1. By the time that Ss have the benefit of experience on some 300 problems, however, Trial 2 performance is almost perfect. Thus, if S is presented with a long series of similar problems, discrimination performance is gradually altered from what might be called a trial-and-error mode of solution to what many would consider "insight."

A similar transition from relatively slow to essentially one-trial learning has been demonstrated for reversal learning (Harlow, 1949), where again Trial 2 performance is close to the 100-percent-correct level after some 100 problems. We have already mentioned in connection with conditional discriminations the fact that rhesus monkeys could eventually learn to reverse to a sign (Riopelle and Copelan, 1954), which constitutes a slightly different form of learning set. Warren (1964), using the conventional conditional discrimination paradigm, has shown that rhesus monkeys, unlike nonprimates, readily form conditional-discrimination LSs.

IMPLICATIONS OF LEARNING-SET PROCEDURES. The major implication from research employing LS procedures is that they provide a means of integrating slow, inefficient, trial-and-error learning and rapid "insightful" learning along a quantitative dimension—amount of relevant past experience. Depending on its past experience, a monkey can require 100 or more trials to solve a simple

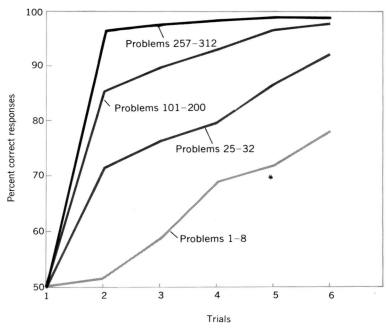

Fig. 11-4. Discrimination learning over the initial six training trials of a problem as a function of blocks of problems (see text). (SOURCE: H. F. Harlow. The formation of learning sets. *Psychological Review,* 1949, **56,** 51–65. Copyright 1949 by the American Psychological Association and used by permission.)

discrimination or, like a human adult, solve it at once. The animal has the capacity not only to learn to solve a particular discrimination problem but also to learn how to go about learning such problems—"learning how to learn," as Harlow has put it.

In the interests of conceptual simplicity, this capacity for higher-order learning was neglected by most learning theorists, who restricted themselves to the single-problem approach. However, it is by no means clear that an accurate theory of how naive animals learn a discrimination problem will be directly relevant to the more significant issue of how they go about learning to learn. There have been efforts, partially successful, to deduce one from the other (e.g., Restle, 1958), but the data from comparative psychology suggest that there are limitations to an organism's ability to form learning sets that are structurally determined.

Learning-set procedures have been extremely important for recent research in comparative psychology. As Warren (1965) points out, "The evidence fails to indicate any meaningful variation among vertebrates in the acquisition of single simple conditioned responses or discrimination habits by experimentally naive subjects [p. 274]." Naive monkeys learn a simple discrimination not differently from naive rats, but there is a vast difference in the ease with which they develop learning sets (Fig. 11-5). Thus, whereas researchers despaired of finding meaningful differences among widely divergent species in single-problem learning, *LS* procedures have provided them with a new set of fruitful analytical tools.

[See Warren (1965) for an informative discussion of this issue. Miles (1965) and Reese (1964) may be consulted for a detailed description of learning-set procedures and results. A mathematical model interpretation in terms of hypothesis behavior has been advanced by Levine (1965), while Restle (1958) has developed a mathematical model based on the conditioning of different classes of cues from which simple discrimination learning emerges as a special case.]

In summary, learning-set procedures tap learning abilities which far exceed those required for mastering a single discrimination problem. Because of its higher demands on the animal's ability to integrate information, the learning-set paradigm has proven extremely valuable in comparative psychology and has provided physiological psychologists with a more sensitive tool with which to analyze the relationships between structure and function. Finally it seems a reasonable assumption that, with regard to animal research, principles arising from *LS* research are far more likely to be relevant to human behavior than generalizations emerging from the single discrimination problem. The innumerable learning situations which the normal human being experiences through the long years of childhood may be conceptualized as leading to the establishment of a wide range of learning sets that contributes greatly to the intellectual

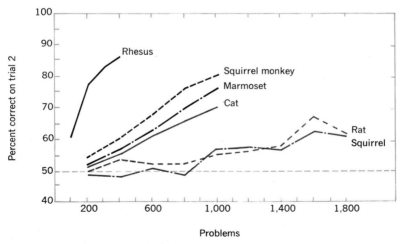

Fig. 11-5. Discrimination learning-set performance by primates, carnivores, and rodents. The dependent variable is the percentage correct responses on the second trial of each (different) discrimination problem. [SOURCE: J. M. Warren. Primate learning in comparative perspective. In A. M. Schrier, H. F. Harlow, and F. Stollnitz (Eds.), *Behavior of nonhuman primates. Vol. I.* New York: Academic, 1965. Used by permission.]

accomplishments which we, as adults, take for granted. Conceivably, a "rich" and "stimulating" early environment is important for proper intellectual and motivational development precisely because it provides the experiences necessary for the formation of a variety of learning sets.

Errorless Discrimination Learning

All the paradigms discussed thus far allow for the occurrence of errors—responding to the negative stimulus—during discrimination acquisition. Such an eventuality has been accepted as inevitable, and in fact many theoretical interpretations of discrimination learning stress heavily the necessity of inhibiting error tendencies in discrimination learning (e.g., Harlow & Hicks, 1957; Spence, 1936, 1937). That the commitment of errors is a necessary accompaniment of the learning process seems to be a generally accepted hypothesis in and out of the laboratory.

ARE ERRORS NECESSARY FOR DISCRIMINATION LEARNING?   This general acknowledgment of the role of errors in the learning process has been accompanied by an only slightly less general recognition that very often a problem could be learned more easily if it was approached in degrees, or gradually, rather than all at once—a point that has been demonstrated experimentally in rats by Lawrence (1952). Indeed, it has even been shown that if one is sufficiently careful, a successive discrimination (Skinner, 1938) as well as a simultaneous discrimination (Schlosberg & Solomon, 1943) can be established with virtually no errors (or responding to $S-$). In spite of the important theoretical and practical consequences suggested by these demonstrations, they remained isolated instances until relatively recently when Terrace, in a series of papers (1963a, b, c; 1964; 1966c), developed a procedure for "errorless" discrimination learning and examined its properties in detail.

Working with pigeons in both a free-operant and a discrete-trials procedure, Terrace (1963a) was able to establish a successive discrimination between red- and green-illuminated keys with few or no responses to $S-$. This was accomplished by introducing $S-$ very early in training and in an attenuated form (i.e., reduced in duration and intensity), then gradually increasing its intensity and duration until they equalled that of $S+$. The birds failed to respond during $S-$ periods for as long as 3 min in the case of the free-operant training and 5 sec in the case of the discrete-trials procedure. [See Lyons (1969) for a variation of this procedure.]

Moreover, by incorporating a "fading" technique it was possible, without errors, to transfer a discrimination formed on a relatively easy color discrimination to the much more difficult problem of discriminating between a vertical and a horizontal line (Terrace, 1963c). The Ss were first trained on a red-green discrimination with the errorless technique, after which the vertical and horizontal lines were superimposed on the colors to form compound stimuli (e.g., a vertical line was superimposed on the red key, which was $S+$). After a number of sessions with the compound stimuli, the color component was gradually faded—its intensity progressively diminished—until the color stimuli were no longer visible, thus leaving the vertical and horizontal stimuli as the discriminanda. In contrast to superimposition alone, which led to considerable errors when the color cues were abruptly removed, the use of fading enabled virtually errorless transfer of discrimination from the color to the line-tilt dimension.

Using much the same technique, but employing a simultaneous discrimination paradigm, Sidman and Stoddard (1967) were able to develop a highly efficient program for training retarded children to discriminate between a circle and an ellipse. The fading technique permitted Schusterman (1966) to train a sea lion under water on a series of three-form discrimination reversals virtually without error (again with simultaneous discrimination). Thus the errorless discrimination technique is applicable to both acquisition and reversal and, in simultaneous discrimination paradigms, to a wide range of organisms.

ERRORLESS DISCRIMINATION TRAINING AND FRUSTRATION. There are a number of results obtained with the errorless discrimination-training technique that can be integrated around the notion that such training averts the frustration normally occasioned by nonreinforced responding to $S-$. Another way of putting this is that with errorless training, $S-$ does not become aversive to S. Recall from Chap. 7 that frustration was conceptualized as an unconditioned response to nonreward in a situation where S was accustomed to receiving reward upon performing a certain response. It follows from this interpretation that with customary discrimination training, anticipatory goal responses (r_G) develop by virtue of the reward associated with $S+$. When r_G is established in some strength and not followed by reward, as occurs when S responds to $S-$, frustration (R_F) results. In time, anticipation of frustration (r_F) should be elicited by $S-$, thus providing the basis for the aversiveness of this stimulus (see Chap. 7). A procedure that averts, almost entirely, responding to $S-$ ought to eliminate frustration as well, and such appears to be the case with the errorless discrimination-training procedure.

The supporting evidence comes from a number of directions. Based on observation and photographs of the pigeons' gross reactions to $S-$, Terrace concluded that following discrimination learning with errors, $S-$ tended to evoke various emotional responses, such as wing flapping and turning away from the response key. "Following errorless discrimination learning, however, the usual response to $S-$ [was] a slow settling down under the response key. . . . In these instances the pigeon quietly [waited] for the next appearance of $S+$ [Terrace, 1966c, p. 316]." Schusterman (1966) reported that sea lions not having the benefit of errorless training showed considerable emotional behavior when, during reversal, they responded repeatedly to $S-$. They bit parts of the apparatus and attempted to escape from the training tank. However, no such emotional behavior was observed during reversal accomplished with errorless techniques.

More important, perhaps, are the different functional relations associated with errorless and conventional discrimination-training procedures. During conventional training on a successive discrimination (multiple schedule), the rate of response to $S+$ increases over what it would have been if no periods of $S-$ had been presented, a phenomenon called "behavioral contrast" (see Chap. 10). A plausible interpretation of this result is that the nonrewarded responding to $S-$ induces frustration which in turn lifts S's motivational level. This increase in drive is manifested during the next $S+$ period by an augmented response rate.

If the reasoning thus far is correct, errorless discrimination training should not be attended by behavioral contrast, inasmuch as, presumably, frustration does not develop in the first place. Such a result has been obtained by Terrace, the relevant data appearing in Fig. 11-6. Further evidence comes from the fact that the peak-shift phenomenon, which as pointed out in the last chapter has been interpreted to be the result of aversiveness developed by $S-$, does not occur when the errorless discrimination-training technique is employed during acquisition (Terrace, 1964). A final bit of evidence concerns the effects on discrimination training of chlorpromazine and imipramine. Using the fading technique described above, Terrace (1963b) trained two pigeons to discriminate between a horizontal and a vertical line, with no "errors" made; two other Ss were trained from the beginning with the same stimuli with no attempt made to reduce responding to $S-$. After 30 sessions of discrimination training, the drugs were introduced; each S was tested on each drug at various dose levels. The results were dramatic. The two Ss given conventional discrimination training averaged approximately 100 responses to $S-$ at the lowest dose level and more than 2,000 responses at the highest dose level. In contrast, the pigeons trained with the errorless procedure failed to make a single response to $S-$ at *any* dose level. The interpretation of this result is that chlorpromazine and imipramine disturb a discrimination established by conventional means because they attenuate the frustration responses ordinarily elicited by $S-$. As a consequence, S's inhibition toward responding to $S-$ is reduced, and his discriminative performance suffers. The Ss trained without errors, on the other hand, presumably withhold their responding to $S-$ for reasons other than frustration. Thus, the drugs are without effect in this case.

If one recalls the effects that sodium amytal and alcohol had on certain aspects of runway performance—interpreted in terms of their effects on frustration (Chap. 7)—one sees that the data presented there and the results just described fall into a neat pattern.

DOES THE $S-$ OF ERRORLESS TRAINING POSSESS INHIBITORY CONTROL? The role played by $S-$ in errorless discrimination training has been the subject of some dispute. Terrace (e.g., 1966b) has maintained that, unlike the $S-$ of a discrimination acquired with errors, the negative stimulus of errorless training does not control the subject's responding; it is essentially a "neutral" stimulus. Among the evidence supporting this view is the fact that postdiscrimination gradients

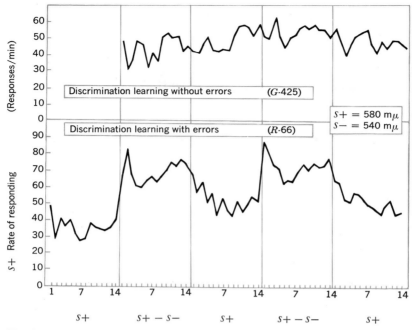

Fig. 11-6. Behavioral contrast as a function of the presence or absence of errors during discrimination acquisition. The ordinate presents rate of responding in $S+$. On the abscissa 14 sessions of $S+$ only alternate with 14 sessions of the $S+$ component of a successive discrimination task. Note that pigeon R-66, who learned with errors, responds at a much higher rate when periods of $S-$ are experienced—an instance of behavioral contrast. When learning occurs without errors, however, there is no evidence of contrast (G-425). The latter S is not represented during the initial 14 sessions (of $S+$ only) because the errorless training technique requires that $S-$ be introduced very early in acquisition. [SOURCE: H. S. Terrace. Stimulus control. In W. K. Honig (Ed.), *Operant behavior: Areas of research and application.* New York: Appleton-Century-Crofts, 1966. Copyright 1966 by Appleton-Century-Crofts and used by permission.]

obtained around $S-$ after errorless training are perfectly flat, whereas those generated after conventional discrimination training usually have a nonzero slope with the point of minimum responding located at $S-$ (Lyons, 1969; Terrace, 1966b). Recall from Chap. 10 that a generalization gradient of zero slope was frequently taken as evidence that the stimulus dimension tested possessed no stimulus control for S's behavior. Applying the same argument to the present case, Terrace concluded that the $S-$ of errorless training does not develop inhibitory control.

Deutsch (1967), however, has contested this position. He points out that the very low level of responding which is observed in generalization tests on the $S-$ dimension after errorless training suggests a very strong degree of inhibitory control (cf. Marsh & Johnson, 1968). Why else does S fail to respond to these stimuli? The counterargument offered by Terrace is based on a distinction between two kinds of discrimination learning. In conventional procedures, where responding to S− is allowed, the subject learns to respond to S+ and *not* to respond to S−; thus both discriminanda gain control over S's behavior. In errorless discrimination training the subject learns to respond to S+ and not to respond to *its absence* (Terrace, 1968). Presumably, in the latter situation it is the absence of S+ that exerts inhibitory control rather than the presence of any particular stimulus.

If Terrace is correct, Ss given conventional discrimination training ought to respond in subsequent generalization tests at a relatively high rate to any stimulus dimension other than one related to S−, because, by assumption, it is only the latter that possesses inhibitory control. On the other hand, Ss trained with errorless techniques ought to withhold responding to all dimensions other than one related to S+ and, other things equal, to the same degree. This follows from the assumption that it is the *absence* of S+ which is exerting inhibitory control. As far as the author knows, there are no studies available that bear directly on this issue.

As noted in the previous chapter, the question of how inhibitory control is best conceptualized is not yet resolved; a solution to this problem is needed as urgently as additional relevant data (cf. Farthing & Hearst, 1968; H. M. Jenkins, 1965a; Lyons, 1969).

THEORETICAL AND PRACTICAL IMPLICATIONS OF ERRORLESS TRAINING PROCEDURES. We have already pointed out that a number of theoretical interpretations of discrimination learning emphasize the role that responding to S− plays in discrimination performance. True enough, discrimination learning in and out of the laboratory normally occurs in such a manner that errors are likely to be made, and eventually these must somehow be inhibited if learning is to take place. But the clear demonstration that responding to S− (errors) is not a *necessary* accompaniment of discrimination learning appears to pull the props out from the argument that errors, and consequently inhibition, is a necessary process in discrimination learning. It renders Spence's (1937) theory of discrimination learning less plausible because it is difficult to see why the "excitatory strength" developed at S+ should not generalize to S− and, having done so, how it could be "neutralized" in the absence of nonreinforced responding to S−.

On the other hand, it is not clear why in the errorless technique S does not respond to S−. After all, not having done so, how can S "know" that responding to S− will not be rewarded? There is a superficial resemblance between the errorless training technique and the learning-set paradigm in that with the latter, S also acquires a discrimination with no errors, or perhaps only one. But it must be remembered that S learns through *LS* training (of the object discrimination type) that one or the other stimulus is correct, and thus he either stays with his first choice if this is correct or switches if it is not. The pigeons of Terrace's experiments had no such previous experimental training; moreover, trained on a successive discrimination, they had to withhold their response for the duration of $S-$, which in one experiment was as long as 3 min. It is one thing for a subject to keep responding to a stimulus which has always provided reward rather than to shift to an alternative that might not; it is quite another thing for S to withhold his response in the presence of $S-$ when he has no information concerning whether responses to this stimulus will be rewarded or not. It would appear that the basis of the success of the errorless training procedure in *multiple* schedules is far from clear, and a question which arises immediately is the degree to which it can be generalized beyond the pigeon.

The belief that errors are a necessary accompaniment of the learning process has deterred educators from devising techniques for their elimination. With the development of programmed instruction and the detailed analysis of teaching strategies which it entailed came the realization that a great many performance failures could be eliminated by proper programming. Skinner (e.g., 1959) long argued on grounds other than technology that not only is the commission of errors an unnecessary accompaniment of learning but that it is detrimental to both learning and the learner's motivational attitude. Given the programming skills acquired over the last decade or so and the capabilities for individualized instruction inherent in computers, there is now the very real possibility that a great deal of the material taught in elementary grades, at least, could be programmed for individuals in such a fashion that for many students errors would decrease to the vanishing point.

One question is whether this is a wise step. Many see virtue in error, in that one learns to persevere in the face of adversity. But as Skinner has pointed out, this may be a misguided notion. Perhaps learning need not be as effortful and demanding of fortitude as it has always been. Man's character seems not to have suffered unduly now that he is no longer required to rub together two sticks each time he needs a light. Nevertheless, the learning achieved in schools must be geared to the "real" world, where control over errors cannot be maintained. One answer to this problem is to shape an individual's resistance to frustration, starting a student out on errorless procedures at the time he confronts new material or new problems and then gradually having him develop a tolerance for nonreinforcement—perhaps by manipulating the schedules associated with correct responses (i.e., intermittent schedules, Terrace, 1966c) or perhaps by permitting the occurrence of certain classes of errors. In any event, recognition of the possibility of virtually error-free learning and the possession of the techniques for its implementation should mean that in the future many fewer children are turned away from academic activities because of needless failures early in their experience.[1]

[1] The "hardware" necessary for individualized instruction is already available commercially in the form of time-sharing on-line computers (e.g., RCA's Instructional 70 System). See Atkinson (1968) for a detailed account of an application of computerized instruction to the teaching of reading to first-grade students, and see Suppes and Morningstar (1969) for a discussion of computer-assisted college-level courses in Russian.

Now that we have completed our brief survey of discrimination learning paradigms, we return to the topics of attention and selective perception, which we touched on earlier in the chapter.

ATTENTION, SELECTIVE PERCEPTION, AND STIMULUS SELECTION

"We can consider attention as the primary process underlying sensory perception, memory, and thinking, without which human life would be comparable to that of lower organisms." Perhaps some would take exception to certain implications of this appraisal by the eminent neurophysiologist Hernández-Peón (1966, p. 122), but it nonetheless reflects the importance with which contemporary investigators in a number of allied areas view the topic of attention.

Although attention has always been a concern of psychologists (e.g., James, 1890, Chap. 11; Pillsbury, 1908), it is only within the last decade or so that the subject has commanded a remarkable degree of interest from psychologists of widely different persuasions. Selective attention (stimulus selection) has been implicated and investigated in animal studies employing rats, pigeons, and monkeys and in the performance of a wide variety of tasks by human adults involving both learning (e.g., Trabasso & Bower, 1968; Underwood, 1963) and "nonlearning" situations (e.g., Egeth, 1967). Attentional processes have entered importantly in the investigation of perceptual development in infants (e.g., Hershenson, 1967) and in the functioning of schizophrenics (e.g., Silverman, 1964). Entire volumes on the subject have begun to appear (e.g., Mostofsky, 1970a; Sanders, 1967), as well as specialized monographs (e.g., Lovejoy, 1968; Trabasso & Bower, 1968). And the topic has not been neglected with respect to possible physiological mechanisms (e.g., Deutsch & Deutsch, 1963; Hernández-Peón, 1966; Horn, 1965; Thompson & Bettinger, 1970; Worden, 1966). Finally the "orienting reflex," investigated in much detail by the Russians (see Lynn, 1966, for a concise presentation of this literature) has been widely interpreted as an attentional mechanism (e.g., Jeffrey, 1968).

Obviously a term that has such a diversified set of referents is not likely to be well defined, and "attention" is no exception (cf. Berlyne, 1970; Mostofsky, 1970b; Treisman, 1969). In this chapter we cannot even briefly consider the data and hypotheses which have arisen in all the areas putatively involving attentional mechanisms. Our emphasis will be on how attention enters into discrimination learning. To expedite our task, we wish to distinguish two senses in which the term is employed, which we shall refer to as "selective perception" and "stimulus selection."

Selective Perception

That not all the stimuli in our immediate environment gain access to our awareness (perception) is a fact known to all of us. We may spend minutes talking to an acquaintance and later be unable to recall the color of his tie because we failed to take note of it. A child intently watching television protests to his irate mother that he did not hear her calls. We drive a familiar route and are astonished to observe suddenly a feature which we must have "seen" before but never noticed. Clearly, that a stimulus strikes one's receptor surface is no guarantee that it will be perceived. Perception, in other words, is selective. This is the sense in which the term "attention" is used most often, and it points to the direction that much of the relevant research has taken.

A subtle distinction must be made between perception and memory. In the first illustration given, our inability to report the color of our acquaintance's tie might reflect a failure of memory rather than of perception, particularly if we were called upon to give this information some time later. It may have gained access to our perception but not to our (long-term) memory. The number which the telephone operator gives us might at that moment be crystal clear in our perception and yet be lost in a matter of seconds if some distraction intervenes. There is, nevertheless, ample evidence that under certain conditions, the stimulus fails to be perceived in the first place, or is perceived only dimly.

In one sense the question of whether or not a stimulus is perceived is a perceptual matter, not necessarily a concern for one interested primarily in the learning process, who could insist as a precondition that perception take place. In fact, just such a precondition was behind the widespread use in discrimination learning studies of "clearly" discriminable stimuli, such as circles versus triangles, white versus black, etc. Yet the fact that a stimulus is perceived—can be reported, is noticed—by no means makes it certain that it will be *utilized* in a discrimination learning situation. There are ample data, some of which we shall review later, which show that out of the stimulus complex perceived by an individual, some aspects will be selected out upon which to base his behavior, whereas other aspects—although perceived—are ignored. Illustrations can be cited which make it extremely difficult to maintain that the individual did not perceive the stimuli he chose to ignore, and, in fact, at times independent evidence can be cited that he did (e.g., Trabasso & Bower, 1968, pp. 85–86). The conclusion, then, is that in the process of employing perceived stimuli in our behavioral adjustments *stimulus selection* often takes place. In a sense, this is "associational" rather than perceptual selectivity.

Although it may be obvious that learning must be intimately involved in the process of stimulus selection, a similar role will have to be conceded to selective perception. Which stimuli "get in" (are perceived) depends greatly on past experience. There are some who feel that learning enters selective perception in a way different from the role it assumes in instrumental behavior, e.g., that reinforcement is unimportant in the first case (Gibson & Gibson, 1955). But whatever one's views with respect to this matter, it seems clear that a thorough understanding of discrimination learning—to return to the topic of this chapter— depends in turn upon a thorough understanding of selective perception and stimulus selection, which is to say, of perception as well as of how the products of perception are utilized.

Let us summarize the preceding paragraphs and expand on them with the aid of Fig. 11-7, which is a schematization of discrimination learning from input stimuli to output behavior.

Out of the enormous flux of stimuli impinging on an organism, only certain aspects are perceived (selective perception—A). However, as later experimental data will show, selective perception is not an all-or-none affair; frequently input stimuli are attenuated rather than completely blocked. The dotted lines are meant to convey this fact. Of the stimuli that are successful in gaining access to perception, not all are utilized as the basis for discriminative behavior (stimulus selection—B). Again attenuation, rather than complete blocking, frequently occurs, which in this case means that perceived stimuli differ in the degree to which they become associated with responses, or in different terminology, in the degree to which they develop stimulus control. Strictly speaking, once we go beyond selective perception (A) we are no longer dealing with stimuli in the sense of physically defined events, but rather with stimuli as perceived, i.e., perceptions. How the latter depend on the former is a topic which has a long history in psychology, but discussing this would take us too far afield. The interested student can consult Gibson (e.g., 1960, 1963, 1966), who has considered the problem extensively (see also Hocutt, 1967, versus Gibson, 1967).

Learning, in one capacity or another, is involved at both A and B. Much of the learning that takes place at A falls within the realm of perceptual learning and concerns how an individual comes to differentiate stimulus properties which

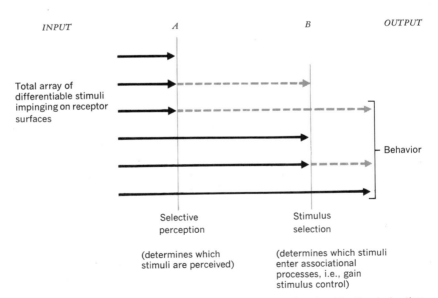

Fig. 11-7. A schematization of some of the processes involved in discrimination learning from input to output. The dashed lines indicate that attenuation rather than complete blockage has taken place (see text).

initially appear equivalent. The variables, learning and otherwise, that control stimulus selection (B) have only recently come under serious investigation.

In the subsequent portions of this chapter we shall discuss some of the data and theoretical hypotheses which are relevant for the processes shown in Fig. 11-7. It should be stressed, however, that the schematization presented in this figure is a gross simplification. For example, certain important processes—such as short-term memory—are omitted, and the processes shown are by no means independent but rather, through receptor adjustments and other mechanisms, often interact upon each other.

ATTENTION AS SELECTIVE PERCEPTION

Perception can be selective in a number of different ways (cf. Treisman, 1969). However, our classification will distinguish only two types. We may fail to perceive certain stimulus aspects because we are insensitive to them; this is a matter of learning to differentiate features in a stimulus array. Or, as shown in a number of previous illustrations, because our perception is focused on one aspect of a stimulus complex, we then fail to perceive—or perceive only dimly—other aspects which ordinarily are perfectly discriminable to us. Over a number of years, James and Eleanor Gibson have addressed themselves to the first problem and have presented a position which has come to be known as "differentiation theory" (Tighe & Tighe, 1966). Selective perception among stimuli that are already well differentiated has received a good deal of attention from British investigators. Much of the relevant data arises from experiments employing selective-listening techniques.

Differentiation Theory of Perceptual Learning

To quote from a recent exposition of differentiation theory (Tighe & Tighe, 1966), it "assumes that the critical change in discrimination learning is *perceptual learning*, defined as an increase in sensitivity to existing but initially undetected or poorly detected variables of stimulation. The process whereby perceptual learning occurs is assumed to be one of differentiation, that is, of coming to see more of what is present in stimulation by progressive analysis, rather than by synthesis, of stimulation; and it is distinguished from the association process which often occurs concurrently in the discrimination experiment [p. 361, italics added]."

A basic assumption of this theory, then, is that there are features—often extremely complex—of the stimulus array confronting S which the individual is initially *incapable* of perceiving. Through some learning process, largely unspecified except that it does not involve reinforcement, the individual becomes capable of detecting such features. The process of differentiation, although "especially important as a rule in the case of young or less experienced organisms . . . is assumed to be a fundamental aspect of all discrimination learning, including that at the adult level [Tighe & Tighe, 1966, p. 361]."

In other words, association of responses to the differentiated aspects of the stimulus takes a back seat, and the process of differentiation itself becomes the prime focus of discrimination learning. The "differentiation theorist assumes that the stimulus properties themselves are the primary determiners of discrimination behavior and he is primarily interested in the role played by increasing sensitivity to stimulation [Tighe & Tighe, 1966, p. 361]."

PREEXPOSURE EXPERIENCE AND DISCRIMINATION LEARNING. Although the theory does not specify precisely how learning—practice—results in perceiving what was formerly unperceivable, there is sufficient substance in the theoretical position to suggest various experimental validations. In one set of experiments it was shown that if rats were reared in a cage containing the stimuli later to serve as discriminanda in a discrimination problem, learning would be facilitated over Ss that did not have the benefit of this visual experience (e.g., Walk, Gibson, Pick, & Tighe, 1959). Rats were reared in cages which contained triangles and circles in the form of metal cutouts until approximately 90 days of age. At this time Ss were trained to discriminate, in a discrimination box, between a black triangle and a black circle. Although faster acquisition of the discrimination was usually obtained for animals having the benefit of the "preexposure" experience, it turned out that the conditions necessary for such facilitation were complex. Cutouts, rather than simple figures painted on the cage walls, were apparently necessary for the preexposure experience to be helpful. Furthermore, even with the use of cutouts, if the preexposure experience was limited to the period before the commencement of discrimination training, no facilitation occurred; neither was it evident when the experience with the figures was limited to the period during which discrimination training was taking place (Gibson, Walk, & Tighe, 1959). Nevertheless the series of experiments seems to suggest that under appropriate conditions, mere experience with stimuli—differential reinforcement being unnecessary—allows S to so differentiate between the latter that subsequent discrimination learning is facilitated.

This interpretation has been challenged, however, by Kerpelman (1965), who found that reinforcement in some form apparently was required for the preexposure experience to be effective. In all the studies conducted by Gibson and her colleagues, the animals received their daily rations of food and water in the same cages in which the stimuli were presented—a "nondifferential" reinforcement procedure. Kerpelman, following the earlier studies closely, evaluated the effects of nondifferential reinforcement by employing preexposure groups in which inspection of the figures could occur in conjunction with reinforcement (food) or not; in the latter groups the forms were removed during feeding periods. His results (as well as those of Bennett and Ellis, 1968) tend to support the view that nondifferential reinforcement is important for facilitation to occur, a result which Kerpelman interpreted within the framework of Spence's (1936) discrimination theory.

It appears, then, that this line of research has not produced unambiguous evidence for differentiation theory, as opposed to an "enrichment" theory of visual perception (cf. Tighe & Tighe, 1966). One difficulty is that the measurements employed, with respect to both the independent and dependent variables, are not sufficiently refined to permit analyses that have a firmer bearing on differentiation theory. We would like to know, for example, what the rats do when the forms are present in their cages. How often do they "manipulate" the forms; are they more likely to do so just before feeding, or perhaps after feeding; do they increase their manipulation of the forms after discrimination training has started? Unfortunately, observations bearing on such questions are rarely reported. Similarly, concerning discrimination training we only have the gross information that Ss with the preexposure experience usually perform better than control subjects. One would like to know how much time was spent by experimental and control Ss in exploring the stimuli (perhaps a measure such as "vicarious trial-and-error" would prove useful), whether irrelevant behaviors drop out first in the experimental Ss, and so forth. Until such refinements occur, it is unlikely that the preexposure experiments will yield decisive information concerning the mechanisms by which exposure to stimuli results in their differentiation.

DIFFERENTIATION VERSUS MEDIATION IN REVERSAL AND EXTRADIMENSIONAL SHIFTS. Another application of differentiation theory concerns the role of comparative and developmental factors in discrimination learning. This illustration also serves as a glimpse of an area of discrimination learning that has received a substantial amount of research effort. [See Wolff (1967) for a detailed review of the discrimination-shift literature, and see Slamecka (1968a) for a penetrating methodological analysis of discrimination-shift paradigms.]

Suppose S learns a discrimination between a triangle and a circle, with color irrelevant. Let us say that on 50 percent of the trials the triangle is red (and the circle is green) and on the remaining trials the triangle is green (and the circle is red); let us assume that the triangle is S+. Reversal learning (often called a reversal shift—RS) consists of having the circle serve as S+ and the triangle as S−, color still irrelevant. There is another shift that is possible in this situation, a "nonreversal" or "extradimensional" shift (EDS). In the latter, S+ is shifted to a value of the formerly irrelevant dimension. For example, red might now be S+ and green S−; form—triangle and circle—becomes the irrelevant dimension.

There is an interesting relationship that holds between type of shift and phylogenetic and developmental status. Rats (Kelleher, 1956), chickens (Brookshire, Warren, & Ball, 1961), and rhesus monkeys (Tighe, 1964) learn an EDS faster than an RS. On the other hand, human adults [including, apparently, illiterate Liberian tribal people (Cole, Gay, & Glick, 1968)] consistently learn the RS faster, even when intermittent reinforcement—of the initial discrimination habit—is controlled (e.g., Harrow & Friedman, 1958). Moreover, there appears to be a relationship (recently challenged by Wolff, 1967) between the developmental status of human subjects and the degree to which *RS* is learned faster than *EDS*. Very young children (about 4 years of age) behave like animals in that they find an *EDS* easier to master than an *RS* (e.g., Kendler, Kendler, & Wells, 1960; Tighe & Tighe, 1967). Older children (5 to 6 years of age) show little difference in the ease of acquiring the two types of shift, and adults generally acquire an *RS* faster than an *EDS*.

One interpretation of the dependence of shift behavior on developmental status is based on "mediation" theory (Kendler & Kendler, 1962; see also Goss, 1961b). Briefly, it is assumed that discrimination learning in animals and in very young children is essentially a single-unit *S–R* affair, much as described by Spence (1936, 1937). By the end of acquisition training the tendency to respond to *S+* is high whereas the tendency to respond to *S−* is low. The response strength accruing to stimuli of the irrelevant dimension will be moderate, inasmuch as responding to stimuli of this dimension is reinforced on only 50 percent of the trials. Reversal learning is relatively difficult because the response strength developed to *S+* must be reduced substantially and the inhibition generated toward *S−* must be overcome (see Fig. 10-11). With extradimensional shifts, on the other hand, it is only necessary to increase an already moderate response strength in the case of *S+* and to reduce response strength to a tolerably low level in the case of *S−*. Consequently, *EDS* should prove easier than *RS* for Ss which operate on the basis of single-unit associations. [It has been shown, however, that for certain special conditions Spence's (1936) model also predicts faster learning for a reversal shift (cf. Wolford & Bower, 1969).]

In older subjects, particularly those in whom the language function is well developed, discrimination learning is presumed to involve an extra "mediation" link; that is, the relevant dimension elicits in S a "mediational" response to which the instrumental behavior becomes associated (Kendler & Kendler, 1962, pp. 6–7). In reversal learning, although the instrumental responses must be reversed, the mediational response is still relevant and thus does not require change. With an *EDS*, *both* the instrumental behavior and the mediating response must be altered. It is maintained, therefore, that where a mediational response is employed, *RS* should prove easier to acquire than *EDS*. However, this conclusion would seem to depend upon, among other things, the learning-rate parameters assumed for the instrumental and the mediating responses. If, for example, mediational responses extinguish and condition much faster than instrumental responses, their use might not result in faster acquisition of a reversal shift.

Working within the framework of differentiation theory, L. S. Tighe (1965) proposed that the constellation of results described above may be explained in terms of the different levels of perceptual learning that are achieved by the end of acquisition of the initial discrimination. Essentially the argument is that if by the end of acquisition S has differentiated out the relevant dimension, *RS* will be easier than *EDS* because the formerly relevant dimension is still relevant and S has "only to learn a relation between one aspect of this feature and reinforcement [Tighe & Tighe, 1966, p. 366]." The *EDS*, on the other hand, requires that S's attention first be redirected to the formerly irrelevant dimension—which possibly might also have to be differentiated out—and that S learn the appropriate stimulus-reward relationships (cf. Tighe & Tighe, 1968a).

If S achieves criterion on the initial discrimination without having differentiated out the relevant dimension, *EDS* should then be easier than *RS*. The basis for this prediction is that, when S has not differentiated the relevant dimension, solution of the initial discrimination must be based on responding to composite properties of the positive objects. For example, S must learn that reward is associated with the red triangle and the green triangle but not with the red circle or the green circle. If it is assumed that S maintains this lack of differentiation, reversal learning can be accomplished only by completely reversing these relationships. For the extradimensional shift, in contrast, only two changes are required: responding positively to the red circle and negatively to the green triangle.

The two theories, mediation and differentiation, are quite similar in several respects. In both, *EDS* is easier to learn than *RS* when the relevant cues are reacted to as unrelated stimuli. And in both cases organizing the relevant stimuli into a single dimension so that they can be manipulated jointly results in *EDS* being more difficult than *RS*. The rationale for these predictions is also similar, namely, that in the case of the extradimensional shift, instrumental responses as well as the "organizing" response must be changed, whereas for the reversal shift only the former need be altered. However, a mediating response provides the means of organization in the case of the first theoretical view, while for the second it is a perceptual process—"differentiation."

If the reasoning behind differentiation theory is correct, one should be able to decrease the difficulty of reversal shifts by ensuring that differentiation of the relevant dimension takes place during initial acquisition. L. S. Tighe (1965) attempted to accomplish this by giving her subjects (children between 67 and 84 months of age) pretraining in the dimensions which were to be used in the experimental discriminations. The pretraining did not, of course, involve reinforcement; Ss simply made judgments as to whether pairs of stimuli from the dimensions to be used later were similar or different. The results were in the expected direction; that is, there was a marked facilitation of *RS* learning in the group which had the benefit of the pretraining experience.

Although the results are suggestive, it is not clear that they are squarely in opposition with a mediational analysis. Despite the absence of experimenter-applied reinforcement, it is conceivable that the pretraining was sufficient to develop the very sort of mediating responses which Kendler and Kendler (1962) invoke in their theoretical analysis. It might be possible to discriminate more sharply between the two theoretical approaches by ascertaining whether facilitation of *RS* learning in animals can be accomplished by analogous pretraining experience.

In his interesting book *The Senses Considered as Perceptual Systems*, Gibson (1966) states, "The 'differentiation theory' of perceptual learning proposed by Gibson and Gibson (1955) was programmatic at the outset, but the mechanisms for this learning are becoming clearer. The process is one of learning what to attend to, both overtly and covertly. For the perception of objects, it is the detection of distinctive features and the abstraction of general properties. This almost always involves the detection of invariance under changing stimulation [pp. 270–271]." Although the theory is promising, before it can hope to gain a wider acceptance, it will have to spell out in more detail how perceptual learning differs from "association" learning and identify with some precision the variables that influence the former process importantly (cf. E. J. Gibson, 1969; Tighe & Tighe, 1968b).

Selective-listening Experiments

As was already pointed out, the selective perception with which differentiation theory concerns itself is largely a matter of becoming sensitive to aspects of the stimulus flux toward which one is initially insensitive. There is little doubt, however, that perception is selective even among stimulus properties that are already fully differentiated. We have provided several illustrations of this variety of selective perception, and now we turn to some experimental data.

"SHADOWING" EXPERIMENTS.   Selective perception of fully differentiable auditory stimuli, such as words and numbers, has been demonstrated, and a number of its properties have been investigated by means of selective-listening experiments. There are a number of pertinent experimental arrangements (see, for example, Broadbent, 1958), but we shall take as our illustrations experiments on "shadowing" with *binaural* and *dichotic* listening.

In dichotic listening, two messages are fed to S independently, one in the right ear and one in the left. The subject is usually given the task of attending to the (relevant) message presented in one ear (the "accepted" ear), and the question of major interest is the extent to which he perceives the (irrelevant) message on the other, "rejected," ear. "Shadowing" is a response technique which assures that S attends to the accepted ear, the task of S being simply to repeat verbatim the relevant message. Essentially S is talking and listening at the same time. According to Cherry (1953), a marked characteristic of S's voice as he shadows (while listening dichotically) is its monotone. "Very little emotional content or stressing of the words occurs at all. Subjectively, the subject is unaware of this fact. Also he may have very little idea of what the message that he has repeated is all about, especially if the subject matter is difficult. But he has recognized every word, as his repeating proves [p. 978]."

In the binaural mode of presentation both messages are presented to both ears. Shadowing (attempting to repeat verbatim the relevant message) is far more difficult under this condition. The difference is rather like trying to attend to one of two individuals speaking simultaneously and sitting next to each other as against attending to one of two individuals speaking simultaneously but sitting on either side of you. Moreover, peripheral auditory masking is much more likely under the binaural mode of presentation.

BINAURAL SHADOWING. In a somewhat informal paper, Cherry (1953), who was among the first to use the shadowing technique, reported that his Ss had a great deal of difficulty repeating one of two messages recorded by the same speaker and presented binaurally. Eventually, after many hearings, they were able to repeat the message with a high degree of accuracy.

In a more rigorous follow-up study in which S was allowed only a single exposure to the two messages, A. M. Treisman (1964b) showed that shadowing of binaural messages could be facilitated greatly by certain manipulations of the irrelevant message. For example, if both messages were recorded by the same (female) voice and came from the same source (an English novel), Ss averaged only 31 percent correct words for the shadowed message, committing an average of 19.5 intrusions from the irrelevant message (Table 11-1). Changing the irrelevant message to a passage of technical English (biochemistry) increased the percentage of correct words repeated from the shadowed message to approximately 40 percent and reduced the average number of intrusions to 12.3.

A dramatic increase in efficiency was obtained by using different voices for the two messages, a female voice for the relevant message and a male for the irrelevant message, even though the messages came from the same source (the English novel). In this case almost 74 percent of the words were shadowed correctly, with less than 1.0 intrusions from the irrelevant message. Interestingly enough, the percentage of correct words shadowed was not increased by changing the character of the irrelevant message (from the English novel to a passage in Latin) in addition to changing the voice.

Treisman also included conditions in which the irrelevant message was delivered by the same (female) voice, but in a foreign language with which S had varying degrees of familiarity, ranging from fluency to no knowledge. For example, the irrelevant message might be a selection of French prose. As one might expect, if S was fluent in the language used in the irrelevant mes-

Table 11-1 Performance in Binaural Shadowing Task with Relevant Message a Passage from an English Novel Spoken in a Female Voice

	CONDITIONS OF IRRELEVANT MESSAGE			
	SAME VOICE SAME NOVEL	SAME VOICE TECHNICAL ENGLISH	MALE VOICE SAME NOVEL	MALE VOICE LATIN
Mean percent words correctly shadowed	31.0	39.8	73.7	73.9
Mean number of intrusions from irrelevant message	19.5	12.3	<1.0	<1.0

SOURCE: A. M. Treisman. Verbal cues, language, and meaning in selective attention. *American Journal of Psychology*, 1964, **77**, 206–219. Copyright by Karl M. Dallenbach, 1964. Used by permission.

sage, shadowing performance was more seriously affected (42.2 percent words shadowed correctly on the average) than if the language in the irrelevant message was completely unknown to S (55.5 percent correct).

Another point of interest is that only 9 of 20 Ss for whom the irrelevant message consisted of Latin spoken by a male voice noticed that this message was not in English. On the other hand, when both messages were delivered by the same voice, but the irrelevant message was in a foreign language, every one of the 44 Ss involved noticed that the irrelevant message was not in English.

These results have a bearing on the mechanisms that underlie selective perception. It appears that selection can take place at a very early stage in the perceptual analysis of sensory input. And when it does, very little information contained in the ignored material is perceived by S. Selection at an early stage of analysis is facilitated by gross physical differences between the relevant and irrelevant material, such as the frequency (pitch) differences that exist between a male and a female voice. If on the basis of "gross" characteristics the irrelevant message is rejected early, aspects of the irrelevant material which require finer analysis, such as discriminating whole words or even discriminating the general linguistic nature of the irrelevant material, will go undetected. It is as though S "tunes in" on the female's voice, and having thus rejected the male's voice becomes unaware of its content.

If a mechanism such as this were actually operating, we should expect that S would perceive very little about the nature of the irrelevant message presented in the male's voice. And indeed this is the case. Recall (Table 11-1) that there were extremely few intrusions from the irrelevant message when a man's voice was employed, *whether the material came from the same novel or from a passage of Latin*. Also, as already noted, only 9 of the 20 Ss in the group presented with the irrelevant message in Latin spoken by a male's voice noticed the obvious fact that the irrelevant message was not in English.

When, however, the relevant and irrelevant messages are in the same voice, analysis of sensory input must proceed to a further point before a difference in input can be detected and the irrelevant message rejected. As a consequence more of the irrelevant message will be perceived, more intrusions from the irrelevant message are likely to occur, and the overall shadowing performance will be lower. These predictions were realized in the poor performance, both in terms of the percentage of correct words shadowed and the number of intrusions, which occurred when the same voice delivered the relevant and irrelevant messages. The somewhat better performance which occurred when the irrelevant message took the form of technical English may be accounted for by the assumption that the wide difference in content of the relevant and irrelevant messages permitted perceptual analysis to terminate earlier than when the content of the messages was highly similar.

DICHOTIC SHADOWING.   As already pointed out, dichotic shadowing is much easier to perform than binaural shadowing. This makes sense because S has an added, and rather potent, cue upon which to base his selective perception, namely, the ear in which the relevant message is received. Thus, even though both messages might be spoken by the same voice and be from the same general material, one would expect that rejection could take place at a relatively low level of analysis and consequently little concerning the structure or nature of the irrelevant message would be perceived by S. Such is the case. Cherry (1953), for example, found that if the irrelevant message to the rejected ear was started in English and while S was shadowing the relevant message (also in English) the material on the rejected ear was switched to German, the subject was not able later to report that the irrelevant message was anything but English. His subjects did recognize that an irrelevant message consisted of normal human speech but they were unable "to make definite identification of the language as being English." On the other hand they always noticed a change in voice from male to female or the difference between speech and a 400-Hz pure tone. Most Ss took reversed male speech (normal speech played backwards) to be normal speech.

Using the dichotic-shadowing technique, Moray (1959) presented a prose passage as the relevant message and a short list of simple words as the irrelevant message, with both messages matched for loudness. Although the list of words was presented for a total of 35 times on the rejected ear, Ss failed in a later test to recognize them. In fact, there was no more recognition for these words than for a comparable set of words presented for the first time.

However, there are exceptions to the principle that when selective perception takes place at a relatively low level of analysis, discriminations based on more refined features of the input message will not occur. As an illustration, Moray (1959) reported that a subject's own name was very likely to be perceived when it occurred as part of the irrelevant message, which suggests that when perception is focused on one "channel" not all stimuli on the rejected channel are equally blocked. This is a result that seems to square with common experience.

Treisman (1960) reported a similar effect for contextual cues. She had subjects shadow dichotically a message on the accepted ear which could be either a selection of prose (relatively strong contextual cues) or a statistical approximation to English (see Miller & Selfridge, 1950). About halfway through the recording, the message on the accepted ear was suddenly switched to the rejected ear and that on the latter was switched to the accepted ear. The Ss had been instructed to shadow only the material coming in on the accepted ear. The question that interested Treisman was the degree to which Ss would continue shadowing the message that had been on the accepted ear after the switch took place and whether this shift to the rejected ear would be a function of the strength of contextual cues in the first message. Indeed she found this to be the case. When the message on the accepted ear consisted of prose from a novel, subjects were far more likely to repeat words from that message after it had been switched to the rejected ear than when the shadowed message was composed of approximations to English. This suggests that another factor which influences the extent to which information can get through the "attention block" is the degree of contextual restraint operating on the information. If certain words are highly probable following previously shadowed words, they are likely to be perceived even though they are transmitted over a rejected channel.

Treisman also reported that most of her subjects described the rejected message as "just noise," "perhaps English," again showing how little of the irrelevant message is perceived in dichotic listening. Most of the subjects had no idea that the passages had been switched to opposite ears, and they were unaware that they had spoken any words from the wrong ear.

If, however, the voices in the two messages were different—one a male's voice and the other a female's—Ss did notice that the voices were switched to opposite ears, and they did not transfer shadowing at the point of switch. This last finding further verifies that if selective perception is based on a rather low level of analysis, very little of the rejected message is transmitted.

As previously noted, one must distinguish between the perception of a stimulus and its retention and take appropriate measures to ensure that inability to report the stimulus is attributable to failure of perception rather than of memory. Unfortunately, most of the relevant experiments in selective listening have permitted a delay to intervene between presentation of the critical stimuli and tests for their perception. It is easy to show, however, that at least in some cases the difficulty lies in perception and not in memory.

To cite one illustration, Treisman and Geffen (1967) presented two prose messages dichotically, requiring S to shadow one of the messages. A secondary task given to S was to indicate by a tapping response the presence of certain "target" words when they occurred in either the relevant or irrelevant message. Thus if S failed to respond to target words which appeared on the rejected ear, it is not likely a result of failure of memory, inasmuch as he was instructed to respond with the tapping response immediately. The results were clear-cut. In the main experiment, 86.5 percent of the target words were detected and responded to when these words occurred in the accepted ear, whereas only 8.1 percent of the target words which occurred in the rejected ear drew a response. Treisman and Geffen interpreted their results to mean that the failure to report various features of stimuli coming in through the rejected ear is a perceptual rather than a memory or motor (response competition) deficit. Though strongly contested (see Deutsch, Deutsch, Lindsay, & Treisman, 1967), subsequent research has provided additional support for this view (Treisman & Riley, 1969).

Interestingly, in a very similar experiment, Lawson (1966) got very different results. She used as target stimuli brief tones or pips, rather than words, and found that S detected such stimuli about equally when they were presented to his accepted and rejected ears (cf. Treisman & Riley, 1969). The implication of this result, as well as a number of related findings in selective listening, is that certain gross discriminations, particularly those involving the physical characteristics of stimuli coming over different channels, are performed *before* the point where mechanisms of selective attention take over, or, in terms of "filter theory" (to be discussed below), before the selective filter.

"FILTER THEORY." One of the first attempts to organize systematically data resulting from experiments on selective listening and other investigations of divided attention was made by Broadbent (1958), who devised a "selective filter" theory based on concepts borrowed from information processing and communication analysis. The general idea is that individuals have limited information-processing capacity; they cannot possibly analyze and process all the information which impinges on their receptor surfaces. Somehow this stream of potential information must be filtered, so that only one "channel" at a time is allowed access to the mechanisms by means of which information is processed. A selective filter chooses from among the various input channels that one whose information will receive (higher) processing. Various factors, such as S's current motivation, operate to "tune" the filter, and certain properties of input signals increase the probability of getting by the filter—for example, strong rather than weak stimuli or high rather than low frequency of sounds.

Originally Broadbent proposed that when a channel was rejected, it was an all-or-none situation, so that if S did not attend to a stimulus, it would have no effect upon him. However, there is now some evidence (e.g., Broadbent & Gregory, 1963; Treisman, 1960) that information coming over a rejected channel may be merely attenuated rather than blocked completely. This forms the basis for the explanation of the result that words of importance to S, or of high affectivity (such as one's name), tend to be perceived when presented to the rejected ear whereas less favored words do not.

Treisman (1960) has proposed a modification of Broadbent's theory which takes the latter result into account (Fig. 11-8). A basic assumption is that the selective filter attentuates rather than blocks completely information coming over a rejected channel. Whether or not the attenuated "signal" will be detected depends upon the "threshold" of the corresponding item in the "store for known words." Thus if the threshold for a word is relatively low, either because the word is highly probable after the immediately preceding words (B and C in Fig. 11-8) or because, like one's name, it has "affective" value, detection of the attenuated signal coming over the rejected channel will take place. Provision is also made in Fig. 11-8 for discriminative functions that presumably occur before the selective filter. There is a good deal of evidence, some of which has been mentioned above, that certain physical aspects of the message coming over the rejected channel are discriminated—are perceived—though other, more refined features are not. Thus as we have seen, in dichotic listening one can discriminate that the irrelevant message consists of speech rather than a pure tone (a discrimination based on differences in the distributions of frequencies) without being aware of the content of the spoken words. Apparently, then, some types of analyses occur whether the signals are received over an accepted or a rejected channel, so presumably this processing takes place "prior" to the point where the selective filter chooses among the "active" channels.

Let us now summarize some of the results we have discussed and point to a number of indicated conclusions. First, there is little question that if an individual attends to information arriving over one channel (such as the accepted

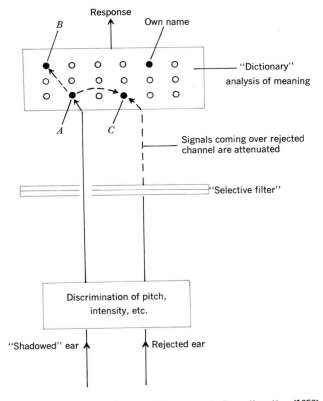

Fig. 11-8. Treisman's modification of Broadbent's (1958) filter theory of selective perception. The thresholds of words B and C are lowered by their high transition probabilities after word A (see text). (SOURCE: A. M. Treisman. Contextual cues in selective listening. *Quarterly Journal of Experimental Psychology,* 1960, **12,** 242–248. Used by permission.)

ear) to the extent that he extracts a large amount of the available information—which must occur if S shadows the relevant message correctly—he then simply does not have sufficient information-processing ability available to perform refined analyses on information arriving over other channels. The evidence on which this conclusion is based comes from the remarkable ignorance which S displays toward the content of the irrelevant message. He does not recognize words or even digits that form part of the irrelevant message, nor can he respond to the simplest words transmitted over the rejected ear.

Second, the degree to which S remains ignorant of—fails to perceive—the contents of the irrelevant message is directly related to the ease with which the latter can be rejected. Other things equal, the less similar the relevant and irrelevant message—in content, in the physical characteristics of the signals, or in the channels over which they are transmitted—the earlier in the hierarchal sequence of discriminative processing S can reject the irrelevant message. The earlier the point at which rejection takes place (and thus the earlier the selective filter is applied to the rejected channel), the less S will perceive of the irrelevant message. With binaural shadowing the accepted and rejected channels are not easily separable. We saw that as a consequence rejection of the irrelevant message was difficult, particularly if both messages were similar in content. And as shown by the large number of intrusions, a substantial amount of information from the irrelevant message was perceived under the latter condition. Tagging the irrelevant message with a salient physical characteristic (e.g., a male rather than a female voice) permitted its rejection at a much earlier point, and consequently less information from the rejected channel was available to interfere with shadowing the relevant message. Similar results were found in the case of dichotic shadowing.

Third, discrimination of certain features of the input signal which comes over the rejected channel—such as frequency characteristics and other physical properties—is very likely to occur, as shown by the fact that a tone coming over the rejected ear is just as likely to be perceived and reacted to appropriately as when it occurs in the accepted ear. For those theorists subscribing to a filter theory of selective perception, results such as these imply that certain discriminations take place *before* the selective filter.

Fourth and last, in some cases the selective filter attenuates rather than blocks completely information coming over the rejected channel. The evidence for this conclusion is the fact that words which have a special meaning to the subject, such as his name, or words which on the basis of immediately preceding items have a high transition probability are likely to breach the attention block and be perceived.

This last conclusion, and the results on which it is based, seems to raise particular difficulties for filter theory. On the one hand it may imply that all analyses of input signals that take place on the accepted channel are performed on the rejected channel as well, but in the latter case, the products of the analyses come through in an attenuated form. If so, the role of the selective filter would seem to be downgraded from a "filter" to an "attenuator," and one would have to search elsewhere for mechanisms to account for most aspects of selective perception (e.g., Deutsch & Deutsch, 1963). Perhaps a more promising interpretation is that some, but by no means all, of the analyses which take place on the relevant message are also applied to the signals coming over the rejected channel; the results of the latter analyses are transmitted in an attenuated form. Some analyses—for example, those by means of which meaning is extracted from a series of words—probably never take place on the rejected channel, so that no amount of lowering of "thresholds" could possibly cause detection of this feature of verbal material. The difficulty with this interpretation is in accounting for the means by which the degree of attenuation varies from one class of information to another, and although some suggestions are available (e.g., A. M. Treisman, 1964a), the solution is by no means evident.

One further point: It turns out that signal detection theory is applicable to the problem of what goes on in the rejected channel. The notion that the filter acts to attenuate rather than to block completely information coming over the rejected channel immediately suggests an analogy with signal detection theory, in that the attenuation may be interpreted as a reduction in the signal-to-noise ratio. In the terminology of signal detection theory (see Chap. 5) d' is reduced for signals coming over the rejected channel. Such signals would still be responded to provided S's criterion is sufficiently low.

There are some data to support this point of view. Broadbent and Gregory (1963) combined a signal detection procedure with dichotic listening. One group of subjects was required to attend to a series of 6 digits, spoken into one ear at the rate of one digit per half-second, and to record these responses immediately afterwards. They had fed into their other ear a burst of white noise, which started just before the first of the six digits and stopped just after the last one. Imbedded in half of these bursts of noise was a pure tone of 1,000 Hz (1 sec in duration). The subjects in this group had the additional task of reporting whether or not the tone occurred in the burst of white noise and of indicating their confidence concerning the decision. However, they first recorded the digits. A control group, whose entire attention was devoted to trying to detect the tone, was instructed to take no notice of the digits. They registered their opinions concerning the presence or absence of the tone immediately, or whenever they wished. This seems a weakness in the experimental design. However it was found that, analyzing the data in terms appropriate to signal detection theory, attending to the digits resulted in a much smaller value of d'; moreover, the β parameter, an indication of S's criterion, was unchanged. In other words, it appears that the effect of directing S's attention to the digits was to decrease the discriminability of the tone, as one might surmise from the attenuation hypothesis.

This conclusion was verified in a more recent study by Moray and O'Brien (1967), which advanced the additional suggestion that, compared to performance when attention is shared, the primary message of a selective-listening task is *amplified*. Working under two sets of experimental conditions, a group of eight Ss was given the task of detecting the occurrence of letters randomly distributed among a larger collection of numbers. In the *shared*-attention condition, S was instructed to listen to the messages coming over both ears. Whenever a letter was heard in the right ear, S was to tap the key near his right hand; whenever a letter was heard in his left ear, S was to press a second key with his left hand. In the *selective*-attention condition, S was instructed to listen only to the primary message fed into his right ear; the secondary message presented to the left ear served only as a distraction. Whenever a letter was heard in the right ear, S was to press the right key, and if, despite his efforts to ignore the secondary message, a letter was heard in the left ear, S was to indicate so by tapping the left key.

Using the proportion of hits and false positives in the manner described in Chap. 5, values of d' and $\log \beta$ were calculated for various features of the data. Table 11-2 summarizes these results. It is clear from the table that in the selective-attention condition, there is only a small difference between the values of log β for the accepted and rejected channels. On the other hand the corresponding values of d' differ widely, suggesting again that attending to the primary message reduces the discriminability of the secondary or rejected message while having little effect on S's response criterion. Neither log β nor d' showed much variation between the left and right ears in the shared-attention condition. Apparently, when attention is shared between two messages, an equal level of detectability is maintained on the two channels as well as an equal criterion.

Note, however, that the d' of both the left and the right ear is substantially (and significantly) less than the corresponding value achieved with the accepted ear in the selective-attention condition. This result suggests that the accepted message is somehow amplified. Because the value of d' calculated for both channels combined differs little for the two attention conditions, the implication is that S has at his disposal a "fixed amount" of attention which he distributes in accordance with the needs of the task at hand. In the shared-attention condition he distributes the available attention equally between the two channels, whereas in the selective-attention condition more is directed to the accepted channel. The result is that the primary message is amplified at the expense of attenuation of the rejected message.

Clearly, in spite of the rather ingenious experimentation which has been conducted in the area of selective listening, theoretical developments are still at a relatively preliminary stage. This is to be expected, since selective attention is an extremely complex process. There seems little question that signal detection theory will play an important role in future developments. It is also likely that a close liaison between the purely behavioral data and results from relevant physiological research (e.g., Milner, Taylor, & Sperry, 1968) will prove particularly fruitful.

As a final comment, it should be pointed out that research in the area of selective perception has by no means been restricted to selective-listening experiments. Selective perception has been demonstrated in the case where the accepted and rejected channels utilize different sensory modalities—vision and audition (see Broadbent, 1958). Moreover there is evidence that selective perception also occurs within the visual modality alone, some data suggesting that different portions of the retina may act as different "channels" (Eriksen &

Table 11-2 Values of d' and log β Obtained in the Shared and Selective Conditions

	SELECTIVE ATTENTION			SHARED ATTENTION		
	ACCEPTED	REJECTED	COMBINED	LEFT	RIGHT	COMBINED
d'	3.712	1.429	2.719	3.001	2.823	2.895
log β	1.473	1.228	1.692	1.569	1.431	1.489

SOURCE: N. Moray, and T. O'Brien. Signal-detection theory applied to selective listening. *Journal of the Acoustical Society of America*, 1967, **42**, 765–772. Used by permission.

Lappin, 1967), other data implying that visual perception can be selectively "pretuned" (Egeth & Smith, 1967). The student interested in the topics discussed in this section should consult the recent review by Treisman (1969).

STIMULUS SELECTION

Stimulus selection, it will be recalled, refers to the fact that from among the numerous stimuli which enter one's perception, only some are utilized whereas others, perhaps equally informative, are not or are utilized to a lesser extent (Fig. 11-7). We turn now to a number of recent illustrations of this process.

Reynolds (1961a) trained two pigeons on a *mult VI* 3 *EXT;* S+ was a compound stimulus formed by superimposing a triangle on a red background, and S— consisted of a circle superimposed on a green background. After Ss acquired the discrimination, they were tested separately on each of the four components, and none of the responses executed during the test phase were reinforced. As Fig. 11-9 shows, both Ss selected out one component of the compound S+ on which to base their responding, or, put differently, only one component of S+ gained stimulus control. Note that in this experiment the rejected component of S+ achieved virtually no stimulus control whatever.

A similar result was obtained by D'Amato and Fazzaro (1966b). Employing the apparatus described earlier (Fig. 11-3), they presented two capuchin monkeys with a simultaneous discrimination task in which a compound S+ (a white vertical line superimposed on a red background) and a compound S— (a horizontal white line superimposed on a green background) served as discriminanda. Twenty of the daily 40 trials were of this nature. However, on 10 other trials only the color component was presented, and S was given two options. He could either respond on the basis of the color cue or he could execute a cue-producing response—pressing the white-illuminated center key—which resulted in the appearance of the bar component. In other words, a cue-producing response (*CPR*) transformed the color component into the compound stimuli. On the remaining 10 of the 40 daily trials, the bar component appeared alone, and S could either respond on the basis of this cue or "call for" the color component by making a *CPR* (converting, therefore, the bar component into the compound stimuli). It was assumed that if a component failed to be utilized by S in mastering the discrimination, S would perform *CPR*s in its presence in order to transform the component into the compound stimuli. The ability of S to perform *CPR*s to obtain additional cues was established by previous pretraining.

The results obtained for one subject are presented in Fig. 11-10. It is evident from the upper panel that although this subject initially responded equally to the color and bar components, it soon entirely gave up responding to the bars. Just the reverse is true for the color component; after the first two sessions, S never transformed it to the compound stimuli. Although S's performance curve for the color component (lower panel) is somewhat erratic,

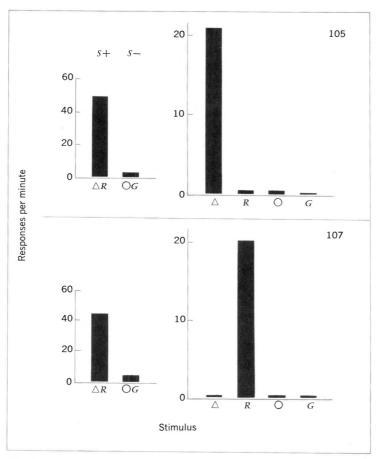

Fig. 11-9. The panels on the left show response rate for each of two pigeons to $S+$ and $S-$ over three training sessions. On the right appear results of test sessions during which each component was presented separately (see text). (SOURCE: G. S. Reynolds. Attention in the pigeon. *Journal of the Experimental Analysis of Behavior,* 1961, **4,** 203–208. Copyright 1961 by the Society for the Experimental Analysis of Behavior, Inc. and used by permission.)

it is a reasonable assumption that S's responses to the compound stimuli were based entirely on the color component.

Further evidence for stimulus selection was obtained from subsequent test trials in which S was forced to respond to the bar component. In this stage 20 of the 40 daily trials consisted of the usual compound stimuli. On 10 other trials the bar component alone was presented with the option of a *CPR* available. On the remaining 10 trials the bars appeared with no option for a *CPR*, and hence S was forced to respond on the basis of this component.

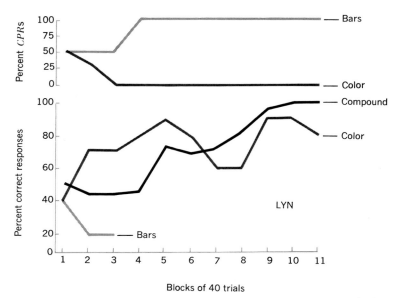

Fig. 11-10. The upper panel depicts the percentage of cue-producing responses made by S to the color and bar components. Note that starting with the fourth block of trials, when confronted with the bar component, S always "called for" the color cue. The lower panel shows S's choice behavior separately for each of the components and the compound stimuli (see text). (SOURCE: M. R. D'Amato and J. Fazzaro. Attention and cue-producing behavior in the monkey. *Journal of the Experimental Analysis of Behavior,* 1966, **9,** 469–473. Copyright 1966 by the Society for the Experimental Analysis of Behavior, Inc. and used by permission.)

As Fig. 11-11 shows, S learned nothing about the significance of the bar component, in spite of the fact that during earlier training (Fig. 11-10) he responded to the compound discriminanda—and hence to the bar component—on more than 320 trials. This component evidently gained no stimulus control whatever. Moreover, even though S eventually mastered the discrimination between the horizontal and vertical bars, he never failed to transform the bar component to compound stimuli when this option was available (top line in Fig. 11-11). In other words, S maintained a strong preference for responding on the basis of the color component.

As a third illustration of the operation of stimulus selection, we turn to an experiment by Underwood, Ham, and Ekstrand (1962). These investigators trained college students on a paired-associate task in which the stimulus items were composed of compound stimuli. In one condition the compound was formed by superimposing a trigram of low association value (e.g., GWS) upon a clearly discriminable color background. For example, one stimulus item was the compound NXQ printed on a yellow background. The response items were single digits. A second condition differed only in that high frequency three-

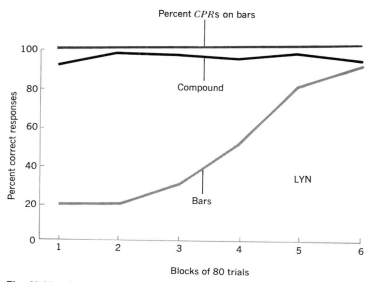

Fig. 11-11. Cue-producing and choice behavior when S was forced to respond to the bar component on 20 of each block of 80 trials (see text). (SOURCE: M. R. D'Amato and J. Fazzaro. Attention and cue-producing behavior in the monkey. *Journal of the Experimental Analysis of Behavior*, 1966, **9**, 469–473. Copyright 1966 by the Society for the Experimental Analysis of Behavior, Inc. and used by permission.)

letter words (e.g., GAS) were used in place of the trigrams. The question at issue was whether the tendency to use color as the "functional" stimulus (the stimulus gaining stimulus control) would depend upon the meaningfulness of the alternative stimulus component.

To test this hypothesis, one group in each of the two conditions was given transfer trials in which only the color component of the stimulus complex was presented. A second group received only the trigram (or word) component, and two control groups—one in each condition—continued during the "transfer" trials to receive the compound stimuli. In all cases transfer trials started when S achieved one perfect recitation on the original list.

It is apparent from Fig. 11-12 (left panel) that with trigrams and color making up the compound stimuli, acquisition of the list was based almost entirely on the color component; the trigrams apparently gained very little stimulus control. With high meaningful words as the alternative to color, this relationship was reversed in that the words gained more stimulus control than color. Nevertheless, it is clear from the figure that the color component achieved a fair degree of effectiveness, and, as if in compensation, the words alone were not as effective a cue as the compound stimuli.

Stimulus selection in concept-identification tasks has been investigated recently by Trabasso and Bower (1968). The subject is required in such tasks

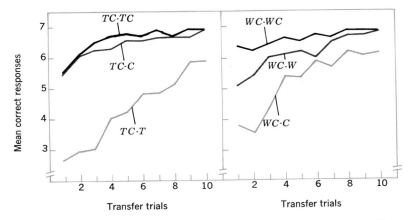

Fig. 11-12. Stimulus selection as shown in transfer trials, which began 45 sec after Ss met criterion on the compound stimuli (trigram plus color, *TC*, or word plus color, *WC*). The data of the left panel show that color was the effective acquisition cue for the *TC* groups, inasmuch as the group tested on this component only (*TC-C*) performed as well as the control (*TC-TC*), who had both cues available. Trigrams apparently gained a small measure of control since the performance of the *TC-T* group is somewhat higher than would be expected on a chance basis. There were seven items in the list, with the response members consisting of the digits 2 to 8; consequently a plausible estimate of the number of correct items expected by chance alone is 1.

From the right panel it is evident that stimulus control was more equally shared by the word (*W*) and color components, with the former being the more effective of the two cues. (SOURCE: B. J. Underwood, M. Ham, and B. Ekstrand. Cue selection in paired-associate learning. *Journal of Experimental Psychology*, 1962, **64,** 405–409. Copyright 1962 by the American Psychological Association and used by permission.)

to sort stimuli in accordance with criteria established by **E**. To take a simple illustration, consider a set of stimuli generated by all possible combinations of three stimulus dimensions, with each dimension possessing two values. Let the dimensions be color (red or blue), shape (circle or triangle), and size (large or small). Since there are three dimensions, each having two values, there are $2^3 = 8$ possible different combinations of the three dimensions (e.g., large-red-triangle). In a typical concept-identification problem, **S** might be told that some of the stimuli (often presented on cards) have the name "A" and others have the name "B," and it is his task to find out which stimuli are associated with which letter. The stimulus cards are presented one at a time, and **S** responds "A" or "B," whereupon **E** informs **S** of the correctness of his response. If color was the relevant dimension and "A" was associated with red, the problem is solved when **S** responds "A" to the red cards and "B" to the blue cards. It is perhaps now clear why such problems are called "concept-identification tasks": the subject has only to identify the concept (or the dimension) which is relevant.

Trabasso and Bower (1968, Chap. 3) trained college students on a concept-identification task in which two dimensions, shape and location of a dot, were the relevant cues; there were in addition three irrelevant dimensions. The subjects were trained to a criterion of 32 consecutive correct responses and then tested for the amount of learning which occurred on the shape and dot-location dimensions. It was found that out of a total of 89 Ss, 76 solved the problem on the basis of only one of the relevant dimensions. The performance of these Ss on the relevant dimension not utilized by them showed no evidence whatever of learning; only about 51 percent correct responses occurred over the first test series. Thirteen of the 89 Ss learned the significance of both relevant dimensions and almost to exactly the same degree, achieving 95 percent correct responses on both shape and dot location during the first test series. This experiment provides a striking illustration of complete stimulus selection, even in the face of what amounts to a fair degree of overtraining. As our later review of the effects of overtraining on stimulus selection will indicate, complete stimulus selection after overtraining is the exception rather than the rule.

Stimulus selection may also occur in classical conditioning paradigms, as our final illustration shows. Investigating "attentionlike" processes in classical conditioning, Kamin (1968) showed that contiguity of CS and UCS is by no means a sufficient condition for classical conditioning to occur. Kamin employed the conditioned-emotional-response (CER) paradigm, in which, it will be recalled, an animal working for positive reinforcement is presented with a CS at the termination of which occurs an unavoidable shock. After a few such pairings of CS and UCS, presentation of the former results in a marked degree of response suppression.

Kamin gave his Ss (rats) 18 CER trials with white noise serving as the CS. Then 8 additional CER trials followed in which the CS was composed of a compound stimulus formed by adding light to the white noise. Finally, Ss were tested with the light stimulus alone to determine the degree of stimulus control gained by this component. There was virtually no sign of a CER on the test trial, which is to say the light failed to achieve even a small measure of stimulus control. The "attention block" shown by Kamin's Ss was interpreted by him in a way not different from our notion of stimulus selection. He concluded that it was not the perception of the CS that was at fault; rather, the difficulty lay in a failure of association.

As is so often the case when discussing phenomena of classical conditioning, the first report of stimulus selection occurring within the classical conditioning paradigm came from Pavlov (1927). He cited experiments from his laboratory in which a compound CS, composed of two stimuli from different sensory modalities, was employed in salivary conditioning studies. After acquisition of the conditioned response, the compound CS and the components were tested for the degree of stimulus control achieved by each. The results were clear-cut, allowing Pavlov to conclude: "When the stimuli making up the compound act upon different analyzers, the effect of one of them when tested singly was found very commonly to overshadow the effect of the others almost completely . . . [p. 141]." The term "overshadow" introduced by Pavlov in the discussion of these experiments is still used to refer to the dominance of stimulus control exerted by one component of a compound stimulus over other components. Pavlov also reported that overshadowing could occur with a compound *CS* formed of components belonging to the same sensory modality but varying in their intensity.

It is of some interest to note that whereas in the studies reported by Pavlov complete overshadowing was obtained with components presented simultaneously, Kamin (1968), in the research discussed above, observed complete stimulus selection only if one component of a compound were first conditioned to the *CER*. The basis of this discrepancy is not known, though it might reside in the nature of the reinforcement employed; conceivably, there is less stimulus selection—a greater breadth of learning—in situations involving negative reinforcement.

Although other illustrations of stimulus selection could be cited (cf. Mackintosh, 1965b; Ray, 1969; Trabasso & Bower, 1968), the previous examples show clearly that such a mechanism operates within a considerable range of learning situations and over a wide class of subjects. It seems apparent that in these illustrations we are not dealing with selective perception. There can be little doubt that the pigeons and monkeys discussed above "perceived" not only the colors but the stimuli making up the forms as well. Similarly, one can hardly doubt that the college students perceived the trigrams as well as the color backgrounds, and, in the concept-identification task, were aware of the existence of both the forms and dots. Nevertheless selective utilization of one or the other component occurred. In view of the ubiquitousness of this mechanism and the powerful effects which it can exert, it is important that the variables controlling stimulus selection be uncovered and investigated thoroughly. As yet only a modest beginning has been made in this direction.

ADDITIVITY OF CUES. Although there are many instances of "complete" stimulus selection, very often "secondary" relevant cues gain partial stimulus control, as in the Underwood et al. (1962) study. Division of stimulus control among two or more stimulus components raises the following interesting issue.

Suppose that with color and form as the relevant stimulus dimensions, one subject learns a discrimination on the basis of the color component alone and a second subject employs both color and form in solving the problem. Did the second *S* learn as much as the first about the color dimension; i.e., did the learning about form come at the "expense" of learning about color? This would be the case if, on any given trial, *S* could attend only to one dimension, so that if *S* attended to form, he could not learn anything about color on that trial. On the other hand, if attention (in the sense of stimulus selection) is not so limited, *S* could possibly attend to both dimensions on a single trial and learn something about each.

Results from experiments on "additivity of cues" bear on this issue. If *S* learns a discrimination faster with two relevant dimensions than with either one of them alone, the cues are said to be additive. Many experiments, employing both animals (e.g., Eninger, 1952; Warren, 1964) and humans (e.g., Bourne & Haygood, 1959), have shown that acquisition of discrimination tasks is faster when more than one relevant dimension is available to S. Indeed, unless one of the relevant cues is especially dominant (e.g., Draper, 1965; Warren, 1953), additivity of cues is likely to be obtained. Although superficially a result of this nature seems to support the notion that S is able to attend to and to learn about more than one stimulus dimension on a single trial, closer analysis shows that this is not necessarily the case. It is possible, as suggested by Sutherland and Holgate (1966), that multiple relevant cues often lead to faster learning in a *group* of Ss merely because, with a wider range of relevant cues available, each S is more likely to find a salient cue on which to focus his attention and with which to solve the problem. With only a single relevant stimulus dimension available, Ss do not enjoy this advantage.

The importance of the issue resides in the fact that certain models of discrimination learning (e.g., Lovejoy, 1966) have embraced the assumptions that (1) S attends to only one dimension on a given trial—"single-look models" as they are sometimes called—and (2) as S learns the discrimination on the basis of a given cue, attending to this dimension gets "locked in," so that it is not possible for S to learn about other dimensions. Thus proponents of these assumptions have found it necessary to show that the result of additivity of cues is not necessarily in conflict with their views.

If, as suggested above, additivity of cues (say in a two-dimension problem) arises because some Ss learn the discrimination on the basis of one cue primarily, whereas others utilize the other dimension, it ought to be the case that the more S learns about one of the relevant dimensions, the less he learns about the other. And if such were the case, the assumption that S attends to only one dimension on a single trial could remain intact. Sutherland and Holgate (1966), investigating the problem in some detail, indeed found that the more individual Ss (rats) learned about one cue of a two-dimension simultaneous discrimination, the less they learned about the other. While this result tends to support a single-look approach, other aspects of their data—such as the fact that Ss performed better with two cues than with one—are in keeping with the view that more than one stimulus dimension can be utilized on a single trial.

Moreover, in a more recent study Mumma and Warren (1968), attempting to replicate with cats Sutherland and Holgate's finding, found no evidence for the kind of negative correlations reported by the latter investigators. It will be recalled from our discussion of stimulus selection in concept-identification tasks that a number of subjects in the Trabasso and Bower (1968) study learned fully about both relevant dimensions of a two-cue task. This result also conflicts with the notion that S learns about one cue at the expense of learning about another. The indicated conclusion from these and other studies appears to be that not all instances of additivity of cues in discrimination acquisition can be attributed to the assumption that different Ss learn about different dimensions. Although the mere manifestation of additivity of cues in discrimination acquisition can easily be handled by single-look models (cf. Trabasso & Bower, 1968, Chap. 1), the evidence for additivity produced by the kinds of transfer tests employed in the previously cited studies of Trabasso and Bower (1968) and Mumma and Warren (1968) requires a modification of either the single-look assumption (cf. Trabasso & Bower for a pertinent "multiple-look" model) or some relaxation of the notion that S learns only about the dimension to which he attends (cf. Lovejoy, 1968).

Additivity of cues in discrimination performance. Additivity of cues has also been shown for discrimination *performance*, both in cats (Hara & Warren, 1961) and rats (McGonigle, 1967; cf. Sutherland & Holgate, 1966). In the Hara and Warren study, psychometric functions (Chap. 5) were first obtained for each S separately on three stimulus dimensions: brightness, size, and form (square versus rectangle). From these psychometric functions the stimulus value that was discriminable from the standard stimulus on 70 percent of the trials was determined for each dimension; this stimulus is referred to as the "subliminal" cue. (Recall from Chap. 5 that in the method of constant stimuli—the psychophysical method employed by Hara and Warren—a comparison stimulus is separated from the standard stimulus by 1 *DL* if it is discriminated from the latter on 75 percent of the trials.) A second stimulus was determined for each dimension such that it was discriminated from the standard on 80 percent of the trials (the "supraliminal" stimulus). The point of these determinations was to achieve equally discriminable pairs of discriminanda along the three stimulus dimensions. Previous tests of the additivity-of-cues hypothesis used arbitrarily selected pairs of stimuli as discriminanda, such as red versus green and circle versus square. And as already pointed out, additivity of cues is less likely to be detected when the discriminability of a pair of discriminanda varies greatly from one stimulus dimension to another.

After the subliminal and supraliminal stimuli of each of the three dimensions was determined for each S, discrimination performance was evaluated in test trials during which each S was exposed to all possible combinations of two and three subliminal or supraliminal cues. As an illustration of tests involving two dimensions, the subliminal cues for brightness occurred together with the supraliminal cues for form. The results showed convincingly that discrimination performance was facilitated by adding additional relevant dimensions. Moreover, facilitation occurred when subliminal discriminanda were combined as well as when supraliminal stimuli were combined. The degree of additivity of cues observed was the same order of magnitude for all dimensions; in other words, adding brightness to form facilitated discriminative performance to approximately the same degree as adding the size cues to form. Substantially the same results were obtained by McGonigle (1967).

The improvement in performance obtained by combining stimulus dimensions was, in some cases, rather surprising. With only a single subliminal dimension available, Hara and Warren's cats responded correctly on approximately 72 percent of the test trials. When the subliminal cues from all three stimulus dimensions were combined, performance increased to approximately 88 percent correct. In the case of supraliminal stimuli the corresponding figures were 82 and 99 percent.

Despite the magnitude of the additive effects obtained in this experiment, such results once again cannot be taken as conclusive evidence against one-look models of stimulus control. As pointed out by Lovejoy (1968) and quantitatively demonstrated by Trabasso and Bower (1968), the Hara and Warren data can be accommodated by a one-look model which simply assumes that the chances of sampling a relevant cue increases with the number of relevant dimensions. From this assumption it follows that S's performance will be positively related to the number of available relevant dimensions. Theoretical implications aside, it is clear that both discrimination acquisition and discrimination performance can use to advantage multiple relevant cues. This comes as no surprise. Multiple relevant cues are the rule in our everyday discriminative behavior. Our recognition of people, for example, is based on a host of multiple cues, such as height, color of hair, voice, and gait. Which characteristics ("dimensions") we employ for recognition will vary from situation to situation. Height and gait are important for recognition at a distance but useless for deciding who is at the other end of the phone. Nevertheless we by no means use all of one's characteristics that could be of service in the recognition task. We select out in various degrees certain dimensions, ignoring others.

ATTENTION VERSUS STIMULUS CONTROL. In the previous chapter we suggested that the concepts of stimulus control and attention, despite having a great deal in common, are not equivalent. We can now be somewhat more explicit about the distinction. Attention is the more general concept—it subsumes both selective perception and stimulus selection. The term "stimulus control" is better reserved for situations in which differential behavioral control comes about through stimulus selection; this appears to be the most common intent of those employing the term. It is true that a stimulus which fails to be perceived cannot gain behavioral control. But it may very well be that the variables which determine selectivity in perception are generally different in nature from the variables that determine stimulus selection. At least the issue should not be prejudged. Thus it is suggested that the term "attention" be the generic label for those processes which exert a selectivity over stimulus functions, whether this be at the level of perception or association. "Selective perception" is the term to be used to refer to the former type of selectivity, with "stimulus selection" and "stimulus control" reserved for the latter. Confining the concept of stimulus control to matters of selectivity in associative control is consistent with the discussion of this concept in Chap. 9.

Some Variables That Influence Stimulus Selection

STRUCTURAL FACTORS. That stimulus selection will be influenced importantly by the structural status of an organism's sensory modalities is a conclusion hardly worth contesting. Birds, for example, have a highly developed visual system, which correlates with a close dependence on visual stimuli. In other species, vision—in structure and in function—plays a secondary role, and other sensory modalities—such as olfaction—dominate.

But even within the same modality there may occur a hierarchal arrangement, perhaps also structurally determined, of the "dominance" of cues, which reveals itself in the stimulus selection process. Thus in pigeons color apparently gains stimulus control more easily than angular tilt (e.g., M. R. Baron, 1965). In rhesus monkeys color is often found greatly superior to size or form cues (e.g., Draper, 1965; Warren, 1953, 1954). And cats were long thought to be completely color-blind because of their extreme tendency to select brightness over color cues (e.g., Sechzer & Brown, 1964).

There is, however, a problem of control involved in many of these experiments that needs to be stressed. Given the experimental result that, for example, color is selected over size, one must somehow take into account the "distance" separating the colors and sizes assigned to the discriminanda before he can safely conclude that the difference in stimulus control exerted by the two stimulus dimensions can be assigned to differences in their "dominance." Clearly if the colors were orange versus orange-red and the sizes of the discriminanda were 2 in. versus 20 in., the latter dimension would emerge as the more discriminable, i.e., display the greater degree of stimulus control. Moreover, when color is employed as a cue, it normally occupies the entire area of the stimuli and hence may often be associated with a larger region of stimulation on the retina. Both these variables need to be assessed carefully if we are to obtain a meaningful ordering of stimulus dimensions with respect to the dominance factor.

In one of the few studies of "cue dominance" which satisfied the first desideratum, Hara and Warren (1961) showed that in cats brightness was a more dominant cue than either size or form. Recall from our earlier discussion of this experiment that, with the discriminability of the various stimuli controlled, additivity of cues occurred in the brightness, size, and form dimensions to approximately the same degree. In the final portion of this experiment, the relative dominance of the three stimulus dimensions was evaluated by presenting S with compound discriminanda in which the S+ of one dimension was pitted against the S− of the other. For example, one compound discriminandum was composed of the brightness that had been S+ and the form cue that had been S−; the other compound stimulus consisted of the brightness that had been S− and the form cue that had been S+. If the various stimulus dimensions were equally dominant, presumably over a series of test trials S would respond equally to the two stimulus compounds. The results revealed a clear preference for the brightness dimension, particularly in the case of the supraliminal stimuli. Form and size were approximately equivalent in this respect. Interestingly, McGonigle (1967) found very nearly the same results for his rats, although in this case the dominance of the brightness dimension was evident only for the supraliminal cues, and, in addition, size turned out to be dominant to form. [It is interesting to observe that more than 55 years ago, Lashley (1912, p. 329) came to a similar conclusion.] These results constitute promising evidence for the operation of a hierarchy of dominance among stimulus dimensions, a hierarchy which cannot be completely accounted for in terms of differences in discriminability. The preference for color (over the bar component) shown by the monkey whose data are presented in Fig. 11-11 may be construed as further supporting evidence.

It should be pointed out, however, that the dominance ordering observed by Hara and Warren may reside in the stimuli rather than in "structural" factors. Because brightness is normally a property of a very substantial portion of the stimulus display, it may require less "observing" behavior than such dimensions as form and size and may be preferred for this reason. Moreover, the possible contributions of past experience, in the ways discussed in the next section, must be reckoned with.

THE ROLE OF PREVIOUS EXPERIENCE.   That the dominance of cues (and hence stimulus selection) can be manipulated by relevant past experience is a reasonable hypothesis for which there are a number of supporting data. Lawrence was one of the first to investigate this issue experimentally and provide demonstrations of what he termed "acquired distinctiveness of cues." In one experiment (Lawrence, 1949) rats were trained on a simultaneous discrimination task with one of three stimulus dimensions relevant (black versus white, smooth versus rough floors, or wide versus narrow goal compartments). The remaining two dimensions were held "constant" at their mid-values. After 40 trials on this initial discrimination, Ss were divided into three groups in accordance with the stimulus conditions prevailing in a second, transfer, task. The latter problem was a spatial conditional discrimination in which S learned to make either a right or a left turn in a T maze, depending upon the status of the conditional cue. For one group the previous relevant dimension again constituted the relevant cue in the conditional discrimination task; one of the other dimensions appeared as an irrelevant cue. Thus, for example, if black-white had been the relevant dimension in the first task, Ss in this group had to learn to turn right when *both* alleys of the T maze were white and to turn left when both were black; variation of the irrelevant cue had to be ignored. For a second group of Ss, the previous relevant dimension was made the irrelevant cue in the conditional discrimination problem, and one of the two cues formerly held constant now served as the relevant dimension. Finally a third group of Ss, the controls, had as their relevant and irrelevant cues the two stimulus dimensions with which they had no previous discriminative experience.

If previous experience with stimuli that are relevant for some discrimination task somehow increases their dominance (perhaps through an increase in "distinctiveness"), the first group of Ss should acquire the conditional discrimination faster than either of the other two groups. Lawrence did indeed find that acquisition of the conditional discrimination was facilitated if the conditional cue had served as the relevant dimension of the initial discrimination task (Fig. 11-13). There was no indication, however, that acquisition of the

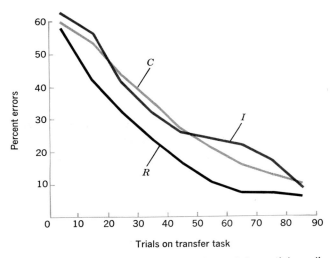

Fig. 11-13. Performance on the transfer task (a spatial conditional discrimination). The relevant dimension of a previous simultaneous discrimination task was again relevant for Group *R* but irrelevant for Group *I*. Group *C* did not have previous discriminative experience with either the current relevant or irrelevant dimensions. (SOURCE: D. H. Lawrence. Acquired distinctiveness of cues: I. Transfer between discriminations on the basis of familiarity with the stimulus. *Journal of Experimental Psychology*, 1949, **39**, 770–784. Copyright 1949 by the American Psychological Association and used by permission.)

transfer task was hindered when the formerly relevant dimension no longer provided reliable information. [See Siegel (1967) for an interpretation of these and related data in terms of the transfer of "overt response tendencies" rather than attentional mechanisms.]

In a more recent study Sutherland and Holgate (1966, Experiment 6) were able to demonstrate both facilitation and inhibition of past experience on stimulus selection. Rats were first trained on a conditional discrimination; Ss learned to jump to the right-hand door (of a Lashley-type jumping stand) when the form on each of the two stimulus cards was black and to jump to the left-hand door when both forms were white. For one group of Ss the forms consisted of squares. A second group was exposed to rectangles that were oriented in either the horizontal or the vertical direction; however, orientation of the rectangles was irrelevant whereas, as with the first group, brightness was the relevant dimension. A control group—actually the group of their Experiment 1—received no experience on the conditional discrimination. A total of 360 trials was given during this phase of the experiment.

In Phase 2 of the experiment, the three groups were given either 60 or 80 trials on a simultaneous discrimination task in which the stimuli were a white horizontal rectangle, the S+, and a vertical black rectangle (S−). Sutherland and Holgate were interested in determining whether the initial experience given to the first two groups would have an effect on which dimension—brightness or rectangle orientation—would be employed to solve the second discrimination problem.

To evaluate which dimension was selected out by the individual animals, a third phase was conducted in which all Ss were tested on the four pairs of stimuli shown in Fig. 11-14 (Phase 3); all responses were rewarded. Forty "re-training" trials on the task of the second phase were interspersed with these test trials.

If S had solved the discrimination of Phase 2 on the basis of brightness, it should respond appropriately when presented with pairs 1 and 2, which differ in brightness but not rectangle orientation. When presented with pairs 3 and 4, however, S should be less likely to be correct because the brightness cue has been eliminated; indeed, if stimulus selection had been complete in Phase 2, S should respond at a chance level. The results of the experiment were that the control group, which received no training during Phase 1, scored 72 percent correct on test pairs 1 and 2 and 86 percent correct on pairs 3 and 4. Thus, in the absence of Phase 1 experience, rectangle orientation was a more salient dimension than rectangle brightness, a result which generally held in this particular situation. The first group of Ss, which did not experience rectangles in Phase 1, presented a different picture in that they scored 72 percent correct on test patterns 1 and 2 and only 71 percent correct on pairs 3 and 4. Phase 1 training with brightness, although not increasing the percentage of Phase 3 responses to the brightness cue, did reduce the saliency of the rectangle-orientation dimension.

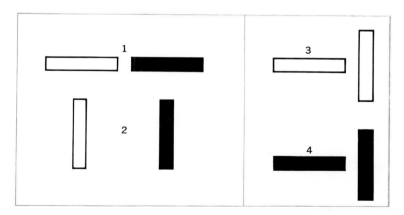

Fig. 11-14. The four test pairs of stimuli employed in Phase 3 (see text). (SOURCE: N. S. Sutherland and V. Holgate. Two-cue discrimination learning in rats. *Journal of Comparative and Physiological Psychology*, 1966, **61**, 198–207. Copyright 1966 by the American Psychological Association and used by permission.)

More decisive results were obtained in the case of the second group, which registered 90 percent correct responses on test pairs 1 and 2 but only 59 percent on pairs 3 and 4. The results of this group nicely show how the previous function of a stimulus dimension can affect stimulus selection on a subsequent task. A dimension that has been relevant in the past tends to be selected out, whereas a dimension that has been irrelevant tends to be ignored. [However, see Gonzalez and Bitterman (1968) for certain limitations concerning the latter conclusion.] The fact that the first group did not select out brightness more often than the control group might be related to their relatively inferior performance on the retraining trials which were given during Phase 3. In any event this experiment and several others employing rats as subjects (e.g., Lawrence, 1950; Mackintosh, 1965b, c), as well as more recent work with cats (Hirayoshi & Warren, 1967; Warren & McGonigle, 1969) and pigeons (Johnson & Cumming, 1968) demonstrate pointedly the influence that previous experience can have on stimulus selection.

Nor are such effects limited to the animal level. Similar results have been reported for children (e.g., Crane & Ross, 1967) and adults. In a recent study, Houston (1967) found that if an item had been used as the stimulus component in previous paired-associate learning, it was much more likely to be utilized in the learning of a subsequent paired-associate task in which it formed part of a compound stimulus. Following the paradigm employed by Underwood et al. (1962), described above, Houston's subjects were given six trials on a first paired-associate learning task. Next, Ss received six trials on a second paired-associate list in which the stimulus items of the first list constituted one of a two-component compound stimulus. For example, in one condition the stimulus items of the first list consisted of digits, and in the second list the same digits occurred as part of a compound stimulus; the other component was the surrounding color. As one might expect, when recall was tested separately for the color and digit components, Houston found that a greater degree of stimulus control was achieved by the component that S had experienced during first-list learning.

A second result of the study (Experiment III) is more unexpected. The responses of the first list were so devised that they could conceivably facilitate or impede second-list learning if first-list stimuli were selected during second-list learning. To illustrate the potential source of facilitation, for some subjects the first list can be designated as A-C' (A is the stimulus item and C' the response item); the second list consisted of the stimulus compound AX to which the response C had to be associated. Inasmuch as C' and C were similar in meaning, one might expect that if S selected the A component out of the AX-compound stimulus, second-list learning would be facilitated because of the previous A-C' association. Other subjects acquired associations of the A-B form during first-list learning and thus for them selecting stimulus item A during second-list learning might be expected to incur negative transfer. The question at issue is whether the nature of the previous association entered into by a stimulus item determines in part whether that item will be selected out during a subsequent learning task. Houston found that this was a relatively minor factor. His subjects tended to select out the stimulus item with which they had had experience, whether or not the earlier association tended to facilitate or retard second-list learning. The suggestion from this result is that recent familiarity with a stimulus item is more important for stimulus selection than the specific associations entered into by that item. However, Houston's results are by no means definitive, and this interesting problem deserves further investigation.

To summarize the last two sections, structural factors and past experience are important determiners of stimulus selection. They cause some stimulus dimensions (or some modalities) to be more "dominant" or perhaps more "distinctive" than others and hence to enter more easily into associative processes. The precise mechanisms through which these effects are mediated—involving perhaps central inhibitory mechanisms or peripheral observing responses—remain to be worked out.

OVERTRAINING.   It seems a reasonable assumption that overtraining on a task should "relax" stimulus selection, allowing more stimulus components to gain stimulus control. If we drive the same route repeatedly, we cannot help but learn different and additional signs by means of which to negotiate our trip. Originally we may have learned to make a left turn at the corner at which there are three service stations; later we may note that a particular house appears on the block before that point and use this as our cue to anticipate the turn.

The notion that overtraining might serve to relax stimulus selection was recently tested by James and Greeno (1967), who employed a paradigm similar to that of Underwood et al. (1962). They presented their subjects with a paired-associate learning task, in which the stimulus portion was a compound consisting of a three-letter word of high association value and a nonsense syllable (trigram) of low association value. The response items were the digits 1 through 8. They found that without overtraining the learning of the paired associates was based almost entirely on the word portion of the compound stimulus; the trigram achieved virtually no stimulus control. With 20 trials of overtraining, however, the trigrams achieved a significant degree of stimulus control. Interestingly, their data also suggest that it is not overtraining on individual paired-associate items that results in a broadening of the associative process but rather overtraining on the entire list. It is as though the subject must learn the entire list before he relaxes his attention and takes note of stimulus characteristics which originally were ignored.

Turning to the animal level, Sutherland and Holgate (1966, Experiment 2) trained rats on a discrimination in which brightness and orientation of rectangles were the correlated cues. Like James and Greeno, they found from subsequent test trials that overtraining resulted in Ss' learning more about the less preferred or "secondary" cue.

In a similar experiment from our laboratory, three groups of capuchin monkeys were trained on the compound discriminanda shown in Fig. 11-15.

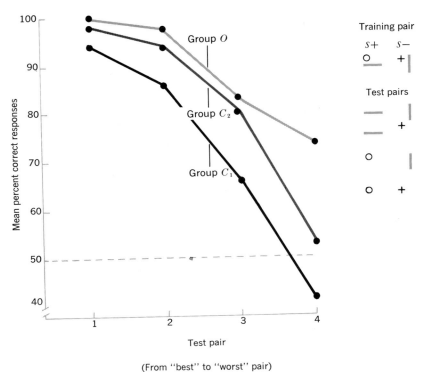

Fig. 11-15. On the right appear the compound discriminanda employed during training and the four stimulus pairs of the testing phase. Mean percent correct responses on the first test day (10 trials on each pair) is shown as a function of the amount learned about each stimulus pair. Group O was overtrained before being exposed to the test pairs, and Groups C_1 and C_2 were control groups that were tested without overtraining experience (see text).

Two groups of Ss were trained to perform cue-producing responses (pressing a lever—Fig. 11-3) in order to present the discriminanda to themselves for brief intervals (.1 sec). Each S was free to make as many cue-producing (or "observing") responses as he wished before making a choice. One of the groups, C_1, was trained to a criterion of 90 percent correct responses and then tested (40 trials per day) on the four pairs of stimuli shown in Fig. 11-15. Group O was given 800 trials beyond criterion before entering the testing phase. There was a third group, C_2, which was treated in the same fashion as Group C_1 except that with each cue-producing response the discriminanda appeared for a period of 10 sec.

To evaluate the degree of stimulus selection shown by the three groups, each S's performance on the four test pairs was arranged in decreasing order with respect to the percentage of correct responses achieved. Group means were obtained for the "best" test pair, the next best, and so on. These values, for the first test day, are plotted in Fig. 11-15. If overtraining has little or no effect on breadth of learning, there ought to be little difference between Group O's curve and those of Groups C_1 and C_2. On the other hand, if overtraining encourages S to learn about cues he might have otherwise ignored, a significant divergence between curves ought to exist, particularly for poorly learned cues.

It is clear from Fig. 11-15 that the second situation prevailed for the first test day; moreover, the pattern shown in the figure maintained itself over the next two test days. Note that there is little difference between the performance of Groups C_1 and C_2, suggesting that the stimulus selection observed in C_1 is not attributable to the short discriminanda duration. The results of this experiment add to the mounting evidence that overtraining can increase, rather markedly, the range of cues that enter associative processes.

On the other hand, in an experiment rather similar to that of James and Greeno, Houston (1967) did not find a comparable amount of overtraining to be effective in relaxing stimulus selection. The discrepancy may lie in the nature of the stimulus items employed in the two experiments. Houston followed Underwood et al. (1962) in employing trigrams and colors as his component stimuli. Color may be such a dominant cue in this situation that a great deal of overtraining might be required before relaxation of stimulus selection is noticeable. Or, put differently, the presence of an "easy" cue may prevent for a considerable time S's learning about a redundant difficult dimension (cf. Lovejoy & Russell, 1967).

In their detailed review of the literature relating to the effects of overtraining on stimulus selection, Trabasso and Bower (1968) point to the lack of consistency in the experimental data. Nevertheless it is beyond question that overtraining *can* increase breadth of learning, though perhaps not under all possible sets of experimental conditions. A model of discrimination learning which does not allow for such a result, such as the model proposed by Trabasso and Bower (1968, Chap. 2), consequently suffers a severe limitation. Trabasso and Bower rightly point out that a theory is needed which can generate graded effects of overtraining on stimulus selection. Perhaps a more urgent need, however, is the unraveling of the variables which, interacting with overtraining, are responsible for the current "inconsistent" pattern of results.

SCHEDULE OF REINFORCEMENT. Appealing to intuition again, one would think that a continuous reinforcement schedule would encourage stimulus selection more than an intermittent schedule, particularly when the reinforcement is biologically significant. A hungry rat that receives food reward each time it makes the correct response is perhaps more likely to become set on a pattern of attending than an animal for which reinforcement comes only occasionally.

In one of the few experiments bearing directly on this issue, Sutherland (1966, Experiment 2) trained rats on a jumping stand to discriminate between two compound stimuli which differed on five visual dimensions (Fig. 11-16). There were also a tactual and an auditory dimension, but these need not concern us. The group trained with CRF (Group C) arrived at the acquisition criterion of

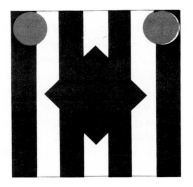

Fig. 11-16. The visual discriminanda, consisting of five different dimensions, of the Sutherland study. (SOURCE: N. S. Sutherland. Partial reinforcement and breadth of learning. *Quarterly Journal of Experimental Psychology,* 1966, **18,** 289–301. Used by permission.)

10 correct trials in a single day in a mean of 7.0 days. The partially reinforced Ss (*VR* 2—Group *P*) required 12.5 days on the average to arrive at the same criterion. Inasmuch as all Ss were given a total of 200 training trials, the first group received more overtraining than the second, and therefore on this account alone the *CRF* Ss should show less stimulus selection than the partially reinforced group.

Nevertheless the results from single-cue transfer tests clearly showed a higher degree of stimulus selection in Group *C*. During these transfer tests one trial daily was given on each of the five stimulus dimensions. Since every other trial was a retraining trial (with all five cues present), Ss received a total of 10 daily trials. On test trials devoted to evaluating the degree of selection of the horizontal-vertical stripe component, the other visual cues were eliminated, and the thickness of the stripes was maintained constant (on half of such trials the stripes were narrow and on the other half they were broad). When the location of the circles was evaluated, the circles were presented on plain gray stimulus cards. The other single dimensions were similarly isolated from the remaining four stimulus dimensions.

The percentage of correct responses on the retraining and test trials are shown in Table 11-3. Note that on the retraining trials Group *C* performed somewhat better than Group *P*. Still, Group *P*'s performance on the individual stimulus components was better than that of Group *C*. Indeed Group *C* responded better than chance on only one component—horizontal versus vertical stripes—whereas Group *P*'s performance on all five components was significantly greater than chance. These results are striking evidence that intermittent reinforcement relaxes stimulus selection, broadening the range of cues to which one attends.

There is one puzzling aspect of the data, however. If Group *C* learned the discrimination between the compound stimuli on the basis of a single com-

Table 11-3 Percentage of Correct Responses on
Retraining and Test Trials

CUES	GROUP P	GROUP C
All (retraining trials)	94	99
Horizontal-vertical	71	67
Narrow-broad	64	51
White-black	59	48
Circles	59	47
Square-diamond	58	48

SOURCE: N. S. Sutherland. Partial reinforcement and breadth of learning. *Quarterly Journal of Experimental Psychology,* 1966, **18,** 289–301. Used by permission.

ponent—orientation of the stripes—one would expect that the performance on this single cue ought to be comparable to that achieved with the compound stimuli themselves. Actually, however, there is a very large difference between the two values, 99 versus 67 percent. In part this difference may be explained by the fact that orientation of stripes was not the most dominant cue for all Ss. Nevertheless when one averages the best performance achieved by each S of Group C, disregarding the nature of the dimension involved, the resulting figure, 70 percent, is still very far from 99 percent. Perhaps Ss were responding to a combination of cues, for example, to the black square with circles on the top of the card. Or perhaps the dimension to which Ss primarily responded interacted with the positive and negative stimulus. For example, S might have learned to avoid vertical stripes and to jump to circles on the bottom of the card. Whatever the explanation, it is clear that despite the fact that Group C appeared to attend to only one stimulus dimension, there must have been additional cues controlling the behavior of this group. Sutherland did include test trials in which two stimulus dimensions were combined. Unfortunately, interpretation of these data is clouded by the circumstance that during this stage of the experiment Ss "tended to develop very strong position habits."

The present data and those reported by McFarland (1966) offer clear support for the view that intermittent reinforcement results in a relaxation of selective attention, or put somewhat differently, in a greater breadth of learning. It appears that schedule of reinforcement might be a more powerful variable than overtraining, taking into consideration both the magnitude of the effects that have been observed with the two variables and the fact that in the Sutherland study, Group C had to its advantage more overtraining on the initial discrimination than Group P.

SUMMARY. A variety of variables, certainly more than have been discussed above (cf. Davis, Brown, & Ritchie, 1968; Johnson & Cumming, 1968; Wagner, Logan, Haberlandt, & Price, 1968) importantly affect the stimulus-selection process. To reiterate a point that has been made several times, the selective attention that is evidenced in stimulus selection does not relate to a failure of perception. Some stimuli, though perceived, are not utilized, or are utilized to a much lesser degree than others in the associative process. A good diagnostician not only "notices" symptoms but also associates them with the appropriate syndrome. Conversely, a poor diagnostician is probably less often guilty of failing to observe symptoms than of failing to take proper account of them.

Although the process of stimulus selection was recognized as operating in animals many years ago (e.g., Lashley, 1912) and although it gave rise to the heated and prolonged continuity-noncontinuity controversy, it is only in very recent years that the variables influencing this process have come under serious study. This postponement seems strange in view of the widespread importance of the topic and in view of the fact that suitable experimental techniques were available decades ago (e.g., Lashley, 1938). Perhaps it is a consequence of the shift in interest away from sensory and perceptual matters that appears to have taken place during the second quarter of this century among many investigators concerned with animal discrimination learning.

OBSERVING BEHAVIOR

Early in the chapter it was pointed out that the continuity-noncontinuity controversy was one issue of perceptual import that survived the transition of interest in discrimination learning from matters of perception to matters of conditioning. Although framed in quite different terms, the major question was whether or not stimulus selection plays a significant role in discrimination learning. Employing a paradigm upon whose relevance proponents of both sides agreed, Krechevsky (1938) showed that if rats were reversed on a pattern discrimination problem before they showed signs of responding systematically to the discriminanda (i.e., during the "presolution" period), no effect of the earlier training was evident; that is, these subjects learned the reversal as fast as control subjects for which $S+$ and $S-$ remained as they were during the presolution phase. This result was embarrassing for continuity theory because even though Ss were not responding systematically to the discriminative stimuli during the presolution period, some degree of appropriate conditioning to $S+$ and $S-$ should have taken place, and this should have been reflected in a retardation of acquisition in the Ss for which $S+$ and $S-$ were subsequently reversed.

Spence's (1940) rebuttal stressed a response mechanism whose importance has been increasingly recognized over the years. His point was that in pattern discrimination learning, the subject has the additional task of learning to look at the appropriate part of the stimulus displays, of learning "receptor-orientation" responses as they later came to be called (Spence, 1945). Until these responses are acquired, differential exteroceptive stimulation arising from the discriminanda may not necessarily result in differential stimulation on the receptor surfaces. Applying this argument to the Krechevsky study, Spence suggested that during

the presolution trials the rats were fixating at the bottom of the stimulus cards—
the point to which their jump would take them—and although the discriminanda
might arrive on the retina as proximal stimuli, they might not be distinguishable
to the animal (presumably because of their distance from the sensitive portion
of the retina). In a sense, then, Spence was asserting that what appeared to be
a case of stimulus selection was really one of selective perception due to faulty
receptor orientation. His interpretation was supported by Ehrenfreund (1948),
who showed that if rats were encouraged to orient toward the center of the
stimulus cards, the expected decrement in performance of the group reversed
after the presolution phase did actually occur.

In addition to Spence's emphasis on receptor-orienting responses, a number of investigators had been taking note of observinglike behavior in the rat
during its attempts to solve a discrimination problem (e.g., Tolman, 1938).
Frequently the animals would be seen to stop at the choice point and orient
toward one alternative and then the other in succession, as if sampling the
relevant stimuli before making their choice. This behavior has been colorfully
referred to as "vicarious trial-and-error," or *VTE*.

It was not until some years later, however, that the concept of observing
behavior received detailed treatment. Wyckoff (1952) presented an explicit theory
of the role of observing responses in discrimination learning in which the
observing response was conceived of as permitting the discriminanda to impinge
on S. As with Spence, Wyckoff viewed the observing response as providing a
mechanism of perceptual rather than associational selectivity. He presented the
interesting idea that the reinforcement for an observing response was the appearance of the discriminanda themselves which, being associated with differential
reinforcement, could be conceived of as conditioned reinforcers, a view which
he subsequently elucidated in some detail (1959). Wyckoff (1952) reported, for
example, that a pigeon would step on a pedal in order to receive the discriminative stimuli of a successive discrimination, even though the observing response
had no effect on the probability of reinforcement.

Subsequently Prokasy (1956) reported similar results for rats run in an
E-maze situation. Food appeared on each side of the apparatus on 50 percent
of the trials so that with respect to reward the two sides were equivalent. However, on one side of the E maze, discriminative cues were provided which indicated when reward was present and when it was not. The animals showed a
marked preference for the side on which this information appeared, a result
subsequently replicated by a number of investigators (e.g., Mitchell, Perkins,
& Perkins, 1965).

Wyckoff's interpretation of these results is that the mean conditioned reinforcing strength of a stimulus associated with 100 percent reward and one
associated with 0 percent reward is greater than the conditioned reinforcing
strength of a stimulus associated with 50 percent reward (see Fig. 11-17). The
Ss consequently show a preference for the side of the E maze on which the
informative cues appear. A possible alternative explanation is that informative
cues are reinforcing because they allow certain "preparatory" responses to occur

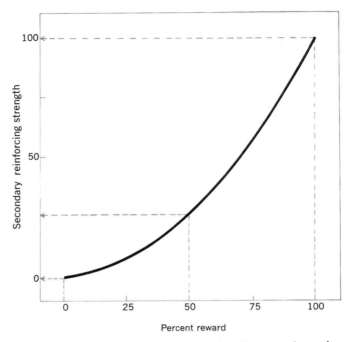

Fig. 11-17. In this figure it is assumed that the secondary reinforcing strength of a stimulus is a positively accelerated function
of the percentage of reward with which the stimulus is correlated. Under this supposition a stimulus associated with a 50
percent reward schedule develops an amount of conditioned
reinforcement substantially less than 0.50. Because a stimulus
associated with 0 percent reward acquires 0 conditioned reinforcement strength and one associated with 100 percent reward
schedule develops the maximum reinforcing strength, 1.0, the
average conditioned reinforcement strength of these two stimuli,
0.50, exceeds that of the stimulus associated with reward on 50
percent of the trials.

A similar analysis can be made for other schedules of reinforcement, for example, variable-interval schedules, and therefore
accounts for the general result that animals prefer multiple to
mixed schedules (e.g., Bower, McLean, & Meacham, 1966; Kelleher, Riddle, & Cook, 1962).

which serve to augment the reinforcing value of the rewards received (Perkins,
1968; Prokasy, 1956).

As conceived of by Spence, Wyckoff, and others (e.g., Stollnitz, 1965),
observing behavior, though perhaps capable of accounting for the selectivity
in discrimination learning that arises from selective perception, seems poorly
suited to deal with associational selectivity, i.e., with stimulus selection. As
pointed out repeatedly, stimulus selection occurs, not because the discriminanda

fail to appear as differential proximal stimuli, but because numerous factors intervene to determine which of the perceived stimulus components will enter ongoing associational processes. It seems likely, moreover, that much of the "interesting" selectivity that occurs in discrimination learning and related activities is associational rather than perceptual in nature. In any event, whether the factors that govern selective perception by means of observing behavior are identical to those which control stimulus selection is a question about which relatively little is known. Although useful applications have been made of observing behavior in a broader context than selective perception (Zeaman & House, 1963), it would seem prudent to maintain the distinction between selective perception and stimulus selection and be more explicit about the role of observing behavior in these two processes.

INFORMATION VERSUS CONDITIONED REINFORCEMENT. Although a substantial amount of evidence can be assembled for the view that observing behavior in discrimination situations is developed and maintained by the differential reinforcement associated with the discriminanda that observing responses produce, there are some relevant data which do not easily lend themselves to this sort of interpretation. As one illustration, D'Amato, Etkin, and Fazzaro (1968) trained monkeys on three separate two-choice discrimination problems in the apparatus of Fig. 11-3. To receive the stimuli of a discrimination, Ss had to make an observing (or cue-producing) response which consisted of pressing the center key, thus presenting S+ and S− on two of the four remaining keys for a period of 0.05 sec. The subject was free to make as many observing responses as he wished before responding. The major point of interest concerned the effect of reversal and extinction on observing behavior. According to the view that the latter is maintained by terminal differential reinforcement, observing responses should be initially depressed by reversal training (Wyckoff, 1952) and abolished by extinction (neither alternative reinforced). Neither of these results were realized, however. In two of the four Ss studied, reversal and extinction both had the result of leading to a rather marked elevation of observing responses in those discriminations which were subjected to these operations (Fig. 11-18).

Note that in the present experiment the additional observing responses which occurred during reversal and extinction did not provide S with useful information. If, as in Fig. 11-18, S required on the average only approximately two observing responses in order to respond correctly to a particular problem, it is clear that observing responses beyond this number (during the reversal trials) provided only redundant information. This fact immediately raises the question of the source of motivation for such responses. A number of writers concerned with perception and related activities assume that one source of motivation for exploratory perceptual behavior, of which the observing responses of the present experiment may be considered a special case, arises from a lack of information. According to Berlyne (1966), for example, "when an animal is disturbed by a lack of information, and thus left a prey to uncertainty and con-

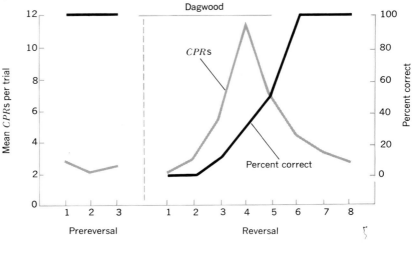

Fig. 11-18. Illustration of increased observing (cue-producing) behavior during reversal learning. Over the three prereversal days *S* responded correctly on 100 percent of the trials and performed few cue-producing responses (*CPRs*). Upon entering reversal *S* showed a marked increase in *CPRs*, followed by a gradual reduction to prereversal levels as *S* mastered the reversal problem. (SOURCE: M. R. D'Amato, M. Etkin, and J. Fazzaro. Cue-producing behavior in the Capuchin monkey during reversal, extinction, acquisition, and overtraining. *Journal of the Experimental Analysis of Behavior,* 1968, **11,** 425–433. Copyright 1968 by the Society for the Experimental Analysis of Behavior, Inc. and used by permission.)

flict, it is likely to resort to . . . exploratory responses" which "supply or intensify stimulation from particular sources [p. 26]." Thus increases in observing responses during reversal and extinction may be interpreted as a "search" for information to resolve the uncertainty which the nonreinforcement encountered during these phases induces (see Gibson, 1968). According to this view, reduction in uncertainty ought to be paralleled by a reduction in observing responses. Figure 11-18 shows that as *S* mastered the reversal problem the number of observing responses rapidly returned to their prereversal level (cf. Premack & Collier, 1966).

Whether one wishes to consider the development and maintenance of observing behavior in discrimination learning in terms of conditioned reinforcement or in the somewhat more "cognitive" concepts of lack of information and uncertainty reduction (cf. Steiner, 1967), there is no doubt that such behavior will continue to play a central role in theoretical accounts of discrimination learning. There is a parallel emphasis on the role of observing-response processes in perceptual learning (e.g., Gibson, 1968), which suggests that this concept may serve as a bridge between these hitherto rather divorced areas.

A MODEL OF DISCRIMINATION LEARNING AND ATTENTION

The wealth of data that exists in the area of discrimination learning has by no means discouraged the theoretical enterprise. The form that such efforts have taken has ranged from rather informal verbal statements to quite explicit and highly rigorous mathematical models. Some theoretical attempts have modestly limited themselves to circumscribed problem areas, while others have been far more ambitious. Spence's theories (1936, 1937) were (quasi) quantitative in nature and were broad with respect to the range of data to which they presumably applied. The long years that these theories have stood as plausible models of discrimination learning and as unrivaled stimulants for productive research is indication of the magnitude of Spence's contribution.

However in this chapter we shall not provide an account of Spence's theories, which are easily accessible to all, nor shall we attempt a survey of theoretical developments in discrimination learning. Rather we shall describe in some detail a mathematical model recently advanced by Lovejoy (1968) that attempts to accommodate a number of the attentional mechanisms which, as we have seen, enter discrimination learning and related activities. A discussion of Lovejoy's model will prove illuminating as an illustration of how such processes as stimulus selection and distinctiveness—unlearned and acquired— can be formulated in a fashion sufficiently precise as to allow their incorporation into a rigorous quantitative model.

Recently, Trabasso and Bower (1968) presented a mathematical model also explicitly devised to accommodate a number of results pertaining to stimulus selection. Their model, though far simpler than Lovejoy's in terms of the number of initial assumptions, does a remarkable job of describing in quantitative detail results from a wide range of experiments. The student with even a rudimentary knowledge of probability theory will find their monograph rewarding, particularly as an illustration of the amount of theoretical "mileage" that can be gotten out of a model formulated from a few, simple assumptions.

Let us consider some of the features which, based on the data presented in this chapter, ought to be incorporated into a model of discrimination learning.

1. Some means must be found to accommodate the fact that not all relevant stimuli are utilized (or utilized to an equal degree) in discrimination learning—the problem of stimulus selection.

2. Some stimuli, because they are more "dominant" or more "distinctive" than others, are more likely to gain stimulus control than stimuli having less of this property.

3. Structural factors and past and current experience all serve to modify the distinctiveness of stimuli; these variables must find representation within the theory.

In addition to these considerations the model must, of course, be able to generate a sufficient number of the more significant results obtained in discrimination learning studies—such as the fact that overtraining and intermittent reinforcement often increase the breadth of learning and the finding that under certain sets of circumstances reversal learning is facilitated by overtraining. Other results which a reasonable model should be able to handle will be discussed later.

One important virtue of a mathematical model is that the assumptions upon which the model is based must be made explicit, a requirement that forces one to think more deeply and analytically about the psychological processes he is attempting to capture than is demanded by relatively informal verbal statements. This, in turn, frequently leads to insights into the basic structure of one's psychological assumptions. Another virtue is the fact that if the mathematical analysis is not in error, predictions—or deductions—flowing from the assumptions are not open to question. As has been repeatedly shown, there is often a great deal of question with theories stated in verbal form as to whether or not putative predictions are actually implied by the initiating hypotheses (cf. Gleitman, Nachmias, & Neisser, 1954).

Unfortunately, however, these are virtues of mathematical models that seem less and less amenable to exploitation. The reason is that as mathematical models of behavior—and discrimination learning is no exception—become more complicated in their attempts to capture a larger piece of reality, it becomes less and less possible to analyze the model mathematically. Thus it may be impossible to obtain a mathematical expression which gives, for example, the group learning curve as a function of the parameters of the model. A completely analyzable model can make detailed predictions about a remarkably wide range of aspects of the data (cf. Atkinson, Bower, & Crothers, 1965), which is of value when it comes to evaluating the appropriateness of a model.

When mathematical analysis is not attainable, as in the case of Lovejoy's "Model III," one must turn to other devices. The major alternate avenue of analysis is computer simulation (cf. Bush & Mosteller, 1955). In computer simulation of a mathematical model one writes a computer program which embodies the mathematical assumptions of the model. One then runs a group of "stat-rats" through the program at fixed values of the parameters which enter the model. The behavior of these stat-rats, which is generated in accordance with the assumptions of the model and the fixed parameter values, then provides estimates of various properties of the model. Several illustrations of this process are given below.

Although this approach is perhaps not as elegant or as esthetically satisfying as explicit mathematical analysis, it seems at present that for many areas of psychology there may be little alternative if a mathematical model is to capture the essential properties of the behavior of interest and at the same time be applicable to a sufficiently wide range of data (cf. Trabasso & Bower, 1968, Chap. 8). Moreover, there are some who believe that information-processing models, in the form of computer-simulation programs, are a preferred source of formal, quantitative models of behavior (Gregg & Simon, 1967). In any event the mathematical model to be described can at present be analyzed only through computer simulation. Accompanying this limitation is the peripheral advantage that in discussing the model there is very little mathematics for us to consider. The Trabasso and Bower (1968) model, which is analyzable, should be examined for an indication of some of the advantages of mathematical tractability.

Selective Control versus Selective Learning

In incorporating stimulus selection into his model, Lovejoy makes a distinction which was not entertained in our earlier discussion of this topic. Essentially stimulus control is differentiated into the two processes of "selective control" and "selective learning." Selectivity may occur with respect to the stimuli that *control* S's behavior and, allowing for the possibility that S does not necessarily *learn* about the stimuli which control his behavior, selectivity in the learning process is also provided for. To take a concrete illustration, suppose that on a given trial S, trained on a discrimination with a red circle as S+ and a green square as S−, attends to color and responds on that basis. We may say that on this trial S is (selectively) controlled by color. According to Lovejoy, however, it does not necessarily follow that whatever S learns on this trial must relate to the color dimension. Perhaps S learns about form instead, as might happen if, after responding, S instantly "forgot" to which dimension he had attended. In our discussion of stimulus selection, we assumed that S learned about those dimensions to which he attended, so that the necessity of distinguishing between selective control and selective learning did not arise. Indeed, in Lovejoy's earlier models (1965, 1966), this distinction did not exist. Let us reserve further discussion of this point until later, when we will present some evidence on which the distinction is based.

SELECTIVE CONTROL. The first task is to devise a system by means of which selective control can occur. We have seen that, perhaps because of structural factors or other reasons, certain dimensions are more dominant or distinctive than others and, consequently, are more likely to control S's behavior. To incorporate this finding into the mechanisms that control behavior, it is assumed that each dimension has a certain amount of "distinctiveness" which may be symbolized as $D(i)$ (for the distinctiveness of the ith dimension). How the distinctiveness of a specific dimension might actually be measured is a vexing problem that presently is far from solution. Let us simply assume that we can assign a nonnegative number to each differentiable stimulus dimension which defines the distinctiveness of that dimension.

We could, if we wished, stop here and allow the *control strength* of a dimension (the strength of its tendency to control behavior) to be its degree of distinctiveness. Although we naturally expect the amount of control exerted by a dimension to be positively related to its distinctiveness, other factors might be influential. For example, suppose S was trained with a square as S+ and a triangle as S−, and after S learned this discrimination, red and green backgrounds were introduced as irrelevant cues. Even assuming that the distinctiveness of the color and form cues were equal, we would nevertheless expect S to continue responding to the circle (i.e., on the basis of form). In other words what S has learned about a stimulus dimension (relating to the associated reinforcement contingencies) ought to have some influence on the degree of control which that dimension exerts.

This feature is incorporated into the model in the following way. Restricting ourselves to two-choice situations (i.e., situations in which only two values of a stimulus dimension are involved), we define a response strength, $V(i)$, which reflects the strength of the tendency of S to choose one of the two stimuli of this dimension. If the dimension in question were form and the two values were circle and triangle, $V(i)$ might refer to the tendency of S to choose the circle. If S had a strong tendency to do so $V(i)$ would be relatively large, whereas if S were strongly disposed to respond to the triangle, $V(i)$ would be small; in the case that S had no preference, $V(i)$ would be intermediate in value. In Model III, $V(i)$ has the restriction that $0 < V(i) < 1$, so that if S's tendency to respond to the circle is strong, weak, or intermediate, the corresponding values of $V(i)$ are in the neighborhood of 1, 0, or 0.5, in that order.

Both quantities—the distinctiveness of a dimension, $D(i)$, and the response strength of a dimension, $V(i)$—combine to determine the dimension's control strength, which is symbolized as $C(i)$. Lovejoy postulates the following relationship:

$$C(i) = \frac{D(i)}{V(i)[1 - V(i)]}$$

Looking at this equation a little closer, it is clear that the tendency of S to be controlled by a given dimension is directly proportional to the distinctiveness of the dimension. Also, the control strength of the dimension is large when S has a strong tendency to choose one of the two alternatives. It should be clear now why $V(i)$ was not permitted to take on the extreme values of 0 or 1; in both these cases the denominator of the above ratio vanishes.

The next task is to state explicitly how the control strength of a dimension, $C(i)$, determines the likelihood that that dimension will actually control S's behavior. Suppose that in a discrimination involving color and form, the control strength of the color dimension is 2.0 and that of form is 4.0. How do we use these values to determine the likelihood or probability that a dimension will control S's responding? Lovejoy's solution is

$$P_c(i) = \frac{C(i)}{\sum_j C(j)}$$

$P_c(i)$ stands for the probability that S's behavior will be *controlled* by the ith stimulus dimension, and is defined to be the proportion of control strength which this dimension has of the total available control strength. In the previous numerical illustration, with the control strengths given, the probability that S's behavior is controlled by the color dimension is 2/6 or 1/3.

A brief review of the previous developments shows that four concepts have been introduced, only two of which are independent: (1) $D(i)$ refers to the distinctiveness of a dimension. As we shall shortly see, $D(i)$ really refers to the *total* distinctiveness, which includes a "preexperimental" component and a component that develops during acquisition training. (2) $V(i)$ stands for the *response strength* of a dimension, which is to say, the strength of S's tendency to choose one of the two values available on a given dimension. (3) $C(i)$, the *control strength* of a dimension, is defined entirely in terms of the previous two quantities and is a measure of the degree to which a dimension is apt to control S's behavior. To say that a dimension "controls" S's behavior means that S's choice is based on the response strength of that dimension. (4) $P_c(i)$, defined in terms of the control strengths, gives the *probability* that a specific dimension will control S's responding.

The two parts of distinctiveness. In accommodation of the requirement that a model of discrimination learning should reflect the fact that the distinctiveness of stimuli arises from both structural factors and past experience, the total distinctiveness of a dimension, $D(i)$, is composed of two parts. It is assumed that before a study begins, a stimulus dimension possesses a degree of distinctiveness, symbolized as $d_0(i)$, which arises either from structural factors or from past learning, but in any case remains constant over the duration of the contemporary learning experience. To this basic level of distinctiveness a certain amount, $d(i)$, may be added by virtue of S's experience during the current learning task. For various reasons the total amount of distinctiveness that is available for distribution during the acquisition of a discrimination task is limited to 1; i.e., $\Sigma d(i) = 1$. The total distinctiveness of a dimension is then defined simply as $D(i) = d_0(i) + d(i)$.

SELECTIVE LEARNING. Thus far we have accounted for selective control as one component of stimulus selection, and now we turn to selective learning. It is assumed that once S has responded and received the outcome of his choice— reward or nonreward—he remembers with probability r the dimension that was used for his choice; with probability $1 - r$ he "forgets" the controlling cue. In the event he remembers, S learns about the controlling cue, which is to say the response strength associated with that dimension changes in accordance with the reward outcome of the trial. If he fails to remember, he resamples the entire class of available dimensions and chooses one to learn. In this resampling scheme the probability that a dimension will be chosen is proportional to its total distinctiveness; that is, given that S has forgotten the controlling cue, the probability that S will sample and therefore learn about dimension i is

$$\frac{D(i)}{\sum_j D(j)}$$

Note that if r is equal to 1, S always learns about the controlling cue, so that the present model is a generalization of that special case.

Having completed the mechanisms that incorporate stimulus selection into the model, we now turn to other features.

How Response Strength Influences Response Probability

So far we have no mechanism for generating a response. Suppose, for example, that on a given trial S is controlled by color (red and green) and $V(i)$ refers to the tendency of S to choose red. Assume $V(i) = 0.8$. All we know is that the absolute tendency of choosing red is rather high, but in a probabilistic model, such as this one, $V(i)$ must somehow be related to the probability of response [symbolized as $P_r(i)$]. This is accomplished by the device of the simple function appearing in Fig. 11-19. Response strength, $V(i)$, and response probability, $P_r(i)$, are shown to be linearly related for values of $V(i)$ between a and $1 - a$. For values of $V(i) < a$, $P_r(i) = 0$, and for values of $V(i) > 1 - a$, $P_r(i) = 1$. There are subtle reasons for choosing a function of this sort rather than using response probabilities in place of response strengths (Lovejoy, 1968, pp. 49–50), but they need not concern us. The important point is that given any value of $V(i)$ between 0 and 1 we can determine the corresponding response probability by the function of Fig. 11-19. The price paid for using response strengths rather than probabilities directly is the addition of one more parameter, a, into the model.

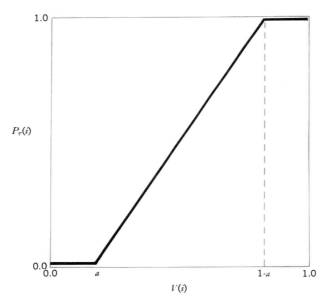

Fig. 11-19. The function which relates response probability, $P_r(i)$, to response strength, $V(i)$. (SOURCE: E. Lovejoy. *Attention in discrimination learning.* San Francisco: Holden-Day, 1968. Used by permission.)

Learning of Responses and Distinctiveness

At this point the model is completely specified except for the means by which learning—of responses and distinctiveness—takes place. Lovejoy uses conventional "linear" operators for this purpose. It is assumed in the following equations that $V(i)$ is the response strength associated with choosing value "1" of the two stimulus values of the ith dimension (the dimension about which S is to learn). If S chooses value 1 and is rewarded,

$$V_{n+1}(i) = V_n(i) + (1 - \alpha_1)[1 - V_n(i)]$$

If S chooses value 2 and is not rewarded,

$$V_{n+1}(i) = V_n(i) + (1 - \alpha_2)[1 - V_n(i)]$$

What these two equations imply is that if S chooses a stimulus value and is rewarded, then the tendency to choose that particular value ought to increase. Similarly if S chooses the other stimulus of the dimension and is not rewarded, the tendency to choose the first value ought likewise to be increased. The fact that α_1 appears in the first equation and α_2 in the second simply provides for the possibility that reward and nonreward have different quantitative effects on learning.

If S chooses value 2 and is rewarded,

$$V_{n+1}(i) = \alpha_1 V_n(i)$$

And finally, if S chooses value 1 and is not rewarded,

$$V_{n+1}(i) = \alpha_2 V_n(i)$$

The first two equations are applicable when reward is consistently associated with stimulus value 1 of a relevant dimension and nonreward with value 2. When these reward contingencies are reversed, as in reversal learning, the second pair of equations are required. All four equations are needed for an irrelevant dimension, because each of the two stimulus values occurs in association with both reward and nonreward.

LEARNING OF DISTINCTIVENESS. It is assumed in the model that changes in distinctiveness occur only when S remembers what cue he used for control. Thus if $r = 1$, learning of distinctiveness occurs on every trial. If on any given trial S fails to remember the controlling cue, the $d(i)$ remain as they were. When S does remember the dimension employed and is rewarded, the distinctiveness of that dimension increases as follows:

$$d_{n+1}(i) = d_n(i) + (1 - \alpha_3)[1 - d_n(i)]$$

All other dimensions have their distinctiveness reduced in the following fashion:

$$d_{n+1}(j) = \alpha_3 d_n(j)$$

When S remembers the controlling cue but is not rewarded, it is assumed that the distribution of modifiable distinctiveness regresses toward the initial distribution, i.e., toward the distribution of $d(i)$ on Trial 1. The exact form of this change is given by

$$d_{n+1}(i) = \alpha_4 d_n(i) + (1 - \alpha_4) d_1(i)$$

Note that if $\alpha_4 = 1$, nonreward leaves the distribution as it was, and if $\alpha_4 = 0$, one nonreward is sufficient to return the distribution of modifiable distinctiveness to its initial state. Obviously, values between these two extremes return the distribution to its initial state with varying degrees of rapidity. The learning-rate parameters which modify response strength, α_1 and α_2, have similar effects on the speed with which response strength changes. Small values of α cause rapid increases or decreases in the value of $V(i)$, whereas large values lead to smaller increments or decrements. The quantitative changes specified in the previous equations are called "linear operators" (because a linear difference equation specifies the rate of change) and are frequently employed in mathematical models of learning processes (cf. Bush & Mosteller, 1955).

PARAMETERS OF THE MODEL. One disadvantage of the present model is that there are a large number of free parameters—quantities which, not specified by the model, must be supplied from other sources, often from the data themselves. In a discrimination problem containing N stimulus dimensions, we must somehow specify for each dimension the initial values of response strength, $V_1(i)$, the initial values of unmodifiable distinctiveness $d_0(i)$, and the initial distribution of modifiable distinctiveness $d_1(i)$, which adds to $3N$ parameters. In addition there are 4 rate parameters (α_1, α_2, α_3, and α_4), plus r and a, for a total of $3N + 6$ parameters.

However, the situation is not quite as bad as it seems. It should be possible to choose stimulus values of each dimension in such a way that S does not have an initial bias, which is to say that for each dimension, $V_1(i) = 0.5$. A somewhat less plausible assumption can be made concerning the initial distribution of modifiable distinctiveness, namely, that the latter be divided among the various dimensions in proportion to their unmodifiable distinctiveness:

$$d_1(i) = \frac{d_0(i)}{\sum_j d_0(j)}$$

Even so, we are left with $N + 6$ parameters, which allows for an enormous amount of play in the model.

The reason why a large number of free parameters is abhorent to theorists is that each parameter is essentially equivalent to an assumption, and the more assumptions a theory requires to explain a set of data, the less impressive is the theoretical accomplishment. The $N + 6$ "residual" parameters of the present model, which under special circumstances might possibly be reduced further, is perhaps not prohibitively large. We shall return to this point when we later evaluate the accomplishments of the model.

Properties of the Model as Revealed by Computer Simulation

The following account shows that there exist various values of the $N + 6$ parameters discussed above from which one may generate a constellation of simulation results that are congruent with corresponding data from actual discrimination experiments. In other words, it is *possible* for the model to predict such empirical findings.

To achieve the simulation data, a computer program (reproduced in Lovejoy's monograph), incorporating the basic assumptions of the model, was assigned actual values of the $N + 6$ parameters and then given the task of training "stat-Ss" on various discrimination problems. To take a specific illustration of how the computer might proceed, consider the first row of Table 11-4, which shows the various parameter values established for 40 stat-rats (Group 1) run on a simple black-white (B-W) discrimination problem with position (L-R) as the irrelevant dimension. Note that the unmodifiable distinctiveness of the position dimension is assumed to be six times greater than that of the brightness dimension. In this illustration (as in the other groups of Table 11-4), inasmuch as $\alpha_1 < \alpha_2$, reward is assumed to be more effective than nonreward in changing response strength. In running a stat-rat through this problem the computer first determines on Trial 1 which dimension is to control the response of the stat-S. Because it is assumed that the initial response strengths, $V_1(i)$, equal 0.5 for both dimensions (i.e., S has no preferences to begin with), control strength will be determined entirely by the distinctiveness of the two

---

Table 11-4 Parameter Values Used in Simulation Studies

GROUP	$d_0(i)$ FOR DIMENSION			α_1	α_2	α_3	α_4	r	a	NO. OF Ss
	(B-W)	(L-R)	(H-V)							
1	0.25	1.50	0.00	0.80	0.98	0.97	0.97	0.70	0.20	40
2	2.00	1.00	0.00	0.80	0.98	0.97	0.97	0.70	0.20	20
3	1.00	1.00	0.25	0.80	0.98	0.97	0.97	0.95	0.20	20
4	1.00	1.00	0.25	0.80	0.98	0.97	0.97	0.95	0.20	20
5	0.50	0.50	0.50	0.80	0.98	0.97	0.97	0.70	0.20	30

SOURCE: E. Lovejoy. *Attention in discrimination learning.* San Francisco: Holden-Day, 1968. Used by permission.

dimensions. If we recall the definition of P_c and the fact that by assumption the modifiable distinctiveness is divided between the dimensions in proportion to their base-level distinctiveness, it is clear that the probability of the stat-rat being controlled by brightness is only $1/7$.

Having made this computation, the computer goes to a table of random numbers and makes a choice between the two dimensions in such a way that the brightness dimension has a probability of $1/7$ of being chosen. Suppose the outcome of that operation is that the stat-S is controlled by position. The computer next looks at the response strength for position, and finding that it is 0.5, it goes back to the table of random numbers and chooses between left and right with probability of 0.5 each (cf. Fig. 11-19). Let us suppose it turns out that the stat-S "chooses" right and that furthermore it happens that reward is on that side. The next task of the computer is to determine whether or not the stat-S is to remember the controlling dimension, so it returns to its table of random numbers and with probability of 0.7 (the value of r) chooses between remembering and forgetting. If we assume that the former takes place, changes in response strength and modifiable distinctiveness are then computed in accordance with the parameters α_1 (letting "right" have the stimulus value 1) and α_3. This having been done the computer repeats the process, only now (1) total distinctiveness is changed because the distribution of modifiable distinctiveness is altered in favor of the position dimension, (2) the response strength of the latter dimension is increased, and (3) owing to (1) and (2) the control strength of position is increased over its previous value.

The computer continues in this manner, keeping a record of the outcome of every trial, until it reaches some criterion established by the "stat-E," such as 18 correct responses out of any 20 successive trials. When the entire group of 40 stat-Ss has been run to completion, one has a mass of data not unlike those that would be collected in an actual experiment. There are, however, some nice advantages to the stat-data. For example, in a real experiment we are not likely to know for a specific trial what the controlling dimension actually was; with stat-data this information is available for each and every trial.

Let us turn now to the kinds of results that can be generated from the model.

ACQUISITION AND REVERSAL LEARNING. The 40 stat-Ss in Group 1 were run to a criterion of 18 correct out of any 20 successive trials on a black-white discrimination using the parameters shown in Table 11-4. Upon reaching acquisition criterion, each stat-S was made to serve as his own control for two different experimental treatments. One was reversal training. All parameters were maintained as they had been in acquisition, except for the $d(i)$ and $V(i)$ of each dimension, which were set at the values achieved at the end of acquisition training. Reversal was carried to the same criterion as acquisition. The second treatment administered to each stat-rat was 150 overtraining trials followed by reversal learning.

The acquisition and reversal learning data of the stat-rats were not unlike those observed with real animals. There was considerable variability in the acquisition data, with the average number of trials to criterion, 121, being what might be expected in such a discrimination situation (of course, this value can easily be manipulated through the rate parameters employed). As one often finds in discrimination experiments with real rats, most of the stat-Ss developed "position habits" even though they began acquisition and reversal without position preferences.

A rather interesting and apparently reliable finding (Lovejoy, 1968) is that when, in the course of learning a visual discrimination, rats develop a position habit, they very often break it by choosing S+. This result suggests, incidentally, that a certain amount of learning about the visual dimension is occurring while the animal is under the control of the position dimension; this is one reason why Lovejoy chose to distinguish between selective control and selective learning. In any event the same result was obtained with the stat-Ss; 80 of 91 runs of 10 or more to one side terminated with the stat-S choosing S+.

Another result of interest was that the stat-Ss reversed faster when they had the benefit of overtraining trials, the so-called "overlearning reversal effect" (ORE). In recent years the ORE has been a topic of intense empirical and theoretical interest. The literature devoted to this issue has grown to sizable proportions and cannot be reviewed here (see Mackintosh, 1965b; Sperling, 1965). It should be pointed out, however, that the ORE is rarely obtained with subhuman mammals other than the rat (e.g., Cross and Boyer, 1966; D'Amato, 1965b; T. J. Tighe, 1965; Warren, Derdzinski, Hirayoshi, & Mumma, 1970), and even on the rat level the ORE frequently fails to appear despite intensive efforts to analyze the conditions responsible for this phenomenon (e.g., D'Amato & Schiff, 1965; Lukaszewska, 1968). Accumulating evidence suggests that the occurrence of the ORE at the rat level depends heavily on two factors, the magnitude of reward employed—which should be large—and task difficulty—which should at least be moderate (Mackintosh, 1969).

The ORE has been important for the kind of attention theory developed in Model III for the simple reason that the theory contains mechanisms which are compatible with such a phenomenon (Lovejoy, 1965, 1966). Viewing discrimination learning as a two-stage process—learning to attend to the relevant dimension and learning to associate the appropriate instrumental responses to the values of that dimension—the ORE is predicted on the basis that if S is reversed immediately after reaching criterion, it is likely that the nonreinforced responding encountered during initial reversal trials will serve to extinguish S's tendency to attend to the relevant dimension. As a consequence, S shifts his attention to another cue, and when this occurs, the response strength associated with the relevant dimension remains intact for as long as S is controlled by a different dimension. When finally S begins attending again to the relevant dimension, he must alter the associated response strength in accordance with the reversal reinforcement contingencies. After overtraining, on the other hand, the control strength of the relevant dimension reaches such a high level that the latter is able to maintain control through the early portions of subsequent reversal learning; consequently the inappropriate response strength of the relevant dimension is not "conserved," and reversal learning proceeds at a faster pace. [We should point out that Wolford and Bower (1969) have reported computer-simulation data which show that for certain parameter values Spence's (1936) theory is also capable of predicting an ORE.]

It follows from this line of reasoning that the ORE is particularly likely to be evident when at least one irrelevant dimension present is highly distinctive (to "attract" S's attention during reversal). Note in Group 1 of Table 11-4 that the position dimension, which is irrelevant, has its unmodified distinctiveness set much higher than that of the brightness dimension. It is of interest, then, that Group 1 did show an ORE; 29 of the 40 Ss reversed faster when given overtraining "experience" than when reversed immediately after reaching criterion.

The dependence in Model III of the ORE on the existence of a highly distinctive irrelevant cue is substantiated by the results obtained from Group 2. Observe that this group operated under precisely the same parameter values as Group 1, except for the distinctiveness variable. The brightness dimension (relevant) was assumed to be twice as distinctive as position (irrelevant). The simulation data showed that reversal learning required 54.1 trials on the average with no overtraining and 51.2 trials with overtraining, this small difference being statistically insignificant. It would appear, then, that the model has sufficient flexibility to generate a pattern of results which is not unlike that found in many experiments that have investigated the ORE on the rat level. The critical roles that problem difficulty and reward magnitude presumably play in the ORE can be accommodated in the model by the distinctiveness parameters and the rate parameters for response strength.

Still it is vexing that even when the required conditions are met, at least to a fair degree, the ORE frequently fails to appear with animals other than rats (e.g., Warren et al., 1970). It may be that despite the present complexity of Model III, it is not complex enough in that it does not include variables which reflect differences in learning processes which occur at different phylogenetic levels. The problem is a fascinating one, and if Model III's accomplishment were "only" to account for discrimination learning in the rat, it would be a first-rate contribution indeed.

INTERMITTENT REINFORCEMENT AND BREADTH OF LEARNING. Recall that intermittent reinforcement had the effect of reducing stimulus selection or, in other terms, of increasing the breadth of learning. To determine whether this result could be generated by Model III, Groups 3 and 4 of Table 11-4 were run with two relevant dimensions, brightness and orientation (horizontal versus vertical), the former being a much more distinctive cue than the latter. Position served as an irrelevant dimension. In Group 3 all correct responses were rewarded, but Group 4 was maintained on a 50 percent partial reinforcement schedule. Note that the nine parameter values are identical in the two groups. After 200 training trials, by which time all stat-Ss met a criterion of at least 18 correct out of 20 successive trials, it was found that the response strength of the secondary dimension (H-V) was greater on the average in the partially reinforced group. The median values of response strength for the orientation dimension in the two groups were 0.85 versus 0.61.

The model generates this kind of behavior because continuous reinforcement quickly builds up the distinctiveness and response strength of the brightness dimension, which causes the control strength of that dimension, $C(i)$, to become quite large. As a result, Ss have little chance to be controlled by orientation and therefore learn little about that dimension. Note that the r values are very high for Groups 3 and 4, so that the chances are small that S will forget about the controlling dimension and thus have an opportunity to learn about the weaker dimension.

OVERTRAINING AND BREADTH OF LEARNING. We have also reviewed a number of experiments in which overtraining led to increased learning about a secondary cue. Although Lovejoy does not present simulation data bearing on this point, it is clear how such a result could be coaxed out of his model. With r sufficiently small, a stat-S would be likely to learn about a secondary dimension even though the probability of control by this dimension might not be large. This follows because there would be a strong tendency for S to forget the dimension which had just controlled his behavior, to resample the available dimensions, and, at least on many occasions, to choose the secondary dimension about which to learn. Presumably this process would continue substantially beyond the attainment of criterion and thus show overtraining to increase S's knowledge about the secondary cue.

Lovejoy presents a number of other results obtained with the model that are in correspondence with at least some empirical work. For example, he is able to produce the negative correlation reported by Sutherland and Holgate (1966) in the amounts learned about two dimensions of a two-cue problem (Group 5). But as pointed out earlier, this result has not been replicated with cats (Mumma & Warren, 1968).

SUMMARY. The simulation data which Model III has produced thus far suggest that there is some validity to its underlying assumptions. True, the number of free parameters is large, but it is difficult to see how this number can be significantly reduced in any model that attempts to capture the basic processes involved in discrimination learning. If we wish to incorporate into a model the fact that not all stimuli are equal in the facility with which they enter discrimination learning, we are forced to introduce a parameter, such as distinctiveness, for each of the available dimensions. Thus for an N-dimensional problem we must have at least N parameters. Moreover if the concept of varying response strength is to be employed, it is hard to see how one can do away with the two rate parameters that control this quantity, inasmuch as the assumption that reward acts in precisely the same manner as nonreward is probably fallacious. A parameter to control the speed with which modifiable distinctiveness is acquired would also seem to be necessary in some situations. Apparently, then, there is not much hope for a marked reduction in the number of parameters needed by a model whose goals are as ambitious as those of Model III.

But the fact that Model III, with appropriate juggling of parameters, can generate such a wide pattern of results renders *post hoc* predictions of empirical data of little or no value. Lovejoy is well aware of this limitation; he writes, "As it stands, Model III cannot be considered a complete theory for discrimination learning. It has given rise to no predictions of new results, and at present it would be difficult to disprove it without actually disproving one of the underlying assumptions which make up the model [1968, pp. 121–122]." Lovejoy offers several suggestions of how constraints can be applied to the model's parameters so as to contain its excess flexibility. But the success of such endeavors remains to be demonstrated.

One of the weakest assumptions in the model, insofar as face validity is concerned, is that which relates to the r parameter. It seems very remote that in the short interval separating response from reward or nonreward, S would forget the controlling dimension and thus possibly learn about a different dimension. Perhaps a more plausible hypothesis is that as S achieves a certain level of learning of the dominant cue, he begins learning more about other dimensions. Possibly there is for each S a constant amount of attention that can be expended on each trial, and early in learning most or all of it is devoted to the dominant dimension. Later, however, when a good bit has been learned about the dominant relevant dimension, there is less that the latter can "absorb" and thus more attention is available to be directed elsewhere. The implication is that the number of dimensions to which S can attend on a single trial increases as S learns more about the experimental task. It is only fair to acknowledge that this hypothesis—which could form the basis of a "variable-look" model—confronts the theorist with added complexities and, probably, additional parameters as well. But the notion that S has at his disposal a fixed amount of attention that he can distribute in various ways is, as we have seen, congruent with certain features of the selective-listening experiments, and for this reason is perhaps worthy of serious consideration.

SUMMARY

In spite of the length of the present chapter we have done little more than scratch the surface of a few areas of contemporary interest in discrimination learning and related topics. As many of the references cited in this chapter show (e.g., Sechzer & Brown, 1964; Slamecka, 1968a), these areas are not immune from methodological problems. Things are not always—alas not even often—as they appear, but it frequently takes acute methodological analysis to set our perceptions and preconceptions straight.

Perhaps nowhere is the need for searching methodological analysis more pressing than in the area of attention. The sheer diversity of processes to which this term is applied, in addition to its "lay" connotations, has imbued attention with far more meaning than a single concept can comfortably carry in the scientific enterprise. With the abundance of relevant data now at hand we are likely to witness increasing efforts aimed at clarifying this proliferating concept.

1. Discrimination learning is affected by both perceptual and nonperceptual variables. Illustrations of these two sources of relevant variables are:

2. A newly discovered organism is run in a two-choice discrimination situation for a large number of trials in an attempt to determine whether the animal possesses color discrimination. What are some of the factors one must consider before concluding from above-chance behavior that the animal does indeed possess the ability to discriminate colors or before concluding from continued chance behavior that it does not?

3. Describe the continuity-noncontinuity controversy and contrast the positions of Lashley and Krechevsky, on the one hand, and Spence, on the other.

4. Matching-to-sample and oddity discrimination paradigms can be employed to investigate concept-formation behavior in the following way:

5. (a) Distinguish between *LS* procedures and the changes in learning proficiency that result from such procedures.
(b) *LS* techniques have been valuable for comparative and physiological psychology because:

6. (a) Some of the theoretical implications of errorless discrimination learning for conventional discrimination theories are:
(b) Some of the practical implications are:
(c) The data that suggest a connection between aspects of errorless learning and frustration are:

7. Distinguish between selective perception and stimulus selection.

8. (a) Describe as best you can the differentiation theory of perceptual learning.
(b) Describe the nature of the "preexposure experience" data that have been brought to bear on this theory.
(c) Do the same for the reversal and extradimensional shift data.
(d) Compare the Kendlers' explanation of the faster acquisition of reversal shifts by adults in terms of their "mediating" mechanism with the approach of Tighe and Tighe which employs differentiation theory.

9. (a) Describe Broadbent's "filter" theory of selective perception as modified by Treisman and apply it to:

i The fact that little information coming over the rejected ear is apparently perceived in dichotic-listening experiments whereas much more is perceived when listening is by the binaural method.

ii The finding that perceptions based on "simple" discriminations occur with ease on the rejected channel.

iii The result that complex discriminations on the rejected channel are nevertheless possible if they involve stimuli of high affectivity.

(b) Why is the distinction between perception and memory so important when considering the selective perception data?

10. Why is it not true that "additivity of cues" necessarily implies that S learns about more than one stimulus dimension on a given trial?

11. Why is stimulus selection assumed to involve "associational" selection rather than perceptual selection?

12. (a) Describe how structural factors and past experience influence stimulus selection.

(b) Do the same for overtraining and intermittent reinforcement.

13. How was the concept of observing responses employed by Spence in the continuity-noncontinuity controversy?

14. Describe some of the evidence which shows that animals will learn a response to receive informative stimuli even though by doing so they do not increase the reward density that they receive?

15. How can S's preference for stimuli that inform him of the reinforcement schedule currently in effect be interpreted in terms of secondary (conditioned) reinforcement?

16. (a) The mechanisms in Lovejoy's Model III that accommodate stimulus selection are:

(b) What is the distinction between selective control and selective learning, and how are these concepts defined in Model III?

(c) What are the means by which differences in the distinctiveness of stimuli based on past experience and structural factors enter the model, and how are the changes in distinctiveness which occur during a contemporary discrimination problem accommodated?

(d) Compare Model III with Models I and II (Lovejoy, 1966).

(e) A very useful and revealing exercise, if possible, is to compare Lovejoy's model with that of Trabasso and Bower (1968, Chap. 2).

12 VERBAL LEARNING AND RETENTION

Norman E. Spear

INTRODUCTION

The study of verbal learning has achieved special prominence in recent years. There has been a dramatic upsurge in the amount of related research and in the involvement of several leading learning theorists whose previous work had concerned other areas of learning. One reason for this is the increasing recognition of the importance of verbal learning for any general account of human learning. This in turn may be traced to the fact that we have not yet found it possible to collect diverse quantities of data on human learning in instances where the possibility of verbal mediation can be dismissed. This is not to say that it cannot be done, and some progress is being made within the context of human classical eyelid conditioning (e.g., Spence, 1966). But the verbal component in human instrumental (e.g., motor) learning is often plainly in view and must be acknowledged.

The converse probably also is true: there may always be some motor component in verbal learning, although this influence appears relatively small. This also should be easier to test, since it is theoretically quite possible to paralyze S so that the implicit motor movements in the throat and tongue, etc., are eliminated during verbal learning. An approximation to this sort of manipulation has been made. Underwood (1964a) presented lists of verbal units varying in their ease of pronunciability to college students and asked them to recall them by writing on a piece of paper. In an effort to disrupt the motor involvement, Underwood had some of the Ss insert a physician's tongue depressor in their mouths and push down while the items were being presented. Others did this while recalling the items. Additional Ss were not given the tongue-depressor treatment. Surprisingly, Ss given the tongue-depressor treatment recalled as many items as those who were not, regardless of how easily the items could be pronounced, implying that the slower learning of items more difficult to pronounce is not a direct result of greater motor difficulty at the level of the tongue or larynx. Rather it may be attributed to processes going on elsewhere, presumably in the central nervous system. This sort of result further implies that the relevance of verbal learning is not limited by the uniqueness of the verbal tasks, and so principles evolved from this area may be expected to have broader applicability.

A Historical Overview

The enterprise of verbal learning may be traced from its beginnings in the early twentieth century with the "functionalists" who were primarily at Columbia University or the University of Chicago. Before 1950, work on verbal learning may be characterized as atheoretical, though there were a few notable exceptions, such as Gibson (1940), Hull et al. (1940), and Melton and Irwin (1940). Consequently the source as well as the subject matter of experiments in verbal learning differed from the more theoretically oriented animal work.

This atheoretical approach may be reflected by the definition of association presented in McGeoch's book on human learning, one of the first to emphasize data from verbal learning. At a time when, within the context of theories based on animal learning, there was much debate over "what is learned," McGeoch defined "association" in this most noncommittal way: "Two or more psychological events will here be said to be associated when, as a function of prior individual experience, one elicits or stands for the other. . . . The essential aspect of association is the relation between or among sequences of events [1942, p. 25]." To neutralize further his position, McGeoch noted that the term "association" was quite arbitrary and, alternatively, "*organization* could be used, since the associated events are organized into a sequence or unit. *Connection, bond, acquired relation* are other possible substitutes [1942, p. 25]." The approach of the functionalists was to select an independent variable likely to influence learning or retention, substantiate the reliability of this effect, and then determine the functional relationship between this variable and learning or retention.

This approach may be contrasted with that employed in the study of animal learning, which emphasized theory during the same period. Psychologists primarily concerned with lower animals as Ss were engrossed with issues relatively removed from the data and concerned with the operation of intervening variables and hypothetical constructs and the evolution of sets of laws or systems of learning applicable to all organisms. Thus most of the leading "animal learners" of the time (e.g., Guthrie, 1935; Hull, 1943; Spence, 1936; Tolman, 1932) asked, for example, whether motivation was a necessary condition for learning and whether discriminations were formed on the basis of the relative or the absolute characteristics of discriminanda. In contrast, the leading "verbal learners" of the period were less concerned with universally applicable constructs or theories and more with concrete manipulations of the task or environment which make a difference in rate of verbal learning, transfer from one such task to another, and amount forgotten. They asked, for example, which particular relationships between verbal units contribute to transfer (e.g., Bruce, 1933) and what changes in number of intrusions occur during relearning of a list as a function of degree of training on an interpolated list (e.g., Melton & Irwin, 1940).

As knowledge of verbal learning accumulated and functional relationships became more secure, theory began to play a more important role in verbal learning. This theoretical concern was not with evolving systems of learning having great generality, as, e.g., Hull (1943) had attempted. Rather, these theoretical issues dealt with learning per se, such as the questions of whether learning is a discrete or a continuous process (see Restle, 1965) and how mechanisms of interference in retention are best conceptualized (e.g., Postman, 1961).

In spite of the concerted attempt by early workers in verbal learning to divorce themselves from speculation, theory, or other means of generalizing much beyond the limits of their data, there are general properties of verbal learning that surely were evident from the beginning. These follow from the fact that human Ss are well experienced with learning in general and verbal learning in particular long before they serve in a verbal learning experiment.

The Subjects

Primarily because of convenience, Ss in most verbal learning experiments have been college students, usually students enrolled in an introductory course in psychology. College students, especially, have had a considerable history of learning assignments, not all well received; it is generally true that including them in an experiment is not viewed as a great favor. It is not being cynical to suppose that most Ss, even those who "volunteer," find the verbal learning task a rather tedious and somewhat stressful venture. The stress is present, of course, because they would like to avoid appearing dull. The result is that S inevitably brings all his skills to bear in trying to succeed in the experimental task or in devising strategies for escaping the situation as soon as possible. The S most distinctly is not a passive organism in whom "associative bonds" are being formed, nor is he simply a human S whose only purpose is to give a representative performance. There are two basic implications of this. The first is that instructions must be clear and straightforward and procedures completely uniform and well worked over to minimize distortions arising from the diverse idiosyncratic learning "strategies" of various Ss given the same experimental conditions. A second implication is that motivation, particularly for college students, is usually fairly high even without special efforts by E to make it so. In fact it would seem that providing additional motivation or incentive for doing well is likely to have little effect on performance in verbal learning, and this generally seems to be the case. Of course, this may not be the only reason why motivational variables have little effect on verbal learning performance, but it does represent one distinct possibility.

A second major aspect in which Ss are well experienced before entering a verbal learning experiment is in "handling" verbal units, including learning them. It has been estimated that the typical S, the college sophomore, has read between 60 and 70 million words by the time he serves in an experiment. The senior will have read nearly 100 million (Underwood & Schulz, 1960, p. 59). In addition, humans are bombarded by auditory verbal stimuli at incessant rates. What and how much of this verbal deluge is *learned* and influential in subsequent verbal learning is an empirical question and a theoretical issue. Nevertheless, it is almost certain that the verbal memory system is formed primarily by this means.

It should be made clear that the study of verbal learning has not exclusively involved college students as Ss. Younger children are being used as Ss with increasing frequency in verbal learning research (see Goulet, 1968; Keppel, 1964b), and other populations of human Ss, such as retardates, have been similarly investigated when appropriate (e.g., Wallace, 1967). At any rate, generalization about verbal processes from college students to other humans usually does not require an unreasonable conceptual leap. Certainly, if one is primarily interested in *verbal* learning, this particular generalization is considerably safer than that from the behavior of our other "most popular S"— the albino rat.

The Materials

The materials to be learned are by definition made up from the fundamental units of the language—letters and, in some cases, numbers. It is not necessary that these letters form words. At the present time, more verbal learning experiments involve words than involve nonwords, but this is a relatively recent development.

It is axiomatic that verbal materials in a verbal learning experiment must be carefully selected. This is so because a set of humans associated with a given language have a predictable commonality of past experience with verbal materials, and this experience importantly influences learning. For example, it is obvious to a literate person that the trigram (any three-letter combination) CAT has more "meaning" than TAC or CTA. "Meaning" is defined in terms of referents or associates: items differ *qualitatively* in meaning if they have referents or associates which are themselves different. Verbal units also may differ in meaning *quantitatively*, which is one way of conceptualizing degree of *meaningfulness*. Operationally, this usually refers to the extent that verbal units differ in the number of referents or associates they elicit (which in fact may have nothing to do with denotative meaning). We shall use the term "meaningfulness" more comprehensively, incorporating a number of different definitions which all seem to tap some aspect of earlier verbal experience. Used in this way, meaningfulness is one of the few variables which may be said to have a profound effect on rate of verbal learning. Another significant variable, the similarity between items within a list (intralist similarity), also is determined by the particular materials selected for learning.

Perhaps the best way to consider the problem of how materials are selected for verbal learning research is to trace their use historically. Hermann Ebbinghaus, who was the first to define verbal learning operationally by deciding what verbal materials should be learned and how learning should be measured, was born in 1850 in what is now West Germany. By the time he was 23, he had studied history, philology, and philosophy at several universities, served in the Franco-Prussian war and completed his Ph.D. dissertation on the philosophy of the unconscious. His early work and subsequent influence on the study of verbal learning have been described and insightfully analyzed by Postman (1968a).

Ebbinghaus's learning and testing procedures were quite simple. First he constructed a pool of 2,300 nonsense syllables consisting of all possible permutations and combinations of consonants and vowels with the restrictions that the first letter be a consonant, the second a vowel, and the third a consonant. Each nonsense syllable was written on a separate card, forming a pool from which he randomly selected 10 to 12 items to be learned at a time. His typical procedure (Watson, 1963, pp. 265–266) was to read through each card at a uniformly rapid rate, pausing for 15 sec after each complete run-through to record the trial. When he believed he could repeat them all in order, he attempted to do so without looking at the cards. On each attempt he recorded all his errors, however few, then repeated the procedure until he was able to recite them all without error. Once the list was "learned," he proceeded with other lists until such time (an hour, a day, or a week later) as his schedule required that he relearn a particular list. As an index of retention, the number of "readings" (trials) required before an errorless recital of the list was compared with the number originally required. For example, if 10 trials were required originally, but he needed only 6 to relearn the list after a week, he recorded his "savings" as $\frac{4}{10}$ or 40 percent.

Ebbinghaus saw three advantages in his use of nonsense syllables. (1) Compared with selections of "real language" from prose or poetry, his nonsense syllables were relatively uniform in difficulty. However, Ebbinghaus was aware of the nonsense syllable's lack of perfection in this respect, as is indicated by his admission that: "These series exhibit very important and almost incomprehensible variations as to the ease or difficulty with which they are learned . . . the predisposition due to the influence of the mother tongue, for certain combinations of letters and syllables must be a very heterogeneous one [Postman, 1968b, p. 152]." (2) The 2,300-item pool provided a large number of comparable combinations from which to draw. (3) The amount of material learned could be efficiently varied.

It is now quite clear that nonsense syllables are far from homogeneous and that the various lists selected by Ebbinghaus differed in the two ways most likely to affect their rate of learning. These are "meaningfulness" and "intralist similarity," which we shall discuss in some detail below. Furthermore, as Postman (1968b) pointed out, nonsense syllables are rarely used in contemporary verbal learning research for the purpose originally intended by Ebbinghaus— the study of associational processes or the factors responsible for formation of associations. Rather, when associative learning is studied, more familiar and readily available verbal units such as words, single letters, or numbers are used. Nonsense syllables and other nonword letter combinations themselves are difficult to learn, and the factors responsible for this difficulty are not easily separated from factors contributing to the learning of an association involving these verbal units.

As we shall see, there are techniques available for separating the learning of a verbal unit from learning to associate it with some other verbal unit. Still, the more efficient and direct way to study formation of associations is to use materials, such as letters, which are well "learned" and familiar to S before the experiment. This realization has been particularly important for understanding the relationship between learning lists of relatively isolated verbal units and the acquisition of verbal materials which more closely approximate everyday language, such as prose (e.g., Deese, 1961).

The Tasks

Learning tasks as well as learning materials generally serve as a compromise between *analytical* and *representative* purposes (cf. Underwood, 1966a). Ebbinghaus originally employed serial learning; he required himself to learn not only the 10 or 12 nonsense syllables in a list but also the exact order in which they were presented. This choice was not accidental, but a direct consequence of the British associationists' influence on Ebbinghaus's thinking. These association-ists, such as Locke and Mills, were primarily interested in how ideas become associated one to the other, and for Ebbinghaus these nonsense syllables repre-sented "ideas" (cf. Postman, 1968b). However, as we shall see, serial learning has little analytical value in contemporary verbal learning research.

There are four major verbal learning tasks: free recall, serial learning, recognition or verbal discrimination learning, and paired-associate learning. We turn now to a brief description of each.

FREE RECALL. The simplest verbal learning task is free recall. In this task verbal units, usually words, are read aloud or presented visually to S. After all the items, usually 10 to 20, have been presented, S's task is to write or say as many as he can. The unique feature is that S is free to give the items in any order: he is given credit for recalling list items regardless of their order.

Although many experiments have been concerned only with the characteristics of recall after a single presentation ("single-trial" free recall), others have dealt with changes in performance over successive presentation-recall trials ("multitrial" free recall). With multitrial free-recall procedures, the order of presentation may differ from trial to trial, but typically S is unrestricted in the order of recall that he chooses on each trial.

To provide an illustration of typical multitrial free-recall procedures, we may consider an experiment by Tulving (1966), who presented his Ss with 22 nouns, each a common word having a relatively high frequency of more than 100 per million words, as recorded in the Thorndike and Lorge (1944) frequency count. This table includes the frequency with which each of 30,000 words occur in a combination of written sources (e.g., newspapers, magazines, etc.; separate tables for each source also are presented). On each of 12 successive trials the items were presented at the rate of 1 per sec, after which S was permitted 60 sec for oral recall. These Ss recalled an average of 9.25 words correctly on the first trial. Their performance progressively improved until on the twelfth trial they recalled more than 18 words on the average.

This task is representative of much of the verbal recall in which we engage in our day-to-day existence, such as that which occurs when making up a list of people to invite to a party or attempting to name all countries in Europe. However, the general analytical value of free recall is limited because the stimuli eliciting the responses are nebulous, especially the stimulus responsible for eliciting the first item recalled. The most likely suggestion seems to be that it is elicited by "contextual" cues, although the specification of these cues currently is vague.

We shall see that much of the interest in free recall has been generated by the fact that Ss reorganize items for recall in an orderly way, and this seems to be related to the improvement shown in multitrial recall from trial to trial. Perhaps this kind of reorganization is representative of a more fundamental set of encoding and response processing behaviors to be found in verbal learning and verbal behavior.

SERIAL LEARNING. Operationally serial learning differs from free recall in two major respects. First, the order of the items typically is held constant in presentation from trial to trial, and items are counted correct only if S recalls them in the same order that they were given. Second, an "anticipation" procedure usually is used in serial learning experiments but never in free recall. With this procedure, S is presented with a list of, say, 8 words. When he sees the first word, he is to respond with (anticipate) the second; when he sees the second, he is to respond with the third, etc.

This requirement of correct order produces two characteristics—the "serial-position" effect and obscurity of the functional stimulus. Both of these are little understood in spite of a large amount of relevant research (see, e.g., Young, 1968).

The serial-position phenomenon is the nearly invariable tendency for S to learn the first few items most rapidly, the last few a little less rapidly, and items just beyond the middle of the list least rapidly (e.g., Glanzer & Peters, 1962). There have been a large number of theoretical attempts to explain this phenomenon, but none have been "successful" in the sense of having wide appeal and theoretical generality. Underwood has stated, somewhat facetiously, "Suffice it to say that the person who originates a theory that works out to almost everyone's satisfaction will be in line for an award in psychology equivalent to the Nobel Prize [Underwood, 1966a, p. 491]."

The functional stimulus in serial learning has been characterized alternatively as the serial position of each item, the immediately preceding item, or some preceding "clump" of items. If the functional stimulus is not serial position, then the implication is that each item is *both* a stimulus and response. If this is so, it obviously is impossible to study stimulus and response characteristics separately to determine the effect of, for example, intralist similarity on the stimulus side, meaningfulness of the responses, or response coding versus stimulus selection. In spite of a wealth of relevant experiments, Young (1968) has concluded that it still is not possible to unconfound or extricate the stimulus from response functions in a serial list "simply because the stimulus in serial learning has not been identified [p. 145]." Because of this limitation, the serial learning task has been found wanting in analytic value.

VERBAL DISCRIMINATION OR RECOGNITION LEARNING. In the most general case of recognition learning S first is exposed to a number of verbal items, then at some later time he is presented with these original items mixed among new items. The S's task is to tell whether each item is from the new list or the original one. It may be helpful to consider three specific instances which fall under this general category.

The simplest case of recognition learning is verbal discrimination in which an arbitrarily selected "correct" item is to be identified from an accompanying, but incorrect, item. A specific example may be taken from a paper by Spear, Ekstrand, and Underwood (1964, Experiment II). A list of 24 low-frequency words (12 pairs) was presented utilizing the anticipation method. For example, BAIL-FIFE was presented for 2 sec on the memory drum; then the "correct" word (e.g., BAIL) was shown alone for 2 sec, followed by another pair, then the correct word for that pair, etc. The S's task was to anticipate and say the correct member of each pair before its appearance, i.e., during the 2-sec presentation of the pair. The Ss of this experiment required an average of 5.88 trials to give two consecutive perfect recitations of the list.

Another special case of recognition learning may be illustrated from one condition of an experiment by Underwood and Freund (1968b). The basic procedure was to present S with 40 high-frequency words, then with 40 4-word sets. In this particular condition, S received the 40 critical words for a single presentation, then immediately was asked to select from each set of 4 words the word that had appeared among the original 40. The Ss correctly identified an average of 32.71 of the critical words.

A third case of recognition learning may be represented by an experiment by Underwood (1965). We need not consider the basic purpose of the experiment at this point, so we can omit elaboration of the design. College students were presented with 200 relatively high-frequency words spoken twice in immediate succession from a tape recorder. Ten sec elapsed between different words. Upon presentation of a word, S's task was to record on a sheet of paper having 200 numbered blanks whether or not it had been read earlier in the list. The intent was to identify instances in which a word was incorrectly identified as having appeared previously—a "false recognition"—as a function of relationships between that word and previous words. These false recognitions did, indeed, depend upon relationships with previous words, a fact we shall return to with reference to effects of intralist similarity.

PAIRED-ASSOCIATE LEARNING.   The greatest opportunity for analysis of verbal learning in general is provided by the paired-associate procedure, and most of the data discussed in this chapter have been gathered using this technique. This task requires S to produce a verbal unit (response term) upon the appearance of another verbal unit (stimulus term) with which it previously had appeared. The most frequent case of the paired-associate procedure—the "anticipation" technique—requires that S learn to anticipate and say the correct response during a period ("anticipation interval") in which only the stimulus is shown before both items are presented ("study interval"). The anticipation and study intervals are carefully controlled and held constant within each experiment, with typical durations of 2 sec each.

Careful consideration must be given to the instructions S receives, as they are likely to influence the learning strategy adopted by him and may importantly affect his performance in other respects as well. Unfortunately, specific instructions are rarely reported in published verbal learning experiments, because of limited journal space. Because the anticipation version of paired-associate learning is so widely used and important to this chapter, we have included a typical set of instructions for a paired-associate task having numbers as stimuli and words as responses (from Runquist, 1966, p. 512). The instructions, always read verbatim to S, are presented in complete form to illustrate the care taken to inform S fully of all details in a clear, even redundant, way while attempting to quell his general anxiety about the task and his performance.

> This is a learning experiment in which you will learn to associate words and numbers. It is very important that you follow the instructions to the best of your ability. Should you fail to follow any instruction, be sure to tell me since the interpretation of the results may be affected.

The list will consist of 8 pairs of items like the pair on this card. (The experimenter gives the subject the example card.) These pairs will be presented in the window in front of you. When we begin, the number will always appear in the window alone, while the word is covered by a piece of metal called a shutter. (The experimenter demonstrates by covering the right-hand item of the card.) After a short time, the shutter will lift and reveal the word. Your task is to associate or connect the word with the number, so that you will be able to say the word while the number is in the window alone, that is, before the shutter goes up. Since the order in which the pairs follow each other will not always be the same, you must learn these pairs *as pairs* and not in the particular order in which the pairs follow each other.

When I start this drum we will go through the list once so that you can study the list and try to make associations between the members of the pairs. After we have gone through the 8 pairs once, another tape, like the one now in the window, will appear. The appearance of the tape means that we are starting another trial, in this case, the second trial. It is on the second trial that, when the number appears, you must begin trying to say the word that goes with it *before* it appears in the window. We will then continue to go through the list while you attempt to anticipate the second members of the pairs before they appear in the window. You will continue through the list, trial after trial, until I stop you.

Always try to anticipate the word just after the number has appeared. If you are able to say the word before the shutter goes up, I will count it as correct; on the other hand, if you say nothing or say the word *after* the shutter goes up, I will count it as incorrect.

Always try to get as many of the pairs correct as you can on each trial. You should try to do the best that you can on each trial, even though you may have them all correct on some of the preceding trials. If you are having trouble anticipating some of the words or are giving some incorrectly, try not to let this discourage you or prevent you from doing the best that you can. We have found that most students find this type of learning a little more difficult than they first thought it would be.

The advantage of the paired-associate task is that it specifies the stimulus, the response, and—to a somewhat lesser extent—the association that occurs between them. Primarily because of these analytical properties, the paired-associate task is by far the one most often used in verbal learning research. Because the term "paired associates" implies that each verbal stimulus item is a unique signal for producing a particular verbal response, steps are taken to ensure that the presentation of this stimulus item is the only basis on which S can consistently give the appropriate response. Thus, there must be at least two pairs in a list; if there were only one, S would have no need to pay attention to the stimulus but could simply give the response whenever a trial occurred. Similarly, care is taken to change the order of pair presentation from trial to trial so S cannot receive credit for responding correctly if he has learned only the serial order of the responses and not their association with each stimulus. The effect of varied versus constant orders of presentation from trial to trial has been studied (e.g., Battig, Brown, & Nelson, 1963). Though little difference in overall performance was found, varied orders of presentation still are necessary to maintain analytical integrity.

In addition to being the most analytical of verbal learning procedures, paired-associate learning also is representative of a large amount of human learning, such as much of that taking place in school—acquiring an answer to a specific question, memorizing the state capitals, or learning the French equivalents of English words. With the presumed importance of teaching technique in mind, it is, therefore, surprising that variation in the method of presenting paired-associate lists does not make much difference in rate of learning (assuming that total time of exposure to the verbal materials is held constant). Let us consider some examples of this surprising fact, which seems counter to intuition.

Variation in ways of presenting paired associates. If there is a standard method of presenting paired associates, it is the anticipation method we already have described. Lockhead (1962) compared learning rate with this method to learning rate with the "alternate study-recall" and "random" methods. With the alternate study-recall method (which Lockhead labeled "blocking"), *S* first is presented with the entire list of stimulus-response pairs; then *S* is given the stimulus members one at a time and instructed to provide the appropriate response. The random method used exactly the same materials as the alternate study-recall and anticipation methods—the stimulus-response pairs and each stimulus alone—but randomized the orders. Thus, *S* sometimes would see a stimulus-response pair and sometimes only the stimulus, but temporally adjacent items were not necessarily related. To the extent that delayed knowledge of results impairs learning, one would expect the anticipation method to yield more rapid learning. Recall that with this method, the correct response is always presented immediately after *S* has attempted to anticipate the response, but presentation of the correct response is relatively delayed in the other two conditions. Surprisingly, Lockhead's results indicated no fundamental differences in learning among the three conditions.

Another variation of presenting paired associates is the prompting method (e.g., Cook & Spitzer, 1960). There are several subvariations possible, but its basic distinction is that the correct response is presented along with the stimulus *before* *S* produces the response. Tests of learning may then be given either before the presentation of the stimulus-response pair or on independent trials in which only the stimuli are presented. Although Cook and Spitzer's results seemed to indicate that prompting led to more rapid learning than anticipation, a subsequent study with slight procedural variation (Hawker, 1964) found no differences in overall learning. Also, it is probable that greater amounts of study time are provided with the prompting technique, because *S* almost certainly will be able to respond correctly immediately after presentation of the paired stimulus-response and so gains added study time compared with the anticipation technique (Sidowski, 1968). It appears safe to conclude that the prompting method per se yields about the same learning rate as the anticipation procedure.

Another variation in presenting paired associates—one with considerable intuitive appeal—is the "cumulative method" studied by Jung (1964). When the typical list of 10 or 12 paired-associate items is presented, some responses are given correctly sooner than others, because such a list exceeds S's memory span. Jung suggested that S probably concentrates on mastering a few items per trial—a trial is defined as one complete presentation of the list—and ignores remaining items temporarily. If this is so, presentation of remaining items on each trial is wasted. Jung's cumulative method was expected to be more economical because it consisted of progressively increasing the number of items on successive trials.

In a five-pair list, Jung presented one pair on the first trial, two pairs on the second trial, three on the third, four on the fourth, and five on the fifth. The first pair presented occurred on each of the five trials, and the last pair presented occurred only on the fifth trial. Separate groups also received the standard anticipation method of presenting all five pairs per trial for three trials. To evaluate learning with a comparable measure, eight standard trials were then given to all Ss. In spite of a very thorough set of experiments, Jung could find no consistent differences in amount of learning between Ss who were given the cumulative method and those given the standard method of presentation. However, it is notable that Postman and Goggin (1966) did find substantial facilitation of learning with a procedure similar to Jung's "cumulative method" (their "repetitive part" condition), which suggests that additional work on this problem may prove more fruitful.

There are two additional modifications of procedure in presenting materials that long have been suspected to influence rate of verbal learning, and both concern how best to distribute S's learning efforts. One is variation in temporal distribution of practice, and the other is learning parts of the material separately, as opposed to learning the whole in one "chunk." Underwood and his students have investigated the former variable, particularly within the context of paired associates, as thoroughly as any problem has been studied in any area of psychology. The conclusion from this research is that the influence of distribution of practice is relatively inconsequential. Summarizing a large number of experiments, Underwood and Ekstrand state, "It may be noted again that with PA [paired-associate] learning the DP [distribution-of-practice] effect is one of small absolute magnitude. It is most likely to occur with high formal similarity but even under optimal conditions there is not much 'room' to work with it experimentally, i.e., to study the influence of other potential interacting variables [1967a, p. 21]."

The question of learning "parts" versus learning "wholes" may be seen in attempts to memorize a long list of French equivalents to English words. Is it more efficient to try to learn the entire list at once or is it better to divide the list into sections, memorize each of these individually, and then combine the sections? Postman and Goggin (1966) are among the most recent investigators of this classic problem. They have concluded that the total time required for learning a paired-associate list by the whole and part methods does not differ.

The advantage of shorter lists which stems from the part method is counteracted by the disadvantages of learning them successively—which results in forgetting of previous parts because of retroactive interference (see below)—and then putting the parts together, at which point S must differentiate items across different parts.

The general conclusion emerging from this discussion is that the method of presenting a paired-associate list does not effectively alter rate of learning. This is surprising for two reasons. First, there is a great deal of wisdom (largely intuitive) which seems to demand that "methods of teaching" are critical determinants of the rate and amount of learning. Moreover, the procedures which do not make much difference in paired-associate learning, such as anticipation versus prompting, have been considered particularly important for teaching machines and programmed instruction. Perhaps they are not, in fact, as critical for programmed instruction as one might think.

This leads into the second a priori reason for expecting presentation procedures to make a difference in rate of paired-associate learning. Analogies, empirical extensions, and other general attempts to draw parallels between paired-associate verbal learning and classical (or in some cases instrumental) conditioning in lower animals predict it. For example, distribution of practice has considerable effect on performance in certain animal learning tasks and in human motor-learning tasks, as does delay of reinforcement (cf. Chap. 7). How successful or useful have these parallels been as devices for analyzing and understanding verbal learning? To gain some perspective on this question, it must be considered along with other conceptions of paired-associate verbal learning.

Conceptualizations of paired-associate verbal learning. Along with most verbal learning tasks, paired-associate learning is representative of certain real-life learning tasks. But its greatest value, as we have emphasized, is analytical. It is particularly useful for what may be termed "S–R theorists" who use "S–R language" and think in these terms (see Kendler, 1965). Indeed, most psychologists conduct S–R research even though they do not agree with the language or the thinking (cf. Asch, 1968). What should be quite clear, however, is that the use to which the paired-associate paradigm is put and its corresponding analytical value are quite dependent upon one's conception of it.

However straightforward the paired-associate technique may appear, its conceptualizations, uses, and consequent interpretation of results have been varied. Theorists who have shaped their systems largely on the basis of intuitions and data from animal-learning literature in the 1930s have differed to a great extent in the way they conceptualized the role of the stimulus, the response, and the association between them. This being the case, many early theorists looked upon paired-associate learning as an ideal way of manipulating stimulus and response variables independently, and they were not especially incorrect in feeling this way. In the 1930s and 1940s, when complex mazes were in common use, the specific stimulus elements controlling an animal's behavior were really quite vague. Thus, Gibson (1940), although a student of Hull, chose the paired-associate verbal-learning paradigm to test theoretical implications regarding the role of stimulus differentiation and generalization on learning and retention.

There also have been some more recent attempts to view verbal learning as a special case of conditioning. For example Goss, Morgan, and Golin (1959) considered the stimulus term in a paired-associate list as analogous to the conditioned stimulus in classical conditioning. They further viewed the physical representation of the response term as analogous to the unconditioned stimulus and S's representational response to this response term as analogous to the unconditioned response. This kind of analogy, although useful in some respects, has not proven very productive, as shown by some representative attempts to follow these analogies through.

Goss and his colleagues noted that if their analogy is correct, then omission of the response terms in the paired-associate list should have the same effect as omission of the unconditioned stimulus in classical conditioning—extinction. However, it has become quite apparent that even with a large number of such simulated extinction trials, the probability of correct responding in paired-associate learning does not decrease. For example, Goss (1965) gave 56 such trials without noticeable decline in correct responding. In fact there is some convincing evidence that the probability of giving a correct response actually increases on these kinds of "extinction" trials.

Jones (1962) was one of the first to see the theoretical importance of related phenomena arising from the "miniature experiments" or "RTT designs" originated by Estes to investigate possible discrete jumps in learning probabilities. Jones gave Ss a single study trial on a single paired-associate item (a consonant as stimulus and a number as response). She followed it with four successive test trials presenting only the stimulus without intervening feedback as to whether or not S was correct. Of those items that were incorrect on the first test trial, 29 percent were correct on the second test trial. This was not purely a "chance" effect, but rather a permanent change in behavior we could call learning, because 18 percent of those originally incorrect on the first test trial also were given correctly on the third, and 14 percent of those originally incorrect items remained correct on the fourth test trial.

Other attempts at analogy have been similarly unprofitable. Kintsch and McCoy (1964) found that delay in presenting the correct response following presentation of the stimulus did not affect learning rate. Although the task was not completely representative of paired-associate verbal learning, the results are quite different from those typically obtained with conditioning procedures. Even the partial reinforcement effect in extinction, perhaps the most robust of all instrumental conditioning phenomena (Chap. 7), has not survived the analogy. A number of studies have varied percentage of occurrence of response members in paired-associate learning (e.g., Schulz & Runquist, 1960), which may be viewed as analogous to variation in percentage reinforcement. Although lower percentage occurrence of response members often has been accompanied by poorer acquisition performance, it has not had its expected effect on "extinction" behavior (e.g., Keppel, Zavortink, & Schiff, 1967).

In spite of these generally negative results, it probably is premature to conclude that there are no common processes between basic classical and instrumental conditioning phenomena and verbal learning phenomena. As might be expected, the analogies have been very loosely drawn so far. Also, most of these attempts have concerned phenomena which are dependent upon variation in conditions of reinforcement, such as delay and percentage of reinforcement, and it is probably true that the widest gap between the behavioral characteristics of verbal learning and those of classical and instrumental conditioning will be found to involve motivational and reinforcement variables. We may expect to see better success with this sort of analogy in situations where motivational considerations are less important, for example, in terms of characteristics of discrimination learning (such as stimulus selection; see Chap. 11) or retention of learned behavior.

Moreover, it is important to keep one's priorities balanced in both directions. Regarding the general failure of analogies like these and the fact that they have not yet proven fruitful, Asch (1968) has made a useful comment: "One should not, however, conclude that the effort was wrong in principle; the inadequacies may be attributable to an insufficiently detailed acquaintance with the area of conditioning [p. 219]."

Although the attempts to explain paired-associate learning phenomena by analogy have not really advanced our understanding of them, other explanatory devices evolved *within* the verbal learning field have had more success in this respect. Perhaps the most popular analytical conception of the general processes involved in paired-associate learning in terms of the frequency of application is the two-stage model introduced by Underwood, Runquist, and Schulz (1959). These researchers were faced with the problem that although high levels of similarity among responses facilitated free recall of the list of responses presented alone, this variable had either the opposite effect or no effect when these same responses were response terms in a paired-associate list. Believing that this was understandable in terms of separate processes in paired-associate learning, Underwood et al. made a distinction between *response learning*—i.e., the capacity of S to give the response with or without the correct stimulus—and a *hook-up* or *associative* phase of learning, in which the responses were paired with the correct stimulus. These processes were generally assumed to occur sequentially, with response learning preceding hook-up learning, although separate items within a list might differ in their stage of progression. This framework led Underwood et al. to the solution that greater interresponse similarity retarded the hook-up stage of paired-associate learning to counteract the advantage found in the response-learning stage.

Additional processes have been suggested, some in two-process theories different from that of Underwood et al. (e.g., Polson, Restle, & Polson, 1965) whereas others simply have added to the two processes already suggested by Underwood et al. (e.g., McGuire, 1961). Alternative or additional processes usually have concerned operations on the stimulus, such as stimulus learning involving mediation mechanisms (e.g., McGuire, 1961), stimulus differentiation

(Polson et al., 1965), and stimulus coding (Atkinson & Crothers, 1964). Underwood and his colleagues subsequently considered various processes involved in Ss' treatment of the stimulus, as well as additional response and associative processes in their analysis of the influence of intralist similarity on paired-associate learning (Underwood, Ekstrand, & Keppel, 1965). Battig (1968), in his review and analysis of these and other conceptualizations of paired-associate learning, suggests that it may be necessary to consider as many as ten separate processes or stages in the learning of a "simple" paired-associate list.

SOME BASIC DETERMINANTS OF VERBAL LEARNING

Predispositions of the Verbal Memory System

The verbal memory system is neatly ordered. One consequence of this is a set of dependable characteristics of memory which influence verbal learning in important respects. That this is no mystery may be seen in the fact that each of the four characteristics listed below has great intuitive appeal as well as sound empirical foundation.

1. Perhaps the fundamental organizer of memory is frequency. Underwood and Schulz (1960) discussed relevant sources of evidence in support of the portion of their "spew hypothesis," which states that "the order of availability of verbal units is directly related to the frequency with which the units have been experienced [p. 86]." For example, Howes (1957) found that the greater the frequency of words according to the word count by Thorndike and Lorge (1944), the more often they were given as responses in a free-association test; the correlation between these measures was nearly perfect, 0.94. The point is that verbal units experienced more frequently in the past may be more readily emitted as responses or more correctly associated in a learning task, or both. But a major problem remains because, as we shall see, the critical specific aspect of frequency of experience (i.e., what kind of experience?) has not been isolated.

Of course, an even better predictor of the specific word given by a human is the stimulus word to which he is asked to respond. This, too, is undoubtedly a function of frequency, although it is not clear whether it is a matter of absolute or situational frequency. In any case, most of us have a fairly strong though intuitive feeling about how most people would respond to a given stimulus word. A number of game shows on television have capitalized on this fact.

One remarkable thing about the regularity of the memory system is the accuracy with which people can judge or predict the learning rate of various verbal units. Underwood (1966b), for example, reported correlations as high as 0.92 between estimated and actual rates of learning three-letter verbal units. Although few of us could be specific about the dimensions underlying this judgment, we probably would agree that some version of experiential frequency dictates them.

2. A second factor acting to determine the verbal output of an individual is recency. It is no secret that forgetting occurs, and it hardly comes as a surprise that the probability that an item will be given back correctly decreases with increasing intervals from the time it was given to S. But the reference here is to the *nature* of the items that will be given, irrespective of their correctness. The fact is that Ss rarely make an error by responding with an item that is not in the list being learned at the moment, a tendency governed by a hypothetical "selector mechanism." Underwood and Schulz (1960) were the first to comment on this "selector mechanism" and on its dependence upon recency. Suppose S is given, say, 12 letters and asked to recall them a minute later. Although he may not recall all 12 original items, it is very unlikely that he will give any letters that were *not* in the original list. Underwood (1964c, p. 58) cites an unpublished study in which 30 Ss made 1,424 overt errors during 15 trials of practice on 16 pairs of common words. *Only one of these errors was a word which did not already appear elsewhere in the list.* Someone said "yellow" when the correct response was "canary."

In a certain sense, the selector mechanism provides a "set" to respond from a restricted pool of items, and this set dissipates as a function of the length of the retention interval that follows exposure to the items. It has recently been suggested by Postman, Stark, and Fraser (1968) that this mechanism might have important general implications for the influence of interference on forgetting. This will be discussed in more detail later.

There are two additional, somewhat obvious, processes which act to restrict verbal responding. They are pointed out here because they are important considerations in the design of experiments. Although they are all too evident after the fact, they frequently are ignored.

3. The memory system has a limited holding capacity, or "memory span," which is a rather rigid one for adults, consisting of about seven items. As Miller (1956) has pointed out, these "items" are best thought of as coded "chunks" of information. By constructing large chunks of information, humans may appear to have greatly expanded memory spans.

This limited holding capacity has been explicitly recognized by experimenters and has determined the list length of verbal units used in verbal learning experiments. To avoid problems introduced by possible differences in memory characteristics when verbal units are "held in memory span" rather than "learned," most verbal learning experiments before the late 1950s employed list lengths that exceeded S's maximum holding capacity. As researchers became explicitly concerned with possible differences between short- and long-term memory processes, the consequences implied by making lists longer than the memory span began to be investigated rather than ignored.

4. Another fundamental fact of the memory system is that S prefers to study and learn certain materials over others (cf. Underwood, 1964c, pp. 67–68). This is not simply a reflection of the fact that S can judge the learning rate of verbal materials and prefers to attack those most rapidly learned. Rather, there undoubtedly are preferences among verbal materials which are equally learnable. For example, Postman and Riley (1957) found that separate groups of Ss learned *like* pairs of two numbers (two digits each) or two trigrams (nonsense syllables) at about the same rate as *unlike* pairs (number-trigram or trigram-number). However, when a single group of Ss were given a mixed list with half like and half unlike pairs, the like pairs were learned more rapidly. Apparently the Ss preferred to start learning the like pairs first and so acquired them before the unlike pairs, although they were, in fact, no easier to learn. Although these sorts of preferences are probably some function of language habits, they also may hold components of esthetic or other perceptual preferences, and the controlling factors have not been studied extensively.

Meaningfulness

We have discussed the variable of meaningfulness in somewhat general terms, noting its functional and conceptual obviousness. Therefore, this section may be brief. More detailed discussion of the history, measurement, and effects of meaningfulness may be found in two detailed research monographs (Goss & Nodine, 1965; Underwood & Schulz, 1960).

The influence of meaningfulness in verbal learning cannot be overestimated. For example, Hall (1966) states, "All things considered, perhaps the most important variable found in the verbal learning task is the meaningfulness of the material that is used [p. 292]." The first index or measure of meaningfulness was "association value," devised by Glaze (1928). Glaze presented a small number of Ss with a large number of nonsense syllables (consonant-vowel-consonant combinations) and asked them to respond, for each syllable, whether it did or did not arouse an association. The association value for a nonsense syllable was taken to be the percentage of Ss reporting an association for it.

A number of variations of this theme subsequently appeared (e.g., Hull, 1933), perhaps the latest and most complete being those of Archer (1960) and Noble (1961). A thorough set of summary tables showing the various scales of association value and other indices of meaningfulness may be found in Goss and Nodine (1965). Some of these indices have included counts of written frequency of nonword letter combinations, rated familiarity of these items, and rated pronunciability. A "feel" for variations in some of these characteristics may be obtained from samples of such ratings presented by Runquist (1966). Examples of variation in trigrams according to association value (Archer, 1960) include CIJ, XEP (low association value); BOH, NEF (medium); and BIM, CAT (high). Similar variation in pronunciability (Underwood & Schulz, 1960) ranges among items such as CFL, GHT (low pronunciability); CYR, QAD (medium); and CUB, BAD (high). Numbers also have been scaled for association value (Battig & Spera, 1962), including 31, 53 (low association value); 76, 44 (medium); and 18, 7 (high).

If indices of this sort were taken for words, there would be certain difficulties. For example, there would be very few words for which *no* association would be aroused in S. Still there is considerable variation in rate of acquiring different words. One index corresponding to something like meaningfulness is Noble's (1952a) measure of the number of verbal associates elicited by a word. Another is *frequency* of appearance of these words in the written language (Thorndike & Lorge, 1944). Still another such index, which is a predictor of the rate of acquiring groups of words, is based on *sequential dependencies*. Miller and Selfridge (1950) found that the more closely a sequence of words approximates the order found in the language, the more rapidly it will be learned. A similar index concerning sequential dependencies of letters within nonwords has been developed by Underwood and Schulz (1960), and it also efficiently predicts the rate of learning nonwords.

In spite of the diversity with which indices of meaningfulness have been derived, they have intercorrelated quite well in most cases. If Glaze's scale, for example, rates a nonsense syllable relatively high in terms of its probability of eliciting an associate, the same syllable is also likely to rate high in Archer's scale, as well as in indices of familiarity, pronunciability, etc.

In addition, these indices of meaningfulness correlate well with the speed of learning. For example, Underwood (1966b) determined the average number of correct responses for each of 27 trigrams (e.g., BGM, IDW, UNH) in a multitrial free-recall task. Then he determined the interrelationships between this learning measure, two indices of meaningfulness, and two estimates of learning rate for each trigram. One meaningfulness index had Ss rate each trigram (assign it a number between 1 and 9) according to the number of associates it elicited, and the other had Ss rate each trigram in terms of how easily it could be pronounced. These meaningfulness measures correlated 0.88 and 0.90, respectively, with actual learning. The Ss' estimates of learning rate also correlated quite highly with actual learning (0.92 and 0.91) and with the indices of meaningfulness (ranging from 0.91 to 0.94).

There are two general points to be drawn from these very high correlations. First, not only do indices of meaningfulness correlate highly with each other, but they also correlate well with S's estimates of how rapidly a trigram will be learned. Second, each of these measures correlates well with how rapidly the trigrams actually are learned.

The size of the correlations would indicate that these different response measures are importantly influenced by a common underlying determinant. In other words, they basically are measuring the same thing. It would appear that each of these response measures, and probably all other indices of meaningfulness, measures how much the average S has learned about a given verbal unit before a laboratory test (see Underwood, 1966a). Certain of S's past experiences have resulted in his learning about nonword verbal units, some more and some less. The question remaining is whether some specific portion of the past experience and/or learning connected with these trigrams is critical, i.e., necessary if this past experience and/or learning is to facilitate subsequent learning.

Answering this question and identifying the necessary experience which is the fundamental basis of meaningfulness are a most difficult task (see Underwood & Schulz, 1960).

Nevertheless, the influence of this aggregate of characteristics (association value, pronunciability, etc.) on learning rate is relatively clear. As is evident from the size of the correlation between rate of learning and some indices of meaningfulness, free recall is a direct function of meaningfulness. Similarly, serial learning is more rapid the greater the meaningfulness of the verbal units to be learned (e.g., Noble, 1952b).

The influence of meaningfulness on paired-associate learning requires more complex consideration because meaningfulness of the stimuli and meaningfulness of the responses may be considered independently of each other. Learning is more rapid with higher meaningfulness on the response side, and it also is more rapid with higher stimulus meaningfulness. However, the influence of variation in response meaningfulness is much greater than the corresponding influence of meaningfulness varied among the stimuli (e.g., Cieutat, Stockwell, & Noble, 1958; L'Abate, 1959). The reason for this is easy to understand. We know that the response terms, as in free recall, must be learned well enough to be recited perfectly by S, so meaningfulness has a large effect on the response side in accord with its large effect on free recall. However, there is no need for the stimuli in paired-associate learning to be learned. Subjects need only discriminate them, one from the other, in order to respond correctly. As you saw in Chap. 11, stimulus items are often subject to "stimulus selection." Thus S may select out a portion, say the first or last letter of a trigram, as the functional stimulus. It is not surprising, then, that the meaningfulness of the entire stimulus term is relatively unimportant for determining rate of paired-associate learning.

Does this imply that meaningfulness influences only response learning but has little influence on acquisition of the association between the stimulus and response? On the contrary, it appears that associative learning is significantly affected by meaningfulness of the potential associates in at least two ways. First, it has been determined that verbal units may become associated under certain conditions simply because they have appeared together in close temporal and spatial contiguity (Spear, Ekstrand, & Underwood, 1964); moreover, such association by contiguity is acquired more rapidly the greater the meaningfulness of the items to be associated (Keppel, 1966a; Spear et al., 1964). It is not entirely clear why this should be so, although Spear et al. suggested this may be a consequence of more meaningful items having more stable representational responses.

Second, meaningfulness of the stimuli, the responses, or both, is known to affect associative learning when mechanisms in addition to simple contiguity are available to S (Martin, Cox, & Boersma, 1965), perhaps in accord with Underwood and Schulz's (1960) associative-probability theory (but see Martin, 1968). This theory simply says that the greater the number of associates possessed by each member of a pair, the greater the probability that one of these associates will provide a mediational link through which the members of the pair may be associated. A mediational link, or mediator, is some third verbal unit already associated with the stimulus and response terms of a pair. For example, the trigrams LOW and BAL may readily be associated if one employs the common associate, HI, as a mediator. Since LOW and BAL each have a number of associates, it is relatively easy to find a common one to serve as a mediator, compared with LGF and BQX.

Intralist Similarity

Aside from meaningfulness, the task variable having the greatest influence on verbal learning is intralist similarity. The effects of intralist similarity are somewhat more complex than those of meaningfulness, primarily because they depend upon how "similarity" is defined. *Formal similarity* is defined in terms of the common letters possessed by verbal items. Manipulation of formal similarity occurs almost exclusively with nonwords, although it also has been manipulated and found to have an effect when words were learned (Heckelman & Spear, 1967). Items such as XBM, BVX, and MVB have relatively high formal similarity, whereas XBM, YVJ, and CFT have zero formal similarity. *Semantic similarity* nearly always is broken down into two types: *meaningful* and *conceptual similarity*. Meaningful similarity usually is indexed in terms of degree of synonymity (e.g., CHILD, KID, YOUNGSTER), although other means have been used (see Runquist, 1968). Conceptual similarity occurs to the extent that items belong to the same concept (e.g., CARROT, RADISH, POTATO).

Perhaps the most general statement that can be made about similarity is that in paired-associate learning, the higher the degree of stimulus similarity, the poorer the rate of learning. This relationship holds whether similarity is formal (e.g., Joinson & Runquist, 1968), meaningful (e.g., Beecroft, 1956), or conceptual (e.g., Underwood, Ekstrand, & Keppel, 1965). After that, a distinction between kinds of similarity is necessary in describing effects. For example, free recall or the response learning phase of paired-associate learning is facilitated by high meaningful similarity (e.g., Underwood, Runquist, & Schulz, 1959) and high conceptual similarity (e.g., Ekstrand & Underwood, 1963) but is retarded by high formal similarity (e.g., Horowitz, 1961; Underwood, Ekstrand, & Keppel, 1964). We mentioned previously that overall paired-associate learning is relatively unaffected by variation in meaningful similarity (Underwood et al., 1959) or conceptual similarity (Underwood et al., 1965) among the response terms.

Underwood et al. (1965), in a study that provides an excellent model for the experimental analysis of the effects of stimulus and response similarity, suggested and investigated two inferred processes thought to mediate the effects of similarity on paired-associate learning. The first is the *representational response*. This is the implicit response "made as the act of perceiving the word [p. 450]." Undoubtedly words are not represented in the central nervous system isomorphically to their physical representation on the screen, card, or window of the memory drum. Nor are they likely to be represented identically for all Ss:

some Ss may represent a given word as a visual image, others as a sound, and still others as a group of written letters. The representational response is a generic term covering all possible representations. The second process, also conceptualized as an implicit response, is particularly important for understanding the operation of conceptual similarity. This is the *implicit associative response (IAR)*, which is assumed to be produced by the stimulus action of the representational response. The *IAR* is often a readily available associate of the representational response, or it may be the conceptual category to which the representational response belongs. Often, it is assumed to be the most frequent associate or associates of the word presented (Underwood, 1965). If the word is DARK, we may expect that the *IAR* will be "night" or "light." When the word presented is a member of some conceptual grouping, e.g., DOG or CARROT, we may expect that the *IAR* elicited will be the name of that concept, e.g., "animal" or "vegetable," and this is where the importance of the *IAR* conceptualization enters considerations of conceptual similarity.

We know that a list containing groups of words having high conceptual similarity (e.g., OCEAN, LAKE, RIVER, APPLE, PEACH, PEAR) will yield better free-recall performance than a similar list having no conceptual similarity (e.g., SNOW, CAR, SUN, APPLE, LAKE, GAS, BED). Now assume that the better free recall with higher conceptual similarity is due to the fact that several items in this list have the same *IAR* ("body-of-water," "fruit"). If so, we should expect that Ss having fewer or less stable *IAR*s available would show less influence of conceptual similarity on learning.

This essentially is the reasoning behind Wallace and Underwood's (1964) attempt to understand the learning characteristics of retarded humans. There are data available supporting the contention that retarded Ss have fewer or weaker *IAR*s than normal Ss (Wallace, 1967). On this basis, one would expect conceptual similarity to influence verbal learning less in retardates than in normals.

Wallace and Underwood (1964) tested this hypothesis with regard to two effects of conceptual similarity previously obtained with normal Ss: in normals the greater the similarity, the better the free recall but the poorer the paired-associate learning. Conceptual similarity was varied simultaneously on the stimulus and response sides. As predicted, Wallace and Underwood found that the influence of conceptual similarity was essentially nil for the retarded Ss in both the free-recall and the paired-associate tasks. This contrasted with the typically strong effects found with normal Ss. Supplementary analyses further supported their contention that *IAR*s were less active (either weaker or fewer) in the retardates. For methodological purposes, it is important to note that Wallace and Underwood were not concerned with the relatively trivial absolute comparisons of rate of learning between retardates and normals, because normals surely would learn more rapidly. Rather, they were concerned with differences in the characteristics of verbal learning as a consequence of specific verbal deficiencies in the retardates.

An immediate extension of this kind of reasoning comes to mind with respect to learning as a function of age. Because *IAR*s are necessarily acquired, we might expect that younger children, having had less opportunity to learn verbal associates, would be less influenced by conceptual similarity than older children. One experiment tested this with children ranging from 7 to 11 years old but failed to find the predicted differences in the effects of similarity (Heckelman & Spear, 1967). However, this may simply reflect the fact that language habits, including *IARs*, are essentially fully developed by 7 years of age (cf. Keppel, 1964b). Perhaps the predicted effects would occur at younger ages.

Other Variables Important in Verbal Learning

There are two additional variables of importance that we have mentioned only in passing. These are motivation and total time permitted *S* for learning. Both of these strike the intuition of most people as important, and this, in itself, makes these variables important enough to consider here.

MOTIVATION AND VERBAL LEARNING. "Motivation" is such a general term that discussion of it is difficult without introduction of additional intervening variables closely tied to operational definitions. Probably the associated intervening variables that come to mind first are those introduced and seen most often within the context of learning by lower animals—reinforcement and drive. We already have seen some instances in which operations taken to reflect reinforcement in verbal learning have failed to have much influence. Similar results have been obtained with variation in magnitude of the reinforcer (e.g., a penny versus a nickel for a correct response). As with instrumental (discrimination) learning generally (see Chap. 7), reinforcer magnitude seems to have little effect on verbal learning, except perhaps in special cases (e.g., Harley, 1965a; Weiner, 1966a, 1966b). When positive effects have been found, they often may be attributed to some indirect consequence of greater reinforcer magnitude such as increased rehearsal (Wickens & Simpson, 1968). Also, almost none of the various operations intended to vary drive have been shown to influence verbal learning; and exceptions were limited to special cases (e.g., Spence, 1958a).

Incidental learning. We speculated briefly in an earlier section about why motivation has so little influence on verbal learning. One possibility is that instructions like "Learn this material" are sufficient and maximal motivators. This would imply that simply eliminating the instructions to learn should result in poor learning rates. When Ss are tested for learning in the absence of explicit instructions to learn, performance above a chance level has been termed *incidental learning.* Two basic types of incidental learning have been considered (McLaughlin, 1965; Postman, 1964a). In the Type-I paradigm, S is instructed such that he presumedly believes that *nothing* about the task involves learning; in the Type-II paradigm, he is instructed to learn a portion of the task but later is tested on the remaining items. For example, S might be presented with a list containing words and nonwords. With a Type-I paradigm, he might be asked to write all the associates he can think of for each item and later tested on how many items he can recall. In a Type-II paradigm, S might be instructed to learn the words for subsequent recall but only write associates for each of the non-words and be tested, subsequently, for how many nonwords he can recall. This distinction has been made because some effects seem to depend upon whether a Type-I or -II paradigm has been used (see McLaughlin, 1965).

The central issue of incidental learning, however, would seem to be whether instructions per se—the presence as opposed to the absence of instructions to learn—influence rate of learning. To answer this it is logically necessary to exclude all other differences between the experimental conditions for incidental and intentional learning. This is difficult, because it means that incidental learners must somehow be tricked into emitting the same overt and covert responses as the intentional learners. When these conditions are approximated (one cannot be certain about covert responses), the differences between incidental and intentional learning begin to vanish (e.g., Mechanic, 1964). This result implies that instructions per se have little motivating effect in verbal learning. Apparently, if you somehow can get S to pay enough attention and respond appropriately, he will learn whether or not he is told to do so.

Arousal and affectivity. A final consideration of motivation in verbal learning concerns a relationship between how well a verbal unit is recalled and how S responds to it physiologically. In this case, the physiological index involved may measure emotionality, arousal, or both.

Kleinsmith and Kaplan (1963) presented college students with an 8-item paired-associate list for a single study trial. The responses were the digits 2 through 9. The stimuli, selected with apparently few considerations except that they were "expected to produce different arousal levels [p. 191]," were KISS, RAPE, VOMIT, EXAM, DANCE, MONEY, LOVE, and SWIM. As each stimulus was presented, deflections in the galvanic skin response were measured as an index of the extent of "arousal" associated with that word. For each S, the three stimulus words showing the greatest deflection and the three showing the least were selected to represent high and low arousal. Recall of the associated digits upon presentation of the stimuli was taken after either 2 min, 20 min, 45 min, 1 day, or 1 week.

The results, shown in Fig. 12-1, indicated poorer recall of responses having high arousal stimuli after 2 min, but this relationship gradually reversed with longer retention intervals until recall was *better* for these high arousal items. It is not really surprising to find differential recall at a given retention interval for items that Ss also respond to differentially in some other respect. Such a result could simply be a reflection of degree of learning, and we have already seen that a variety of responses to verbal units correlate highly with how well the units are learned. Unfortunately, the verbal materials employed by Kleinsmith and Kaplan (1963) severely restrict generalization beyond this specific experiment. Also, these items were particularly subject to the high correlations implied by such a result because they were so heterogeneous, although the investigators subsequently corrected this aspect of their design (Kleinsmith & Kaplan, 1964).

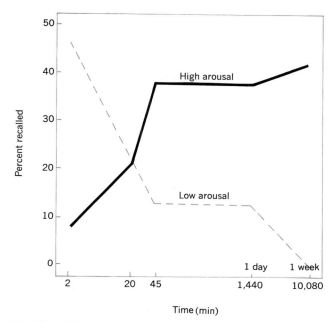

Fig. 12-1. Differential recall of paired associates as a function of arousal level, with arousal level defined by the extent of deflection in the *GSR*. (SOURCE: L. J. Kleinsmith and S. Kaplan. Paired-associate learning as a function of arousal and interpolated interval. *Journal of Experimental Psychology*, 1963, **65**, 190–193. Copyright 1963 by the American Psychological Association and used by permission.)

Nevertheless, their finding of an *interaction* between galvanic-skin-response deflection to a verbal unit and retention interval to determine recall is impressive. It does not seem wise to dismiss such an interaction as an instance of a relatively trivial response-response law. Moreover, this kind of interaction has been replicated (e.g., Kleinsmith & Kaplan, 1964; Walker & Tarte, 1963) and extended to other situations (Weiner & Walker, 1966).

The conclusion about motivation in general must be that it does not have much influence on verbal learning, just as it had little effect on discrimination learning within separate-groups designs (Chap. 7). Studies such as Kleinsmith and Kaplan (1963) may imply some important special influences. Further investigation of the characteristics and generality of these effects (e.g., to what extent are they tied to motivational-personality differences between Ss or momentary motivational differences within S?) appear to present important targets for future research.

TIME FOR LEARNING. It is difficult to conceive of circumstances in which performance on a verbal learning task will not improve with successive trials, given some room for improvement after the first trial and sufficient exposure of items per trial to permit perception. Is this improvement a consequence of the repeated trials themselves? Is there some special advantage to studying a verbal list again and again in a trial-by-trial procedure, or is the improvement over trials simply a consequence of the accumulation of study time as trials progress? We already have seen a hint that there is no great general advantage in leaving a task and coming back to it on successive trials, because there is no simple facilitation of learning attributable to greater distribution of practice.

That *total learning time*—not total number of learning trials—is the critical determinant of amount learned, is one of the most consistently documented and general of verbal learning phenomena (cf. Cooper & Pantle, 1967). The basic idea is as simple as it appears, so that little need be added here. Suffice it to say that, with some relatively minor qualifications (see Cooper & Pantle, 1967), equal amounts of learning of a paired-associate, free-recall, and to some extent, serial-learning task would occur if verbal items are presented at the rate of $\frac{1}{2}$ sec per trial for 20 trials, as if they are presented at the rate of 1 sec per trial for 10 trials, or as if they are presented at the rate of 2 sec per trial for 5 trials. Except for some special cases of free recall involving slow rates of presentation (cf. Underwood, 1969b), amount learned will be determined by total time spent learning, regardless of how this total time is broken up into separate trials.

SUMMARY. The verbal memory system has some distinctive and predictable characteristics determining its organization and use. These include (1) a verbal repertoire with structure and availability based upon some version of frequency of experience, (2) a tendency toward restrictive availability of items recently learned, (3) a limit to the number of discrete items held in a state of immediate availability, and (4) a preferential system probably based upon past experience but not always related to ease of learning.

Although it does not necessarily follow from these characteristics, there are only a few variables that make a considerable difference in rate of verbal learning. These are meaningfulness (some conglomerate of characteristics determining the extent to which an item is consonant with S's past experience), intralist similarity, and, of course, S himself. Also, amount learned generally increases with total time spent learning. Other variables (e.g., motivational variables, distribution of practice, etc.) have a relatively minor influence on learning and then only in special cases.

"S–R PSYCHOLOGY," "ASSOCIATION," AND VERBAL LEARNING

We have now considered essentially all the variables that have significant effects on acquisition of verbal units. Related questions that come to mind are: What does it mean to say that verbal learning has occurred, that a verbal "association" has been acquired? What has changed about S's behavior as a consequence?

Does the acquisition of a verbal association imply a physical link somewhere in the central nervous system between isomorphic representations of the verbal stimulus and the verbal response?

Of course, these questions require complex and detailed answers, most of which are not available as yet. We shall consider two portions of one type of answer. First we shall confront the question, What is an association? We shall do this by examining the relevant thoughts of some outstanding contemporary investigators of verbal learning. Whenever we discuss an association between a stimulus and response, we implicate something called "S–R psychology," and we also shall consider this. Then in the following section, we shall consider some of the specific changes in S's behavior during a verbal learning task. We have claimed that human Ss are not passive organisms upon whom associations may be inscribed, and we shall see that recent S–R conceptualizations of the term "association" have taken this into account. On the other hand, the variables we cited as most important for learning, e.g., physical aspects of the task itself and total time permitted to learn, could as easily apply to the learning of rats or computers. The following section considers some operations S may perform on verbal material during the course of learning and the extent to which these kinds of activities do, indeed, facilitate rate of learning.

Thus far and throughout the remainder of this chapter, most of our discussion centers on independent consideration of stimuli, responses, and the associations between them. The terms "stimulus" and "response" create relatively little difficulty because, at least in paired-associate tasks, they have readily identifiable representations in the real world. But developing a firm grasp on the term "association" is a difficult conceptual task, perhaps especially so because its use carries with it philosophical overtones of S–R associationism or S–R psychology.

For a proper perspective on verbal learning, it is useful to consider these issues. Is the term still used in verbal learning in the strictly descriptive sense employed by McGeoch (1942)? The answer must be an unequivocal "no," largely because the verbal learning data gathered in the past 30 years have created a greatly enriched "association." For most scientists dealing with verbal learning, the term "association" has expanded its connotations in correspondence with the expanded understanding of conditions and processes surrounding it. On the other hand, some have suggested that the term may have outlived its usefulness even in an operationally descriptive sense, and still others doubt that it was ever as useful as it was used.

Although the issues cannot be considered in depth here, some flavor of the related thinking may be acquired by sampling the views of representative scientists.

"S–R Psychology"

Perhaps first consideration should be given to the terms "S–R psychology," "S–R tradition," or "S–R associationism." What do they mean? Kendler (1965,

1968) analyzed *S–R* associationism as a multifaceted concept consisting of four primary components: (1) a technical language, (2) a methodological orientation, (3) a pretheoretical model, and (4) a group of theories. The term has been used as an instance of each of these, sometimes implying considerable overlap across classifications, but Kendler suggests that the four are at least relatively independent. The gist of Kendler's components is as follows:

1. The *S–R* language conceivably can be used in the fairly neutral sense of a tool of representation, neither implicating specific processes nor excluding others. It is perfectly appropriate to apply *S–R* associationism in this sense, though assuming, as in Kendler's illustrative statement, that "we do not *find* behavior atomized into individual *S–R* associations; we represent it as consisting of such associations [1965, p. 11]."

2. As a methodological orientation, *S–R* associationism involves operationism. In this sense, the term ties together psychologists who require data obtained with the experimental method as their major, perhaps exclusive, basis for argument and decisions among characteristically data-bound theories.

3. Stimulus-response associationism may be employed as a pretheoretical model when one makes a conceptual leap between a specific concrete learning situation and the functional stimulus or response presumedly associated in that situation. This use differs from that of simple *S–R* language in that in addition to simply specifying the functional stimulus and response, the pretheoretical model adds assumptions about conditions controlling the acquisition of the association, often by analogy with other learning situations.

4. Finally, *S–R* associationism may be used as one label for a class of theories having different degrees of agreement in terms of structure, assumptions, and constructs.

The major point is that there is no *S–R* psychology or *S–R* associationism per se. There are instead four scientific tools, any of which might be employed with equal efficiency by "*S–R* psychologists" or "non-*S–R* psychologists."

A CRITICISM OF ASSOCIATIONISM IN VERBAL LEARNING.   Historically, the group of psychologists least likely to employ *S–R* tools—although they often conduct research closely parallel to those who do—have preferred the language and concepts originated in Gestalt psychology. Application of the Gestalt point of view to verbal learning recently has been capably championed by Asch (e.g., Asch, 1968).

Asch finds a great deal to criticize about the paired-associate approach, viewing it as symptomatic of a general failure of non-Gestaltists to see the learning world as consisting of anything but associative bonds between specific stimuli and responses. Asch suggests that a central mistake was the equation of learning with "association by contiguity." The parties responsible are not specified, but the leading theorists of the 1930s are the likely referents. If they were alive to respond, Asch might receive an abrupt denial from Hull or Tolman but probably a shrug from the most influential researcher of verbal learning in that era, John McGeoch. It is reasonable to argue that the functionalistic verbal learners of the 1930s and 1940s behaved as if they believed this were correct. But their more likely response would be that this sort of issue is irrelevant. Asch's implication that investigators got locked into the rote-learning paradigm by ignoring perceptual relationships and sequential linguistic characteristics is largely accurate, but descriptively so, rather than philosophically. Once the complications of the functional properties of this "simple" paradigm became apparent, there was little to do but ride them out, hopefully to solution. Such behavior is rather typical in all sciences throughout history (Kuhn, 1962).

Thus it may be correct, as Asch suggested, that the paradigm of rote learning was so designed that it "eliminated as far as possible the presence of relations other than contiguity [p. 216]." But it is difficult to imagine that such men as McGeoch, Robinson, Melton, and others were unaware of the *possibility* of other kinds of relations. If there is awareness of alternatives, there would seem to be nothing wrong with biasing research toward a particular theoretical orientation. According to Kuhn (1962), science has always progressed in this way, and the viewpoint most successful in this dominates until a more convincing one gains sufficient strength to prevail. In this respect, one might ask by what sort of historical accident did Gestalt psychologists *fail* to develop and pursue a corresponding paradigm, eliminating all relations save those of *their* philosophical preference, i.e., "organization, which is based on relational determination . . . the antithesis of association by contiguity [p. 215]."

Asch's primary point perhaps is that the structure of the paired-associate task is a "set-up" for interpretation by contiguity, and, in Asch's terms, the S–R formulations have "served to entrench the associationistic premise by protecting it from examination [p. 223]." This assertion contains a great deal of truth and it requires—and is receiving (e.g., Jenkins, 1968)—attention. This is not to say that the extensive investigation of paired-associate learning was necessarily a mistake: the progress in understanding verbal learning, which should not be underestimated, otherwise may have amounted to a great deal less.

Similarly, Asch appears correct in stating that "there has been no fundamental inquiry of the ways in which events become psychologically contiguous [p. 224]." This is so even within the realm of rote learning, where association by contiguity plays an important, if not a central, role. Perhaps the major reason for this is that the underlying nature of the association and of psychological contiguity is not ready for further explanation because its fundamental properties have not yet been described. Nevertheless, Asch's cogent arguments call attention to the need to do exactly that. The recent advances in linguistic research suggest that "association" as a concept may need to be updated and perhaps broadened to accommodate some fundamental characteristics of language behavior.

What is the contemporary thinking regarding association as a concept? First, we shall consider some views of two leading verbal learning theorists who make some use of tools of S–R language, methodology, and pretheoretical concepts. Then we shall turn to the views of Deese, an eminent psychologist who has switched from these tools to others.

Contemporary Views of "Association"

Underwood (1966b) has suggested that modern associationism assigns six basic characteristics to the association. These characteristics are of no small importance, because Underwood views an association as the "basic unit of analysis in verbal learning [p. 492]." They may be paraphrased as follows:

1. It is inevitable that the paired-associate technique would be identified with the ambiguous program referred to as "S–R theory" in view of its reference to a specific stimulus term and a specific response term. But the S–R *language* may be more misleading than informative, because one need not conceptualize the association acquired by this technique as a *theoretical* S–R association. The conceptual jump from paired associate to theory may go in any of several directions. One may even choose an "R–R" (response-response) theory, because it is clear that "no one is so naive as to believe that an association is formed between two verbal units apart from the responses a subject makes to these units [Underwood, 1966b, p. 492]."

2. The stimulus and response items of the paired-associate list may bear only vague resemblance to S's representation of these verbal units. The college-age S will operate on the stimulus term, representing it perhaps as a single letter. Similar transformations of the response term will be tried and sometimes employed (see below). The association is formed between S's *representations* of the stimuli and responses, not between the stimuli and responses appearing in the window of the memory drum or projection screen.

3. The stimulus is not necessarily hooked up directly to the response. Rather, the stimulus and response may be connected by one or more mediators or perhaps by a chain of mediators, including some items associated previously only with the stimulus and some associated only with the response (see Kjeldergaard, 1968).

4. Associations in general must be contextually dependent (cf. Lashley, 1950). Thus it can readily be shown that a list of paired associates is more rapidly relearned in a room *different* from one in which a contradictory list has just been learned (e.g., Greenspoon & Ranyard, 1957).

5. There can be no doubt that there is some tendency acquired for the response to evoke the stimulus, as well as the more commonly diagramed tendency for the stimulus to evoke the response. The questions of theoretical importance concern the relative strength and characteristics of the "backward" compared with the "forward" association.

6. The construct "association" is purely an intervening variable and implies no specific events in the central nervous system. Underwood states that it is "a functional unit and simply reflects the observation that under certain specified conditions one event will be followed by another—that learning will occur [p. 493]."

A comparable, but somewhat different, analysis of "association" has been made by Postman (1968a). Postman distinguishes six general cases that have used association as a concept. The first use is as a descriptive term, such as that employed by McGeoch (1942). Next, Postman makes a distinction between the "association" implied within the concept of "preexperimental associative hierarchies" and that referred to in the case of "implicit mediators." The former is an independent variable which refers to the extra-experimental associations which S brings to the experimental situation. These may be specified in advance and manipulated to determine their influence. The latter, on the other hand, is a dependent variable under the control of S: so far, it has not been possible to guarantee the production of implicit mediators. Therefore, they remain a part of the behavior being measured.

Another use of association has occurred in consideration of contextual associations, implying a capacity for nonspecific situational cues—some aspect of the experimental apparatus, room, or internal condition of S during the time of learning—to elicit verbal responses acquired within that context. If a list of verbal items is presented to S with a free-recall procedure, it may be argued that S recalls the list in the form of a chain of items with each response eliciting the subsequent response. Even so, it is necessary to refer to some aspect of the context in order to answer the question of what elicited the *first* response. It is not enough simply to say that the first response was elicited by E's instructions to begin recalling because, after all, none of the responses previously were associated with this instruction. In addition to the association implied by the elicitation of verbal responses by nonverbal contextual cues, Postman recognizes the converse—elicitation of nonverbal responses by verbal stimuli. As a final use of the concept of association, Postman cites models and theories implicating underlying physiological mechanisms of association.

An important point that Postman makes is to emphasize that association is distinctly a *dispositional* concept. To say that A is associated with B is not to say that A inevitably follows B. Rather, this implies only that *given the appropriate circumstances* A will follow B. This is simply to say that what is performed is not a perfect and one-to-one reflection of what is learned. This distinction between learning and performance has long been a source of concern in animal conditioning, where motivational variables play a considerably greater role than in verbal learning, but it has been relatively ignored in verbal learning work until recently. Postman emphasizes that there are instances in which it is profitable for verbal learning theorists to be reminded of this distinction.

It may be seen that Underwood and Postman make a common point: an association is not simply an irrevocable requirement that a "bonded" response follow presentation of the stimulus. Rather, it is a statement of conditional probability: the response has a certain probability of occurring upon presentation of the stimulus, given the appropriate context. This is a considerably more flexible conception of "association" than is generally recognized, especially historically. In a sense it was anticipated by Skinner's view that a (discriminative) stimulus "sets the occasion for the response" (see Chap. 9). There are, however, some students of verbal learning who go further in liberalizing the concept of association, some to the point of abandoning it entirely.

SOME CONTEMPORARY PROBLEMS WITH "ASSOCIATION." Deese (1968) has recently stated that, because the fundamental assumptions of associationism have escaped empirical scrutiny, it "is by no means obvious to many students of verbal behavior that radically different assumptions about the nature of associations are even possible [p. 97]." He suggests that the classical conception of an association and its accompanying characteristics of spatial, temporal, and logical sequences is inadequate, perhaps to the point of having retarded progress in verbal learning, and that it has particular shortcomings in accounting for language behavior. Indeed, he suggests that more rapid progress in linguistics has occurred because such concepts were discarded, and the same could be true for verbal learning.

Deese takes issue, for example, with the general notion that individual items in a free-recall list should be the basic unit of analysis: in this instance, he questions the idea that the predictable organizational patterns in which Ss recall words in a free-recall task are a consequence of item-to-item association (see below). Rather, he believes that memory is ordered in terms of *structures* rather than items. In this he seems to imply that the *object* stored in memory is the intersection—a point in multidimensional space—of various defining characteristics of an item, presumably including class, category, etc. (cf. Underwood, 1969a). He sees no need to limit the concept of "what one knows" to spatial or temporal stimulus-response sequences simply because original associationists conceptualized ideas as flowing in this way.

Thus, Deese rejects the notion that there is, as he says, "a one-to-one correspondence between the manifest verbal elements emitted in recall and the form of storage in the head [p. 101]," dismissing as well the doctrine of contiguous associations. For him, the central issue of memory is the question of what is stored. The immediate association that this tends to arouse is the question, "What is learned?", which was so much hacked over in the context of animal learning during the period of controversies of the great systems of learning and behavior. One would hope that the question "What is stored?" will not lead to as many blind alleys as the question "What is learned?" Nevertheless, Deese's (1968) points have a great deal of appeal and are presented with a thoroughness that cannot be duplicated here. His message, and related views (e.g., Jenkins, 1968), may be expected to have increasingly important impact on verbal learning in future years.

SUMMARY. *S–R* associationism does not refer to a single philosophy; rather, it incorporates four tools which may be used regardless of one's scientific ideology. These include a language, a methodological orientation, a pretheoretical model, and a class of theories. These tools are likely to appear in studies of verbal learning, arousing the suspicion that the results obtained may have propagated *S–R* associationism, particularly the concept of association by contiguity, only because the verbal learning tasks and variables permitted no alternative conclusions. However, contemporary theorists in verbal learning take a more liberal view of association than is often supposed, specifying particularly that an association is not an ironclad, irrevocable bond but instead represents a disposition to respond given certain circumstances. Moreover, the "*S–R*" association itself may, in fact, involve many other items as mediators, strategies, etc. Still there are some who question the usefulness of even a liberalized "association." This question has arisen mainly from a failure to handle complex linguistic phenomena with most current conceptualizations of association.

ORGANIZATIONAL PROCESSES IN VERBAL LEARNING

One of the more significant developments in verbal learning in recent years has been an increasing realization that the subject in a verbal learning experiment is far more than an associative mechanism. To understand verbal learning is not merely to comprehend some analogy to a welding torch which solidifies a connection between a stimulus and response, although something like this may sometimes occur. Reactive rather than passive, *S* brings to bear complex organizational processes which serve to transform in diverse ways the stimulus materials presented to him. In this brief section we can only deal with a few of the ways in which the subject, in his efforts to learn and remember, has been recognized to transform verbal learning material. Generally speaking, the kinds of transformations imposed by *S* on the items presented to him may be classified as transformations of the order of the items (e.g., clustering), transformations effected on the items themselves (coding), and finally, transformations which depend heavily on associations or features that lie outside of the items—"extra-item" transformations.

Transformations of Item Order

When *S* is presented with a list of words to memorize, a number of predictable events occur which are interesting in themselves and relevant to theories of free recall. The most prominent event common to both multitrial and single-trial free-recall tasks is that *S* can be depended upon to recall the words in a different order from the order in which they were presented.

When some of the words are mutual associates (e.g., BOY, GIRL) or members of a common category or concept (e.g., CARROT, LETTUCE), they are likely to be recalled together. This phenomenon has been labeled "clustering" and sometimes, but not inevitably, the degree of clustering is positively related to the amount recalled. Clustering has been well studied, and a good discussion of some of the relevant issues may be found in Cofer (1965) and Jung (1968, pp. 152–164). For our part, clustering will be considered as a special case of S's general tendency to rearrange or transform items for recall in a relatively predictable way.

SINGLE-TRIAL FREE RECALL. The organizational characteristics of free-recall behavior are readily illustrated by the following experiment. Underwood (1964c) read two different kinds of lists of 16 words each to 37 college students. Immediately after each list was presented, Ss wrote down all the words from the list that they could remember. One type of list, said to have high conceptual similarity, consisted of four concept categories, each including four instances of the category (e.g., RABBI, BISHOP, MINISTER, PRIEST). The second list consisted of 16 unrelated words, in the sense that they belonged to no obvious common conceptual grouping (e.g., DAISY, KNIFE, BUS).

As expected, Ss recalled more of the conceptually similar words than items from the "unrelated" lists, 14.57 versus 11.35 on the average. Moreover, 38 percent of the Ss got all 16 items correct from the lists with high conceptual similarity, but only 3 percent got all items correct in the lists with unrelated items. Another result of interest was that with the high-conceptual-similarity list, all 37 Ss showed "extreme clustering," in that all four items from a given concept were recalled before any items of another concept were given, and no S gave more than four items per cluster or less than three. The "selector mechanism" also functioned well. Of 1,184 opportunities for responding, only 16 words were given that were not in the list, and of these, 14 were members of a concept that *was* in the list. In general, the memory for concepts was remarkable: from a total of 296 opportunities to recall one or more members of a concept category, there were only three cases in which no member was recalled.

These results demonstrate two basic characteristics of free recall and, more generally, of verbal learning. First, Ss actively operate on the material which is to be learned, reorganizing it in such a way as might serve to facilitate recall. Second, Ss learn a great deal more, when presented with a list, than simply the items which are to be learned. In the case of the high-conceptual-similarity lists, for example, Ss clearly learned the number of concepts contained in the list, the number of items within each concept, the concepts themselves, and which items belonging to a concept were *not* in the list.

Organization of the items of the list may also occur even when the items are apparently unrelated. Suppose, for example, that Ss are presented with a list of 15 to 20 well-integrated verbal items which are not interrelated. That is to say, taking into account association norms, conceptual similarity, or number of common letters between words, there is no a priori reason to believe that these items—say, words—are related in any way. Under these conditions, two characteristics of S's recall are almost inevitable. First, S will not recall the words in the same order in which they were given; second, the order in which these words are recalled will be relatively consistent from one S to another in a number of ways.

There are two general interpretations explaining why this commonality of selected recall order might occur. First, it is possible that the transformed order is unrelated to efficiency of recall but only reflects, for example, consistencies in preexperimental item strength or linguistic preferences. The other possibility is that a transformed order is actively selected because it does, in fact, improve recall. Tulving (1965) conducted two simple but illuminating experiments which bear on these alternatives. From an earlier experiment Tulving constructed 16-word lists of "high" and "low" organization. The high-organization list embodied the order in which a previous group of Ss had recalled the 16-word list, and the low-organization list was, according to Tulving's index, approximately the antithesis of the transformed order most often observed in Ss' recall. In two experiments, one employing a free-recall task and the other a serial-learning task, Tulving found that the high-organization list led to far faster learning than the comparable low-organization list. These results show clearly that items are learned more readily when they are presented in an order preferred for recall by most Ss than when a different order is imposed.

The advantage of a particular item order could be due to more efficient input and storage by S, or it could arise from the fact that when words are stored in a particular way, they are more readily retrieved at recall. The results from free-recall experiments in which interitem similarity has been manipulated bear on these alternatives. Let us turn now to a few relevant studies.

ORGANIZATION AND CONCEPTUAL SIMILARITY IN RECALL. The general fact that free recall is better the higher the conceptual similarity among items (assuming that these are well integrated) has been mentioned earlier. This effect, as well as the influence of transformations of order, may have its basis either in input or output processes. Assume for the moment that the facilitating effect of interitem similarity arises during the retrieval process. Imagine that, in attempting to recall a list in which several items belong to a common concept, S completes a multistep editing operation. First, he covertly recalls one item from any given concept. Then he searches through the remaining items available to him until he gathers together all possible items that he can remember as belonging to that concept. Next he searches through these, separating items from inside and outside the list. Finally, he overtly recalls the *list* items belonging to this concept before beginning on another concept.

Such editing processes (of which the above is one remote possibility) would seem to require relatively large amounts of time at recall and, perhaps, varying times for different items. If S is not limited in recall time he can devote to the various items, it would seem that S could more effectively employ an editing process than if E "paced" S's recall by allowing a constant responding time for each item. Moreover, when similarity among items of the list is high and such editing is presumably more useful, one might expect the superiority of unpaced over paced recall to be even greater. Ekstrand and Underwood (1963) were not able to support these predictions, however. They found only a slight advantage of unpaced over paced recall—a superiority, moreover, which did not increase with greater similarity of items.

An alternative to the "editing at retrieval" process is one in which the facilitation of free recall by greater interitem similarity occurs during *input* into memory storage, that is, while the words are being presented to S. This interpretation was investigated in detail by Wood and Underwood (1967).

In order to discuss Wood and Underwood's theory and experiments, it is necessary to recall the two theoretical constructs representing two kinds of implicit responses made by humans upon presentations of a word. The first is the "representational response [Bousfield, Whitmarsh, & Danick, 1958]," which is simply the act of perceiving the word. The second implicit response produced by the stimulus action of the representational response is the implicit associative response (*IAR*). In a sense, to say that two words elicit a common *IAR* is to say that they have conceptual similarity.

Wood and Underwood suggest that the fundamental process mediating better free recall with higher conceptual similarity is a common one—frequency. Their hypothesis contains two basic assumptions: (1) each presentation of a word elicits an *IAR*, most likely the concept name (their specific procedure essentially excluded the possibility that words within a conceptual grouping would elicit one another); and (2) each time the concept name is elicited, each concept member previously presented in the list will in turn be elicited by way of a backward association from the concept. If four items in a list are FRANCE, ENGLAND, ITALY, and POLAND, presentation of FRANCE will elicit the *IAR*, "country"; presentation of ENGLAND will elicit "country," which in turn will elicit FRANCE; presentation of ITALY will elicit "country," which will elicit both ENGLAND and FRANCE, etc. In effect, list members of a common conceptual group receive more *functional* trials per *nominal* trial than members of a list having no other items of the same concept. Moreover, a word should get more *functional* trials—and so be better learned—the greater the number of items falling under the same conceptual category in the list and the earlier it is presented in the list.

This theory yields readily testable predictions, but the most fundamental of these requires some means for controlling the appearance of *IAR*s. For a single set of words, it is necessary to find one set of circumstances in which common conceptual categories (*IAR*s) are elicited and another in which they are not. If this were accomplished, recall should be better with than without *IAR*s, because the latter presumably mediate the beneficial aspects of conceptual similarity. Moreover, *IAR*s are assumed to increase learning, so they should be more facilitory when they occur during presentation of the list than when they occur during recall.

Wood and Underwood accomplished the previous objective by selecting words which possess some commonality of sense impression but which *ordinarily* do not elicit a common *IAR*. For example, DERBY, COFFEE, and SKUNK are not ordinarily thought of as belonging to a common conceptual grouping. But if BLACK is included in the list or otherwise presented to S, then all of these words will elicit "black" as an *IAR* (Underwood, 1965). By including or not including the "cue"—the word, or in this case, the color indicating the common-sense impression which subsequently would be elicited as a common *IAR*—Wood and Underwood effectively manipulated the presence or absence of an *IAR* while holding constant all other aspects of the tasks. When common *IAR*s are present, conceptual similarity is higher than when they are absent.

The first experiment reported by Wood and Underwood, an extensive one including 18 experimental conditions with 20 Ss in each, tested a number of more or less subtle predictions from the theory. Although not all predictions were strongly verified, the results consistently reflected better recall when the *IAR* cue was present than when it was not. The theory, you will recall, attributes this to the effectively greater number of learning trials during *presentation* of the list.

An alternative explanation is that this "cueing" phenomenon might be the consequence of a *retrieval* mechanism. If so, the overall benefit to recall, and perhaps more subtle effects of conceptual similarity as well, should be replicable when the appropriate cue is presented at recall, regardless of its presence or absence during the learning trial. The second experiment reported by Wood and Underwood tested this possibility.

Two groups of college students were given a free-recall task as in the first experiment. One group was presented with the relevant cue color during learning (i.e., presentation of the list), but the other group received no cue during learning. Both groups were given the appropriate cue at recall; this was accomplished by presenting them with answer sheets consisting of five columns with eight blank spaces under each column. At the heading of each column was one of the words BLACK, RED, GREEN, YELLOW, and WHITE. These colors were the appropriate cue, the common-sense impression, of the eight words in each set. Because all Ss had the relevant cues available at recall, they could not be expected to differ in recall performance if the better recall attributable to conceptual similarity is primarily a retrieval, not a learning, phenomenon. The results were as predicted: Ss presented with the cues only at recall but not during learning recalled significantly fewer words than comparable Ss of Experiment I who had the relevant cue presented only during learning (16.38 words in the former group compared to 18.70 in the latter). This suggests that providing the common *IAR* at recall does not facilitate performance to the extent that providing it during learning does.

Therefore, the results of Experiment II supported Wood and Underwood's learning interpretation of the influence of conceptual similarity on free recall. Further confirmation is provided by an experiment by Wood (1968).

MULTITRIAL FREE RECALL. When Ss are presented with a list of nominally unrelated words for recall on successive trials, we can safely predict that the items will be recalled in a different order from that in which they were presented and that Ss will recall more items correctly on each successive trial. Moreover, subjects will stick fairly closely to their own reordering from trial to trial; i.e., Ss tend to repeat items recalled on successive trials in the same contiguous order. They will tend to show each of these behaviors whether the items are presented in the same order or successively different orders, a variation in procedure which does not seem to have much effect on the number of items recalled correctly (Waugh, 1961; but see Jung & Skeebo, 1967). At this point, however, we are concerned with the typical case in which items are presented in a different order from trial to trial and Ss may recall in any order they choose.

It is not completely accurate to say that Ss maintain their chosen reorganization of words from trial to trial. Obviously if they get more items correct on each trial, there is likely to be some change in organization; but this is not the point. The point, with important implications for learning, is that Ss seem to *improve* their organizations from one block of trials to the next. The meaning of "improved organization" will become clear after a brief description of how "organization" is measured.

Tulving (1962) has developed an index of such organization ("subjective organization") based upon information-theory concepts. Briefly, the extent to which items are recalled in the same relative (adjacent, in this case) ordinal position from one trial to the next is quantified for a block of two or more trials. This quantity then is divided by the maximum value it could have taken, i.e., by a number indicating identical orders of recall for all trials within the block. The resultant quotient, always a number between zero and one, is the index of subjective organization. The larger the number, the more consistently Ss recall items together in the same ordinal positions.

Tulving (e.g., 1962) has discovered that Ss do improve their organization from one block of trials to the next (see Fig. 12-2). Furthermore, they do so in correspondence with the improvement in number of words recalled, such that the better S's organization at any given point, the better his recall. Note that these are statements of correlation which cannot by themselves make much of a case for a cause-effect relationship. Nevertheless Tulving (1964, 1968a), in an extension of some suggestions by Miller (1956), has theorized that the improvement in subjective organization from trial to trial *is* the cause of the improvement in performance.

We should quickly add that Tulving has based his argument upon much evidence in addition to the simple fact of correlation between these events (e.g., Tulving, 1965). The basis of his argument begins with the recognition that humans are biologically restricted in how many chunks of information one can hold in one's immediately retrievable memory—the "memory span." Nevertheless, Tulving suggests that humans may increase the number of *nominally* independent information chunks even though the number of *functional* information chunks remains the same. This may be accomplished by appropriately grouping, coding, and generally reorganizing items as they are presented to the memory system. Tulving refers to each nominally separate verbal unit

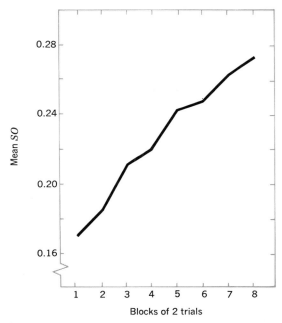

Fig. 12-2. Mean subjective organization scores (*SO*) for 16 subjects on 8 successive blocks of two trials. (SOURCE: E. Tulving. Subjective organization in free recall of "unrelated" words. *Psychological Review*, 1962, **69**, 344–354. Copyright 1962 by the American Psychological Association and used by permission.)

(usually a word) presented to *S* as an "*E* unit." The *E* unit may be thought of as an "experimenter unit" because it is counted as a single unit by the experimenter. Several *E* units may be incorporated within a single "*S* unit," the core information chunk which is the functional element stored in *S*'s memory. It is important to note that the use of such a higher-order memory unit for storage of a group of *E* units does not *guarantee* that the *E* units will be more likely to be recalled. In fact, it is unlikely that an *E* unit will be recalled with the same probability as *S* units. We shall see later that this potential difficulty in decoding has a parallel in organizational processing within individual response units (see below).

Other theoretical mechanisms have been suggested to account for the trial-to-trial improvement on a multitrial free-recall task. These have considered learning as due to, e.g., increases in response "availability" (Asch & Ebenholtz, 1962b) or increases in the associative strength between contextual stimuli and responses (e.g., McGovern, 1964). Tulving (1968a) has presented a clear consideration of these possibilities along with a defense of his own ideas, and it is unnecessary to repeat them here (see especially Tulving, 1964, 1968a).

It cannot be denied that reorganization is a fundamental feature in the free recall of words. But is the organization only *incidental* to learning? Some special cases seem to show that it is more than that. We have seen that one sort of reorganization appears to operate during item presentation to facilitate subsequent recall (e.g., Wood & Underwood, 1967) and another may improve recall performance by means of a coding-reorganization-decoding combination operating on storage and retrieval (e.g., Tulving, 1968a). Whether words are generally reorganized on their way *into* or *out of* memory is not completely clear, although Slamecka (1968b) has argued convincingly for the latter. Also, how much reorganization really aids recall in the general case remains a question. It is perhaps tempting to ask why Ss would bother reorganizing words if it did *not* facilitate their recall. The answer may be simply that Ss—perhaps even college students—do not always know what is best for them for learning purposes and may reorganize on other bases. We shall observe in the next section that a similar case of reorganization occurs which actually impairs learning rate.

Transformation of Individual Items (Coding)

We have seen that if Ss are presented with a list of familiar, well-integrated verbal units, such as words, they will reorganize them—transform their order—into groups of words that apparently "fit together" better. Indeed, we have seen that some theorists believe that learning—trial-to-trial improvement—in multitrial free recall simply reflects improved organizational techniques on the part of S. An analogous situation may exist in the case of single, multiletter items which are not words. To what extent are these reorganization principles and strategies applied when Ss set about to learn an item like QXR?

There are two general ways in which a nonword letter combination is learned and made available for later recall. First, if the items have only a vague resemblance to words, if they are difficult to pronounce, or if they have appeared infrequently in S's past experience (items such as NDF, GXK, KBV), then it is likely that something like "raw learning," such as association by contiguity, takes place. A second way these nonword letter combinations may be acquired is by being transformed by S, "coded" into some more familiar verbal or nonverbal form which S is more facile at storing and retrieving.

Underwood and Schulz (1960) have extensively investigated acquisition of responses in a paired-associate list when the response items are nonwords, items such as QTX. This particular trigram occurs with zero frequency in written materials, does not sound like a word, is difficult to pronounce, and probably does not immediately elicit an association. How then does S operate on such a trigram during the response-learning stage to make it available for association with the stimulus? At a descriptive level, Underwood and Schulz (1960) have shown (see Fig. 12-3) that the integration of the trigram letters is, on the average, a gradual process, such that the first letter becomes available, then the first two, and then all three. After a few more trials, all three are given consistently in the proper order as an integrated response unit.

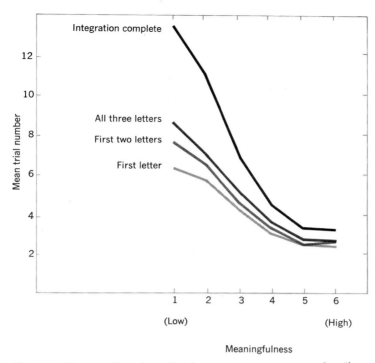

Fig. 12-3. Stages of learning with trigrams as responses as a function of meaningfulness (as indexed by Underwood and Schulz's "generated values"). It can be seen that the higher the meaningfulness, the fewer the trials required for complete integration once the letters have been given by S. (SOURCE: B. J. Underwood and R. W. Schulz. *Meaningfulness and verbal learning.* Philadelphia: Lippincott, 1960. Copyright 1960 by Lippincott & Co. and used by permission.)

Such a trigram may be conceived of as a miniature serial list in which the verbal units consist of individual letters. In terms of learning processes, however, it probably is quite different from the typical serial list because it is well within nearly everyone's memory span, at least to the extent that the letters themselves are well integrated and serve as the units of memory rather than the individual phonetic units.

There are a number of processes which may be involved in the simple acquisition of such a verbal unit. First, it is possible that existing associations between letters which conflict with those in this trigram must be suppressed or "unlearned" if present ones are to be acquired. Thus in the case of QTX, Q is almost invariably followed by U in the written language, so this U response and perhaps the association between U and Q must be suppressed if QT is to be acquired. Once this sort of suppression has taken place, it is necessary for the letters to become associated by some raw learning technique, perhaps by simple contiguity (see Spear, Ekstrand, & Underwood, 1964).

Alternatively, S might approach the response-learning task somewhat more strategically and attempt to rearrange the letters so they acquire functionally greater meaningfulness. For example, if the trigram to be acquired were DWE, S might code it as DEW or WED, which are more compatible with previous experience and so more readily stored. Perhaps the item also may be more available at recall with this technique. The effectiveness of this kind of strategy was first investigated by Underwood and Keppel (1963a).

RESPONSE CODING.   Underwood and Keppel (1963a) presented college students with a multitrial free-learning task consisting of 10 trigrams. Each of these (e.g., TPA, BSU, UTB) can be transformed into at least two different words by rearranging the letters. The assumption was that if S transformed the items into words, thus increasing their meaningfulness, they would be more readily acquired. Four of the eight groups of Ss were instructed about these coding possibilities; the remaining four groups were not. Pilot work had shown that without explicit instructions to do so, about 50 percent of the Ss would code by transforming the trigram into a word.

Underwood and Keppel reasoned that although it might be easier to store the item as a word, which might also be more available at recall than the nonword form, a major difficulty during recall could be *decoding* the word back to the appropriate trigram. To the extent that this is true, performance ought to be greatly facilitated if the requirement of exact letter order was removed and Ss were credited for giving the correct letters without regard to order. Therefore, within each of the four instructed and noninstructed groups, one group was permitted to recall the letters in any order from the beginning, one group in any order after one trial with exact letter order required, one group after three trials, and one group after five trials.

Underwood and Keppel found that coding instructions facilitated learning only if Ss were free to recall trigram letters in any order; otherwise, coding instructions were a deterrent to learning. With no letter-order requirements, Ss instructed on coding possibilities gave 38.9 items back correctly over all five trials, and those not instructed gave 34.2. However, when Ss were required to give the letters back in correct order, those instructed on coding possibilities got only 22.7 items correct over all five trials; those not instructed got 28.1 items correct. In the latter two groups (given all five trials with exact letter order required) the trouble was apparently in the decoding, as expected. When "coders" were excluded from the instructed group (coders were determined in terms of the kind of errors produced), the differences between Ss not instructed and those instructed on coding disappeared. These results indicate that coding may impair learning under some circumstances, though otherwise it might help.

Forrester and Spear (1967) suggested that the seemingly high level of coding (56 percent) in Ss not instructed about it and the tendency for Underwood and Keppel's Ss to show the "stupid" behavior of attempting to code even though it interfered with performance, were consequences of the low level of meaningfulness of Underwood and Keppel's trigrams. They expected that Underwood and Keppel's effects might be decreased if the items had a higher initial degree of integration between the letters or if some other code, such as pronouncing ("sound coding"), had been available for items in their uncoded form.

Forrester and Spear replicated a portion of Underwood and Keppel's experiment, comparing trigrams having low pronunciability with trigrams composed of the identical letters but in arrangements which resulted in higher pronunciability. The eight groups of their experiment consisted of all combinations of high pronunciability versus low, instructions on coding versus no instructions, and exact letter-order requirements at recall versus no restrictions on order. Overall, they found that removing letter-order requirements at recall facilitated performance only if the items were of low pronunciability to begin with. Moreover, when there were no letter-order requirements, more low-pronunciability items were coded than high-pronunciability items. Finally, there was a general inverse relationship between pronunciability and the probability that an item would be coded.

One of the implications of these results was that pronunciation—"sound coding"—might be a more useful code than rearranging letters into words. The potential importance of sound coding previously had been suggested in one of several experiments by Underwood and Erlebacher (1965), which is the most thorough work to date on response coding. Their general strategy was to induce coding to various degrees in Ss, coding which, if used, should alter learning rates. They caution, however, that finding no differences as a function of some treatment does not imply that Ss were not coding: each S may be using a coding system of his own rather than the one presumably induced, or the coding strategy may not actually affect learning even though it is used as intended. This point is applicable to the study of verbal learning strategies in general whenever E is concerned with effects of an imposed strategy.

The first experiment reported by Underwood and Erlebacher studied the effect of having various numbers of rules applicable for coding trigrams in a multitrial free-recall task. They did this by the following technique: First assume that the numbers, 1, 2, 3 represent the three letters in each of the words SIX, DAY, BIG, MEN, GET, FEW, LOT, JOB, TAX, CAN, WIN, and ROW. They rearranged the letters of these words in four orders—1-3-2, 2-1-3, 2-3-1, and 3-1-2. One group then was given a list of twelve items all having the same nonword order, e.g., 1-3-2 or 2-1-3. Another group had half their items of one order and half of a different order. The third group had one-fourth of their items in each order. Thus, the groups had one, two, or four rearranging rules to learn if they were to rearrange letters into words for storage.

In addition to the typical instructions for a multitrial free-recall task, the Ss were told that if the letters of each item were properly rearranged, a common word would result.

The results indicated better recall with fewer coding rules: Ss given items all codable by the same rule recalled about two items per trial more than Ss with two or four rules. This advantage was maintained about uniformly throughout all six trials. However, various aspects of their results, such as overt errors, did not produce a clear picture as to whether or not the Ss with two and four rules were, in fact, coding the items into words. Perhaps it was so troublesome to remember different coding rules that they had abandoned coding entirely. Therefore, Underwood and Erlebacher ran a subsidiary experiment. One group received the Experiment I list to which two coding rules were applicable, and another group received 12 comparable items which were not codable to words at all. Although they found no significant difference in number of items learned throughout six free-recall trials (40.75 items correct on the average for the codable list and 40.40 for the noncodable list), the overt errors provided conclusive evidence that the group given the codable list did, in fact, code, and the other Ss did not. This suggested that all the groups in Experiment I coded, but only the group with a single rule did so to advantage. Apparently difficulty in recalling multiple rules contributed problems in *decoding*, since exact letter-order requirements held at recall.

Altogether, Underwood and Erlebacher reported six major experiments, four dealing with response coding and two with stimulus coding. Each of these makes important points and warrants brief mention.

In Experiment II, they asked whether the one-rule list in Experiment I involved such simple coding-decoding processes that they would have been learned no more rapidly if the letters actually had been presented in the form of words. They found that this was not so: learning the nonword trigrams with a single coding rule required nearly three times as many trials as when the items were given as words in the first place. They also asked in Experiment II whether they might devise a situation such that Ss could employ a general *decoding* rule at recall, thus reducing the difficulty with multi-rule lists. They were able to do this with the two-rule lists but not the four-rule lists.

Response coding during paired-associate learning was studied in Experiment III. The general procedure was the same as Experiment I, incorporating responses which could be decoded at recall by one, two, or four different rules. Again they found learning considerably more rapid when a single rule was sufficient to decode all the response items at recall. As in Experiment I, they concluded that all Ss were coding, but the Ss with two or four rules to handle had more difficulty at decoding.

Finally, Experiment VI studied the possibility of sound coding. Basically, one group received a list with items that sounded like previously learned items, but the control learned a list of equivalent items which did not. The first group showed better learning than the second. Underwood and Erlebacher concluded that sound coding did occur. The effect, however, was relatively small.

The response-coding experiments by Underwood and Erlebacher yielded three general principles. Generally, these principles accord surprisingly little importance to coding in verbal learning: (1) the response-coding operation must be very simple if it is to influence learning at all; (2) the influence of response coding on learning is not always facilitatory; and (3) when response coding does facilitate learning, the effect is small. Existing evidence suggests that these principles may generalize to other forms of learning strategies and mediational devices as well.

Finally, it is notable that response items in a paired-associate list may be transformed not only to facilitate the availability of the responses for hook-up but in certain special cases to facilitate hook-up itself. Podd and Spear (1967) found that if paired-associate lists were such that transformation of responses into words resulted in an item which already had a high preexperimental association with the stimulus, then variables which induced Ss to response-code facilitated overall paired-associate learning as well as response learning. A somewhat analogous result has been found in an experiment by Tulving (1968b). Tulving found that the second member of pairs of words, such as TOOTH-ACHE, FLOOR-SHOW, HOME-SICK, were better *recalled* upon presentation of the first member than *recognized* from among other second members. Obviously, this relationship between recall and recognition is opposite that typically obtained. In a sense, Tulving's result is the converse of those in the Podd and Spear experiment. Tulving showed that something about the association between the members made the responses more available, whereas the results of Podd and Spear indicated that something about the responses had made the associations more available.

STIMULUS CODING.   Stimuli in a paired-associate list do not themselves need to be *learned*. Therefore, they may be transformed without concern for subsequent retrieval in their original form, and the nature and function of these transformations have achieved increasing importance (e.g., Martin, 1968). A special case of stimulus transformation—stimulus selection—has already been discussed in Chap. 11. Recall that S may, for example, select a single letter of the nominal stimulus to associate with the response. In this way, efficiency of learning *may* be increased because S need not concern himself with recognizing the entire stimulus item as a whole.

However, there is little reason to believe that individual letters are more easily discriminated than trigrams, assuming low formal similarity (which is an optimal condition for stimulus selection anyway). So the actual benefit to learning from stimulus selection probably is not great. Moreover, it is known that although response meaningfulness has a great deal of influence on rate of learning in a paired-associate list, stimulus meaningfulness does not. Therefore, one might not ordinarily expect to see a great deal of benefit from coding stimuli into more meaningful units, relative to that found when coding responses, even if such stimulus coding were tried.

Suppose, however, that the stimuli in a paired-associate list were highly similar, to the extent that differential aspects could not be readily selected— that is, they all had the same letters, etc. For example, suppose two stimuli in a list are ESMOK and EMSUO (Underwood & Erlebacher, 1965). These would be difficult to differentiate from trial to trial as they stand. But if they are coded as

SMOKE and MOUSE, they are more readily differentiated and associated with their respective responses. In such a case, Underwood and Erlebacher (1965, Experiment IV) expected that coding stimuli into readily differentiable words would facilitate learning. Upon testing, they did find facilitation from coding in this kind of situation. However, they did so only when the anagram solutions were fairly obvious; otherwise, Ss using such coding did no better than a control group given comparable stimuli not rearrangeable into words.

In the previous experiment (Experiment IV), Underwood and Erlebacher had only *assumed* that varying the orders of letters within stimuli from trial to trial would make stimulus selection more difficult. They tested this in Experiment V and verified their assumption. They found, however, that most of the effect of shifting letters involved shifting the first two letters of the stimulus. Apparently, these are the elements of the nominal stimulus to which Ss most often attend in selecting a functional stimulus.

SUMMARY. Much of the behavior accompanying transformations of individual items parallels that concerning transformations of entire lists of items. In both cases, the extent to which transformations are used may depend upon initial relationships among the elements (words or letters) and whether or not S is made aware of the transformation possibilities. Also, in both cases the extent to which these transformations *generally* provide a net aid to learning, if they provide any aid at all, is in doubt. It is fairly clear that there are instances where learning is aided by these transformations (e.g., Podd & Spear, 1967; Tulving, 1965); in others, however, learning may proceed with little, if any, transformation activity (e.g., Underwood & Keppel, 1963a; Waugh, 1961). The inconclusiveness concerning the effect of each kind of transformation on learning reflects the correlational nature of most of the relevant evidence. When it is found among Ss treated alike that those most likely to use transformations also learn most rapidly, the former clearly cannot be said to have necessarily caused the latter. Better control over the occurrence of transformations is essential for more conclusive experimental evidence.

Extra-item Transformations

In some cases efforts at restructuring the material to be acquired go far beyond mere transformations of item order or transformations of the items themselves. Relatively complex strategies may be involved, making use of sources of external prompting and even bizarre visual imagery. For lack of a more descriptive term, we have referred to these reorganizations as "extra-item transformations." Many of the well-known mnemonic devices fall under this heading.

MNEMONIC IMAGERY AND THE "PEG-WORD" TECHNIQUE. Is it generally true that the efficiency of memory may be readily increased by a few simple instructions on storage or retrieval strategies? We all have seen entertainers perform amazing feats of recall, sometimes involving hundreds of items of information. Do these people have supernormal brains with supernormal storage capacities, or are they super-strategists? Recently, an interest in the effectiveness of mnemonic strategies has been revived within the context of "legitimate" problems and theories of verbal learning.

The most widely employed systems of mnemonic devices or "memory tricks" have a common basis. First a set of "peg" words is acquired by associating these readily available words with numbers; for example, "one is a bun, two is a shoe, etc." Next, the response words are acquired by connecting them with the peg words through bizarre imagery. Thus, if the words in a list presented for subsequent recall include PEN and DOG, one might imagine a pen taking the place of a hot dog in a hot dog bun, a tiny dog sitting in a shoe, etc. Another technique might be to use as peg words the labels of objects found in a sequence of familiar places. Thus, one might imagine himself starting from his bedroom, walking downstairs to the living room, dining room, kitchen, and garage, paying particular attention to discrete objects along the way, such as the bedroom door, the railing on the stairs, the vase on the table, etc. These objects become the peg words. Then to acquire PEN and DOG for later recall, one might imagine a huge pen writing on the door of the bedroom, a dog sliding down the railing, etc. Once the bizarre images are formed, it is believed that further learning is unnecessary and the readily available peg words will consistently elicit the bizarre images, and, in turn, the critical words to be recalled are elicited.

Wood (1967) described some studies showing better recall using these mnemonic systems than without. One is a study by Wallace, Turner, and Perkins (1957) in which Ss were instructed to form visual images between two words. Each pair of words was presented only once, but there was no time limit on how long Ss could study each pair. Beginning with 25 pairs at a time and working up to 700, amazing accuracy in recalling the response words occurred when the stimulus word was presented. With 500 pairs, recall was about 99 percent accurate; with 700 pairs, recall was 95 percent accurate. Also, as Ss became more practiced, the time they took to study each pair decreased rather markedly from a mean of 20.4 sec on the first list to a mean of 3 sec on lists 6, 7, and 8.

There have been other studies showing similar advantages of mnemonic systems over uninstructed attempts to recall. However, before Wood's study there had been no systematic attempts to determine which aspects of the mnemonic devices were primarily responsible for the improved recall. There also had been no indication whether the use of such memory systems represent a different kind of learning, "different" in that variables typically influencing free recall might have other influences when mnemonic devices are used. Wood (1967) considered these problems in a set of five experiments.

In Wood's first experiment (1967), college students were asked to recall lists of 40 relatively high-frequency, concrete nouns (e.g., KITTEN, ACTOR, CLOSET). The 40 words were presented by a tape recorder with 5-sec intervals between successive items. After the 40 words were presented, Ss were immediately asked to write as many as they could on an answer sheet given to them at the start of the experiment. In four of the seven experimental conditions, the answer sheet included peg words to which they could associate the response words. The peg words had the same characteristics as response words (e.g., WHEEL, FLEA, ARMOR). One of these four groups was instructed to form a bizarre image associating the peg word and the response. Wood's instructions suggested to Ss, "For example, if *automobile* was the first [peg] word printed on your answer sheet and *salt-shaker* was the first taped [response] word, you might imagine a huge *salt-shaker* driving an *automobile* [p. 26]." Another group was given essentially the same instructions except that they were told to rehearse the bizarre images whenever possible, whereas the first group had been instructed not to rehearse them. A third group was given the same instructions as the first group except they were told to form common, rather than bizarre, images. The fourth group was given standard verbal-mediation instructions—that is, they were told to form a *verbal* association between the response word and the peg word.

All groups given the peg words recalled more words than two of the groups not presented with peg words. One of the latter groups had been instructed simply to form a bizarre image for each response word, and the other group had received only standard recall instructions and otherwise were left to their own devices.

The final group not given peg words were "told to link response words with a bizarre image. For example, if the first, second, and third response words were *automobile*, *salt-shaker*, and *dog*, respectively, S might form an image of a large *salt-shaker* driving an *automobile* shaped like a *dog* [p. 3]." This group did about as well as the first group, better than the other two not given peg words, but more poorly than the remaining three groups given peg words.

In a second experiment, Wood found that by shortening the presentation rate from one word every 5 sec to one every 2 sec, the advantage of using a mnemonic system was significantly reduced. This suggests it takes a little more time to use efficiently the mnemonic system than devices a typical S might otherwise use if not instructed in mnemonic techniques. This fact seems to parallel the probable role of length of study interval in paired-associate learning involving mediation (see below and Richardson, 1968; Richardson & Brown, 1966).

Wood's remaining three experiments investigated possible differences between mnemonic systems in which Ss are instructed to form *bizarre-image* associations between the peg and response words (as in the first condition of the first experiment) and those in which Ss are instructed simply to form *verbal* associations between the peg and response words. He found that this difference in instructed strategy made no difference in number recalled in two types of transfer conditions, nor when abstract words were used instead of concrete words. These results seem to imply that bizarre imagery has no special qualities as a mnemonic agent distinguishing it from simple verbal mediation. Wood did find, however, that a little better recall was obtained with concrete, rather than abstract, items for peg words as well as response words, which Paivio (1969) has linked to imagery in general.

One difference between the mnemonic systems studied by Wood and the more general pattern described above is that Wood *supplied* S with peg words, whereas the more general mnemonic systems permit the learner to select his own. It is not clear what this effect should be, if indeed there should be any effect at all, but this does tend to restrict generalization from Wood's results to mnemonic systems in general.

Wood suggests that there are these three advantages of employing the peg-word method for free recall: "(a) the amount of recall of concrete and perhaps abstract words is increased when a peg list is used; (b) the correct serial ordering of recall seems to be an inherent result of a peg list approach; (c) material in the middle of a list does not appear to be any more difficult to learn than material at the ends of the list [p. 20]." However, he cautions against the general application of the peg-word approach to learning in the "real world." First, it is obvious that some time is required to acquire the peg list itself—time that could be applied to working on the more important items that one wishes to acquire. Moreover, if the same peg list continues to be used, performance is likely to decline over successive uses. Second, Wood points out that there are really no indications of how applicable this kind of mnemonic system is to material having greater structural complexity than a list of unrelated high-frequency words. Finally, there is no evidence available on long-term retention after using the peg-word approach. Moreover, as we shall see in the section on retention, a great deal of interference with retention (that is, increased forgetting) may result if the same set of peg words is used to memorize several different lists.

OTHER CONSIDERATIONS OF IMAGERY IN MEMORY. We already have seen evidence that the "numerical-rhyme" mnemonic system (one is a bun, two is a shoe) facilitates response learning of words to some extent (for another example, see Bugelski, Kidd, & Segmen, 1968). Recall that the basic strategy of this mnemonic technique is to form an image between one of the peg words, such as bun, and the response word to be recalled. Paivio (1969) has suggested that this technique surely is not simple. Rather, it is psychologically complex, involving a great deal of transformation from images to words and words to words, and vice versa. Indeed, under general conditions these complex transformations might be expected to contribute enough interference to detract from, rather than add to, recall. Paivio (1969) suggests that the complexity is enhanced by the use of images, implying some advantage for memory not possessed by words—otherwise, why should Ss increase the complexity? We have seen, though, that Ss do not always use learning strategies to advantage. However, Paivio's argument makes a number of solid points, which need not be elaborated here. It is well documented with empirical evidence of his own and others, and the article provides the reader with an extensive reference list relevant to the general problems of response transformations and coding. One particular point, however, is especially pertinent to our present discussion.

Paivio essentially dismisses the fact that Wood found no differences when verbal mediators and images were used, a result contrary to his professed importance of imagery, per se. His basis for this is a belief that Wood's procedure of *providing* S with peg words really is not representative of the general mnemonic system. Instead, Paivio emphasizes the possibility that differences in the capacity to arouse images may be an important determinant of the effectiveness of peg words and stimuli in general, so he expects that concrete images may function as mnemonic mediators more effectively than do their verbal representations. Paivio does not deny that verbal mediators have important effects; his general argument, rather, emphasizes the possibilities for employing imagery as an active explanatory concept in verbal learning.

Certainly subjective experience makes it difficult to deny the apparent importance of imagery in memory, although independent verification of its use presents a critical problem of experimental design. The important question for verbal learning is whether variations in imagery functionally affect the characteristics of acquisition and retention of verbal materials. For example, are differences in the vividness of images per se responsible for differential rates of verbal learning or for differential susceptibility to forgetting? The work of Paivio and others, and the apparently general revival of theoretical interest in imagery (e.g., Hebb, 1968), promises increased activity concerning these potentially important processes.

TRANSFER PROCESSES IN VERBAL LEARNING

Essentially all the verbal learning we accomplish as adults makes use of our previous learning in some way. This, of course, is one pleasant feature of having a memory: it relieves us of the necessity of starting from scratch whenever new verbal material is to be acquired. If we can read or speak German, it is easier for us to learn a Dutch vocabulary than if we read or speak only English. Occasionally, however, one may incorrectly respond with a German word when asked for its Dutch equivalent and wonder whether it might not have been less difficult to have started without the previous knowledge of German. The question then becomes different from simply asking whether there is or is not "transfer." The question now is concerned with whether the past learning has a "negative" or "positive" effect on current learning.

One can become still more analytical and ask whether some aspect of having learned the first language hinders learning the second, and if so, what it is. The study of transfer in verbal learning is at this stage. It is no longer useful to ask whether there is transfer or whether the transfer is positive or negative from one verbal learning task to another. Rather, the question is which elements acquired in learning one verbal task are assets and which are liabilities in a subsequent verbal learning task.

Generally speaking, coding and item organization are processes of transfer. Previous learning determines the extent and kind of rearranging of "new" verbal materials one uses to make them more efficiently stored or recalled. Usually these new materials are simply new orders or arrangements of old verbal units with which S is already well acquainted; and, as we have seen, sometimes these coding or organizational processes help performance, and sometimes they do not. In present terminology, transfer is sometimes positive and sometimes neutral or negative.

A distinction must be drawn between *specific* and *nonspecific* transfer. Given a verbal learning task, S acquires specific knowledge about the nature of the verbal units—the letters they consist of, the stimuli to which they are associated, etc.—but he also learns something about how to perform in the task. The subject's behavior has been changed just by the general activity of learning as well as by the specific materials learned.

Two special cases of nonspecific transfer are *warm-up* and *learning-to-learn*. Schwenn and Postman (1967) have defined these in a generally accepted way: "Warm-up refers to the establishment of an effective set for the performance of the learning task. Such a set is assumed to include appropriate postural adjustments and optimal rhythm of responding. Learning-to-learn encompasses the development of instrumental habits which facilitate the acquisition of prescribed verbal associations, e.g., the use of coding devices and mediators [p. 565]."

Many special cases of specific transfer have been suggested and still more are possible. It probably is obvious that the fundamental determinant of specific transfer is similarity: similarity between the stimuli or responses of the initially learned list and the stimuli or responses of the subsequently learned list. The primary cases may be seen in terms of the paired-associate transfer paradigms used to study them. In the representations that follow, the first two letters stand for the first list to be learned, and the next two stand for the second list. Within each pair, the first letter represents the stimuli and the second letter the response term. Thus in the *A-C, A-B* paradigm, the stimuli of the two successive lists are identical, but the responses are different and unrelated. The remaining paradigms are as follows: *A-B', A-B*—the stimuli are the same and the responses to a common stimulus term are related, i.e., synonyms, antonyms, etc.; *A-B_r, A-B* —the stimuli and responses remain the same in both lists but they are re-paired, hence the "r"; *C-D, A-B*—both the stimuli and responses in the first list are unrelated to those in the second; *C-B, A-B*—the stimuli are different but the responses remain the same for the two lists.[1]

There are a number of potential sources of specific transfer in the preceding and other transfer paradigms. Generally these include transfer of first-list stimulus characteristics, response characteristics, and associations. Before examining some of these specific sources in detail, we shall consider the influence of various nonspecific transfer factors.

[1] In many sources the successive lists are symbolized conversely to the sequence used here, i.e., as *A-B, A-B'; A-B, A-C*; etc. However, when transfer paradigms are compared in practice, the common list always is given as the second (transfer) list in order to eliminate the confounding of transfer effects by subtle differences in list difficulty. Hence, the present symbolism conforms more closely to actual practice.

Nonspecific Transfer

Inspired primarily by an experiment by Bruce (1933), a principle concerning the effect of degree of first-list learning on transfer to a subsequent list has held up through several experimental studies. This is the generalization that there is an increasing tendency toward positive transfer—transfer becoming more positive or less negative—the greater the degree of learning of the first task. Of course, in the case of negative transfer, this logically must be a curvilinear relationship, since with no learning on a first list, performance on a second list is by definition better than after some learning has occurred on the first list. Aside from this, the generalization has stood up well and is still accurate as a statement of empirical fact. The *explanation* of it, however, has been sharpened by considering the role of nonspecific factors.

When transfer is separated into nonspecific and specific factors, the general conclusion has been that the effect of degree of learning is mediated entirely by nonspecific factors. Postman (1962b) and Jung (1962) compared changes in transfer with various paradigms against comparable changes for groups given a *C-D, A-B* sequence, i.e., a sequence of two lists with unrelated verbal units. They found that changes in the other paradigms paralleled those in the non-specific-transfer control condition. There have been some theoretical arguments suggesting that if enough learning is given on a first list, items on that list may, in effect, enter a different *kind* of memory storage (cf. Jung, 1965; Mandler, 1965). However, no solid empirical principles have evolved to substantiate this possibility, and other "negative" results have appeared in addition to those of Postman and Jung (e.g., Spence & Schulz, 1965).

LEARNING-TO-LEARN. This term is already familiar from the discussion of learning sets given in Chap. 11. Perhaps some of the same mechanisms contribute to learning-to-learn in verbal learning as in animals' acquisition of learning sets, but probably not. In any event, the histories of the respective problems differ in that there never really has been any doubt about the average human's ability to demonstrate learning-to-learn; the question in verbal learning has concerned the nature of the mechanisms employed to do so. Let us first consider a mechanism associated with learning-to-learn which potentially is quite exciting, although it probably has relatively limited generality.

Webb (1962) paid Ss $2 an hour to learn successive lists of pairs of English and Russian words for six successive hours or until 121 six-item lists each had been learned to a criterion of one perfect recitation. As soon as one list was learned, a new list was presented without any rest. The Ss were informed before the experiment that they would not be paid unless they continued serving in the experiment until E excused them. Most Ss completed at least 77 lists massed in a single session. Some idea of the changes in performance that occurred as learning progressed may be seen in Fig. 12-4. The six points on the abscissa represent six equal portions for each S of the total trials given over a period of at least 5 hr and $\frac{1}{4}$ of continuous learning. Perhaps the most interesting aspect

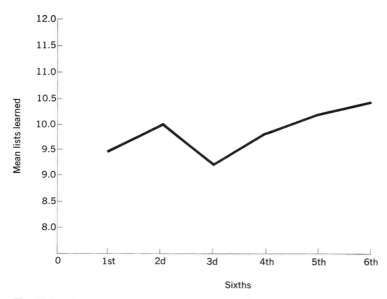

Fig. 12-4. Mean number of lists learned in each sixth of total learning. (SOURCE: W. B. Webb. The effects of prolonged learning on learning. *Journal of Verbal Learning and Verbal Behavior,* 1962, **1,** 172–182. Used by permission.)

of this experiment is Webb's interpretation of the apparent improvement in learning near the end after an apparent decrement at about the middle of the learning session. Webb suggested the interesting possibility that in the latter portions of this grueling learning session Ss engaged in a different kind of behavior that facilitated their learning. Specifically, he suggested that a "mechanization" of learning seemed to have taken place. He illustrated this by a subjective description of what Ss did while learning the lists:

> A "typical" S's behavior would be somewhat as follows in the later part of learning: While grumbling at the E about the length of the time he had been at the task, or asking, "How long is this ——— experiment going to go on?", he may be lighting a cigarette or standing up from the chair, yet he would glance at the stimulus word and apparently involuntarily give a response word and glance at the correct response word. He then may comment on the English word or the Russian word as to its associated meaning to him. Then a glance at the next stimulus word with a response to it with a response word. Other Ss would interject varying kinds of schema such as replacing the response words ideationally on the screen with three at the top and three at the bottom or concentrate on never missing, for example, the fourth word. Yet within the schema (which would typically last only for a few lists) the stimulus word would seem to be "picked off" when it appeared and a response word elicited with little hesitation. In essence, learning seemed to proceed independently of motivation or irrelevant responses, such as side comments, or stretching, or cigarette light-

ing, or self-induced schema, or perhaps more critically, prior list interference. In short, it seemed that an intrinsically autonomous process had developed and was operating in a mechanical fashion (hence, the term "mechanization") (pp. 180–181).

Perhaps this mechanization of learning, which has its precedents (cf. Webb, 1962), is primarily an input phenomenon operating on attention mechanisms. For example, it may occur only after complete habituation to other aspects of the experimental situation. Whatever its basis, its investigation would appear to provide some exciting possibilities for an *E* of considerable research energy, utmost patience, and persuasive abilities with *S*s (cf. Keppel, Postman, & Zavortink, 1968).

Now let us turn to a consideration of some more fundamental work on learning-to-learn. In the first report of a series of papers, Postman and Schwartz (1964) asked "What is learned?" about learning-to-learn. In other words, what is the nature of the relatively permanent response tendencies that make verbal materials easier to learn if unrelated verbal materials previously have been learned? Postman and Schwartz had college students learn two lists of unrelated adjectives on a memory drum. For some *S*s, the first and second lists were either both paired-associate or both serial-learning tasks. Other *S*s had a paired-associate task as the first list and a serial task as the second, and still other *S*s had the reverse order. First-list items were trigrams for some *S*s and adjectives for others; the second list always consisted of adjectives.

Generally they found that the kind of task used for the first list influenced learning of the second list more than the class of materials learned. Second-list learning was better when both tasks were alike than when they differed, but it did not depend upon the kind of items in the first list. However, the latter does not imply that *S*'s learning operations on a particular class of materials generally do not become more efficient with practice. Indeed, Postman, Keppel, and Zacks (1968) found better learning of a paired-associate list with trigram-response terms after learning a list with unrelated trigram responses than a list with highly available words. Apparently, learning experience with a given class of materials does aid in learning otherwise unrelated materials of the same class, but perhaps only for materials requiring special coding or other integration skills.

The results of this experiment indicate that learning-to-learn clearly does occur, and probably with great regularity. Subsequently Postman and his associates concerned themselves with the specific nature of the skills which produced learning-to-learn, their generality, and the variables governing them.

One set of studies was addressed to what might be called *learning-to-transfer*. Does transfer from one task to another improve with increasing experience of this kind? We can mention these experiments only in general terms because they deal with the possibility of an increase in skills involving specific transfer processes, a topic which we have not yet considered in any detail. After discovering that such learning-to-transfer does occur, with greater gain in a positive- than a negative-transfer paradigm (Postman, 1964b), Keppel and

Postman (1966) asked whether this improvement was due to acquired skills applicable *only* to the transfer conditions specifically practiced or whether a more general set of transfer skills was learned. Their results supported the latter view. They found that training under any of four transfer paradigms (*A-B'*, *A-B*; *A-C*, *A-B*; *A-B_r*, *A-B*; or *C-D*, *A-B*) uniformly facilitated subsequent transfer with an *A-B'*, *A-B* or *A-C*, *A-B* paradigm. In other words, improvement in transfer occurred about equally whether the same paradigm or some other paradigm had provided the earlier transfer experience. This acquisition of quite generalizable transfer skills does not preclude the possibility that more specific skills also might be demonstrated under more complex circumstances of transfer. Accordingly, Postman (1968c) found that Ss did acquire transfer skills specific to a complex three-list paradigm—*A-C*, *C-B*, *A-B*, in which list 3 may be acquired by using the *A-C-B* chain (see section on mediation).

Postman and his colleagues have also found that Ss acquire special skills applicable to integrating nonword trigrams which are different from those used to learn words (Postman, Keppel, & Zacks, 1968) and that positive transfer from a serial to a paired-associate list may be facilitated by previous practice on transfer from serial learning to paired-associate learning (Postman & Stark, 1967). We already have had reason to cite other work from their learning-to-learn series (Keppel, Postman, & Zavortink, 1968; Schwenn & Postman, 1967). Taken as a whole, this work emphasizes the wide variety of means by which Ss may improve their verbal learning performance, means considerably more subtle and complex than simply strengthening an associative bond between verbal units. To understand verbal learning, one certainly must gain control over these many ways in which S may operate on verbal material.

WARM-UP. Perhaps the standard reference experiment giving evidence for warm-up was reported by Thune (1950). His experimental design separated learning-to-learn from warm-up on the basis of two apparently reasonable assumptions. The first was that the effect of warm-up is transient, dissipating over intervals of, say, 24 hr. Second, he assumed that in accord with the general definition of learning, learning-to-learn is relatively permanent, so rather little of these acquired skills should be lost over 24 hr.

Most of Thune's Ss learned part of their first list on day 1 and got their remaining first-list training on day 2, just before learning the second. All Ss were given 10 trials on the first list. Separate groups received either 10, 8, 6, 4, 2, or 0 of these trials on day 1 and the balance of the 10 trials on day 2, just before learning the second list. Therefore, before learning the second list, all Ss had 10 trials of (permanent) learning-to-learn, but differed in the number of warm-up trials before learning list 2. The results were quite clear in showing better performance with more warm-up trials.

Thune (1950) also reported a second experiment indicating that a nonverbal learning task, guessing which of five colors (order unpredictable) would appear, could also serve as warm-up and facilitate learning accordingly, an important point to which we now turn. Is it possible that the effect of warm-up is general and unrelated to associative processes? If so, it would be far less interesting for purposes of understanding verbal learning.

Schwenn and Postman (1967) were concerned that Thune had used well-practiced Ss in his second experiment, i.e., Ss with previous experience at verbal learning tasks. They also preferred to design an experiment that would not require Thune's two assumptions about the relative transiency of warm-up and learning-to-learn. Schwenn and Postman correctly pointed out that little is known about the rate of forgetting learning-to-learn. Also it is possible that the modifications of responses mediating the warm-up effect might be conditioned to the experimental situation and so not as transient as Thune had supposed.

Therefore, Schwenn and Postman used five groups of college students who were naive to verbal learning experiments. Each group received a paired-associate test list of 10 pairs of two-syllable adjectives. One group received no training before the test list; two groups previously had performed a number-guessing task presented in the same way as the verbal paired-associate task; and the final two groups had been given training on a paired-associate list of adjectives unrelated to the test list. The previous number-guessing and paired-associate tasks were given for either 4 or 10 trials to the different groups before the test list.

The results indicated considerably less influence from warm-up on a nonverbal learning task than had Thune's. The Ss given 4 number-guessing trials learned the test list no more readily than Ss given no warm-up task at all, and Ss given 10 such trials did only a little better. These were particularly minimal effects compared with the Ss given the previous verbal learning task. Schwenn and Postman suggest that their results, indicating that learning-to-learn benefited paired-associate learning substantially more than warm-up (in contrast to Thune's results showing approximately equal benefit from both), were attributable to the fact that their Ss had not previously experienced paired-associate learning in the experimental context, whereas Thune's had. Apparently, when Ss are generally experienced with verbal learning in the context of the laboratory, initial tasks of either a verbal or nonverbal nature provide adequate warm-up. But for Ss new to laboratory-style verbal learning, substantial benefit from warm-up depends upon its having verbal content.

Specific Transfer

The question of what specific elements contribute to transfer effects between verbal tasks, particularly paired-associate tasks, has been thoroughly analyzed in a number of cogent reviews of the topic (e.g., Jung, 1968; Kjeldergaard, 1968; Martin, 1965, 1968; Underwood, 1966a). It is generally agreed that the primary processes influenced by having learned an earlier list are response learning, acquisition of the forward association from stimulus to response, acquisition of the backward association from response to stimulus, and various processes involved in applying the functional stimulus, such as stimulus selection and general coding of the stimulus term. The roles of the first three have been analyzed thoroughly by Martin (1965), and the latter has been emphasized in a subsequent paper by Martin (1968; also, see Underwood & Ekstrand, 1968a), who suggested some subprocesses of transfer which previously had not been considered.

As an illustration of some factors involved in specific transfer, consider the case in which the response members of two successive lists are identical. Under these transfer circumstances, the more difficult the responses are to acquire, the greater will be the benefit of having accomplished this in a previous list. Thus, if S learns first a list of items like GIRL-CAT and subsequently a list with items like CHAIR-CAT, the specific advantage of having experienced the previous list (compared with a group exposed to an unrelated previous list) would be relatively small compared to Ss first given lists with items like GIRL-QCT, followed by a list with CHAIR-QCT. In the former, the advantage of having learned the responses in the previous list is so small that it will be outweighed by the disadvantage of learning the backward association CAT-GIRL (see Ekstrand, 1966), which interferes with the acquisition of the backward association in the second list, CAT-CHAIR. In the latter case (GIRL-QCT, CHAIR-QCT) it is so difficult for S to integrate the low meaningful trigram that there is considerable advantage in having previously completed this. This advantage outweighs the difficulties with competing backward associations, a conclusion well supported by empirical study (e.g., Jung, 1963; Merikle & Battig, 1963).

The role of similarity in determining specific transfer will not be detailed here. Some of the rather complex issues involved are discussed in the references listed above. However, the extreme cases of response similarity will be considered, because their analysis implicates two very important phenomena: mediation and generalization.

COMPARING TRANSFER PROCESSES IN A-C, A-B AND A-B', A-B PARADIGMS. The classic experiment by Barnes and Underwood (1959) is cited most often for its results with the *A-C, A-B* paradigm—a negative-transfer paradigm, i.e., *A-B* is learned more slowly than with a comparable *C-D, A-B* nonspecific-transfer control paradigm—particularly for their demonstration of "unlearning" phenomena (see below). However, they also reported data useful for understanding mediation and generalization. Several groups of college students learned successive paired-associate lists consisting of nonsense syllables as stimuli and adjectives as responses. For one set of conditions, the eight items in the second list had the same stimuli as in the first list, and the second-list response was a synonym of the first-list response (e.g., DEX-PEACEFUL, DEX-TRANQUIL). This represents the *A-B', A-B* transfer paradigm which, in most cases, yields positive transfer compared to the *C-D, A-B* control paradigm (e.g., Postman, 1966).

After Ss had learned the first list and been given some training on the second list (either 1, 5, 10, or 20 trials for different groups of Ss), they were presented the stimulus items on a sheet of paper and given 4 min during which they were to write down all the responses which occurred to them. The S's performance on this "modified modified free-recall" test was surprisingly accurate in terms of recalling first-list items, regardless of how many trials they experienced with the second list. Of the eight first-list items possible, averages of between 6.92 and 7.67 first-list responses were both written correctly and paired with their appropriate stimulus terms.

This suggests that learning the second list tended to maintain rather than decrease the availability of responses and associations from the first list. Moreover, it is well established that initial learning of the second list in an A-B', A-B paradigm is better than that obtained if the first list had been unrelated to the second. Both these facts imply that some mutually facilitating interaction occurs between the first and second list response having a common stimulus in the A-B', A-B paradigm. The question is, "What is the nature of this interaction?"

Underwood (1951) had suggested a response generalization mechanism termed "parasitic reinforcement" to account for the positive transfer found in an A-B', A-B paradigm. He hypothesized that as the associative strength between stimuli and responses in the first list (e.g., DEX-PEACEFUL) increases, there is a corresponding though smaller increase in the associative strength between this stimulus and all other responses similar to that response term (e.g., DEX-TRANQUIL, DEX-QUIESCENT, DEX-SERENE). The greater the similarity, the greater this generalized associative strength. With this reasoning, acquisition of A-B in the A-B', A-B paradigm is relatively rapid because the association between A and B has been partially formed during acquisition of A-B'. However, additional data collected by Barnes and Underwood (1959) suggested that mediation, rather than parasitic reinforcement, was more likely the mechanism employed in transferring from an A-B' to an A-B list.

Three pieces of evidence argue for mediation in the Barnes-Underwood experiment. First, in 63 percent of the items recalled, first-list responses were recalled before the second-list response, i.e., B' then B. This may be seen to be consistent with the possibility that Ss learn the second list by mediating through B'; i.e., they acquire B with the mediation link going A to B' to B. Second, when the 96 Ss serving in the A-B', A-B conditions were asked whether they mediated in this way, 94 of them said they did. Third, when measured with their free-recall method, learning of the second list after only one anticipation trial appeared to be "too good" to be accounted for in terms of parasitic reinforcement. In fact, when Ss were stopped after one anticipation trial and asked to write their responses, an average of 7.75 responses of a possible 8 were given correctly. After a comparable number of second-list trials, the Ss given only 2 sec in which to respond averaged 5.04 correct responses. This suggests that amount of time permitted for S to "think" about what response to give makes a great deal of difference in his performance in the A-B' paradigm.

Because there is no conceivable way that parasitic reinforcement should depend upon anticipation time permitted for recall of A-B—this mechanism is supposed to operate on strength of A-B associations during learning of A-B'— and because it is reasonable to assume that mediation is affected by anticipation time, these results argue for operation of a mediation mechanism. Note that

the underlying assumption is that the increase in anticipation time benefited the
A-B', A-B paradigm more than it would have benefited some other paradigm
in which mediation is not involved. Indeed, this appeared to be the case comparing the A-B', A-B and A-C, A-B paradigms in the Barnes and Underwood
experiment, although they did not comment on this. We shall return to this
point later.

Barnes and Underwood were quite aware that their arguments for mediation in the A-B', A-B paradigm could not be considered conclusive. For example, the fact that Ss almost unanimously reported that they mediated may
merely have reflected the fact that they implicitly (and perhaps unavoidably)
responded with the first-list response when the stimulus was presented during
learning of the second list. This may have had nothing at all to do with the
actual mechanisms of transfer from A-B' to A-B.

Perhaps more important for an understanding of transfer processes is
Barnes and Underwood's conclusion that the mediation employed in the A-B',
A-B paradigm constitutes a different mechanism from that employed in lists
where the stimuli remain the same but responses are unrelated (A-C, A-B). In
the latter case, Barnes and Underwood demonstrated that many first-list responses are actively suppressed—"unlearned"—during learning of the second
list and the degree of this suppression increases the greater the number of second-
list trials. Thus, Ss were quite unable to give about half of their first-list responses
after 20 trials on the second list, even though only about 12 to 15 min had
elapsed since they had given and paired all of them correctly.

Assume for the moment that Barnes and Underwood were completely
correct about the transfer mechanisms involved in the A-B', A-B and A-C, A-B
paradigms. When Ss are faced with a transfer task in which the stimuli in the two
lists are the same but the responses differ, what determines which of these two
quite different mechanisms—mediation or unlearning—will occur? Apparently
there is little difficulty when, as in the Barnes and Underwood experiment, the
responses in the two lists are clearly similar and interassociated, or when the
responses in the two lists are clearly unrelated. But what if the C and B terms are
intermediate in terms of similarity and interassociation? Furthermore, can we
expect S to select a strategy and stay with it for all items within the list, or will
he mix strategies such that some of the items are operated on with mediation
and others with unlearning? And if strategies are mixed, requiring S to associate
a strategy as well as a response with each stimulus, will this not disrupt learning?
Postulating two such different mechanisms for apparently similar transfer
paradigms requires that these matters of continuity be resolved. Although the
characteristics of transfer under conditions of response similarity or interassociation intermediate between A-B' and A-C are not well understood as yet, there
are data showing the influence of mixing transfer strategies within a task.

EFFECTS OF MULTIPLE TRANSFER STRATEGIES. An experiment by Postman
(1966) considered the relative efficiency of learning a list with mixed strategies.
Postman compared the learning on the second list for Ss having transfer con-

ditions which were homogeneous within a list (i.e., all pairs in the second list bore the same relation to pairs in the first list) with that of Ss having a mixture of such relationships within the lists. For the latter Ss, equal portions of their second-list items had the same stimuli but different and unrelated responses than some items in the first list (A-C, A-B), the same stimuli but different and related responses (A-B', A-B), or items having no relationship to the stimuli and responses of the first list (C-D, A-B). Thus, for the second-list pairs conforming to the A-C, A-B paradigm, S's strategy might be to "suppress or unlearn the response previously associated with this item"; but the second-list items having an A-B', A-B relationship with the first list would elicit this strategy: "keep available; don't suppress the first-list responses associated with this stimulus and use it as a mediator to acquire the second-list response."

It can be seen that if different strategies for different transfer paradigms actually are employed, Ss in the mixed-list condition had a lot more to think about while learning the second list. These Ss theoretically had to also "keep in mind" a different strategy for each type of pair in addition to sorting out types of relationships with the first list and implementing the strategy. As might be expected on this basis, Ss given the unmixed list did better on their transfer list than Ss given the mixed list. However, the magnitude of the difference was small—surprisingly small only to the extent to which one believes that articulated strategies are of great importance in verbal learning.

Within paradigms, the biggest difference found between transfer under mixed- and unmixed-list conditions was only about one item of a possible twelve. This difference was considerably smaller than differences found between response paradigms. For example, on the first transfer trial, Ss with the A-B' unmixed-list condition got about four more items correct than Ss with the unmixed A-C list, and Ss with the mixed-list condition got about three more A-B' items correct than A-C items.

It seems possible, though it could not be determined from Postman's experiment, that Ss in the mixed-list conditions did not really vary strategy among items but simply stuck with the same strategy for all items. Thus, learning of some items may have proceeded in spite of, rather than because of, a strategy. Notice that this conclusion regarding the use of explicit strategies on transfer—that they have only a small influence on rate of learning—is consistent with the conclusion by Underwood and Erlebacher (1965) regarding strategies of coding in response integration.

MEDIATION AS A MECHANISM OF TRANSFER. The suggestion from Barnes and Underwood's data that mediation in general, and transfer in an A-B', A-B paradigm in particular, is facilitated by greater length of anticipation interval (i.e., time to respond) is intuitively agreeable. Furthermore, a subsequent study by Katz (1963) indicated that Ss had longer reaction times when their responses apparently required longer mediation chains, and Schulz and Lovelace (1964) found better mediation effects with a 4-sec anticipation interval than with

2 sec. It is not surprising, therefore, that several investigators independently began to study the influence of anticipation time on transfer performance.

Spear, Mikulka, and Podd (1966) based their experiment on the following reasoning. Suppose that under normal paired-associate conditions, Ss employ a mediation strategy in an A-B', A-B paradigm but an unlearning strategy in the A-C, A-B paradigm. Suppose further that a 1-sec anticipation interval is simply too short for effective mediation from A to B' to B and that a 4-sec anticipation interval provides for more effective mediation than does a 2-sec interval. We would expect, then, that Ss given a 1-sec anticipation interval during learning of A-B after learning A-B' would be forced to suppress the first-list responses rather than maintain their availability as mediators. This would be necessary if second-list responses were to be given quickly enough to be counted correct. In other words, these A-B' Ss should switch to an unlearning strategy when only a 1-sec anticipation interval was permitted, and, in terms of characteristics of learning the second list and recalling the first, these Ss should be no different than those given an A-C, A-B transfer paradigm.

Suppose further that Ss given an A-C, A-B transfer paradigm and permitted 4 sec in which to anticipate each second-list response find it at least as efficient to employ mediation as an unlearning strategy. If so, the only additional learning required is an association between C and B, which should be no more difficult than starting "from scratch" to learn an association between A-B. And if they chose the latter, they would in addition have to suppress the C response. Therefore, with sufficient time to respond, Ss given an A-C, A-B paradigm may behave the same as Ss given an A-B', A-B transfer paradigm.

Spear et al. employed essentially the same materials and procedures as Barnes and Underwood (1959). The major differences were that Spear et al. gave all Ss ten trials to learn the second list, and three groups representing each transfer condition (A-B', A-B; A-C, A-B; and C-D, A-B) were given their transfer list with anticipation intervals of 1, 2, or 4 sec.

The results agreed quite well with those of Barnes and Underwood at comparable points, but variation in anticipation interval had no apparent effect on the transfer processes chosen by S. For example, 95 percent of Ss given the A-B' paradigm reported using mediation in learning the second list (including all 20 Ss given this paradigm with a 1-sec anticipation interval). In contrast, only 13 percent of Ss given the A-C paradigm reported that they did so, and for only one or two of the items in the eight-item list. Moreover, neither free recall of first-list responses nor any index of second-list learning revealed differential influence of anticipation interval on A-B' and A-C transfer. The results indicated that if mediation is a basic mechanism for transfer between lists with identical stimuli, it "runs off" in less than 1 sec when the responses are associates; but mediation is essentially ignored, even under optimal mediational conditions, if the responses are not associates. This places a great deal of importance on the speed of mediation and S's capacity for rather rigidly adhering to a process in accord with the relationships between responses, neither of which would be important characteristics if the basic transfer process really were parasitic reinforcement.

A similar experiment with slightly different anticipation intervals (0.75, 1.50, and 3.00 sec) was reported by Richardson (1967b). His conclusions were essentially identical to those of Spear et al.: anticipation interval does not influence the transfer behavior of Ss given an A-B', A-B paradigm differently from those given an A-C, A-B paradigm. Together these studies suggest that mediation may not be the primary mechanism employed in transfer between the A-B', A-B lists. They leave the door open for explanation in terms of a mechanism such as Underwood's parasitic reinforcement, perhaps with response "generalization" defined in terms of associative similarity or conceptual grouping instead of similarity as Underwood originally intended (cf. Bastian, 1961; Schwenn & Underwood, 1965). Another alternative is that the basic process involved in the positive transfer with A-B', A-B does not facilitate the *association* between A and B, but instead acts to increase the *availability* of B—an effect on the response, not the hook-up, stage. However, complete evaluation of these possibilities requires more knowledge about the general influence of anticipation time on mediational processes.

THE ROLE OF TEMPORAL FACTORS IN MEDIATION. A number of investigators have been concerned with length of the study interval as well as length of the anticipation interval, noting that mediating responses must be discovered and probably also rehearsed before they can be used effectively. If these activities are curtailed by insufficiently long study intervals, mediation will be limited as a strategy regardless of the length of the anticipation interval. Conversely, if the anticipation interval is too short to permit mediators to "run off," length of the study interval is relatively inconsequential for mediational purposes.

Richardson has used anticipation and study time as independent variables, controlling the temporal interval and recording S's consequential use of potential mediators for learning. In at least one case, Richardson (1966a) found some influence of these variables on mediation, but most often, at least in his early studies, he did not (e.g., Richardson, 1966b).

Subsequently, Richardson employed anticipation time as a *dependent* variable. He varied the amount of mediation presumedly required of S between presentation of a stimulus and S's response. Then he measured the time required for S to give the response upon presentation of the stimulus, providing a precise estimate of the time required to run off a chain of implicit associative responses of a given length. Richardson accomplished this with a simple, but ingenious technique. He reasoned that if S is given a letter of the alphabet, say, J, and then asked to give the letter two places beyond, most Ss would have to respond implicitly with the intermediate K before overtly responding with L. This provides a mediational chain of specifiable length, which can be timed.

In one study (Richardson, 1967a), upon presentation of a letter one group of Ss was required simply to repeat the letter shown; another group was to say the *next* letter in the alphabet; and the third was to say the letter *two* letters beyond the one shown. The instructions emphasized that S should respond as quickly as possible. Each S responded for a number of trials on each of three successive days. It may be seen in Fig. 12-5 that, although all Ss initially improved their speed of responding with practice, there remained a substantial difference among response latencies with 0, 1, or 2 implicit verbal responses (abbreviated *IVR* in Fig. 12-5) interspersed between presentation of a letter and the response. These results permitted Richardson to set anticipation intervals which would, or would not, permit mediation.

Richardson (1967a) next presented college students with two successive lists having the same nonsense syllables as stimuli but different responses (*A-C, A-B*). For 32 Ss, the responses of the first list were letters which preceded those with a common stimulus in the second list by two (e.g., if the first-list pair was BAV-H, the second-list pair was BAV-J). Another set of 32 Ss had exactly the *same* letter responses for the first-list stimulus as in the second list (BAV-K, BAV-K), and 32 other Ss had a *number* as a response in the first list (BAV-5, BAV-K). Richardson assumed that each S in the first condition would have to make an implicit verbal response—say each item covertly to himself—for each letter: the stimulus

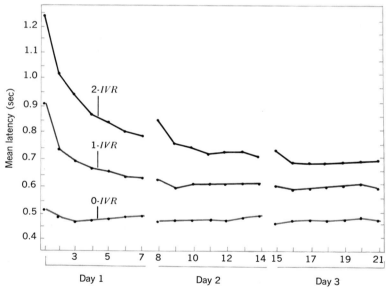

Fig. 12-5. Mean latency before the correct verbal response over 7 blocks of 24 trials on each of 3 practice days for Ss having 0, 1, or 2 implicit verbal responses (*IVR*) intervening between the signal to respond and the verbal response. In this case a "trial" refers to a single presentation of a letter to which S responded. (SOURCE: J. Richardson. Latencies of implicit verbal responses and the effect of the anticipation interval on mediated transfer. *Journal of Verbal Learning and Verbal Behavior*, 1967, **6**, 819–826. Used by permission.)

term and the two letters intervening between the first- and second-list responses, a total of three implicit responses. The first experiment had shown that when *two* implicit verbal responses were required, 79 percent of the responses given by his Ss took longer than 0.9 sec and about 2 percent took longer than 2.5 sec. On this basis, he concluded that a 1-sec anticipation interval would not be long enough to permit a sequence of *three* implicit verbal responses to be run off, but 3 sec would. Before the transfer test, all Ss were informed of the nature of the change in responses, and the Ss with the mediation opportunity were informed how they could evolve the correct second-list response from the first. The task, then, was analogous to *A-B'*, *A-B* transfer with Ss informed of the interrelationship between lists.

As predicted, Richardson found that having a 3-sec instead of a 1-sec anticipation interval on the second list benefited those Ss who theoretically could use mediation to advantage more than those who could not. On the first presentation of the list, the "mediating" Ss given the 1-sec anticipation interval gave a mean of 0.69 correct responses; those given the 3 sec gave 5.94 correct responses.

Apart from showing conclusively that implicit verbal responses such as mediators take a measurable amount of time to be run off, Richardson's data suggest that "1 sec is simply not enough time for two *IVR*s [implicit verbal responses] to mediate the overt response [p. 826]." Why, then, have no differences been found between presumably mediated transfer in *A-B'*, *A-B* and non-mediated transfer with a 1-sec as compared with a 4-sec anticipation interval? Perhaps something similar to "parasitic reinforcement"—i.e., a generalization construct—may be as likely a process, in transfering from *A-B'* to *A-B*, as mediation.

To complicate the situation further, Richardson (1968) reported a similar study appearing to implicate mediational processes in this transfer paradigm, this time using words as implicit verbal responses to tighten the analogy with *A-B'* experiments. The first two experiments in this study replicated his findings with alphabetical sequences, except that chained sequences of three words were involved. Richardson trained college students to give a second word upon presentation of the first, then a third word upon presentation of the second. He then established how long it took Ss to say the third word upon presentation of the first, compared with the time required after presentation of the second, or of the same (third) word, and found that appropriately long anticipation intervals benefited Ss more the longer their chain of implicit associative responses.

Now Richardson had a case in which S could immediately give the correct responses in a transfer list by running through the established word chain. This is exactly the behavior presumed to occur in the *A-B'*, *A-B* paradigm, *if* mediation is the basic transfer process. For his third experiment he selected anticipation intervals of 1 and 3 sec on the basis of his latency data. Compared with a *C-D* group having no similar specific elements between the first and second list, the results indicated that the longer anticipation interval benefited Ss in the *A-B'* condition more. In fact there was some indication that Ss showed *negative* transfer when permitted only a 1-sec anticipation interval, suggesting further that their mediating strategy actually *interfered* with their learning when there was not enough time for it to be employed properly. Taken together, Richardson's results demonstrate that mediational processes of the sort presumed operative in the *A-B'* paradigm may or may not facilitate transfer, depending upon anticipation interval. Furthermore, the range of anticipation intervals he found effective were comparable to those found *ineffective* in several direct tests of *A-B'* transfer.

The basis of the remaining discrepancy is not clear, but we may consider some possibilities. Perhaps the extra-experimental association assumed between *B'* and *B* is stronger than, or otherwise different from, associations acquired in the laboratory. As another possibility, Richardson suggested that his use of a short study interval (1 sec) was the probable factor contributing to the differences between his results and previous failures to find differential benefit from longer anticipation intervals in the *A-B'* paradigm. However, the latter is not entirely consistent with his earlier data (cf. Richardson & Brown, 1966), and *why* the study interval should make the critical difference has not been determined. The function of the study interval in such mediation paradigms is thought to be to permit discovery of mediational relationships, and Richardson (1968) found equivalent results whether or not *S*s in the *A-B'* paradigm were informed of the nature of the relationships between the lists. Perhaps rehearsal of the mediational relationships during the study interval is critical, or as Richardson suggested perhaps longer study intervals gave control *S*s (*C-D, A-B*) sufficient opportunity to contrive mediational devices as effective as those in *A-B'*. Alternatively, it simply may be that Richardson was more careful than others had been in selecting his materials and precisely estimating the length of time required to run off the theoretically necessary mediational chains.

Direct Study of Associative Mediation

Whenever *S* interjects a third term between the stimulus and response of a paired-associate list, we say that associative mediation, or just "mediation," has occurred. This term essentially always implicates the associative phase of learning. A special case of mediation already has been considered as a possible mechanism in transfer from *A-B'* to *A-B*.

Mediating processes have served important roles in considerations of learning processes in general since the earliest associationists. In spite of this relatively ancient concern, direct study of the role of mediation in verbal learning did not really begin in earnest until the mid-1950s. Perhaps the earliest influential paper in this regard was that of Russell and Storms (1955), although in retrospect Cofer and Foley (1942) anticipated many of the issues and might have been an impetus to this work were it not for World War II. Goss (1961a) attributed this delay to the emphasis on nonverbal mediators placed by theorists (e.g., Hull, 1943) concerned with general behavioral theories which potentially incorporated subhuman species.

Once begun, the study of mediation in verbal learning flourished (see Kjeldergard, 1968) with emphasis on two basic sources of verbal mediators—mediators assumed on the basis of association norms and mediators which S has been specifically trained to associate with the stimulus and/or the response term. Each of these sources of mediation may function in three generally distinct ways referred to as "mediation paradigms."

Each paradigm includes a final test of learning a paired-associate list with items of the form A-B subsequent to acquiring separate associations between a common term, C, and each of A and B. There are a number of ways this may be accomplished, assuming backward as well as forward associations. The "chaining" paradigm requires, in one instance, learning A-C and C-B before A-B. The "response equivalence" paradigm involves learning C-A and C-B before A-B, and the "stimulus equivalence" paradigm includes learning of A-C and B-C before A-B. It is obvious that the paradigms have been descriptively labeled. In the first case, C forms the middle link of a "chain," A-C-B; in the second, A and B have attained equivalent status as stimuli for their response and subsequent mediator, C; and in the third case, A and B have served equally as responses to their stimulus and subsequent mediator, C. By forming all possible permutations of the associations acquired before learning A-B, eight mediation paradigms may be constructed (see Horton & Kjeldergard, 1961).

For a brief period there was some controversy over the status of mediation in three-stage paradigms. Mandler and Earhard (1964) correctly pointed out that the designs employed (e.g., Horton & Kjeldegaard, 1961) ostensibly to demonstrate mediation often were inadequate to do so. They generally lacked proper control over potential nonmediational influences. Mandler and Earhard demonstrated that in the A-C, C-B, A-B chaining paradigm, changes in the extent of negative transfer from learning A-C to learning A-B were not adequately controlled or accounted for in terms of traditional control conditions. Subsequent papers argued that the importance of Mandler and Earhard's particular point probably depends upon certain methodological details such as materials being learned or anticipation interval (e.g., Schulz, Weaver, & Ginsberg, 1965), transfer effects which were somewhat inconsistent with typical results (J. J. Jenkins, 1965), and some unknown subtle effects which made their basic data difficult to replicate (Jenkins & Foss, 1965; Schulz et al., 1965; but see Earhard & Mandler, 1965).

There seems to be general agreement at the present time, however, that the question "Does mediation occur in verbal learning?" is as distracting and misleading as "Does one-trial learning occur in verbal learning?" The argument has shifted to a consideration of the variables affecting mediation (cf. J. J. Jenkins, 1965). Thus, the study of mediation in verbal learning has progressed toward answering two major questions. First, what are the circumstances which determine when mediators will be used; and second, under what circumstances do mediators actually influence learning rate, and what is the direction of this influence?

As regards the first question, we have seen that there is essentially no doubt that mediation may occur in associating a response to a stimulus. On the other hand, it is equally certain that not *all* verbal associations are acquired by mediation through a third mutually associated verbal unit. Obviously, at least one and probably many more verbal associations have to be acquired by infants without mediation. It is possible that nonverbal mediators, such as images (see Hebb, 1968), are used from the beginning; but this seems a remote possibility. We also know that verbal associations may be acquired by adults without mediation (Keppel, 1966a; Spear, Ekstrand, & Underwood, 1964), so the capacity to do so is not lost with increasing verbal experience.

Concerning the second question, special cases have appeared in which learning is facilitated by using mediators (see Horton & Kjeldergard, 1961), others in which it is not (e.g., Jenkins, 1963), and some in which the use of mediators appears to retard learning (e.g., Richardson, 1968, Experiment III). There have been some gains concerning the question of what circumstances determine the influence of mediators. When mediators are "built into" S by special training, learning is more likely to be facilitated when the verbal materials have high meaningfulness (Horton, 1964; Peterson, Colavita, Sheahan, & Blattner, 1964). To say that in another way, mediators are more likely to facilitate learning if, for example, they are readily familiar words than if they are nonsense syllables.

Horton (1964) concluded that only the meaningfulness of the mediator itself is important. This advantage of greater meaningfulness could be due to stronger or more stable associative strength between mediational links or to increased availability of the mediator. The latter influence could be simply one of availability versus nonavailability, or it might occur because the mediator of higher meaningfulness is implicitly produced more readily by S, creating an effectively longer anticipation interval for employing the mediator.

Other variables investigated include S's native learning ability and S's awareness that mediation is possible (e.g., Horton, 1964). Neither appear to have clear-cut effects, at least not as clear as the effect of meaningfulness.

It probably is obvious that an important concern for the role of mediation in verbal learning is the case in which mediators are neither built in nor explicitly inferred. When a single paired-associate list is acquired, it is known that "natural language mediators" often occur to S during associative learning. Montague, Adams, and their colleagues (e.g., Adams, 1967; Montague, Adams, & Kiess, 1966) have suggested and studied the occurrence and use of mediation in these circumstances.

NATURAL LANGUAGE MEDIATORS.   It has been known for some time that when Ss are asked how they learn paired-associate items, they often report that they use mediators as associative aids. Underwood and Schulz (1960) reported some examples of this based upon an experiment by Arthur Mattocks. In this experiment, Ss learned a list of paired-associate items composed of trigrams as stimuli and three-letter words as responses. After reaching criterion, Ss were asked to describe how they associated each response to its stimulus. Overall, they reported using mediational devices to associate 73 percent of the responses to their stimuli.

Three general kinds of mediational devices were reported by Mattocks's Ss: single-step associates, multistep mediation, and complex mediators for which the complete associative rationale could not be reported. As examples of the first kind, to associate DSU and CAT, Ss reported associating the sequence D to "dog" to "cat." To associate RZL to KID, an S reported that RZL suggested "Russell" and "Russell is a kid." As examples of multistep mediation, to associate TPM with AND, S reported transforming TPM to WPM or "words per minute" on the typewriter, and further that AND is a word commonly written on a typewriter. To associate IGW to FAN, S transformed IGW to "igloo" to "cold" to FAN. As examples of the third case of mediation, to associate IGW with AND, S reported that IGW elicited "International Geophysical Year," but he could not report how this suggested AND. To associate DSU with HAT, S reported that DU means "fraternity house" and associated this with HAT.

Natural language mediators vary from one S to another, but if they have a common characteristic, it is a trend toward simplicity. It is likely that Ss do not use, or do not gain from using, long, complex chains of mediators. We already have mentioned the importance of temporal factors with long chains of mediators; another obvious problem would be the potential increase in "intralist similarity" among mediators. This would seem almost inevitable when mediators are derived from a class of materials having a finite number of members, for example, letters, words, or common phrases. As the numbers of these units employed in a mediational chain increase, we might expect that Ss would eventually run out of sufficiently different ones and get them "mixed up," thus interfering with learning. However, as Adams (1967) argued, it is also possible that other interference effects may be *decreased* by using certain types of mediation (see below).

What kind of evidence may one turn to in order to evaluate the role of natural language mediators in learning? We shall consider three different procedures which derive the same kind of evidence with similar results.

Underwood and Schulz (1960) considered this problem in terms of Mattocks's data by comparing the learning performance within various Ss on items for which mediators were reported with items for which no mediators were reported. Considering the 21 Ss whose data included enough mediated and nonmediated items to be applicable, they found that one-third more items were given correctly when mediators were reportedly used than when they were not, a difference of considerable statistical reliability. Nineteen of the twenty-one Ss got more mediated items correct than nonmediated items. This correlation between correct responding and the use of natural language mediators is the fact of central interest here.

Runquist and Farley (1964) found better paired-associate learning of paired adjectives for which Ss reported mediational devices than for pairs for which Ss reported no mediators. In one experimental condition, Ss were given a single exposure to each of the pairs before testing. In this case, 73.5 percent of the pairs learned with the reported mediators were correct compared to only 10.9 percent of the nonmediated pairs.

Montague, Adams, and Kiess (1966) gave Ss a single presentation of 25 pairs of nonsense syllables and asked them to report the natural language mediators, if any, they used to learn them. Twenty-four hr later the Ss returned to the laboratory and were asked to recall both the response terms of each pair and the natural language mediators they had used on the previous day. Montague et al. then compared the recall of items for which Ss did or did not also recall their original natural language mediator. They counted a natural language mediator as correctly recalled if it was judged by independent judges to be sufficiently similar to the original natural language mediator. Combining across their various experimental conditions, they found that when the natural language mediator was recalled correctly, 72.6 percent of the nonsense syllables were recalled and paired with the appropriate stimulus. In contrast, when the natural language mediator was recalled incorrectly or when no natural language mediator had been reported during original learning, only 1.8 percent and 5.8 percent of the nonsense syllables were recalled and paired correctly. Subsequently, Adams and Montague (1967) reported data suggesting that one advantage of natural language mediators under these circumstances is that they increase the resistance of learned associations to subsequent interference-induced forgetting.

What can these data tell us about mediational devices as actual aids to learning and retention? First, as will become clear in the next section, it is not possible to conclude clearly about retention as long as the appearance of natural language mediators is consistently accompanied by better learning: better retention of items with mediators could be due to the mediators *or* the better original learning. Next, it should be made clear that in all the cited experiments, decisions about whether natural language mediators did or did not occur were based on what Ss *said* they did. Even discounting the typical unreliability of such reports by relatively inexperienced Ss, there obviously are alternative ways of interpreting the meaning of these S reports. As Adams (1967, p. 91) has pointed out, natural language mediators may not really occur to S until he is quizzed about them, or possibly they may be emitted during learning but are only correlates, not causes, of the associative strength measured between the nominal stimulus and nominal response. The alternative preferred by Adams is that natural language mediators are in fact the cause, not merely a correlate, of associative strength.

These difficulties in interpreting the role of natural language mediators in learning are not easily dismissed. Furthermore, an additional question must arise even if it could be shown that the natural language mediators reported by Ss do causally contribute to associative strength. Underwood and Schulz (1960) phrased this most clearly: "It is not inconceivable that those items for which associates are reported would be learned more rapidly than those for which no associations are reported even if associates had not been used [p. 305]." To date, adequate experimental procedures have not been devised to permit a completely satisfactory decision among these alternatives.

SUMMARY. There is little doubt that subjects may employ mediators as aids in associating stimuli and responses. The effect of mediation on learning has been studied by training S to have mediators available, by inferring specific mediators on the basis of assumed previous verbal experience, and by interrogating Ss about their "natural" use of mediators in learning. In the first and second cases, the influence of mediation on learning sometimes appears to be facilitatory, sometimes neutral, and sometimes an impairment, depending upon, e.g., meaningfulness of the verbal materials and time permitted for responding. In the last case, items for which mediators are reported are learned more rapidly than items for which no mediators are reported, but strong conclusions about cause and effect are not possible given only this sort of (correlational) evidence.

RETENTION AND FORGETTING OF VERBAL LEARNING

We already have considered strategies and coding devices that may be said to affect memory. In that discussion we were concerned simply with the correctness of recall at some given point in time following input. This section concerns memory in a somewhat different sense. Our interest now is in how recall, or any other performance measure, changes with increasing time since input.

The title of this section was chosen because we will think of forgetting as a special case of retention, with retention referring to *any change in performance which occurs as a function of time after input.* Usually the change observed is a decrease in performance, which we call "forgetting." On other, relatively rare, occasions, there may be no change in retention performance, or there may even be an increase in performance called "reminiscence" (e.g., Keppel & Underwood, 1967; Peterson, 1966a).

By using these operational definitions, we escape for the time being such problems as distinguishing between simple changes in performance and changes in "learning," the more basic disposition to perform, and whether changes over time in the learned performance ever mean that learning is lost forever from the organism's repertoire. But escaping them does not eliminate them, and we shall be forced to partial consideration of these problems later. Adams (1967, Chaps. 2 and 3) presents an interesting discussion of these and other general problems of retention.

A final note of introduction concerns experimental design. When retention is studied with two or more levels of an independent variable, e.g., meaningfulness, magnitude of the reinforcer, S's age, etc., it is necessary to be certain that the groups assigned different values of the independent variable do not differ in degree of learning before the retention tests. Of course, it is necessary to control all known relevant variables in an experiment, as the reader is surely aware by now (cf. Chap. 2). But the confounding influence of degree of learning on retention is a particularly subtle one, and the best of us need to be rewarned of it from time to time. One need only refer to Underwood's (1964b) methodological article on this problem to see how some of the most competent investigators of verbal learning have been caught in this trap.

There are two general ways in which uncontrolled degree of learning may become a source of misinterpretation and incorrect conclusion. The first is the relatively trivial circumstance in which unequal learning precedes a single retention test. In this case "unequal retention" scores may only reflect the fact that there was, to begin with, less to retain. Moreover, strong conclusions about retention would be impossible even if the dependent variable employed is the percentage of terminal acquisition performance lost over the retention interval. The reason is that degree of original learning is known to influence importantly both absolute and percentage loss over a retention interval (cf. Joinson & Runquist, 1968). A similar methodological issue arose in Chap. 7 in connection with the problem of assessing differences in extinction performance when performance differences existed at the end of acquisition training.

The second, and more insidious, problem arises when E employs operations which appear to equate degree of learning but, in fact, do not. One such operation is to continue training each subject until all Ss attain a common performance criterion before the retention interval. This does not guarantee equivalent learning because additional learning occurs on the last (criterion) test trial of the training session (and with the anticipation procedure, an additional study trial also occurs). Therefore, if two groups differ in how rapidly their performance attains criterion level, the group with the more rapid learning rate will, in fact, have learned somewhat more before the retention interval because of the greater amount they learned on the criterion trial. The simplest, though least economical, way around this problem is to include for each experimental condition at least two groups tested at different retention intervals: one immediately after attaining criterion, and the other at some later time (see Runquist & Joinson, 1968; Underwood, 1964b; and Underwood & Keppel, 1962, for other procedures).

However, even this procedure is not completely safe if the criterion represents the best level of performance measurable. This entails a difficulty also encountered when all Ss are given the same number of trials and they all perform "perfectly" at the end of training. When all Ss give 100 percent correct responses, it is likely that some Ss have *overlearned* the task. Such overlearning cannot be detected, because performance better than 100 percent cannot be measured, and it is known that the greater the overlearning, the better the retention performance (see Underwood, 1964b). Clearly, this problem cannot be cured simply by adding additional groups given an immediate retention test. Therefore, it is advisable in retention experiments to bring Ss to a common performance level at the end of training, but a level less than the maximum performance measurable (e.g., to a criterion of 70 or 80 percent correct responding).

By correcting the methodological errors of uncontrolled degree of learning, Underwood and his colleagues (e.g., Underwood, 1954) have corrected the oft-published misconception that individual differences (e.g., fast learners versus slow learners), meaningfulness, and intralist similarity affect rate of forgetting. In fact, although all these variables have profound influences on rate of learning, they have little, if any, effect on retention performance.

With this background, let us briefly examine four areas of interest concerning retention of verbal learning. First we shall consider briefly the proposition that there are two separate memory systems, one for relatively recent events and one for events occurring in the more distant past. Next we shall look at some of the factors which influence retention of recent events, and then we shall consider the (partially overlapping) set of factors which affect retention of learning acquired in the more distant past. Finally, a theory of forgetting will be described, with particular attention to recent modifications.

Are There Two Systems of Memory?

Some theorists have suggested that two separate memory systems exist, one of which controls memory over short periods (*short-term memory, STM*) and one over longer periods (*long-term memory, LTM*). In doing so, they have assigned differentiating properties to *STM* and *LTM*. But have differentiating sets of laws been *empirically* determined to justify the theoretical distinction between *STM* and *LTM*? We shall see that some theorists believe they have, but others do not, maintaining that it is unnecessary at this point to consider two different systems. It is useful to consider the kinds of reasoning that have led theorists to their respective positions on this matter.

Hebb (1949), in his influential speculations about the physiological basis of learning and memory, suggested that different physiological processes underlie *STM* and *LTM*. He suggested that *STM* was a consequence of the activity of groups of neurons through which neural impulses circulated and continued to reverberate throughout the period of *STM*. If this reverberation lasted long enough, or if it were reinstated from time to time, a permanent pathway would be established representing permanent storage or *LTM*. This kind of formulation not only stimulated a great deal of physiological research on memory concerning such topics as retrograde amnesia (e.g., Glickman, 1961; Lewis & Maher, 1965), but it also helped to stimulate workers in verbal learning into considering the possibility of two separable systems of memory. Such a distinction had been most strenuously defended in the 1950s by several English psychologists (e.g., Broadbent, 1957; Brown, 1958; Conrad & Hille, 1958). These psychologists also suggested that the fundamental mechanism of forgetting in *STM* and *LTM* is simple decay, which begins whenever rehearsal stops, although they generally did not disagree with the contention that some forgetting in *LTM* also may be due to mechanisms of associative interference.

Melton (1963) has pointed out that the *STM-LTM* distinction is not to be taken lightly in view of the past 30 to 40 years of work in relevant areas. During this period interference mechanisms were thoroughly documented as the basic mechanisms of forgetting in *LTM*, beginning about the time of McGeoch's (1932) insightful theoretical attack on the "Law of Disuse." Melton argues for a *continuum* of memory processes—a single system of memory of which *STM* and *LTM* are special cases differing only in degree, not in kind. His paper presents a clear statement of the fundamental issues in memory as well as a thorough review of the relevant literature up to 1962.

Other verbal learning theorists have taken a position for or against a distinction between *STM* and *LTM* on a variety of empirical grounds. For example, Tulving (1968a) argues that although certain free-recall phenomena seem to imply separate *STM* and *LTM* memory systems, they may be more efficiently interpreted in terms of the different retrieval cues available to recent and remote events. On the other hand, Adams (1967) suggests that the following three factors argue for an *STM-LTM* distinction: (1) *STM* has a smaller storage capacity (i.e., memory span) than *LTM*; (2) acoustic, but not semantic, interference seems primarily responsible for forgetting in *STM*, but the converse is apparently true for *LTM*; (3) certain hippocampal lesions leave humans with no capacity for transfering information from immediate storage (*STM*) to *LTM*, even though these Ss do well on *STM* tasks and demonstrate essentially normal memory for remote events which occurred *before* the lesion. [A summary of the physiological evidence favoring an *STM-LTM* distinction has been presented by John (1967).]

Regardless of whether one does or does not accept a functional distinction between *STM* and *LTM*, it appears wise to consider them separately in this chapter for two reasons. First, they do differ operationally—nearly all *STM* studies have used retention intervals less than 1 hr (usually less than a minute), and nearly all *LTM* studies have used retention intervals longer than 24 hr—and although there is some overlap, the methodological problems associated with each differ somewhat (see Keppel, 1965). Second, partially because of the methodological differences and partially because of theoretical distinctions between *STM* and *LTM*, the questions underlying *STM* and *LTM* experiments often differ. For these reasons, we first shall consider some of the research and facts of *STM*, then those of *LTM*. Finally, we shall concern ourselves with some theoretical interpretations of these phenomena.

Short-term Memory

You probably have had the experience of being introduced to a stranger, exchanging a few sentences, and then saying as you separate, "Very nice to have met you, ———." You cannot remember his name even though you heard it only a few minutes before. Or perhaps you have looked up a phone number, dialed it, found a busy signal, and then been immediately unable to remember it to dial again. Are these experiences fundamentally different from being unable to remember the name of a friend you have not seen for 3 years or the "old" telephone number you had before you moved a few years ago? These two cases do differ operationally, of course, in two important ways. The former case concerns retention after relatively short intervals and after relatively low degrees of original learning. These features characterize procedures for the study of

STM. The reason for the short retention interval, usually measured in seconds or a few minutes, is obvious. The low degree of learning is necessary because better original learning may facilitate subsequent retention to such a degree that no loss may be measurable over the short retention interval.

Historically the study of *LTM* preceded that of *STM*, and this dominance, beginning with Ebbinghaus (1913), continued until the now classic article by Peterson and Peterson (1959). Peterson and Peterson's work represented a departure from the previous major concern involving *STM*, characteristics of the memory span (e.g., Blankenship, 1938; Broadbent, 1957). Their technique was unique in that it permitted assessment of retention of a single item (in their case, a nonword consisting of three consonants) outside of the usual context of an entire list of items. They accomplished this in the following way. When S saw a green light, E spoke the three letters of one of the consonant syllables and then a three-digit number. The S previously had been instructed as follows: "You are to repeat the number immediately after I say it and begin counting backwards by 3's . . . from that number in time with the ticking that you hear . . . When you see this red light come on, stop counting immediately and say the letters that were given at the beginning of the trial [p. 194]." Each S was tested in this way on 48 different consonant syllables, a factor which, as we shall see, turned out to have great importance. Each S was tested with six retention intervals: 3, 6, 9, 12, 15, and 18 sec.

Peterson and Peterson found surprisingly rapid forgetting, progressing in a negatively accelerated function between 3- and 18-sec retention intervals, similar to that of the one-repetition group shown in Fig. 12-6. Assuming that the consonant syllables always would have been given correctly if tested immediately after their presentation, Peterson and Peterson's results indicated nearly 50 percent forgetting after only 6 sec and more than 90 percent forgetting after 18 sec.

What could account for this huge quantity of forgetting over such short periods? Is it simply a matter of rapid disintegration, i.e., spontaneous decay of a relatively lightly formed memory trace (see Brown, 1958), or has interference somehow contributed to this rapid forgetting? We shall pursue these theoretical alternatives in a moment, but let us first examine some additional characteristics of *STM* in tasks similar to that of Peterson and Peterson.

EMPIRICAL CHARACTERISTICS OF STM. Two variables which seem to have the greatest influence on *STM* are degree of original learning and characteristics of other materials learned by S under the same circumstances. Although these are variables which also have the greatest impact on *LTM*, by themselves such commonalities are insufficient grounds for considering *LTM* and *STM* as variants of a single system.

Degree of learning and STM. We have mentioned that the most common methodological error in retention studies is the failure to equate the terminal level of original learning, and this continues to be so in *STM* (cf. Keppel,

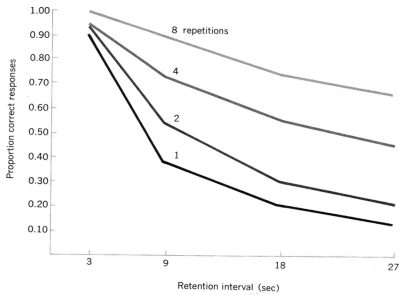

Fig. 12-6. Proportion of items correctly recalled as a function of retention interval after 1, 2, 4, or 8 visual presentations and overt repetitions by *S* of a single trigram. (SOURCE: S. Hellyer. Supplementary report: Frequency of stimulus presentation and short-term decrement in recall. *Journal of Experimental Psychology*, 1962, **64,** 650. Copyright 1962 by the American Psychological Association and used by permission.)

1965). This is especially a problem in cases in which all conditions result in perfect immediate recall, as in the Melton (1963) experiment (cf. Underwood, 1964b).

The influence of degree of learning on *STM* has been shown in three ways. The most clear-cut demonstration of this effect has appeared in experiments such as Hellyer's (1962). Hellyer's procedures were similar to Peterson and Peterson's, including the same kind of verbal materials and retesting of *S*s in a number of conditions. Hellyer varied degree of original learning simply by varying the number of times *S* repeated aloud the verbal unit (1, 2, 4, or 8 repetitions) immediately after presentation. Then *S* counted backward by threes, as in the Peterson and Peterson experiment, before being asked to recall the item either 3, 9, 18, or 27 sec later. The results are shown in Fig. 12-6. The more repetitions the better the retention, i.e., the less the loss over a given retention interval. It may be seen that after one repetition, Hellyer's *S*s retained somewhat more than Peterson and Peterson's *S*s had. This might be due to the fact that Peterson and Peterson's *S*s gave *no* repetitions. Another possibility is that the latter *S*s learned and recalled 48 trigrams, compared with 16 for Hellyer's *S*s, which may have contributed more interference and so more forgetting (see below).

The two other ways in which degree of learning has been varied in *STM* are a little more indirect. Variation in duration of the time a verbal unit is exposed may be analogous to variation in degree of practice, assuming the number of implicit repetitions by S are related to this duration. Accepting this, it may be said that retention in *STM* is directly related to degree of learning since it is improved by increasing the duration of item exposure (see Peterson, 1966b, p. 201).

A final way that degree of learning may be said to be increased is by increased rehearsal during the retention interval. When the retention interval is filled with backward-counting activity, rehearsal is assumed to be minimal. However, it is important to note that when Ss are asked whether anything like rehearsal occurs during backward counting, over 60 percent report that it does (Groninger, 1966, p. 135). To the extent that these S reports are reliable, we would expect that the more the rehearsal, the better the learning and so the better the retention. And this is exactly what Groninger found. We must, of course, be cautious about any conclusions concerning this latter statement, because this is a statement of correlation, and those Ss who rehearsed more might have retained better even though they had not rehearsed.

Effect of prior and subsequent interference on retention in STM. The procedure of Peterson and Peterson (1959) included a test for retention of each individual item before presentation of the next. Since the interpolated experience involves a different class of materials (numbers) which does not involve learning, it has seemed unreasonable to attribute the observed forgetting to interfering materials acquired during the retention interval. Peterson and Peterson recognized that because their Ss learned 48 different items, learning *before* the presentation of any item might have caused the forgetting. This source is termed "proactive interference" and is discussed in greater detail in a later section. Their evaluation of this possibility suggested to them that proactive interference was not an important factor. However, subsequent studies have seemed to show that proactive interference did contribute to the forgetting that Peterson and Peterson measured (e.g., Keppel & Underwood, 1962a; Loess, 1964; Wickens, Born, & Allen, 1963; but see Conrad, 1967).

The increase in forgetting with increasing numbers of verbal units previously learned and recalled is shown in Fig. 12-7. It may be seen that the difference in performance after 3 and 18 sec (i.e., forgetting) is absent on the first test but becomes more sizeable the greater the number of earlier tests. In this respect it is important to note that similarity between the previous items and the item to be recalled is not necessary for the production of proactive interference in this context. In fact, the data represented in Fig. 12-7 are based upon six trigrams, composed of 18 different letters with no duplication between trigrams. This is not to say that the influence of proactive interference may not be varied by manipulating similarity of items. However, similarity of *class* of items (i.e., single letters, digits, and words are different classes) seems to be more important than similarity *within* the class. This has been shown for *STM*

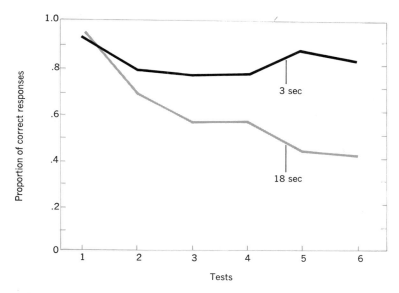

Fig. 12-7. Retention as a function of number of syllables previously presented and duration of retention interval. A single syllable was experienced by *S* on each test. (SOURCE: G. Keppel and B. J. Underwood. Proactive inhibition in short-term retention of single items. *Journal of Verbal Learning and Verbal Behavior,* 1962, **1,** 153–161. Used by permission.)

(Wickens et al., 1963), and it also is consistent with the influence of proactive interference in *LTM* (cf. Underwood, 1957a).

Additional *STM* experiments have been designed specifically to estimate the impact of interfering materials learned during the retention interval ("retroactive interference"). Forgetting in *STM* has been shown to increase as a consequence of retroactive interference (Houston, 1968). However, as in the case of proactive interference, control over degree of learning in *STM* studies is extremely important in investigating retroactive interference (cf. Crowder, 1968; Goggin, 1966).

Two additional variables may be mentioned because they seem to have relatively robust effects in *STM* and because they have counterparts in data from *LTM* studies. The first is similarity within a class of interfering materials which does, in some cases, appear to influence retention in *STM*, particularly acoustical interference (e.g., Wickelgren, 1965). Furthermore, an experiment by Bruce and Murdock (1968) indicates that most of the forgetting found with their materials and *STM* procedures was produced by *proactive* acoustical interference. Another important variable for *STM* seems to be the distribution with which the items are presented. Keppel (1964a) found results indicating better retention after more widely spaced practice between multiple presentations of a single item before a single, short, retention interval. His results nicely paralleled the *LTM* experiment he reported in the same paper (described below), indicating better retention the longer the intertrial interval. Other experiments also have indicated some influence of time between repetitions of a single item, although this often is confounded by number of different items presented between each repetition (see Peterson, 1966b). Each of these effects may have rather special boundary conditions, however. Keppel's results may be limited to conditions in which high degrees of proactive interference are present; and in the latter studies, length of the interval between repetitions of single items seems to interact with length of retention interval to determine forgetting (Peterson, 1966b, p. 202).

DOES "DECAY" CAUSE FORGETTING IN STM? We have noted that some theorists argue for "trace decay" as the primary contributor to forgetting in *STM* to the exclusion of interference. They have argued, among other things, that decay occurs independently of interference, that number of repetitions in the original presentation does not affect the rate of later decay but only serves to delay its onset, and that decay proceeds whenever rehearsal stops (e.g., Brown, 1958). They have argued further that the kinds of intrusion errors, which seem to imply interference, are really only a *consequence* of the forgetting that has occurred, not a cause of this forgetting (e.g., Conrad, 1960).

One basic test for the simplest form of decay theory is whether amount forgotten in *STM* is independent of the nature of material learned previously or during the retention interval. We have seen that although there is not a great deal of evidence of this sort, there is some which indicates that the nature of the intervening materials does determine how much is forgotten (e.g., Houston, 1968).

Of course there exists physiological evidence (e.g., John, 1967) which may be cited in support of a decay process in forgetting, and the influence of decay is not completely excluded in *STM* studies of retroactive and proactive interference. For example, we know that little, if any, forgetting occurs in *STM* if S experiences only a single item; but substantial forgetting occurs if he has experienced many other items. If rehearsal occurs during the filler task to the extent that Groninger's data have implied, this may simply reflect the fact that rehearsal is easier in the former case. On the other hand, some behavioral data purporting to support a decay position have been difficult to replicate or interpret. Conrad and Hille (1958) varied retention interval (hence, opportunity for decay) while holding constant the number of potentially interfering items intervening between item presentation and the recall test. They did this by varying the speed of presentation of items. Although their results indicated that less forgetting occurred with the faster rates in spite of the apparently equal opportunities for interference, others have failed to confirm this result (e.g., Mackworth, 1962). Still, it should be noted that clear conclusions about forgetting can hardly be drawn with this procedure since rate of presentation surely affects degree of learning as well (see Keppel, 1965). At best, it appears that the role of decay in short-term memory of verbal learning is uncertain. It also appears that a decision will ultimately be based upon a network of evidence rather than one or two "critical" experiments. Such a network has been presented by Peterson (1966b) in support of a decay component in *STM*.

Peterson (1966b) argues for separate *LTM* and *STM* systems of memory. In this paper he has included some cogent arguments for the considering decay in *STM* in a more restricted sense than had been implied by most previous decay theorists (see also Conrad, 1967). Peterson suggests that a learning mechanism operates in *STM* experiments even after a single presentation of an item, and it is common to both *STM* and *LTM*. In addition, however, Peterson suggests there is a recency mechanism, particularly important to *STM*, which is "conceptualized as a post-perceptual mechanism whose effectiveness decreases through time and the action of other information [p. 206]." He distinguishes this from the more permanent *LTM* on the basis of data showing that initial and later portions of a retention curve are affected differently by variables such as duration or number of presentations of items and length of the interval between repetitions. This recency mechanism is thought to mask the learning mechanism for a short period and contribute to the unique phenomena occurring within short retention intervals of a few seconds.

The major portion of Peterson's paper describes some of these interesting phenomena and their implications for the existence of this recency mechanism. Peterson suggests that recall might be a composite function including this rapidly decaying *STM* mechanism superimposed on the relatively permanent learning mechanism. The effectiveness of the learning mechanism, he suggests, may even increase with time to account for some evidence of reminiscence.

His model is shown in Fig. 12-8. It is a relatively explicit model, and he outlines the general mathematical form it might take. It cannot be said how this particular model will fare in the future. This kind of approach, however, may serve to reconcile some of the concern over the extent to which decay contributes to forgetting—if it contributes at all—and the boundary conditions for the mechanisms of *STM* and *LTM*, if indeed they are separate.

SUMMARY.   Short-term memory (*STM*) is distinguished operationally by lower degrees of original learning and shorter retention intervals than long-term memory (*LTM*). It is not yet clear whether functional differences between *STM* and *LTM* justify separate theoretical treatment. Functional similarities appear to include some common influences of degree of learning and interference on forgetting, but some differences also have been determined; e.g., interference by acoustical similarity seems to influence *STM* but not *LTM*, and semantic similarity apparently affects *LTM* more than *STM*. Some theorists have suggested that the heavier influence of simple decay processes in *STM* than *LTM* provides a critical distinction, but the decay process itself is difficult to establish, and there is no general agreement concerning its influence on retention of verbal learning.

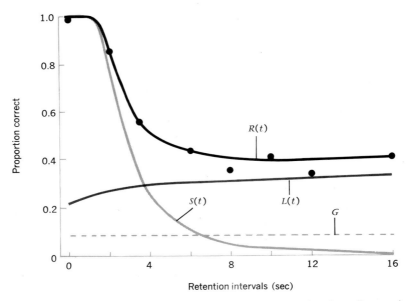

Fig. 12-8. The course of three hypothetical components of recall over short retention intervals. The components are symbolized as follows: $S(t)$ indicates the short-term component, $L(t)$ indicates the learning component, and G indicates the guessing component. These components are assumed to combine to produce probability of recall, symbolized as $R(t)$. (SOURCE: L. R. Peterson. Short-term verbal memory and learning. *Psychological Review*, 1966, **73**, 193–207. Copyright 1966 by the American Psychological Association and used by permission.)

Long-term Memory

If you are presented with a list of words today, how many will you be able to recall tomorrow? This obviously is a foolishly worded question, which almost certainly will be answered by anyone with the words, "It depends." However, you may be surprised to learn that a rather accurate answer may be given which actually depends on very few conditions. We shall see that the only conditions of real importance are (1) how well you learned the items today and (2) how often you previously have learned these kinds of items under the same circumstances or will do so between today and tomorrow. Compared with these factors, it would not matter much whether the items to be learned were words or nonwords, whether there was a lot of similarity among them or whether they were all different, or whether you are a slow or fast learner. If the list learned today were such that an immediate recall test would show nearly perfect recall (but little, or no, overlearning) and if you learned no other lists of this kind under similar circumstances at any other time prior to recall, then tomorrow you would be able to recall correctly about 80 percent of the items.

The above paragraph carries four implicit messages. The first is that human competence at retention really is not bad and certainly presents a rosier picture than the earlier generally accepted estimate of about 25 percent retention. Underwood (1957a) showed that the massive amount of forgetting which had been reported so often in the past—75 percent over 24 hr—was highly inflated. The Ss that had shown this extent of forgetting also had learned many other verbal associations in the same situation before being presented with their critical learning and retention tests. They were victims, in other words, of heavy proactive interference.

The second point implicit in the above paragraph is that there are a large number of intuitively important factors which do not seem to influence retention much, such as meaningfulness (e.g., Underwood & Keppel, 1963b; Underwood & Richardson, 1956), intralist similarity (e.g., Joinson & Runquist, 1968; Underwood & Richardson, 1956), and unique characteristics of S himself (e.g., Underwood, 1964b, p. 117). It is, however, scientifically awkward to become overly involved with those things that do *not* seem to make much of a difference. The remaining points in the above paragraph, therefore, concern things that *do* make a difference in *LTM*. These are that retention is importantly influenced by degree of original learning and by other verbal learning which has occurred within the same context as the list to be retained. We have noted previously that retention is directly related to original degree of learning, a fact which has been thoroughly documented in verbal learning (e.g., Underwood, 1964b; Underwood & Keppel, 1963b). Therefore, we shall concern ourselves primarily with the role of interfering associations in retention and forgetting. We already have seen something of their influence in *STM*, but it is within the context of *LTM* that interference has been most extensively studied.

The two sources of interference include (1) learning that has occurred prior (*prior learning*, *PL*) to the learning to be retained (*original learning*, *OL*) and (2) learning interpolated (*interpolated learning*, *IL*) between *OL* and the retention test. Descriptively, the former is referred to as *proactive interference* (*PI*) and the latter as *retroactive interference* (*RI*). Although these often are referred to as proactive "inhibition" and retroactive "inhibition," we prefer the term "interference" because its more neutral theoretical character serves to remind us of the fact that *RI* and *PI* simply describe empirical phenomena and research paradigms. Because the term "inhibition" has so many theoretical overtones, there may be inappropriate tendencies to treat *RI* and *PI* as complete explanations of the forgetting that occurs, thus ignoring more basic mechanisms of the forgetting.

FACTORS INFLUENCING RI AND PI. The impact of *RI* and *PI* on retention may be softened or enhanced by manipulating certain key conditions. We shall consider a few of these which are particularly important for interference theory. Further discussion of these and other factors relevant to understanding *RI* and *PI* may be found in several sources, among them Slamecka and Ceraso (1960), Postman (1961), Hall (1966, Chap. 17), and Keppel (1968).

Effects of absolute and relative degrees of learning on RI and PI. The defining conditions of *RI* are met when Ss recall *OL* more poorly following *IL* than control Ss who received no *IL*. In the sense of something versus nothing, then, forgetting due to *RI* is greater the greater the degree of *IL*. When this variable has been parametrically examined, the more general increase in *RI* with increasing degrees of *IL* has been confirmed. Moreover, this is so whether recall requires S to give only those responses from *OL* (e.g., Thune & Underwood, 1943), the first response S thinks of during a short anticipation interval (Briggs, 1957), or responses from both *OL* and *IL*, with plenty of time to think about it before responding (Barnes & Underwood, 1959). The increase in *RI* begins to level off at high degrees of *IL* or whenever degree of *IL* begins to exceed degree of *OL*.

On the other side of the coin, *RI* decreases when degree of *OL* is increased and degree of *IL* held constant. Note that this is consistent with the fact that forgetting in general decreases the greater the degree of learning, even without specifically built-in sources of interference.

The influence of degree of learning on *PI* is equally straightforward, at least from low to moderate degrees of learning. As degree of prior learning increases, forgetting due to *PI* also increases (Underwood & Ekstrand, 1966). There are two reasons why this phenomenon is perhaps not as tightly established as is the effect of degree of interpolated learning on *RI*. First, earlier studies that have shown this relationship suffered from failure to control degree of original learning to the extent required by current standards (e.g., Underwood, 1949). Second, a study which has appropriately controlled degree of original learning found that *PI* increases with increasing prior learning only when prior learning is acquired under conditions of massed practice (original learning also was given under massed practice) and only between 0 and 48 prior learning trials, after which there was a slight decline in *PI* at a higher level (80 trials) of prior learning (Underwood & Ekstrand, 1966). These exceptions require that our conclusions be somewhat restricted. Within these boundaries, however, we may conclude that forgetting occurs the greater the degree of learning the interfering material for both *RI* and *PI*.

Effect of distributed practice on original learning and interfering material. For reasons we shall discuss shortly, Underwood and Ekstrand (1966) compared forgetting attributable to *PI* for Ss differing in their distribution of practice on prior learning (*PL*). Some Ss acquired *PL* in four sessions distributed over 4 days (distributed practice). Others were given their *PL* in a single session just before original learning (*OL*) and with the same 4-sec intertrial interval (massed practice). It is significant that *OL* occurred with massed practice for all Ss, because considerably more forgetting of *OL* occurred when *PL* also had been acquired by massed practice. In one condition, percentage forgetting at recall was nearly twice as great for Ss given *PL* with massed, compared with distributed, practice.

Another experiment showing massive effects of distribution of practice on forgetting has been reported by Keppel (1964a). This experiment was similar to that of Underwood and Ekstrand, but it differed in that Keppel varied the distribution of practice on *OL* rather than *PL*. Keppel's experiment was an extensive one, but for our purposes two conditions are particularly important. In both conditions, Ss learned four successive paired-associate lists having the same stimuli but different responses. Subsequently, Ss were given retention tests on the fourth list (*OL*), either 1 or 8 days after it was learned. All Ss learned their three *PL* lists with a 4-sec intertrial interval and just before presentation of the fourth list (*OL*), but they differed in the distribution in which the eight *OL* trials were given. In the massed-practice condition, Ss received all eight trials on the same day as their *PL* and with the same 4-sec intertrial interval. The distributed-practice Ss were given two of their *OL* trials immediately after *PL*, then two additional *OL* trials on each of the next 3 days. Thus, for Ss in the distributed-practice condition, each block of two *OL* trials was separated by a 24-hr intertrial interval.

The influence of this manipulation on forgetting was astonishing. After the 1-day retention interval, percentage recall was nearly five times as great for Ss in the distributed-practice condition as for Ss in the massed-practice condition. To state this more dramatically, in contrast to the 16 percent retention shown in the massed-practice condition after a single day's retention interval, Ss in the distributed-practice condition showed 72 percent retention over an 8-day retention interval. Furthermore, other Ss run by Keppel under the distributed-practice condition and given a 29-day retention interval, showed about 34 percent retention. Thus, it may be said that retention under the distributed-practice condition was better after a *month* than retention under the massed-practice condition after a *day*. In fact, it was about twice as good.

We shall return to their theoretical significance, but for now it is sufficient to point out the similarity of the Keppel (1964a) and Underwood and Ekstrand (1966) experiments. Here we have two experiments showing dramatic differences in rate of forgetting under conditions in which *PI* is the major source of the forgetting. Both experiments found great facilitation of retention when the distribution of practice on the primary source of interference, *PL*, differed vastly from the distribution of practice on the material to be recalled, *OL*.

A final experiment varied distribution of practice in a *PI* design differently from the above two studies. But as we shall see, it may reflect the same theoretical principles.

Before the experiment in question, Underwood and Ekstrand (1967b) had suggested that the decreased forgetting in the distributed-practice condition of the Underwood and Ekstrand (1966) experiment might be due to better *list differentiation* at recall. By list differentiation we mean S's recall of whether an item occurred in the first or the second list previously presented (cf. Winograd, 1968). Perhaps the difference in the temporal distribution under which the lists were experienced in this condition (spaced practice on *PL*, massed practice on *OL*) might have facilitated S's differentiation of the lists at recall. Accordingly, Underwood and Ekstrand (1967b) were able to eliminate about two-thirds of the effect by having some *PL* items appear in *OL* as well. Presumably this manipulation further decreased list differentiation in a way different from that of distribution of practice, thus minimizing the benefit of list differentiation on the latter basis.

Underwood and Freund (1968a) then investigated another manipulation expected to decrease *PI* on a similar list-differentiation basis. In this experiment, Ss again received *PL* followed by *OL* and were asked to recall *OL* 24 hr after learning it. In one condition, *PL* was given just before *OL* and on the same day; in another condition, *PL* was given on Monday and *OL* on Thursday, which separated the two learning tasks by 3 days. When the learning tasks were separated by 3 days, 65 percent of the *OL* items were recalled correctly 24 hr later compared with 38 percent when both *PL* and *OL* had been learned on the same day. This recall advantage due to the 3-day separation of *PL* from *OL* was almost the same as that found previously when *PL* had been distributed about equally over 3 days (Underwood & Ekstrand, 1966, 1967b). Furthermore, the advantage of the 3-day separation in the Underwood and Freund experiment was essentially eliminated when list differentiation was made very difficult for all conditions by including some *PL* items in *OL*. Therefore, these results imply that the reduction in *PI*-induced forgetting found by Underwood and Freund was due to the same process contributing to that found by Underwood and Ekstrand (1966, 1967b) and by Keppel (1964a), and that process seems to be list differentiation.

Influence of sleep during the retention interval. If S sleeps during most of the retention interval, and if we believe that *RI* from extra-experimental sources otherwise experienced during a retention interval contributes to forgetting, then we would expect S to retain more than a similar S who did not sleep during the retention interval. Indeed, this prediction was apparently verified by experiments conducted long ago (Jenkins & Dallenbach, 1924; Van Ormer, 1932). However, the methods employed in these early studies were inadequate by today's standards. The primary problem was that Ss in the earlier experiments were given multiple testing sessions, which, as Underwood (1957a) has shown, inflate amount forgotten by uncontrolled *PI*. This fact detracts from a clear interpretation of the early sleep studies; it is possible, for example, that the sleep did not decrease *RI* effects but, instead, decreased *PI* effects (Underwood, 1957a).

Ekstrand (1967) completed a tightly controlled set of experiments designed to clarify the effects of sleep during the retention interval. To replicate the earlier studies, he had some experimentally naive Ss learn a single list of paired associates, then tested them for retention 8 hr later. Based upon careful estimates of original degrees of learning, Ss who slept during most of the retention interval recalled about 89 percent of the items correctly, i.e., forgot about 11 percent. The Ss who stayed awake during this period and presumably engaged in more verbal behavior recalled about 77 percent correctly, i.e., forgot about 23 percent. To say this another way, percentage forgetting was about twice as great for Ss who stayed awake as for Ss who slept during the retention interval.

Was the reduced forgetting in the sleep condition due to decreased *RI* or decreased *PI*? Ekstrand had other Ss learn two lists (*A-C, A-B*) before the 8-hr retention interval, during which some Ss slept and others were awake. With appropriate control conditions, he was able to estimate changes in the relative influence of *PI* and *RI* during intervals filled with sleep- or awake-type activity. His results indicated that lesser forgetting by sleeping Ss was more likely due to a decrease in *RI* than a decrease in *PI*. In fact, he found some indication of an increase during sleep in the magnitude of one mechanism which has been theorized to account for increases in *PI* over time—spontaneous recovery. We shall consider some theoretical mechanisms of this sort in a moment.

Other characteristics of RI and PI. Clearly, the above discussion does not exhaust the properties of *RI* and *PI*. Thus, for example, the influence of *RI* decreases the longer the retention interval, but the influence of *PI* increases (see Keppel, 1968), a fact of theoretical importance. Also, both *RI* and *PI*, particularly *PI*, are very transient in their effect. For example, *PI* rarely is measurable after the first recall trial (e.g., Underwood & Ekstrand, 1966; 1967b).

However, most other variables influencing *RI* and *PI* generally do so to a lesser extent than those noted above, with the possible exception of degree of similarity between the interfering materials and the material to be retained. A complete account of the effect of this variable becomes immensely complex (see Keppel, 1968; Martin, 1965). However, considering the extremes of response similarity in terms of the *A-B'* and *A-C* paradigms, it seems safe to conclude that more interference to retention occurs in the *A-C* than the *A-B'* paradigm in the case of *RI* (e.g., Barnes & Underwood, 1959) and perhaps also with *PI* (Postman, 1962a).

SUMMARY.   The major determinants of long-term memory are degree of original learning and interference from prior or subsequent learning. Within limits, more forgetting occurs the higher the degree of learning the interfering material relative to the material to be retained. Forgetting attributable to interference from prior learning is a transient effect which increases the longer the retention interval and is decreased when there is considerable temporal separation between the learning of the interfering material and the material to be retained. Sleep decreases forgetting, apparently by decreasing interference which would have been acquired if awake, because the influence of previously acquired interference tends to increase during sleep.

Interference Theory

It is misleading to speak of interference theory without qualification. Probably everyone who has thought seriously about it would agree that interference of some sort plays a major role in determining retention loss, i.e., forgetting. It follows that there are a number of different ideas about how this interference works, incorporated in a number of different "interference theories" (e.g., Shiffrin & Atkinson, 1969; Slamecka, 1969).

But there is no disagreement as to what has been the most influential theory of interference. This is the theory evolved from McGeoch's work of the 1930s and subsequently expanded upon by Melton (e.g., Melton & Irwin, 1940), and, still later, developed and refined by Underwood, Postman, and their colleagues.

Slamecka and Ceraso (1960) emphasized four sources of development in this theory beginning with Melton and Irwin's (1940) suggestion that an unlearning process needed to be added to the response-competition factor. A second development in this theory was Gibson's (1940) work, which implicated the role of generalization and discrimination among stimuli in a paired-associate task. The third important theoretical development before 1960 was Underwood's introduction of the concept of list differentiation (e.g., Underwood, 1945), along with his analysis of some of the properties accompanying unlearning, such as spontaneous recovery (e.g., Underwood, 1948). Finally, Slamecka and Ceraso cite the importance of Osgood's analysis of the commonalities between transfer and the effects of *RI* (Osgood, 1948, 1949).

In anticipation of material below, it may be noted that, with the exception of Underwood's list-differentiation concept, all these developments in interference theory cited by Slamecka and Ceraso (1960) dealt with processes which assigned the focus of the interference effects to individual verbal items. The concepts of response competition, unlearning, and spontaneous recovery were applied to single responses or associations, and the fact that they were one item of many in the list was incidental so far as the concepts were concerned. We mention this now because we soon will describe a more recent emphasis on interference mechanisms which uses the entire list of items as the unit of analysis, with the fate of individual items perhaps incidental to their membership in the list.

RECENT DEVELOPMENTS IN INTERFERENCE THEORY. The critical events for interference theory occurring after 1960 have been thoroughly discussed by Keppel (1968), which is a good reference for further elaboration on related material.

Perhaps the most formal statement of interference theory has been given by Underwood and Postman (1960). From the implications of the Underwood (1957a) paper—that the 15 to 25 percent forgetting shown over 24 hr by a naive S is due mainly to language habits acquired before learning the material presented in the laboratory—Underwood and Postman set out to delineate the nature of these interfering language habits and the mechanism by which they interfered with retention. They identified two sources of interference: previously learned associations between individual letters, e.g., *Q-U* (*letter-sequence interference*), and previously learned associations between integrated groups of letters, such as words, e.g., ICE-COLD, (*unit-sequence interference*). Briefly, these earlier habits were thought to interfere with retention of subsequent learning in this way: To learn a unit sequence like ICE-DOG, *unlearning* of responses such as

COLD to ICE had to occur. However, over the retention interval the response of COLD to ICE would undergo *spontaneous recovery* and thus *compete* with the response, DOG, resulting in the observed forgetting.

It should be clear that this theory predicted differential forgetting for items differing in meaningfulness. However, only the extreme cases of meaningfulness were implicated: low-meaningfulness letter groupings with so little integration (e.g., QTX) that they are learned by associating adjacent letters and are subject to letter-sequence interference, and high-meaningfulness letter groupings forming frequent words which are subject to unit-sequence interference. We already have seen that variation within the intermediate range of meaningfulness (e.g., easily pronunciable nonwords such as nonsense syllables) has no influence on forgetting (e.g., Underwood & Richardson, 1956). Again it was believed that the most probable sources of extra-experimental interference were previously well-formed language habits involving associations between individual verbal units, either between single letters involving nonwords or between single words.

Being readily testable as all good theories are, the Underwood-Postman theory soon was found wanting in several respects. Before considering these difficulties, it will be useful to consider subsequent work dealing directly with the unlearning-recovery and response-competition factors of interference theory.

What is unlearned and how does unlearning occur? With Underwood and Postman's statement of their theory, unlearning began to play a more central role than ever in interference theory. We already have seen that Barnes and Underwood (1959) clearly demonstrated unlearning as a fundamental source of *RI*, apparently independent of competition. Now Underwood and Postman had employed unlearning and subsequent recovery to account for forgetting due to extra-experimental sources. Underwood (e.g., 1949) previously had suggested such a mechanism to account for the increase in *PI* with increasing retention interval when the source of *PI* was learned in the laboratory. It is, therefore, not surprising that questions arose concerning the generality of the unlearning phenomenon.

Before the appearance of the Underwood-Postman theory, unlearning had been specifically demonstrated only when the source of *RI* had the same stimuli as, but different responses from, *OL* (*A-C, A-B*). It was important to establish exactly what aspect of *OL* had been unlearned as a consequence of *IL*. It also was important to determine whether the factors unlearned with this paradigm were similarly unlearned with other paradigms and whether additional factors might be found.

McGovern (1964) looked for evidence of two sources of unlearning, the association between the *OL* stimulus and response and the *OL* response itself, in each of four transfer paradigms: *A-C, A-B*; *C-D, A-B*; *A-B$_r$, A-B*; and *C-B, A-B*. All groups were compared in recall against a standard *RI* control given *OL* but no *IL*. McGovern assessed unlearning of the association by asking some Ss at recall to match the appropriate *OL* stimuli and responses when all were presented in random order. Unlearning of the *OL* responses was assessed by asking other Ss at recall to write down the appropriate *OL* responses upon presentation of the stimuli. Her results, along with those of subsequent studies (e.g., Houston, 1964; Keppel & Underwood, 1962b), indicated that three sources of unlearning may be identified as contributing to *RI*: (1) unlearning of the forward association between the stimulus and the response of *OL*; (2) unlearning of the backward association between response and stimulus of *OL*; and (3) unlearning of the *OL* response itself, which McGovern conceptualized as unlearning of the association between contextual stimuli and the response. Subsequently, unlearning was shown to have considerable generality across tasks as well as across associations within tasks. Its existence has also been documented as a source of the *RI* obtained in serial learning (e.g., Keppel, 1966b) and in free recall (e.g., Postman & Keppel, 1967).

To understand the boundary conditions which limit the operation of unlearning, it is necessary to delineate the mechanisms responsible for its occurrence. By rough analogy with classical and instrumental conditioning data, it seemed likely to some theorists that unlearning will occur to the extent that *OL* responses are given by *S* during acquisition of *IL*, with these unreinforced "response elicitations" resulting in something like experimental extinction. Because so very few overt errors occur during *IL* of even the most potent *RI* designs (*A-C, A-B; C-D, A-B*), the elicitation of covert as well as overt *OL* responses during *IL* was assumed responsible for unlearning. A series of experiments has tested this "response elicitation theory" (e.g., Goggin, 1967; Keppel & Rauch, 1966; Postman, 1965; Postman, Keppel & Stark, 1965), generally with positive results.

A different, though not mutually exclusive, mechanism underlying unlearning has been reemphasized by Postman. On the basis of an extensive series of studies concerned with changes in *PI* and *RI* over retention intervals (Postman, 1967a; Postman, Stark, & Fraser, 1968), Postman has concluded that the relative unavailability of *OL* responses in free recall immediately after *IL*—operationally defined "unlearning"—represents the maintenance of a set to respond in terms of the list most recently learned. He implicates the selector mechanism, through which *S* restricts himself to the responses of the current list, as the fundamental mechanism of unlearning and, hence, *RI*.

It is important to note that in addition to changing emphasis from a learning phenomenon at *IL* to a performance phenomenon at recall, Postman has shifted the locus of interference sources and effects from individual responses to entire repertoires or systems of responses. This view asserts that entire lists of responses, not individual stimulus-response items, are the primary foci of unlearning. It also is important to realize that this particular emphasis on entire systems of responses is not necessarily incompatible with previous interference theory notions dealing with individual responses and associations. It does not seem unlikely, for example, that response elicitation of some form may still be a necessary condition of unlearning and may determine its degree. It may well be that the selector mechanism functions only to the extent that inappropriate responses have been overtly or covertly emitted and then suppressed.

Spontaneous recovery of verbal learning. It is a fact that *RI* nearly always decreases and *PI* nearly always increases the longer the retention interval between *OL* and the recall test (see Keppel, 1968). In other words, relative to their control groups, the first-list or *OL* responses in an *RI* paradigm seem to get stronger the longer the time since the second (*IL*) list was learned. Similarly, in the *PI* paradigm, the first-list or *PL* responses seem to get stronger the longer the retention interval following the *OL*. This fact inspired the interpretation that spontaneous recovery of these unlearned, first-list responses was occurring the longer the interval (e.g., Underwood, 1948). However, because the potential influence of competition was not even partially divorced from that of unlearning until the study by Barnes and Underwood (1959), only studies subsequent to this one, employing something analogous to Barnes and Underwood's modified-modified free-recall technique, can really be said to study spontaneous recovery of unlearned responses and associations.

When proper tests for spontaneous recovery of verbal learning have been made, the results often have been discouraging for the Underwood-Postman theory. In fact, results of these tests taken as a whole have formed one of the two major factors contributing to extensive revisions in interference theory. The several studies that have or have not obtained absolute spontaneous recovery in long-term retention tests have been summarized elsewhere (see Keppel, 1968; Postman, Stark, & Fraser, 1968). The consequent status of spontaneous recovery may be aptly summarized with the statement by Postman et al. (1968), "It is clear that long-term spontaneous recovery is not a dependable phenomenon [p. 673]."

Postman et al. (1968) consistently were able to obtain absolute spontaneous recovery over short intervals (less than 60 min), and it is likely that this interval may be lengthened under certain conditions. The critical point is that long-term spontaneous recovery is not nearly as dependable and robust as the phenomena which it had been supposed to explain. These include, especially, changes in the effects of *RI* and *PI* over long retention intervals and the long-term forgetting attributable to extra-experimental sources of interference in the Underwood-Postman theory.

CONCEPTUAL MODIFICATIONS OF INTERFERENCE THEORY. Two generalizations have evolved empirically since 1960 which have caused theorists to rethink the basic tenets of Underwood and Postman (1960). We have just discussed one of these—the failure of spontaneous recovery of verbal learning to emerge as a phenomenon with sufficient robustness to account for the fundamental characteristics of *RI* and *PI*, particularly their changes over retention intervals. The second is the fact that meaningfulness—the central task variable supposed to determine the extent of extra-experimental interference by Underwood and Postman—has been found to have little, if any, influence on rate of simple forgetting. Most often it has had none, and in those cases where some effects have appeared, they have not seemed sufficiently large or consistent to account for all the forgetting which occurs. This has been true both in the case of unit-sequence interference (e.g., Postman, 1961) and in the case of letter-sequence interference (Underwood & Keppel, 1963b).

These events have produced a change in conceptual emphasis within interference theory rather than any substantial movement discarding interference in favor of some other source of forgetting. This seems appropriate in view of the overwhelming evidence that interfering habits acquired in the laboratory dramatically affect rates of forgetting. Also, it is entirely consistent with the reaction of scientists in general to breakdowns in theory (Kuhn, 1962). These modifications of interference theory may be categorized in terms of four "movements" which are neither mutually exclusive nor exhaustive. We shall discuss briefly how Underwood has reemphasized list differentiation, rather than spontaneous recovery and competition of individual items, as the primary source of *PI*. Postman has emphasized generalized competition as the basic mechanism in *RI*. On the other hand, Keppel has come to believe that events occurring during the retention interval are more important than previous events for determining forgetting, and Adams has argued for serious consideration of natural language mediators within the context of interference theory.

Before considering these ideas separately, it might be well to state explicitly the questions which elicited them. Underwood and Postman had delineated the kind of previously acquired, extra-experimental linguistic habits that might interfere with habits acquired in the laboratory, and the mechanisms by which these extra-experimental habits might cause the laboratory habits to be forgotten. From the long history of research on *RI* and *PI*, there could be no doubt that if the presumedly conflicting extra-experimental habits had been learned in the laboratory, they would have caused a great deal of forgetting. But these extra-experimental habits (letter-sequence and unit-sequence associations) did not, in fact, appear to affect forgetting of the laboratory habits. This raised the questions of why interfering linguistic habits acquired *outside* the laboratory do not interfere with retention of laboratory habits as much as those acquired *in* the laboratory and whether the primary source of extra-experimental habits interfering with subsequent retention really are those acquired *before* learning.

The role of list differentiation. Underwood and Ekstrand (1966) considered two potential reasons why previously acquired extra-experimental linguistic habits are less likely to influence forgetting than habits previously acquired in the laboratory. They tested the hypotheses that extra-experimental associations are more heavily overlearned or are acquired with longer intervals between learning "trials." They concluded, as noted above, that previously acquired habits were less likely to influence the forgetting of laboratory learning completed in one day if these habits had been learned under conditions of widely distributed practice. This implied that previously acquired extra-experimental associations have little effect on retention of laboratory learning because these tasks usually differ in distribution of practice. Degree of learning the previously acquired habits was relatively unimportant.

In the above section on *PI* and *RI* we discussed these results, along with those of Keppel (1964a), which also showed dramatically less forgetting of *OL* when the distribution of practice on the *OL* differed widely from that on *PL*. We also mentioned the Underwood and Freund (1968a) results, which indicated less forgetting from *PI* when prior learning and original learning were separated by several days. Each of these effects seems to implicate list differentiation. The more divergent the conditions under which *PL* and *OL* occur, the less the forgetting of *OL* due to *PL*, the reason being that *OL* and *PL* are better differentiated at recall. To the extent that this is so, we may expect previously acquired language habits to have little influence on forgetting of habits acquired in the laboratory even without differential distributions of practice, because these previously acquired language habits almost certainly were acquired under quite different conditions from those encountered in the laboratory. However, if the previously acquired learning also has occurred in laboratory situations, it may be expected to influence forgetting of laboratory associations a great deal (e.g., Underwood, 1957a). This kind of reasoning seems to exemplify Underwood's more recent views of forgetting due to previously acquired language habits (e.g., Underwood & Ekstrand, 1968b).

How, then, do we account for the 15 to 25 percent forgetting that does occur over 24 hr after learning of a single list in a laboratory? Underwood and Ekstrand (1968b) have suggested that it is due to interference, but not to interference involving individual items within the list in the sense of specific response competition. As alternatives they suggest generalized competition of the sort espoused by Postman (see below) or nonspecific sources of unlearning occurring during the retention interval suggested by Keppel (see below).

Finally, it is notable that Underwood (1969b) has restated his views on interference and retention within a broader conception of memory than before, and it seems safe to predict that these views will provide a stimulus for future research in this area.

Conservation versus interference mechanisms. Postman's major modifications of interference theory have taken two directions. The first, a relatively early response to the shortcomings of the Underwood-Postman theory, was a suggestion that the operations and effects of interference were correctly represented in the Underwood-Postman theory but were, in effect, masked by opposing "conservation mechanisms" which acted to deter forgetting (Postman, 1963). Among these mechanisms are S's reorganization and transformation of learned material, which might effectively change the meaningfulness of the learned materials and alter the ability of human Ss to keep interfering materials separate from those to be retained (via list differentiation, etc.). Postman (1963) also suggested an imbalance in the "associative paradox" favoring facilitation over interference (cf. Underwood & Schulz, 1960). The associative paradox is this: Interference theories generally predict that the more associations are attached to a stimulus, the more difficult it should be to acquire new associations to this stimulus and the greater its forgetting because of the higher probability of interference; but is also seems to be true that the more associates a stimulus has, the more efficiently it will enter into new associations. Postman (1963) suggested that in long-term retention of verbal units, those with the greater number of previously acquired associates receive greater gain than loss—the associates facilitate more than they interfere. Some subsequently published data cited by Postman (1963) and additional work (e.g., Postman, 1967b; Postman, Fraser, & Burns, 1968) generally have supported his interpretation of "conservation mechanisms."

Generalized competition. A second direction taken by Postman has included an intense pursuit of the nature of spontaneous recovery of verbal learning and a consequent modification of concepts underlying "unlearning." As with Underwood's list differentiation, Postman's revision de-emphasizes the role of individual stimulus and response items as the primary causes and victims of interference and accentuates the role of the entire list as a fundamental unit of interference.

His most extensive early statements with this emphasis occurred in two closely reasoned papers which overlap somewhat in content (Postman, 1967a; Postman et al., 1968). Postman rejects the view that RI is primarily due to experimental extinction of individual responses or of individual associations between stimuli and responses. Rather, the fundamental unit on which the mechanisms underlying RI operate is viewed as the entire repertoire of first-list responses in, say, an A-C, A-B paradigm. He suggests that when A-B is learned under these circumstances, the selector mechanism functions to exclude from S's immediate response repertoire all items (including those from A-C) except those in the A-B list. Thus excluded, items from the first list (A-C) are unavailable for immediate recall. This "set" to continue responding with the list most recently learned—generalized competition—has particular characteristics detailed by Postman et al. (1968, pp. 689–691).

Essentially, Postman's work suggests that "true" absolute spontaneous recovery of first-list items in, say, an A-C, A-B paradigm generally occurs over very short periods, less than 1 hr. A further suggestion of this work is that retention changes occurring over longer periods are due to mechanisms other than this sort of spontaneous recovery. Generally, changes in RI or changes in unlearning over intervals are due to the dissipation of generalized competition. In the case of PI, Postman believes the fundamental underlying mechanism is associated with "the simultaneous activation of two or more response systems at the time of the test [Postman, 1967a, p. 21]."

Generally, then, Postman has realigned the basis of interference theory. As Underwood, he has not "invented" entirely new concepts but has modified his use of previous ones. Perhaps Postman and Underwood's current view may be best expressed by this quote from Postman: "There are growing indications that the mechanisms of interference operate as much or more on repertoires or systems of responses as on specific stimulus-response associations [1967a, p. 22]."

In retrospect, data reported by Runquist (1957) forewarned of the apparently mistaken emphasis on the individual item within a list as the fundamental recipient of interference effects. He found that the amount of *RI* on each *OL* item could not be predicted in terms of the strength of the corresponding *IL* item which was, presumably, in direct competition with it. Similarly, the *PI* effect on individual *OL* items was uninfluenced by the strength of the corresponding *PL* items.

Further reconsiderations of interference theory. We shall consider two additional variations of interference theory which may contribute to a more satisfactory account of the facts. The first, like Underwood and Postman's, modifies certain extant interference-theory constructs and shifts their relative importance.

Keppel (1968) documents some inconsistencies between theory and data when previously acquired linguistic habits are assumed to produce interference in retention and cites the several failures to find absolute spontaneous recovery over long retention intervals. To reconcile these difficulties within the context of interference theory, Keppel (1968) suggests that the primary source of interference may be in the general linguistic activity occurring during the retention interval. Keppel views the specific nature of the interpolated linguistic activity as relatively unimportant. The basic mechanism of forgetting in Keppel's system is unlearning—unlearning of the list acquired in the laboratory and attributable to essentially *any kind* of linguistic activity which occurs during the retention interval. This nonspecific unlearning is analogous to that occurring in a *C-D*, *A-B* paradigm, which has been interpreted as unlearning of the association between the responses and the contextual stimuli. This implies, for example, that similarity of the context associated with original and interpolated learning may be even more important than similarity of materials themselves. Generally, Keppel's interesting theory seems to be consistent with available data (Keppel, Henschel, & Zavortink, 1969), and some extensions of these ideas have been empirically confirmed (Zavortink & Keppel, 1969).

Finally, it is of interest to note suggestions by Adams (1967) for revision of the Underwood-Postman theory, because these include concepts not previously associated with interference theory. Adams suggests that whenever *S* uses natural language mediators, the functional characteristics of the material to be retained are no longer consonant with the nominal characteristics. Therefore, Underwood and Postman's predictions in terms of nominal meaningfulness and accompanying susceptibility to extra-experimental interference become inappropriate. Adams apparently believes that the basic ideas of interference theory probably are sound but that they need to be expanded to incorporate the operation of natural language mediators. In passing, it may be noted that Adams's concern for natural language mediators in this respect is very similar to Postman's (1963) suggestions that organizational and mediational devices employed by *S* may have conservation effects on retention, thus masking otherwise predicted interference effects.

SUMMARY.   The first conceptualization of the role of interference in forgetting focused upon individual items within a list. Presumably, retroactive interference was due primarily to the unlearning of individual responses and associations from the first list, perhaps determined by the number of unreinforced elicitations of first-list items during second-list learning. Proactive interference was thought to be due to competition among individual response items occurring upon spontaneous recovery of previously unlearned (e.g., first-list) responses, and extra-experimental interference was primarily proactive and dependent upon meaningfulness. Subsequently long-term spontaneous recovery of verbal learning, and the supposed dependence of simple forgetting upon meaningfulness, were found to be weak and unreliable phenomena of limited generality. Modifications of interference theory have emphasized entire lists or repertoires of verbal units as the vehicles and victims of interference, with generalized competition and list differentiation viewed as the basic mechanisms underlying retroactive and proactive interference, respectively.

SUMMARY

This chapter has covered several aspects of verbal learning and retention broadly, rather than fewer aspects in depth. Obviously severe selectivity still was in order, a task made particularly difficult by the huge and growing literature. As is true of many other areas of experimental psychology, the number of published studies devoted to verbal learning and retention has shown an enormous increase during the past 15 years or so. It cannot be denied that this is partially attributable to an elementary fact of research difficulty: it is easier to *conduct* verbal learning experiments than many other kinds of experimental research, even restricting consideration to *significant* experiments. This does not imply that it is easier to *conceptualize* and *design* a significant verbal learning experiment; indeed, there is reason to believe this task is more difficult than in many other areas.

The actual selections of reference experiments and other papers may appear insular. However, although a large number of truly important works probably have not been cited, it seems difficult to deny that of the many scientists concerned with this area, there are a few to whom one continually returns for significant ideas and data. This should come as no surprise, and it is generally true of other areas of psychology and other sciences as well.

1. In what ways might characteristics attributed to subjects in a verbal learning task (e.g., college students) influence the design and procedure of related experiments?

2. Describe a nonsense syllable, including an assessment of its earliest and present uses in verbal learning research.

3. What are the characteristics and major uses of free-recall, serial, and paired-associate learning tasks? Describe their relative advantages and disadvantages.

4. Variation in method of presenting paired associates has not seemed to have as much influence on learning rates as variations in the specific verbal materials involved. Upon what sort of evidence is this conclusion based?

5. Describe some of the ways in which paired-associate verbal learning has been conceptualized, and evaluate these conceptualizations in light of their contribution to the understanding of learning in general and verbal learning in particular.

6. Describe some aspects of method and procedure in verbal learning research that have been dictated by general characteristics of the memory system.

7. Discuss the concept and measurement of meaningfulness, along with a description of its effect on learning rate.

8. What is the relationship between intralist similarity and rate of verbal learning?

9. On what grounds might one account for the influence of motivation on verbal learning?

10. What are some characteristics of the concept "association" in terms of its contemporary use in verbal learning?

11. What sorts of criticisms have been made of the use of the concept "association" in verbal learning?

12. Describe four or five reliable characteristics of free-recall behavior with and without high conceptual similarity.

13. Contrast the theoretical positions of Tulving and Wood and Underwood concerning the role of conceptual similarity in free recall.

14. Describe the conditions under which transformations of verbal materials facilitate, retard, or have no effect on rate of learning.

15. Why might subjects employ transformations, even though they do not facilitate learning?

16. List the advantages and disadvantages associated with the use of extra-item transformations, such as the "peg-word" technique, for learning and retention of verbal materials.

17. What kinds of factors are involved in nonspecific transfer? How may these factors be controlled in order to evaluate the role of specific transfer?

18. (a) Compare the relative effectiveness of transfer to an A-B list from a list of the form A-C with that found in transfer from a list of the form A-B'.

(b) Describe some of the tests that have been made to identify the processes which underlie the transfer differences obtained under these two circumstances.

19. What is the role of mediation in verbal learning, and what sorts of conditions modify its effectiveness?

20. Describe some difficulties encountered in designing experiments to answer the question, Do natural language mediators facilitate learning? Include a description of the sorts of evidence presently available.

21. On what bases have theorists distinguished between short-term memory and long-term memory? Include a description of methodological and functional distinctions.

22. Describe some instances in which conclusions about the effects of an independent variable on forgetting may be confounded by unintentional differences in degree of learning.

23. Contrast the variables which importantly influence rate of learning with those that influence rate of forgetting.

24. Compare proactive interference with retroactive interference, both operationally and in terms of their distinctive functional characteristics.

25. Cite evidence concerning the role of proactive interference and retroactive interference in short-term memory experiments and corresponding evidence in long-term memory experiments. What sort of variables may modify the influence of proactive and retroactive interference?

26. What was the major contribution of the paper by Underwood (1957a) entitled, "Interference and forgetting"?

27. Describe the primary components of the Underwood-Postman (1960) theory of forgetting. Cite subsequent evidence relevant to an evaluation of the theory.

28. Describe the conceptual changes in interference theory since the Underwood-Postman paper, including the empirical bases of these modifications.

REFERENCES

* Entries ending with an asterisk were not yet published at the time this book went to press.

Adams, J. A. *Human memory*. New York: McGraw-Hill, 1967.

Adams, J. A., & Montague, W. E. Retroactive inhibition and natural language mediation. *Journal of Verbal Learning and Verbal Behavior*, 1967, **6**, 528–535.

Amsel, A. Frustrative nonreward in partial reinforcement and discrimination learning: Some recent history and a theoretical extension. *Psychological Review*, 1962, **69**, 306–328.

Amsel, A. Partial reinforcement effects on vigor and persistence. In K. W. Spence & J. T. Spence (Eds.), *The psychology of learning and motivation. Vol. I.* New York: Academic, 1967. Pp. 1–65.

Amsel, A., & Roussel, J. Motivational properties of frustration: 1. Effect on a running response of the addition of frustration to the motivational complex. *Journal of Experimental Psychology*, 1952, **43**, 363–368.

Anant, S. S. Verbal aversion therapy with a promiscuous girl: Case report. *Psychological Reports*, 1968, **22**, 795–796.

Anderson, D. C., Cole, J., & McVaugh, W. Variations in unsignaled inescapable preshock as determinants of responses to punishment. *Journal of Comparative and Physiological Psychology Monograph Supplement*, 1968, **65** (3, Pt. 2).

Anderson, N. H. Comparison of different populations: Resistance to extinction and transfer. *Psychological Review*, 1963, **70**, 162–179.

Anger, D. The role of temporal discriminations in the reinforcement of Sidman avoidance behavior. *Journal of the Experimental Analysis of Behavior*, 1963, **6**, 477–506.

Appel, J. B. Punishment in the squirrel monkey *Saimiri sciurea*. *Science*, 1961, **133**, 36.

Appel, J. B., & Peterson, N. J. Punishment: Effects of shock intensity on response suppression. *Psychological Reports*, 1965, **16**, 721–730.

Archer, E. J. A re-evaluation of the meaningfulness of all possible CVC trigrams. *Psychological Monographs*, 1960, **74** (10, Whole No. 497).

Armus, H. L. Effect of magnitude of reinforcement on acquisition and extinction of a running response. *Journal of Experimental Psychology*, 1959, **58**, 61–63.

Asch, S. E. The doctrinal tyranny of associationism: Or what is wrong with rote learning. In T. R. Dixon & D. L. Horton (Eds.), *Verbal behavior and general behavior theory*. Englewood Cliffs, N.J.: Prentice-Hall, 1968. Pp. 214–228.

Asch, S. E., & Ebenholtz, S. M. The principle of associative symmetry. *Proceedings of the American Philosophical Society*, 1962, **106**, 135–163. (a)

Asch, S. E., & Ebenholtz, S. M. The process of free recall: Evidence for nonassociative factors for acquisition and retention. *Journal of Psychology*, 1962, **54**, 3–31. (b)

Atkinson, R. C. Computerized instruction and the learning process. *American Psychologist*, 1968, **23**, 225–239.

Atkinson, R. C., & Crothers, E. J. A comparison of paired-associate learning models having different acquisition and retention axioms. *Journal of Mathematical Psychology*, 1964, **1**, 285–315.

Atkinson, R. C., Bower, G. H., & Crothers, E. J. *An introduction to mathematical learning theory*. New York: Wiley, 1965.

Avery, G. C., & Day, R. H. Basis of the horizontal-vertical illusion. *Journal of Experimental Psychology*, 1969, **81**, 376–380.

Ayllon, T., & Azrin, N. *The token economy*. New York: Appleton-Century-Crofts, 1968.

Ayllon, T., & Haughton, E. Control of the behavior of schizophrenic patients by food. *Journal of the Experimental Analysis of Behavior*, 1962, **5**, 343–352.

Azrin, N. H. A technique for delivering shock to pigeons. *Journal of the Experimental Analysis of Behavior*, 1959, **2**, 161–163.

Azrin, N. H. Effects of punishment intensity during variable-interval reinforcement. *Journal of the Experimental Analysis of Behavior*, 1960, **3**, 123–142. (a)

Azrin, N. H. Sequential effects of punishment. *Science*, 1960, **131**, 605–606. (b)

Azrin, N. H., & Holz, W. C. Punishment. In W. K. Honig (Ed.), *Operant behavior: Areas of research and application*. New York: Appleton-Century-Crofts, 1966. Pp. 380–447.

Azrin, N. H., Hutchinson, R. R., & Hake, D. F. Extinction-induced aggression. *Journal of the Experimental Analysis of Behavior*, 1966, **9**, 191–204.

Azrin, N. H., Rubin, H. B., & Hutchinson, R. R. Biting attack by rats in response to aversive shock. *Journal of the Experimental Analysis of Behavior*, 1968, **11**, 633–639.

Badia, P. Effects of drive, reinforcement schedule, and change of schedule on performance. *Journal of Experimental Psychology*, 1965, **69**, 292–297.

Badia, P., McBane, B., Suter, S., & Lewis, P. Preference behavior in an immediate versus variably delayed shock situation with and without a warning signal. *Journal of Experimental Psychology*, 1966, **72**, 847–852.

Badia, P., Suter, S., & Lewis, P. Preference for warned shock: Information and/or preparation. *Psychological Reports*, 1967, **20**, 271–274.

Baer, D. M. Laboratory control of thumbsucking by withdrawal and representation of reinforcement. *Journal of the Experimental Analysis of Behavior*, 1962, **5**, 525–528.

Baker, K. E., & Dudek, F. J. Weight scales from ratio judgments and comparisons of existent weight scales. *Journal of Experimental Psychology*, 1955, **50**, 293–308.

Bandura, A. Psychotherapy as a learning process. *Psychological Bulletin*, 1961, **58**, 143–159.

Banks, R. K., & Vogel-Sprott, M. Effect of delayed punishment on an immediately rewarded response in humans. *Journal of Experimental Psychology*, 1965, **70**, 357–359.

Barnes, J. M., & Underwood, B. J. "Fate" of first-list associations in transfer theory. *Journal of Experimental Psychology*, 1959, **58**, 97–105.

Baron, A. Delayed punishment of a runway response. *Journal of Comparative and Physiological Psychology*, 1965, **60**, 131–134.

Baron, M. R. The stimulus, stimulus control, and stimulus generalization. In D. I. Mostofsky (Ed.), *Stimulus generalization*. Stanford: Stanford University Press, 1965. Pp. 62–71.

Barry, H., III. Effects of drive strength on extinction and spontaneous recovery. *Journal of Experimental Psychology*, 1967, **73**, 419–421.

Barry, H., III, & Miller, N. E. Effects of drugs on approach-avoidance conflict tested repeatedly by means of a "telescope alley." *Journal of Comparative and Physiological Psychology*, 1962, **55**, 201–210.

Barry, H., III, Wagner, A. R., & Miller, N. E. Effects of alcohol and amobarbital on performance inhibited by experimental extinction. *Journal of Comparative and Physiological Psychology*, 1962, **55**, 464–468.

Bastian, J. Associative factors in verbal transfer. *Journal of Experimental Psychology*, 1961, **62**, 70–79.

Battig, W. F. Paired-associate learning. In T. R. Dixon & D. L. Horton (Eds.), *Verbal behavior and general behavior theory*. Englewood Cliffs, N.J.: Prentice-Hall, 1968. Pp. 149–171.

Battig, W. F., & Spera, A. J. Rated association values of numbers from 0–100. *Journal of Verbal Learning and Verbal Behavior*, 1962, **1**, 200–202.

Battig, W. F., Brown, S. C., & Nelson, D. Constant vs. varied serial order in paired-associate learning. *Psychological Reports*, 1963, **12**, 695–721.

Beck, J., & Shaw, W. A. Ratio-estimations of loudness-intervals. *American Journal of Psychology*, 1967, **80**, 59–65.

Beecroft, R. S. Verbal learning and retention as a function of the number of competing associations. *Journal of Experimental Psychology*, 1956, **51**, 216–221.

Beecroft, R. S. *Classical conditioning*. Goleta, Cal.: Psychonomic Press, 1966.

Bennett, T. L., & Ellis, H. C. Tactual-kinesthetic feedback from manipulation of visual forms and nondifferential reinforcement in transfer of perceptual learning. *Journal of Experimental Psychology*, 1968, **77**, 495–500.

Berlyne, D. E. Curiosity and exploration. *Science*, 1966, **153**, 25–33.

Berlyne, D. E. Attention as a problem in behavior theory. In D. I. Mostofsky (Ed.), *Attention: Contemporary theory and analysis*. New York: Appleton-Century-Crofts, 1970.*

Bernbach, H. A. Decision processes in memory. *Psychological Review*, 1967, **74,** 462–480.

Bevan, W. The contextual basis of behavior. *American Psychologist*, 1968, **23,** 701–714.

Birch, D., Allison, J. K., & House, R. F. Extinction performance following discrimination training. *Journal of Experimental Psychology*, 1963, **65,** 148–155.

Bitterman, M. E. Techniques for the study of learning in animals: Analysis and classification. *Psychological Bulletin*, 1962, **59,** 81–93.

Black, R. W. On the combination of drive and incentive motivation. *Psychological Review*, 1965, **72,** 310–317.

Black, R. W. Shifts in magnitude of reward and contrast effects in instrumental and selective learning: A reinterpretation. *Psychological Review*, 1968, **75,** 114–126.

Blankenship, A. B. Memory span: A review of the literature. *Psychological Bulletin*, 1938, **35,** 1–25.

Bloomfield, T. M. A peak shift on a line-tilt continuum. *Journal of the Experimental Analysis of Behavior*, 1967, **10,** 361–366.

Blough, D. S. A method for obtaining psychophysical thresholds from the pigeon. *Journal of the Experimental Analysis of Behavior*, 1958, **1,** 31–43.

Blough, D. S. Generalization and preference on a stimulus-intensity continuum. *Journal of the Experimental Analysis of Behavior*, 1959, **2,** 307–317.

Blough, D. S. The reinforcement of least-frequent interresponse times. *Journal of the Experimental Analysis of Behavior*, 1966, **9,** 581–591. (a)

Blough, D. S. The study of animal sensory processes by operant methods. In W. K. Honig (Ed.), *Operant behavior: Areas of research and application*. New York: Appleton-Century-Crofts, 1966. Pp. 345–379. (b)

Blough, D. S. Stimulus generalization as signal detection in pigeons. *Science*, 1967, **158,** 940–941.

Blough, D. S. Generalization gradient shape and summation in steady-state tests. *Journal of the Experimental Analysis of Behavior*, 1969, **12,** 91–104.

Boe, E. E. Bibliography on punishment. In B. A. Campbell & R. M. Church (Eds.), *Punishment and aversive behavior*. New York: Appleton-Century-Crofts, 1969. Pp. 531–587.

Boe, E. E., & Church, R. M. Permanent effects of punishment during extinction. *Journal of Comparative and Physiological Psychology*, 1967, **63,** 486–492.

Bolles, R. C. Species-specific defense reactions. In F. R. Brush (Ed.), *Aversive conditioning and learning*. New York: Academic, 1970.*

Bolles, R. C., & Grossen, N. E. Effects of an informational stimulus on the acquisition of avoidance behavior in rats. *Journal of Comparative and Physiological Psychology*, 1969, **68,** 90–99.

Bolles, R. C., & Warren, J. A., Jr. The acquisition of bar press avoidance as a function of shock intensity. *Psychonomic Science*, 1965, **3,** 297–298.

Bolles, R. C., Stokes, L. W., & Younger, M. S. Does CS termination reinforce avoidance behavior? *Journal of Comparative and Physiological Psychology*, 1966, **62,** 201–207.

Boneau, C. A., & Cole, J. L. Decision theory, the pigeon, and the psychophysical function. *Psychological Review*, 1967, **74,** 123–135.

Boren, J. J. The study of drugs with operant techniques. In W. K. Honig (Ed.), *Operant behavior: Areas of research and application*. New York: Appleton-Century-Crofts, 1966. Pp. 531–564.

Boren, J. J., Sidman, M., & Herrnstein, R. J. Avoidance, escape, and extinction as functions of shock intensity. *Journal of Comparative and Physiological Psychology*, 1959, **52**, 420–425.

Boring, E. G. *Sensation and perception in the history of experimental psychology*. New York: Appleton-Century-Crofts, 1942.

Boring, E. G. *A history of experimental psychology*. (2d ed.) New York: Appleton-Century-Crofts, 1950.

Boring, E. G. The nature and history of experimental control. *American Journal of Psychology*, 1954, **67**, 573–589.

Born, D. G. Resistance of a free operant to extinction and suppression with punishment as a function of amount of training. *Psychonomic Science*, 1967, **8**, 21–22.

Bourne, L. E., Jr., & Haygood, R. C. The role of stimulus redundancy in concept identification. *Journal of Experimental Psychology*, 1959, **58**, 232–238.

Bousfield, W. A., Whitmarsh, G. A., & Danick, J. J. Partial response identities in verbal generalization. *Psychological Reports*, 1958, **4**, 703–713.

Bower, G. H. Partial and correlated reward in escape learning. *Journal of Experimental Psychology*, 1960, **59**, 126–130.

Bower, G. H. A contrast effect in differential conditioning. *Journal of Experimental Psychology*, 1961, **62**, 196–199.

Bower, G. H. The influence of graded reductions in reward and prior frustrating events upon the magnitude of the frustration effect. *Journal of Comparative and Physiological Psychology*, 1962, **55**, 582–587.

Bower, G., & Grusec, T. Effect of prior Pavlovian discrimination training upon learning an operant discrimination. *Journal of the Experimental Analysis of Behavior*, 1964, **7**, 401–404.

Bower, G. H., & Trapold, M. A. Reward magnitude and learning in a single-presentation discrimination. *Journal of Comparative and Physiological Psychology*, 1959, **52**, 727–729.

Bower, G. H., Fowler, H., & Trapold, M. A. Escape learning as a function of amount of shock reduction. *Journal of Experimental Psychology*, 1959, **58**, 482–484.

Bower, G., McLean, J., & Meacham, J. Value of knowing when reinforcement is due. *Journal of Comparative and Physiological Psychology*, 1966, **62**, 184–192.

Bower, G., Starr, R., & Lazarovitz, L. Amount of response-produced change in the CS and avoidance learning. *Journal of Comparative and Physiological Psychology*, 1965, **59**, 13–17.

Breger, L., & McGaugh, J. L. Critique and reformulation of "learning-theory" approaches to psychotherapy and neurosis. *Psychological Bulletin*, 1965, **63**, 338–358.

Briggs, G. E. Retroactive inhibition as a function of the degree of original and interpolated learning. *Journal of Experimental Psychology*, 1957, **53**, 60–67.

Broadbent, D. E. A mechanical model for human attention and immediate memory. *Psychological Review*, 1957, **64**, 205–215.

Broadbent, D. E. *Perception and communication*. New York: Pergamon, 1958.

Broadbent, D. E., & Gregory, M. Division of attention and the decision theory of signal detection. *Proceedings of the Royal Society B*, 1963, **158**, 222–231.

Brody, S. *Bioenergetics and growth*. New York: Reinhold, 1945.

Broen, W. E., Jr., Storms, L. H., & Goldberg, D. H. Decreased discrimination as a function of increased drive. *Journal of Abnormal and Social Psychology*, 1963, **67,** 266–273.

Brookshire, K. H., Warren, J. M., & Ball, G. G. Reversal and transfer learning following overtraining in rat and chicken. *Journal of Comparative and Physiological Psychology*, 1961, **54,** 98–102.

Brown, J. Some tests of the decay theory of immediate memory. *Quarterly Journal of Experimental Psychology*, 1958, **10,** 12–21.

Brown, J. S. Generalization and discrimination. In D. I. Mostofsky (Ed.), *Stimulus generalization*. Stanford: Stanford University Press, 1965. Pp. 7–23.

Brown, J. S. Factors affecting self-punitive locomotor behavior. In B. A. Campbell & R. M. Church (Eds.), *Punishment and aversive behavior*. New York: Appleton-Century-Crofts, 1969. Pp. 467–514.

Brown, J. S., Martin, R. C., & Morrow, M. W. Self-punitive behavior in the rat: Facilitative effects of punishment on resistance to extinction. *Journal of Comparative and Physiological Psychology*, 1964, **57,** 127–133.

Brown, R. T., & Logan, F. A. Generalized partial reinforcement effect. *Journal of Comparative and Physiological Psychology*, 1965, **60,** 64–69.

Brown, R. T., & Wagner, A. R. Resistance to punishment and extinction following training with shock or nonreinforcement. *Journal of Experimental Psychology*, 1964, **68,** 503–507.

Bruce, D., & Murdock, B. B., Jr. Acoustic similarity effects on memory for paired associates. *Journal of Verbal Learning and Verbal Behavior*, 1968, **7,** 627–631.

Bruce, R. W. Conditions of transfer of training. *Journal of Experimental Psychology*, 1933, **16,** 343–361.

Bruning, J. L. Effects of magnitude of reward and percentage of reinforcement on a lever movement response. *Child Development*, 1964, **35,** 281–285.

Brush, F. R. The effects of shock intensity on the acquisition and extinction of an avoidance response in dogs. *Journal of Comparative and Physiological Psychology*, 1957, **50,** 547–552.

Brush, F. R. (Ed.) *Aversive conditioning and learning*. New York: Academic, 1970.*

Brush, F. R., Brush, E. S., & Solomon, R. L. Traumatic avoidance learning: The effects of CS–US interval with a delayed-conditioning procedure. *Journal of Comparative and Physiological Psychology*, 1955, **48,** 285–293.

Brush, F. R., Bush, R. R., Jenkins, W. O., John, W. F., & Whiting, J. W. M. Stimulus generalization after extinction and punishment: An experimental study of displacement. *Journal of Abnormal and Social Psychology*, 1952, **47,** 633–640.

Bugelski, B. R. Presentation time, total time, and mediation in paired-associate learning. *Journal of Experimental Psychology*, 1962, **63,** 409–412.

Bugelski, B. R. Images as mediators in one-trial paired-associate learning. II: Self-timing in successive lists. *Journal of Experimental Psychology*, 1968, **77,** 328–334.

Bugelski, B. R., Kidd, E., & Segmen, J. Image as a mediator in one-trial paired-associate learning. *Journal of Experimental Psychology*, 1968, **76,** 69–73.

Bull, J. A., III, & Overmier, J. B. Additive and subtractive properties of excitation and inhibition. *Journal of Comparative and Physiological Psychology*, 1968, **66,** 511–514.

Burstein, K. R., Epstein, S., & Smith, B. Primary stimulus generalization of the GSR as a function of objective and subjective definition of the stimulus dimension. *Journal of Experimental Psychology*, 1967, **74,** 124–131.

Bush, R. R., & Mosteller, F. *Stochastic models for learning.* New York: Wiley, 1955.

Camp, D. S., Raymond, G. A., & Church, R. M. Response suppression as a function of the schedule of punishment. *Psychonomic Science,* 1966, **5,** 23–24.

Camp, D. S., Raymond, G. A., & Church, R. M. Temporal relationship between response and punishment. *Journal of Experimental Psychology,* 1967, **74,** 114–123.

Camp, W., Martin, R., & Chapman, L. F. Pain threshold and discrimination of pain intensity during brief exposure to intense noise. *Science,* 1962, **135,** 788–789.

Campbell, B. A., & Church, R. M. (Eds.) *Punishment and aversive behavior.* New York: Appleton-Century-Crofts, 1969.

Campbell, B. A., & Kraeling, D. Response strength as a function of drive level and amount of drive reduction. *Journal of Experimental Psychology,* 1953, **45,** 97–101.

Campbell, B. A., & Teghtsoonian, R. Electrical and behavioral effects of different types of shock stimuli on the rat. *Journal of Comparative and Physiological Psychology,* 1958, **51,** 185–192.

Campbell, S. L. Resistance to extinction as a function of number of shock-termination reinforcements. *Journal of Comparative and Physiological Psychology,* 1959, **52,** 754–758.

Capaldi, E. J. Partial reinforcement: A hypothesis of sequential effects. *Psychological Review,* 1966, **73,** 459–477.

Capaldi, E. J., & Bowen, J. N. Delay of reward and goal box confinement time in extinction. *Psychonomic Science,* 1964, **1,** 141–142.

Capaldi, E. J., & Lynch, D. Repeated shifts in reward magnitude: Evidence in favor of an associational and absolute (noncontextual) interpretation. *Journal of Experimental Psychology,* 1967, **75,** 226–235.

Carlin, S., Ward, W. D., Gershon, A., & Ingraham, R. Sound stimulation and its effect on dental sensation threshold. *Science,* 1962, **138,** 1258–1259.

Carterette, T. S. An application of stimulus sampling theory to summated generalization. *Journal of Experimental Psychology,* 1961, **62,** 448–455.

Catania, A. C. Concurrent operants. In W. K. Honig (Ed.), *Operant behavior: Areas of research and application.* New York: Appleton-Century-Crofts, 1966. Pp. 213–270.

Catania, A. C. (Ed.) *Contemporary research in operant behavior.* Glenview, Ill.: Scott, Foresman, 1968.

Catania, A. C., & Reynolds, G. S. A quantitative analysis of the responding maintained by interval schedules of reinforcement. *Journal of the Experimental Analysis of Behavior,* 1968, **11,** 327–383.

Champion, R. A., & Smith, L. R. Predicting discrimination learning from differential conditioning with amount of reinforcement as a variable. *Journal of Experimental Psychology,* 1966, **71,** 529–534.

Cherry, E. C. Some experiments on the recognition of speech, with one and with two ears. *Journal of the Acoustical Society of America,* 1953, **25,** 975–979.

Church, R. M. The varied effects of punishment on behavior. *Psychological Review,* 1963, **70,** 369–402.

Church, R. M. Systematic effect of random error in the yoked control design. *Psychological Bulletin,* 1964, **62,** 122–131.

Church, R. M. Response suppression. In B. A. Campbell & R. M. Church (Eds.), *Punishment and aversive behavior.* New York: Appleton-Century-Crofts, 1969. Pp. 111–156.

Cieutat, V. J., Stockwell, F. E., & Noble, C. E. The interaction of ability and amount of practice with stimulus and response meaningfulness (m, m') in paired-associate learning. *Journal of Experimental Psychology*, 1958, **56**, 193–202.

Clifford T. Extinction following continuous reward and latent extinction. *Journal of Experimental Psychology*, 1964, **68**, 456–465.

Coate, W. B. Effect of deprivation on postdiscrimination stimulus generalization in the rat. *Journal of Comparative and Physiological Psychology*, 1964, **57**, 134–138.

Cofer, C. N. On some factors in the organizational characteristics of free recall. *American Psychologist*, 1965, **20**, 261–272.

Cofer, C. N., & Foley, J. P., Jr. Mediated generalization and the interpretation of verbal behavior: I. Prolegomena. *Psychological Review*, 1942, **49**, 513–540.

Cole, M., Gay, J., & Glick, J. Reversal and nonreversal shifts among Liberian tribal people. *Journal of Experimental Psychology*, 1968, **76**, 323–324.

Collins, J., & D'Amato, M. R. Magnesium pemoline: Effects on avoidance conditioning mediated by anticipatory responses. *Psychonomic Science*, 1968, **12**, 115–116.

Conrad, R. Serial order intrusions in immediate memory. *British Journal of Psychology*, 1960, **51**, 45–48.

Conrad, R. Interference or decay over short retention intervals? *Journal of Verbal Learning and Verbal Behavior*, 1967, **6**, 49–54.

Conrad, R., & Hille, B. A. The decay theory of immediate memory and paced recall. *Canadian Journal of Psychology*, 1958, **12**, 1–6.

Cook, J. O., & Barnes, L. W., Jr. Choice of delay of inevitable shock. *Journal of Abnormal and Social Psychology*, 1964, **68**, 669–672.

Cook, J. O., & Spitzer, M. E. Supplementary report: Prompting versus confirmation in paired-associate learning. *Journal of Experimental Psychology*, 1960, **59**, 275–276.

Cooper, E. H., & Pantle, A. J. The total-time hypothesis in verbal learning. *Psychological Bulletin*, 1967, **68**, 221–234.

Cornsweet, T. N. The staircase-method in psychophysics. *American Journal of Psychology*, 1962, **75**, 485–491.

Cornsweet, T. N. *The design of electrical circuits in the behavioral sciences*. New York: Wiley, 1963.

Cornsweet, T. N., & Pinsker, H. M. Luminance discrimination of brief flashes under various conditions of adaption. *Journal of Physiology*, 1965, **176**, 294–310.

Corso, J. F. A theoretico-historical review of the threshold concept. *Psychological Bulletin*, 1963, **60**, 356–370.

Couch, J. V., & Stanley, L. R. Consistent delay of reward vs consistent nonreward in the alley. *Psychonomic Science*, 1967, **9**, 497–498.

Cowey, A., & Ellis, C. M. Visual acuity of rhesus and squirrel monkeys. *Journal of Comparative and Physiological Psychology*, 1967, **64**, 80–84.

Crane, N. L., & Ross, L. E. A developmental study of attention to cue redundancy introduced following discrimination learning. *Journal of Experimental Child Psychology*, 1967, **5**, 1–15.

Cronbach, L. J. The two disciplines of scientific psychology. *American Psychologist*, 1957, **12**, 671–684.

Cross, H. A., & Boyer, W. N. Influence of overlearning on single habit reversal in naive rhesus monkeys. *Psychonomic Science*, 1966, **4**, 245–246.

Crowder, R. G. The relation between interpolated-task performance and proactive inhibition in short-term retention. *Journal of Verbal Learning and Verbal Behavior*, 1968, **7**, 577–583.

Cumming, W. W. A bird's eye glimpse of men and machines. In R. Ulrich, T. Stachnik, & J. Mabry (Eds.), *Control of human behavior*. Glenview, Ill.: Scott, Foresman, 1966. Pp. 246–256.

D'Amato, M. R. Secondary reinforcement and magnitude of primary reinforcement. *Journal of Comparative and Physiological Psychology*, 1955, **48**, 378–380.

D'Amato, M. R. Direct programming of multiple stimuli—the tape block reader. *Journal of the Experimental Analysis of Behavior*, 1965, **8**, 230. (a)

D'Amato, M. R. The overlearning reversal effect in monkeys provided a salient irrelevant dimension. *Psychonomic Science*, 1965, **3**, 21–22. (b)

D'Amato, M. R., & Fazzaro, J. Discriminated lever-press avoidance learning as a function of type and intensity of shock. *Journal of Comparative and Physiological Psychology*, 1966, **61**, 313–315. (a)

D'Amato, M. R., & Fazzaro, J. Attention and cue-producing behavior in the monkey. *Journal of the Experimental Analysis of Behavior*, 1966, **9**, 469–473. (b)

D'Amato, M. R., & Gumenik, W. E. Some effects of immediate versus randomly delayed shock on an instrumental response and cognitive processes. *Journal of Abnormal and Social Psychology*, 1960, **60**, 64–67.

D'Amato, M. R., & Jagoda, H. Age, sex, and rearing conditions as variables in simple brightness discrimination. *Journal of Comparative and Physiological Psychology*, 1960, **53**, 261–263.

D'Amato, M. R., & Schiff, D. Long-term discriminated avoidance performance in the rat. *Journal of Comparative and Physiological Psychology*, 1964, **57**, 123–126.

D'Amato, M. R., & Schiff, D. Overlearning and brightness discrimination reversal. *Journal of Experimental Psychology*, 1965, **69**, 375–381.

D'Amato, M. R., Etkin, M., & Fazzaro, J. Cue-producing behavior in the Capuchin monkey during reversal, extinction, acquisition, and overtraining. *Journal of the Experimental Analysis of Behavior*, 1968, **11**, 425–433.

D'Amato, M. R., Fazzaro, J., & Etkin, M. Discriminated bar-press avoidance maintenance and extinction in rats as a function of shock intensity. *Journal of Comparative and Physiological Psychology*, 1967, **63**, 351–354.

D'Amato, M. R., Fazzaro, J., & Etkin, M. Anticipatory responding and avoidance discrimination as factors in avoidance conditioning. *Journal of Experimental Psychology*, 1968, **77**, 41–47.

D'Amato, M. R., Keller, D., & Biederman, G. Discriminated avoidance learning as a function of parameters of discontinuous shock. *Journal of Experimental Psychology*, 1965, **70**, 543–548.

D'Amato, M. R., Lachman, R., & Kivy, P. Secondary reinforcement as affected by reward schedule and the testing situation. *Journal of Comparative and Physiological Psychology*, 1958, **51**, 737–741.

D'Amato, M. R., Schiff, D., & Jagoda, H. Resistance to extinction after varying amounts of discriminative or nondiscriminative instrumental training. *Journal of Experimental Psychology*, 1962, **64**, 526–532.

Davenport, J. W. Choice behavior as a function of drive strength and rate of learning. Unpublished Ph.D. dissertation, State University of Iowa, 1956.

Davenport, J. W., & Hagquist, W. W. Intermixture of positive and negative trials in instrumental discrimination. *Psychonomic Science*, 1968, **10**, 173–174.

Davis, S. F., & North, A. J. The effect of number of large reward training trials on behavior following incentive reduction. *Psychonomic Science*, 1968, **11**, 311–312.

Davis, W. L., Brown, S. C., & Ritchie, E. Cue selection as a function of degree of learning and response similarity. *Journal of Experimental Psychology*, 1968, **78,** 323–328.

Deese, J. From the isolated verbal unit to connected discourse. In C. N. Cofer (Ed.), *Verbal learning and verbal behavior.* New York: McGraw-Hill, 1961. Pp. 11–38.

Deese, J. Association and memory. In T. R. Dixon & D. L. Horton (Eds.), *Verbal behavior and general behavior theory.* Englewood Cliffs, N.J.: Prentice-Hall, 1968. Pp. 97–108.

Deutsch, J. Discrimination learning and inhibition. *Science*, 1967, **156,** 988.

Deutsch, J. A., & Deutsch, D. Attention: Some theoretical considerations. *Psychological Review*, 1963, **70,** 80–90.

Deutsch, J. A., Deutsch, D., Lindsay, P. H., & Treisman, A. M. Comments and reply: "Selective attention: Perception or response?" *Quarterly Journal of Experimental Psychology*, 1967, **19,** 362–367.

Dews, P. B. The effect of multiple S^Δ periods on responding on a fixed-interval schedule: V. Effect of periods of complete darkness and of occasional omissions of food presentations. *Journal of the Experimental Analysis of Behavior*, 1966, **9,** 573–578.

Dews, P. B. The theory of fixed-interval responding. In W. N. Schoenfeld (Ed.), *Theory of reinforcement schedules.* New York: Appleton-Century-Crofts, 1970.*

DiCara, L. V., & Miller, N. E. Changes in heart rate instrumentally learned by curarized rats as avoidance responses. *Journal of Comparative and Physiological Psychology*, 1968, **65,** 8–12.

DiLollo, V. Runway performance in relation to runway-goal-box similarity and changes in incentive amount. *Journal of Comparative and Physiological Psychology*, 1964, **58,** 327–329.

Dinsmoor, J. A. The effect of hunger on discriminated responding. *Journal of Abnormal and Social Psychology*, 1952, **47,** 67–72.

Doll, T. J., & Thomas, D. R. Effects of discrimination training on stimulus generalization for human subjects. *Journal of Experimental Psychology*, 1967, **75,** 508–512.

Dollard, J., & Miller, N. E. *Personality and psychotherapy.* New York: McGraw-Hill, 1950.

Donnelly, M. B., & Rimoldi, H. J. A. Experimental considerations concerning category and magnitude scaling. *American Journal of Psychology*, 1967, **80,** 602–607.

Draper, W. A. Cue dominance in oddity discriminations by rhesus monkeys. *Journal of Comparative and Physiological Psychology*, 1965, **60,** 140–141.

Dunham, P. J. Contrasted conditions of reinforcement: A selective critique. *Psychological Bulletin*, 1968, **69,** 295–315.

Dyal, J. A. "On the combination of drive and incentive motivation:" A critical comment. *Psychological Reports*, 1967, **20,** 543–550.

Earhard, B., & Mandler, G. Mediated associations: Paradigms, controls, and mechanisms. *Canadian Journal of Psychology*, 1965, **19,** 346–378.

Ebbinghaus, H. *Memory.* (Trans. by H. A. Ruger & C. E. Bussenius.) New York: Teachers College, Columbia University, 1913.

Edwards, A. L. *Experimental design in psychological research.* (3d ed.) New York: Holt, Rinehart and Winston, 1968.

Egan, J. P., & Clarke, F. R. Psychophysics and signal detection. In J. B. Sidowski

(Ed.), *Experimental methods and instrumentation in psychology*. New York: McGraw-Hill, 1966. Pp. 211–246.

Egeth, H. Selective attention. *Psychological Bulletin*, 1967, **67**, 41–57.

Egeth, H., & Smith, E. E. Perceptual selectivity in a visual recognition task. *Journal of Experimental Psychology*, 1967, **74**, 543–549.

Egger, M. D., & Miller, N. E. Secondary reinforcement in rats as a function of information value and reliability of the stimulus. *Journal of Experimental Psychology*, 1962, **64**, 97–104.

Ehrenfreund, D. An experimental test of the contiguity theory of discrimination learning with pattern vision. *Journal of Comparative and Physiological Psychology*, 1948, **41**, 408–422.

Eisler, H. Magnitude scales, category scales, and Fechnerian integration. *Psychological Review*, 1963, **70**, 243–253.

Eisman, E., Asimow, A., & Maltzman, I. Habit strength as a function of drive in a brightness discrimination problem. *Journal of Experimental Psychology*, 1956, **52**, 58–64.

Ekman, G. Measurement of moral judgment: A comparison of scaling methods. *Perceptual and Motor Skills*, 1962, **15**, 3–9.

Ekman, G., & Gustafsson, U. Threshold values and the psychophysical function in brightness vision. *Vision Research*, 1968, **8**, 747–758.

Ekstrand, B. R. Backward associations. *Psychological Bulletin*, 1966, **65**, 50–64.

Ekstrand, B. R. Effect of sleep on memory. *Journal of Experimental Psychology*, 1967, **75**, 64–72.

Ekstrand, B., & Underwood, B. J. Paced versus unpaced recall in free learning. *Journal of Verbal Learning and Verbal Behavior*, 1963, **2**, 288–290.

Ellis, N. R. Amount of reward and operant behavior in mental defectives. *American Journal of Mental Deficiency*, 1962, **66**, 595–599.

Engen, T. Psychophysical analysis of the odor intensity of homologous alcohols. *Journal of Experimental Psychology*, 1965, **70**, 611–616.

Eninger, M. U. Habit summation in a selective learning problem. *Journal of Comparative and Physiological Psychology*, 1952, **45**, 604–608.

Epstein, S., & Fenz, W. D. Steepness of approach and avoidance gradients in humans as a function of experience: Theory and experiment. *Journal of Experimental Psychology*, 1965, **70**, 1–12.

Eriksen, C. W., & Lappin, J. S. Selective attention and very short-term recognition memory for nonsense forms. *Journal of Experimental Psychology*, 1967, **73**, 358–364.

Estes, W. K. An experimental study of punishment. *Psychological Monographs*, 1944, **57** (3, Whole No. 263).

Estes, W. K. The problem of inference from curves based on group data. *Psychological Bulletin*, 1956, **53**, 134–140.

Estes, W. K. The statistical approach to learning theory. In S. Koch (Ed.), *Psychology: A study of a science*. Vol. 2. New York: McGraw-Hill, 1959. Pp. 380–491.

Estes, W. K. Transfer of verbal discriminations based on differential reward magnitudes. *Journal of Experimental Psychology*, 1966, **72**, 276–283.

Estes, W. K. Outline of a theory of punishment. In B. A. Campbell & R. M. Church (Eds.), *Punishment and aversive behavior*. New York: Appleton-Century-Crofts, 1969. Pp. 57–82.

Evans, S. Failure of the interaction paradigm as a test of Hull vs Spence. *Psychological Reports*, 1967, **20**, 551–554.

Eyman, R. K. The effect of sophistication on ratio- and discriminative scales. *American Journal of Psychology*, 1967, **80**, 520–540.

Fagot, R. F., Eskildsen, P. R., & Stewart, M. R. Effect of rate of change in physical intensity on bisection and fractionation judgments of brightness. *Journal of Experimental Psychology*, 1966, **72**, 880–886.

Fallon, D. Resistance to extinction following learning with punishment of reinforced and nonreinforced licking. *Journal of Experimental Psychology*, 1968, **76**, 550–557.

Farthing, G. W., & Hearst, E. Generalization gradients of inhibition after different amounts of training. *Journal of the Experimental Analysis of Behavior*, 1968, **11**, 743–752.

Fazzaro, J., & D'Amato, M. R. Resistance to extinction after varying amounts of nondiscriminative or cue-correlated escape training. *Journal of Comparative and Physiological Psychology*, 1969, **68**, 373–376.

Fechner, G. *Elements of psychophysics*. (Trans. by H. E. Adler.) New York: Holt, Rinehart and Winston, 1966.

Fehrer, E. Effects of amount of reinforcement and of pre- and postreinforcement delays on learning and extinction. *Journal of Experimental Psychology*, 1956, **52**, 167–176.

Feldman, M. P. Aversion therapy for sexual deviations: A critical review. *Psychological Bulletin*, 1966, **65**, 65–79.

Fellows, B. J. Chance stimulus sequences for discrimination tasks. *Psychological Bulletin*, 1967, **67**, 87–92.

Felton, M., & Lyon, D. O. The post-reinforcement pause. *Journal of the Experimental Analysis of Behavior*, 1966, **9**, 131–134.

Ferraro, D. P. Response suppression and recovery under some temporally defined schedules of intermittent punishment. *Journal of Comparative and Physiological Psychology*, 1967, **64**, 133–139.

Ferster, C. B. Positive reinforcement and behavior deficits of autistic children. *Child Development*, 1961, **32**, 437–456.

Ferster, C. B. Classification of behavioral pathology. In L. Krasner & L. P. Ullmann (Eds.), *Research in behavior modification*. New York: Holt, Rinehart and Winston, 1965. Pp. 6–26.

Ferster, C. B., & DeMeyer, M. K. A method for the experimental analysis of the behavior of autistic children. *American Journal of Orthopsychiatry*, 1962, **32**, 89–98.

Ferster, C. B., & Hammer, C. E., Jr. Synthesizing the components of arithmetic behavior. In W. K. Honig (Ed.), *Operant behavior: Areas of research and application*. New York: Appleton-Century-Crofts, 1966. Pp. 634–676.

Ferster, C. B., & Skinner, B. F. *Schedules of reinforcement*. New York: Appleton-Century-Crofts, 1957.

Ferster, C. B., Nurnberger, J. I., & Levitt, E. B. The control of eating. *Journal of Mathetics*, 1962, **1**, 87–109.

Findley, J. D. An experimental outline for building and exploring multioperant behavior repertoires. *Journal of the Experimental Analysis of Behavior*, 1962, **5**, 113–166.

Findley, J. D. Programmed environments for the experimental analysis of human behavior. In W. K. Honig (Ed.), *Operant behavior: Areas of research and application*. New York: Appleton-Century-Crofts, 1966. Pp. 827–848.

Findley, J. D., & Brady, J. V. Facilitation of large ratio performance by use of conditioned reinforcement. *Journal of the Experimental Analysis of Behavior*, 1965, **8**, 125–129.

Findley, J. D., Migler, B. M., & Brady, J. V. A long-term study of human performance in a continuously programmed experimental environment. *Technical Report*, 1963, Space Research Laboratory, University of Maryland.

Fletcher, H. J. The delayed-response problem. In A. M. Schrier, H. F. Harlow, & F. Stollnitz (Eds.), *Behavior of nonhuman primates. Vol. I.* New York: Academic, 1965. Pp. 129–165.

Forrester, W. E., & Spear, N. E. Coding processes in verbal learning as a function of response pronounciability. *Journal of Experimental Psychology*, 1967, **74,** 586–588.

Fowler, H. Suppression and facilitation by response contingent shock. In F. R. Brush (Ed.), *Aversive conditioning and learning.* New York: Academic, 1970.*

Fowler, H., & Trapold, M. A. Escape performance as a function of delay of reinforcement. *Journal of Experimental Psychology*, 1962, **63,** 464–467.

Fowler, H., & Wishner, G. J. The varied functions of punishment in discrimination learning. In B. A. Campbell & R. M. Church (Eds.), *Punishment and aversive behavior.* New York: Appleton-Century-Crofts, 1969. Pp. 375–420.

Freeman, F., & Thomas, D. R. Attention vs. cue utilization in generalization testing. Paper presented at the meeting of the Midwestern Psychological Association, Chicago, May, 1967.

French, G. M. Associative problems. In A. M. Schrier, H. F. Harlow, & F. Stollnitz (Eds.), *Behavior of nonhuman primates. Vol. I.* New York: Academic, 1965. Pp. 167–209.

Friedman, H., & Guttman, N. Further analysis of the various effects of discrimination training on stimulus generalization gradients. In D. I. Mostofsky (Ed.), *Stimulus generalization.* Stanford: Stanford University Press, 1965. Pp. 255–267.

Galanter, E., & Holman, G. L. Some invariances of the isosensitivity function and their implications for the utility function of money. *Journal of Experimental Psychology*, 1967, **73,** 333–339.

Galanter, E., & Messick, S. The relation between category and magnitude scales of loudness. *Psychological Review*, 1961, **68,** 363–372.

Galbraith, K., Rashotte, M. E., & Amsel, A. Within-subjects partial reinforcement effects varying percentage of reward to the partial stimulus between groups. *Journal of Experimental Psychology*, 1968, **77,** 547–551.

Ganz, L., & Riesen, A. H. Stimulus generalization to hue in the dark-reared Macaque. *Journal of Comparative and Physiological Psychology*, 1962, **55,** 92–99.

Gardner, W. J., Licklider, J. C. R., & Weisz, A. Z. Suppression of pain by sound. *Science*, 1960, **132,** 32–33.

Garner, W. R. An argument for the use of discriminability scaling procedures in scaling sensory intensities. *Acta Psychologica*, 1959, **15,** 94–97.

Gavalas, R. J. Operant reinforcement of an autonomic response: Two studies. *Journal of the Experimental Analysis of Behavior*, 1967, **10,** 119–130.

Geldard, F. A. *The human senses.* New York: Wiley, 1953.

Gescheider, G. A., & Wright, J. H. Effects of sensory adaptation on the form of the psychophysical magnitude function for cutaneous vibration. *Journal of Experimental Psychology*, 1968, **77,** 308–313.

Gibson, E. J. A systematic application of the concepts of generalization and differentiation to verbal learning. *Psychological Review*, 1940, **47,** 196–229.

Gibson, E. J. Trends in perceptual development. Paper presented at Eastern Psychological Association Convention, Washington, D.C., April, 1968.

Gibson, E. J. *Perceptual learning and development.* New York: Appleton, 1969.

Gibson, E. J., Walk, R. D., & Tighe, T. J. Enhancement and deprivation of visual stimulation during rearing as factors in visual discrimination learning. *Journal of Comparative and Physiological Psychology*, 1959, **52,** 74–81.

Gibson, J. J. The concept of the stimulus in psychology. *American Psychologist*, 1960, **15,** 694–703.

Gibson, J. J. The useful dimensions of sensitivity. *American Psychologist*, 1963, **18,** 1–15.

Gibson, J. J. *The senses considered as perceptual systems.* Boston: Houghton Mifflin, 1966.

Gibson, J. J. On the proper meaning of the term "stimulus." *Psychological Review*, 1967, **74,** 533–534.

Gibson, J. J., & Gibson, E. J. Perceptual learning: Differentiation or enrichment? *Psychological Review*, 1955, **62,** 32–41.

Gilbert, R. M., & Sutherland, N. S. (Eds.) *Animal discrimination learning.* New York: Academic, 1969.

Glanzer, M., & Peters, S. C. Re-examination of the serial position effect. *Journal of Experimental Psychology*, 1962, **64,** 258–266.

Glaze, J. A. The association value of non-sense syllables. *Journal of Genetic Psychology*, 1928, **35,** 255–269.

Gleitman, H., Nachmias, J., & Neisser, U. The S-R reinforcement theory of extinction. *Psychological Review*, 1954, **61,** 23–33.

Glickman, S. E. Perseverative neural processes and consolidation of the memory trace. *Psychological Bulletin*, 1961, **58,** 218–233.

Goggin, J. Retroactive and proactive inhibition in short-term retention of paired associates. *Journal of Verbal Learning and Verbal Behavior*, 1966, **5,** 526–535.

Goggin, J. First-list recall as a function of second-list learning method. *Journal of Verbal Learning and Verbal Behavior*, 1967, **6,** 423–427.

Goldiamond, I. Self-control procedures in personal behavior problems. *Psychological Reports*, 1965, **17,** 851–868. (a)

Goldiamond, I. Stuttering and fluency as manipulatable operant response classes. In L. Krasner & L. P. Ullman (Eds.), *Research in behavior modification.* New York: Holt, Rinehart and Winston, 1965. Pp. 106–156. (b)

Goldstein, H., & Spence, K. W. Performance in differential conditioning as a function of variation in magnitude of reward. *Journal of Experimental Psychology*, 1963, **65,** 86–93.

Gollin, E. S. Solution of conditional discrimination problems by young children. *Journal of Comparative and Physiological Psychology*, 1966, **62,** 454–456.

Gonzalez, R. C., & Bitterman, M. E. Partial reinforcement effect in the goldfish as a function of amount of reward. *Journal of Comparative and Physiological Psychology*, 1967, **64,** 163–167.

Gonzalez, R. C., & Bitterman, M. E. Two-dimensional discriminative learning in the pigeon. *Journal of Comparative and Physiological Psychology*, 1968, **65,** 427–432.

Goodrich, K. P., Ross, L. E., & Wagner, A. R. An examination of selected aspects of the continuity and noncontinuity positions in discrimination learning. *Psychological Record*, 1961, **11,** 105–117.

Gormezano, I. Yoked comparisons of classical and instrumental conditioning of the eyelid response; and an addendum on "voluntary responders." In W. F. Prokasy (Ed.), *Classical conditioning: A symposium.* New York: Appleton-Century-Crofts, 1965. Pp. 48–70.

Gormezano, I. Classical conditioning. In J. B. Sidowski (Ed.), *Experimental methods and instrumentation in psychology*. New York: McGraw-Hill, 1966. Pp. 385–420.

Gormezano, I., & Moore, J. W. Classical conditioning. In M. Marx (Ed.), *Learning: Processes*. New York: Macmillan, 1969. Pp. 121–203.

Goss, A. E. Early behaviorism and verbal mediating responses. *American Psychologist*, 1961, **16**, 285–298. (a)

Goss, A. E. Verbal mediating responses and concept formation. *Psychological Review*, 1961, **68**, 248–272. (b)

Goss, A. E. Manifest strengthening of correct responses of paired-associates under postcriterion zero per cent occurrence of response members. *Journal of General Psychology*, 1965, **72**, 135–144.

Goss, A. E., & Nodine, C. F. *Paired-associates learning: The role of meaningfulness, similarity, and familiarization*. New York: Academic, 1965.

Goss, A. E., Morgan, C. H., & Golin, S. J. Paired-associates learning as a function of percentage of occurrence of response members (reinforcement). *Journal of Experimental Psychology*, 1959, **57**, 96–104.

Goulet, L. R. Verbal learning in children: Implications for developmental research. *Psychological Bulletin*, 1968, **69**, 359–376.

Grant, D. A. Classical and operant conditioning. In A. W. Melton (Ed.), *Categories of human learning*. New York: Academic, 1964. Pp. 1–31.

Gray, J. A. Relation between stimulus intensity and operant response rate as a function of discrimination training and drive. *Journal of Experimental Psychology*, 1965, **69**, 9–24.

Green, D. M., & Swets, J. A. *Signal detection theory and psychophysics*. New York: Wiley, 1966.

Greenspoon, J., & Ranyard, R. Stimulus conditions and retroactive inhibition. *Journal of Experimental Psychology*, 1957, **53**, 55–59.

Gregg, L. W., & Simon, H. A. Process models and stochastic theories of simple concept formation. *Journal of Mathematical Psychology*, 1967, **4**, 246–276.

Grice, G. R. Dependence of empirical laws upon the source of experimental variation. *Psychological Bulletin*, 1966, **66**, 488–498.

Grice, G. R. Stimulus intensity and response evocation. *Psychological Review*, 1968, **75**, 359–373.

Grice, G. R., & Hunter, J. J. Stimulus intensity effects depend upon the type of experimental design. *Psychological Review*, 1964, **71**, 247–256.

Grimsley, D. L., & McDonald, R. D. Effect of varied magnitude of reward on runway performance. *Psychological Reports*, 1964, **14**, 199–202.

Groninger, L. D. Natural language mediation and covert rehearsal in short-term memory. *Psychonomic Science*, 1966, **5**, 135–136.

Grossen, N. E., & Bolles, R. C. Effects of a classical conditioned "fear signal" and, "safety signal" on nondiscriminated avoidance behavior. *Psychonomic Science*, 1968, **11**, 321–322.

Grossman, S. P. Eating or drinking elicited by direct adrenergic or cholinergic stimulation of the hypothalamus. *Science*, 1960, **132**, 301–302.

Grusec, T. The peak shift in stimulus generalization: Equivalent effects of errors and noncontingent shock. *Journal of the Experimental Analysis of Behavior*, 1968, **11**, 239–249.

Guilford, J. P. *Psychometric methods*. (2d ed.) New York: McGraw-Hill, 1954.

Guilford, J. P. Three faces of intellect. *American Psychologist*, 1959, **14**, 469–479.

Guilford, J. P. Intelligence: 1965 model. *American Psychologist*, 1966, **21**, 20–26.

Guilford, J. P., & Dingman, H. F. A validation study of ratio-judgment methods. *American Journal of Psychology*, 1954, **67**, 395–410.

Gulliksen, H. Louis Leon Thurstone, experimental and mathematical psychologist. *American Psychologist*, 1968, **23**, 786–802.

Guthrie, E. R. *The psychology of learning.* New York: Harper & Row, 1935.

Guttman, N. Generalization gradients around stimuli associated with different reinforcement schedules. *Journal of Experimental Psychology*, 1959, **58**, 335–340.

Guttman, N., & Kalish, H. I. Discriminability and stimulus generalization. *Journal of Experimental Psychology*, 1956, **51**, 79–88.

Haber, A., & Kalish, H. I. Prediction of discrimination from generalization after variations in schedule of reinforcement. *Science*, 1963, **142**, 412–413.

Hake, D. F., Azrin, N. H., & Oxford, R. The effects of punishment intensity on squirrel monkeys. *Journal of the Experimental Analysis of Behavior*, 1967, **10**, 95–107.

Hall, J. F. *The psychology of learning.* Philadelphia: Lippincott, 1966.

Halpern, J., Schwartz, J. A., & Chapman, R. Simultaneous and successive contrast effects in human-probability learning. *Journal of Experimental Psychology*, 1968, **77**, 581–586.

Hansel, C. E. M. *ESP A scientific evaluation.* New York: Scribner, 1966.

Hanson, H. M. Effects of discrimination training on stimulus generalization. *Journal of Experimental Psychology*, 1959, **58**, 321–334.

Hara, K., & Warren, J. M. Stimulus additivity and dominance in discrimination performance by cats. *Journal of Comparative and Physiological Psychology*, 1961, **54**, 86–90.

Harker, G. S. Delay of reward and performance of an instrumental response. *Journal of Experimental Psychology*, 1956, **51**, 303–310.

Harley, W. F., Jr. The effect of monetary incentive in paired associate learning using a differential method. *Psychonomic Science*, 1965, **2**, 377–378. (a)

Harley, W. Jr. The effect of monetary incentive in paired associate learning using an absolute method. *Psychonomic Science*, 1965, **3**, 141–142. (b)

Harlow, H. F. The formation of learning sets. *Psychological Review*, 1949, **56**, 51–65.

Harlow, H. F. Learning set and error factor theory. In S. Koch (Ed.), *Psychology: A study of a science. Vol. 2.* New York: McGraw-Hill, 1959. Pp. 492–537.

Harlow, H. F., & Hicks, L. H. Discrimination learning theory: Uniprocess vs. duoprocess. *Psychological Review*, 1957, **64**, 104–109.

Harper, R. S., & Stevens, S. S. A psychological scale of weight and a formula for its derivation. *American Journal of Psychology*, 1948, **61**, 343–351.

Harrell, R. F., Woodyard, E., & Gates, A. I. *The effect of mothers' diets on the intelligence of the offspring.* New York: Teachers College, Columbia University, 1955.

Harris, J. D. Pitch discrimination. *Journal of the Acoustical Society of America*, 1952, **24**, 750–755.

Harris, S. J., Smith, M. G., & Weinstock, S. Effects of nonreinforcement on subsequent reinforced running behavior. *Journal of Experimental Psychology*, 1962, **64**, 388–392.

Harrow, M., & Friedman, G. B. Comparing reversal and nonreversal shifts in concept formation with partial reinforcement controlled. *Journal of Experimental Psychology*, 1958, **55**, 592–598.

Hawker, J. R. The influence of training procedure and other task variables in paired-associate learning. *Journal of Verbal Learning and Verbal Behavior*, 1964, **3**, 70–76.

Hayes, K. J. The backward curve: A method for the study of learning. *Psychological Review*, 1953, **60**, 269–275.

Hays, W. L. *Statistics for psychologists*. New York: Holt, Rinehart and Winston, 1963.

Hearst, E. Concurrent generalization gradients for food-controlled and shock-controlled behavior. *Journal of the Experimental Analysis of Behavior*, 1962, **5**, 19–31.

Hearst, E. Discrimination learning as the summation of excitation and inhibition. *Science*, 1968, **162**, 1303–1306.

Hearst, E. Aversive conditioning and external stimulus control. In B. A. Campbell & R. M. Church (Eds.), *Punishment and aversive behavior*. New York: Appleton-Century-Crofts, 1969. Pp. 235–277.

Hearst, E., & Koresko, M. B. Stimulus generalization and amount of prior training on variable-interval reinforcement. *Journal of Comparative and Physiological Psychology*, 1968, **66**, 133–138.

Hearst, E., Koresko, M. B., & Poppen, R. Stimulus generalization and the response-reinforcement contingency. *Journal of the Experimental Analysis of Behavior*, 1964, **7**, 369–380.

Hebb, D. O. *The organization of behavior*. New York: Wiley, 1949.

Hebb, D. O. Concerning imagery. *Psychological Review*, 1968, **75**, 466–477.

Heber, R. F. Motor task performance of high grade mentally retarded males as a function of the magnitude of incentive. *American Journal of Mental Deficiency*, 1959, **63**, 667–671.

Heckelman, S. B., & Spear, N. E. Effect of interitem similarity on free learning in children. *Journal of Verbal Learning and Verbal Behavior*, 1967, **6**, 448–450.

Heinemann, E. G., & Rudolph, R. L. The effect of discriminative training on the gradient of stimulus-generalization. *American Journal of Psychology*, 1963, **76**, 653–658.

Heinemann, E. G., Chase, S., & Mandell, C. Discriminative control of "attention." *Science*, 1968, **160**, 553–554.

Hellyer, S. Supplementary report: Frequency of stimulus presentation and short-term decrement in recall. *Journal of Experimental Psychology*, 1962, **64**, 650.

Helson, H. *Adaptation-level theory*. New York: Harper & Row, 1964.

Hendry, D. P. (Ed.) *Conditioned reinforcement*. Homewood, Ill.: Dorsey Press, 1969.

Hernández-Peón, R. Physiological mechanisms in attention. In R. W. Russell (Ed.), *Frontiers in physiological psychology*. New York: Academic, 1966. Pp. 121–147.

Herrick, R. M., & Bromberger, R. A. Lever displacement under a variable ratio schedule and subsequent extinction. *Journal of Comparative and Physiological Psychology*, 1965, **59**, 392–398.

Herrnstein, R. J. Superstition: A corollary of the principles of operant conditioning. In W. K. Honig (Ed.), *Operant behavior: Areas of research and application*. New York: Appleton-Century-Crofts, 1966. Pp. 33–51.

Herrnstein, R. J. Method and theory in the study of avoidance. *Psychological Review*, 1969, **76**, 49–69.

Herrnstein, R. J., & Hineline, P. N. Negative reinforcement as shock-frequency reduction. *Journal of the Experimental Analysis of Behavior*, 1966, **9**, 421–430.

Herrnstein, R. J., & van Sommers, P. Method for sensory scaling with animals. *Science*, 1962, **135**, 40–41.

Hershenson, M. Development of the perception of form. *Psychological Bulletin*, 1967, **67**, 326–336.

Hilgard, E. R., & Bower, G. H. *Theories of learning*. (3d ed.) New York: Appleton-Century-Crofts, 1966.

Hill, W. F. An attempted clarification of frustration theory. *Psychological Review*, 1968, **75**, 173–176.

Hill, W. F., & Spear, N. E. Resistance to extinction as a joint function of reward magnitude and the spacing of extinction trials. *Journal of Experimental Psychology*, 1962, **64**, 636–639.

Hill, W. F., & Wallace, W. P. Effects of magnitude and percentage of reward on subsequent patterns of runway speed. *Journal of Experimental Psychology*, 1967, **73**, 544–548. (a)

Hill, W. F., & Wallace, W. P. Reward magnitude and number of training trials as joint factors in extinction. *Psychonomic Science*, 1967, **7**, 267–268. (b)

Hillman, B., Hunter, W. S., & Kimble, G. A. The effect of drive level on the maze performance of the white rat. *Journal of Comparative and Physiological Psychology*, 1953, **46**, 87–89.

Hirayoshi, I., & Warren, J. M. Overtraining and reversal learning by experimentally naive kittens. *Journal of Comparative and Physiological Psychology*, 1967, **64**, 507–509.

Hiss, R. H., & Thomas, D. R. Stimulus generalization as a function of testing procedure and response measure. *Journal of Experimental Psychology*, 1963, **65**, 587–592.

Hocutt, M. On the alleged circularity of Skinner's concept of stimulus. *Psychological Review*, 1967, **74**, 530–532.

Hoffeld, D. R. Primary stimulus generalization and secondary extinction as a function of strength of conditioning. *Journal of Comparative and Physiological Psychology*, 1962, **55**, 27–31.

Hoffman, H. S. Stimulus generalization versus discrimination failure in conditioned suppression. In R. M. Gilbert & N. S. Sutherland (Eds.), *Animal discrimination learning*. New York: Academic, 1969. Pp. 63–82.

Hoffman, H. S., & Fleshler, M. Discrimination and stimulus generalization of approach, of avoidance, and of approach and avoidance during conflict. *Journal of Experimental Psychology*, 1963, **65**, 280–291.

Hoffman, H. S., & Fleshler, M. Stimulus aspects of aversive controls: The effects of response contingent shock. *Journal of the Experimental Analysis of Behavior*, 1965, **8**, 89–96.

Hoffman, H. S., Selekman, W., & Fleshler, M. Stimulus aspects of aversive controls: Long term effects of suppression procedures. *Journal of the Experimental Analysis of Behavior*, 1966, **9**, 659–662. (a)

Hoffman, H. S., Selekman, W. L., & Fleshler, M. Stimulus factors in aversive controls: Conditioned suppression after equal training to two stimuli. *Journal of the Experimental Analysis of Behavior*, 1966, **9**, 649–653. (b)

Holland, J. G., & Skinner, B. F. *The analysis of behavior*. New York: McGraw-Hill, 1961.

Holway, A. H., & Hurvich, L. M. Differential gustatory sensitivity to salt. *American Journal of Psychology*, 1937, **49**, 37–48.

Holz, W. C. Punishment and rate of positive reinforcement. *Journal of the Experimental Analysis of Behavior*, 1968, **11**, 285–292.

Holz, W. C., & Azrin, N. H. Discriminative properties of punishment. *Journal of the Experimental Analysis of Behavior*, 1961, **4**, 225–232.

Homzie, M. J., & Ross, L. E. Runway performance following a reduction in the concentration of a liquid reward. *Journal of Comparative and Physiological Psychology*, 1962, **55**, 1029–1033.

Honig, W. K. Generalization of extinction on the spectral continuum. *Psychological Record*, 1961, **11**, 269–278.

Honig, W. K. (Ed.) *Operant behavior: Areas of research and application*. New York: Appleton-Century-Crofts, 1966. (a)

Honig, W. K. The role of discrimination training in the generalization of punishment. *Journal of the Experimental Analysis of Behavior*, 1966, **9**, 377–384. (b)

Honig, W. K., Thomas, D. R., & Guttman, N. Differential effects of continuous extinction and discrimination training on the generalization gradient. *Journal of Experimental Psychology*, 1959, **58**, 145–152.

Honig, W. K., Boneau, C. A., Burstein, K. R., & Pennypacker, H. S. Positive and negative generalization gradients obtained after equivalent training conditions. *Journal of Comparative and Physiological Psychology*, 1963, **56**, 111–116.

Horenstein, B. R. Performance of conditioned responses as a function of strength of hunger drive. *Journal of Comparative and Physiological Psychology*, 1951, **44**, 210–224.

Horn, G. Physiological and psychological aspects of selective perception. In D. S. Lehrman, R. A. Hinde, & E. Shaw (Eds.), *Advances in the study of behavior. Vol. I*. New York: Academic, 1965. Pp. 155–215.

Horowitz, L. M. Free recall and ordering of trigrams. *Journal of Experimental Psychology*, 1961, **62**, 51–57.

Horton, D. L. The effects of meaningfulness, awareness, and type of design in verbal mediation. *Journal of Verbal Learning and Verbal Behavior*, 1964, **3**, 187–194.

Horton, D. L., & Kjeldergaard, P. M. An experimental analysis of associative factors in mediated generalization. *Psychological Monographs*, 1961, **75** (11, Whole No. 515).

Houston, J. P. Verbal R-S strength following S-R extinction. *Psychonomic Science*, 1964, **1**, 173–174.

Houston, J. P. Stimulus selection as influenced by degrees of learning, attention, prior associations, and experience with the stimulus components. *Journal of Experimental Psychology*, 1967, **73**, 509–516.

Houston, J. P. Unlearning and spontaneous recovery in short-term memory. *Journal of Verbal Learning and Verbal Behavior*, 1968, **7**, 251–253.

Hovland, C. I. The generalization of conditioned responses. IV. The effects of varying amounts of reinforcement upon the degree of generalization of conditioned responses. *Journal of Experimental Psychology*, 1937, **21**, 261–276.

Howe, E. S. The effect of an increased versus a decreased reduction in shock used as incentive. *American Journal of Psychology*, 1961, **74**, 462–466.

Howes, D. On the relation between the probability of a word as an association and in general linguistic usage. *Journal of Abnormal and Social Psychology*, 1957, **54**, 75–85.

Hull, C. L. The meaningfulness of 320 selected nonsense syllables. *American Journal of Psychology*, 1933, **45**, 730–734.

Hull, C. L. *Principles of behavior*. New York: Appleton-Century-Crofts, 1943.

Hull, C. L. *A behavior system*. New Haven: Yale University Press, 1952.

Hull, C. L., Hovland, C. I., Ross, R. T., Hall, M., Perkins, D. T., & Fitch, F. B. *Mathematico-deductive theory of rote learning*. New Haven: Yale University Press, 1940.

Hulse, S. H., Jr. Amount and percentage of reinforcement and duration of goal confinement in conditioning and extinction. *Journal of Experimental Psychology*, 1958, **56**, 48–57.

Hunt, H. F., & Brady, J. V. Some effects of punishment and intercurrent "anxiety" on a simple operant. *Journal of Comparative and Physiological Psychology*, 1955, **48**, 305–310.

Hunter, W. S. The delayed reaction in animals and children. *Behavior Monographs*, 1913, **2**, 1–86.

Hunter, W. S. The auditory sensitivity of the white rat. *Journal of Animal Behavior*, 1914, **4**, 215–222.

Hutchinson, R. R. Azrin, N. H., & Renfrew, J. W. Effects of shock intensity and duration on the frequency of biting attack by squirrel monkeys. *Journal of Experimental Analysis of Behavior*, 1968, **11**, 83–88.

Huxley, J. S. *Problems of relative growth.* New York: Dial, 1932.

Ison, J. R. Experimental extinction as a function of number of reinforcements. *Journal of Experimental Psychology*, 1962, **64**, 314–317.

Ison, J. R., & Cook, P. E. Extinction performance as a function of incentive magnitude and number of acquisition trials. *Psychonomic Science*, 1964, **1**, 245–246.

Ison, J. R., & Northman, J. Amobarbital sodium and instrumental performance changes following an increase in reward magnitude. *Psychonomic Science*, 1968, **12**, 185–186.

Ison, J. R., & Rosen, A. J. The effects of amobarbital sodium on differential instrumental conditioning and subsequent extinction. *Psychopharmacologia*, 1967, **10**, 417–425.

Ison, J. R., & Rosen, A. J. Extinction and reacquisition performance as a function of sucrose-solution rewards and numbers of acquisition trials. *Psychological Reports*, 1968, **22**, 375–379.

James, C. T., & Greeno, J. G. Stimulus selection at different stages of paired-associate learning. *Journal of Experimental Psychology*, 1967, **74**, 75–83.

James, W. *The principles of psychology. Vol. II.* New York: Holt, 1890.

Jeffrey, W. E. The orienting reflex and attention in cognitive development. *Psychological Review*, 1968, **75**, 323–334.

Jenkins, H. M. The effect of discrimination training on extinction. *Journal of Experimental Psychology*, 1961, **61**, 111–121.

Jenkins, H. M. Resistance to extinction when partial reinforcement is followed by regular reinforcement. *Journal of Experimental Psychology*, 1962, **64**, 441–450.

Jenkins, H. M. Generalization gradients and the concept of inhibition. In D. I. Mostofsky (Ed.), *Stimulus generalization.* Stanford: Stanford University Press, 1965. Pp. 55–61. (a)

Jenkins, H. M. Measurement of stimulus control during discriminative operant conditioning. *Psychological Bulletin*, 1965, **64**, 365–376. (b)

Jenkins, H. M. Sequential organization in schedules of reinforcement. In W. N. Schoenfeld (Ed.), *Theory of reinforcement schedules.* New York: Appleton-Century-Crofts, 1970.*

Jenkins, H. M., & Harrison, R. H. Effect of discrimination training on auditory generalization. *Journal of Experimental Psychology*, 1960, **59**, 246–253.

Jenkins, H. M., & Harrison, R. H. Generalization gradients of inhibition following auditory discrimination learning. *Journal of the Experimental Analysis of Behavior*, 1962, **5**, 435–441.

Jenkins, J. G., & Dallenbach, K. M. Obliviscence during sleep and waking. *American Journal of Psychology*, 1924, **35,** 605–612.

Jenkins, J. J. Mediated associations: Paradigms and situations. In C. N. Cofer & B. S. Musgrave (Eds.), *Verbal behavior and learning: Problems and processes.* New York: McGraw-Hill, 1963. Pp. 210–245.

Jenkins, J. J. Comments on pseudomediation. *Psychonomic Science*, 1965, **2,** 97–98.

Jenkins, J. J. The challenge to psychological theorists. In T. R. Dixon & D. L. Horton (Eds.), *Verbal behavior and general behavior theory.* Englewood Cliffs, N.J.: Prentice-Hall, 1968. Pp. 538–549.

Jenkins, J. J., & Foss, D. J. An experimental analysis of pseudomediation. *Psychonomic Science*, 1965, **2,** 99–100.

Jenkins, W. O., Pascal, G. R., & Walker, R. W., Jr. Deprivation and generalization. *Journal of Experimental Psychology*, 1958, **56,** 274–277.

Jensen, G. D., & Cotton, J. W. Running speed as a function of stimulus similarity and number of trials. *Journal of Comparative and Physiological Psychology*, 1961, **54,** 474–476.

John, E. R. *Mechanisms of memory.* New York: Academic, 1967.

John, E. R., & Killam, K. F. Electrophysiological correlates of avoidance conditioning in the cat. *Journal of Pharmacology and Experimental Therapeutics*, 1959, **125,** 252–274.

Johnson, D. F., & Cumming, W. W. Some determiners of attention. *Journal of the Experimental Analysis of Behavior*, 1968, **11,** 157–166.

Joinson, P. A., & Runquist, W. N. Effects of intra-list stimulus similarity and degree of learning on forgetting. *Journal of Verbal Learning and Verbal Behavior*, 1968, **7,** 554–559.

Jones, J. E. All-or-none versus incremental learning. *Psychological Review*, 1962, **69,** 156–160.

Jones, L. V. Some invariant findings under the method of successive intervals. In H. Gulliksen & S. Messick (Eds.), *Psychological scaling: Theory and application.* New York: Wiley, 1960. Pp. 7–20.

Jung, J. Transfer of training as a function of degree of first-list learning. *Journal of Verbal Learning and Verbal Behavior*, 1962, **1,** 197–199.

Jung, J. Effects of response meaningfulness (*m*) on transfer of training under two different paradigms. *Journal of Experimental Psychology*, 1963, **65,** 377–384.

Jung, J. A cumulative method of paired-associate and serial learning. *Journal of Verbal Learning and Verbal Behavior*, 1964, **3,** 290–299.

Jung, J. Comments on Mandler's "From association to structure." *Psychological Review*, 1965, **72,** 318–322.

Jung, J. *Verbal learning.* New York: Holt, Rinehart and Winston, 1968.

Jung, J., & Skeebo, S. Multitrial free recall as a function of constant versus varied input orders and list length. *Canadian Journal of Psychology*, 1967, **21,** 329–336.

Kalish, H. I. The relationship between discriminability and generalization: A re-evaluation. *Journal of Experimental Psychology*, 1958, **55,** 637–644.

Kalish, H. I. Stimulus generalization. In M. Marx (Ed.), *Learning: Processes.* New York: Macmillan, 1969. Pp. 207–297.

Kalish, H. I., & Guttman, N. Stimulus generalization after equal training on two stimuli. *Journal of Experimental Psychology*, 1957, **53,** 139–144.

Kalish, H. I., & Guttman, N. Stimulus generalization after training on three stimuli: A test of the summation hypothesis. *Journal of Experimental Psychology*, 1959, **57,** 268–272.

Kalish, H. I., & Haber, A. Prediction of discrimination from generalization following variations in deprivation level. *Journal of Comparative and Physiological Psychology*, 1965, **60**, 125–128.

Kamin, L. J. Traumatic avoidance learning: The effects of CS–US interval with a trace-conditioning procedure. *Journal of Comparative and Physiological Psychology*, 1954, **47**, 65–72.

Kamin, L. J. The effects of termination of the CS and avoidance of the US on avoidance learning. *Journal of Comparative and Physiological Psychology*, 1956, **49**, 420–424.

Kamin, L. J. The gradient of delay of secondary reward in avoidance learning. *Journal of Comparative and Physiological Psychology*, 1957, **50**, 445–449.

Kamin, L. J. "Attention-like" processes in classical conditioning. In M. R. Jones (Ed.), *Miami symposium on the prediction of behavior, 1967: Aversive stimulation.* Coral Gables, Fla.: University of Miami Press, 1968. Pp. 9–31.

Kamin, L. J., Brimer, C. J., & Black, A. H. Conditioned suppression as a monitor of fear of the CS in the course of avoidance training. *Journal of Comparative and Physiological Psychology*, 1963, **56**, 497–501.

Kamin, L., Campbell, D., Judd, R., Ryan, T., & Walker, J. Two determinants of the emergence of anticipatory avoidance. *Journal of Comparative and Physiological Psychology*, 1959, **52**, 202–205.

Karsh, E. B. Effects of number of rewarded trials and intensity of punishment on running speed. *Journal of Comparative and Physiological Psychology*, 1962, **55**, 44–51.

Karsh, E. B. Punishment: Effect on learning and resistance to extinction of discrete operant behavior. *Psychonomic Science*, 1964, **1**, 139–140.

Katkin, E. S., & Murray, E. N. Instrumental conditioning of autonomically mediated behavior: Theoretical and methodological issues. *Psychological Bulletin*, 1968, **70**, 52–68.

Katz, S. The reaction time of mediated responses. *Psychological Record*, 1963, **13**, 57–64.

Kaufman, A., & Baron, A. Suppression of behavior by timeout punishment when suppression results in loss of positive reinforcement. *Journal of the Experimental Analysis of Behavior*, 1968, **11**, 595–607.

Keehn, J. D. The effect of a warning signal on unrestricted avoidance behaviour. *British Journal of Psychology*, 1959, **50**, 125–135.

Keehn, J. D. Temporal alternation in the white rat? *Journal of the Experimental Analysis of Behavior*, 1965, **8**, 161–168.

Keehn, J. D. Avoidance responses as discriminated operants. *British Journal of Psychology*, 1966, **57**, 375–380.

Keesey, R. E., & Kling, J. W. Amount of reinforcement and free-operant responding. *Journal of the Experimental Analysis of Behavior*, 1961, **4**, 125–132.

Keidel, W. D., & Spreng, M. Neurophysiological evidence for the Stevens power function in man. *Journal of the Acoustical Society of America*, 1965, **38**, 191–195.

Kelleher, R. T. Discrimination learning as a function of reversal and nonreversal shifts. *Journal of Experimental Psychology*, 1956, **51**, 379–384.

Kelleher, R. T. Chaining and conditioned reinforcement. In W. K. Honig (Ed.), *Operant behavior: Areas of research and application.* New York: Appleton-Century-Crofts, 1966. Pp. 160–212.

Kelleher, R. T., & Fry, W. T. Stimulus functions in chained fixed-interval schedules. *Journal of the Experimental Analysis of Behavior*, 1962, **5**, 167–173.

Kelleher, R. T., & Morse, W. H. Schedules using noxious stimuli. III. Responding maintained with response-produced electric shocks. *Journal of the Experimental Analysis of Behavior*, 1968, **11**, 819–838.

Kelleher, R. T., Riddle, W. C., & Cook, L. Observing responses in pigeons. *Journal of the Experimental Analysis of Behavior*, 1962, **5**, 3–13.

Keller, F. S., & Schoenfeld, W. N. *Principles of psychology.* New York: Appleton-Century-Crofts, 1950.

Kellicutt, M. H. Response duration during an operant discrimination. *Journal of Experimental Psychology*, 1967, **73**, 56–60.

Kendler, H. H. Motivation and behavior. In D. Levine (Ed.), *Nebraska symposium on motivation: 1965.* Lincoln: University of Nebraska Press, 1965. Pp. 1–23.

Kendler, H. H. Some specific reactions to general S-R theory. In T. R. Dixon & D. L. Horton (Eds.), *Verbal behavior and general behavior theory.* Englewood Cliffs, N.J.: Prentice-Hall, 1968. Pp. 388–403.

Kendler, H. H., & Kendler, T. S. Vertical and horizontal processes in problem solving. *Psychological Review*, 1962, **69**, 1–16.

Kendler, T. S., Kendler, H. H., & Wells, D. Reversal and nonreversal shifts in nursery school children. *Journal of Comparative and Physiological Psychology*, 1960, **53**, 83–88.

Keppel, G. Facilitation in short- and long-term retention of paired associates following distributed practice in learning. *Journal of Verbal Learning and Verbal Behavior*, 1964, **3**, 91–111. (a)

Keppel, G. Verbal learning in children. *Psychological Bulletin*, 1964, **61**, 63–80. (b)

Keppel, G. Problems of method in the study of short-term memory. *Psychological Bulletin*, 1965, **63**, 1–13.

Keppel, G. Association by contiguity: Role of response availability. *Journal of Experimental Psychology*, 1966, **71**, 624–628. (a)

Keppel, G. Unlearning in serial learning. *Journal of Experimental Psychology*, 1966, **71**, 143–149. (b)

Keppel, G. Retroactive and proactive inhibition. In T. R. Dixon & D. L. Horton (Eds.), *Verbal behavior and general behavior theory.* Englewood Cliffs, N.J.: Prentice-Hall, 1968. Pp. 172–213.

Keppel, G., Henschel, D. M., & Zavortink, B. Influence of nonspecific interference on response recall. *Journal of Experimental Psychology*, 1969, **81**, 246–255.

Keppel, G., & Postman, L. Studies of learning to learn: III. Conditions of improvement in successive transfer tasks. *Journal of Verbal Learning and Verbal Behavior*, 1966, **5**, 260–267.

Keppel, G., Postman, L., & Zavortink, B. Studies of learning to learn: VIII. The influence of massive amounts of training upon the learning and retention of paired-associate lists. *Journal of Verbal Learning and Verbal Behavior*, 1968, **7**, 790–796.

Keppel, G., and Rauch, D. S. Unlearning as a function of second-list error instructions. *Journal of Verbal Learning and Verbal Behavior*, 1966, **5**, 50–58.

Keppel, G., & Underwood, B. J. Proactive inhibition in short-term retention of single items. *Journal of Verbal Learning and Verbal Behavior*, 1962, **1**, 153–161. (a)

Keppel, G., & Underwood, B. J. Retroactive inhibition of R-S associations. *Journal of Experimental Psychology*, 1962, **64**, 400–404. (b)

Keppel, G., & Underwood, B. J. Reminiscence in the short-term retention of paired-associate lists. *Journal of Verbal Learning and Verbal Behavior*, 1967, **6**, 375–382.

Keppel, G., Zavortink, B., & Schiff, B. B. Unlearning in the A-B, A-C paradigm as a function of percentage occurrence of response members. *Journal of Experimental Psychology*, 1967, **74**, 172–177.

Kerpelman, L. C. Preexposure to visually presented forms and nondifferential reinforcement in perceptual learning. *Journal of Experimental Psychology*, 1965, **69**, 257–262.

Kimble, G. A. *Hilgard and Marquis' conditioning and learning.* New York: Appleton-Century-Crofts, 1961.

Kimmel, E., & Kimmel, H. D. Instrumental conditioning of the GSR: Serendipitous escape and punishment training. *Journal of Experimental Psychology*, 1968, **77**, 48–51.

Kimmel, H. D. Instrumental conditioning of autonomically mediated behavior. *Psychological Bulletin*, 1967, **67**, 337–345.

Kimmel, H. D., & Terrant, F. R. Bias due to individual differences in yoked control designs. *Behavior Research Methods and Instrumentation*, 1968, **1**, 11–14.

Kintsch, W. Runway performance as a function of drive strength and magnitude of reinforcement. *Journal of Comparative and Physiological Psychology*, 1962, **55**, 882–887.

Kintsch, W., & McCoy, D. F. Delay of informative feedback in paired-associate learning. *Journal of Experimental Psychology*, 1964, **68**, 372–375.

Kjeldergaard, P. M. Transfer and mediation in verbal learning. In T. R. Dixon & D. L. Horton (Eds.), *Verbal behavior and general behavior theory.* Englewood Cliffs, N.J.: Prentice-Hall, 1968. Pp. 67–96.

Kleinsmith, L. J., & Kaplan, S. Paired-associate learning as a function of arousal and interpolated interval. *Journal of Experimental Psychology*, 1963, **65**, 190–193.

Kleinsmith, L. J., & Kaplan, S. Interaction of arousal and recall interval in nonsense syllable paired-associate learning. *Journal of Experimental Psychology*, 1964, **67**, 124–126.

Klüver, H. *Behavior mechanisms in monkeys.* Chicago: University of Chicago Press, 1933.

Knapp, R. K., Kause, R. H., & Perkins, C. C. Immediate versus delayed shock in T-maze performance. *Journal of Experimental Psychology*, 1959, **58**, 357–362.

Kobrick, J. L. The relationships among three measures of response strength as a function of the numbers of reinforcements. *Journal of Comparative and Physiological Psychology*, 1956, **49**, 582–585.

Koffka, K. *Principles of gestalt psychology.* New York: Harcourt, Brace, 1935.

Koh, S. D. Scaling musical preferences. *Journal of Experimental Psychology*, 1965, **70**, 79–82.

Kraeling, D. Analysis of amount of reward as a variable in learning. *Journal of Comparative and Physiological Psychology*, 1961, **54**, 560–565.

Krasner, L., & Ullmann, L. P. (Eds.) *Research in behavior modification.* New York: Holt, Rinehart and Winston, 1965.

Krechevsky, I. A study of the continuity of the problem-solving process. *Psychological Review*, 1938, **45**, 107–134.

Krippner, R. A., Endsley, R. C., & Tacker, R. S. Magnitude of G_1 reward and the frustration effect in a between subjects design. *Psychonomic Science*, 1967, **9**, 385–386.

Kuhn, T. S. *The structure of scientific revolution.* Chicago: University of Chicago Press, 1962.

L'Abate, L. Manifest anxiety and the learning of syllables with different associative values. *American Journal of Psychology*, 1959, **72**, 107–110.

LaBerge, D. Generalization gradients in a discrimination situation. *Journal of Experimental Psychology*, 1961, **62**, 88–94.

LaBerge, D., & Martin, D. R. An analysis of summated generalization. *Journal of Experimental Psychology*, 1964, **68**, 71–79.

Lachman, R. The influence of thirst and schedules of reinforcement-nonreinforcement ratios upon brightness discrimination. *Journal of Experimental Psychology*, 1961, **62**, 80–87.

Lashley, K. S. Visual discrimination of size and form in the albino rat. *Journal of Animal Behavior*, 1912, **2**, 310–331.

Lashley, K. S. The mechanism of vision. I. A method for rapid analysis of pattern-vision in the rat. *Pedagogical Seminary and Journal of Genetic Psychology*, 1930, **37**, 453–460.

Lashley, K. S. The mechanism of vision. XV. Preliminary studies of the rat's capacity for detail vision. *Journal of Genetic Psychology*, 1938, **18**, 123–193.

Lashley, K. S. In search of the engram. *Symposia of the Society for Experimental Biology*, 1950, **4**, 454–482.

Lashley, K. S., & Wade, M. The Pavlovian theory of generalization. *Psychological Review*, 1946, **53**, 72–87.

Lawrence, D. H. Acquired distinctiveness of cues: I. Transfer between discriminations on the basis of familiarity with the stimulus. *Journal of Experimental Psychology*, 1949, **39**, 770–784.

Lawrence, D. H. Acquired distinctiveness of cues: II. Selective association in a constant stimulus situation. *Journal of Experimental Psychology*, 1950, **40**, 175–188.

Lawrence, D. H. The transfer of a discrimination along a continuum. *Journal of Comparative and Physiological Psychology*, 1952, **45**, 511–516.

Lawrence, D. H., & Festinger, L. *Deterrents and reinforcement*. Stanford: Stanford University Press, 1962.

Lawson, E. A. Decisions concerning the rejected channel. *Quarterly Journal of Experimental Psychology*, 1966, **18**, 260–265.

Lawson, R. Brightness discrimination performance and secondary reward strength as a function of primary reward amount. *Journal of Comparative and Physiological Psychology*, 1957, **50**, 35–39.

Leaf, R. C. Acquisition of Sidman avoidance responding as a function of S–S interval. *Journal of Comparative and Physiological Psychology*, 1965, **59**, 298–300.

Leary, R. W. Analysis of serial-discrimination learning by monkeys. *Journal of Comparative and Physiological Psychology*, 1958, **51**, 82–86.

Leff, R. Behavior modification and the psychoses of childhood: A review. *Psychological Bulletin*, 1968, **69**, 396–409.

Leib, J. W., Cusack, J., Hughes, D., Pilette, S., Werther, J., & Kintz, B. L. Teaching machines and programmed instruction: Areas of application. *Psychological Bulletin*, 1967, **67**, 12–26.

Leung, C. M., & Jensen, G. D. Shifts in percentage of reinforcement viewed as changes in incentive. *Journal of Experimental Psychology*, 1968, **76**, 291–296.

Levine, M. Hypothesis behavior. In A. M. Schrier, H. F. Harlow, & F. Stollnitz (Eds.), *Behavior of nonhuman primates. I*. New York: Academic, 1965. Pp. 97–127.

Levine, S. UCS intensity and avoidance learning. *Journal of Experimental Psychology*, 1966, **71**, 163–164.

Levison, M., & Restle, F. Invalid results from the method of constant stimuli. *Perception & Psychophysics*, 1968, **4**, 121–122.

Lewis, D. *Quantitative methods in psychology*. New York: McGraw-Hill, 1960.

Lewis, D. J. Partial reinforcement: A selective review of the literature since 1950. *Psychological Bulletin*, 1960, **57**, 1–28.

Lewis, D. J., & Maher, B. A. Neural consolidation and electroconvulsive shock. *Psychological Review*, 1965, **72**, 225–239.

Lindsley, O. R. A behavioral measure of television viewing. *Journal of Advertising Research*, 1962, **2**, 2–12.

Lockard, J. S. Choice of a warning signal or no warning signal in an unavoidable shock situation. *Journal of Comparative and Physiological Psychology*, 1963, **56**, 526–530.

Lockhead, G. R. Methods of presenting paired associates. *Journal of Verbal Learning and Verbal Behavior*, 1962, **1**, 62–65.

Loess, H. Proactive inhibition in short-term memory. *Journal of Verbal Learning and Verbal Behavior*, 1964, **3**, 362–368.

Logan, F. A. The Hull-Spence approach. In S. Koch (Ed.), *Psychology: A study of a science. Vol. 2*. New York: McGraw-Hill, 1959. Pp. 293–358.

Logan, F. A. *Incentive*. New Haven: Yale University Press, 1960.

Logan, F. A. Continuously negatively correlated amount of reinforcement. *Journal of Comparative and Physiological Psychology*, 1966, **62**, 31–34.

Logan, F. A., Beier, E. M., & Ellis, R. A. Effect of varied reinforcement on speed of locomotion. *Journal of Experimental Psychology*, 1955, **49**, 260–266.

Lovass, O. I., Schaeffer, B., & Simmons, J. Q. Building social behavior in autistic children by use of electric shock. *Journal of Experimental Research in Personality*, 1965, **1**, 99–109.

Lovejoy, E. An attention theory of discrimination learning. *Journal of Mathematical Psychology*, 1965, **2**, 342–362.

Lovejoy, E. Analysis of the overlearning reversal effect. *Psychological Review*, 1966, **73**, 87–103.

Lovejoy, E. *Attention in discrimination learning*. San Francisco: Holden-Day, 1968.

Lovejoy, E., & Russell, D. G. Suppression of learning about a hard cue by the presence of an easy cue. *Psychonomic Science*, 1967, **8**, 365–366.

Luce, R. D. *Individual choice behavior*. New York: Wiley, 1959.

Luce, R. D. A threshold theory for simple detection experiments. *Psychological Review*, 1963, **70**, 61–79.

Luce, R. D., & Edwards, W. The derivation of subjective scales from just noticeable differences. *Psychological Review*, 1958, **65**, 222–237.

Luce, R. D., & Galanter, E. Psychophysical scaling. In R. D. Luce, R. R. Bush, & E. Galanter (Eds.), *Handbook of mathematical psychology. Vol. I*. New York: Wiley, 1963. Pp. 245–307.

Luce, R. D., Bush, R. R., & Galanter, E. (Eds.) *Handbook of mathematical psychology. Vol. I, II*. New York: Wiley, 1963.

Luce, R. D., Bush, R. R., & Galanter, E. (Eds.) *Handbook of mathematical psychology. Vol. III*. New York: Wiley, 1965.

Ludvigson, H. W., & Gay, R. A. An investigation of conditions determining contrast effects in differential reward conditioning. *Journal of Experimental Psychology*, 1967, **75**, 37–42.

Lukaszewska, I. Some further failures to find the visual overlearning-reversal effect in rats. *Journal of Comparative and Physiological Psychology*, 1968, **65**, 359–361.

Lynn, R. *Attention, arousal and the orientation reaction*. New York: Pergamon, 1966.

Lyons, J. Stimulus generalization as a function of discrimination learning with and without errors. *Science*, 1969, **163**, 490–491.

MacKinnon, J. R. Interactive effects of the two rewards in a differential magnitude of reward discrimination. *Journal of Experimental Psychology*, 1967, **75**, 329–338.

Mackintosh, N. J. Extinction of a discrimination habit as a function of overtraining. *Journal of Comparative and Physiological Psychology*, 1963, **56**, 842–847.

Mackintosh, N. J. Incidental cue learning in rats. *Quarterly Journal of Experimental Psychology*, 1965, **17**, 292–300. (a)

Mackintosh, N. J. Selective attention in animal discrimination learning. *Psychological Bulletin*, 1965, **64**, 124–150. (b)

Mackintosh, N. J. The effect of attention on the slope of generalization gradients. *British Journal of Psychology*, 1965, **56**, 87–93. (c)

Mackintosh, N. J. Further analysis of the overtraining reversal effect. *Journal of Comparative and Physiological Psychology Monograph Supplement*, 1969, **67** (2, Pt. 2).

Mackworth, J. F. Presentation rate and immediate memory. *Canadian Journal of Psychology*, 1962, **16**, 42–47.

Maier, S. F., Seligman, M. E. P., & Solomon, R. L. Pavlovian fear conditioning and learned helplessness: Effects on escape and avoidance behavior of (a) the CS-US contingency and (b) the independence of the US and voluntary responding. In B. A. Campbell & R. M. Church (Eds.), *Punishment and aversive behavior*. New York: Appleton-Century-Crofts, 1969. Pp. 299–342.

Malott, M. K. Stimulus control in stimulus-deprived chickens. *Journal of Comparative and Physiological Psychology*, 1968, **66**, 276–282.

Mandler, G. Subjects do think: A reply to Jung's comments. *Psychological Review*, 1965, **72**, 323–326.

Mandler, G., & Earhard, B. Pseudomediation: Is chaining an artifact? *Psychonomic Science*, 1964, **1**, 247–248.

Margolius, G. Stimulus generalization of an instrumental response as a function of the number of reinforced trials. *Journal of Experimental Psychology*, 1955, **49**, 105–111.

Markowitz, J., & Swets, J. A. Factors affecting the slope of empirical ROC curves: Comparison of binary and rating responses. *Perception & Psychophysics*, 1967, **2**, 91–100.

Marks, L. E., & Stevens, J. C. Individual brightness functions. *Perception & Psychophysics*, 1966, **1**, 17–24.

Marsh, G. D. Inverse relationship between discriminability and stimulus generalization as a function of number of test stimuli. *Journal of Comparative and Physiological Psychology*, 1967, **64**, 284–289.

Marsh, G., & Johnson, R. Discrimination reversal following learning without "errors." *Psychonomic Science*, 1968, **10**, 261–262.

Martin, B. Reward and punishment associated with the same goal response: A factor in the learning of motives. *Psychological Bulletin*, 1963, **60**, 441–451.

Martin, C. J., Cox, D. L., & Boersma, F. J. The role of associative strategies in the acquisition of P-A material: An alternate approach to meaningfulness. *Psychonomic Science*, 1965, **3**, 463–464.

Martin, E. Transfer of verbal paired associates. *Psychological Review*, 1965, **72**, 327–343.

Martin, E. Stimulus meaningfulness and paired-associate transfer: An encoding variability hypothesis. *Psychological Review*, 1968, **75**, 421–441.

Martin, R. C., & Melvin, K. B. Vicious circle behavior as a function of delay of punishment. *Psychonomic Science*, 1964, **1**, 415–416.

Marx, M. H., & Tombaugh, J. W. The frustration vigor effect (FVE) as a function of number of rewarded barpress trials. *Psychonomic Science*, 1967, **8**, 105–106.

McAllister, W. R., & McAllister, D. E. Drive and reward in aversive learning. *American Journal of Psychology*, 1967, **80**, 377–383.

McAllister, W. R., & McAllister, D. E. Behavioral measurement of conditioned fear. In F. R. Brush (Ed.), *Aversive conditioning and learning*. New York: Academic, 1970.*

McBurney, D. H. Magnitude estimation of the taste of sodium chloride after adaptation to sodium chloride. *Journal of Experimental Psychology*, 1966, **72**, 869–873.

McFarland, D. J. The role of attention in the disinhibition of displacement activities. *Quarterly Journal of Experimental Psychology*, 1966, **18**, 19–30.

McGeoch, J. A. Forgetting and the law of disuse. *Psychological Review*, 1932, **39**, 352–370.

McGeoch, J. A. *The psychology of human learning*. New York: Longmans, Green, 1942.

McGill, W. J., & Goldberg, J. P. A study of the near-miss involving Weber's law and pure-tone intensity discrimination. *Perception & Psychophysics*, 1968, **4**, 105–109.

McGonigle, B. Stimulus additivity and dominance in visual discrimination performance by rats. *Journal of Comparative and Physiological Psychology*, 1967, **64**, 110–113.

McGovern, J. B. Extinction of associations in four transfer paradigms. *Psychological Monographs*, 1964, **78** (16, Whole No. 593).

McGuigan, F. J. The experimenter: A neglected stimulus object. *Psychological Bulletin*, 1963, **60**, 421–428.

McGuire, W. J. A multi-process model for paired-associate learning. *Journal of Experimental Psychology*, 1961, **62**, 335–347.

McHose, J. H., and Ludvigson, H. W. Role of reward magnitude and incomplete reduction of reward magnitude in the frustration effect. *Journal of Experimental Psychology*, 1965, **70**, 490–495.

McKearney, J. W. Maintenance of responding under a fixed-interval schedule of electric shock presentation. *Science*, 1968, **160**, 1249–1251.

McKelvey, R. K. The relationship between training methods and reward variables in brightness discrimination learning. *Journal of Comparative and Physiological Psychology*, 1956, **49**, 485–491.

McLaughlin, B. "Intentional" and "incidental" learning in human subjects: The role of instructions to learn and motivation. *Psychological Bulletin*, 1965, **63**, 359–376.

McMillan, D. E. A comparison of the punishing effects of response-produced shock and response-produced time out. *Journal of the Experimental Analysis of Behavior*, 1967, **10**, 439–449.

Mechanic, A. The responses involved in the rote learning of verbal materials. *Journal of Verbal Learning and Verbal Behavior*, 1964, **3**, 30–36.

Mechner, F. A notation system for the description of behavioral procedures. *Journal of the Experimental Analysis of Behavior*, 1959, **2**, 133–150.

Mednick, S. A., & Freedman, J. L. Stimulus generalization. *Psychological Bulletin*, 1960, **57**, 169–200.

Melton, A. W. Implications of short-term memory for a general theory of memory. *Journal of Verbal Learning and Verbal Behavior*, 1963, **2**, 1–21.

Melton, A. W., & Irwin, J. M. The influence of degree of interpolated learning on retroactive inhibition and the overt transfer of specific responses. *American Journal of Psychology*, 1940, **53**, 173–203.

Melvin, K. B. Escape learning and "vicious-circle" behavior as a function of percentage of reinforcement. *Journal of Comparative and Physiological Psychology*, 1964, **58**, 248–251.

Melvin, K. B., & Martin, R. C. Facilitative effects of two modes of punishment on resistance to extinction. *Journal of Comparative and Physiological Psychology*, 1966, **62**, 491–494.

Mentzer, T. L. Comparison of three methods for obtaining psychophysical thresholds from the pigeon. *Journal of Comparative and Physiological Psychology*, 1966, **61**, 96–101.

Merikle, P. M., & Battig, W. F. Transfer of training as a function of experimental paradigm and meaningfulness. *Journal of Verbal Learning and Verbal Behavior*, 1963, **2**, 485–488.

Meyer, D. R. Food deprivation and discrimination reversal learning by monkeys. *Journal of Experimental Psychology*, 1951, **41**, 10–16.

Meyer, D. R., Cho, C., & Wesemann, A. F. On problems of conditioning discriminated lever-press avoidance responses. *Psychological Review*, 1960, **67**, 224–228.

Meyer, D. R., Treichler, F. R., & Meyer, P. M. Discrete-trial training techniques and stimulus variables. In A. M. Schrier, H. F. Harlow, & F. Stollnitz (Eds.), *Behavior of nonhuman primates. Vol. I.* New York: Academic, 1965. Pp. 1–49.

Migler, B. Effects of averaging data during stimulus generalization. *Journal of the Experimental Analysis of Behavior*, 1964, **7**, 303–307.

Miles, R. C. Discrimination in the squirrel monkey as a function of deprivation and problem difficulty. *Journal of Experimental Psychology*, 1959, **57**, 15–19.

Miles, R. C. Discrimination-learning sets. In A. M. Schrier, H. F. Harlow, & F. Stollnitz (Eds.), *Behavior of nonhuman primates. Vol. I.* New York: Academic, 1965. Pp. 51–95.

Miller, G. A. The magical number seven plus or minus two: Some limits on our capacity for processing information. *Psychological Review*, 1956, **63**, 81–96.

Miller, G. A., & Selfridge, J. A. Verbal context and the recall of meaningful material. *American Journal of Psychology*, 1950, **63**, 176–185.

Miller, L. K. Escape from an effortful situation. *Journal of the Experimental Analysis of Behavior*, 1968, **11**, 619–627.

Miller, N. E. Experimental studies of conflict. In J. McV. Hunt (Ed.), *Personality and the behavior disorders.* New York: Ronald, 1944. Pp. 431–465.

Miller, N. E. Liberalization of basic S-R concepts: Extensions to conflict behavior, motivation, and social learning. In S. Koch (Ed.), *Psychology: A study of a science. Vol. 2.* New York: McGraw-Hill, 1959. Pp. 196–292.

Miller, N. E. Learning resistance to pain and fear: Effects of overlearning, exposure, and rewarded exposure in context. *Journal of Experimental Psychology*, 1960, **60**, 137–145.

Miller, N. E. Some recent studies of conflict behavior and drugs. *American Psychologist*, 1961, **16**, 12–24.

Miller, N. E. Learning of visceral and glandular responses. *Science*, 1969, **163**, 434–445.

Miller, N. E., & Banuazizi, A. Instrumental learning by curarized rats of a specific visceral response, intestinal or cardiac. *Journal of Comparative and Physiological Psychology*, 1968, **65**, 1–7.

Miller, N. E., & Carmona, A. Modification of a visceral response, salivation in thirsty dogs, by instrumental training with water reward. *Journal of Comparative and Physiological Psychology*, 1967, **63**, 1–6.

Miller, N. E., & DiCara, L. Instrumental learning of heart rate changes in curarized rats: Shaping, and specificity to discriminative stimulus. *Journal of Comparative and Physiological Psychology*, 1967, **63**, 12–19.

Miller, N. E., & Kraeling, D. Displacement: Greater generalization of approach than avoidance in a generalized approach-avoidance conflict. *Journal of Experimental Psychology*, 1952, **43**, 217–221.

Milner, B., Taylor, L., & Sperry, R. W. Lateralized suppression of dichotically presented digits after commissural section in man. *Science*, 1968, **161**, 184–186.

Mitchell, K. M., Perkins, N. P., & Perkins, C. C., Jr. Conditions affecting acquisition of observing responses in the absence of differential reward. *Journal of Comparative and Physiological Psychology*, 1965, **60**, 435–437.

Montague, W. E., Adams, J. A., & Kiess, H. O. Forgetting and natural language mediation. *Journal of Experimental Psychology*, 1966, **72**, 829–833.

Moray, N. Attention in dichotic listening: Affective cues and the influence of instructions. *Quarterly Journal of Experimental Psychology*, 1959, **11**, 56–60.

Moray, N., & O'Brien, T. Signal-detection theory applied to selective listening. *Journal of the Acoustical Society of America*, 1967, **42**, 765–772.

Morse, W. H. Intermittent reinforcement. In W. K. Honig (Ed.), *Operant behavior: Areas of research and application*. New York: Appleton-Century-Crofts, 1966. Pp. 52–108.

Morse, W. H., & Kelleher, R. T. Schedules using noxious stimuli. I. Multiple fixed-ratio and fixed-interval termination of schedule complexes. *Journal of the Experimental Analysis of Behavior*, 1966, **9**, 267–290.

Morse, W. H., & Kelleher, R. T. Schedules as fundamental determinants of behavior. In W. N. Schoenfeld (Ed.), *Theory of reinforcement schedules*. New York: Appleton-Century-Crofts, 1970.*

Morse, W. H., Mead, R. N., & Kelleher, R. T. Modulation of elicited behavior by a fixed-interval schedule of electric shock presentation. *Science*, 1967, **157**, 215–217.

Moskowitz, H., & Kitzes, L. A comparison of two psychophysical methods using animals. *Journal of the Experimental Analysis of Behavior*, 1966, **9**, 515–519.

Mostofsky, D. I. (Ed.) *Stimulus generalization*. Stanford: Stanford University Press, 1965.

Mostofsky, D. I. (Ed.) *Attention: Contemporary theory and analysis*. New York: Appleton-Century-Crofts, 1970. (a)*

Mostofsky, D. I. Semantics of attention. In D. I. Mostofsky (Ed.), *Attention: Contemporary theory and analysis*. New York: Appleton-Century-Crofts, 1970. (b)*

Mowrer, O. H. On the dual nature of learning—A re-interpretation of "conditioning" and "problem-solving." *Harvard Educational Review*, 1947, **17**, 102–148.

Mowrer, O. H. *Learning theory and personality dynamics*. New York: Ronald, 1950.

Mowrer, O. H. *Learning theory and behavior*. New York: Wiley, 1960.

Mowrer, O. H., & Lamoreaux, R. R. Avoidance conditioning and signal duration—

a study of secondary motivation and reward. *Psychological Monographs*, 1942, **54** (5, Whole No. 247).

Mowrer, O. H., & Lamoreaux, R. R. Conditioning and conditionality (discrimination). *Psychological Review*, 1951, **58**, 196–212.

Moyer, K. E., & Korn, J. H. Effect of UCS intensity on the acquisition and extinction of an avoidance response. *Journal of Experimental Psychology*, 1964, **67**, 352–359.

Moyer, K. E., & Korn, J. H. Effect of UCS intensity on the acquisition and extinction of a one-way avoidance response. *Psychonomic Science*, 1966, **4**, 121–122.

Mumma, R., & Warren, J. M. Two-cue discrimination learning by cats. *Journal of Comparative and Physiological Psychology*, 1968, **66**, 116–121.

Munn, N. L. *Handbook of psychological research on the rat*. New York: Houghton Mifflin, 1950.

Murdock, B. B., Jr. The serial position effect in free recall. *Journal of Experimental Psychology*, 1962, **64**, 482–488.

Murdock, B. B., Jr. Signal-detection theory and short-term memory. *Journal of Experimental Psychology*, 1965, **70**, 443–447.

Myer, J. S., & Ricci, D. Delay of punishment gradients for the goldfish. *Journal of Comparative and Physiological Psychology*, 1968, **66**, 417–421.

Myers, A. K. Avoidance learning as a function of several training conditions and strain differences in rats. *Journal of Comparative and Physiological Psychology*, 1959, **52**, 381–386.

Nachmias, J., & Steinman, R. M. An experimental comparison of the method of limits and the double staircase-method. *American Journal of Psychology*, 1965, **78**, 112–115.

Nakamura, C. Y., & Krudis, B. R. Evaluation of a response speed measure of incentive value of reward. *Journal of Experimental Psychology*, 1967, **74**, 44–49.

Newman, F. L., & Baron, M. R. Stimulus generalization along the dimension of angularity: A comparison of training procedures. *Journal of Comparative and Physiological Psychology*, 1965, **60**, 59–63.

Newman, F. L., & Benefield, R. L. Stimulus control, cue utilization, and attention: Effects of discrimination training. *Journal of Comparative and Physiological Psychology*, 1968, **66**, 101–104.

Newman, J. R., & Grice, G. R. Stimulus generalization as a function of drive level, and the relation between two measures of response strength. *Journal of Experimental Psychology*, 1965, **69**, 357–362.

Nissen, H. W. Analysis of a complex conditional reaction in chimpanzee. *Journal of Comparative and Physiological Psychology*, 1951, **44**, 9–16.

Noble, C. E. An analysis of meaning. *Psychological Review*, 1952, **59**, 421–430. (a)

Noble, C. E. The role of stimulus meaning (*m*) in serial verbal learning. *Journal of Experimental Psychology*, 1952, **43**, 437–446. (b)

Noble, C. E. Measurements of association value (*a*), rated associations (*a'*), and scaled meaningfulness (*m'*) for the 2100 CVC combinations of the English alphabet. *Psychological Reports*, 1961, **8**, 487–521.

Nodine, C. F. Temporal variables in paired-associate learning: The law of contiguity revisited. *Psychological Review*, 1969, **76**, 351–362.

Norman, D. A. A comparison of data obtained with different false-alarm rates. *Psychological Review*, 1964, **71**, 243–246.

North, A. J., & Stimmel, D. T. Extinction of an instrumental response following a large number of reinforcements. *Psychological Reports*, 1960, **6**, 227–234.

North, A. J., Maller, O., & Hughes, C. Conditional discrimination and stimulus patterning. *Journal of Comparative and Physiological Psychology*, 1958, **51**, 711–715.

Notterman, J. M. A study of some relations among aperiodic reinforcement, discrimination training, and secondary reinforcement. *Journal of Experimental Psychology*, 1951, **41**, 161–169.

Notterman, J. M., & Mintz, D. E. *Dynamics of response*. New York: Wiley, 1965.

Osgood, C. E. An investigation into the causes of retroactive interference. *Journal of Experimental Psychology*, 1948, **38**, 132–154.

Osgood, C. E. The similarity paradox in human learning: A resolution. *Psychological Review*, 1949, **56**, 132–143.

Osgood, C. E. Studies on the generality of affective meaning systems. *American Psychologist*, 1962, **17**, 10–28.

Osgood, C. E., & Suci, G. J. Factor analysis of meaning. *Journal of Experimental Psychology*, 1955, **50**, 325–338.

Overmier, J. B. Interference with avoidance behavior: Failure to avoid traumatic shock. *Journal of Experimental Psychology*, 1968, **78**, 340–343.

Owens, W. A. Toward one discipline of scientific psychology. *American Psychologist*, 1968, **23**, 782–785.

Paivio, A. Mental imagery in associative learning and memory. *Psychological Review*, 1969, **76**, 241–263.

Parker, N. I., & Newbigging, P. L. Decrement of the Müller-Lyer illusion as a function of psychophysical procedure. *American Journal of Psychology*, 1965, **78**, 603–608.

Parks, T. E. Signal-detectability theory of recognition-memory performance. *Psychological Review*, 1966, **73**, 44–58.

Pavlik, W. B., & Carlton, P. L. A reversed partial-reinforcement effect. *Journal of Experimental Psychology*, 1965, **70**, 417–423.

Pavlik, W. B., Carlton, P. L., Lehr, R., & Hendrickson, C. A reversed PRE. *Journal of Experimental Psychology*, 1967, **75**, 274–276.

Pavlov, I. P. *Conditioned reflexes*. (Trans. by G. V. Anrep.) London: Oxford University Press, 1927.

Peckham, R. H., & Amsel, A. Within-subjects demonstration of a relationship between frustration and magnitude of reward in a differential magnitude of reward discrimination. *Journal of Experimental Psychology*, 1967, **73**, 187–195.

Pennes, E. S., & Ison, J. R. Effects of partial reinforcement on discrimination learning and subsequent reversal or extinction. *Journal of Experimental Psychology*, 1967, **74**, 219–224.

Penney, R. K. Children's escape performance as a function of schedules of delay of reinforcement. *Journal of Experimental Psychology*, 1967, **73**, 109–112.

Perkins, C. C., Jr. An analysis of the concept of reinforcement. *Psychological Review*, 1968, **75**, 155–172.

Perkins, C. C., Jr., & Weyant, R. G. The interval between training and test trials as a determiner of the slope of generalization gradients. *Journal of Comparative and Physiological Psychology*, 1958, **51**, 596–600.

Perloe, S. I. The relation between category-rating and magnitude-estimation judgments of occupational prestige. *American Journal of Psychology*, 1963, **76**, 395–403.

Peterson, L. R. Reminiscence in short-term retention. *Journal of Experimental Psychology*, 1966, **71**, 115–118. (a)

Peterson, L. R. Short–term verbal memory and learning. *Psychological Review*, 1966, **73**, 193–207. (b)

Peterson, L. R., & Peterson, M. J. Short-term retention of individual verbal items. *Journal of Experimental Psychology*, 1959, **58**, 193–198.

Peterson, M. J., Colavita, F. B., Sheahan, D. B., III, & Blattner, K. C. Verbal mediating chains and response availability as a function of the acquisition paradigm. *Journal of Verbal Learning and Verbal Behavior*, 1964, **3**, 11–18.

Peterson, N. Effect of monochromatic rearing on the control of responding by wavelength. *Science*, 1962, **136**, 774–775.

Pillsbury, W. B. *Attention*. New York: MacMillan, 1908.

Podd, M. H., & Spear, N. E. Stimulus relatedness and response coding. *Journal of Verbal Learning and Verbal Behavior*, 1967, **6**, 55–60.

Pollack, I. Iterative techniques for unbiased rating scales. *Quarterly Journal of Experimental Psychology*, 1965, **17**, 139–148.

Pollack, I., & Decker, L. R. Confidence ratings, message reception, and the receiver operating characteristic. *Journal of the Acoustical Society of America*, 1958, **30**, 286–292.

Pollack, I., & Norman, D. A. A non-parametric analysis of recognition experiments. *Psychonomic Science*, 1964, **1**, 125–126.

Polson, M. C., Restle, F., & Polson, P. G. Association and discrimination in paired-associates learning. *Journal of Experimental Psychology*, 1965, **69**, 47–55.

Porter, J. J. Stimulus generalization as a function of UCS intensity in eyelid conditioning. *Journal of Experimental Psychology*, 1962, **64**, 311–313.

Postman, L. The present status of interference theory. In C. N. Cofer (Ed.), *Verbal learning and verbal behavior*. New York: McGraw-Hill, 1961. Pp. 152–196.

Postman, L. Retention of first-list associations as a function of the conditions of transfer. *Journal of Experimental Psychology*, 1962, **64**, 380–387. (a)

Postman, L. Transfer of training as a function of experimental paradigm and degree of first-list learning. *Journal of Verbal Learning and Verbal Behavior*, 1962, **1**, 109–118. (b)

Postman, L. Does interference theory predict too much forgetting? *Journal of Verbal Learning and Verbal Behavior*, 1963, **2**, 40–48.

Postman, L. Short-term memory and incidental learning. In A. W. Melton (Ed.), *Categories of human learning*. New York: Academic, 1964. Pp. 145-201. (a)

Postman, L. Studies of learning to learn: II. Changes in transfer as a function of practice. *Journal of Verbal Learning and Verbal Behavior*, 1964, **3**, 437–447. (b)

Postman, L. Unlearning under conditions of successive interpolation. *Journal of Experimental Psychology*, 1965, **70**, 237–245.

Postman, L. Differences between unmixed and mixed transfer designs as a function of paradigm. *Journal of Verbal Learning and Verbal Behavior*, 1966, **5**, 240–248.

Postman, L. Mechanisms of interference in forgetting. Vice-Presidential Address given at the Annual Meeting of the American Association for the Advancement of Science. New York, 1967. (a)

Postman, L. The effect of interitem associative strength on the acquisition and retention of serial lists. *Journal of Verbal Learning and Verbal Behavior*, 1967, **6**, 721–728. (b)

Postman, L. Association and performance in the analysis of verbal learning. In T. R. Dixon & D. L. Horton (Eds.), *Verbal behavior and general behavior theory*. Englewood Cliffs, N.J.: Prentice-Hall, 1968. Pp. 550–571. (a)

Postman, L. Hermann Ebbinghaus. *American Psychologist*, 1968, **23**, 149–157. (b)

Postman, L. Studies of learning to learn: VI. General transfer effects in three-stage mediation. *Journal of Verbal Learning and Verbal Behavior*, 1968, **7**, 659–664. (c)

Postman, L., & Goggin, J. Whole vs. part learning of paired-associate lists. *Journal of Experimental Psychology*, 1966, **71**, 867–877.

Postman, L., & Keppel, G. Retroactive inhibition and free recall. *Journal of Experimental Psychology*, 1967, **74**, 203–211.

Postman, L., & Phillips, L. W. Short-term temporal changes in free recall. *Quarterly Journal of Experimental Psychology*, 1965, **17**, 132–138.

Postman, L., & Riley, D. A. A critique of Köhler's theory of association. *Psychological Review*, 1957, **64**, 61–72.

Postman, L., & Schwartz, M. Studies of learning to learn: I. Transfer as a function of method of practice and class of verbal materials. *Journal of Verbal Learning and Verbal Behavior*, 1964, **3**, 37–49.

Postman, L., & Stark, K. Studies of learning to learn. IV. Transfer from serial to paired-associate learning. *Journal of Verbal Learning and Verbal Behavior*, 1967, **6**, 339–353.

Postman, L., Fraser, J., & Burns, S. Unit-sequence facilitation in recall. *Journal of Verbal Learning and Verbal Behavior*, 1968, **7**, 217–224.

Postman, L. Keppel, G., & Stark, K. Unlearning as a function of the relationship between successive response classes. *Journal of Experimental Psychology*, 1965, **69**, 111–118.

Postman, L., Keppel, G., & Zacks, R. Studies of learning to learn: VII. The effects of practice on response integration. *Journal of Verbal Learning and Verbal Behavior*, 1968, **7**, 776–784.

Postman, L., Stark, K., & Fraser, J. Temporal changes in interference. *Journal of Verbal Learning and Verbal Behavior*, 1968, **7**, 672–694.

Poulton, E. C. Population norms of top sensory magnitudes and S. S. Stevens' exponents. *Perception & Psychophysics*, 1967, **2**, 312–316.

Poulton, E. C. The new psychophysics: Six models of magnitude estimation. *Psychological Bulletin*, 1968, **69**, 1–19.

Poulton, E. C., & Freeman, P. R. Unwanted asymmetrical transfer effects with balanced experimental designs. *Psychological Bulletin*, 1966, **66**, 1–8.

Pradhan, P. L., & Hoffman, P. J. Effect of spacing and range of stimuli on magnitude estimation judgments. *Journal of Experimental Psychology*, 1963, **66**, 533–541.

Premack, D., & Collier, G. Duration of looking and number of brief looks as dependent variables. *Psychonomic Science*, 1966, **4**, 81–82.

Pribram, K. H., Gardner, K. W., Pressman, G. L., & Bagshaw, M. An automated discrimination apparatus for discrete trial analysis (DADTA). *Psychological Reports*, 1962, **11**, 247–250.

Price, R. H. Signal-detection methods in personality and perception. *Psychological Bulletin*, 1966, **66**, 55–62.

Price, R. H., & Eriksen, C. W. Size constancy in schizophrenia: A reanalysis. *Journal of Abnormal Psychology*, 1966, **71**, 155–160.

Prokasy, W. F., Jr. The acquisition of observing responses in the absence of differential external reinforcement. *Journal of Comparative and Physiological Psychology*, 1956, **49**, 131–134.

Prokasy, W. F. (Ed.) *Classical conditioning: A symposium*. New York: Appleton-Century-Crofts, 1965.

Prokasy, W. F. Do *D* and *H* multiply in determining performance in human conditioning? *Psychological Bulletin*, 1967, **67**, 368–377.

Prokasy, W. F., & Hall, J. F. Primary stimulus generalization. *Psychological Review*, 1963, **70**, 310–322.

Pubols, B. H., Jr. The acquisition and reversal of a position habit as a function of incentive magnitude. *Journal of Comparative and Physiological Psychology*, 1961, **54**, 94–97.

Rachlin, H. Recovery of responses during mild punishment. *Journal of the Experimental Analysis of Behavior*, 1966, **9**, 251–263.

Rachlin, H., & Herrnstein, R. J. Hedonism revisited: On the negative law of effect. In B. A. Campbell & R. M. Church (Eds.), *Punishment and aversive behavior*. New York: Appleton-Century-Crofts, 1969. Pp. 83–109.

Rachman, S. Introduction to behaviour therapy. *Behaviour Research and Therapy*, 1963, **1**, 3–15.

Rachman, S. Aversion therapy: Chemical or electrical? *Behaviour Research and Therapy*, 1965, **2**, 289–299.

Rashotte, M. E. Resistance to extinction of the continuously rewarded response in within-subject partial-reinforcement experiments. *Journal of Experimental Psychology*, 1968, **76**, 206–214.

Ray, B. A. The course of acquisition of a line-tilt discrimination by rhesus monkeys. *Journal of the Experimental Analysis of Behavior*, 1967, **10**, 17–33.

Ray, B. A. Selective attention: The effects of combining stimuli which control incompatible behavior. *Journal of the Experimental Analysis of Behavior*, 1969, **12**, 539–550.

Ray, B. A., & Sidman, M. Reinforcement schedules and stimulus control. In W. N. Schoenfeld (Ed.), *Theory of reinforcement schedules*. New York: Appleton-Century-Crofts, 1970.*

Razran, G. H. S. A quantitative study of meaning by a conditioned salivary technique (semantic conditioning). *Science*, 1939, **90**, 89–90.

Razran, G. Stimulus generalization of conditioned responses. *Psychological Bulletin*, 1949, **46**, 337–365.

Reese, H. W. Discrimination learning set in rhesus monkeys. *Psychological Bulletin*, 1964, **61**, 321–340.

Reese, H. W. *The perception of stimulus relations*. New York: Academic, 1968.

Reese, T. S., & Stevens, S. S. Subjective intensity of coffee odor. *American Journal of Psychology*, 1960, **73**, 424–428.

Renner, K. E. Delay of reinforcement: A historical review. *Psychological Bulletin*, 1964, **61**, 341–361.

Renner, K. E., & Houlihan, J. Conditions affecting the relative aversiveness of immediate and delayed punishment. *Journal of Experimental Psychology*, 1969, **81**, 411–420.

Rescorla, R. A. Inhibition of delay in Pavlovian fear conditioning. *Journal of Comparative and Physiological Psychology*, 1967, **64**, 114–120. (a)

Rescorla, R. A. Pavlovian conditioning and its proper control procedures. *Psychological Review*, 1967, **74**, 71–80. (b)

Rescorla, R. A. Pavlovian conditioned fear in Sidman avoidance learning. *Journal of Comparative and Physiological Psychology*, 1968, **65**, 55–60.

Rescorla, R. A., & LoLordo, V. M. Inhibition of avoidance behavior. *Journal of Comparative and Physiological Psychology*, 1965, **59**, 406–412.

Rescorla, R. A., & Solomon, R. L. Two-process learning theory: Relationships between Pavlovian conditioning and instrumental learning. *Psychological Review*, 1967, **74**, 151–182.

Restle, F. Toward a quantitative description of learning set data. *Psychological Review*, 1958, **65**, 77–91.

Restle, F. *Psychology of judgment and choice*. New York: Wiley, 1961.

Restle, F. Significance of all-or-none learning. *Psychological Bulletin*, 1965, **64**, 313–325.

Reynolds, B. The relationship between the strength of a habit and the degree of drive present during acquisition. *Journal of Experimental Psychology*, 1949, **39**, 296–305.

Reynolds, G. S. Attention in the pigeon. *Journal of the Experimental Analysis of Behavior*, 1961, **4**, 203–208. (a)

Reynolds, G. S. Behavioral contrast. *Journal of the Experimental Analysis of Behavior*, 1961, **4**, 57–71. (b)

Reynolds, G. S., & Limpo, A. J. Negative contrast after prolonged discrimination maintenance. *Psychonomic Science*, 1968, **10**, 323–324.

Richardson, J. Facilitation of mediated transfer by instructions, B-C training, and presentation of the mediating response. *Journal of Verbal Learning and Verbal Behavior*, 1966, **5**, 59–67. (a)

Richardson, J. The effect of B-C presentation and anticipation interval on mediated transfer. *Journal of Verbal Learning and Verbal Behavior*, 1966, **5**, 119–125. (b)

Richardson, J. Latencies of implicit verbal responses and the effect of the anticipation interval on mediated transfer. *Journal of Verbal Learning and Verbal Behavior*, 1967, **6**, 819–826. (a)

Richardson, J. Transfer and the A-B anticipation interval in the A-B', A-B paradigm. *Journal of Verbal Learning and Verbal Behavior*, 1967, **6**, 897–902. (b)

Richardson, J. Latencies of implicit associative responses and positive transfer in paired-associate learning. *Journal of Verbal Learning and Verbal Behavior*, 1968, **7**, 638–646.

Richardson, J., & Brown, B. L. Mediated transfer in paired-associate learning as a function of presentation rate and stimulus meaningfulness. *Journal of Experimental Psychology*, 1966, **72**, 820–828.

Riesz, R. R. Differential intensity sensitivity of the ear for pure tones. *Physical Review*, 1928, **31**, 867–875.

Riley, D. A. *Discrimination learning*. Boston: Allyn and Bacon, 1968.

Riopelle, A. J., & Copelan, E. L. Discrimination reversal to a sign. *Journal of Experimental Psychology*, 1954, **48**, 143–145.

Rohles, F. H., Jr. Operant methods in space technology. In W. K. Honig (Ed.), *Operant behavior: Areas of research and application*. New York: Appleton-Century-Crofts, 1966. Pp. 677–717.

Rosen, A. J. Incentive-shift performance as a function of magnitude and number of sucrose rewards. *Journal of Comparative and Physiological Psychology*, 1966, **62**, 487–490.

Rosen, A. J., Glass, D. H., & Ison, J. R. Amobarbital sodium and instrumental performance changes following reward reduction. *Psychonomic Science*, 1967, **9**, 129–130.

Rosenbaum, G. Stimulus generalization as a function of level of experimentally induced anxiety. *Journal of Experimental Psychology*, 1953, **45**, 35–43.

Rosenthal, R. *Experimenter effects in behavioral research.* New York: Appleton-Century-Crofts, 1966.

Ross, J., & DiLollo, V. A vector model for psychophysical judgment. *Journal of Experimental Psychology Monograph Supplement,* 1968, **77** (3, Pt. 2).

Rudolph, R. L., Honig, W. K., & Gerry, J. E. Effects of monochromatic rearing on the acquisition of stimulus control. *Journal of Comparative and Physiological Psychology,* 1969, **67,** 50–57.

Runquist, W. N. Retention of verbal associates as a function of strength. *Journal of Experimental Psychology,* 1957, **54,** 369–375.

Runquist, W. N. Mediation speed, reported mediators and recall as related to presentation rate. *Psychonomic Science,* 1965, **3,** 51–52.

Runquist, W. N. Verbal behavior. In J. B. Sidowski (Ed.), *Experimental methods and instrumentation in psychology.* New York: McGraw-Hill, 1966. Pp. 487–540.

Runquist, W. N. Functions relating intralist stimulus similarity to acquisition performance with a variety of materials. *Journal of Verbal Learning and Verbal Behavior,* 1968, **7,** 549–553.

Runquist, W. N., & Farley, F. H. The use of mediators in the learning of verbal paired associates. *Journal of Verbal Learning and Verbal Behavior,* 1964, **3,** 280–285.

Runquist, W. N., & Joinson, P. A. Predictions of terminal acquisition performance for individual subjects. *Journal of Verbal Learning and Verbal Behavior,* 1968, **7,** 98–105.

Russell, W. A., & Storms, L. H. Implicit verbal chaining in paired-associate learning. *Journal of Experimental Psychology,* 1955, **49,** 287–293.

Ryan, T. J., & Watson, P. Frustrative nonreward theory applied to children's behavior. *Psychological Bulletin,* 1968, **69,** 111–125.

Sanders, A. F. (Ed.) *Attention and performance.* Amsterdam: North-Holland, 1967.

Savage, C. W. Introspectionist and behaviorist interpretations of ratio scales of perceptual magnitudes. *Psychological Monographs,* 1966, **80** (19, Whole No. 627).

Schiff, D. Resistance to extinction as a function of level of acquisition training and altered stimulus conditions during extinction. *Psychonomic Science,* 1965, **2,** 23–24.

Schlosberg, H., & Solomon, R. L. Latency of response in a choice discrimination. *Journal of Experimental Psychology,* 1943, **33,** 22–39.

Schoenfeld, W. N. An experimental approach to anxiety, escape and avoidance behavior. In P. H. Hoch & J. Zubin (Eds.), *Anxiety.* New York: Grune & Stratton, 1950. Pp. 70–99.

Schoenfeld, W. N. "Avoidance" in behavior theory. *Journal of the Experimental Analysis of Behavior,* 1969, **12,** 669–674.

Schoenfeld, W. N. (Ed.) *Theory of reinforcement schedules.* New York: Appleton-Century-Crofts, 1970.*

Schoonard, J., & Lawrence, D. H. Resistance to extinction as a function of the number of delay of reward trials. *Psychological Reports,* 1962, **11,** 275–278.

Schrier, A. M. Comparison of two methods of investigating the effect of amount of reward on performance. *Journal of Comparative and Physiological Psychology,* 1958, **51,** 725–731.

Schrier, A. M., & Harlow, H. F. Effect of amount of incentive on discrimination learning by monkeys. *Journal of Comparative and Physiological Psychology,* 1956, **49,** 117–122.

Schulz, R. W., & Lovelace, E. A. Mediation in verbal paired-associate learning: The role of temporal factors. *Psychonomic Science*, 1964, **1**, 95–96.

Schulz, R. W., & Runquist, W. N. Learning and retention of paired adjectives as a function of percentage occurrence of response members. *Journal of Experimental Psychology*, 1960, **59**, 409–413.

Schulz, R. W., Weaver, G. E., & Ginsberg, S. Mediation with pseudomediation controlled: Chaining is not an artifact! *Psychonomic Science*, 1965, **2**, 169–170.

Schuster, R., & Rachlin, H. Indifference between punishment and free shock: Evidence for the negative law of effect. *Journal of the Experimental Analysis of Behavior*, 1968, **11**, 777–786.

Schusterman, R. J. Serial discrimination-reversal learning with and without errors by the California sea lion. *Journal of the Experimental Analysis of Behavior*, 1966, **9**, 593–600.

Schwartzbaum, J. S., & Kellicutt, M. H. Inverted generalization gradients about a nonreinforced stimulus. *Psychological Reports*, 1962, **11**, 791–792.

Schwenn, E., & Postman, L. Studies of learning to learn. V. Gains in performance as a function of warm-up and associative practice. *Journal of Verbal Learning and Verbal Behavior*, 1967, **6**, 565–573.

Schwenn, E., & Underwood, B. J. Simulated similarity and mediation time in transfer. *Journal of Verbal Learning and Verbal Behavior*, 1965, **4**, 476–483.

Sechzer, J. A., & Brown, J. L. Color discrimination in the cat. *Science*, 1964, **144**, 427–429.

Seligman, M. E. P. Chronic fear produced by unpredictable electric shock. *Journal of Comparative and Physiological Psychology*, 1968, **66**, 402–411.

Seligman, M. E. P. Control group and conditioning: A comment on operationism. *Psychological Review*, 1969, **76**, 484–491.

Seligman, M. E. P., & Maier, S. F. Failure to escape traumatic shock. *Journal of Experimental Psychology*, 1967, **74**, 1–9.

Seligman, M. E. P., Maier, S. F., & Solomon, R. L. Unpredictable and uncontrollable aversive events. In F. R. Brush (Ed.), *Aversive conditioning and learning.* New York: Academic, 1970.*

Sellin, T., & Wolfgang, M. E. *The measurement of delinquency.* New York: Wiley, 1964.

Senf, G. M., & Miller, N. E. Evidence for positive induction in discrimination learning. *Journal of Comparative and Physiological Psychology*, 1967, **64**, 121–127.

Sgro, J. A., & Weinstock, S. Effects of delay on subsequent running under immediate reinforcement. *Journal of Experimental Psychology*, 1963, **66**, 260–263.

Sgro, J. A., Dyal, J. A., & Anastasio, E. J. Effects of constant delay of reinforcement on acquisition asymptote and resistance to extinction. *Journal of Experimental Psychology*, 1967, **73**, 634–636.

Sherman, J. G., Hegge, F. W., & Pierrel, R. Discrimination formation as related to the amount of S^Δ training. *Psychonomic Science*, 1964, **1**, 43–44.

Shiffrin, R. M., & Atkinson, R. C. Storage and retrieval processes in long-term memory. *Psychological Review*, 1969, **76**, 179–193.

Shnidman, S. R. Extinction of Sidman avoidance behavior. *Journal of the Experimental Analysis of Behavior*, 1968, **11**, 153–156.

Sidman, M. A note on functional relations obtained from group data. *Psychological Bulletin*, 1952, **49**, 263–269.

Sidman, M. Avoidance conditioning with brief shock and no exteroceptive warning signal. *Science*, 1953, **118**, 157–158.

Sidman, M. *Tactics of scientific research.* New York: Basic Books, 1960.

Sidman, M. Reduction of shock frequency as reinforcement for avoidance behavior. *Journal of the Experimental Analysis of Behavior*, 1962, **5**, 247–257.

Sidman, M. Avoidance behavior. In W. K. Honig (Ed.), *Operant behavior: Areas of research and application*. New York: Appleton-Century-Crofts, 1966. Pp. 448–498.

Sidman, M., & Boren, J. J. A comparison of two types of warning stimulus in an avoidance situation. *Journal of Comparative and Physiological Psychology*, 1957, **50**, 282–287.

Sidman, M., & Stoddard, L. T. The effectiveness of fading in programming a simultaneous form discrimination for retarded children. *Journal of the Experimental Analysis of Behavior*, 1967, **10**, 3–15.

Sidowski, J. B. Response prompting: The practice time variable. *Psychonomic Science*, 1968, **13**, 311–312.

Sidowski, J. B., & Smith, M. J. Basic instrumentation. In J. B. Sidowski (Ed.), *Experimental methods and instrumentation in psychology*. New York: McGraw-Hill, 1966. Pp. 33–114.

Siegel, S. Overtraining and transfer processes. *Journal of Comparative and Physiological Psychology*, 1967, **64**, 471–477.

Silverman, J. The problem of attention in research and theory in schizophrenia. *Psychological Review*, 1964, **71**, 352–379.

Singh, D. Resistance to extinction as a function of differential levels of drive and effortfulness of response. *Psychological Reports*, 1967, **21**, 189–193.

Skinner, B. F. *The behavior of organisms*. New York: Appleton-Century-Crofts, 1938.

Skinner, B. F. "Superstition" in the pigeon. *Journal of Experimental Psychology*, 1948, **38**, 168–172. (a)

Skinner, B. F. *Walden two*. New York: Macmillan, 1948. (b)

Skinner, B. F. Are theories of learning necessary? *Psychological Review*, 1950, **57**, 193–216.

Skinner, B. F. The experimental analysis of behavior. *American Scientist*, 1957, **45**, 343–371.

Skinner, B. F. Diagramming schedules of reinforcement. *Journal of the Experimental Analysis of Behavior*, 1958, **1**, 67–68.

Skinner, B. F. *Cumulative record*. New York: Appleton-Century-Crofts, 1959.

Skinner, B. F. Pigeons in a pelican. *American Psychologist*, 1960, **15**, 28–37.

Skinner, B. F. Operant behavior. In W. K. Honig (Ed.), *Operant behavior: Areas of research and application*. New York: Appleton-Century-Crofts, 1966. Pp. 12–32. (a)

Skinner, B. F. The phylogeny and ontogeny of behavior. *Science*, 1966, **153**, 1205–1213. (b)

Skinner, B. F. *Contingencies of reinforcement: A theoretical analysis*. New York: Appleton-Century-Crofts, 1969.

Slamecka, N. J. A methodological analysis of shift paradigms in human discrimination learning. *Psychological Bulletin*, 1968, **69**, 423–438. (a)

Slamecka, N. J. An examination of trace storage in free recall. *Journal of Experimental Psychology*, 1968, **76**, 504–513. (b)

Slamecka, N. J. A temporal interpretation of some recall phenomena. *Psychological Review*, 1969, **76**, 492–503.

Slamecka, N. J. & Ceraso, J. Retroactive and proactive inhibition of verbal learning. *Psychological Bulletin*, 1960, **57**, 449–475.

Snyder, C., & Noble, M. Operant conditioning of vasoconstriction. *Journal of Experimental Psychology*, 1968, **77**, 263–268.

Solomon, R. L. Punishment. *American Psychologist*, 1964, **19**, 239–253.

Solomon, R. L., & Lessac, M. S. A control group design for experimental studies of developmental processes. *Psychological Bulletin*, 1968, **70**, 145–150.

Solomon, R. L., & Turner, L. H. Discriminative classical conditioning in dogs paralyzed by curare can later control discriminative avoidance responses in the normal state. *Psychological Review*, 1962, **69**, 202–219.

Solomon, R. L., & Wynne, L. C. Traumatic avoidance learning: The principles of anxiety conservation and partial irreversibility. *Psychological Review*, 1954, **61**, 353–385.

Spear, N. E. Retention of reinforcer magnitude. *Psychological Review*, 1967, **74**, 216–234.

Spear, N. E., & Spitzner, J. H. PRE within Ss: Conventional effect on differential speeds, reverse effect on choices. *Psychonomic Science*, 1967, **7**, 99–100.

Spear, N. E., Ekstrand, B. R., & Underwood, B. J. Association by contiguity. *Journal of Experimental Psychology*, 1964, **67**, 151–161.

Spear, N. E., Mikulka, P. J., & Podd, M. Transfer as a function of time to mediate. *Journal of Experimental Psychology*, 1966, **72**, 40–46.

Spence, J. T., & Schulz, R. W. Negative transfer in paired-associate learning as a function of first-list trials. *Journal of Verbal Learning and Verbal Behavior*, 1965, **4**, 397–400.

Spence, K. W. The nature of discrimination learning in animals. *Psychological Review*, 1936, **43**, 427–449.

Spence, K. W. The differential response in animals to stimuli varying within a single dimension. *Psychological Review*, 1937, **44**, 430–444.

Spence, K. W. Continuous versus non-continuous interpretations of discrimination learning. *Psychological Review*, 1940, **47**, 271–288.

Spence, K. W. An experimental test of the continuity and non-continuity theories of discrimination learning. *Journal of Experimental Psychology*, 1945, **35**, 253–266.

Spence, K. W. *Behavior theory and conditioning*. New Haven: Yale University Press, 1956.

Spence, K. W. A theory of emotionally based drive (*D*) and its relations to performance in simple learning situations. *American Psychologist*, 1958, **13**, 131–141. (a)

Spence, K. W. Behavior theory and selective learning. In M. R. Jones (Ed.), *Nebraska symposium on motivation: 1958*. Lincoln: University of Nebraska Press, 1958. Pp. 73–107. (b)

Spence, K. W. Anxiety (drive) level and performance in eyelid conditioning. *Psychological Bulletin*, 1964, **61**, 129–139.

Spence, K. W. Cognitive and drive factors in the extinction of the conditioned eye blink in human subjects. *Psychological Review*, 1966, **73**, 445–458.

Spence, K. W., Goodrich, K. P., & Ross, L. E. Performance in differential conditioning and discrimination learning as a function of hunger and relative response frequency. *Journal of Experimental Psychology*, 1959, **58**, 8–16.

Sperling, S. E. Reversal learning and resistance to extinction: A review of the rat literature. *Psychological Bulletin*, 1965, **63**, 281–297.

Spiker, C. C. The effects of number of reinforcements on the strength of a generalized instrumental response. *Child Development*, 1956, **27**, 37–44.

Staats, A. W., & Staats, C. K. *Complex human behavior*. New York: Holt, Rinehart and Winston, 1963.

Staats, A. W., Staats, C. K., & Heard, W. G. Language conditioning of meaning to meaning using a semantic generalization paradigm. *Journal of Experimental Psychology*, 1959, **57**, 187–192.

Stahl, W. R. Organ weights in primates and other mammals. *Science*, 1965, **150,** 1039–1041.

Stebbins, W. C. Relation of amount of primary reinforcement to discrimination and to secondary reinforcement strength. *Journal of Comparative and Physiological Psychology*, 1959, **52,** 721–726.

Steiner, J. Observing responses and uncertainty reduction. *Quarterly Journal of Experimental Psychology*, 1967, **19,** 18–29.

Steinhardt, J. Intensity discrimination in the human eye. I. The relation of $\Delta I/I$ to intensity. *Journal of General Physiology*, 1936, **20,** 185–209.

Stevens, J. C. Applications of power functions to perceptual-motor learning. *Journal of Experimental Psychology*, 1964, **68,** 614–616.

Stevens, J. C., & Mack, J. D. Scales of apparent force. *Journal of Experimental Psychology*, 1959, **58,** 405–413.

Stevens, J. C., & Marks, L. E. Apparent warmth as a function of thermal irradiation. *Perception & Psychophysics*, 1967, **2,** 613–619.

Stevens, J. C., & Savin, H. B. On the form of learning curves. *Journal of the Experimental Analysis of Behavior*, 1962, **5,** 15–18.

Stevens, J. C., & Stevens, S. S. Warmth and cold: Dynamics of sensory intensity. *Journal of Experimental Psychology*, 1960, **60,** 183–192.

Stevens, J. C., & Stevens, S. S. Brightness function: Effects of adaptation. *Journal of the Optical Society of America*, 1963, **53,** 375–385.

Stevens, S. S. Mathematics, measurement and psychophysics. In S. S. Stevens (Ed.), *Handbook of experimental psychology*. New York: Wiley, 1951. Pp. 1–49.

Stevens, S. S. Decibels of light and sound. *Physics Today*, 1955, **8,** 12–17.

Stevens, S. S. The direct estimation of sensory magnitudes—loudness. *American Journal of Psychology*, 1956, **69,** 1–25.

Stevens, S. S. On the psychophysical law. *Psychological Review*, 1957, **64,** 153–181.

Stevens, S. S. Problems and methods of psychophysics. *Psychological Bulletin*, 1958, **55,** 177–196.

Stevens, S. S. Tactile vibration: Dynamics of sensory intensity. *Journal of Experimental Psychology*, 1959, **57,** 210–218.

Stevens, S. S. The psychophysics of sensory function. *American Scientist*, 1960, **48,** 226–253.

Stevens, S. S. To honor Fechner and repeal his law. *Science*, 1961, **133,** 80–86.

Stevens, S. S. The surprising simplicity of sensory metrics. *American Psychologist*, 1962, **17,** 29–39.

Stevens, S. S. The basis of psychophysical judgments. *Journal of the Acoustical Society of America*, 1963, **35,** 611–612.

Stevens, S. S. On the uses of poikilitic functions. In D. I. Mostofsky (Ed.), *Stimulus generalization*. Stanford: Stanford University Press, 1965. Pp. 24–29.

Stevens, S. S. A metric for the social consensus. *Science*, 1966, **151,** 530–541. (a)

Stevens, S. S. Matching functions between loudness and ten other continua. *Perception & Psychophysics*, 1966, **1,** 5–8. (b)

Stevens, S. S., & Galanter, E. H. Ratio scales and category scales for a dozen perceptual continua. *Journal of Experimental Psychology*, 1957, **54,** 377–411.

Stevens, S. S., & Greenbaum, H. B. Regression effect in psychophysical judgment. *Perception & Psychophysics*, 1966, **1,** 439–446.

Stevens, S. S. & Guirao, M. Loudness, reciprocality, and partition scales. *Journal of the Acoustical Society of America*, 1962, **34,** 1466–1471.

Stevens, S. S. & Guirao, M. Subjective scaling of length and area and the matching of length to loudness and brightness. *Journal of Experimental Psychology*, 1963, **66**, 177–186.

Stevens, S. S., & Harris, J. R. The scaling of subjective roughness and smoothness. *Journal of Experimental Psychology*, 1962, **64**, 489–494.

Stevens, S. S., & Poulton, E. C. The estimation of loudness by unpracticed observers. *Journal of Experimental Psychology*, 1956, **51**, 71–78.

Stevens, S. S., & Stone, G. Finger span: Ratio scale, category scale, and JND scale. *Journal of Experimental Psychology*, 1959, **57**, 91–95.

Stevens, S. S., & Volkmann, J. The relation of pitch to frequency: A revised scale. *American Journal of Psychology*, 1940, **53**, 329–353.

Stevens, S. S., Carton, A. S., & Shickman, G. M. A scale of apparent intensity of electric shock. *Journal of Experimental Psychology*, 1958, **56**, 328–334.

Stewart, M. R., Fagot, R. F., & Eskildsen, P. R. Invariance tests for bisection and fractionation scaling. *Perception & Psychophysics*, 1967, **2**, 323–327.

Stollnitz, F. Spatial variables, observing responses, and discrimination learning sets. *Psychological Review*, 1965, **72**, 247–261.

Storms, L. H., & Broen, W. E., Jr. Drive theories and stimulus generalization. *Psychological Review*, 1966, **73**, 113–127.

Storms, L. H., Boroczi, G., & Broen, W. E., Jr. Punishment inhibits an instrumental response in hooded rats. *Science*, 1962, **135**, 1133–1134.

Suboski, M. D. The analysis of classical discrimination conditioning experiments. *Psychological Bulletin*, 1967, **68**, 235–242.

Suppes, P., & Morningstar, M. Computer-assisted instruction. *Science*, 1969, **166**, 343–350.

Suppes, P., & Zinnes, J. L. Basic measurement theory. In R. D. Luce, R. R. Bush, & E. Galanter (Eds.), *Handbook of mathematical psychology. Vol I.* New York: Wiley, 1963. Pp. 1–76.

Sutherland, N. S. Partial reinforcement and breadth of learning. *Quarterly Journal of Experimental Psychology*, 1966, **18**, 289–301.

Sutherland, N. S., & Holgate, V. Two-cue discrimination learning in rats. *Journal of Comparative and Physiological Psychology*, 1966, **61**, 198–207.

Sutherland, N. S., Mackintosh, N. J., & Wolfe, J. B. Extinction as a function of the order of partial and consistent reinforcement. *Journal of Experimental Psychology*, 1965, **69**, 56–59.

Swets, J. A. Is there a sensory threshold? *Science*, 1961, **134**, 168–177.

Switalski, R. W., Lyons, J., & Thomas, D. R. Effects of interdimensional training on stimulus generalization. *Journal of Experimental Psychology*, 1966, **72**, 661–666.

Tanner, W. P., Jr., & Swets, J. A. A decision-making theory of visual detection. *Psychological Review*, 1954, **61**, 401–409.

Tanner, W. P., Jr., Swets, J. A., & Green, D. M. Some general properties of the hearing mechanism. *Technical Report No. 30*, 1956, Electronic Defense Group, University of Michigan.

Taub, E., Bacon, R. C., & Berman, A. J. Acquisition of a trace-conditioned avoidance response after deafferentation of the responding limb. *Journal of Comparative and Physiological Psychology*, 1965, **59**, 275–279.

Teitelbaum, P. The use of operant methods in the assessment and control of motivational states. In W. K. Honig (Ed.), *Operant behavior: Areas of research and application.* New York: Appleton-Century-Crofts, 1966. Pp. 565–608.

Terman, M., & Kling, J. W. Discrimination of brightness differences by rats with food or brain-stimulation reinforcement. *Journal of the Experimental Analysis of Behavior*, 1968, **11,** 29–37.

Terrace, H. S. Discrimination learning with and without "errors." *Journal of the Experimental Analysis of Behavior*, 1963, **6,** 1–27. (a)

Terrace, H. S. Errorless discrimination learning in the pigeon: Effects of chlorpromazine and imipramine. *Science*, 1963, **140,** 318–319. (b)

Terrace, H. S. Errorless transfer of a discrimination across two continua. *Journal of the Experimental Analysis of Behavior*, 1963, **6,** 223–232. (c)

Terrace, H. S. Wavelength generalization after discrimination learning with and without errors. *Science*, 1964, **144,** 78–80.

Terrace, H. S. Behavioral contrast and the peak shift: Effects of extended discrimination training. *Journal of the Experimental Analysis of Behavior*, 1966, **9,** 613–617. (a)

Terrace, H. S. Discrimination learning and inhibition. *Science*, 1966, **154,** 1677–1680. (b)

Terrace, H. S. Stimulus control. In W. K. Honig (Ed.), *Operant behavior: Areas of research and application*. New York: Appleton-Century-Crofts, 1966. Pp. 271–344. (c)

Terrace, H. S. Discrimination learning, the peak shift, and behavioral contrast. *Journal of the Experimental Analysis of Behavior*, 1968, **11,** 727–741.

Terrace, H. S., & Stevens, S. S. The quantification of tonal volume. *American Journal of Psychology*, 1962, **75,** 596–604.

Terris, W., & Wechkin, S. Learning to resist the effects of punishment. *Psychonomic Science*, 1967, **7,** 169–170.

Theios, J., & Brelsford, J. Overlearning-extinction effect as an incentive phenomenon. *Journal of Experimental Psychology*, 1964, **67,** 463–467.

Theios, J., & McGinnis, R. W. Partial reinforcement before and after continuous reinforcement. *Journal of Experimental Psychology*, 1967, **73,** 479–481.

Thomas, D. R., & King, R. A. Stimulus generalization as a function of level of motivation. *Journal of Experimental Psychology*, 1959, **57,** 323–328.

Thomas, D. R., & Lopez, L. J. The effects of delayed testing on generalization slope. *Journal of Comparative and Physiological Psychology*, 1962, **55,** 541–544.

Thomas, D. R., & Switalski, R. W. Comparison of stimulus generalization following variable-ratio and variable-interval training. *Journal of Experimental Psychology*, 1966, **71,** 236–240.

Thompson, D. M. Escape from S^D associated with fixed-ratio reinforcement. *Journal of the Experimental Analysis of Behavior*, 1964, **7,** 1–8.

Thompson, R. F. Primary stimulus generalization as a function of acquisition level in the cat. *Journal of Comparative and Physiological Psychology*, 1958, **51,** 601–606.

Thompson, R. F. Effect of acquisition level upon the magnitude of stimulus generalization across sensory modality. *Journal of Comparative and Physiological Psychology*, 1959, **52,** 183–185.

Thompson, R. F., & Bettinger, L. A. Neural substrates of attention. In D. I. Mostofsky (Ed.), *Attention: Contemporary theory and analysis*. New York: Appleton-Century-Crofts. 1970.*

Thorndike, E. L. *Animal intelligence*. New York: Macmillan, 1911.

Thorndike, E. L. *Educational psychology. Vol. II. The psychology of learning*. New York: Teachers College, Columbia University, 1913.

Thorndike, E. L. Reward and punishment in animal learning. *Comparative Psychology Monographs*, 1932, **8** (4, Whole No. 39).

Thorndike, E. L., & Lorge, I. *The teacher's word book of 30,000 words*. New York: Columbia University Press, 1944.

Thune, L. E. The effect of different types of preliminary activities on subsequent learning of paired-associate material. *Journal of Experimental Psychology*, 1950, **40**, 423–438.

Thune, L. E. Warm-up effect as a function of level of practice in verbal learning. *Journal of Experimental Psychology*, 1951, **42**, 250–256.

Thune, L. E., & Underwood, B. J. Retroactive inhibition as a function of degree of interpolated learning. *Journal of Experimental Psychology*, 1943, **32**, 185–200.

Thurstone, L. L. A law of comparative judgment. *Psychological Review*, 1927, **34**, 273–286. (a)

Thurstone, L. L. Psychophysical analysis. *American Journal of Psychology*, 1927, **38**, 368–389. (b)

Thurstone, L. L. The phi-gamma hypothesis. *Journal of Experimental Psychology*, 1928, **11**, 293–305.

Thurstone, L. L. Psychophysical methods. In T. G. Andrews (Ed.), *Methods of psychology*. New York: Wiley, 1948. Pp. 124–157.

Tighe, L. S. Effect of perceptual pretraining on reversal and nonreversal shifts. *Journal of Experimental Psychology*, 1965, **70**, 379–385.

Tighe, L. S., & Tighe, T. J. Discrimination learning: Two views in historical perspective. *Psychological Bulletin*, 1966, **66**, 353–370.

Tighe, T. J. Reversal and nonreversal shifts in monkeys. *Journal of Comparative and Physiological Psychology*, 1964, **58**, 324–326.

Tighe, T. J. Effect of overtraining on reversal and extradimensional shifts. *Journal of Experimental Psychology*, 1965, **70**, 13–17.

Tighe, T. J., & Tighe, L. S. Discrimination shift performance of children as a function of age and shift procedure. *Journal of Experimental Psychology*, 1967, **74**, 466–470.

Tighe, T. J., & Tighe, L. S. Differentiation theory and concept-shift behavior. *Psychological Bulletin*, 1968, **70**, 756–761. (a)

Tighe, T. J., & Tighe, L. S. Perceptual learning in the discrimination processes of children: An analysis of five variables in perceptual pretraining. *Journal of Experimental Psychology*, 1968, **77**, 125–134. (b)

Tinbergen, N. *The study of instinct*. London: Oxford University Press, 1951.

Tolman, E. C. *Purposive behavior in animals and men*. New York: Appleton-Century-Crofts, 1932.

Tolman, E. C. The determiners of behavior at a choice point. *Psychological Review*, 1938, **45**, 1–41.

Tombaugh, T. N. Resistance to extinction as a function of the interaction between training and extinction delays. *Psychological Reports*, 1966, **19**, 791–798.

Torgerson, W. S. *Theory and methods of scaling*. New York: Wiley, 1958.

Torgerson, W. S. Quantitative judgment scales. In H. Gulliksen & S. Messick (Eds.), *Psychological scaling: Theory and application*. New York: Wiley, 1960. Pp. 21–31.

Trabasso, T., & Bower, G. H. *Attention in learning: Theory and research*. New York: Wiley, 1968.

Trapold, M. A., & Winokur, S. Transfer from classical conditioning and extinction to acquisition, extinction, and stimulus generalization of a positively reinforced instrumental response. *Journal of Experimental Psychology*, 1967, **73**, 517–525.

Trapold, M. A., Lawton, G. W., Dick, R. A., & Gross, D. M. Transfer of training from differential classical to differential instrumental conditioning. *Journal of Experimental Psychology*, 1968, **76**, 568–573.

Treisman, A. M. Contextual cues in selective listening. *Quarterly Journal of Experimental Psychology*, 1960, **12**, 242–248.

Treisman, A. M. Selective attention in man. *British Medical Bulletin*, 1964, **20**, 12–16. (a)

Treisman, A. M. Verbal cues, language, and meaning in selective attention. *American Journal of Psychology*, 1964, **77**, 206–219. (b)

Treisman, A. M. Strategies and models of selective attention. *Psychological Review*, 1969, **76**, 282–299.

Treisman, A., & Geffen, G. Selective attention: Perception or response? *Quarterly Journal of Experimental Psychology*, 1967, **19**, 1–17.

Treisman, A. M., & Riley, J. G. A. Is selective attention selective perception or selective response? A further test. *Journal of Experimental Psychology*, 1969, **79**, 27–34.

Treisman, M. Noise and Weber's law: The discrimination of brightness and other dimensions. *Psychological Review*, 1964, **71**, 314–330. (a)

Treisman, M. Sensory scaling and the psychophysical law. *Quarterly Journal of Experimental Psychology*, 1964, **16**, 11–22. (b)

Treisman, M., & Watts, T. R. Relation between signal detectability theory and the traditional procedures for measuring sensory thresholds: Estimating d' from results given by the method of constant stimuli. *Psychological Bulletin*, 1966, **66**, 438–454.

Trowill, J. A. Instrumental conditioning of the heart rate in the curarized rat. *Journal of Comparative and Physiological Psychology*, 1967, **63**, 7–11.

Tulving, E. Subjective organization in free recall of "unrelated" words. *Psychological Review*, 1962, **69**, 344–354.

Tulving, E. Intratrial and intertrial retention: Notes towards a theory of free recall verbal learning. *Psychological Review*, 1964, **71**, 219–237.

Tulving, E. The effect of order of presentation on learning of "unrelated" words. *Psychonomic Science*, 1965, **3**, 337–338.

Tulving, E. Subjective organization and effects of repetition in multi-trial free-recall learning. *Journal of Verbal Learning and Verbal Behavior*, 1966, **5**, 193–197.

Tulving, E. Theoretical issues in free recall. In T. R. Dixon & D. L. Horton (Eds.), *Verbal behavior and general behavior theory*. Englewood Cliffs, N.J.: Prentice-Hall, 1968. Pp. 2–36. (a)

Tulving, E. When is recall higher than recognition? *Psychonomic Science*, 1968, **10**, 53–54. (b)

Turner, L. H., & Solomon, R. L. Human traumatic avoidance learning: Theory and experiments on the operant-respondent distinction and failures to learn. *Psychological Monographs*, 1962, **76** (40, Whole No. 559).

Uhl, C. N., & Young, A. G. Resistance to extinction as a function of incentive, percentage of reinforcement, and number of nonreinforced trials. *Journal of Experimental Psychology*, 1967, **73**, 556–564.

Ullmann, L. P., & Krasner, L. (Eds.) *Case studies in behavior modification*. New York: Holt, Rinehart and Winston, 1965.

Ulrich, R. E., Holz, W. C., & Azrin, N. H. Stimulus control of avoidance behavior. *Journal of the Experimental Analysis of Behavior*, 1964, **7**, 129–133.

Ulrich, R., Stachnik, T., & Mabry, J. (Eds.) *Control of human behavior*. Glenview, Ill.: Scott, Foresman, 1966.

Underwood, B. J. The effect of successive interpolations on retroactive and proactive inhibition. *Psychological Monographs*, 1945, **59** (3, Whole No. 273).

Underwood, B. J. 'Spontaneous recovery' of verbal associations. *Journal of Experimental Psychology*, 1948, **38,** 429–439.

Underwood, B. J. Proactive inhibition as a function of time and degree of prior learning. *Journal of Experimental Psychology*, 1949, **39,** 24–34.

Underwood, B. J. Associative transfer in verbal learning as a function of response similarity and degree of first-list learning. *Journal of Experimental Psychology*, 1951, **42,** 44–53.

Underwood, B. J. Speed of learning and amount retained: A consideration of methodology. *Psychological Bulletin*, 1954, **51,** 276–282.

Underwood, B. J. Interference and forgetting. *Psychological Review*, 1957, **64,** 49–60. (a)

Underwood, B. J. *Psychological research.* New York: Appleton-Century-Crofts, 1957. (b)

Underwood, B. J. An evaluation of the Gibson theory of verbal learning. In C. N. Cofer (Ed.), *Verbal learning and verbal behavior.* New York: McGraw-Hill, 1961. Pp. 197–223.

Underwood, B. J. Stimulus selection in verbal learning. In C. N. Cofer & B. S. Musgrave (Eds.), *Verbal behavior and learning.* New York: McGraw-Hill, 1963. Pp. 33–48.

Underwood, B. J. Articulation in verbal learning. *Journal of Verbal Learning and Verbal Behavior*, 1964, **3,** 146–149. (a)

Underwood, B. J. Degree of learning and the measurement of forgetting. *Journal of Verbal Learning and Verbal Behavior*, 1964, **3,** 112–129. (b)

Underwood, B. J. The representativeness of rote verbal learning. In A. W. Melton (Ed.), *Categories of human learning.* New York: Academic, 1964. Pp. 47–78. (c)

Underwood, B. J. False recognition produced by implicit verbal responses. *Journal of Experimental Psychology*, 1965, **70,** 122–129.

Underwood, B. J. *Experimental psychology.* (2d ed.) New York: Appleton-Century-Crofts, 1966. (a)

Underwood, B. J. Individual and group predictions of item difficulty for free learning. *Journal of Experimental Psychology*, 1966, **71,** 673–679. (b)

Underwood, B. J. Motor-skills learning and verbal learning: Some observations. In E. A. Bilodeau (Ed.), *Acquisition of skill.* New York: Academic, 1966. Pp. 489–516. (c)

Underwood, B. J. Attributes of memory. *Psychological Review*, 1969, **76,** 559–573. (a)

Underwood, B. J. Some correlates of item repetition in free-recall learning. *Journal of Verbal Learning and Verbal Behavior*, 1969, **8,** 83–94. (b)

Underwood, B. J., & Ekstrand, B. R. An analysis of some shortcomings in the interference theory of forgetting. *Psychological Review*, 1966, **73,** 540–549.

Underwood, B. J., & Ekstrand, B. R. Effect of distributed practice on paired-associate learning. *Journal of Experimental Psychology Monograph Supplement*, 1967, **73** (4, Pt. 2). (a)

Underwood, B. J., & Ekstrand, B. R. Studies of distributed practice: XXIV. Differentiation and proactive inhibition. *Journal of Experimental Psychology*, 1967, **74,** 574–580. (b)

Underwood, B. J., & Ekstrand, B. R. Differentiation among stimuli as a factor in transfer performance. *Journal of Verbal Learning and Verbal Behavior*, 1968, **7,** 172–175. (a)

Underwood, B. J., & Ekstrand, B. R. Linguistic associations and retention. *Journal of Verbal Learning and Verbal Behavior*, 1968, **7**, 162–171. (b)

Underwood, B. J., & Erlebacher, A. H. Studies of coding in verbal learning. *Psychological Monographs*, 1965, **79** (13, Whole No. 606).

Underwood, B. J., & Freund, J. S. Effect of temporal separation of two tasks on proactive inhibition. *Journal of Experimental Psychology*, 1968, **78**, 50–54. (a)

Underwood, B. J., & Freund, J. S. Errors in recognition learning and retention. *Journal of Experimental Psychology*, 1968, **78**, 55–63. (b)

Underwood, B. J., & Keppel, G. An evaluation of two problems of method in the study of retention. *American Journal of Psychology*, 1962, **75**, 1–17.

Underwood, B. J., & Keppel, G. Coding processes in verbal learning. *Journal of Verbal Learning and Verbal Behavior*, 1963, **1**, 250–257. (a)

Underwood, B. J., & Keppel, G. Retention as a function of degree of learning and letter-sequence interference. *Psychological Monographs*, 1963, **77** (4, Whole No. 567). (b)

Underwood, B. J., & Postman, L. Extraexperimental sources of interference in forgetting. *Psychological Review*, 1960, **67**, 73–95.

Underwood, B. J., & Richardson, J. The influence of meaningfulness, intralist similarity and serial position on retention. *Journal of Experimental Psychology*, 1956, **52**, 119–126.

Underwood, B. J., & Schulz, R. W. *Meaningfulness and verbal learning*. Philadelphia: Lippincott, 1960.

Underwood, B. J., Ekstrand, B. R., & Keppel, G. Studies of distributed practice: XXIII. Variations in response-term interference. *Journal of Experimental Psychology*, 1964, **68**, 201–212.

Underwood, B. J., Ekstrand, B. R., & Keppel, G. An analysis of intralist similarity in verbal learning with experiments on conceptual similarity. *Journal of Verbal Learning and Verbal Behavior*, 1965, **4**, 447–462.

Underwood, B. J., Ham, M., & Ekstrand, B. Cue selection in paired-associate learning. *Journal of Experimental Psychology*, 1962, **64**, 405–409.

Underwood, B. J., Runquist, W. N., & Schulz, R. W. Response learning in paired-associate lists as a function of intralist similarity. *Journal of Experimental Psychology*, 1959, **58**, 70–78.

Urban, R. M. *The application of statistical methods to the problems of psychophysics*. Philadelphia: Psychological Clinic Press, 1908.

Valenstein, E. S., & Beer, B. Continuous opportunity for reinforcing brain stimulation. *Journal of the Experimental Analysis of Behavior*, 1964, **7**, 183–184.

Van Ormer, E. B. Retention after intervals of sleep and of waking. *Archives of Psychology*, 1932, No. 137.

Verhave, T. Technique for the differential reinforcement of rate of avoidance responding. *Science*, 1959, **129**, 959–960.

Verhave, T. The pigeon as a quality-control inspector. *American Psychologist*, 1966, **21**, 109–115.

Vogel–Sprott, M., & Thurston, E. Resistance to punishment and subsequent extinction of a response as a function of its reward history. *Psychological Reports*, 1968, **22**, 631–637.

Wagner, A. R. Sodium amytal and partially reinforced runway performance. *Journal of Experimental Psychology*, 1963, **65**, 474–477.

Wagner, A. R. Frustration and punishment. In R. N. Haber (Ed.), *Current research in motivation*. New York: Holt, Rinehart & Winston, 1966. Pp. 229–239.

Wagner, A. R., Siegel, L. S., & Fein, G. G. Extinction of conditioned fear as a function of percentage of reinforcement. *Journal of Comparative and Physiological Psychology*, 1967, **63**, 160–164.

Wagner, A. R., Logan, F. A., Haberlandt, K., & Price, T. Stimulus selection in animal discrimination learning. *Journal of Experimental Psychology*, 1968, **76**, 171–180.

Wald, A. *Statistical decision functions*. New York: Wiley, 1950.

Walk, R. D., Gibson, E. J., Pick, H. L., Jr., & Tighe, T. J. The effectiveness of prolonged exposure to cutouts vs. painted patterns for facilitation of discrimination. *Journal of Comparative and Physiological Psychology*, 1959, **52**, 519–521.

Walker, E. L., & Tarte, R. D. Memory storage as a function of arousal and time with homogeneous and heterogeneous lists. *Journal of Verbal Learning and Verbal Behavior*, 1963, **2**, 113–119.

Wallace, W. H., Turner, S. H., & Perkins, C. C. Preliminary studies of human information storage. *Signal Corps Project No. 1320*, 1957, Institute for Cooperative Research, University of Pennsylvania.

Wallace, W. P. Implicit associative response occurrence in learning with retarded subjects: A supplementary report. *Journal of Educational Psychology*, 1967, **58**, 110–114.

Wallace, W. P., & Underwood, B. J. Implicit responses and the role of intralist similarity in verbal learning by normal and retarded subjects. *Journal of Educational Psychology*, 1964, **55**, 362–370.

Waller, T. G. Effects of magnitude of reward in spatial and brightness discrimination tasks. *Journal of Comparative and Physiological Psychology*, 1968, **66**, 122–127.

Warren, J. M. Additivity of cues in visual pattern discrimination by monkeys. *Journal of Comparative and Physiological Psychology*, 1953, **46**, 484–486.

Warren, J. M. Perceptual dominance in discrimination learning by monkeys. *Journal of Comparative and Physiological Psychology*, 1954, **47**, 290–292.

Warren, J. M. Additivity of cues in conditional discrimination learning by rhesus monkeys. *Journal of Comparative and Physiological Psychology*, 1964, **58**, 124–126.

Warren, J. M. Primate learning in comparative perspective. In A. M. Schrier, H. F. Harlow, & F. Stollnitz (Eds.), *Behavior of nonhuman primates. Vol. I.* New York: Academic, 1965. Pp. 249–281.

Warren, J. M., & McGonigle, B. Attention theory and discrimination learning. In R. M. Gilbert & N. S. Sutherland (Eds.), *Animal discrimination learning*. New York: Academic, 1969. Pp. 113–136.

Warren, J. M., Derdzinski, D., Hirayoshi, I., & Mumma, R. Some tests of attention theory with cats. In D. I. Mostofsky (Ed.), *Attention: Contemporary theory and analysis*. New York: Appleton-Century-Crofts, 1970.*

Warren, R. M., & Warren, R. P. A critique of S. S. Stevens' "New Psychophysics." *Perceptual and Motor Skills*, 1963, **16**, 797–810.

Watson, R. I. *The great psychologists: From Aristotle to Freud*. Philadelphia: Lippincott, 1963.

Waugh, N. C. Free vs. serial recall. *Journal of Experimental Psychology*, 1961, **62**, 496–502.

Webb, W. B. The effects of prolonged learning on learning. *Journal of Verbal Learning and Verbal Behavior*, 1962, **1**, 173–182.

Weiner, B. Effects of motivation on the availability and retrieval of memory traces. *Psychological Bulletin*, 1966, **65**, 24–37. (a)

Weiner, B. Motivation and memory. *Psychological Monographs*, 1966, **80** (18, Whole No. 626). (b)

Weiner, B., & Walker, E. L. Motivational factors in short-term retention. *Journal of Experimental Psychology*, 1966, **71**, 190–193.

Weiss, J. M., Krieckhaus, E. E., & Conte, R. Effects of fear conditioning on subsequent avoidance behavior and movement. *Journal of Comparative and Physiological Psychology*, 1968, **65**, 413–421.

Weissman, A. Nondiscriminated avoidance behavior in a large sample of rats. *Psychological Reports*, 1962, **10**, 591–600.

Weitzman, B. Behavior therapy and psychotherapy. *Psychological Review*, 1967, **74**, 300–317.

Werner, G., & Mountcastle, V. B. Neural activity in mechanoreceptive cutaneous afferents: Stimulus-response relations, Weber functions, and information transmission. *Journal of Neurophysiology*, 1965, **28**, 359–397.

Wickelgren, W. A. Acoustic similarity and retroactive interference in short-term memory. *Journal of Verbal Learning and Verbal Behavior*, 1965, **4**, 53–61.

Wickelgren, W. A., & Norman, D. A. Strength models and serial position in short-term recognition memory. *Journal of Mathematical Psychology*, 1966, **3**, 316–347.

Wickens, D. D., & Simpson, C. K. Trace cue position, motivation, and short-term memory. *Journal of Experimental Psychology*, 1968, **76**, 282–285.

Wickens, D. D., Born, D. G., & Allen, C. K. Proactive inhibition and item similarity in short-term memory. *Journal of Verbal Learning and Verbal Behavior*, 1963, **2**, 440–445.

Wike, E. L. (Ed.) *Secondary reinforcement: Selected experiments.* New York: Harper & Row, 1966.

Wike, E. L., & Farrow, B. J. The effects of magnitude of water reward on selective learning and habit reversal. *Journal of Comparative and Physiological Psychology*, 1962, **55**, 1024–1028.

Wike, E. L., & McWilliams, J. The effects of long-term training with delayed reward and delay-box confinement on instrumental performance. *Psychonomic Science*, 1967, **9**, 389–390.

Willems, E. P., & Raush, H. L. (Eds.) *Naturalistic viewpoints in psychological research.* New York: Holt, Rinehart and Winston, 1969.

Wilton, R. N., & Strongman, K. T. Extinction performance as a function of reinforcement magnitude and number of training trials. *Psychological Reports*, 1967, **20**, 235–238.

Winer, B. J. *Statistical principles in experimental design.* New York: McGraw-Hill, 1962.

Winograd, E. Escape behavior under different fixed ratios and shock intensities. *Journal of the Experimental Analysis of Behavior*, 1965, **8**, 117–124.

Winograd, E. List differentiation as a function of frequency and retention interval. *Journal of Experimental Psychology Monograph Supplement*, 1968, **76** (2, Pt. 2).

Wolff, H. G., & Wolf, S. *Pain.* Springfield, Ill.: Charles C Thomas, 1948.

Wolff, J. L. Concept-shift and discrimination-reversal learning in humans. *Psychological Bulletin*, 1967, **68**, 369–408.

Wolford, G., & Bower, G. H. Continuity theory revisited: Rejected for the wrong reasons? *Psychological Review*, 1969, **76**, 515–518.

Wolpe, J., & Lazarus, A. A. *Behavior therapy techniques.* New York: Pergamon, 1966.

Wolpe, J., Salter, A., & Reyna, L. J. (Eds.) *The conditioning therapies.* New York: Holt, Rinehart and Winston, 1964.

Wood, G. Mnemonic systems in recall. *Journal of Educational Psychology Monograph,* 1967, **58** (6, Pt. 2).

Wood, G. Implicit responses and conceptual similarity: A repetition. *Journal of Verbal Learning and Verbal Behavior,* 1968, **7,** 838–840.

Wood, G., & Underwood, B. J. Implicit responses and conceptual similarity. *Journal of Verbal Learning and Verbal Behavior,* 1967, **6,** 1–10.

Woods, P. J. A bibliography of references relevant to instrumental escape conditioning. Distributed privately, 1965.

Woods, P. J. Performance changes in escape conditioning following shifts in the magnitude of reinforcement. *Journal of Experimental Psychology,* 1967, **75,** 487–491.

Woods, P. J., & Holland, C. H. Instrumental escape conditioning in a water tank: Effects of constant reinforcement at different levels of drive stimulus intensity. *Journal of Comparative and Physiological Psychology,* 1966, **62,** 403–408.

Woods, P. J., Davidson, E. H., & Peters, R. J. Instrumental escape conditioning in a water tank: Effects of variations in drive stimulus intensity and reinforcement magnitude. *Journal of Comparative and Physiological Psychology,* 1964, **57,** 466–470.

Woodworth, R. S., & Schlosberg, H. *Experimental psychology.* (Rev. ed.) New York: Holt, 1954.

Worden, F. G. Attention and auditory electrophysiology. In E. Stellar & J. M. Sprague (Eds.), *Progress in physiological psychology. Vol. I.* New York: Academic, 1966. Pp. 45–116.

Wright, D. C., French, G. M., & Riley, D. A. Similarity responding by monkeys in a matching to sample task. *Journal of Comparative and Physiological Psychology,* 1968, **65,** 191–196.

Wyckoff, L. B., Jr. The role of observing responses in discrimination learning: Part I. *Psychological Review,* 1952, **59,** 431–442.

Wyckoff, L. B. Toward a quantitative theory of secondary reinforcement. *Psychological Review,* 1959, **66,** 68–78.

Wynne, L. C., & Solomon, R. L. Traumatic avoidance learning: Acquisition and extinction in dogs deprived of normal peripheral autonomic function. *Genetic and Psychological Monographs,* 1955, **52,** 241–284.

Yarczower, M., Dickson, J. F., & Gollub, L. R. Some effects on generalization gradients of tandem schedules. *Journal of the Experimental Analysis of Behavior,* 1966, **9,** 631–639.

Yarczower, M., Gollub, L. R., & Dickson, J. F. Some effects of discriminative training with equated frequency of reinforcement. *Journal of the Experimental Analysis of Behavior,* 1968, **11,** 415–423.

Young, R. K. Serial learning. In T. R. Dixon & D. L. Horton (Eds.), *Verbal behavior and general behavior theory.* Englewood Cliffs, N.J.: Prentice-Hall, 1968. Pp. 122–148.

Zajonc, R. B., & Cross, D. V. Stimulus generalization as a function of drive shift. *Journal of Experimental Psychology,* 1965, **69,** 363–368.

Zajonc, R. B., & Dorfman, D. D. Perception, drive, and behavior theory. *Psychological Review,* 1964, **71,** 273–290.

Zaretsky, H. H. Learning and performance in the runway as a function of the shift in drive and incentive. *Journal of Comparative and Physiological Psychology*, 1966, **62,** 218–221.

Zavortink, B., & Keppel, G. Retroactive inhibition for lists learned under interference conditions. *Canadian Journal of Psychology*, 1969, **23,** 245–253.

Zeaman, D. Response latency as a function of the amount of reinforcement. *Journal of Experimental Psychology*, 1949, **39,** 466–483.

Zeaman, D., & House, B. J. The role of attention in retardate discrimination learning. In N. R. Ellis (Ed.), *Handbook of mental deficiency: Psychological theory and research.* New York: McGraw-Hill, 1963. Pp. 159–223.

APPENDIX

Table A Random Digits

	00-04	05-09	10-14	15-19	20-24	25-29	30-34	35-39	40-44	45-49
00	83474	29226	28313	50047	48885	15141	09967	41583	16311	37427
01	03923	12282	93819	58928	25273	21305	34912	25859	36556	32280
02	14513	51745	25987	46116	32723	14553	01890	75123	77090	86182
03	89813	75362	13801	71825	45502	43603	00528	03315	80797	51954
04	32167	08652	49524	24791	84877	71892	44795	32077	76302	40872
05	41419	10395	90389	94960	98682	26763	41593	75984	36920	10095
06	92598	05485	47358	39840	33510	40603	50204	80801	21792	01742
07	44370	61741	80259	65432	47900	29031	91048	40456	62170	19789
08	60770	74345	45182	15639	53398	85816	76665	24022	50982	52449
09	18885	55615	59863	07591	03824	11293	91288	22314	33136	49537
10	95977	99943	27874	65452	24880	52721	11748	97489	25505	95311
11	13948	24893	90727	72819	73147	73969	69684	45497	43388	53054
12	39828	87021	32726	45085	53523	75128	24268	12765	66799	41394
13	32736	29722	43545	60914	53862	41737	86544	40180	33924	27858
14	22844	77742	71572	07617	05136	09287	66488	47731	64881	53030
15	69694	11080	15759	09183	85138	81561	42286	83489	62109	30034
16	34176	42271	70176	16320	07336	39747	02510	96462	52222	96490
17	97147	69734	68047	37417	69690	70957	64654	54441	15633	24937
18	51396	58500	26926	31821	01710	33137	09045	62171	85939	22096
19	61072	38873	20627	53366	57474	98386	56765	48994	87359	00194
20	74153	72232	59491	53355	94270	06993	25306	80985	94216	19045
21	43826	91447	33560	13859	87473	70388	90742	21200	26763	95272
22	06081	03049	95964	54648	65039	68453	93891	68985	19932	73134
23	86584	09836	82703	69606	68055	70436	72572	08402	53232	75154
24	73158	59948	82129	22767	85068	61835	79218	64601	59854	43637
25	65929	54411	47087	27745	35924	53146	90280	73174	51987	21585
26	95847	62612	19969	52243	81078	51215	17581	42364	16496	12368
27	04676	69361	00065	64381	04068	20584	13768	84957	37497	73988
28	03462	12273	85723	80945	14509	60281	24731	37852	34272	85003
29	84994	42334	72269	98383	71589	10078	40046	96418	25271	28251
30	46058	46944	82021	95088	28425	53576	31766	98136	63861	41579
31	79369	42575	44260	23557	28077	38159	12850	56267	52301	93777
32	47619	63272	16060	49389	02296	27358	10203	78476	13620	06070
33	91936	46600	40241	82240	27313	17378	50813	42093	04975	33514
34	31243	70172	85247	02430	21072	41513	76442	14620	90890	73587
35	96046	48680	10662	69950	50120	10001	22292	60895	96131	55097
36	97992	81395	19071	44288	17955	31596	57292	88164	68103	85081
37	59160	85187	66887	49709	30070	02666	76745	94570	58940	52746
38	85919	38263	70617	39025	14090	24346	29285	64554	94188	59964
39	10529	17903	03444	34875	17918	60255	25574	05170	72397	21948
40	56367	93527	21720	34389	76432	80791	80439	03236	24115	53200
41	24715	21324	49067	35552	48193	10830	22090	62157	57003	98094
42	58543	87341	22903	24735	60537	86466	69156	55159	96945	37613
43	01975	45181	46760	30200	93843	16941	72660	36059	34037	56202
44	76410	49033	82143	61042	30948	00738	77290	58414	01386	69725
45	91975	00277	43514	33696	10583	60683	53147	01880	50756	68078
46	68365	07355	38251	13864	66333	35803	51901	18910	66097	19087
47	70233	78620	16528	33752	91647	18647	53531	47462	75575	27458
48	10396	81046	04540	37692	87303	07304	01051	92710	90874	92322
49	33035	86608	45741	91437	05579	43612	58883	73264	09915	51373

SOURCE: J. E. Wert, C. O. Neidt, & J. S. Ahmann. *Statistical methods in education and psychological research.* New York: Appleton-Century-Crofts, 1954. Copyright 1954 by Appleton-Century-Crofts. Used by permission.

Table B Areas of a Unit Normal Distribution

An entry in the table is the proportion under the entire curve which is between $z = 0$ and a positive value of z. Areas for negative values of z are obtained by symmetry.

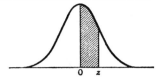

z	.00	.01	.02	.03	.04	.05	.06	.07	.08	.09
0.0	.0000	.0040	.0080	.0120	.0160	.0199	.0239	.0279	.0319	.0359
0.1	.0398	.0438	.0478	.0517	.0557	.0596	.0636	.0675	.0714	.0753
0.2	.0793	.0832	.0871	.0910	.0948	.0987	.1026	.1064	.1103	.1141
0.3	.1179	.1217	.1255	.1293	.1331	.1368	.1406	.1443	.1480	.1517
0.4	.1554	.1591	.1628	.1664	.1700	.1736	.1772	.1808	.1844	.1879
0.5	.1915	.1950	.1985	.2019	.2054	.2088	.2123	.2157	.2190	.2224
0.6	.2257	.2291	.2324	.2357	.2389	.2422	.2454	.2486	.2517	.2549
0.7	.2580	.2611	.2642	.2673	.2703	.2734	.2764	.2794	.2823	.2852
0.8	.2881	.2910	.2939	.2967	.2995	.3023	.3051	.3078	.3106	.3133
0.9	.3159	.3186	.3212	.3238	.3264	.3289	.3315	.3340	.3365	.3389
1.0	.3413	.3438	.3461	.3485	.3508	.3531	.3554	.3577	.3599	.3621
1.1	.3643	.3665	.3686	.3708	.3729	.3749	.3770	.3790	.3810	.3830
1.2	.3849	.3869	.3888	.3907	.3925	.3944	.3962	.3980	.3997	.4015
1.3	.4032	.4049	.4066	.4082	.4099	.4115	.4131	.4147	.4162	.4177
1.4	.4192	.4207	.4222	.4236	.4251	.4265	.4279	.4292	.4306	.4319
1.5	.4332	.4345	.4357	.4370	.4382	.4394	.4406	.4418	.4429	.4441
1.6	.4452	.4463	.4474	.4484	.4495	.4505	.4515	.4525	.4535	.4545
1.7	.4554	.4564	.4573	.4582	.4591	.4599	.4608	.4616	.4625	.4633
1.8	.4641	.4649	.4656	.4664	.4671	.4678	.4686	.4693	.4699	.4706
1.9	.4713	.4719	.4726	.4732	.4738	.4744	.4750	.4756	.4761	.4767
2.0	.4772	.4778	.4783	.4788	.4793	.4798	.4803	.4808	.4812	.4817
2.1	.4821	.4826	.4830	.4834	.4838	.4842	.4846	.4850	.4854	.4857
2.2	.4861	.4864	.4868	.4871	,4875	.4878	.4881	.4884	.4887	.4890
2.3	.4893	.4896	.4898	.4901	.4904	.4906	.4909	.4911	.4913	.4916
2.4	.4918	.4920	.4922	.4925	.4927	.4929	.4931	.4932	.4934	.4936
2.5	.4938	.4940	.4941	.4943	.4945	.4946	.4948	.4949	.4951	.4952
2.6	.4953	.4955	.4956	.4957	.4959	.4960	.4961	.4962	.4963	.4964
2.7	.4965	.4966	.4967	.4968	.4969	.4970	.4971	.4972	.4973	.4974
2.8	.4974	.4975	.4976	.4977	.4977	.4978	.4979	.4979	.4980	.4981
2.9	.4981	.4982	.4982	.4983	.4984	.4984	.4985	.4985	.4986	.4986
3.0	.4987	.4987	.4987	.4988	.4988	.4989	.4989	.4989	.4990	.4990

SOURCE: P. G. Hoel. *Elementary statistics.* New York: Wiley, 1960. Copyright 1960 by John Wiley & Sons, Inc. Used by permission.

SYMBOLS
AND
ABBREVIATIONS

A-B′, *A-B*: A transfer paradigm in which the stimulus items of the two lists are identical and the responses are related (e.g., synonyms).

A-B$_r$, *A-B*: A transfer paradigm in which the stimulus and response items of the two lists are identical but the response items are re-paired.

A-C, *A-B*: A transfer paradigm in which the stimulus items of the two lists are identical but the response items are unrelated.

AD: Average deviation of a group of scores, i.e., $\Sigma|X_i - \bar{X}|/n$.

AD$_m$: Average deviation taken around the median, i.e., $\Sigma|X_i - m|/n$.

AL: Absolute limen; in the method of limits $AL = \bar{T}$.

C-B, *A-B*: A transfer paradigm in which the response items of the two lists are identical but the stimulus items are unrelated.

C-D, *A-B*: A transfer paradigm in which the stimulus and response items of the two lists are unrelated.

CER: Conditioned emotional response.

cm: Centimeter.

CR:	Conditioned response.
CRF:	Continuous (regular) reinforcement schedule.
CS:	Conditioned stimulus.
D:	Drive (motivation).
d':	In TSD a measure of S's sensitivity
db:	Decibel.
DL:	Difference limen.
DRH:	Differential reinforcement of high rate schedule.
DRL:	Differential reinforcement of low rate schedule.
DRO:	Differential reinforcement of other behavior.
DT:	Difference threshold (on a single series, as in the method of limits).
E:	Reaction potential.
$\mathbf{E}$:	Experimenter.
E_N:	In TSD the distribution of central neural effects arising from N.
E_{SN}:	In TSD the distribution of central neural effects arising from SN.
EDS:	Extradimensional shift in discrimination studies.
EXT:	Extinction schedule.
f:	Frequency
FI:	Fixed-interval schedule of reinforcement.
FR:	Fixed-ratio schedule of reinforcement.
GSR:	Galvanic skin response.
H:	Habit strength.
Hz:	Cycles per second, named in honor of the physicist Heinrich Hertz.
IAR:	Implicit associative response.
IL:	Interpolated learning.
IRT:	Interresponse time, i.e., the interval separating two adjacent responses.
IU:	Interval of uncertainty.
JND:	Just noticeable difference.
K:	Incentive motivation.
l:	Likelihood ratio.
LDL:	Lower difference limen; $S_t - LL$.
LDT:	Lower difference threshold (on a single series in the method of limits).
LL:	Lower limen; $\overline{LT}$ in the method of limits.
LT:	Lower threshold (on a single series of the method of limits).
LTM:	Long-term memory.
m:	The median of a group of scores.
m_0:	The mode of a group of scores.
ma:	Milliampere.
mm:	Millimeter.
msec:	Millisecond.
$m\mu$:	Millimicron, a billionth of a meter; also nanometer (nm).
n:	In TSD a response signifying that N occurred.
N:	The noise stimulus of TSD.
$N(\mu, \sigma)$:	Symbolic representation of a normal distribution.
OL:	Original learning.
ORE:	Overlearning reversal effect.
P_x:	The score whose percentile is X.
PDG:	Postdiscrimination generalization gradient.
PI:	Proactive interference.

PL:	Prior learning.
PR_X:	The percentile rank of the score X.
PRE:	The partial reinforcement effect.
PSE:	Point of subjective equality.
$P(n\|N)$:	In TSD, the probability of a correct rejection.
$P(n\|SN)$:	In TSD, the probability of a false rejection.
$P(s\|N)$:	In TSD, the probability of a false alarm.
$P(s\|SN)$:	In TSD, the probability of a hit.
Q:	The semi-interquartile range, i.e., $(Q_3 - Q_1)/2$.
Q_1:	The first quartile, i.e., the score below which 25 percent of the distribution lies.
Q_2:	The second quartile, i.e., m.
Q_3:	The third quartile, i.e., the score below which 75 percent of the distribution lies.
r_F:	Fractional anticipatory frustration response.
r_G:	Fractional anticipatory goal response.
r_P:	Fractional anticipatory pain or discomfort response.
R:	Response.
R_F:	Primary or unconditioned frustration response.
R_G:	Primary or unconditioned goal response.
R_j:	A judgmental response based on R_s and perhaps other factors.
R_0:	The sensory response corresponding to the AL; the origin of the sensory continuum.
R_P:	Primary or unconditioned pain or discomfort response.
R_s:	The sensory response or sensation evoked by a stimulus.
RI:	Retroactive interference.
RS:	Reversal shift in discrimination studies.
RT:	Reaction time.
RV:	Relevant variable.
s:	In TSD, a response signifying that SN occurred.
S:	Stimulus.
$\mathbf{S}$:	Subject or observer.
$S+$:	Positive stimulus in discrimination learning task.
$S-$:	Negative stimulus in discrimination learning task.
S^D:	Discriminative stimulus of operant conditioning, similar to $S+$.
S^{R+}:	A primary or unconditioned positive reinforcer.
S^{R-}:	A primary or unconditioned negative reinforcer.
S^Δ:	The negative stimulus of operant conditioning.
S_t:	Standard stimulus of psychophysical tasks.
S_v:	Variable stimulus of psychophysical tasks.
SD:	Standard deviation, i.e., $\sqrt{\Sigma(X_i - \bar{X})^2/n}$.
SD^2:	The variance of a group of scores, i.e., $\Sigma(X_i - \bar{X})^2/n$.
SN:	The signal-plus-noise stimulus of TSD.
STM:	Short-term memory.
T:	Absolute threshold obtained on a single series of the method of limits.
$\dot{T}$:	Momentary absolute threshold, i.e., the absolute threshold on a single trial.
TSD:	Signal detection theory.
UCS:	Unconditioned stimulus.
UDL:	Upper difference limen; $UL - S_t$.

UDT: Upper difference threshold (on a single series in the method of limits).

UL: Upper limen; $\overline{UT}$ in the method of limits.

UT: Upper threshold (on a single series of the method of limits).

VI: Variable-interval schedule of reinforcement.

VR: Variable-ratio schedule of reinforcement.

$\bar{X}$: The arithmetic mean of a group of scores, i.e., $\Sigma X_i / n$.

z: A score measured in terms of the number of *SD* units from the distribution mean.

β: In *TSD* a measure of **S**'s criterion.

β_0: In *TSD* the optimal criterion for a given objective.

σ: The standard deviation of a population or of a theoretical distribution.

μ: The mean of a population or of a theoretical distribution.

μa: Microampere.

%cf: Percent cumulative frequency, $(cf/n) \times 100$.

%f: Percent frequency, $(f/n) \times 100$.

NAME INDEX

NAME INDEX

Adams, J. A., 609–612, 615, 635, 639, 668
Allen, C. K., 618, 619, 687
Allison, J. K., 302, 642
Amsel, A., 278, 287, 292, 295, 296, 639, 651, 670
Anant, S. S., 335, 640
Anastasio, E. J., 283, 676
Anderson, D. C., 325, 640
Anderson, N. H., 293, 640
Anger, D., 365, 640
Appel, J. B., 334, 335, 640

Archer, E. J., 560, 640
Armus, H. L., 290, 291, 640
Asch, S. E., 555, 557, 570, 571, 581, 640
Asimow, A., 305, 649
Atkinson, R. C., 62, 483, 528, 558, 627, 640, 676
Avery, G. C., 149, 640
Ayllon, T., 384, 385, 415, 640
Azrin, N. H., 318, 331, 333, 334, 339, 340, 348, 353, 370, 415, 640, 654, 656, 658, 683

Brush, F. R., 318, 331, 357, 359, 423, 644
Bugelski, B. R., 591, 644
Bull, J. A., III, 363, 644
Burns, S., 634, 672
Burstein, K. R., 422, 443, 444, 447, 644, 657
Bush, R. R., 4, 423, 528, 534, 644, 645, 664

Camp, D. S., 330, 334, 337–339, 645
Camp, W., 132, 133, 645
Campbell, B. A., 318, 319, 321, 331, 645
Campbell, D., 362, 660
Campbell, S. L., 326, 645
Capaldi, E. J., 278, 279, 294, 295, 320, 645
Carlin, S., 133, 645
Carlton, P. L., 30, 296, 670
Carmona, A., 264, 668
Carterette, T. S., 448, 645
Carton, A. S., 224, 225, 243, 680
Catania, A. C., 384, 392, 393, 397, 645
Ceraso, J., 628, 677
Champion, R. A., 306, 645
Chapman, L. F., 132, 133, 645
Chapman, R., 280, 654
Chase, S., 430, 655
Cherry, E. C., 492, 493, 495, 645
Cho, C., 366, 667
Church, R. M., 24, 45, 46, 318, 330–332, 334, 337–339, 346, 347, 642, 645
Cieutat, V. J., 562, 645
Clarke, F. R., 165, 648
Clifford, T., 292, 646
Coate, W. B., 435, 646
Cofer, C. N., 576, 607, 646
Colavita, F. B., 609, 671
Cole, J., 325, 640
Cole, J. L., 164, 183, 642

Cole, M., 489, 646
Collier, G., 526, 672
Collins, J., 373, 646
Conrad, R., 614, 618, 620, 621, 646
Conte, R., 364, 687
Cook, J. O., 337, 553, 646
Cook, L., 524, 661
Cook, P. E., 291, 658
Cooper, E. H., 568, 646
Copelan, E. L., 472, 475, 674
Cornsweet, T. N., 129, 156, 319, 646
Corso, J. F., 119, 181, 232, 233, 646
Cotton, J. W., 427, 659
Couch, J. V., 284, 646
Cowey, A., 150, 646
Cox, D. L., 562, 665
Crane, N. L., 516, 646
Cronbach, L. J., 6, 7, 646
Cross, D. V., 435, 688
Cross, H. A., 537, 646
Crothers, E. J., 62, 528, 558, 640
Crowder, R. G., 619, 646
Cumming, W. W., 415, 516, 521, 647, 659
Cusack, J., 414, 663

Dallenbach, K. M., 626, 659
D'Amato, M. R., 18, 30, 289, 290, 302, 326, 327, 337, 338, 356, 366–374, 430, 471, 502, 504, 505, 525, 526, 537, 646, 647, 650
Danick, J. J., 578, 643
Davenport, J. W., 282, 301, 647
Davidson, E. H., 319, 321, 688
Davis, S. F., 279, 288, 647
Davis, W. L., 521, 647
Day, R. H., 149, 640
Decker, L. R., 175, 671
Deese, J., 548, 572, 574, 648
DeMeyer, M. K., 414, 650
Derdzinski, D., 537, 538, 686
Deutsch, D., 484, 496, 499, 648
Deutsch, J. A., 484, 496, 499, 648

McGeoch, J. A., 544, 569, 571, 573, 614, 628, 666
McGill, W. J., 156, 666
McGinnis, R. W., 303, 681
McGonigle, B., 510, 512, 516, 666, 686
McGovern, J. B., 581, 629, 630, 666
McGuigan, F. J., 43, 666
McGuire, W. J., 557, 666
McHose, J. H., 288, 666
Mack, J. D., 236, 237, 679
McKearney, J. W., 345, 666
McKelvey, R. K., 304, 305, 666
MacKinnon, J. R., 298, 665
Mackintosh, N. J., 296, 303, 305, 467, 468, 508, 516, 537, 665, 680
Mackworth, J. F., 620, 665
McLaughlin, B., 565, 566, 666
McLean, J., 524, 643
McMillan, D. E., 318, 343, 351, 666
McVaugh, W., 325, 640
McWilliams, J., 283, 687
Maher, B. A., 614, 664
Maier, S. F., 323–325, 665, 676
Maller, O., 472, 670
Malott, M. K., 429, 665
Maltzman, I., 305, 649
Mandell, C., 430, 655
Mandler, G., 594, 608, 648, 665
Margolius, G., 431, 432, 665
Markowitz, J., 177, 665
Marks, L. E., 225, 239, 240, 665, 679
Marsh, G. D., 461, 482, 665
Martin, B., 347, 665
Martin, C. J., 562, 665
Martin, D. R., 448, 663
Martin, E., 587, 598, 599, 627, 665, 666
Martin, R., 132, 133, 645
Martin, R. C., 328, 329, 644, 666, 667
Marx, M. H., 292, 666
Meacham, J., 524, 643
Mead, R. N., 345, 668

Mechanic, A., 566, 666
Mechner, F., 409, 666
Mednick, S. A., 458, 667
Melton, A. W., 544, 545, 571, 614, 617, 628, 667
Melvin, K. B., 328, 329, 666, 667
Mentzer, T. L., 150, 667
Merikle, P. M., 599, 667
Messick, S., 212, 250, 651
Meyer, D. R., 305, 366, 468, 667
Meyer, P. M., 468, 667
Migler, B. M., 62, 404, 407, 651, 667
Mikulka, P. J., 603, 678
Miles, R. C., 305, 477, 667
Miller, G. A., 495, 559, 561, 580, 667
Miller, L. K., 318, 667
Miller, N. E., 263–265, 302, 336, 339, 349, 350, 353, 414, 434, 439–441, 641, 648, 649, 667, 668, 676
Milner, B., 501, 668
Mintz, D. E., 387, 670
Mitchell, K. M., 523, 668
Montague, W. E., 609, 611, 639, 668
Moore, J. W., 261, 653
Moray, N., 495, 500, 501, 668
Morgan, C. H., 556, 653
Morningstar, M., 483, 680
Morrow, M. W., 328, 644
Morse, W. H., 330, 339–345, 384, 387, 397, 661, 668
Moskowitz, H., 129, 150, 668
Mosteller, F., 528, 534, 645
Mostofsky, D. I., 418, 484, 668
Mountcastle, V. B., 245, 246, 687
Mowrer, O. H., 329, 331–333, 353, 356, 357, 377, 414, 668
Moyer, K. E., 366, 669
Mumma, R., 509, 510, 537–539, 668, 686
Munn, N. L., 396, 399, 466, 669
Murdock, B. B., Jr., 184, 619, 644, 669

Sgro, J. A., 283, 284, 676
Shaw, W. A., 229, 641
Sheahan, D. B., III, 609, 671
Sherman, J. G., 300, 676
Shickman, G. M., 224, 225, 243, 680
Shiffrin, R. M., 627, 676
Shnidman, S. R., 370, 676
Sidman, M., 52, 61, 356, 363, 365–367, 370, 373, 387, 390, 391, 412, 440, 479, 643, 673, 676, 677
Sidowski, J. B., 319, 553, 677
Siegel, L. S., 368, 686
Siegel, S., 514, 677
Silverman, J., 484, 677
Simmons, J. Q., 335, 664
Simon, H. A., 4, 528, 653
Simpson, C. K., 565, 687
Singh, D., 289, 677
Skeebo, S., 580, 659
Skinner, B. F., 263, 331, 346, 381, 383, 385–388, 390, 392–395, 397, 398, 402, 409–411, 414, 478, 483, 574, 650, 656, 677
Slamecka, N. J., 489, 540, 582, 623, 627, 628, 677
Smith, B., 422, 644
Smith, E. E., 502, 649
Smith, L. R., 306, 645
Smith, M. G., 352, 654
Smith, M. J., 319, 677
Snyder, C., 264, 677
Solomon, R. L., 24, 38, 315, 325, 331, 332, 357–359, 362, 363, 366, 374–376, 478, 644, 665, 674–678, 683, 688
Spear, N. E., 278, 290, 291, 296, 550, 562, 563, 565, 583–585, 587, 588, 603, 609, 651, 655, 656, 671, 678
Spence, J. T., 594, 678
Spence, K. W., 275, 298, 300, 306–310, 312, 376, 410, 411, 432–435, 442, 448–450, 461, 463, 467, 468, 478, 482, 488, 490, 522–524, 527, 537, 541–543, 545, 565, 652, 678

Spera, A. J., 560, 641
Sperling, S. E., 296, 537, 678
Sperry, R. W., 501, 668
Spiker, C. C., 431, 678
Spitzer, M. E., 553, 646
Spitzner, J. H., 296, 678
Spreng, M., 245, 660
Staats, A. W., 419, 678
Staats, C. K., 419, 678
Stachnik, T., 381, 683
Stahl, W. R., 242, 243, 679
Stanley, L. R., 284, 646
Stark, K., 559, 630, 631, 672
Starr, R., 373, 643
Stebbins, W. C., 297, 679
Steiner, J., 526, 679
Steiner, S. S., 277
Steinhardt, J., 155, 679
Steinman, R. M., 124, 669
Stevens, J. C., 225, 236, 237, 239, 240, 242, 665, 679
Stevens, S. S., 191, 209–214, 217, 219, 220, 222–227, 229–232, 236–239, 241–246, 248–253, 256, 654, 673, 679–681
Stewart, M. R., 229, 650, 680
Stimmel, D. T., 289, 669
Stockwell, F. E., 562, 645
Stoddard, L. T., 387, 479, 677
Stokes, L. W., 362, 372, 642
Stollnitz, F., 477, 524, 680
Stone, G., 225, 680
Storms, L. H., 334, 434, 435, 607, 644, 675, 680
Strongman, K. T., 291, 687
Suboski, M. D., 183, 680
Suci, G. J., 419, 670
Suppes, P., 191, 483, 680
Suter, S., 337, 338, 641
Sutherland, N. S., 303, 467, 509, 510, 514, 515, 517, 519–521, 539, 652, 680
Swets, J. A., 157, 158, 164, 165, 168–174, 177, 182, 183, 653, 665, 680

SUBJECT INDEX

SUBJECT INDEX

Analysis of variance, 34, 36, 37, 41, 46, 59
Anxiety (*see* Fractional anticipatory pain responses)
Arithmetic mean, 72, 73
  (*See also* Mean)
Association:
  contemporary views of, 572–574
  in verbal learning, 568–572
  (*See also* Stimulus control; Stimulus generalization)
Attention:
  filter theory, 497–499
  in Lovejoy's model, 527–539
  overshadowing, 507–508
  range of application, 484
  role in generalization, 427–431
  in selective-listening experiments, 492–502
  as selective perception, 487–502
  selective perception versus stimulus selection, 484–487
  and signal-detection theory, 500, 501
  versus stimulus control, 511
  as stimulus selection, 502–540
  (*See also* Observing behavior; Stimulus selection)
Average deviation, 94, 95
  from median, 114
Averages, caution against, 61, 62
Aversion therapy, 335
Avoidance conditioning:
  conservation and partial irreversibility, 357–360
  defined, 272, 273
  as discriminative behavior, 368–374
  extinction of, 357–359
  modified by Pavlovian conditioning, 362–364
  role of anticipatory responses in, 372, 373
  and shock intensity, 366, 367

Avoidance conditioning:
  termination of *CS* and avoidance of *UCS* as factors in, 360–362
  two-factor theory of, 354–360, 362–371

Bar graph, 74, 75
Behavior therapy, 336, 414, 415
Behavioral contrast:
  and contrast effects, 453, 455
  defined, 453
  and peak shift, 453–456
Between-subjects design (*see* Separate-group design)
Binaural listening, defined, 492
Bisection (*see* Psychophysical scaling methods, partition, interval production)

Carry-over effects, 49, 50
Category rating (*see* Psychophysical scaling methods, partition, category estimation)
Classical conditioning:
  backward conditioning, 262
  defined, 262
  versus instrumental conditioning, 263, 264
  of nonautonomic nervous system responses, 263
  pairing relations of *CS* and *UCS*, 262, 263
  proper controls in, 262, 263
Clustering, 575, 576
Coding (*see* Verbal learning)
Computer-based instruction, 483
Computer simulation, 528, 529, 535, 536
Conditioned emotional response (*CER*), 330
  generalization of, 445–447

Conditioning:
  defined, 265–269, 271
  Hull-Spence theory of, 307–310
  (*See also* Classical conditioning; Instrumental conditioning; Operant conditioning; *and* specific types)
Constant sum method (*see* Psychophysical scaling methods, proportionality, ratio estimation)
Continuity-noncontinuity controversy, 467, 522
Contrast effects (*see* Behavioral contrast; Reward magnitude)
Control group, defined, 13
Counterbalancing, 25
  complete, 52–55
  incomplete, 55–57
  intragroup, 52–57
  intrasubject, 50–52
  randomized, 57
Cross-modality matching, 233–239
Cumulative frequency distributions, 83

Decibel:
  defined, 223
  and Fechner's law, 223
Delay of reward:
  in appetitive conditioning: effect on acquisition asymptote, 283, 284
    effect on extinction, 293, 294
    shift effects, 284
    varied, 284, 285
  in escape conditioning, 322, 323
Delayed-response learning, 474
Depression effect (*see* Reward magnitude)
Dichotic listening, defined, 492
Differential conditioning, defined, 274
  (*See also* Instrumental conditioning)

Differentiation theory (*see* Discrimination learning)
Discriminanda:
  defined, 273
  role of proportion of $S+$ trials, 300, 301
Discrimination learning:
  attention model, 527–539
  conditional, 471–473
  and differentiation theory, 487–492
  versus discriminative conditioning, 273, 274, 464, 465
  errorless, 478–483
  learning sets in, 475–478
  nonperceptual variables in, 465, 466
  oddity, 473, 474
  paradigms, 468–479
  perceptual processes in, 466–468
  and preexposure experience, 488, 489
  shift behavior in, 489–491
  single- and multiple-look models, 510, 511
  Spence's theories of, 448–451, 488, 490, 527
  and transposition behavior, 449
Discriminative behavior, predicted from generalization gradients, 432, 461
  (*See also* Discrimination learning; Instrumental conditioning)
Drive (motivation) level:
  in appetitive conditioning: effect on acquisition asymptote, 281, 282
    effect on discriminative behavior, 298–300
    effect on extinction, 288, 289
    shift effects in, 282
  effect on discrimination learning, 305, 306
  effect on generalization gradients, 432–435

Drive (motivation) level:
in escape conditioning, 321, 322
in Hull-Spence theory, 307–310
perceptual effects, 435
role in verbal learning, 565

Elation effect (*see* Reward magnitude)
Error of anticipation, 124
Error of habituation, 124
Errorless discrimination learning, 478
effects of chlorpromazine and imipramine on, 480
and frustration, 479, 480
and inhibitory control, 480–482
and peak shift, 451–453
Escape conditioning:
acquisition, 319–325
aversive stimuli used in, 318
defined, 271, 272
parallels with appetitive conditioning, 319–323, 325–327, 329, 330
Experimental designs, 30, 31
Experimental group, defined, 13
Extinction:
of avoidance behavior, 357–359
below zero, 359
in discriminative conditioning, 273, 301–303
in escape conditioning, 325–329
generalization of, 442–444
in nondiscriminative conditioning, 286–297
of punishment effects, 345–353
as response suppression, 353, 354

Factorial designs, 58–61
Fear (*see* Fractional anticipatory responses, pain)
Fechner's law, 157, 205, 206, 230, 253

Fechner's law:
derivation of, 206–208
evaluation of, 209, 210
Filter theory, 497–499
Forgetting (*see* Retention)
Fractional anticipatory responses:
common conceptual status, 315, 348–353
frustration, 287, 288, 315
role in Hull-Spence theory, 308
in general two-factor theory, 374–378
goal, 286–288, 315
pain, 345, 346, 355, 363
in escape conditioning, 328, 329
as fear, 314, 315
in punishment, 332, 338
relief, 377, 378
Fractionation (*see* Psychophysical scaling methods, proportionality, ratio production)
Free recall, defined, 548, 549
Frequency polygon, 79–82
Frustration:
defined, 286–288
and errorless discrimination training, 479, 480
as explanation of extinction data, 292, 293, 295, 296
and the peak shift, 451–456

Gaussian distribution (*see* Normal distribution)
Generalization (*see* Response generalization; Stimulus generalization)
Geometric mean, use in psychophysical scales, 226

Habit strength in Hull-Spence conditioning theory, 307–310
Histogram, 78–82

Hull-Spence theory of conditioning, 307–310
  and generalization gradients, 432–435

Illusions:
  horizontal-vertical, 149
  Müller-Lyer, 150
Implicit associative responses, 564, 565, 578, 579
Incidental learning, 565, 566
Instrumental conditioning:
  appetitive: defined, 269
    discriminative, 270, 297–307
    nondiscriminative, 270, 274–297
  of autonomic nervous system responses, 263–265
    implications for psychosomatic medicine, 264
  aversive: defined, 269
    discriminative, 272, 273
    nondiscriminative, 271, 272
  versus classical conditioning, 263, 264
  classification of procedures, 269–273
  discriminative: defined, 268
    derived from nondiscriminative case, 303, 306, 307
    and intensity of $S+$, 300
    role of proportion of $S+$ trials, 300, 301
  Hull-Spence theory of, 307–310
  nondiscriminative, defined, 268
  (*See also* Avoidance conditioning; Escape conditioning; Punishment)
Instrumental learning, 273, 274
Interaction of variables, 34
  in Hull-Spence theory, 309, 310
  in instrumental conditioning, 290–293, 298–300, 309, 310

Interference theory of retention, 627–635
Intervening variables in Hull-Spence theory, 307, 308

Just noticeable difference:
  and the difference limen, 153, 154
  and psychophysical scaling method, 249
  and Weber's law, 151–154

Lashley jumping stand, 468, 469
Latin square, 57
Law of effect, 383
Learned helplessness, 323–325
Learning sets, 475–478
Limen:
  absolute, 118, 119
    determined by method of constant stimuli, 129–133
    determined by method of limits, 121–123
  difference, 118, 119
    determined by method of average error, 149, 150
    determined by method of constant stimuli, 144–148
    determined by method of limits, 125–128
    and the just noticeable difference, 153, 154
  (*See also* Threshold)
Line graph, 76
Linear functions, 66–69
Linear interpolation, 85, 86
Logarithmic functions, 196–200
  use of semilogarithmic paper in, 200
Logarithms, 196, 197

Matched conditions, 43–46
Matched groups, 33–39

Matching, 25
to sample, 473
Mean:
arithmetic, 72, 73
deviations from, 114
geometric, 73, 74
Meaning, 546, 547
Meaningfulness, 547, 548, 560–563
and mediation, 562, 563
Median, 72
Mediation:
in discrimination learning, 489–491
temporal factors in, 604–607
in transfer, 602–604
use of natural language in, 609–612
Memory:
long-term, 622–627
role of frequency, 558
short- versus long-term, 614, 615
short-term, 487, 615–621
(*See also* Retention)
Memory span, 559
Metathetic continua, 209, 210, 230, 250, 251
Method of adjustment (*see* Method of average error)
Method of average error, 118, 148–150
Method of averages, 141, 142, 199
Method of constant stimuli, 118, 129–148
Method of just noticeable differences (*see* Method of limits)
Method of least squares, 140
Method of limits, 118, 121–129
modifications of, 128, 129
Method of minimal changes (*see* Method of limits)
Method of reproduction (*see* Method of average error)
Method of serial exploration (*see* Method of limits)

Mode, 72
Motivation (*see* Drive level)
Motive-incentive conditions with negative reinforcement, 313–315

Nonfactorial designs, 61
Nonlinear functions, 196–205
Normal distribution, 101–107
area relations in, 107–110
cumulative, 110–112
linear transformation of, 105
as a model for thresholds, 135–140
in signal-detection theory, 158, 159, 166, 168, 173, 179, 184
unit, 105–107

Observing behavior, 522–526
Ogive (*see* Cumulative frequency distributions)
Operant Conditioning:
attitude toward applied problems, 413–415
behavior control in, 409–415
central concepts of, 382–387
versus respondent conditioning, 382, 383
technology, 409
Order effects, 49
linear, 69
Orienting reflex, 484
Overlearning-reversal effect, 537, 538

Paired-associate learning, 551–558
two-stage model, 557
Parameters, population, 102
Partial reinforcement effect, 294–296
Partial reinforcement schedule and contrast effects, 352
Percentile rank, 87
Percentiles, 86, 87
Perceptual learning, 486–492, 526

Performance versus learning and magnitude of reward, 281, 282
Poikilitic functions, 212
Point of subjective equality:
in method of average error, 149, 150
in method of constant stimuli, 145–147
in method of limits, 128
Power functions, 200–204
in biology, 242, 243
in learning, 242
in mechanoreceptors, 245, 246
and sensation, 222, 223, 225, 226, 228, 230, 232, 236, 237
use of logarithmic paper in, 203–204, 226
Power law:
applications of, 247, 248, 253
criticisms of, 243–247
generalized, 230–234, 243
for individual subjects, 239–241
pervasiveness of, 242, 243
and reciprocality of an attribute, 241, 242
validation of, 233–242
(*See also* Power functions)
Proactive interference:
in long-term memory, 623–627
in short-term memory, 618–620
Programmed environment, 404–409
Prothetic continua, 209, 210, 230, 250, 251
Psychometric function, 138, 145, 179–181, 212
Psychophysical function, 215, 226, 231, 232, 234, 240
versus psychometric function, 212
Psychophysical methods:
applications of, 150
in signal detection, 174–177
(*See also* Method of average error; Method of constant stimuli; Method of limits)

Psychophysical scaling:
category versus interval judgments, 211–212
estimation versus response procedures, 211, 217
regression effect in, 226, 227
Psychophysical scaling methods:
direct versus indirect, 248–250
partition: category estimation, 212–214, 217, 218, 228
category production, 213, 214, 217, 218
common features of, 216, 217
interval estimation, 214, 215, 217, 218
interval production, 215–218
proportionality: cross-modality matching, 239
magnitude estimation, 217, 222–225, 228
magnitude production, 217, 225–227
ratio estimation, 217–219, 225
ratio production, 217, 219–222
use of modulus in, 224, 225
Punishment:
compared to *CER*, 330
cue effects of, 339, 340
behavior maintained by, 340–345
defined, 271, 272
facilitatory effects of, 339–345, 347, 348
factors affecting degree of response suppression in, 333–339
generalization of, 444, 445
immediate versus delayed, 337, 338
implications for behavioral control, 334, 336
versus noncontingent shock, 346
as passive avoidance conditioning, 331–333
resistance to, 336, 339
similarities with extinction, 348–353

Random digits, 25–27
Randomization, 25
  of known subject relevant varia-
    bles, 41, 42
  residual, 39–41
Randomized blocks method, 36–39
Randomized conditions, 46–48
Randomized groups, 39–41
Range, 93
Recognition learning (*see* Verbal
  discrimination learning)
Reinforcement:
  negative: motive-incentive condi-
    tions in, 313–315, 323
    versus positive, 315–317
  response-contingent, 263, 267, 268
  response-noncontingent, 263
  role in Operant Conditioning, 383,
    384
Research:
  correlational, 6, 7, 15–19
  employing type-E independent var-
    iables, 14–16
  experimentation, 7–10, 14–18
  observation, 5, 6, 14–18
  theoretical, 4
Response differentiation, 384, 385
Response generalization, 420
Response magnitude (intensity), 266,
  267
  versus response direction, 265–267
Retention:
  defined, 612
  interference theory of, 627–635
  (*See also* Memory)
Retroactive interference:
  in long-term memory, 623–627
  role of unlearning, 629, 630
  in short-term memory, 618, 619
Reward (*see* Reinforcement)
Reward magnitude:
  in appetitive conditioning: con-
    trast effects, 278–281

Reward magnitude:
  in appetitive conditioning: effect
    on acquisition asymptote, 274–
    277
  effect on discriminative behav-
    ior, 297, 298
  effect on extinction, 290–292
  effect of varied, 281
  shift effects, 277, 278
  effect on discrimination learning,
    304, 305
  in escape conditioning, 319–321
  contrast effects, 319–321

Scales:
  interval, 193–195
  nominal, 191
  ordinal, 192, 193
  partition, 216, 250–252
  ratio, 195, 196
  sensory: consistency of, 228–230
    interval, 211–217, 228–230
    proportionality, 217, 227, 250–
      253
    ratio, 217–230
  unit of measurement in, 193
  zero point of, 194, 195, 217
Schedules of reinforcement:
  applications of, 398–409
  compound: sequential, 394–396
    simultaneous, 396–398
  effect on generalization gradients,
    435–438
  role in Operant Conditioning, 387,
    388
  role in stimulus selection, 519–522,
    538, 539
  simple, 388–391
    behavior generated by, 391–393
Selective-listening experiments, 492–
  502
Selective perception (*see* Attention;
  Stimulus selection)

Semantic generalization, 418, 419, 460

Semi-interquartile range, 93, 94

Separate-group design:
   and method of manipulating variables, 9, **10**
   in reward magnitude studies, 276
   versus single-group design, 29, 30
      in drive level effects, 306
      in partial reinforcement effect, 295, 296
      in reward magnitude effects, 304, 305

Sequence variables (*see* Variables)

Serial learning, defined, 549, 550

Serial-position effect, 549, 550

Shaping (*see* Response differentiation)

Short-term memory (*see* Memory)

Sidman avoidance procedure, 272, 365–391

Signal-detection theory:
   applications of, 182–184
   and attention, 500, 501
   and classical psychophysics, 121, 177–181
   and ideal observer, 164, 165
   optimal criteria in, 160–164, 168–172
   psychophysical methods of, 174–177
   and receiver-operating-characteristic curves, 165–174
   sensitivity versus response criterion, 157–160

Simultaneous discrimination, defined, 270

Single-group design:
   and method of manipulating variables, 9, 10
   versus separate-group design, 29, 30

Single-subject design, 51, 52

Situational variables (*see* Variables)

Sodium amytal, effects on extinction and punished behavior, 349–351, 480

Standard deviation, 95–100

Statistical designs, 30, 31

Stevens' power law (*see* Power law)

Stimulus control, 385, 386
   versus attention, 511
   exteroceptive versus interoceptive, 437, 438
   (*See also* Stimulus generalization)

Stimulus error, 120

Stimulus generalization:
   versus discrimination, 459–462
   failure-of-association hypothesis, 457–459
   failure-of-discrimination hypothesis, 459, 460
   primary versus mediated, 418, 419
   process versus phenomenon, 420
   theoretical issues in, 456–462
   gradients: absolute versus relative, 423–426
      and amount of acquisition training, 431, 432
      avoidance, 439–441
      and conflict, 440, 441
      defined, 420–422
      and drive level, 432–435
      and early discriminative experience, 429
      effect of schedule of reinforcement, 435–438
      effect of training-test interval, 438, 439
      excitatory, 426–441
      extinction, 442–444
      inhibitory, 441–447
      and orthogonal discrimination training, 427–430, 445
      postdiscrimination, 448–456
      and stimulus control, 427–431

Stimulus generalization:
gradients: summation of, 448
techniques for studying, 422, 423
Stimulus selection, 502–540
addivity of cues, 508–511
role of overtraining, 517–519, 539
role of previous experience, 513–517
role of structural factors, 511–513
schedule of reinforcement, 519–522, 538, 539
Subject variables (*see* Variables)
Successive discrimination, defined, 270

t test, 34, 38
Theory of signal detectability (*see* Signal-detection theory)
Threshold:
determination by operant methods, 399–402
sensory versus response, 181, 182
variability of, 123, 142, 143
(*See also* Limen)
Time error, 128
Transfer:
nonspecific, 594–598
specific, 598–602
in verbal learning, 592–594
(*See also* Learning sets)
Two-factor theory:
of avoidance conditioning, 354–360, 362–371
general, 374–378

Variables:
continuous and discrete, 20, 21
defined, 10, 11
dependent, 11, 67
independent, 11, 67
interdependence of independent and dependent, 12, 13

Variables:
manipulation of: direct, 7–10
by selection, 6–10
measurability of, 196
operational definition of, 21, 22
quantitative and qualitative, 19, 20
relevant, 13, 14
sequence, 29
situational, 28, 29
subject, 28
sequence, control of: in separate-groups designs, 57, 58
in single-group designs, 49–57
situational, control of: in separate-groups designs, 42–48
in single-group designs, 48, 49
subject, control of: in separate-groups designs, 33–42
in single-group designs, 42
type-E, 11
type-S, 11
(*See also* Interaction of variables)
Variance (*see* Standard deviation)
Veg, 220–222, 228
Verbal discrimination learning, 474, 550, 551
Verbal learning:
conditioning, 556, 557
organizational processes in: coding, 582–588
extra-item transformations, 588–592
transformations of item order, 575–582
role of imagery, 588–592
role of intralist similarity, 563–565
role of meaningfulness, 560–563
role of motivation, 565–567
role of total learning time, 567, 568
Vicarious trial-and-error, 523
Vicious-circle behavior, 328, 329

Warm-up, 597, 598
Weber's law, 154, 155, 157, 181
    generalizations of, 156, 188, 210
    related to Fechner's law, 206–208
    validity of, 155, 156
Wisconsin General Test Apparatus,
    468, 470

Within-subjects design (*see* Single-
    group design)

Yoking, 44–46

z scores, 106
z transformation, 98, 105, 106